C000018719

Where on Earth is Heaven?

JONATHAN STEDALL

Foreword by Richard Tarnas

HAWTHORN PRESS

Published by Hawthorn Press, Hawthorn House,
1 Lansdown Lane, Stroud, Gloucestershire, GL5 1BJ, UK
Tel: 01453 757040   Fax: 01453 751138
Email: info@hawthornpress.com
Website: www.hawthornpress.com

Cover image © Miriam Macgregor
Cover design and typesetting by Bookcraft Ltd, Stroud, Gloucestershire

Printed by Cromwell Press Group in the UK

Printed on FSC approved paper

British Library Cataloguing in Publication Data applied for

ISBN   978-1-903458-90-7

For Thomas and Ellie

Jonathan Stedall by Saied Dai, 2004

Contents

Foreword

To read this book is like sitting by a fire on a long winter's evening, listening with delight to a friend of many years who has thought deeply about life's mysteries, and who is now looking back on his life's journey to share, modestly and without pretension, its accumulated wisdom. This is a deeply humane book, by a deeply humane man. But it is also more than that.

For in his unassuming way, Jonathan Stedall explores questions and realities, and intimations of realities, that take courage to speak of in an age long ruled by that confident mindset which still believes it has more or less fully and objectively revealed the true nature of the universe. In many ways this is an old-fashioned book—unhurried in its reminiscences and reflections, rather like an intimate essay, full of treasured quotations, courteous to the reader, and sympathetic to its subjects. Yet it is also a strangely new book, radical in its willingness to push the conventional boundaries of received knowledge about what is real. It engages the big questions of life and death, of immortality and love, drawing on sources of insight that have not been accommodated within the narrow empiricism and rationalism of the orthodox modern mind. Without fanfare, without vaulting ambition, Stedall quietly seeks to understand those many more things in heaven and earth than have been dreamt of in our modern philosophy.

Ours is a time between world views, when the powerful assumptions that have shaped the modern understanding of the world and of the human being are undergoing a radical change. It is a time that C.G. Jung called the *kairos*: the ancient Greek term for the 'right moment' for a changing of the fundamental symbols and principles. Jung saw this change as happening with a kind of evolutionary necessity, beyond our conscious choice. Yet he also viewed the outcome of this great shift as in some way depending on how well we consciously participated in its unfolding. At the heart of this shift is a transformation in the spiritual condition of the modern self, which has long been grappling with the paradox of being a purposeful, meaning-seeking oddity of consciousness in a randomly evolving material universe lacking in intrinsic meaning, purpose, or soul.

In the conventional scientific world picture, the spiritual dimension of being must ultimately be seen as nothing but an idiosyncratic projection of the human subject. To preserve consistently this world picture requires the metaphysical dismissal of most of what is most intimate and precious to the human being. Yet to confront that contradiction is to take on an enormous existential task, a tension of opposites not easily resolved. That task, Jung recognized, and Stedall recognizes, defines the spiritual adventure of the modern self.

Jonathan Stedall takes on that adventure, and brings certain special gifts to the task: a calm integrity and warmth of spirit, a breadth of human empathy, an appreciation of the different stages of human life, of different kinds of human beings, of different perspectives, of the different cultures and religions of the world. Throughout this unique narrative of a life's seeking and learning is an engaging transparency, a self-deprecating modesty, that is linked to an extraordinary moral and metaphysical imagination.

It could also be said that this book was made possible by the unusually enlightened working environment of the BBC in an earlier age. There, an intelligent creative producer like Stedall could follow his own intellectual and spiritual curiosity, propose a topic he found of real interest, and in all likelihood be given the green light to make a program or even a series. In such propitious circumstances, Stedall became well-travelled in both the world of people and places and the world of spirit and ideas. This book is the fruit of those explorations. He draws here on the great influences who have shaped his vision of life—Steiner, Jung, Teilhard de Chardin, Gandhi and Tolstoy, Emerson and Wordsworth, Eckhart and Plato. He describes the many remarkable men and women he has met in his life's journey and distills for us their insights – Fritz Schumacher, John Betjeman, Laurens van der Post, Cecil Collins, Malcolm Muggeridge, Bernard Lovell, Theodore Roszak, the men and women of the Camphill movement. He gently but firmly takes on the inevitable antagonists, such as Richard Dawkins. He shares his observations and intuitions without dogmatism, without inflation. Above all, he draws on his own profound experience of being human, a thoughtful person fully engaged in contemporary culture, in a life of wide horizons and poignant losses. This is a gift made possible by a lifetime of reflections and discoveries, tendered with the lightness of spirit of a good friend sharing a very interesting story indeed.

Richard Tarnas

Preface

What is essential is invisible to the eye, the little prince repeated,
so that he would be sure to remember.

Antoine de Saint-Exupéry, *The Little Prince*

My title *Where on Earth is Heaven?* is a question that my son Thomas asked nearly twenty years ago, when he was seven years old. It's a good and reasonable question whatever age you happen to be. He went on to become a physicist and is, I believe, asking it still – albeit using different words and concepts. This book is an attempt to address that question, for what lies behind those words has long interested me.

I'm sure that I didn't ignore or evade my son's curiosity all those years ago, but now I would like to share with him and his equally inquiring sister, Ellie, some thoughts I have had in the meantime; thoughts, too, about immortality. It is a decision partly prompted by the growing awareness that I won't be around forever, at least not in my present shape and form – an awareness heightened for me by a recent and potentially serious illness.

Thomas and Ellie 1989

All of us have had parents and most people become parents themselves. Such relationships can be a bond of extraordinary power, and the prospect of their severance is deeply disturbing. Yet despite this underlying fear, and the overwhelming sense of separation and loss that most people initially experience on the death of someone they love, I do believe that our relationships with one another, all relationships, survive as more than just memories. The story of how I came to this conviction is what I want to share not only with my son and daughter, but also with anyone else who might find this journey of mine of interest and perhaps of help.

Many people are content to say that we simply cannot know what lies beyond death, yet have faith there is more to life than meets the eye. Others dismiss the whole notion of a spiritual existence as fanciful and escapist. For me personally faith is not enough; I am more curious. I am also someone for whom the idea of a supersensible dimension to reality makes a great deal of sense. Yet I am very aware that however deep one's questions, the great mysteries of existence are not instantly forthcoming or easily accessible. I will only hear and understand what I am ready to understand.

I am also aware that the word 'survive' in relation to some sort of after-life may be misleading. People talk about life after death. What about life before birth? Or is there, perhaps, a timeless level of existence – neither past nor future – which itself is the source of what we call life? My physical body is certainly mortal, but this other aspect of my being – the very core of my existence – may not be bound by the laws of time and space. Are we, therefore, both mortal and immortal? The 19th-century American writer and lecturer Ralph Waldo Emerson called his body 'the office where I work'.

Nevertheless, death can seem very final. Eternity and infinity are words we've coined, but are concepts of which we have very little, if any, experience or understanding. Yet perhaps we already live in this eternal dimension of existence to a far greater extent than we experience consciously – above all in that third of our life we spend asleep – and where the notion of life and death may have a quite different meaning. If so, are heaven and earth perhaps not as separate as some people imagine? These are some of the questions that I have lived with for a long time and which I want to explore in the pages that follow.

Picasso once wrote to his friend Matisse: 'We must talk to each other as much as we can. When one of us dies, there will be some things that the other will never be able to talk of with anyone else.' Perhaps Picasso needn't have worried, and after Matisse's death their dialogue did continue, and does so still.

For years I have kept a notebook in which I have written what for me have been helpful and inspiring quotations, along with various thoughts of my own. I make no apology that what follows will at times seem like an anthology. (The bibliography contains details of all books mentioned in the text.) I am an observer and a listener by nature, and my work has been about selecting and editing the words, deeds and images that have touched me, and then turning them into films. A recent entry in my notebook reads: 'Each time we fall asleep we awaken to eternity.' I have a strong feeling that at death we face a similar threshold, but on a far larger scale. And perhaps this will not come as such a surprise if, as I have already suggested, we expand into that reality every night when we fall sleep.

However, in describing what have been meaningful awakeners for me, I am well aware that what I have found helpful may not necessarily be so for someone else. I am also aware that history is littered with examples of people attempting to impose their views and beliefs on others, whether at the point of a sword, from the nib of a pen, or nowadays at the touch of a keyboard. Nor is what follows intended to be an autobiography, though at times it may appear so. It is the story of an inner rather than outer journey, though frequently the two have intertwined.

As a documentary film director for forty years, more than half of which were spent with the BBC, I have been fortunate to be able to pursue much of this quest of mine through my actual work; and it is this work which I shall be drawing on extensively, taking you into the African bush, to the hill temples of northern India, into the streets of San Francisco, to a Taiwanese funeral, by train to Arcadia and by bicycle into the lanes of Cornwall – and above all into the minds and imaginations of some distinguished observers of our human condition; for in making these films I have worked alongside an extraordinary range of interesting and thoughtful people including the poet and broadcaster John Betjeman, astronomer Bernard Lovell, writer and explorer Laurens van der Post, playwright Alan Bennett, cultural historian Theodore Roszak, novelist Alexander Solzenhitsyn, writer and broadcaster Malcolm Muggeridge, poet Ben Okri, philosopher Jacob Needleman, physicist Fritjof

Capra, politician Michael Portillo, economist E.F. Schumacher, broadcaster and writer Mark Tully, and artist Cecil Collins – all of whom cast their light on these pages.

And on this journey my life has also been enormously enriched by encounters with hundreds of other men, women and children whose names will almost certainly never find their way into the history books – a peasant farmer in the Indian state of Bihar, a Russian cameraman, an American Sikh, a night-nurse in Birmingham, a Romanian bishop, the inhabitants of a Quaker Home for the elderly in Bristol, and many of those classed as having special needs – people who, in my experience, often have as much to give and to teach the world as they need help and support from us. I have also been fortunate to make films about the lives of several outstanding individuals from the past including Leo Tolstoy, Mahatma Gandhi and Carl Gustav Jung; and films, too, about the educational, curative and medical work inspired by the research and insights of Rudolf Steiner.

As a film-maker I have always seen myself as a bridge between the subjects that I have found interesting and a largely anonymous audience 'out there' who may happen to be watching television on a particular evening, at a particular time – some out of choice, some by chance. I suppose in the end what has guided me is trust – trust in life, and in what I have found meaningful while at the same time respecting what has meaning for others; and also trust that in their hearts everyone is a searcher like myself, with the same sort of questions, fears and hopes.

I approach the writing of this book in much the same spirit that I have made my films. In this case the rushes, the raw material, are some of the experiences and ideas that I have had in response to the questions I have asked of life along the way, and some of the thoughts that life has whispered back to me. The venture has been much helped and inspired by a quotation often attributed to Goethe, but in fact written by the Scottish mountaineer W.H. Murray: 'Until one is committed, there is hesitancy, the chance to draw back, always ineffectiveness. Concerning all acts of initiative there is one elementary truth, the ignorance of which kills countless ideas and splendid plans: that the moment one definitely commits oneself, then Providence moves too … Whatever you can do or dream you can, begin it.'

This courage to simply take the plunge was once demonstrated to me by the theatre director and dear friend Ron Eyre. We had worked together in the 1970s on a BBC series called *The Long Search* that Ron wrote and presented, and in which we attempted to understand something about other people's beliefs and faith, and the age-old search for meaning. That task was challenging enough, but what followed some eight years later was in many ways more daunting. Our plan was to make a series of seven films exploring the seven phases of life as outlined in Jacques's famous speech 'All the world's a stage' in Shakespeare's *As You Like It*. The canvas was huge. All the sixty or so million inhabitants of Great Britain were qualified to take part. How and where should we select participants, and what should we film for that all-important introductory sequence?

Sometime earlier Ron had told me the story of a summer holiday he had as a small boy with his parents at Scarborough. His father had been unsuccessfully trying to persuade and encourage his somewhat timid son to go into the sea. Apparently Ron's final response, confronted by all those waves, was 'I'll go in when it stops'. Thus Scarborough became the setting for our opening sequence to the series. This time it was a grown-up and courageous Ron Eyre standing on the beach at the edge of the sea with a film crew in tow. He briefly outlined the idea of *Seven Ages* and the enormity of our task. He then told the story of his childhood fear of the sea. But this time he took the plunge: he ran into the sea, and so began the series.

So I too will simply dive in. Above all I want to try and share my sense that our existence in some mysterious way transcends what we experience as time; and that the essence of this existence is a web of relationships. And for reasons which I hope will become clear as this story unfolds, I believe it is vital – both for those of us who are alive, as well as for those who are seemingly no longer present – that this communion is both acknowledged and fostered; indeed that we keep in touch. You can simply call it unfinished business. Another word that springs to mind is love – the love that Philip Larkin hints at in his poem 'An Arundel Tomb'. In Chichester Cathedral an Earl and his Countess are commemorated side by side in the hard formality of stone; but then the poet notices 'with a sharp tender shock' that they are holding hands. Is it, he wonders, a confirmation of what we hardly dare believe: 'What will survive of us is love.'

Tomb of Richard FitzAlan, tenth Earl of Arundel, and his wife
Eleanor of Lancaster in Chichester Cathedral

Chapter 1

What I do is Me

'Where shall I begin?' the White Rabbit asked the King during the trial in *Alice in Wonderland*. 'Begin at the beginning', the King said gravely, 'and go on till you come to the end; then stop.' That's easier said than done if you are trying to trace an inner journey and a search, the roots of which seem to be buried beyond the reach of consciousness. When did I begin? I shall simply have to rely on memory and in doing so I'm going to begin my story not quite at the beginning, but with one particular encounter I had as a film-maker which raises some challenging questions about themes such as love, heaven and eternity.

In 1965, in the early days of BBC2, I made a film for a series called *World of a Child* about a ten-year-old girl, Anne-Marie, in the care of nuns at the Convent of the Good Shepherd in Edinburgh. All the children at the convent had been through disruptive and often traumatic experiences in their early years, and were too emotionally damaged to be adopted or fostered. Most of them, including Anne-Marie, had never formed a close bond with their mothers, and therefore found it very difficult to establish relationships, trust another person or even form friendships among themselves.

When I asked the nun in charge of the home, Sister Therese – the children called her Mother Therese – how they brought religion into the children's lives, she said to me 'I think religion with these children is one of the most difficult things to get across, because again it comes down to a question of love. Now if a child has not known love, and hasn't loved being loved, then they can't love. And if you can't love a human being, then you can't love God.'

Anne-Marie 1966

Sister Therese

The nuns were certainly doing their best to surround the children with as much love as possible, but the wounds were deep, and the protective shells that Anne-Marie and the others had created around themselves were hard to penetrate. Despite this, however, everyone seemed to enjoy the novelty and excitement of our visit, and it was hard to leave again. This can be one of the sad things about filming – making new and very real bonds with people, and then having to say goodbye.

Over twenty years later, for a series called *Second Sight*, the BBC in Bristol where I now worked suggested to several producers that we might retrace and update some stories from old programmes with which we'd been connected. One of the Edinburgh nuns with whom I had kept in touch, Maeve Segrave, helped me to track down Anne-Marie to a council flat in Roehampton, where she lived with her partner Steve and their three children. She was now thirty-three years old.

During the filming that followed Anne-Marie spoke to me a great deal about her early childhood, and about being sent to live with an old man whom she called Grandad, and his two sisters; but no memory of any parents. At one point she actually used the word 'hatred' when speaking of this mother she never knew. 'If it wasn't for her,' she said, 'I wouldn't have done the things I've done. I made a muck-up of my life from nineteen to twenty-five. My life was a mess.'

From a very early age Anne-Marie had truanted from school and was eventually taken into care. She was then sent to the convent where she lived from the age of nine to sixteen. She described to me her reason for truanting as simply wanting to get back home and to get to the bottom of things. 'I thought they didn't want me there and I wanted to know why. I thought they'd be talking about me when I got back home, so I'd find out why they didn't want me ... I always thought they put you in school, not for your benefit, but just for their sake ... When I was young I believed I wasn't wanted.'

The 'mess' she spoke of largely referred to the five other children she'd had by three different and apparently problematic men before she met Steve. The first three children, she told me, were taken into care in Ireland because of their father's violence. She'd been to see them quite recently, but was told that they wouldn't be allowed to visit her until they were sixteen. The last of those first five children was taken away shortly after birth, again because of the father's history of violence. Her efforts to get this baby back were thwarted by bureaucracy and red tape. Social Services said she had to have a home before the child could be returned. The Council said she wasn't eligible to have a house without a child. Not surprisingly she took refuge in a drug and alcohol induced flight from reality.

Anne-Marie spoke well of the nuns, confirming my own impression at the time. When I asked her about religion she replied: 'I know for a fact there's somebody upstairs and he's looking down watching you. And when your day comes he'll either take you away or throw you away. That's basically religion for me.'

'At the moment life's good', she said to me a little later, as Steve and their three children played together in the background – in the sunshine – in their local park. I was therefore very distressed to learn the following year that Anne-Marie had left her family; and I have been unable to find out where she went. Those wounds from early childhood were clearly so deep that not even the love of her children and their father was going to convince her she was wanted.

Such stories can make talk of a spiritual dimension to existence seem somewhat abstract and even insensitive. Some people, it appears, are simply dealt rotten cards and they suffer accordingly. I only hope and pray that Anne-Marie, wherever she is, is not wholly mired in that trough in which she found herself almost from day one. It's true that there are many examples of people overcoming incredible obstacles and hardship, but they are the very strong ones. What I do believe, though, is that achievement in life is ultimately nothing to do with whether you become Prime Minister, write successful plays, accumulate great wealth or even simply stay out of trouble. In any judgement about achievement, a person's starting point – and the degree to which they have edged forward from that – is what matters. Perhaps, also, we are constantly being challenged to have more faith in what Vernon Watkins, in his poem 'The Broken Sea', calls 'the truth that abides in tears'. This is easy to say, though, when it's someone else's tears and not your own.

Another example of the complexity of this word 'achievement' was brought home to me recently when an old friend of mine, Jim Hodgetts, died. He and I were floor managers together at ATV in the early sixties, but he then took himself off to Paris to become a film director on the crest of the Nouvelle Vague.

I was asked by several of his friends to write an obituary. At first I felt somewhat stymied, as Jim never did become a film director, and ended up living alone in rather reduced circumstances on the edge of Madras, India being a country where he had connections and the only place where he could finally afford to live. Most obituaries celebrate achievement, and quite rightly so. But there is a particular achievement that is frequently overlooked. Most people don't become feature-film directors or famous in any other way. Yet most of us, like Jim, have to face, in varying degrees, the inevitable gap between our aspirations and what we actually achieve. And it was Jim's courage in doing just that, always with good humour and without a trace of bitterness or self-pity, which I then decided to celebrate in words and on behalf of the millions of others who do the same.

Although *The Guardian* publishes many obituaries of unknown or less well-known people, in a column entitled 'Other lives', I can understand why they never published mine of Jim – they have so many extraordinary and inspiring lives to acknowledge. But I hope that Jim was somehow aware of what I wrote. I ended with an affectionate description of an Englishman abroad, caring for a collection of stray cats, writing a book about his adopted city, craving marmite and marmalade, and going country dancing on Thursday evenings overlooking the Bay of Bengal. Long may he dance.

In the pages that follow I'm going to be writing about some pretty lofty ideas, as outlined in my preface, but throughout my life I have always tried to keep in mind the down-to-earth things that are happening every day – from the seeming humdrum to the downright tragic – in the lives and experiences of so-called ordinary people, myself included. That is why I have begun with Anne-Marie and Jim. Without bearing them and their stories in mind, much of what I explore in the pages that follow will be in constant danger of sounding like an intriguing but ultimately speculative abstraction, rather than a quest that is, I believe, highly relevant for all our lives.

In relation to this dual interest of mine, the heavenly and the earthly, the subject of biography is one that has absorbed me increasingly. I believe it offers a window into the deeper questions I am asking. When contemplating the pattern and signature of a human life as it unfolds – one's own or that of another person – how do we identify the starting point and the origin of its momentum?

A three-year-old boy I know asked his father recently 'Did you buy me?' When told that he wasn't bought, Tom then came up with another gem. 'I know how I started. I grew.' Charles Darwin couldn't have put it better. But neither Darwin nor Tom knew what he grew from. Darwin called his celebrated book *On the Origin of Species*, and not *On the Origin of Life*. Over two-and-a-half thousand years earlier the Greek philosopher Parmenides offered a clue of sorts when he said: 'Nothing comes out of nothing, and nothing becomes nothing.'

In his poem 'As kingfishers catch fire' Gerard Manley Hopkins celebrates the uniqueness of each creature, clearly implying that all of us have our own individual identity and tasks:

Each mortal thing does one thing and the same:
… *myself* it speaks and spells,
Crying *What I do is me: for that I came*.

If this is so, what are the origins and where is the source of that uniqueness to which Parmenides likewise alludes? Emerson wrote: 'Man is a stream whose source is hidden.' How hidden is that source? How unique are we, once the conditioning and the masks are stripped away?

The debate about how and why we are as we are still tends to revolve around the over-simplified question of nature versus nurture. In one camp people believe that our genetic inheritance is the all-important influence. Others attach more significance to the particular environment in which we find ourselves, and to the psychological, physical and cultural influences that surround us as we grow up. In his famously gloomy poem 'This be the Verse', Philip Larkin warns against having children at all for the simple reason that 'Man hands on misery to man'. This is certainly true in the case of Anne-Marie. But it is equally clear that some very fine gifts can also be passed on, either genetically or through imitation and example. Yet is there, perhaps, still more to this crucial question?

Thomas Weihs, a Viennese doctor who eventually came to work in Scotland with children 'in need of special care', and with whom I made several films, used to say that children not only grow up but also grow down. In other words we already have an existence and a biography before birth; and our childhood is a time when this spiritual essence unites with the body we inherit from our parents. Genetics is therefore a very important factor, as is the environment in which we grow up and also down. But if there is any reality to this process which Dr Weihs and others have described – what I think of as the third ingredient, whether one calls it soul, spirit, or something else – then any explanations about why we are as we are need to be radically altered. Psychological insight into individual human behaviour assumes a whole new dimension if you are prepared to live with the possibility that we come into life not only trailing what William Wordsworth called 'clouds of glory', but also baggage of a less glorious nature; what in the East is called karma. Another English poet, John Bunyan, hints at such a reality in the opening paragraph of *Pilgrim's Progress*: 'I dreamed, and behold I saw a man clothed with rags, standing in a certain place, with his face from his own house, a book in his hand and a great burden upon his back.' Perhaps the house to which Bunyan refers represents our 'divine origin'; while the great burden consists of the unresolved conflicts and failings accumulated on our journey through many lifetimes.

Another helpful though quite different insight into this notion of what I've called a third ingredient, in addition to inherited nature and environmental nurture, is provided by James Hillman in his book *The Soul's Code*. 'We believe', he writes, 'we come empty into this world.' He then describes Plato's concept of a daimon, a sort of companion to the soul who accompanies us through life, reminding us of who we really are, why we came to earth, what tasks we have set ourselves and what we need to learn. 'Remember who you are' was a line in the film *The Lion King* that I scribbled into my notebook some years ago.

'Man's daimon is his destiny', wrote Heraclitus in the 5th century BC. The Romans referred to this companion as a person's 'genius'. In Christianity the daimon became known as a guardian angel. The stirrings of what we call our conscience could also be seen as our interaction with our daimon; but not the conscience that is nagging us to conform to parental and social habits. In other words stop worrying about what the neighbours think. I find the word 'authentic' helpful in this respect – a concept that has its roots in the Greek notion of being author of one's own deeds. 'What does our conscience tell us?' asked Nietzsche: 'You are to become the person you really are.'

For me one of the most perceptive insights into this whole question of conscience and remembering who you are came many years ago from my daughter, Ellie, when I told her about Jacques' speech in *As You Like It*:

All the world's a stage
And all the men and women merely players:
They have their exits and their entrances;
And one man in his time plays many parts,
His acts being seven ages.

Ellie, who was ten at the time, responded by saying 'sometimes we forget our lines, and then we're horrid to people.'

Like most of us, I certainly didn't grow up automatically accepting all the thoughts and values expressed by those around me. I, too, had my inner voice. With parents divorcing when I was only eight there was plenty of conflict in the air; but strangely enough I have only magical memories of my early childhood, mostly associated with nature – a garden blessed with butterflies, our cherry orchard, and the surrounding woods and lanes, all still quiet and empty in those relatively innocent days for a child during and after World War II. Everywhere around me were the miracles we so easily take for granted – a caterpillar turning into a chrysalis and eventually becoming a butterfly, tadpoles growing into frogs, and tiny seeds producing radishes in my own little patch of garden. For a small boy these were miracles indeed.

I have vivid memories, too, of the beautiful house and garden of my grandparents – the fish in their pond, particular flowers that I loved, birds' nests that my sister and I discovered in the hedges, mushrooms we collected, haystacks we played on, and the sounds and scents of nature in spring and autumn. All these experiences gave me such joy, the intensity of which I can still experience not only as a memory but whenever I now encounter a brimstone butterfly, a goldfish, a cowslip – or when I step outdoors in the early morning.

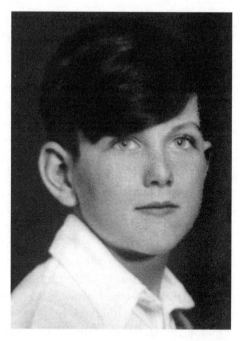

Author aged ten

I also had an imaginary friend whom I called Doyky. His existence feels so private and profound that I feel hesitant about mentioning him at all. In fact this is the first time I've ever written his name. In many ways my memory of Doyky is more vivid than of the human beings who surrounded me in my early childhood, yet his existence had and still has the quality of a dream. Nevertheless I knew exactly where he lived: in an overgrown copse beside the lane along which we went for walks. Doyky felt sacred – far more so than the church and Sunday School I attended. I suppose like many children I was, at heart, a pagan, and in many ways have remained so. Doyky was as magical as the nature that surrounded him.

Yet why do I remember so clearly these enchanted aspects of my childhood and not the trauma of being separated from my mother for much of three years while she recovered from tuberculosis, and then struggled to establish a new home for us? Is it simply temperament? If so, what is temperament? Perhaps, unlike Anne-Marie, I wasn't so deeply wounded because I knew that my sister and brother and I hadn't really been abandoned and were still loved – and loved each other. Children, I'm sure, sense very clearly the reality of a situation. They know the truth of things.

Nevertheless I imagine that some of those negative influences – even if not consciously remembered – have not disappeared entirely. Only to a certain extent can we pick and chose what sticks to us, depending, I suppose, on our own inherent character and sense of purpose. And perhaps my experiences in childhood were not mere chance, but willed by a wiser part of my being in order to learn what I needed to learn.

'Each of our souls', writes Hillman in elaborating on Platonic philosophy, 'is guided by a daimon to that particular body and place, these parents and circumstances, by Necessity – and none of us has an inkling of this because it was eradicated on the plains of forgetting.' It's a beautiful phrase – 'on the plains of forgetting' – reminiscent of Wordsworth's line: 'Our birth is but a sleep and a forgetting.'

I have, in fact, become increasingly convinced that we need to forget, or rather are ill-equipped to remember, the underlying transcendental dimension of existence in order to develop new faculties and arrive at new insights through our own efforts. Forgetting is not just having a bad memory. It is, perhaps, a meaningful phase in our evolution.

For me a revealing example of this 'forgetting' was a powerful experience I had as a boy when I was given gas for a tooth extraction. I remember very well the moment leading up to the experience – moving away from the earth and out into space; and then came an illumination of great profundity, but it was a truth that I was unable to retain consciously. Yet I knew for certain that a revelation had occurred. Perhaps I have been nourished by it ever since, despite having no specific memory of it.

A different but equally profound insight into the mysterious process of forgetting is tucked away in the pages of that beautifully written book *The Wind in the Willows* by Kenneth Grahame. In the chapter entitled 'The Piper at the Gates of Dawn', Mole and Ratty, rowing in their boat early one morning, have had an overwhelming experience of the god Pan:

> As they stared blankly, in dumb misery deepening as they slowly realised all they had seen and all they had lost, a capricious little breeze, dancing up from the surface of the water, tossed the aspens, shook the dewy roses, and blew lightly and caressingly in their faces, and with its soft touch came instant oblivion. For this is the last best gift that the kindly demigod is careful to bestow on those to whom he has revealed himself in their helping: the gift of forgetfulness. Lest the awful remembrance should remain and grow, and overshadow mirth and pleasure, and the great haunting memory should spoil all the after-lives of little animals helped out of difficulties, in order that they should be happy and light hearted as before.

This gift of forgetfulness is indeed precious, for it allows you to remember consciously only what you can make conscious use or sense of, and therefore what is helpful in the process of becoming 'the person you really are'. But to be truly 'happy and light hearted' as human beings we cannot just stay asleep. We do, I suspect, gradually have to wake up, and try to remember more.

What I call my 'awakeners' are a crucial element in the journey I want to describe – a quest to try and understand the relationship between what we call heaven and earth. These awakeners can appear throughout one's life and are, I believe, intimately connected with the notion of a daimon and with the law of karma. One's early awakeners also seem to belong to what Thomas Weihs called our 'growing down'.

During the latter part of my childhood my mother became interested and involved in spiritualism. It was not a trivial interest, and the small gatherings in our home were conducted with the reverence and solemnity of a religious service. We three children were included, but there was no compulsion. It is significant, I feel, that none of us dismissed it as nonsense. After my intimate and inspiring experiences of nature, spiritualism became another great awakener and gave me, at an important stage of my development, a strong sense that there is more to life than meets the eye. It is an awareness that I have carried with me very strongly ever since.

The actual messages from what spiritualists call 'the other side' were, as I remember them, benign but lacking in any great profundity. The dead were alive and well, and seemingly living in a heavenly equivalent of a cosy town like Tunbridge Wells. Largely through something called a ouija board these communications gave no real insight into what a purely spiritual existence might be like. That, anyway, is my memory. For someone asking serious questions about the nature of reality, as I was gradually beginning to do, spiritualism became ever more unsatisfactory.

The best joke I've come across in relation to spiritualism, and indeed to the controversial subject of reincarnation – and I'm always on the lookout for jokes that help undermine our spiritual follies and pretensions – is told by Philip Toynbee in *Part of a Journey*, his wonderfully honest autobiography:

> Wife, in touch with dead husband through medium: 'Well, dear, what do you do over there?' 'Oh, we run about a bit; then we eat a bit; then we have a bit of sex; then we run about a bit again; have a bit more to eat, and a bit more sex … ' Wife: 'Goodness. I never knew heaven was like that.' Husband: 'Oh, I'm not in heaven. I'm a rabbit in Australia.'

Practices like spiritualism are, it seems to me, an example of our attempt to drag profound matters down to our level rather that developing our latent capacities for new forms of perception and experience. Physical proof of a purely spiritual dimension of existence is a contradiction in terms. In 'The Everlasting Gospel', the visionary poet and artist William Blake describes our challenge as seeing beyond physical things:

> This life's dim windows of the soul
> Distorts the heavens from pole to pole
> And leads you to believe a lie
> When you see with, not through, the eye.

This capacity or faculty that Blake points to requires much hard work. Our Home Circle, as it was called, was comforting – particularly for my mother and her two friends, all of whom knew people who had died, some tragically young – but it was in no way challenging, either morally or intellectually.

It is interesting to reflect that spiritualism arose during the 19th century, parallel to the early development of the telecommunications industry. By mid-century, sixty per cent of Americans claimed spiritualism as their religion. As the telegraph started to tap away, so too, it seems, did the spirits. In our gatherings, table-tapping was the other form of communication – one tap for A, two for B and so on. Given that somebody in New York could suddenly and miraculously speak to someone in London, it is perhaps not surprising that some people thought contact between the living and the dead a relatively straightforward possibility. It reminds me of the prophetic remark by that American free spirit, Henry Thoreau, who, when told it was now possible for someone in Texas to speak to someone in England, asked what would happen if they had nothing to say to each other!

Despite my reservations, however, I do think the whole phenomenon of spiritualism warrants more serious investigation and should not be dismissed because of the many instances of fraud. None of us in that little Buckinghamshire sitting room were fooling each other, making money or playing tricks, and that table certainly tipped and tapped without our assistance. If it wasn't the spirit of a Red Indian guide called Morning Cloud, or my grandmother assuring us that she was well and at peace, then who or what was it?

During his university years as a medical student in Basel, the pioneer psychiatrist Carl Gustav Jung was amazed that the academic community refused to even acknowledge, let alone study, psychic phenomena with which he, as a young man from the countryside, was very familiar. Peasants had known about and accepted these occurrences for hundreds, if not thousands of years – not out of ignorance but from experience.

In the early years of the 20th century a number of eminent and open-minded people such as the psychologist William James, writer Conan Doyle and physicist Oliver Lodge did attempt a serious investigation of psychic phenomena. In our own time the biologist Rupert Sheldrake has also made a number of studies of telepathic communications between people, and between people and animals. Among other things, Sheldrake's work raises questions about where and what is this 'other side' that spiritualists speak about. Where are the boundaries, or are there potentially none at all?

Despite this seeming transparency, however, the general blandness of the messages we received in our Home Circle and at the local Spiritualist Church – a blandness that I have also observed more recently in tapes that I've watched of channelling, when so-called higher entities speak through people in a trance-like state – all prompt me to suspect that the origins of these communications are often more human, or even sub-human, than celestial.

This conclusion leaves me asking why wiser souls, or even angelic beings, don't tap us out their wisdom across the threshold we call death? Or do they, but in much subtler ways, providing we are open enough to listen? We spend nearly a third of our lives asleep. Is that period really so blank and void as it seems to our conscious minds?

My early contact with spiritualism did prevent me from going ahead with what, at my Public School, was the almost automatic procedure of Confirmation around the age of fourteen. I liked and respected the Chaplain, Philip Bryant, very much, but he was unable to provide a rather naïve but sincere schoolboy with any satisfying link between the Christian dogma we were meant to absorb, on the one hand, and my experiences of spiritualism on the other. The so-called Divinity lessons were somewhat more interesting. A young and enthusiastic master, Raymond Venables, varied our studies of the Old and New Testaments with a book called *Moral Problems*. At that time it was a bold and radical initiative, particularly in a very traditional school like Harrow. I don't remember what the moral problems actually were, but I am sure I'm still wrestling with them. I also studied French literature under Venables. The questions he asked us to consider in all these lessons certainly stirred in me an interest in human relationships.

Another great awakener for me was something seemingly very different. I read a biography of Leo Tolstoy by an American called Ernest J. Simmons. Aged twenty, in an effort to better educate myself, I had asked my mother to bring me back *War and Peace* from the library. Somebody else had taken it out, but not the biography. One interesting aspect of such awakeners, whether it be a book, an encounter, music or a painting, is the experience you have of recognition, of familiarity. It is almost as though you know the place, the person, the insight already. In that sense I would describe it as a form of homecoming.

What touched me particularly on first reading this biography was Tolstoy's fascination as a child with something called 'The Green Stick'. His elder brother, Nikolai, had told him that a green stick was buried in the forest near their home and that on it was carved a secret which, when known to mankind, would bring about a Golden Age on earth. Then all human misery and evil would vanish, said Nikolai, 'and everyone under the wide dome of heaven would be happy and love one another.'

When he was an old man Tolstoy wrote in his *Recollections*:

As I then believed that there was a little green stick whereon was written something that would destroy all evil in men and give them great blessings, so I now believe that such truth exists among people and will be revealed to them and will give them what it promises.

Leo Tolstoy in old age

At his own request Tolstoy was buried 'at the place of the green stick'. Some ten years after reading the biography I was filming that grave at his family estate, Yasnaya Polyana, deep in the Russian countryside, for a programme I made about Tolstoy's life.

Returning to Simmons' biography all these years later I can see why, as someone already starting to ask serious questions about life, I was so attracted to the book. Some of the chapter headings alone – 'My hero is truth', 'Spirit versus matter', 'Life is beyond space and time', 'To seek, always to seek' – were clear signposts for the journey I had embarked on in becoming a documentary film-maker.

Reading about Tolstoy's life also stimulated my own idealism and encouraged me to hold onto my youthful belief that the world itself could be a better and happier place. Like Tolstoy I have not lost faith in that dream. I also felt inspired to go on asking the questions stirring so strongly within me, not just questions about immortality, but about the nature and potential of human life on earth, and our problems in living up to that potential.

In one of his many moments of self-loathing Tolstoy wrote in his diary: 'I cannot get away from myself.' For me such a statement reveals a very profound insight of which we are barely conscious but which is echoed again and again in our daily speech. When I say, for example, that I am ashamed of myself, I am acknowledging that I am in fact two people.

It is an observation that seems to me clearly though paradoxically confirmed in the work of the behaviourist B.F. Skinner, whose book *Beyond Freedom and Dignity* I read around this time. Skinner made a study of pigeon behaviour in particular, and his experiments with punishment and reward convinced him that human beings behave in much the same way: we are really no different from birds, rats, and the like. What he fails to acknowledge is that by making this observation he is actually transcending the very behaviour he has quite rightly recognised. We may indeed often behave like Skinner's pigeons in our daily lives, but as soon as we are capable of even a modicum of self-knowledge we are no longer merely a pigeon – even if we go on behaving as such, jumping through all sorts of absurd hoops for the sake of some juicy reward. Our recognition of the situation is a first step; to do something about it clearly involves a great many more.

In his book *The Divided Self*, the psychiatrist R.D. Laing suggests that insanity – in particular schizophrenia – is not a medical disease but the result of a person struggling with two separate identities: the one defined by family, culture and so on, and the other by the experience we all have of being uniquely ourselves.

'The poet takes the best out of his life and puts it into his writings', Tolstoy once declared, 'which is the reason his writing is beautiful and his life bad.' The best in each of us, be it only potential, resides perhaps in this capacity for self-reflection. Like Tolstoy we are never quite at peace with the way we live our daily lives. We cannot seem to get away from ourselves, as Tolstoy experienced so powerfully; but we can undertake the long, slow struggle to transform that self – a task I can imagine taking many lifetimes – so that we are no longer in such conflict with our conscience.

Tolstoy lurched from crisis to crisis throughout his life. Aged thirty-nine he wrote to a friend: 'I have loved truth more than anything; I do not despair of finding it, and I am still searching and searching.' The riddle of existence haunted him; and the question that brought him to the verge of suicide some ten years later was, writes Simmons, 'the simplest of questions lying in the soul of every man: Why should I live, why wish for anything or do anything? In short, has life any meaning that the inevitable death awaiting one does not destroy?'

This, of course, is one of the key questions underlying this book. My early ponderings and dilemmas were enormously enriched by Tolstoy's lonely and courageous quest, and by the honesty with which he confronted the world around him and his own complex make-up. His moral dualism, suggests his biographer, was the conflict of all mankind: a struggle between conscience and appetites. As a young army cadet in the Caucasus Tolstoy wrote, ' ... the voice of conscience is what distinguishes good from evil'. This conscience of his was to lead him into a lifetime of conflicts – with his wife, who could never share his extreme and at times utopian idealism; with the Orthodox Church, and with the whole apparatus of government; and finally with his own inherited wealth and privileged life.

Yet in his final dramatic act of protest at the age of eighty-two, when accompanied by his doctor he fled his home and family to live as a peasant, there is in this almost absurd and futile gesture a redemptive triumph. On October 28th 1910 he wrote in his diary, on the train journey that was to be his last, that he had no doubt he had done what he had to do: 'Perhaps I am mistaken and am merely justifying my actions. But it seems to me that I have saved myself – not Leo Nikolayevich, but something of which there is still a bit left in me.'

There is another extract from his diary, written a few years earlier, that stands out for me as powerfully as it did all those years ago, and that is profoundly relevant for all our journeys, inner and outer; for it gives very beautiful expression to the notion that what matters is our life in the here and now, whatever views we might have about eternity and life after death. 'No, this world is not a joke', he wrote, 'and not a vale of trials or a transition to a better, everlasting world, but this world here is one of the eternal worlds that is beautiful, joyous, which we can and must make more beautiful and more joyous for those living with us and for those who will live in it after us.'

CHAPTER 2

Quest and Questions

When I showed my brother David a first draft of this book he told me it conjured up for him the image of a sturdy old galleon returning from a very long and interesting journey around the world and laden with treasure – but with its hull encrusted with barnacles! The implication being that the book needed editing. Since then I have been scraping away, but it's not always easy to know what will be interesting for others – one person's barnacle may be another person's treasure.

My intention was to write very little about myself, but rather to describe the people and ideas that have helped me in my search for the answer to the question 'Where on Earth is Heaven?' Other people, however, on reading my first draft, asked for more about me. What was I feeling and thinking along the way? They wanted more of my reactions to those treasures in my hold. And so this deep interest of mine in biography that I have already declared will extend into moments from my own bumpy journey – the downs as well as the ups.

By the time I was twenty-one I was a few steps up the ladder to becoming a film-maker, working as an assistant film editor at Pinewood studios. I had already worked as a stage manager in a repertory theatre in Croydon, and then managed to get the all-important union card (which the film industry required in those days) by working in a film laboratory as a lowly technician. It wasn't an easy journey; there was no prescribed route to becoming a film director, nor is there still. At that laboratory in Soho Square in London I had to wear a white coat. At lunch time I would go out to buy my sandwiches still wearing my 'uniform'; and in those moments when I felt I was getting nowhere, I would pretend to myself that I was a medical student. At another low point I explored the possibility of going to live for a while on a Kibbutz in Israel. Then, that same summer, I responded to an advertisement for an overland trip to India, which at that time was a very bold and new type of adventure. In the end my determination to work with film kept me at home – a decision that paradoxically paved the way for the many journeys that lay ahead.

In those days it was still the cinema that attracted me, in particular the work of French directors such as Francois Truffaut, and the Swedish director Ingmar Bergman. I loved Bergman's masterpiece *Wild Strawberries*, in which an old man makes a journey across Sweden to receive an honorary degree, and on the way stops off at various places connected with his life. In some of these scenes he is a silent spectator as the events of long ago unfold once again before his eyes. Later I was to become interested in the idea that after death we relive our past life just like Bergman's old professor, only this time from the receiving end, as it were; according to some, we journey through the same events, the same encounters and relationships, but now experience each moment from the other person's point of view, and thus all the joy and all the pain we brought to others.

It was exciting to be at Pinewood, though the films being made there at the end of the fifties were nothing like the ones from Sweden, France and Italy that had so touched me. Apart from one other young assistant film editor, most of the people working at the studios didn't seem to share my particular interests. He and I were nicknamed Sight and Sound, after the highbrow film magazine produced by the British Film Institute.

Nevertheless, several important things happened to me during my time at Pinewood. The most difficult to convey, because it can easily sound somewhat crazy, was a dialogue I started to have with myself as I walked at lunchtime in the beautiful grounds surrounding the studios. Despite the fact that this dialogue was usually conducted out loud, I don't remember thinking that my lunch time ritual was in any way strange.

Looking back on that episode now I realise that it was probably deeply connected with this sense that each of us is, in fact, two people. I talked to myself. About what, I have no memory; but I know it was serious and that it revolved around the question of what my life was to be about, and the mystery of existence altogether.

During this time I had several conversations with one of the film editors, Gerry Hambling, about a Rudolf Steiner School his children were attending at Kings Langley in Hertfordshire. I don't remember having a particular interest in education in those days, but obviously something in me was sufficiently stirred for him to lend me a booklet by a man called Francis Edmunds outlining Rudolf Steiner's educational ideas. Later I realised that a few months previously someone had lent me a book of lectures by Steiner called *Theosophy of the Rosicrucians* which I only read much later on. Clearly, the work of this Austrian educationalist and philosopher (1861–1925), who once described his life's work as awakening the spiritual in the human being to the spiritual in the universe, was knocking at my door.

In the introduction to his booklet, Francis Edmunds writes of Steiner as 'someone making a direct appeal for a greater effort of consciousness in contemplating the world'. Although thoroughly grounded in the science of his time, that 'world' for Steiner was not just all the solid bits, along with the sounds and smells we experience through our five senses, but also what he referred to as invisible and dynamic realities that permeate our surroundings and indeed each one of us. This insight and experience was one he shared with other esotericists of the 19th and 20th centuries, such as Madame Blavatsky and some of the theosophists who came in her wake, as well as her fellow Russian, P.D. Ouspensky. This other layer of existence is not, as I understand it, somewhere else – Ouspensky called it the Fourth Dimension. Steiner frequently uses the expression *geistige Welt*, translated as 'spiritual world', which for me is somewhat unhelpful since it tends to imply, in English at least, not only some other location but also somewhere essentially holy, in the religious sense. In the pages that follow I shall be writing as much about *this* world as I do about the so-called spiritual world because I have come to believe that in essence they are one.

In fact the German word *Geist*, as well as meaning 'spirit', can also be translated as 'mind'. In English we come closer to this definition in phrases like 'I shall be with you in spirit'. We also speak about entering into the spirit of things, and about the spirit of the law; for however sceptical many of us might have become about religion in all its manifestations, our sense of the transcendent is far from dead, and our everyday language reveals this constantly. We talk, too, about the spirit of the age – even the *Zeitgeist* – or the spirit of a place, without thinking twice. Neither thought implies something strange or surreal. Rather, it seems, these phrases embody our instinctive but subconscious recognition that life is indeed many-layered.

For Jung the word 'numinous' was helpful in this debate, for it was free of the clutter associated with religion, yet for him conveyed 'the feeling that one is encountering a dimension which is sacred, holy and radically different from everyday life, and which belongs to a superior order of reality.' The Indian sage, Sri Aurobindo, once said: 'If you are embarrassed by the word "spirit", think of spirit as the subtlest form of matter. But, if you are embarrassed by the word "matter", you can think of matter as the densest form of spirit.' In other words matter and spirit are essentially interwoven, which may offer a clue to understanding what we experience as consciousness; and it is the mystery of consciousness that I shall be exploring as I approach, from many different angles, this question of the meaning and whereabouts of heaven.

One of the most interesting books that I subsequently read on this whole subject is *The Secret History of Consciousness* by Gary Lachman. In it he points out that, over the last four centuries, science has increasingly tried to account for everything – including more recently our own inner worlds – in terms of atoms and molecules and the physical laws they obey. Another approach, which interested not only pioneers like Steiner, but also more mainstream figures such as the French philosopher Henri Bergson, the psychologist William James and the Swiss philosopher Jean Gebser, is to invert the relationship and see consciousness not as the result of neurons and molecules, but as responsible for them.

Lachman writes in great detail and from various perspectives about the notion of 'cosmic consciousness', a phrase that first appeared in 1901 as the title of a book by an American doctor called Richard Maurice Bucke, a close friend and disciple of the poet Walt Whitman. The phrase was prompted by a sudden and overwhelming experience late one evening during a visit to London – 'an intellectual illumination quite impossible to describe'. Bucke wrote his account in the third person:

> All at once, without warning of any kind, he found himself wrapped around, as it were, by a flame-coloured cloud. For an instant he thought of fire – some sudden conflagration in the great city. The next instant he knew that the light was within himself ... he saw and knew that the cosmos is not dead matter but a living Presence, that the soul of man is immortal ...

Such spontaneous illuminations are increasingly experienced, particularly by people undergoing some traumatic moment in their lives like a near-death experience. Steiner, as far as I know, is unique in pointing to ways in which it is possible, after much hard work, to achieve these revelations in full consciousness and at will. Francis Edmunds, in his introduction to Steiner's educational ideas, wrote of 'a progressive training towards the enhancement of thought itself so that it may reach out beyond the accepted limits of cognition.' This may all sound somewhat austere and cerebral, but what I did grasp all those years ago and what has increasingly interested me ever since is this recognition of our potential as human beings to know and experience more – above all in realms that were traditionally the preserve of initiates alone, and then usually in trance-like states. Such teachings are, of course, in direct opposition to Immanuel Kant's hugely influential utterances on the limits to human knowledge; though at that stage of my journey I had barely heard of Kant.

Central to Steiner's teaching on the subject of epistemology – the study of how we know what we know – is the notion of the evolution of consciousness. What we grasp clearly today and how we think about ourselves and the world around us is very different from a hundred, five hundred or five thousand years ago – different, and not always wiser. This theme, human consciousness in constant transition, is one which Owen Barfield explores with great insight in his book *Saving the Appearances*. In his massive work *The Ever-Present Origin*, Jean Gebser shares this view, believing we live in a period between two worlds, one dead and one trying to be born.

In trying to convey the changes that take place as human consciousness evolves, my Austrian friend Thomas Weihs used to evoke in his public lectures the image of early man alone at night with a candle in a huge dark forest. His overwhelming experience was of the forest surrounding him. Nowadays, so Weihs suggested, each one of us is equipped with a powerful beam of light which, wherever we point it, illuminates the details of the world with a sharp, clear focus. But by doing so we have lost all sense of the forest. 'Not seeing the wood for the trees' is an everyday expression that reveals our recognition of the same danger. The word 'blinkered' is also helpful in this respect because blinkers don't blind a horse, but simply ensure that it only looks in one direction and is not distracted by other stimuli. Consciousness has even been compared to a prison. When the sun shines we don't see the stars.

If there is any truth to this idea of an evolving consciousness and the notion that we have latent and as yet undeveloped faculties to see not just with, but through the eye, as William Blake suggested, then clearly it is very short-sighted and even arrogant to assume that evolution has come to a halt with us, either during the last years of the 18th century when Kant was alive or in our own time, at the start of the 21st century; arrogant, too, to assume there is nothing more evolved than us in the universe at large.

Reflecting on Bucke's illumination over a hundred years ago, Gary Lachman writes: 'Nowadays Bucke's experience would be chalked up to the brain's reported "God spot" or, less generously, to temporal lobe epilepsy. For Bucke it was the first glimpse of the future of humanity.'

Weihs's message, in that image of our ancestor armed only with a candle, was not that we should extinguish the powerful beam of light now available to us, but should try to bring the same clarity and insight we have about all the solid realities that surround us, to a rediscovery and contemplation of the whole, of the forest, and thus of the 'new world' that Gebser sensed was trying to be born. It is a task beautifully summed up in T.S. Eliot's much quoted lines from 'Little Gidding':

> We shall not cease from exploration
> And the end of all our exploring
> Will be to arrive where we started
> And know the place for the first time.

As a result of reading Edmunds' booklet on Steiner education, I visited one of the schools, in Sussex, in the autumn of 1959. It was a crucial decision in terms of the quest I had already begun, and through the encounters that followed there awoke in me what I can only describe as a recognition of how that quest might unfold. Meanwhile I was immediately impressed by the relaxed and friendly atmosphere at Michael Hall School. It was co-educational and non-streamed long before comprehensive schools came into existence. Each class was regarded as a little society in miniature, where everyone, whatever their strengths and weaknesses, was seen to have something to contribute.

What also struck me very favourably on that first visit to a Steiner school was that art was not just a separate and somewhat marginal subject, but permeated the whole curriculum. The children created their own textbooks, and in science, for example, these books contained not only all the facts and figures you would expect, but also beautiful drawings and diagrams of the human heart and lungs, a flower, the belly of a whale, a Greek temple and a volcano. Those are the images I still remember from that visit long ago. One of the teachers at the school, Christopher Mann, invited me to return, and through him, his family and his colleagues, I became increasingly interested in Steiner's work generally.

Three years after reading his booklet I was to meet Francis Edmunds himself. It was one of the most decisive encounters of my early adult life and led me along all sorts of helpful paths in my search for a better understanding of these riddles and mysteries that confront us. Edmunds was one of the pioneer teachers at the first Rudolf Steiner School in Britain, founded in 1925. This world-wide educational movement started in 1919 in Stuttgart, where the owner of the Waldorf cigarette factory, Emil Molt, asked Steiner to help found a school that would give the children of his factory workers a really meaningful and inspiring education. The term Waldorf School originates from this early initiative. Steiner developed the fundamentals of the curriculum and worked closely with the pioneer teachers.

Another aspect of the curriculum that I remember interesting me was the notion that the growing child's development recapitulates the whole cultural evolution of humanity. History in Steiner Waldorf schools is therefore taught chronologically, with an understanding for the natural affinity that children feel for the period of history that corresponds to their own stage of development. Myths and fairy stories inspire and nourish young children as they did our distant ancestors. Pupils will learn to build and create in the same way and in the same sequence that these skills unfolded in human history.

Puberty, so Edmunds suggests, can be compared historically to the passage from the Middle Ages into modern times:

> ... an entry into a totally new relationship with the world ... for the first time life becomes a personal affair, an individual questioning of existence in all things big and small ... The wish arises to make one's life one's own ... to question all things: oneself, the world, authority of parent and teacher ... It is a moment of release; yet it brings with it added loneliness.

The theory is that by the time they leave school, pupils can step into today's world having lived through and experienced, as well as studied, the journey that has made this world as it is, for better and for worse. In growing up they have also grown down – have 'fully incarnated', as some describe it. The evolution of consciousness can thus continue with a clearer awareness of what has so far formed it.

Theories are, of course, easier than practice. I have more to relate about Waldorf education and about Steiner himself, but at this stage I will only add that although I continue to take a great interest in this form of education I have a number of reservations, some of which are based on my own subsequent experience as a parent at a Steiner school.

Around this time I started to read the novels of Charles Morgan, a writer who seems almost forgotten these days – though not in France, which he knew well and where some of his stories are set; in fact it was a French friend who told me about his work. The novel I remember particularly well is called *The Riverline*, which Morgan subsequently rewrote as a play, and which is largely set in France during World War II. 'The Riverline' was the code name for an organisation run by the Belgians and the French to help British and American airmen who had been shot down in enemy-occupied territory to get home. They were passed through a series of safe houses into Spain, and for security reasons a strict set of rules was imposed on all those involved. One of these rules was that nothing written should be kept or carried by any of the airmen. One of the main characters, an enigmatic and mysterious officer called Heron, writes a poem which has to be completely destroyed almost immediately because of an imminent raid by the Germans. Later one of his companions asks him what the point was of writing a poem now lost and forgotten. 'I haven't the least desire', says Heron, 'to keep it or anything. It makes no difference what you keep. The thing was there before you had it and is still there when it seems to have gone.' Loss without losing becomes a crucial theme in the story that unfolds; it is a wonderful and profound piece of writing, like so much of Charles Morgan's work, and relates very closely to one of the major themes of this book – the apparent loss and separation when someone dies.

Another inspiration during my time at Pinewood was seeing Arnold Wesker's play *Roots* performed at The Royal Court Theatre in London. I write about it now because its central message strongly relates to the line 'What I do is me, for that I came' in Hopkins's poem. In *Roots* a young girl called Beatie returns for a visit to her Norfolk farming family from whom she has grown apart. She has been studying in London and is full of the ideas and passions of her socialist boyfriend Ronnie whom she quotes endlessly. But because they are not her ideas they carry no real power or conviction. Meanwhile she no longer shares the values and the interests of her family. She has lost her roots but not yet found her own voice, only Ronnie's. After two fractious weeks the whole family assemble to meet him.

As so often happens in life, it is tragedy that wakes her up. A letter arrives from Ronnie saying he doesn't think their relationship will work. Beatie is suddenly on her own, with no Ronnie behind her. But in that moment, instead of collapsing, she speaks for herself. She finds her tongue, as we say. This magnificent soliloquy at the end of the play, first performed by Joan Plowright, is above all a celebration of the birth of the individual. Like the kingfisher in Hopkins poem, she is unique – 'What I do is me.' She has discovered her identity. 'Listen to me someone', she cries out, 'God in heaven, Ronnie! It does work, it's happening to me, I can feel it's happened, I'm beginning, on my own two feet – I'm beginning ...'

In recalling these various beacons that I remember from my early twenties it seems as though each one of us, at that period of our lives in particular, is looking, sometimes unwittingly, for support and confirmation of what already lives strongly just below the surface of our conscious existence. I have already used the word 'awakener', which is another way of trying to describe this mysterious process of discovering our tasks and indeed our destiny; during these years, especially, we often meet the people who will inspire and help us along the way. It was certainly true in my case. You could call them my gurus, and I meet them still. And they are not only old men with long white beards. Years later, while filming in California for the television series *The Long Search*, the American writer and philosopher Jacob Needleman suggested to us that a true guru is not someone who dishes out answers, but rather someone who deepens your questions. It is an insight that I have never forgotten, though I am also secretly in sympathy with that taxi-driver who, on recognising Bertrand Russell settling into the back of his cab, is said to have asked: 'So, Guv – what's it all about then?'

John Betjeman, whom I was soon to meet, was a good example of a wise and undogmatic human being who, although he had strong views on subjects like architecture and poetry, was reluctant to hold forth on deeper issues and on 'what's it all about'. He distrusted certainty to his very fingertips, and because of his openness and vulnerability he was able, I believe, to record his intimations in a number of profound yet deceptively simple poems, as well as on film.

As I touched on in Chapter One, this whole process of finding and recognising signposts for one's life can be experienced as a kind of remembering; and certainly some of the ideas we encounter can seem very familiar, hence their attraction. Plato said that all learning is a process of remembering. Yet, when it comes to understanding and knowledge, I am tempted to ask why, if we know something already, do we have to go through it all again? I am more drawn to the idea that these awakeners are premonitions of what we have yet to learn.

Another book that attracted my attention at this time was *The Phenomenon of Man* by the Jesuit biologist and palaeontologist Pierre Teilhard de Chardin

Pierre Teilhard de Chardin

(1881–1955). It's interesting for me to see the passages that I marked then, and the fact that it is these same passages that resonate for me still.

Teilhard, who spent many years in China on scientific research, devoted his whole life to forging a philosophy that would relate the facts of religious experience to those of natural science, and in particular that would reconcile his deep spiritual faith with the scientific theory of evolution. *The Phenomenon of Man* only became available after Teilhard's death, as the Roman Catholic Church had been seriously concerned by many of the implications in his writings and vetoed their publication. He referred to evolution as 'a light illuminating all facts'.

Teilhard agreed with Friedrich Nietzsche, whose tragic but courageous life deeply touched the young Rudolf Steiner, that the human being is 'unfinished'. He also believed that the brain alone is not responsible for mind; and like Jung, about whom I am soon to write, he attached great importance and significance to our potential for conscious participation in the whole evolutionary process. In his foreword to *The Phenomenon of Man*, Teilhard writes about the significance of vision in this respect, and of our visionary potential: '… the history of the living world can be summarised as the elaboration of ever more perfect eyes within a cosmos in which there is always something more to be seen.'

In her book *Towards a New Mysticism*, subtitled *Teilhard de Chardin and Eastern Religions*, the theologian Ursula King writes: 'Science, religion, and mysticism are part of one and the same longing in the hearts and minds of men. To see this, Teilhard felt, it is necessary to break the boundaries of a narrowly understood science and remove the fetters of outworn creeds.' The passage in *The Phenomenon of Man* that has my heaviest lines beside it, little faded after forty-five years, reads:

> In its early, naïve stage, science, perhaps inevitably, imagined that we could observe things in themselves, as they would behave in our absence. Instinctively physicists and naturalists went to work as though they could look down from a great height upon a world which their consciousness could penetrate without being submitted to it or changing it. They are now beginning to realise that even the most objective of their observations are steeped in the conventions they adopted at the outset and by forms or habits of thought developed in the course of their research; so that, when they reach the end of their analyses, they cannot tell with any certainty whether the structure they have made is the essence of the matter they are studying, or the reflection of their own thought … object and subject marry and mutually transform each other in the act of knowledge; and from now on man willy-nilly finds his own image stamped on all he looks at.

In other words, our ideas and theories about everything – including such sublime subjects as the Divinity itself – probably tell us as much, if not more, about ourselves as they do about whatever we are contemplating. It is this realisation that must have prompted the physicist Werner Heisenberg to write in *Physics and Philosophy*: 'Natural science does not simply describe and explain nature; it is a part of the interplay between nature and ourselves; it describes nature as exposed to our method of questioning.'

I wasn't, however, just reading difficult books in these years. My love affair with the cinema continued and I also started to take a serious interest in television, especially in documentaries. Here, perhaps, was a chance to combine my love of films with my growing interest in philosophical and spiritual questions. I remember being particularly struck by an interview with the German psychoanalyst and writer Erich Fromm. At one point in the conversation he paid tribute to the pioneering work of Sigmund Freud and in particular to Freud's observations of people's tendency to repress their sexual fantasies and emotions. Fromm went on to imply that there was now a far more open and healthy attitude to such matters. The interviewer then asked him what he thought people repress today. There was one of those wonderful pauses when you sense that the person is really thinking and not just trotting out their often repeated opinions. A truly creative encounter was taking place between two people and we, the audience, were privileged to eavesdrop on the process. For me this was television at its most exciting. 'Their sense of the truth', was Fromm's eventual reply. I have never forgotten those words and the profundity of his insight. We repress our sense of the truth. On another occasion Fromm expressed much the same thought when he wrote that the heart knows more than the head admits. These observations do, of course, relate to the idea of a daimon and to that inner voice which I read about much later in James Hillman's book *The Soul's Code*.

A similar point was made by the hugely influential Dr. Spock whose book on the bringing up of children became a bible for many mothers in the years after World War II, especially in America. Then came his renunciation, not because he had changed his mind but rather because he felt there was an increasingly unhealthy dependency on his theories and insights, and not enough trust in our own instincts as parents. Once again, his message was: 'We are wiser than we know'. By all means read Spock or whoever helps you along the way, but in the end do what you instinctively feel is right, irrespective of what the experts say. All such teachers or gurus face this challenge: how to impart what you feel inspired and even obliged to communicate, without creating dependency.

And the challenge to us, the pupils of these teachers, is beautifully summed up by the 19th-century poet Robert Browning in his poem 'Paracelsus':

Truth is within ourselves; it takes no rise
From outward things, what'er you may believe.
There is an inmost center in us all,
Where truth abides in fullness; and around,
Wall upon wall, the gross flesh hems it in,
This perfect, clear perception – which is truth;
A baffling and perverting carnal mesh
Binds it, and makes all error: and, to KNOW,
Rather consists in opening out a way
When the imprisoned splendour may escape,
Than in effecting entry for a light
Supposed to be without.

Another encounter on television that I remember well at this time was John Freeman's interview with Jung for the series *Face to Face*. Particularly relevant in terms of this quest of mine was something Jung said about death. Freeman reminded Jung about his assertion that death is psychologically as important as birth and that like birth is an integral part of life. He then asked Jung how death can be compared to birth if death is an end. 'Yes, if it's an end,' replied Jung, 'and there we are not quite certain about this end.' Jung went on to describe the peculiar and well documented faculties of the psyche to have dreams and visions of the future –' to see round corners'. The psyche or soul is not, according to Jung, entirely confined by time and space. 'Only ignorance denies these facts', he asserted. The implication for Jung is a continuation of a psychical existence beyond time and space, beyond death.

Freeman then asked Jung what advice he would give people in later life, many of whom believe that death is an end. 'I've treated many old people', Jung replied, 'and it's quite interesting to watch and to see what the unconscious does when apparently threatened with a complete end. It disregards it. Life behaves as if it's going on forever'. Jung's advice to old people was to look forward to the next day as though they would live for centuries. 'Then they live properly', he said. I have never thought that Jung was suggesting we should pretend this inevitable deterioration and death of the physical body is not happening; but rather that we should trust the inner voice which disregards the notion of an end. As Woody Allen said: 'I'm not frightened of death. I just don't want to be there when it happens!'

My own 'inner voice' was certainly starting to make itself heard in my early twenties. The people, books, films and ideas that were coming towards me, or that I was hunting out, were all, in their different ways, presenting me with what I have called my 'awakeners'. And like most young people I too felt that life was going on forever; and it was my experience of life, in all its wonderful variety and complexity, that was starting to inspire my own creativity.

CHAPTER 3

Take One

In my search for an understanding of what might lie beyond the threshold we call death, my contact with art and with artists has often been as helpful as the rummaging about that I've done into philosophy, science and theology. Literature, paintings, and the cinema in particular, have long inspired me and helped to deepen my questions. I have always liked the word 'intimation' and all that it evokes. I feel drawn to statements that are tentative and modest, and I identify with Nietzsche's description of himself as 'a lonely ponderer and friend of riddles'. Poems, paintings and music are on the whole undogmatic; they depend for their existence on inspiration. In the wise and entertaining stories by A.A. Milne there is a moment when Pooh Bear is himself searching for inspiration, struggling to write a poem about Owl's house which has just been blown down in a gale: 'But it isn't easy', he says, 'because Poetry and Hums aren't things which you get, they're things which get you. All you can do is to go where they can find you!'

A side of us, however, longs for certainty, not intimations. We are often not patient enough to wait, as Pooh Bear knows he must. Here I am in sympathy with the doubters, for there is an honesty and humility about their position. Certainty stops us in our tracks. It can prevent us from exploring further. Doubt challenges us to come up with our own answers rather than leaning on the efforts of others. The subtitle of broadcaster John Humphrys' book *In God We Doubt* says it all: *Confessions of a Failed Atheist*. After a long journey of enquiry he is not afraid to call himself an agnostic. The book ends up as an honest celebration of doubt in the face of certainty.

In another book, *Feet of Clay: A Study of Gurus*, the psychiatrist Anthony Storr writes: 'All authorities, whether political or spiritual, should be distrusted … the charisma of certainty is a snare which entraps the child who is latent in us all.' In this sense the atheist, as Humphrys discovers on his search, is on no less shaky ground than the religious fundamentalist. We may not yet be able to prove that God or the gods exist, but nor can we prove that they don't – despite the fact that the early Russian astronauts proudly proclaimed on behalf of the USSR that they had seen absolutely no sign of angels on their travels.

In a series of films I was to make many years later about Westminster Abbey, with the playwright Alan Bennett, there is a scene in Poets' Corner where, having paid respects to Shelley, Keats, Wordsworth and Auden, Bennett then says: 'Probably the most beautiful feature of the South Transept which houses Poets' Corner are these 13th-century wall paintings… This is the Incredulity of St Thomas, putting his hand into the side of Christ. Writers deal in doubts rather than certainties, and it's a nice accident that this picture of the most famous of doubters should be revealed as the background for so many memorials to the literary life.'

One of the most important encounters that I've experienced along the way, not just in relation to the literary life, was my friendship and long working relationship with another great doubter, the poet John Betjeman (1906–1984).

After Pinewood, and then nearly two years as a floor manager in television, I was given my first directing job at the age of twenty-three by an ITV company in Cardiff and Bristol called Television Wales and the West (TWW). It was a happy and friendly company, and I already felt very much at home in the young, exciting world of television. One of my first tasks was to make a series of

John Betjeman, by Julia Whatley

Author with film crew, Tony Impey, Mike Greenhalgh and Iain Bruce

films in the West Country with John Betjeman, and in South Wales with the writer Gwyn Thomas.

Although a deeply religious man, Betjeman was extremely suspicious of certainties. Another way to describe this is to say that he too had the courage to live with doubt. What I love and admire most of all in his famous poem 'Christmas' are not just the words he uses, but all those question marks towards the end:

> And is it true? And is it true?
> This most tremendous tale of all,
> Seen in a stained-glass window's hue,
> A baby in an ox's stall?
> The Maker of the stars and sea
> Become a child on earth for me?

What Betjeman taught me was to be wary of trying to pin down things of a profound nature merely to satisfy our longing for order and clarity. Thus over the years he helped me to balance the other side of my nature which was drawn to the Germanic precision and intellectual rigour of men like Jung and Steiner.

A certain professional rivalry existed between John Betjeman and the German architectural historian Nikolaus Pevsner. The latter, having settled in Britain in the thirties, wrote guide books to our historic towns and buildings which are treasured by those who admire his thoroughness and attention to detail. Betjeman himself was equally knowledgeable, but his style was very different. Pevsner is somewhat dry and scholarly. Betjeman's writing is full of quirky insights, humour and a deep interest in people. In his company he would not only tell you all about the architecture, and the character and life of the architect himself, but would also fantasise about those who used to live or work in a particular building, who lived there now and what, for example, they might be having for breakfast.

In his book *Stylistic Cold Wars: Betjeman versus Pevsner*, Timothy Mowl describes how Pevsner worked steadily through the English counties, recording every building of architectural significance. 'He saw it as his business', writes Mowl, 'to record facts and banish obscurities. But obscurities were what Betjeman, the romantic, relished most.'

Betjeman had a word to describe our tendency to dissect and sometimes, in his opinion, to over-analyse whatever catches our interest, be it architecture, theology or cooking. The verb he used was 'pevsnerise'. I will do my best in the pages that follow not to 'pevsnerise' the deeply mysterious subjects of life and death, and heaven and earth. I recognise, however, that balance, as so often, is the ideal position; in this case balance between analysis on the one hand, and intuition and imagination on the other.

Intuition versus analysis; faith versus reason – all this has, I know, been endlessly written about and debated, and understandably so. As I go deeper into the subject of a possible supersensible existence, outside of time and space – particularly as explored by both Steiner and Jung – we will be increasingly brought face to face with the question of whether there are actual limits to human knowledge; or if not, then what are the faculties we need to develop further in our quest for this knowledge; and what role do faith and intuition still have to play?

In my own search, my inspiration has often come from what I call the Pevsner camp, but I am deeply grateful for the influence of John Betjeman and others for a very different kind of inspiration. With his very English sense of humour and his preference for understatement, Betjeman seldom used the word 'God', but would often refer instead to what he called the Management. Far from trivialisation of such a mighty topic, this came over as a recognition of the inadequacy of language when pondering what is, in truth, incomprehensible to our everyday consciousness.

For similar reasons – because a poetic approach is better suited to express the inexpressible, and not because Betjeman was simply a traditionalist, stuck in the past – he, like Alan Bennett, far preferred the traditional King James version of the Bible and also Cranmer's Prayer Book to any modernised version. Our tendency to want things clearly explained – miracles and all – was a trap he instinctively avoided.

'I used to know large chunks of the Prayer Book by heart', said Bennett during Evensong in Westminster Abbey, as he hovered owl-like on the edge of things, 'but that of course is not much use these days. To go into a church knowing the Book of Common Prayer is about as useful as going into a disco knowing how to dance the Veleta.' On a conciliatory note Bennett then added: 'For the clergy it's a working text; and if I loathe what has been done to the Prayer Book, I loathe fanaticism more; and many of the supporters of the old Prayer Book are, or are allied with fanatics. This great building is a monument to tolerance and magnanimity and I value that more than a text, even a text as imbued with history as the comfortable words of the prayer book.'

John Betjeman also loved Westminster Abbey. But just as he was interested in every single person, so too he took delight in every church, great or small, cathedral or chapel, that came into view. His daughter Candida Lycett Green remembers long interrupted car journeys to Cornwall as a child and her repeated protests: 'Oh, no! Not another church!'

Betjeman often used the adjective 'dim', but in his terms it was a compliment – something abandoned or forgotten, something or someone who didn't hit the headlines but, in his eyes, deserved to be treasured. Also, despite his deep attachment to Christian ritual, he was in many ways more interested in the here and now than in the hereafter. Towards the end of his life we had several interesting conversations in which we pondered this notion that they may after all be one and the same thing.

There is a book that I like very much called *The Story of the Other Wise Man*, by Henry van Dyke, which points in this direction, to the interconnectedness of what we call heaven and earth. It tells of a fourth wise man, Artaban, who has sold his house and possessions and purchased three precious stones – a sapphire, a ruby and a pearl – as gifts for the child Jesus. But on his way to Bethlehem he is delayed by attending to the needs of a dying man on the roadside. By the time he arrives, the Holy Family have fled and Herod's soldiers have begun their slaughter of the male babies. Artaban uses one of his jewels to bribe a soldier and thus save the life of at least one child, whose mother has given him shelter.

The story then describes Artaban's many years of wandering (see colour plate 3) and of helping others, his search for Jesus and the underlying feeling that haunts him of having failed in his mission. Finally he arrives in Jerusalem, an old and troubled man, at the time of the Crucifixion. He has one jewel left, the pearl. This he gives to a young girl who is being dragged off by soldiers to be sold as a slave. 'This is thy ransom', he tells her. 'It is the last of my treasures which I kept for the King.' Then comes the earthquake and darkness, and a silent dialogue between the 'other wise man' and the dying Christ. All doubt and conflict disappear when Artaban then hears the words: 'Verily I say unto thee, in as much as thou hast done it unto one of the least of these my brethren, thou hast done it unto me.'

The author, Henry van Dyke, was an American writer and Presbyterian Minister, and his story about Artaban was originally read as a Christmas sermon in his church over a hundred years ago. A similar idea is the subject of James Leigh Hunt's poem 'Abou Ben Adhem', written in 1834, in which Hunt describes how Abou wakes in the night 'from a deep dream of peace' to discover an angel in his room, writing in a book of gold:

> Exceeding peace had made Ben Adhem bold,
> And to the presence in the room he said
> 'What writest thou?' The vision raised its head
> And with a look made all of sweet accord,
> Answered, 'The names of those who love the Lord'.
> 'And is mine one?' said Abou. 'Nay, not so,'
> Replied the angel. Abou spoke more low,
> But cheerly still, and said, 'I pray thee, then,
> Write me as one who loves his fellow men.'
> The angel wrote, and vanished. The next night
> It came again, with a great wakening light,
> And showed the names whom love of God had blest,
> And lo! Ben Adhem's name led all the rest.

Working with John Betjeman was a wonderful experience in all sorts of ways; for example, you could never imagine him being bored. Years later, during a trip we made together to Romania and in the middle of a tiring four-hour coach journey through a very dull part of the country, his voice suddenly broke the silence: 'I am enjoying the boredom'; and I truly believe he was. In fact he loved Romania despite his very English and rather old-fashioned suspicion of 'abroad'. For all of us it was rather like stepping back into the Middle Ages; Betjeman loved the fact that sheep grazed in the churchyards: 'much nicer than an Atco'. I was in Romania preparing to shoot an episode of *The Long Search* on the Orthodox Christian Church and Betjeman had come along for the ride.

Fifteen years earlier, as a young film-maker in the West of England, Betjeman had begun to teach me much, encouraging me to look and then look again, and for longer. He was a poet with a painter's eye, and knew instinctively when images speak for themselves and need no words. He loved the comradeship of filming, the jokes and the jargon. The lights we used all had nicknames like Blondies and Redheads. He often expressed disappointment that our productions weren't grand enough to warrant a huge 100kw lamp known as a Brute. We were fortunate that the film crews with whom we worked were artists as well as technicians; John knew and loved them all. In fact this rich combination of talents among film crews and editors with whom I have worked throughout my career has been a constant inspiration to me too, and I owe a great deal to the companionship and creativity of them all, and initially to those colleagues of mine at TWW, all of us trusted and respected by our colourful boss Bryan Michie and his deputy Wyn Roberts.

Author with John Betjeman and film crew at Weston-super-Mare

In the West Country, over a period of two years, I made twelve short films about places that Betjeman loved – towns like Devizes, Malmesbury, Weston-super-Mare, Bath and Sidmouth. In Clevedon we made a film about an old-fashioned Victorian hotel in winter, largely occupied by old people whose home it had become – characters rather like the Major and those two genteel sisters in the television comedy series *Fawlty Towers*.

Betjeman had a great ability to imagine himself into the skin of others, and he was also a wonderful mimic. In Bath the commentary for our film was a dialogue between Betjeman and an imaginary developer who had outrageous plans for modernising the town. Betjeman wrote and recorded both voices; needless to say the developer was seen to win the argument in the name of progress, crowned by his lucrative scheme to turn the architectural masterpiece known as The Circus into a motorcycle track.

In Clevedon I encouraged him to write a commentary imagining what the hotel residents were thinking or saying to one another as the long winter day unfolded. It was something he often did in life anyway, particularly in restaurants or stuck behind a car in the days before head restraints, when the backs of people's heads in the car in front were clearly visible and you could have a guess at the sort of types they were.

After tea, in the lounge of that seaside hotel, we filmed an elderly couple looking at photographs of their granddaughter on some far away beach. 'Could we both go there – go out next summer?' Betjeman imagined them saying. 'It would be such a change. Or do you think (*pause*) we'd be in the way?' Then as darkness and silence gradually enveloped the hotel, he spoke the last words as himself. 'Bedtime. The long, long corridor. Another long, long night. Do the old sleep well or badly?'

Betjeman had a great fear of old age and death, and many of his poems reflect his gloom and unease, and his awareness of the inevitability of decay. 'Death in Leamington Spa' is one example:

> She died in the upstairs bedroom
> By the light of the ev'ning star
> That shone through the plate-glass window
> From over Leamington Spa.

In the poem the nurse is at first unaware that her patient has died:

> Do you know that the stucco is peeling?
> Do you know that the heart will stop?
> From those yellow Italianate arches
> Do you hear the plaster drop?

Later I will write more about John Betjeman, about how he came to terms with his own physical decline, and about a poignant and inspiring reminder of Jung's remark: 'Life behaves as if it's going on forever.'

———————•—•———————

If life does, in fact, go on forever, why do we – as onlookers – experience death as so final? Why is so much seemingly hidden from our sight and experience? Are we doomed to blindness in relation to these great mysteries – confused into seeing the world not as it is, but as what the Hindus call 'maya'; not necessarily illusion, but only half the picture? Plato drew attention to this situation of being only partially awake, when he wrote in the *Republic* about our tendency to become transfixed by the shadows on the wall of our cave, whereas if we bothered to turn round and look into the real world, we would see what was creating those shadows. Our potential for seeing in a wider sense is what I want to explore in the rest of this chapter.

In my mid-twenties I read a book called *Scientist of the Invisible*. It was written by a canon in the Church of England, A.P. Shepherd, as an introduction to the life and work of Rudolf Steiner. For a long time it seemed to me an excellent title. The realms, or dimensions, of existence that Steiner explored through a systematic training of his natural clairvoyant abilities are indeed invisible. The word 'occult', which has such dubious connotations these days, simply means 'secret' or 'hidden'. The artist Paul Klee spoke of his ambition to make visible the invisible; and Jonathan Swift wrote that 'vision is the ability to see the invisible.' I remember being intrigued as a small boy when my grandfather, who loved Emmental cheese, said that it was the holes that tasted best!

Gradually, however, I have become aware that many of the underlying realities explored by modern scientists are – somewhat like the taste of those holes in my grandfather's cheese – themselves hidden, yet nonetheless real. In the past one could more or less understand how a steam engine worked by simply looking at it. Now our technology is such that this is no longer the case, especially in the realm of electronics. It is a hidden, occult world – yet it exists, and it works.

The physicist Arthur Zajonc, in his book *Catching the Light*, reminds us that light itself is actually invisible without an object to reflect it. And if you dissect the seed of a plant, no miniature 'plant-in-waiting' is revealed. Where, for example, is what we know as the buttercup during the long winter months? Certainly not curled up in the ground; its roots maybe, but not the flower.

What we recognise and understand as life is perhaps the greatest mystery of all, and is certainly invisible. We are perfectly aware of its presence or absence through our encounter with living or dead matter. But the life force itself cannot be weighed, measured, photographed or recorded. All these phenomena are as occult as angelic beings, and just as mysterious.

In his book *The Devil's Doctor*, on the medieval healer Paracelsus, Philip Ball confirms this observation:

> Today 'occult' is equated with superstition, irrationality, charlatanism, but much of contemporary science is itself occult 'in the Renaissance sense', in so far as it is 'hidden' from our senses ... We explain phenomena in terms of atoms or molecules too small for us to see, or electromagnetic fields that are truly (for the most part) invisible, or other fields and forces (such as gravity) that we still struggle to understand. By Renaissance standards, these things are no less occult than the astrological 'emanations' of a star or the causative agency of demons.

Whether we be Paracelsus or Einstein, what is revealed through our senses and through the instruments we create as intermediaries, as extensions of those senses – telescopes, microscopes and the like – tells us something about ourselves and the world only because we have a mind and an imagination that interacts with this data and attempts to make sense of it; a mind that can also engage with what is hidden as concept. 'The senses alone make no judgements,' writes Nick Thomas in his book *Space and Counterspace*, 'only the thinking human being makes judgements.' And it is through the enhancement of our capacity to think and through the faculties we already possess that Steiner and other esotericists such as Swedenborg and Ouspensky believed we have the potential to 'see' and experience invisible realities – to see, as in the word 'seer'.

Once again our everyday language – in phrases like 'I see what you mean' – reveals an instinctive understanding of these subtleties; and in that sense we are all seers of varying ability. The poet Coleridge wrote in his *Biographia Literaria*: 'All the organs of sense are framed for a corresponding world of sense, and we have it. All the organs of spirit are framed for a correspondent world of spirit; though the latter organs are not developed in all alike.' In the view of Steiner in particular – and to a certain extent of Teilhard de Chardin – our future evolution may well depend on our ability to awaken this dormant capacity to be aware, in full consciousness, of more than meets the eye.

There's an interesting and important scene in Carlos Castaneda's book *A Separate Reality* in which his teacher, the Yaqui Indian Don Juan, tries to explain to him the difference between looking and seeing: 'When I want to look at the world', Don Juan tells him, 'I see it in the way you do. Then when I want to see it I look at it the way I know and I perceive it in a different way.' He goes on to tell Castaneda that whenever you just look at things, you don't see them: 'You just look at them', he says, 'I suppose to make sure that something is there. Since you're not concerned with seeing, things look very much the same every time you look at them. When you learn to see, on the other hand, a thing is never the same every time you see it, and yet it is the same.' In answer to the question: What's the advantage of learning to see if you won't be able to recognise anything, since nothing is the same? Don Juan replies: 'You can tell things apart. You can see them for what they really are.'

Another insight into this difference between looking and seeing is conveyed by the artist Frederick Franck in his book *The Zen of Seeing*. 'What I haven't drawn', he writes, 'I have never really seen.' He goes on to describe an exercise in a workshop he gave in which he invited the participants to follow him outdoors, to lie on the grass and let their eyes fall on whatever happened to be in front of them; then, having closed their eyes for five minutes, to open them and focus again on whatever they had previously observed – a plant, a leaf, for instance. 'Look it in the eye', he said to them, 'until you feel it is looking back at you. Feel that you are alone with it on Earth. That it is the most important thing in the universe, that it contains all the riddles of life and death. It does! You are no longer looking, you are *seeing* ...' In the same book Franck writes: 'It is no accident that Zen is being discovered in the West at a time of realisation that we are fast becoming strangers to our inner life, and that we are all too easily confused about what is real and authentic and what is phoney, about what we truly like and what we think we must like because it happens to be required.'

In his 'Lines composed a few miles above Tintern Abbey', the poet William Wordsworth uses a beautiful phrase when describing the serenity that can give rise to ecstatic visions of reality:

> ... with an eye made quiet by the power
> Of harmony, and the deep power of joy,
> We see into the life of things.

To the extent that we remain out and out materialists we are, in the eyes of some teachers, only half alive. Perhaps that word 'blinkered' is a kinder and more accurate word to use. One such teacher, and another explorer of these latent human faculties, was the controversial teacher and visionary, Georgei Gurdjieff (1866–1949). I had several friends in my twenties who, like me, were lifting up various stones in an effort to understand what was going on behind the scenes, as it were, and who were studying one or other offshoot of Gurdjieff's work and teachings.

The writer Colin Wilson calls Gurdjieff 'that strange man of genius'. In a book called *The Secret History of the World* – a comprehensive study of esoteric teachings from the Mystery Schools of Ancient Greece, through the Gnostics, the Kabbala and the Rosicrucians to the present day – its author Jonathan Black refers to Gurdjieff as 'perhaps the most charismatic and disconcerting initiate of the 20th century'. Gurdjieff did most of his teaching in Moscow and St Petersburg, and later in Europe and America. In his opinion most people are largely asleep, with no free will whatsoever.

One aspect of Gurdjieff's elaborate system of waking people up was a method of observing oneself and other people, and recognising how many actions are habitual and mechanical. In *Feet of Clay* Anthony Storr writes: 'Complete concentration on whatever was being carried out at the time was an essential part of Gurdjieff's message and of his own behaviour.' Storr then adds: 'Insistence on living intensely in the present moment and discarding the concern with a past or future which interferes with fully experiencing the here-and-now, is not confined to Gurdjieff's teaching. Zen also treats the past and future as fleeting illusions. It is only the present which is eternally real.' This reminds me of a paradoxical statement by the German medieval mystic Johannes Tauler: 'Eternity is the everlasting now.'

From the little I know and have experienced indirectly of the Gurdjieff movement, I have a somewhat uneasy feeling about him and his legacy; for me, a certain elitism and coldness surround what is called 'The Work'. Some of his insights may be interesting and even profound, but he could be ruthless and even cruel to some of his 'sleeping' disciples – though I suppose if you do keep falling asleep, like the dormouse in *Alice in Wonderland*, you may deserve to be put in a teapot.

Gurdjieff's one-time disciple, P.D. Ouspensky, about whom Lachman also writes in his book on consciousness, was in many ways a more sympathetic character. Like Bucke, Ouspensky had a fleeting experience of a higher form of consciousness, in his case while on a journey by ship across the Sea of Marmora in Turkey. In his book *Tertium Organum* he describes how, while watching the play of huge waves against the ship, he suddenly felt 'the waves drawing me to themselves'. Now it was he, Ouspensky, who was battering the ship. 'At that moment I became all', he writes, 'The waves – they were myself. The wind – it was myself … It was a moment of extraordinary liberation, joy and expansion. A second – and the spell was broken'. This is similar to the experience that the psychiatrist Stanislav Grof describes, having taken LSD: 'I had the feeling I became all there was.'

Like Gurdjieff, Ouspensky travelled widely but it was ultimately his inner journey and the eight years as a pupil of Gurdjieff, described in his book *In Search of the Miraculous*, that yielded the most fruitful insights; his realisation, for example, that our experience of time and space is not so much an illusion, but rather the consequence of limited perception. There is, for example, a strange contradiction – one that has long intrigued me – in the way we nowadays speak about space as being infinite, and yet locate ourselves at some insignificant spot towards the edge of our particular galaxy. If, however, infinity is a reality, then it would seem quite justified and in no way arrogant for each one of us to actually experience ourselves at the centre of the universe; for in whichever direction we gaze, probe or point our gadgets, the distances are not only vast and ultimately infinite, but must also be identical. Indeed the astronomer Bernard Lovell called his 1978 book on the latest developments in physics and astronomy *In the Centre of Immensities*.

One of Gurdjieff's mottos was: 'Take the understanding of the East and the knowledge of the West, and then seek.' But to seek without being sufficiently sensitive to the aches and pains of ordinary human beings is, in my opinion, a perilous path. Steiner, as a western-trained scientist and philosopher who studied these subjects in Vienna and then spent seven years in Weimar editing the scientific writings of Goethe, also drew on sources from the East, particularly on Hinduism through his early connection with the theosophists. But there is an ingredient in Steiner's teaching that is significantly absent from Gurdjieff's utterances and those of many other gurus of recent times. In one of his most important books, *Knowledge of the Higher Worlds*, written in the early years of the 20th century, Steiner repeatedly emphasises how important it is for our moral development to keep pace with any enhancement of these other dormant faculties of cognition: 'For every one step forward that you take in seeking knowledge of occult truths', he wrote, 'you should aim to take three steps in the improvement of your own character.' In other words inner work on its own is no guarantee of virtue and can easily become as egotistical as many of our other pursuits.

In *The Faerie Queen*, by the Elizabethan poet Edmund Spenser, there are three lines which sum up very clearly what can happen when we continue to explore, either spiritually or physically, with a faulty map, inadequate information, and essentially ill-equipped:

Once a man hath lost the way
The further he doth go
The further he doth stray

In other words if the flaws in our character, however small, are not addressed they will almost inevitably become more pronounced the further we soar into the dizzy heights of spiritual exploration and practice – and the further we will stray. It is clear warning to those of us who become obsessed with so-called other worlds at the expense of what can be learned in the here and now, to keep our feet firmly on the ground and honour our obligations to one another – particularly to those who suffer or are vulnerable. For the tree to grow tall it needs to put down sufficient roots to support it.

These dangers are something Steiner understood very well, for – as Nick Thomas points out in *Space and Counterspace* – Steiner was not only a pioneer in adopting a scientific approach to what had previously been regarded as

Rudolf Steiner

territory for philosophy and religion, but also unique in 'his appreciation of the importance of avoiding the sources of illusion inherent in it'.

Although Steiner wrote and lectured on an extraordinary range of subjects – education, medicine, agriculture, as well as angelic beings, reincarnation and karma, and, indeed, the spiritual evolution of the cosmos itself – I feel that his really important contribution and legacy is his focus on our human potential, and on the fact that knowledge in its deepest sense is inseparable from morality, or what Buddhists call 'right action'.

In his celebrated book *The Outsider*, Colin Wilson wrote of visionaries that 'the essentials of what they saw died with them. Their value for us does not lie in the "visions" their words can conjure up for us, but in the instructions they left for anyone who should want to see the same things that they saw. It lies, in other words, in the discipline they recommend.'

Meditation is central to the discipline that Steiner recommended. 'Don't just do something; sit there!' is a light-hearted slogan that resonates increasingly for our hurried and overloaded lives. Modern technology allows us to travel and be in touch with one another in ways that not long ago were quite unthinkable. There are undoubtedly huge advantages in all this, but the danger is that we fill up our lives to such an extent that we do nothing properly or in any depth. As W.H. Davies wrote in his poem 'Leisure':

What is this life if
Full of care
We have no time
To stand and stare?

A few random sentences from the early pages of *Knowledge of the Higher Worlds*, which I began to study alongside my early efforts as a film-maker, give a flavour of the quiet seriousness of Steiner's suggestions: 'A certain fundamental attitude of the soul must be the starting-point ... the path of veneration, of devotion to truth and knowledge.' A little later he writes: 'If we do not develop within ourselves the deeply rooted feeling that there is something higher than ourselves, we shall never find the strength to evolve to a higher stage.'

At this preparatory stage Steiner encourages us to look for whatever can capture our admiration and respect, to look for the good in all things, and to fill our consciousness with thoughts that imbue us with wonder, respect and veneration for the world and for life: 'It is not enough that I show respect to a person in my outward bearing; I must have this respect in my thoughts.'

In my own life I am slowly learning to recognise the subtle and important dividing line between observation and awareness on the one hand, and criticism – particularly unspoken criticism, often leading to irritation – on the other. The latter can be lethal not only because it may have a potentially crippling effect on the person criticised – who is likely to know subliminally what we are thinking – but because it also exerts what Steiner's describes as a paralysing, withering effect on the faculty of cognition. He continues:

> Reverence awakens a power of sympathy in the soul through which we draw towards us qualities in the beings around us, qualities which would otherwise remain concealed. Only what we experience within ourselves gives us the key to the beauties of the outer world ... The outer world is filled with divine splendour, but we must first have experienced the Divine within ourselves if we are to discover it in the surrounding world.

The actual exercises that Steiner suggests, once one has started to work in this spirit of humility and with the attitude of mind outlined above, begin very simply and are echoed in the esoteric traditions of all the great cultures – in particular in Buddhism and Hinduism. 'Provide for yourself moments of inner tranquillity', he writes, 'and learn in these moments to distinguish the essential from the non-essential.' This reminds me of Blake's line: 'There's a moment in each day that Satan cannot find.' Steiner challenges us to confront ourselves with the inner calmness of a judge, to contemplate and assess our experiences and actions as though they were those of others, not our own. It's an important aspect of what the Buddhists call 'mindfulness'. How pure are one's motives, for example? What role does egotism play in one's search? Am I driven by mere curiosity? 'The pupil does not learn in order to accumulate learning as his own treasure of knowledge', writes Steiner, 'but in order to place this learning in the service of the world.'

One result of practising these exercises will be our gradual ability to stand firm, not to be blown hither and thither by distractions of all sorts, but to steer our own ship. It is 'I' who begins to take charge, to make decisions, and not that self which so often disappoints and at times shames me. 'Meditation', writes Steiner, 'is what leads each person to knowledge and vision of the eternal, indestructible core of their being.' It is a statement with which I imagine most teachers of the inner life would agree. Likewise the exercises that Steiner goes on to suggest in *Knowledge of the Higher Worlds* and in some of his lectures will have their parallels in other cultures and spiritual movements, both eastern and western.

After many years, perhaps many lifetimes, Steiner tells us, 'the invisible will become visible'. Then too, he writes, we will take the first steps towards penetrating the mystery of birth and death through our own vision:

For the outer senses a being comes into existence at birth and passes away at death. But that is only because these senses do not perceive the hidden spirit of the being. For the spirit, birth and death are merely transformations, just as the sprouting of the flower from the bud is a transformation enacted before our physical eyes.

But, whether writing or speaking about actual clairvoyance, Steiner was at pains to point out on many occasions that we can only prepare ourselves to cross the threshold into what he calls the spiritual world –'the rest is an affair of that world itself'. The manifestation and experience of the spiritual realities that underpin all existence are therefore an act of grace. 'Wait. Wait. Wait', he says, 'That is the golden rule – to be able to wait in restfulness of soul.'

In a lecture he gave in Dornach, Switzerland on October 3rd 1914, he spoke about how, in our everyday world, if we want to see something we must go to it. 'Those who want to see Rome must go to Rome', he says, 'That is quite natural in the physical world, for Rome will not come to them. In the spiritual world it is just the reverse'.

In that same lecture he emphasised that although the thinking we use to investigate the external world is of little help in penetrating the purely spiritual realm of existence – where, instead of approaching things as we do in the physical world, we must wait for them to approach us – that thinking is of the utmost significance in that we are exercising and strengthening the powers of our own minds through inner activity: 'The soul becomes more capable of living its own life, of activating its own forces'; in other words, thinking helps us to mature inwardly and independently.

In *Knowledge of the Higher Worlds* there is a reference to daily life, to the world that we all inhabit, which has always interested me:

> For many human beings, everyday life is itself a more or less unconscious process of Initiation … Such people have passed through manifold experiences of such a kind that their self-confidence, courage and fortitude have been enhanced in a healthy way, and they learn to bear sorrow, disappointment and failure in undertakings with greatness of soul, and above all with equanimity and unbroken strength. Whoever has undergone experiences of this kind is often an Initiate without definitely knowing it, and then only a little is needed to open his spiritual ears and eyes so that he becomes a seer.

I feel instinctively in sympathy with this idea, that life itself is ultimately the great teacher. My friend Jim Hodgetts may not have been an initiate – nor, I believe, did he meditate – but despite the knocks and disappointments that came his way he kept afloat and always looked ahead, and with good humour.

Likewise Anne-Marie, although she made many mistakes and couldn't, for very understandable reasons, quite ever believe that she really was wanted, did manage to bounce back from each new disaster – her humanity, if not her judgement, enriched rather than undermined.

I am aware, too, of this danger of pursuing a so-called 'spiritual path' safely insulated from the trials and tribulations of the world. It is a theme that particularly interested the German writer Hermann Hesse, whose novels I along with many others of my generation devoured in the sixties. For me – as I've already mentioned – the notion of spirituality is not ultimately to do with somewhere else. 'The real voyage of discovery', wrote Proust, 'is not in seeking new landscapes but in looking through new eyes.'

In his novel *Siddhartha* and still more so in *Narziss and Goldmund*, Hesse explores the two paths open to us all, inner and outer. With Siddartha this dilemma takes place within one person, whereas in the story of Narziss and Goldmund we have two friends who choose alternative paths in life, in their search for understanding and ultimate enlightenment. Narziss is a monk. Goldmund, having been a young novice, goes out into the world and experiences it to the full, its joy and its pain. Yet in the story that unfolds it is clear that both Narziss and Goldmund need each other and their friendship, and what each brings to that friendship, in order to experience life in its ultimate wholeness. As the two journeys come to an end, Hesse, in imagining the thoughts of the old monk Narziss, writes:

> perhaps it is not merely simpler and more human to live a Goldmund-life in the world. Perhaps in the end it was more valiant, and greater in God's sight, to breast the currents of reality, sin, and accept sin's bitter consequence, instead of standing apart, with well-washed hands, living in sober, quiet security, planting a pretty garden of well-trained thoughts, and walking then, in stainless ignorance, among them – the sheltered beds of a little paradise. It was harder perhaps, and needed a stouter heart to walk with broken shoes through forest glades, to trudge the roads, suffer rain and snow, want and drought, playing all the games of the senses, and paying for one's losses with much grief.

In these years I myself was certainly more a Goldmund than a Narziss, more interested in engaging with the world than in meditating. But the Narziss in me was stirring, and soon I was to take both of them with me to London, the monk and the adventurer. There, in 1963, I joined the BBC, where I then worked for twenty-seven years.

I was twenty-five years old, and already my inner life had been deeply enriched by my encounter with Steiner's work, in particular. Meanwhile my interest in, and affection for the world around me had been greatly stimulated by my meeting with John Betjeman and through the films we made together. As someone with many questions I was also learning about the trap of latching onto certainties; learning, too, that the word 'occult' applied as much to science as to spirituality; that looking was not the same as seeing; and that meditation and self-development could be a dangerous cul-de-sac if pursued for one's own salvation alone, without concern for one's fellow human beings.

Author aged twenty-five

CHAPTER 4

Footprints

'Don't die dear master', says Sancho Panza in tears, 'take my advice and live many years.' Don Quixote replies: 'There are no birds this year in last year's nests.' In nature the pattern we witness is cyclical. In human life the image of a spiral seems more appropriate than a circle. The idea that everything is in a constant and dynamic state of change became closely linked to my interest in biography. Our individual stories, I was beginning to sense, will play themselves out not only far into the future, but have their origins way back before our present birth. Biography is therefore a journey in which the words 'beginning' and 'end' have less and less meaning. Now, as a young BBC producer, I was about to start exploring these ideas through film.

Alongside my own inner journey I was also keen to travel. I hadn't been abroad until I was nineteen – not unusual in those somewhat austere and unhurried years after the war. Now I could also start to search for answers to my many questions not only in books and on my own doorstep – enriching as that doorstep was – but also further afield.

The Lean and Foolish Knight, based on the story of Don Quixote, was my first film for the BBC. It was also the start of my interest in the figure of the fool and in the wisdom that only fools can convey. In the very first pages of Cervantes' novel there is a splendid warning to fools like me, when he writes that his hero's brain dried up 'from little sleep and much reading … and he lost his wits'. My own remedy, when I sometimes get too stuck in my head, is simply to go for a long walk – which is, in a sense, what Don Quixote did too! In his introduction to the new translation of the book by Edith Grossman, Harold Bloom writes that Cervantes wants Don Quixote 'to be a new kind of hero, neither ironic nor mindless, but one who wills to be himself'.

In Jonathan Black's *The Secret History of the World* he mentions Don Quixote as an important example of the role of imagination in the forming of the world. And like Harold Bloom, Black sees Cervantes's creation as 'not just a buffoon. He is somebody who has the strongest desire to have his innermost questions answered. He is being shown that material reality is just one of many layers of illusions, and that it is our deepest imaginings that form them.' As

Black implies, the power of thought, and indeed of prayer is greatly underestimated, for it is thus that we influence and indeed change the world, and above all ourselves and each other. If we think well of someone they feel enhanced, whereas those we despise are diminished by our disdain. Black continues:

> A similar choice confronts us when we contemplate the cosmos as a whole. Cervantes was writing at a turning point in history when people no longer knew for sure that the world is a spiritual place with goodness and meaning at its heart. What Cervantes is saying is that if, like Don Quixote, we good-heartedly decide to believe in the essential goodness of the world, despite the brickbats of fortune, despite the slapstick tendency in things that seem to contradict such spiritual beliefs and make them look foolish and absurd, then that decision to believe will help transform the world – and in a supernatural way, too.

Filming in Spain in 1964, once you left the main roads, was in many ways like stepping back into the 17th century. On the great plateau of La Mancha, south of Madrid, farmers ploughed with horses, transport was largely by mule and donkey, and women did their washing in the rivers. With these images, interwoven with Gustav Doré's illustrations, I told a simple and abbreviated version of this wonderful story. The Spanish exile and scholar, Rafael Nadal, who had been a close friend of the poet Lorca, wrote the script with me, but was unwilling to visit Spain while Franco was still alive; Nadal's artist friend Gregorio Prieto, a citizen of La Mancha, became my local guide.

Don Quixote, by Gustav Doré

Don Quixote dreamt of a golden age when the words 'mine' and 'thine' did not yet exist, 'an age when all things were held in common'. The existence of this golden age, whether imaginary, nostalgic or prophetic, was to feature in some of my subsequent films. So too, of course, was the subject of death about which Cervantes writes so movingly at the end of his hero's seemingly hopeless quest.

After his final humiliation Don Quixote was condemned to retire to his own village in the hope that he'd come to his senses. 'Since his defeat', wrote Cervantes, 'he spoke on all matters with a sounder judgment ... Although conquered by another, he conquered himself which is, as I have heard him say, the very best kind of victory …. It was his great good fortune to live a madman and die sane.'

Does this mean that it's mad to tilt at windmills and at the developments and trends that continue to threaten our precious humanity? I think not. Rather, it seems, the author is acknowledging the importance of a little humility, acceptance and self-knowledge before we exit, pause and then, perhaps, return to the fray for another incarnation – armed, as ever, with a faith in this power of the imagination to change the world.

This film was part of a series called *Footprints* that I worked on with another director, Richard Taylor, over a period of two years. We made fourteen films in all, each one an attempt to evoke through landscape, and through paintings and drawings, the lives or a key moment in the lives of people we admired and whose biographies interested us – moments, perhaps, when they were most in touch with their daimons. Don Quixote was the only fictitional subject in the series, though in many ways he feels to me just as real as all the others. He has been called the Spanish Christ. Jonathan Black describes him as 'reckless in his good-heartedness' and writes that 'the effect of his journey on world history has been quite as great as if he had really lived'.

I had been knocking at the door of the BBC for some time but, without a university degree, was not considered eligible for production work. (Family complications had determined that I went straight from school to work in the family business – a long-established firm of building and engineering merchants where I stayed for nearly two years.) Now, at the launch of BBC2 in 1963, and with five years of theatre, film and television experience behind me, the Corporation was prepared to overlook my academic deficiencies.

I was based at Lime Grove in Shepherds Bush, a place bustling with interesting, creative and eccentric people. The building, too, was eccentric in the extreme, with endless passages, tunnels and staircases. It was once the Gainsborough Film Studios, and was thoroughly conducive to the production of imaginative and pioneering programmes such as *Panorama*, presided over by Richard Dimbleby and his fine team of reporters; *Monitor*, and the early films of Ken Russell; *Tonight* with Cliff Michelmore and his talented band of colleagues; and the satire show *That Was the Week that Was*. All this was championed by the wise and liberal Director-General Hugh Carlton-Greene, whose enlightened leadership and vision inspired us all. Producers were trusted and given their head. 'Always assume your audience is uninformed', the arts supremo Huw Wheldon later told us, 'but also assume they are intelligent.' My first boss was Anthony Jay, who went on to write the *Yes, Minister* series. Then came Gordon Watkins, who had been one of the two producers on the pioneering documentary series *The Great War*.

The meditative discipline that I mentioned – of trying to separate the essential from the non-essential – was not altogether dissimilar to the skills that Betjeman, Jay, Watkins and my later boss Richard Cawston all taught me in relation to film-making. Partly it is simply good journalism, with the added challenge of working with images. Keeping things relatively short and simple, I also learned, doesn't have to mean becoming superficial or trivial.

Some other early 'footprints' that I followed were those of Byron and Shelley when they spent the summer of 1816 by the lake of Geneva. It was on that trip that Mary Godwin, not yet married to Shelley, dreamed up her novel *Frankenstein*. In the story that she told her companions, and later wrote down, a scientist called Victor Frankenstein creates a living being which, because of its hideous appearance, he then rejects. What follows illustrates the danger of simply walking away from what we've done or said just because we don't like it. If we do, it is likely to haunt us, to hunt us down – not just in life or beyond the grave, but also perhaps in future incarnations. Our deeds remain essentially part of us; we are responsible for them and remain so. 'You are my creator', the monster tells Frankenstein, 'but I am your master.' In many ways this monster is what Jung described as the 'shadow' – that part of ourselves that we hate, fear and despise; and it is our master so long as we refuse to recognise and acknowledge it. That people now often think the monster is called Frankenstein is interesting and significant – perhaps they sense unconsciously that the creator and his creature are indeed one.

At another level the story can be understood as a warning in relation to our technological creations in general: that we are increasingly in danger of becoming enslaved by the machines that were meant to serve us. The story also offers insight into how lack of love can form a delinquent or criminal mentality. Frankenstein's creation is at first only outwardly ugly. He wants to fit in, to be accepted and to be part of society. He is lonely and wants a companion, a mate. Only gradually, after abuse and rejection – not only from Frankenstein himself – does he gradually become a monster, bitter and revengeful.

The American writer and historian Theodore Roszak, whom I met in London several years later, has long been interested in *Frankenstein*. The fact that this story has been told and retold in every shape and form, and often vulgarised in the process, is a clear indication to Roszak of its power as myth. And he means 'myth' not in its modern usage, as something essentially untrue, but as a story conveying profound insight and wisdom in symbolic form. 'The job of the myth', he wrote, 'is to tell the truth so simply, so deeply that the truth survives, no matter who tells the story, no matter how crudely they tell it.'

During that eventful summer long ago, Byron and Shelley, with their lady friends in tow, had been on a pilgrimage to places associated with their hero, Jean Jacques Rousseau who, in the 18th century, epitomised the Enlightenment's emphasis on self-expression and individual human fulfilment, and whose philosophy – particularly in its emphasis on the inner life as a source of truth – had a profound influence on the Romantic movement of the following century.

Reading about Rousseau's faith in the idea of the 'noble savage', and in the essential goodness of the human being must, at the time, have encouraged my own instinctive idealism. Now, many years later, although far from being a cynic, I have come to realise that things are probably far more complicated than Rousseau's starry-eyed vision. He believed, for example, that children should be left to their own devices and not polluted by education from corrupt adults in institutions; if so, then all would be well. I don't know what he would have made of William Golding's *Lord of the Flies*, a deeply disturbing story that tells of the rapid transformation of childhood innocence into something infinitely more primitive and savage, and something far from noble: a regression from the thin veneer of civilization that the adult world has slowly created and is creating still.

The footprints that I traced in Denmark were those of Hans Christian Andersen, whose stories I had always loved. 'It seems to me', he wrote, 'as if every little flower, every object is saying "Look at me, just for a moment, and then my story will go right into you."' A butterfly, a teapot, an oak tree – all these so-called ordinary things made up the cast of my film, transformed in Andersen's imagination from the everyday world around him.

In *The Last Dream of the Old Oak Tree*, Andersen explores in deceptively simple style the theme of time and eternity that interests me so much: '"Poor little mayfly!" said the Oak Tree, "What a short life that was."' And so every summer, year after year, the oak tree talks briefly to the mayflies, amazed that despite the shortness of their lives none of them are remotely sad:

> 'Everything's so wonderfully bright and warm and lovely, and I'm so happy,' says one mayfly.
> 'But only for one day, and then it's all over and done with' said the

oak tree.

'Done with!' said the mayfly. 'What's done with? Will you be done with, too?'

'No, I shall live for perhaps thousands of your days, and my day is whole seasons long. That's something so long that you simply can't reckon it out.'

'No, because I don't understand you. You may have thousands of my days, but I have thousands of moments to be pleased and happy in. Does all this world's loveliness come to an end when you die?'

'No,' said the tree. 'I expect it goes on longer – far, far longer – than I can imagine.'

Andersen's strong faith in providence and in his own innate talent sustained him through his early life. When he left his humble home at the age of fourteen to seek fame and fortune in Copenhagen, initially as an actor, it seems that providence did indeed protect the naïve and clumsy youth that he was – and in many ways remained.

Yet eventually he became a world-famous writer, though he was less fortunate in love. He mocked himself in his story *The Butterfly*. Flitting from flower to flower all summer, the butterfly couldn't make up its mind which one to marry. Finally it was autumn:

> ... and the flowers now put on their loveliest dresses, but what was the good of that? The fresh fragrance of youth had all gone. Fragrance it is that the heart's in search of, as the years go by; and it can't be said there's much of that in dahlias and hollyhocks. So the butterfly flew down to the mint.
>
> 'She hasn't any blossoms, I know, but she's a whole flower in herself, scented from root to crown, with fragrance in every leaf. She's the one I'll choose.'
>
> And so at last he proposed.
>
> But the mint stood stiff and silent, and at last she said, 'Friendship, but nothing more! I am old, and you are old, I dare say we might live for one another, but marry – no! Don't lets make fools of ourselves at our time of life.'
>
> So the butterfly got no one at all. He had been too 'choosy', and that doesn't do. The butterfly remained a bachelor, as they're called.

(I myself nearly went the way of the butterfly but finally, aged forty-two, I found a very lovely flower who luckily wanted more than friendship!)

The Ugly Duckling is the most autobiographical of all Andersen's tales – the ugly duckling who, after much ridicule and suffering, discovers that he is in fact a swan: 'It doesn't matter about being born in a duck yard, as long as you hatched from a swan's egg.'

We are all, I suppose, born into one sort of duck yard or another; some infinitely more squalid, more challenging than others. 'We are all in the gutter', wrote Oscar Wilde in *The Importance of Being Ernest*, 'but some of us are looking at the stars.' For Hans Andersen the swan is symbolic of our true nature, our deepest potential: what Beatie Bryant discovered in the play *Roots*; what the daimon constantly wants to remind us of, if we are prepared to pause and listen; what Gerald Manley Hopkins celebrates as the kingfisher's essential nature when it cries out: 'What I do is me: for that I came'.

The footprints of T.E. Lawrence – Lawrence of Arabia – are all over the Middle East. The ones I followed were made in 1909 while he was still an undergraduate at Oxford. Lawrence had long been interested in castles, and was writing a thesis on the influence of Saracen architecture on the Crusaders. Little research was available and so, aged twenty-one, he sailed to Beirut and then walked 1250 miles in the heat of summer through Syria, sketching and photographing the remains of the magnificent Crusader castles, visiting thirty-six in all. It was an extraordinary, courageous and in many ways reckless journey to make. He spoke virtually no Arabic, was frequently ill, and as a lone European was often in great danger. Yet he fell in love with the land and with the people, returned to the Middle East after graduating from Oxford and worked intermittently on an archaeological site near Aleppo for three years. In 1912 he was also excavating in Egypt, and in the early months of 1914 conducted a survey of the Sinai peninsular. By the time World War I came Lawrence knew the land, the people and the language. Of the Bedouin he was later to write, '... in his life he had air and winds, sun and light, open spaces and a great emptiness ... There unconsciously he came near God. He could not look for God within him. He was too sure that he was within God.'

We called the story of this walk *Road to a Legend*. My previous head of department, Anthony Jay, wrote the script. Lawrence is, in my experience, one of the most striking examples of a person consciously or unconsciously putting himself in the right place at the right time to fulfil a particular destiny. One can, of course, view it all as chance. What was clearly not chance was the bond Lawrence felt instinctively with the Arabs. I have long been interested in people like Lawrence who feel a particular affinity with another part of the world, or some other period of history – for example historians, archaeologists, biographers. Are their single-minded efforts intimations, perhaps, of a connection from past lives? And is their karma in relation to those places and people still working itself out? In this sense, could the pleasure that many people experience in things old and picturesque be an unconscious nostalgia for a world we once knew?

Another aspect of Lawrence's life that I feel is relevant to this exploration of mine is conveyed in the opening lines of the poem he wrote as a dedication 'To S.A.' in his book *Seven Pillars of Wisdom*. (Nobody seems to know whether S.A. was a person, a place or a cause; there are plenty of theories, but like much of Lawrence's life it remains a mystery.)

I loved you, so I drew these tides of men into my hands
and wrote my will across the sky in stars

What interests me is this confidence, almost arrogance, which no longer accepts that our lives are somehow and mysteriously influenced and even guided by the stars. T.E. Lawrence turns that idea on its head. The stars are influenced, even created as a result of what we do on earth, and not the other way round. It's what Jonathan Black suggests that Cervantes believed. Our imagination is a more creative and powerful force than we sometimes realise.

This same thought – that things are increasingly in our hands – is echoed in a scene in David Lean's film *Lawrence of Arabia* when Lawrence comes up against the obstinate and unshakable faith that many Arabs have in fate. The word Islam means submission. 'It is written', his Arab companion tell him, in an attempt to block some new and outrageous plan. Then comes Lawrence's exasperated response: 'Nothing is written.' In other words we, not the gods, are now in charge. This doesn't necessarily deny their existence, but it does suggest that the ball is in our court. Human evolution, if seen as the unfolding of our journey towards maturity, demands it. God is not dead, as some people have suggested. He – and maybe the gods in general – have simply stepped aside so we can grow up as free beings, with all the risks and perils that inevitably ensue. Parents too, if they are wise, let their children go – out of the cosy nest and into the world. Maybe, ever since that seventh day of Creation as described in Genesis, when God rested from his efforts, we have been increasingly on our own. It is our turn to be creative. It is still Sunday, and the silence is sometimes unbearable.

This thought was vividly brought home to me while I was filming in Westminster Abbey with Alan Bennett. Periodically we, the visitors, were quite rightly asked to pause and remember we were in a place of worship and not a museum. The priest would say a few words, followed by a prayer. On this occasion he ended with these words: 'Dear God, we ask you to remember those less fortunate than ourselves. Be with them and comfort them in their suffering.' My immediate reaction was to imagine God's reply: 'You do it.'

There is a verse by Rudolf Steiner which seems to be making this same point; and although I don't respond to a lot of Steiner's meditative writings – perhaps because I am too steeped in the poetry of the Anglican Church, or maybe because the material simply doesn't translate very satisfactorily into

English – I do find this one both helpful and profound, as I do his suggestions for meditation itself. In this particular verse he speaks of the fragile human condition and the loneliness we increasingly feel:

> The stars once spoke to us.
> It is world destiny
> That they are silent now.
> To be aware of the silence
> Can become pain for human beings on earth.
> But in the deepening silence
> There grows and ripens
> What we speak to the stars

One such response to this silence is exemplified by that extraordinary band of explorers who emerged in the 15th and 16th centuries – men of great courage, with minds of striking originality, and all of them stimulated by a new type of consciousness that concerned itself far more than previously with the ground upon which we stand. One such person was the Portuguese prince known as Henry the Navigator. He was the subject of the last of my films for the series *Footprints*. It was also the first film that I made in colour. I well remember with what excitement the cameraman, John Baker, loaded up those magical rolls of 16mm film as we explored the shores of Portugal in our attempt to evoke Prince Henry's extraordinary life.

Henry's task and his great achievement was to persuade simple Portuguese fisherman that the horizon was not the end of the world, and that by sailing south they would not disappear over the edge into oblivion. It was his vision and their courage that opened up the globe for exploration and thus for all the other discoveries and achievements that followed in their wake. But Henry's plans and initiative met with a great deal of opposition and cynicism in his day. In the commentary I wrote of these opponents as 'unwilling to accept that their small, easily comprehended world might be part of something infinitely greater' – a thought which I feel is enormously relevant today as more and more people again become open to the idea that we may not be alone in the universe, though perhaps we will need to probe those spaces with instruments more subtle than telescopes.

Antoine de Saint-Exupéry, the French writer and pioneer aviator, was the subject of another film in the *Footprints* series, made by my colleague Richard Taylor. The planets in Saint-Exupéry's celebrated tale of *The Little Prince* were certainly inhabited – one by a solitary, proud and autocratic king, in urgent need of subjects, whose magnificent ermine robe took up so much space on his small planet that there was nowhere for the Little Prince to sit down. I remain so grateful to Richard for introducing me to this wonderful and profound story. Another planet, on the little prince's long journey from his star to our earth, was home to *un buveur*, a tippler:

'Why are you drinking?' demanded the Little Prince.
'So that I may forget,' replied the tippler.
'Forget what?' enquired the Little Prince, who already was sorry for him.
'Forget that I am ashamed,' the tippler confessed, hanging his head.
'Ashamed of what?' insisted the Little Prince, who wanted to help him.
'Ashamed of drinking...'

Yet another planet was occupied by a solitary businessman 'concerned with matters of consequence'. He claimed to own the stars and was totally absorbed in counting and re-counting them.

For me one of the most memorable elements in the story is the Little Prince's encounter and relationship with the desert fox, once he finally arrives on earth; and the most memorable sentence that the fox utters: 'It is only with the heart that one can see rightly; what is essential is invisible to the eye.'

St Exupéry's fox and William Blake are not, of course, the only ones to have expressed this opinion. My friend, the visionary artist Cecil Collins, often spoke about 'the eye of the heart', and many of his paintings are beautiful confirmations of this other way of seeing. The journey that the Little Prince makes is certainly the most profound of all the stories we touched upon in the series, and his death the most moving: 'He did not cry out. He fell as gently as a tree falls. There was not even any sound, because of the sand.'

My own journey was heading not so much towards a crisis as a turning point. I was inwardly restless. My new imaginary friend, Don Quixote, was there to remind me that one couldn't hang around in last year's nests, and certainly not with last year's ideas. The move I was soon to make could, at the time, have appeared foolish. In retrospect it certainly wasn't. Like Alice in Wonderland, I was finding the world around me 'curiouser and curiouser', and asking myself and others ever more questions, including one of the most important of all: Is there a meaning not just to our individual lives, but to the life of the universe itself?

During these early years as a film-maker, amid the glamour and excitement of it all, I had also been reading more about Jung and in particular his autobiography *Memories, Dreams, Reflections* which was published in English in 1963, the year I joined the BBC. It is one of the books I return to periodically and am always newly inspired. In it Jung writes about the loneliness that all of us experience from time to time:

> As a child I felt myself to be alone, and I am still, because I know things and must hint at things which others apparently know nothing of, and for the most part do not want to know. Loneliness does not come from having no people about one, but from being unable to communicate the things that seem important to oneself, or from holding certain views which others find inadmissible.

This loneliness was experienced to an even greater degree by the young Rudolf Steiner. 'Must I remain silent?' was the question that increasingly plagued him as he approached mid-life – and it was his life and his experiences I was finding the most helpful and interesting of all.

At this stage of my own life I wasn't experiencing the degree of loneliness that Jung writes about. In ways that seemed to be appreciated I had already started to communicate ideas and stories I felt were important and meaningful. Nor had I, therefore, been silent. Nevertheless another side of me felt increasingly in need of another sort of silence so that some of those ideas could deepen and mature – ideas that were, and still are, strange and even inadmissible to many people.

The worldly Goldmund in me had very much enjoyed travelling all over Europe, as well as being part of a creative and dynamic organisation like the BBC. But my other half – Narziss the monk – had been deeply inspired by quiet talks with the educationalist Francis Edmunds, and others, who seemed to understand the role of silence and the importance of an inner dialogue if communication is to have real power and substance. Through these encounters, along with my continued reading, I felt a growing urge to explore the invisible threads that held together the outer world that I was also exploring, and which I loved and enjoyed so much.

I had kept up my connection with the Steiner school in Sussex that I had visited while still working at Pinewood, and had begun to wonder whether I should perhaps take the plunge in that direction. I talked about my dilemma with John Betjeman with whom I had stayed in close touch – we'd worked together again, this time on a film about the great engineer, Isambard Kingdom Brunel, for *Footprints*. Betjeman had written the commentary in verse, in the first person, as though Brunel himself was narrating the story of his life.

My own story was greatly helped when John Betjeman then wrote me a letter, the words of which have comforted and inspired me ever since: 'My dear Jonathan – Do what you want to do and what you feel is your vocation. If it's teaching then do it. Only you can know. It really is this difficult business of discovering how best one can go on in one's search for God, whether by instructing others or making films or writing – or weaving or carpentry – it doesn't really matter so long as it helps in the search for who made us. Don't hurry.'

CHAPTER 5

A Fork in the Road

I took John Betjeman's advice and didn't hurry my decision about the future direction of my life and my career. Instead I made another documentary series for BBC2, again with Richard Taylor, called *World of a Child*. We each made three films in which we attempted to look at the world through the eyes of ten-year-old children – Anne-Marie being one of my subjects.

Perhaps the most difficult thing I have to write about in this book happened at this time. While making my film at the convent in Edinburgh I had a telephone call from my brother to say that my mother, aged only forty-nine, had committed suicide. I was at least able to express my profound grief in the arms of Sister Therese, at the altar of their church, without inhibition and without words. Never have I felt so close to another human being as to that nun, as my masks fell away and the deep sorrow and shock overwhelmed me. 'Grief is the price we pay for love' were the Queen's words to the mourners of the 9/11 catastrophe in New York.

My mother aged forty

My mother had experienced many difficulties and sorrows in her life – the death of her own mother at a very young age, and a year in a TB sanatorium soon after the birth of my younger brother. Then came the divorce from my father and the struggles of bringing up three children on her own; and finally, despite our closeness as a family, the loneliness she felt as we all moved out into the world. On top of all this she became ill and was in a lot of pain. Yet the state of mind that causes a person to take their own life is hard to understand if you have never experienced such extreme despair yourself.

To say that my search for an understanding of what might lie beyond the threshold of death intensified after my own mother's death might sound obvious and even clumsy. How can one begin to understand such mysteries? Yet it was a search prompted by far more than curiosity. I could not accept, and still don't, that she had ceased to exist except as a fond memory among those of us who knew her. The writer Beryl Bainbridge wrote on the death of her friend, Anna Haycraft: 'I don't think of her as dead…more that she's just not answering the phone.' I again take comfort from those words of Parmenides: 'Nothing can come out of nothing; and nothing that exists can become nothing.'

A few days after my mother's death I did have an experience as I was waking up one morning that had a quality quite different from a dream. It's difficult to describe, except to say that I felt myself in her presence, and that it was a huge comfort. It was as though a veil had been briefly lifted – a gift that I desperately needed.

Almost every day I think about her – a sense of her presence is a constant humanising influence in my life – and increasingly I try not to just pin her down in my mind as the person I knew so well for twenty-eight years. Instead I try and imagine her as someone who continues to grow and learn, as she would have done if she had lived longer – but now from a perspective that is hard for us to imagine. Perhaps she is simply digesting the ups and downs of her life, which must in itself be an extraordinary learning process. What I do believe is that we are, in some mysterious way, in touch – her essence and my essence; and it is at a level that goes far deeper than personality or anything to do with the name I carry at present, or the name and physical form by which I knew her.

I have never been tempted to return to séances, table-tapping and the like, but have come to trust that what goes on unconsciously in our lives, above all in sleep, is a web of communion quite different from our earthly sense of time and space. The spiritual world, heaven – call it what you like – has become something very present for me and not as somewhere else, somewhere we go only when we die. We participate in it all the time, I believe, but not yet consciously. At a funeral service I attended recently the Roman Catholic priest referred to this world as 'just a stopping-off place'. It is a view with which I disagree most strongly. There is only one world, one universe, but it is many-layered, as we are ourselves. The fact that we don't remember aspects of this many-layered existence does not surprise me in the least. Think how vivid and powerful our dreams can be, and yet we don't on the whole retain them for long. Within an hour or so they are forgotten. It is as though our consciousness at this stage in our evolution is simply not equipped to hold onto them. And if we experience our dreams as so ephemeral, it is not surprising that we have no conscious memory of the time we spend asleep, let alone a possible pre-birth existence, and indeed previous incarnations.

Before I leave the subject of my mother's death I would like to mention the expression 'time heals'. A cynical reaction to that thought might be that the pain and sorrow we feel when someone dies gradually fades because, as basically selfish creatures, we simply get on with our own lives and have no deep and lasting concern for others. I believe, however, that time heals because unconsciously we experience this contact I have tried to describe. In our heart of hearts we know that all is well, that nothing is lost and that we can wipe away our tears and get on with life. Erich Fromm described our sense of the truth as being repressed. That may be so, but not completely.

By now I had decided to take a break from television in order to explore Steiner's work in more depth. I was not sure that I wanted to remain in the spectator role of a film-maker – always on the outside, looking on. I was twenty-eight years old. Should I not be rolling up my sleeves and doing a proper job? My head of department at the BBC, Gordon Watkins, was a most thoughtful and sensitive man, and completely understood my need to have this space. Although I hadn't expected it, he even indicated that my job would be kept open if I wanted to return.

My plan was to do a nine-month course at Emerson College, at Forest Row in Sussex. Francis Edmunds, its founder, had been a teacher himself and was later responsible for the teacher-training course for Steiner education. Out of this experience he recognised that many adults of different ages experience a need to pause, take stock and reassess the direction of their lives. Such a need was often prompted by an encounter with some sort of spiritual teaching like that initiated by Steiner. 'Judge a person not by his answers, but by his questions' was one of Edmunds' favourite sayings.

In the first prospectus for the college, Edmunds identified as potential students 'those who feel an acute sense of contradiction between their

Francis Edmunds

intuitive regard for life and the current views, theories and events they have to meet'. As a scientist by training, he repeatedly returned in his lectures at Emerson College to that most central and challenging question of all: 'What is the human being?' Over the centuries many wise people have said that if we truly know and understand ourselves we will understand the whole universe – and vice versa; it's sometimes referred to as the Hermetic Law: 'As above, so below.' We are, each one of us, a microcosm of the macrocosm. And certainly when I read about stars and galaxies, and the unimaginable distances and quantities involved, I am constantly reminded of equally awe-inspiring information about the human body and about the number of cells in the brain alone.

One of the lessons I remember best from those early weeks at the college was learning from Edmunds some extraordinary facts about this relationship we human beings have with the cosmos at large. For example we take an average of 18 breaths every minute. That means that, in 24 hours, we breathe 25,920 times. It takes exactly the same number of years for the vernal point of the sun – the point on the ecliptic at which the sun rises on March 21st – to journey once through the zodiac; a period called the Platonic cosmic year.

Our connection with the rhythms of nature and the heavens is therefore not just a philosophical or spiritual matter, but is reflected in every aspect of our organism and being. As day gives way to night, so do we fall asleep – expanding, as it were, from our sharply focused daytime consciousness. Likewise through the seasons, from winter into summer, we experience a psychological rhythm passing from contraction to expansion. And, as the ancients taught, this is all embedded in the most profound rhythm of all, for at death – as they would have expressed it – we leave our isolated and contracted existence in an earthly body altogether, and expand far into the realm of the stars.

From many different directions Edmunds returned again and again to this theme of the human being as a universe in miniature; and, aided by others, he confronted us with facts and phenomena that we so often take for granted, whether studying science, history, philosophy, religion or art – facts that stimulate a feeling of awe and wonder so often thwarted in the hurried and shallow atmosphere of the modern world.

However, it wasn't all talk during these nine most stimulating months. We dug the garden, and made things from clay and wood. We even learned to weave. Some people performed new and strange movements called eurythmy, but being an inhibited Englishman I boycotted these lessons to read my newspaper – anxious not to completely lose contact with that other reality that we call daily life. At the time I hadn't connected sufficiently with eurythmy to understand that it represents an important aspect of the microcosm/macrocosm theme; the movements correspond to archetypal movements in the cosmos at large, and mirror formative influences that are at work in the interplay between us and the heavens. However, even that awe-inspiring thought doesn't make me any more comfortable about actually performing them!

We also produced a play called *This Way to the Tomb* by Ronald Duncan, whom I had met through his daughter Briony while working at the BBC. Duncan was a prickly genius, living in a remote hideaway on the North Devon coast. He was co-founder with George Devine of the English Stage Company; his friend Ezra Pound called him 'the lone wolf of English letters'. He managed to quarrel with most of his friends and collaborators including Benjamin Britten, for whose opera *The Rape of Lucretia* he wrote the libretto. The second volume of his autobiography is aptly titled *How to Make Enemies*. And in defiance of John Donne's famous line in his *Devotions*: 'No man is an island, entire of itself', Duncan gave the first volume of his autobiography the provocative title *All Men are Islands*. In saying this he is, in my opinion, both profoundly right and profoundly wrong. I will return later to why I think this is so. Towards the end of Duncan's life, inspired by his friendship with the physicist Hermann Bondi, he wrote a mammoth poem simply called 'Man', which opens as follows:

I am: God I could become
If I could remember my future
As I have forgotten my past
I am: God I will become
When I can imagine the whole
As I have remembered a part.
I am: God I shall become;
For I am the only conscious thing
In an unconscious universe;
I am the dreamer who can dream
He is dreaming;
I am the miracle: man.

This Way to the Tomb is also written in verse, and explores among other things the theme of reincarnation. The first Act – The Masque – unfolds on the island of Zante in the Mediterranean during the

Ronald Duncan

14th century. Here Antony, recent Abbot of Santa Ferrata and later to become St Antony, has been living for three years as a hermit together with three young novices – Marcus, a peasant; Julian, a poet; and Bernard, a scholar. As he struggles on his path of purification, Antony meets aspects of himself that have still to be overcome – failings that are mirrored for him in the three young novices. Pride in his own achievement is the sin he is unable to shed completely and is thus prompted to declare:

> Perhaps God has no permanent reality
> But exists as and when we create Him,
> Through the labour of humility
> He is born in the death of pride.

The poet Vernon Watkins expresses a similar thought in his unpublished essay 'A Note on my Poetry' where he writes: 'I had died the death of ambition, and found that death was only a beginning.' In Duncan's play, Antony – in the realisation that his journey is far from over – says to one of his companions:

> You see, Marcus, as old men we face death
> With our souls in pawn to our business
> And none of our business accomplished.
> For living is an endless chain of interlocking actions,
> Distractions disguised as important actions.
> I will do this, when I have done that.
> I will do that, when I have done this.
> And so on and so on and so on.
> The Abbots's wealth was the Abbot's distraction.
> The Hermit's poverty is the Hermit's distraction.
> For here on Zante, our poverty and simplicity
> Can be made a distraction also.

The second Act – the Anti-Masque – takes place on the same island in the present day. Here we meet an assortment of characters – a radio producer and his slick presenter Father Opine, a New Age group of pilgrims, a postcard-seller and other islanders. From this disparate group the characters we met in Act One slowly emerge. Duncan doesn't mention the words karma or reincarnation, but that is the phenomenon we are witnessing. His play is an interesting and bold creation, though dramatically this second Act doesn't work quite as well as the first. Nevertheless Duncan communicates some profound thoughts, as in Antony's speech at the close of the play:

> If the wheel did not revolve and all life upon this earth
> Died in death
> and did not quicken,
> Nor reawaken,

and the severed lay forever fallen
And the buried body were forever broken,

Then in time all life would lie absorbed in greedy death
And no birth
from the tomb could quicken
Nor from the womb awaken.
From life our death is taken,
From death our life is drawn. So with our souls. Amen.

Ronald Duncan also edited a publication that he called *The Encyclopedia of Ignorance*. 'Compared to the pond of knowledge, our ignorance remains atlantic', he wrote in the preface; and he concluded with this sentence: 'Perhaps some answers depend on asking the correct question.' It was such questions that Francis Edmunds and others were encouraging us to ask at Emerson College.

At that time nearly half the students at the college were from the USA. Edmunds much admired and respected the American 'folk soul' as exemplified by that wise and courageous essayist and lecturer Ralph Waldo Emerson (1803–1882) who, in his opinion, shared the same ideals that inspired Rudolf Steiner in the early years of the 20th century.

In his book *The Spiritual Teachings of Ralph Waldo Emerson*, Richard Geldard writes: 'His [Emerson's] intellectual and spiritual journey, like that of Odysseus before him, began with the challenge of avoiding the rocks of fixed doctrine on the one side and the whirlpools of mysticism on the other, in an effort to chart a clear passage to spiritual knowledge.'

At the age of twenty-three Emerson, like his father before him, was ordained as a Minister in the Unitarian Church, but five years later he resigned, convinced of his fundamental unsuitability for the formalities of religion. He then dedicated his life to those who, in Geldard's words, 'were in spiritual and intellectual bondage'. Around him in New England grew what came to be known as American Transcendentalism, 'a conscious seeking of a reality which lay behind and beyond the surfaces of the manifest world'.

Ralph Waldo Emerson

For Emerson and his friends one of the fundamental problems with religion was, according to Geldard, that 'it espoused the complete otherness of God and his Kingdom. The dualism inherent in New England Puritan thought dominated even the Unitarian thinking of Emerson's day. Emerson's instincts were to find a true Unitarianism, a vision of the universe and human life and culture as a whole. Such unity was only to be found in esoteric doctrines, particularly the Eastern variety, and also in the works of Plato and his close followers.'

Another wise American, Jacob Needleman – whose definition of a true guru I mentioned earlier – writes in his endorsement of Geldard's book of how 'Emerson shows a new generation of Americans that it is possible and necessary to bring to the spiritual search an open heart joined to a critical mind.' This is exactly what Edmunds was trying to bring to us students, and not only to the ones from America.

At one time Edmunds had actually wanted to base his college in America, and although it ended up on the edge of the Ashdown Forest in England, it bore the name of his hero, the man who also wrote: 'Though we travel the world over to find the beautiful, we must carry it with us or we find it not.' Another thought of Emerson's that I like: 'When Nature has work to be done, she creates a genius to do it.'

So what did I learn at Emerson College? I certainly learnt more about Rudolf Steiner who, like Teilhard de Chardin, was trying, above all, to reconcile those sensibilities of a more intuitive and imaginative nature with the experience of modern consciousness, which leads quite naturally to the rationality and objectivity that characterises science.

I also learnt at the college to be wary of that tendency we have to form cults around a strong and charismatic leader, whether alive or not. I had glimpsed signs of this unhealthy dependency already, and perhaps it is inevitable in any such movement. Jung is reputed to have said: 'Thank God I'm Jung and not a Jungian'. Krishnamurti was surrounded by adoring followers who recorded his every word, despite the fact that his central message was 'Stand on your own two feet.'

The hapless Brian, in the Monty Python film *The Life of Brian*, is the most obvious victim of this unhealthy adoration. 'Go away', he says to the crowd that has suddenly gathered around him. 'Only the true Messiah denies his Divinity', is their response. A firmer discouragement is clearly needed. 'Fuck off', he tells them. 'How shall we fuck off, Master?' Brian then tries a gentler approach. 'You don't need to follow anybody.' 'We don't need to follow anybody', they repeat in unison.

Even in his lifetime Steiner was troubled by this same uncritical adoration that inevitably plagues anyone with charisma who chooses to stick their head above the parapet. He did his best to diffuse it. Andrew Welburn, in his book *Rudolf Steiner's Philosophy*, writes: 'Those who seek from him ready-made answers to all life's problems will seek in vain, or at best make of him another idol.' Another obvious result of this over-dependency on another person is a tendency to bypass the work and effort oneself, so that the revelations and insights one cherishes are all second-hand. It was the trap into which Beatie Bryant had fallen in the play *Roots*.

If things became too intense, or too reverential at Emerson College, my friend and fellow student Pierre della Negra and I used to write and deliver imaginary lectures by Steiner on all sorts of obscure and absurd subjects. Pierre was French, and although his English was initially pretty ropey we were both blissfully united under the fine banner of humour. Pierre, with his wife Vivien, eventually went on to found a similar college in France – the Foyer Michael – that flourishes to this day, and where learning and laughter, I know, are intertwined.

I was heartened to read later in the reminiscences of the Russian artist Andrei Belyi, who spent some years working alongside Rudolf Steiner, that Steiner himself would at times storm against 'the exalted spirituality' of some of his followers as they flocked to his centre at Dornach in Switzerland. 'It just won't do', Belyi remembers him saying, 'to have you running about constantly with such blissful faces and meditating, meditating, meditating! You could at least organise a group to further your education! Or simply sit down together and laugh a little and parody each other!'

Despite my reservations about the tendency that some of us have to huddle into cosy little groups, I went to Emerson College because Francis Edmunds – and several other people I had met who had a deep commitment to working creatively with Steiner's legacy – were among the most interesting and inspiring people I had encountered. I was not disappointed. Having not been to university it was also a luxury to sit and listen to lectures – even to write essays. In particular I remember the insightful and entertaining courses on history by Cecil Harwood, one of the founders of the first Steiner school in Britain back in 1925. He was also the author of another excellent book on Steiner's educational ideas, *The Recovery of Man in Childhood*.

Harwood's history courses were based on a notion of the evolution of consciousness – still a radical idea – which proposes that not only do the contents of the mind change and evolve, but also the mind itself. 'Evolution has become conscious' as the eminent biologist Julian Huxley put it. If we really want to understand how and why history has unfolded in the way it has, then we need to study not only the actions of individuals who shaped and influenced events, but also how these individuals thought and felt. And it is a great mistake, I have come to realise, to imagine that they thought and felt as we do. Indeed, if you travel far enough back, humanity's relationship with the gods and our divine origin was perhaps not yet determined by doctrine but by actual experience.

In the mid-sixties, Jacob Bronowski made an influential series of documentary films for the BBC entitled *The Ascent of Man*. It was billed as the history of science, but of science in the broadest terms: 'Invention from the flint tool to geometry, from the arch to the theory of relativity, are shown to be expressions of man's specific ability to understand nature, to control it, not to be controlled by it'. A somewhat arrogant statement, one might think, from the perspective of our more uncertain times, some thirty years later. Who controls what? Perhaps partnership is a more appropriate word to use. We, after all, are part of nature. If we harm or exploit her, we harm ourselves. This much we seem to have learned. Our ancestors, I suspect, knew it instinctively.

This flowering of human intelligence has of course been an extraordinary achievement – but at what cost? I shall explore the concerns and reservations that some people have about this 'ascent' in later chapters, particularly in relation to one of the main themes of this book – our attitude to death, and to all that cannot be measured or quantified in our lives.

Meanwhile, in relation to Bronowski's title, I will only add that one can also look at human evolution as a descent. Like the child who grows down as well as up, so human beings have gradually awoken to their physical surroundings. This idea does, of course, presuppose an archetypal, spiritual existence – an idea that underpins the 'idealistic philosophy' explored so comprehensively in Jonathan Black's *The Secret History of the World*. Some people see this 'descent' as a loss, and are nostalgic for some golden age when, in all humility, we knew our place and lived in harmony with all creation. Later I will address in more detail why I believe this journey of ours – as both descent and ascent – is, in fact, profoundly meaningful and not some awful mistake.

At Emerson College I tried to keep an open mind about all these things, and to trust the philosopher Henri Bergson's definition of intuition as 'the faculty for knowledge which results from instinct that is illumined by reason'. In other words, I was attempting to have a rational conversation with my daimon – a continuation of that dialogue begun in the woods around Pinewood Film Studios seven years earlier.

Thus I slowly became comfortable with what in many ways is a very uncompromising yet clear statement by Rudolf Steiner, written in a letter in 1903, when he was forty-two years old: 'I can truly say that for me the spiritual is absolutely real – not a whit less real than is the table at which I am now writing.'

CHAPTER 6

Seen and Unseen

During my time at Emerson College, because of my interest in biography, I took a particular interest in the story of how Steiner's life unfolded. He describes how as a child he lived in two different worlds, distinguishing between things which are seen and those which are not seen. In other words, alongside normal sensory experience of an outer world he was aware from an early age of an inner dimension of experience not based on sense perception. This is why, in his attempt to describe these two areas of experience, he later used the term 'spiritual world' to differentiate it from the 'sense world'. Most small children have these intimations of other levels of existence – the presence of my friend Doyky being one example. In Steiner's case, it seems, these experiences did not fade.

In *Rudolf Steiner: An Introduction to his Life and Work*, Gary Lachman describes Steiner as 'a dweller on the threshold'. It is, perhaps, what we all are during the first year or so of our lives, of which we have no memory. Likewise in old age – when our sensory faculties start to fade – we can also seem to be only partly present. And it is often then that people are apparently aware of, and even in conversation with those long dead.

An early experience of Steiner's faculty for seeing what others did not see occurred when he was seven. He 'saw' an unknown woman come through the door, stop in the middle of the room and then communicate to him, but not in words. 'Now and always, try to do for me whatever you can' was her message. Days later he learned that a relative had committed suicide on the same day and at the precise time he had this experience. He was in no doubt that it was this woman who had asked him for help. But there was no one with whom he felt able to share this experience, knowing he would be rebuked for foolish superstition. Some hundred years earlier William Blake was less inhibited when, as a small boy, he experienced the presence of an angel. He told his father and was beaten for telling lies.

Steiner was born in 1861 and grew up on the fringes of the Austro-Hungarian Empire, where his father held a relatively humble position as a railway official. Despite his instinctive connection to what lay hidden behind the sense-perceptible world, Steiner took a keen interest in all that was mechanical, and in trains in particular. At the time those steaming iron monsters would, I imagine, have been as exciting as a space rocket for a child today. He also felt a deep connection with nature and in particular with the woods surrounding his home.

The family lived in simple circumstances; austere, but healthy would be one way to describe their life. In his autobiography *Chapters in the Course of My Life*, Steiner wrote: 'My parents were assigned near the station a little orchard of fruit trees and a small patch for potatoes. Gathering cherries, taking care of the orchard, preparing the potatoes for planting, cultivating the soil, digging the potatoes – all this work fell to my sister and brother and me.' He wrote too, of his love for the distant mountains and of one particular walk, at first with his parents and later alone. In those woods were blackberries, raspberries and strawberries, 'a delicious contribution to the family supper, which otherwise consisted merely of a piece of buttered bread or bread and cheese for each of us.'

The breakthrough in his dilemma regarding two worlds came for Steiner around the age of eight when he discovered a book on geometry at school: 'I plunged into it with enthusiasm', he wrote over fifty years later:

> For weeks at a time my mind was filled with coincidences, similarities between triangles, squares and polygons; I racked my brain over the question: Where do parallel lines actually meet? The theorem of Pythagoras fascinated me. That one can live within the mind in the shaping of forms perceived only within oneself, entirely without impression upon the external senses – this gave me the deepest satisfaction ... To be able to lay hold upon something in the spirit alone brought to me an inner joy. I am sure that I learned first in geometry to experience this joy.

In other words Steiner realised that although the triangles and circles on the paper in front of him could only ever be approximations, the ideas or theories in themselves, as internalised in his mind, were true, and indeed perfect. And if something like geometry could be grasped with such precision in the mind alone, perhaps he could eventually speak with equal precision about his own inner world and so communicate to others the totality of his experiences, including that world 'which is not seen'. But his 'spiritual world' was for him not somewhere else; it was our world, experienced in greater depth and in full consciousness.

In *Feet of Clay*, Anthony Storr points out that although Steiner had little in common with either Bertrand Russell or Albert Einstein, all three became infatuated with geometry in childhood. Russell later described the experience, aged eleven, as being as dazzling as first love. And Einstein, aged twelve, was overwhelmed by the realisation that 'man was capable, through the force of thought alone, of achieving the degree of stability and purity which the Greeks, before anybody else, demonstrated to us in geometry'.

By the age of twenty Steiner had clarified for himself this early and liberating experience of geometry:

> The objects and occurrences which the senses perceive are in space.
> But, just as this space is outside of us, so there exists also within
> us a sort of soul-space which is the arena of spiritual realities and
> occurrences ... I felt that one must carry the knowledge of the spiritual
> world within oneself after the fashion of geometry. For the reality of
> the spiritual world was to me as certain as that of the physical.

For those who have traumatic memories of their maths lessons at school and couldn't perhaps even spell isosceles triangle, let alone understand what it meant, this may all sound somewhat abstract and obscure. But I want to try and clarify, as best I can, the process by which Steiner was gradually able to make the pronouncements that he did, before I try to share something of their content. To say 'clarify' is perhaps over-optimistic, but at least I have indicated the sober and rational nature of Steiner's efforts – unlike so many spiritual teachings that give the word 'occult' a bad name.

But how does one even start to express in these precise terms what to most people is inexpressible? And isn't it all subjective anyway? '... one of the most difficult aspects of "transcendent", "mystical" or "spiritual" experiences', writes Andrew Welburn in *Rudolf Steiner's Philosophy*, 'has always been precisely the problem of knowing how to interpret them. It is not just the question of what they mean, but how we would know whether our interpretation was right or wrong at all.'

It is a problem Fritjof Capra acknowledges in his book *The Tao of Physics*, where he writes about eastern mystics. They too have been aware that verbal descriptions of the reality they experience risk being either inaccurate or incomplete. 'The direct experience of reality', writes Capra, 'transcends the realm of thought and language, and, since all mysticism is based on such a direct experience, everything that is said about it can only be partly true.'

Steiner, however, wanted to investigate spirituality, even spiritual phenomena, scientifically. It is, says Welburn, the approach of the modern, self-reliant thinker: 'Indeed, what he means by "scientific" in this spiritual context is firstly that he does not ask for a prior act of belief.'

This was the plea that Steiner constantly expressed to those interested in his ideas: not to follow him blindly but to test all he said through their own experience – not necessarily by his clairvoyant means, but by using their own unprejudiced intelligence and powers of observation. Life itself, so he believed, would confirm in time the truth of his research. But essentially, as I understand it, we all have this latent capacity to 'see' more, if we are prepared to do the work.

But what does this word 'clairvoyance' really mean? Steiner spoke of our potential capacity to detect 'the deeper laws beneath the everyday surface of things ... The promptings of the spirit, first in the form of hunches and intuitions, begin to invade our waking life.' Clearly this has nothing to do with going into some kind of trance, which is how the word 'clairvoyance' is usually understood. Perhaps it would be helpful for a moment to ponder the senses we are aware of. The eye, for example, has the capacity to see that out of which it is constituted – no more, no less. The eye and the world that it sees are in essence one; but the eye doesn't see sounds, for example. And if there are indeed realities that are hidden, not just from our sight but from all our five senses, then we need an organ of perception that corresponds to that reality. It is this organ to which Steiner refers and which is of a non-material nature, as is the realm to which it relates, which it 'sees'. And such an organ, as I understand it, is intimately related to something we are very familiar with: our capacity to think.

Is the idea that there are limits to human knowledge therefore about to crumble? There are, in fact, many indications – and not just among Steiner's followers – that it is crumbling already. Scientists, in fact, rather than theologians or philosophers, are in the vanguard of this shift – scientists honest and humble enough to recognise that the phenomenal world, and the paradoxes that confront them, increasingly require a new and deeper way of comprehending the data. For paradoxes are not pointing to insoluble problems, but rather are a challenge to rearrange how we think about things. Our willingness to be sufficiently open-minded, without spiralling into some New Age fantasy, will be the ultimate challenge. It will also be the test of whether Steiner was just an eccentric but highly gifted one-off, or a key figure in indicating a further turning point in our human journey; a herald, maybe, of what the American writer Thomas Kuhn has called a 'paradigm shift' – a complete change in what we take for granted and the assumptions we make about reality.

During the last two decades of the 19th century, between the ages of eighteen and thirty-six, Steiner immersed himself in science and philosophy, first in Vienna and later at the Goethe Institute in Weimar. His resolve, it seems, was to ground himself thoroughly in the thinking of his day and to develop his intellectual abilities fully. In 1891 he gained the degree of Doctor of Philosophy at the University of Rostock. He also felt that the sense-perceptible world had something to tell him that only it could reveal. Above all – through the discipline of his academic work – he was developing the all-important faculty of discrimination. For if a spiritual dimension of reality does exist, I suspect it is, like the everyday world we inhabit, full of voices clamouring to be heard – some wise, some not wise at all. In a book called *In the Belly of the Beast*, which challenges us to take note of what lies behind our contemporary culture, both good and bad, Sevak Gulbekian writes: 'There is an assumption by some New Age practitioners that whatever is received from metaphysical sources is by definition "good" and "true". That position is naïve, to say the least.'

However, many voices have something to say worth listening to, whether you agree with them or not, and if you listen carefully enough. In Vienna, at the end of the 19th century, there were plenty of ideas flying about, not least – as in other European capitals – a revival of interest in occult and mystical ideas.

One of the reasons I found Lachman's biography of Steiner so enjoyable is that, unlike some other books about Steiner which tend to be somewhat over-reverential, it brings him to life as a vulnerable as well as gifted human being, and particularly as a young man from a humble background struggling to find his way amid the buzz of a great city. In a chapter entitled 'At the Megalomania Café', Lachman writes of the young Rudolf Steiner at the Café Griensteidl: 'He could nurse a cup of coffee for hours, enjoying the warm fire his student's room lacked, discussing the serious questions of the day with fellow aspiring geniuses.' And it was here, amidst the noise and bustle, that the diligent young man was already writing his introduction to Goethe's scientific writings.

Lachman suggests, however, that it would be a mistake to imagine Steiner solely as a reclusive introvert 'grimly preparing to do battle with the spirit of the age'. The place was nicknamed the Megalomania Café by the young artists and poets who frequented it, and for a time Steiner gave the café as his address, being the one place where he was sure to be found. It sounds somewhat like a modern-day Starbucks, but with conversation as well as coffee, and in a city that was bubbling with new ideas and creativity. A closer parallel might have been Les Deux Magots in Paris, which became home to the Surrealist Movement in the 1930s and later to Jean-Paul Sartre and his fellow Existentialists.

It is also important to note that during Steiner's early years as a student in Vienna, where he was increasingly to mix with the intellectual and artistic élite of the Austro-Hungarian Empire, he had close contact with someone very different, whom he acknowledges in his autobiography as playing a crucial role in his destiny; someone, in other words, who became for Steiner what I have called an 'awakener' in the very deepest sense.

Felix Koguzki gathered herbs and medicinal plants in the countryside and sold them to apothecaries in Vienna. Steiner had met him on his regular train journey into the city, and in his autobiography writes:

On his back were his bundles of herbs; but in his heart was the knowledge of the spiritual aspects of nature that had come to him through his gathering of them. And so gradually I came to feel that I was in the company of a soul from ancient times, who, untouched by civilisation, science, or the contemplation of the present, brought close to me the intuitive knowledge of former times.

Above the entrance to Koguzki's home were the words: 'With the blessing of God, all things are good.' Steiner describes the pleasure of being in the company of simple country people like Felix Koguzki and his family:

I always had to drink coffee there, not from a cup, but from a porridge bowl which held nearly a litre; with this I had to eat a piece of bread of enormous dimensions. Nor did the villagers by any means look upon the man as a dreamer. There was no occasion for jesting at his behaviour in his village ... There was no one who smiled like those persons that watched him and me going together through the streets of Vienna ...

In *The Secret History of Consciousness*, Lachman goes so far as to suggest that 'Steiner's conversations with this strange man helped plant the seeds of what would later flower as one of the most successful and influential alternative teachings in the world today.'

During this early period Steiner wrote, among other things, his key book *The Philosophy of Freedom*, published in 1894. Welburn calls it his philosophical testament and 'still the proper starting point for a comprehension of his subsequent less academically orthodox line ... a far-reaching new approach to such issues as human freedom, evolution and the sources of moral value.'

I, personally, have always found it a difficult book; but then no philosophy is easy. In the preface to his book *The Great Philosophers* – based on his BBC television series of interviews in 1987 – Bryan Magee refers to a certain 'Anglo-Saxon pride at not being too concerned with abstract ideas'. For me, however – and perhaps for many Englishmen – the problem is not to do with lack of concern or interest, but rather the difficulty of thinking philosophically.

In *Romanticism Comes of Age*, Owen Barfield suggests that the English Romantics of the early 19th century failed to leave their mark on the cultural and philosophical trends of their time because they, too, had experienced this difficulty and had therefore not sufficiently absorbed and immersed themselves in what had been nurtured in Germany, particularly by Goethe. Shelley and Byron travelled to Italy and Greece without making that detour. In other words they too were less inclined to think philosophically.

Barfield mentions the poet Coleridge as the notable exception, with his ten months of wandering in Germany as a young man. There he learnt the language, studied science and metaphysics, and took a life-long interest in the more conscious Romanticism of German Idealistic philosophy. In his two-volume biography of Coleridge, Richard Holmes calls him 'a hero for a self-questioning age', who through his travels, both inner and outer 'found something Teutonic in his own soul'. Rather than the mystic charlatan and opium addict of legend, Holmes suggests that this immersion in the cultural life of Europe 'distinguished him sharply from the purely provincial aspect of English thought'.

Reading Steiner's *The Philosophy of Freedom* is not only difficult, but also feels like a spiritual exercise in itself, which I gather is what the author intended. What I have termed 'mental press-ups' would be another way to describe what seems to be demanded. However I have understood enough of the book to recognise and appreciate what Gertrude Reif Hughes describes in her introduction to the centennial edition – retitled *Intuitive Thinking as a Spiritual Path*: 'Steiner designed all his books to discourage passive collecting of information and to encourage instead conscious pondering and questioning, particularly of hitherto unexamined notions.'

Mere curiosity and an urge to devour all sorts of intriguing bits of occult knowledge are temptations that affect many of us. I recognise it in myself; it's what I call 'spiritual gluttony' – wanting the treats without doing any of the work. Reading *The Philosophy of Freedom* is certainly hard work; but perhaps it is also a treat in disguise, in the same way that people speak of suffering as a secret blessing – since we tend to grow only in the process of overcoming obstacles.

The concentration and meditative exercises suggested by Steiner and other serious spiritual teachers are also, of course, hard work; as is the exhortation 'Know Thyself', which has echoed down the centuries from the oracle of Apollo in Ancient Greece through all the teachings of the 'secret societies', and into the daylight of the 20th and 21st centuries. It is, in Steiner's opinion, the basis for all knowledge. 'Who am I?' is the question at the heart of the practices taught by all the great spiritual traditions.

What I value and respect most of all in the process of answering this question is that element which challenges us to put our own house in order, especially in our relations with other people. All striving for enlightenment and perfection, in whatever sphere of human endeavour, is vain in both senses if pursued for oneself alone. This is what Ronald Duncan's Abbot finally recognises in the play *This Way To The Tomb*. Self-knowledge requires great honesty and rigour, and a recognition of where we are not truly free in the thoughts we have and in the deeds we undertake because of ulterior motives, prejudice and ignorance. In *The Philosophy of Freedom* Steiner singles out the thought process itself as needing the same rigorous purging of egotistical elements in order to arrive at true knowledge.

Many people have difficulty, initially at least, with the emphasis that Steiner placed on thinking. 'Thinking has a bad reputation with many people,' says Hughes in her introduction to the book, 'perhaps especially with those who incline toward a spiritual path.' I suppose Steiner's appeal might have been greater had he, for example, set out what he had to give in mythological form, as did Tolkien and C.S. Lewis, and more recently Philip Pullman. Steiner did, in fact, write four Mystery plays, but in my experience they belong as much in the realm of philosophy as art – certainly, at times, more head than heart.

Although Francis Edmunds loved the theatre, and Shakespeare's plays in particular, he repeatedly reminded us that we live in an age where the intellectual faculty is paramount; an age that prides itself on knowledge based on independent observation and thought. This was, he said, the rock on which Steiner felt he had to build. I don't believe that in saying this Edmunds was dismissing the crucial role played by art in its broadest sense, and above all by music, as a bridge into what is largely inexpressible in any other form. Rather I understand it as a plea for the intellect to deepen in such a way that it does not clash with all that is imaginative and intuitive in our nature.

In fact Steiner himself, in his autobiography, acknowledges that the artistic image is better able to convey what underlies all existence than the rationalistic concept. Even the great physicist Werner Heisenberg, in an address in Athens on June 3rd 1964 (published as *Natural Law and the Structure of Matter*), concluded by acknowledging: 'If harmony in a society finally depends on the common interpretation of the "one", of the unity behind the multitude of phenomena, the language of the poets may be more important than that of the scientists.'

———————

So where was I, a twenty-eight year old student in all this? There were moments, I have to admit – and occasionally there are still – when I wondered whether we don't create or cling to stories about a heavenly world, either elsewhere or potentially here on earth, as a comfort that simply enables us to cope with the difficulties of being a conscious human being in the here and now. In the philosophy classes, for example, my mind would sometimes drift into wondering not whether I really was a microcosm of the macrocosm, but who was filming what at the BBC, or whether I would skip tomorrow's weaving class. Such thoughts had nothing to do with any eternal essence in me or in the cosmos at large. Yet I can also see that my ability to stand back and make such observations and judgements about myself – whether they be wise or absurd – is already an indication of what Steiner is pointing to in *The Philosophy of Freedom*. The extent to which I am aware of my own shortcomings is the first step in overcoming them. As Nelson Mandela once said: 'The truth is we are not yet free; we have merely achieved the freedom to be free.'

Here I want to emphasise Steiner's conviction that thought is an integral part and product of the universe, and belongs to reality as much as the realm accessible to our senses. We tend to experience thoughts as our own private creations, as subjective, in the same way that we experience our physical separation from everything not contained within our individual skins. But if each human being is, in reality, a microcosm of the macrocosm, and if that macrocosm contains not just the stuff of which all things physical, including ourselves, are made, but also contains thought itself, then by fusing our sense perceptions and our thoughts we restore, and thereby mirror, the original unity of the universe. 'Thinking has the same significance in relation to ideas', wrote Steiner, 'as the eye has for light, the ear for sound; it is the organ of perception.' The expression 'the mind's eye' makes the same point.

Rudi Lissau, in *Rudolf Steiner: Life, Work, Inner Path and Social Initiatives*, further elucidates this complex subject in a chapter entitled 'A Philosopher of Freedom'. 'The true act of knowing', he writes, 'is tantamount to a communion in which the world and man are reunited.' In other words the creative forces out there have their correspondences in us. And embedded in those creative forces is a morality with which we are connected. To be good, or at least to strive to be good, is to be true to an essential part of our nature, thereby mirroring an essential element of the cosmos of which we are expressions, and out of which we are born.

Lissau also underlines the important influence that Goethe's writings had on Steiner, in particular the emphasis on

> a meticulous, patient observation of the physical aspect of reality that leads gradually to an awareness of its spiritual reality. Such observation needs utter concentration and imagination, a freeing of sensual reality from its usual conceptual mould. This combination of concentration and imagination is, however, very close to meditation as Steiner later came to teach it.

This notion of the need to look harder and longer at the world around us is likewise expressed in Goethe's suggestion that alongside our study of physical phenomena using microscopes or telescopes, in conjunction with our unprejudiced intelligence and in a spirit of open-mindedness, we should also at times become quiet and still, 'allowing Nature to whisper her secrets to us'. One way to characterise such an approach would be to see it as a balance between the masculine and feminine sensibilities within each of us – action and receptivity.

Steiner's philosophical work thus pins us down well and truly to the here and now. 'It does not suggest', writes Andrew Welburn, 'that we must believe in some "metaphysical" reality beyond what we can see and know, a "thought-out" spiritual world in the beyond. It seeks rather to make us aware of the spirit through our own activity, interpreting and transforming the world around us.'

The dualistic notion of a spiritual world as somewhere essentially separate from the physical world is also tackled by Bryan Magee in *The Great Philosophers*, in a chapter in which he talks to Myles Burnyeat – at that time, in 1967, Professor of Ancient Philosophy at Cambridge University – about one of the greatest of all philosophers, Plato. Burnyeat tells Magee of a passage in *Phaedo* where Socrates maintains that to do philosophy is to rehearse for death. It is in fact to practise being dead because, says Burnyeat, 'being dead is having one's soul separate from the body, and in doing philosophy you are, so far as you can, separating the soul from the body, precisely because you are not thinking about the here and now where the body is.'

If, for example, you are asking the question 'What is justice?' with reference to justice at all times, and not 'Who wronged me yesterday or last week?' or if you are asking 'What is beauty?' and not 'Who is the most beautiful person in this room?' then, says Burnyeat, 'if you are not thinking about the here and now ... you are not here and now. You are where your mind is, not because you are in some other particular place but a better one, but because you are not in a place in that sense at all.'

Steiner, it seems to me, in his emphasis on thought as the unifying factor between the human being and the cosmos at large, is reaffirming the insights of Plato in relation to an archetypal realm that potentially corresponds to our own deepest nature and is not some other place.

Gary Lachman calls Steiner 'a passionate idealist, trying to throw a monkey-wrench into the machinery of materialism' and, in his opinion, *The Philosophy of Freedom* does just that. Lachman goes on to point out that Steiner was working out of the same tradition as Blake, Coleridge, Swedenborg, Husserl and many others in trying to counteract the dominant view of consciousness pioneered by René Descartes, and further articulated by John Locke in his famous pronouncement that at birth our mind is a blank slate on which the world will slowly make its mark. The experience of most parents contradicts this notion, since very small children and even babies clearly have their own unique inner life and character long before the world starts to influence them. 'What Steiner and his fellow idealists are saying', writes Lachman, 'is that you would not even have an outside world unless you first had something inside ... Far from a passive recipient of impressions from an inaccessible outside world, consciousness is a kind of hand, reaching out and giving shape and form to what would remain mere empty chaos.'

In the face of criticism by his contemporaries that he was simply harking back to old, religion-based theories of knowledge, Steiner insisted that his ideas arose out of the modern theory of evolution as pioneered by Darwin, and that he was simply spelling out the consequences of taking evolution seriously. 'The human being', he wrote, 'is not an idle onlooker before the pageant of the world, mirroring back in his spirit what is going on in the universe without involving him; he is an active participant in a cosmic creative process, and his knowledge is actually the most highly evolved part of the organism of the universe.'

Teilhard de Chardin was edging towards the same insight in *The Phenomenon of Man*. As a scientist also deeply influenced by the theory of evolution, he singles out our capacity for reflection, the power of consciousness to turn its gaze inward upon itself, as profoundly significant: 'No longer merely to know, but to know oneself; no longer merely to know, but to know that one knows …' The consequences of such a transformation – this doubling back upon ourselves – Teilhard calls 'immense'. 'In reality another world is born', he writes. 'Abstraction, logic, reasoned choice and inventions, mathematics, art, calculation of space and time, anxieties and dreams of love – all these activities of 'inner life' are nothing else than the effervescence of the newly-formed centre as it explodes onto itself.' Again he is confirming that my ability to mock my own inattention in the philosophy class is, despite its essential triviality, of significance in that I recognise it as trivial.

––––––––––•–•––––––––––

Very early in his life Steiner marked out his task to reunite religion and science; to bring God into science and nature into religion. In a chapter entitled 'The Ultimate Earth' in *The Phenomenon of Man*, Teilhard addresses the same issue of science in relation to religion: 'To outward appearance, the modern world was born of an anti-religious movement: man becoming self-sufficient and reason supplanting belief.' But he goes on to suggest that the conflict needs to be resolved in terms of an entirely different form of equilibrium:

> … not in elimination, nor duality but in synthesis. After close on two centuries of passionate struggles, neither science nor faith has succeeded in discrediting its adversary. On the contrary, it becomes obvious that neither can develop normally without the other. And the reason is simple: the same life animates both.

Steiner chose to study science, as did Teilhard and his Swiss contemporary Jung. In the imagination of Johannes Hemleben, another of Steiner's biographers, the student Steiner spoke to himself as follows, as perhaps did Jung and Teilhard:

If you wish to bring your own inner experience into harmony with the intellectual consciousness of your environment, so as effectively to overcome the constantly growing power of materialism as a world philosophy and a way of life, you must first assume the intellectual attitude of 19th-century man. You must get inside the dragon's skin. Only when you have mastered the method of natural science and have perceived the limited extent to which the view of the world built up by natural science conveys the truth, will you be able to bring into operation in the West a spiritual philosophy of the world.

For the young Rudolf Steiner, writes Hemleben, 'a long, wearisome road lay ahead.'

By now I myself was feeling the urge to explore further that 'world around us' that Andrew Welburn mentions – my own road ahead. As the psychiatrist R.D. Laing once wrote: 'The map is not the territory; the menu not the meal'. Indeed Francis Edmunds himself frequently expressed the thought: 'Let your ideas become your ideals'; in other words go out into the world and try to change it for the better.

I had been enormously helped and inspired by my time at Emerson College and by learning more about Steiner's life and ideas; but I now felt the need not only to do something worthwhile but also to seek confirmation and clarification in life itself of what I had absorbed, and in many instances found either still too difficult or too abstract. The film-maker in me was also re-awakening.

I had met some very fine people during those nine months, not least my fellow students who had come from all over the world, from many different backgrounds and at different stages of their lives. But I was still wary of anything that smacked of a cult – not at Emerson College in particular but anywhere – and of anything that inhibits us from asking awkward questions and rocking the boat; and wary, too, of any ideology that isolates us from what other people are thinking and doing.

Having said that, I recognise that it is both natural and indeed helpful for like-minded people to seek each other out. None of us can function effectively in isolation. I remember once witnessing a rather extreme example of this need we all have for support and encouragement, however sure we feel. While I was editing one of my films at a cutting-room in Soho, I often passed a solitary man on the same street corner declaiming to the world about the glory of Jesus. The world, however, was either far too busy or far too embarrassed to stop and listen. How mad do you have to be to persist against such odds, I wondered. Sometimes I would watch him from the window where I was working, and then I gradually noticed that he was not in fact alone. On the opposite street corner, amid all the passers-by, stood another man, not obviously listening to the tirade, yet always there. Then I understood how this character could keep going in such seeming isolation. He had a friend, a disciple perhaps. Someone believed in him. Someone was on his side. We all need such a friend. The danger comes, I suppose, if we only surround ourselves with like-minded people, with nobody to say: 'Hang on, a moment – explain what you mean.'

One of the most significant meetings for me personally during this time away from films was with Thomas Weihs, whom I have already mentioned. He certainly enjoyed asking awkward questions and rocking the boat. Although he would sometimes refer to himself as a pupil of Rudolf Steiner, he moved in a wide variety of psychiatric and educational circles, with a particular interest in those who, like Steiner, were questioning the whole foundation of epistemology and its obsession with objectivity.

With the Tuesday philosophy class over, and our patch of garden dug, a small group of us from Emerson College travelled to London every week to attend a course of lectures that Thomas gave on embryology, interwoven with the legend of the Stork that brings the baby, and set against the story of Creation as described in the book of Genesis. Quite a theme! Thomas ultimately wrote a book on the subject, *Embryogenesis in myth and science*, and some years later we made a film together for the BBC called *In Defence of the Stork*.

As a result of this meeting in London I visited Thomas Weihs in Scotland, at the school near Aberdeen where he worked with children 'in need of special care'. It was my first encounter with Camphill, now a worldwide network of schools and villages for children and adults with special needs. Thomas, together with a small group of refugees, most of whom were Jewish, had escaped from Austria just before the war, and destiny or chance – whichever you happen to believe in – had led them to Britain and to the creation of one of the most interesting and important social and therapeutic initiatives I have ever encountered.

It was also for me a meeting with both children and adults whose special needs seemed to be dwarfed by their special gifts – gifts of courage, tolerance and, in very many cases, a great open-heartedness. Treasures, all of them; no barnacles here, to be scraped off the hull of my experience.

CHAPTER 7

In Need of Special Care

I returned to the BBC in the autumn of 1967. John Betjeman wrote me a lovely letter saying how pleased he was that I was back in business: 'I daresay the BBC won't be perfection – but, my goodness, I'm glad to think you're there.' Not quite perfection, of course, but at that time it was certainly a remarkable and humane institution, when a producer's enthusiasm for a subject was usually enough to get the go-ahead for a project. There were no committees or focus groups debating the nature and habits of our target audience, and no pressure to produce projected viewing figures. 'If it's a good idea and you believe in it, then do it' was the attitude. The danger of such an approach is, I suppose, that it can open the door to self-indulgence. But I wasn't interested in making films for me to then sit and stare at. I felt instinctively that if I found a subject interesting it was bound to be of interest to at least some other people. If it wasn't, then I was in the wrong job and would sooner or later be told so.

My first initiative was to make two films about Camphill – one at the school near Aberdeen where Thomas Weihs was Superintendent, and the other at a village community for adults with special needs in North Yorkshire. I had the support of my head of department, Gordon Watkins, who had taken an interest in my studies at Emerson College and who could also understand what had so touched me on my visits to those two idealistic and pioneering Camphill communities. The controller of BBC2, David Attenborough, trusted Watkins's judgement, and so I was underway. It was to be one of the most important experiences of my life.

Camphill had its roots in a series of lectures on curative – what we would nowadays call 'special needs' – education, which Steiner gave in Switzerland in 1924. What he said drew in part on his own experience, while a student in Vienna, of working as a tutor to a boy who was severely handicapped with hydrocephalus. Through the young Rudolf Steiner's patient and insightful efforts, Otto Specht gradually improved and was eventually able to qualify as a doctor. Tragically he died during World War I.

In the ten years or so before Steiner's death in 1925, he was approached by an increasing number of people interested in his philosophical and spiritual ideas and insights, and who also wanted help in deepening and strengthening their own work as doctors, farmers, artists and educators of all sorts. A picture may have emerged from what I have written so far of Steiner as someone essentially inward-looking. This would be quite wrong. The whole thrust of his inner, meditative work was to arrive at insights that would be helpful in our day-to-day struggles as human beings on earth. From the Goethe archives in Weimar, which had been a lonely time for him – he referred to the place as 'a huge graveyard' – Steiner moved to Berlin in 1897, and it was there he began to find audiences with whom he could break his 'silence'. His reputation as a lecturer grew rapidly, and from 1913 until his death in 1925 he made his other base at Dornach in Switzerland.

Dr Karl König, a devoted pupil of Steiner, had been the moving spirit behind the founding of Camphill and was somewhat older than his ten fellow pioneers – all in flight from the horrors that were about to overwhelm their homeland. Thomas Weihs, for example, had only just qualified as a doctor when he joined König in Scotland in 1939. Two of the others had also been pursuing medical careers; one of these, Peter Roth, had a sister, Alix, who was a photographer. Carlo Pietzner, who eventually helped establish Camphill first in Northern Ireland and then in the United States, was an artist. Thomas Weihs's future wife, Anke, was a dancer. In the chapter he wrote for the book *The Builders of Camphill*, Friedwart Bock remarks that as a group they were not

Dr Karl König with a Camphill pupil

initially 'like-minded', though they all shared a deep interest in Steiner's work and some had been members of Karl König's study group in Vienna. König, unlike all but one of the others, already had considerable experience of work with children with special needs in Steiner-inspired institutions in Switzerland, Germany and Austria, though he never actually met Rudolf Steiner himself. He died in 1966, the year before my first visit to the school in Aberdeen.

In the film I was about to make, Thomas Weihs spoke to me about those early days in Scotland: 'We were a group of young people determined to start life quite anew, as if there had been no human being on this earth before. A bit arrogant, but also very willing to serve, very willing to do what we believed to be the good, the right and the necessary thing.'

In the simple ceremony to consecrate their first home in Scotland, which took place on Whit Sunday, May 28th 1939, König spoke these words:

> We should not feel that we are bearers of a mission, but should rather try to bring about a meeting of the British Spirit with the Spirit of Middle Europe. A uniting of what within the German language is dreamt and thought, with what the British person is able to put into deed.

I remember Thomas saying to me on several occasions that he and his colleagues recognised how meaningful it was that the Camphill movement came to birth on British soil and was thus able to evolve in the way it had. Likewise, of course, we in Britain could probably never have created this particular beacon without the unique input from the German-speaking world – what König called the spirit of Middle Europe. I have been impressed over the years, particularly through my contact with Camphill, at the way in which different nationalities can interact and complement one another in all sorts of positive ways. It reminds me of the creativity and energy that came out of Vienna itself before the rising tide of nationalism and anti-semitism tore that society and the Habsburg Empire apart.

The relationship between Britain and the German-speaking world was certainly complicated during the 20th century. Perhaps we clashed because in essence we secretly needed one another, needed what the other has to offer as a balance to our own strengths and weaknesses – as in Britain's relationship and conflicts with Spain and then with France in previous centuries. Camphill also struck me as a wonderful example of what can happen when people transcend personal and national differences in pursuit of a higher goal.

From the outset the Camphill pioneers decided to try to exist as a community without wages and to live and work not just *for* but *with* the children in their care. Each household was looked after by houseparents – usually a couple, and often with children of their own – and, as with parents in normal family life, there was no going 'on' and 'off' duty. The focus of their attention was not the 'handicapped child' but rather the child who happened to be handicapped. Their approach is summed up in the opening sequence of my film, *In Need of Special Care*, which I made at that Camphill school in Aberdeen in the autumn of 1967. Christof-Andreas Lindenberg, one of the housefathers, is seen walking along a corridor playing the recorder. It is early morning, and this is his routine for waking the children. 'Our main aim', he says, 'is to realise that each child is not only potentially educable, but has within himself something which is as whole and sound as that something in me or in you. And we hold on to the fact that what appears to be ill or handicapped or in need of special care is not the very child himself but his make-up.'

In his own attempts to convey Camphill's approach to the children in their care, Thomas Weihs would sometimes describe this scene: Imagine, he would say, that you are at a concert and on the platform is someone seated at a piano. As he starts to play a very unharmonious sound emerges. There will be some in the audience who might simply think, 'What a terrible pianist'. Others will realise that there is a serious fault with the piano. But one or two, said Thomas, might recognise that despite the terrible sound, a highly gifted pianist is at work.

He was not, of course, trying to imply that all children with special needs are geniuses in disguise. But the story is a reminder that all of us have faulty pianos of one sort or another, some in poorer shape than others. To the extent that we both acknowledge this fact and try to understand what truly lives in the other person, so will we help that spiritual essence and potential in the other to emerge. For we are, each one of us, deeply affected by what others think of us and how we are judged, however unfairly. Perhaps we should be stronger, but it's not easy. As I mentioned earlier, if someone thinks I am ugly, I may start to feel ugly. If someone thinks I am stupid, I will tend to feel stupid.

In *The Builders of Camphill*, Marianna Sander quotes a description by Thomas Weihs's future wife Anke of her first meeting with Karl König. It clearly indicates this capacity to recognise the individuality behind the persona, behind the masks that we all tend to carry:

> His eyes were very big and grave. When they rested on you, they did not only see through you, they seemed to create you anew. Something dormant in yourself responded whether you wanted to or not; you seemed to become what you really were, beneath the layers of habit, inhibition and illusion. He not only saw what you were but what you were meant to be.

One of the most powerful memories I have of making the film at the Aberdeen Camphill school was the experience of the children's relationship to one another. At that time Camphill took in children with a very wide range of disabilities, often multiple; most of the children, not surprisingly, had behavioural problems as well. They were children whom the various local authorities were unable to place elsewhere. Nowadays there is an increasing tendency whenever possible keep children in their own locality and preferably in mainstream education. In those early days after World War II there was little support as yet for the idea that such children were educable at all. In fact not until 1970 did an Education Act give every child of school age the legal right to an education. There was certainly no recognition that such children might be able to help one another. Nor was that a particular insight among those Camphill pioneers; rather it was something they observed as taking place quite naturally, and so gradually they adopted this policy of taking a broad intake of children. They even educated their own children up to the age of ten or eleven alongside those with special needs.

One striking example of this help that such children can give one another was a relationship between two teenage girls, Julia and Paula. Julia was a severely spastic girl who could do nothing whatsoever for herself. She needed to be fed, washed, dressed and undressed, and was unable to speak. Those who looked after Julia, however, were very aware of the being trapped in that crippled body. Her eyes were extraordinary and it was through her eyes that she spoke. Sad, grateful, happy – her housemother, Gisela Schlegel, as well as her teacher, therapist and doctor, all knew that Julia was a person who in essence was just like everyone else. We small team of film-makers experienced this too.

Paula, who shared a room with Julia, was severely autistic. Besides not speaking she avoided eye contact with everyone – indeed all human contact. Yet after a year or so the carers noticed that Paula had started very slowly to become aware of and take an interest in Julia; no interest in anyone else, just in Julia. Gradually she joined in the bedtime routine, and at meals would help to feed her. By the time we were filming, an even greater miracle had taken place. Paula would sometimes talk to Julia at bedtime, quietly whispering to her about the ups and downs of her day.

Julia had thus done what no doctor or therapist had been able to achieve. She had awoken Paula's interest and concern for a fellow human being, and even prompted her to speak. We witnessed and filmed many similar situations during those extraordinary autumn days over forty years ago. And there seems to me to be a very important message here in relation to those whom we pity, but also for whom we feel that life can't have much purpose or meaning. Julia was thought to be what is sometimes rather crudely referred to as a 'vegetable'. Wouldn't it have been kinder, some people might understandably think, if she hadn't been allowed to survive? Yet if our lives are not only about what we can achieve for ourselves, but also about what we can bring to others, then Julia's life was a triumph. Not only was Paula's narrow and crippled existence enlarged, but all those who came in contact with Julia were deeply inspired and their lives enormously enriched. Time and again I have come across this reaction from parents and from those who work with both children and adults with special needs: that they have learned as much from those in their care as they have been able to give in practical and loving help.

One aspect of this learning process was described in my film by the same person who woke the children each morning with his recorder. 'It's very strange,' said Christof-Andreas, while attending a termly clinic for one of the children, 'when we sit together discussing a particular child I come away with the feeling that we've actually described something that I've got myself. And that's not a philosophical thought; it's a direct experience. And by and by you find out, as this experience recurs, that maybe you have what these children exhibit in an extreme and exaggerated form also in yourself. And through that, I believe, a kind of key is given to understand this very, very complicated human being that each one of us presents a little more.'

This 'complicated human being' was the subject of a talk we filmed by Thomas Weihs to the seminar students at Camphill. It was a different and more detailed angle on his 'damaged piano' story:

I'd like to explain to you the specific way we look at the handicapped child. The testable intelligence is not the criterion. The physical handicap is also not the criterion. That the child is blind or perhaps paralysed is not the all-important aspect to us. The important aspect to us is the child's development, the child's becoming.

Now we must realise that the physical body, magnificent and highly developed and complicated as it is, because it is physical and material can never be absolutely perfect; always only relatively perfect. But there is in each one of us something we call 'I', which is of a non-material nature – because I don't say 'I' to my body. I can be very unhappy about my body because it can be slow or lazy, or too fat or too thin or too weak. We are hardly ever at one with our body. But I do not even completely identify with my soul. I've often been very ashamed of some of my feelings. But who then was ashamed?

So you see there is something in all of us that is our actual identity which is of a purely spiritual nature – the individuality, the ego, the self – it is called by various names, and which we therefore unavoidably experience as perfect. Now Rudolf Steiner has helped us to look at child development imaginatively as the integration of an eternal, always perfect, purely spiritual entity into a physical organism provided for us by hereditary forces, out of environmental forces; and what we call the soul of the child – the way the child thinks, feels, speaks, behaves, learns and plays – all this is the manifestation of the integration of these two entities – the spiritual mind entity with the bodily, physical entity.

Autism is obviously a severe disruption to this process that Thomas Weihs described. Fixated and obsessional behaviour, avoidance of human contact – many people see autism as very much an illness of our time. As we become more individualised, more private, it is easy to recognise milder versions of these tendencies within ourselves. The children with Downs Syndrome at Camphill – at that time still referred to as Mongol children – were a great help, because of their warm and friendly personalities, in lightening the heavy atmosphere created by the psychotic behaviour of the autistic children.

We filmed one such autistic child, Peter, in that seemingly isolated world that he inhabited. One scene that lasted almost fifteen minutes was of Peter putting the chairs back in place after the dining-room floor had been swept after lunch. All went well until the last chair; then Peter became stuck. Retreating more deeply into his other world, he dangled the chair in the air while his housefather worked around him, coaxed him, teased him – all to no avail. From Peter there was no response, and seemingly no awareness of other people – and virtually no speech. Only when Peter's housefather completed his work did Peter put that last chair in place. There didn't seem to be anything remotely obstinate or naughty about his behaviour – rather sheer oblivion.

The next day Peter's whole character and behaviour changed dramatically as he sat with his class watching a puppet show – one of the therapies employed at Camphill. As the story unfolded he became totally absorbed, his face expressing a whole range of emotions. Human contact, human speech was not direct, but via the puppets, and therefore acceptable to him.

We witnessed similar miracles when children who never spoke would slowly start to sing in response to music. 'Speech is very direct confrontation,' said the music-therapist Christof-Andreas, 'to some children not even a means of communication, but just something that acts like a shock.' We were filming him singing simple questions to a small group of disturbed and withdrawn children: 'Music softens the shock, or takes that confrontation away altogether, and they are apt to forget that they are answering a question when they sing.'

At Peter's clinic they discussed his tendency to call the other person 'I'. In Thomas Weihs's opinion it was not because he didn't experience his own individuality but rather because he was so frightened of admitting that he was himself. Over twenty years later I filmed Peter again, but that is a story for later.

Thomas Weihs

It was during the filming of these clinics, and seeing Thomas Weihs and his colleagues in action, that I came to be aware of the word 'empathy'. 'An important aspect of the attitude to really all handicapped children', said Thomas in my interview with him for the film, 'is the ability to feel oneself into their situation; what is called in psychiatric circles "empathy". Now that is of great importance in really any human contact. It is the necessary way of overcoming one's normal attitude of reacting purely to the behaviour of the other person, rather than attempting to experience what lies behind the behaviour.'

I shall never forget the very special way that Thomas spoke to the children at that Camphill School. His words had a magical quality about them, for they seemed to convey so much more than we can ever articulate. He was so very gentle, and yet there was nothing remotely sentimental about his manner. He listened to the children with his whole being. Indeed it was clear that he truly loved them. John Betjeman had an expression he used to describe those who had this ability both to feel themselves into someone else's situation and also to sense and be aware of the effect they themselves were having on others; he spoke about people having 'finger-tips'.

In an interview that the novelist Ian McEwan gave in *The Guardian* a few days after the collapse of the Twin Towers in New York he said this:

> If the hijackers had been able to imagine themselves into the thoughts and feelings of the passengers, they would have been unable to proceed … Imagining what it is like to be someone other than yourself is at the core of our humanity. It is the essence of compassion and the beginning of morality.

And in a lecture that Jung gave in 1932 – reproduced in his book *Modern Man in Search of a Soul* – he describes very much the same approach that Thomas Weihs and his colleagues took in that Camphill School:

> If the doctor wants to offer guidance to another, or even to accompany him a step of the way, he must feel in touch with this other person's psychic life. He is never in touch when he passes judgement. Whether he puts his judgements into words, or keeps them to himself, makes not the slightest difference.

Jung goes on to say that taking the opposite position, of simply going along with whatever the patient says or does, is as unhelpful as condemnation. What he advocates is 'a deep respect for the facts', and above all respect for the secret and the riddle of each human life.

One of Thomas Weihs's Camphill colleagues, Graham Calderwood, has written of how Thomas came to consider empathy the most important force in curative and remedial education:

> He traced it in both the works of Rudolf Steiner and in the publications of R.D. Laing. What is perhaps unique in Thomas's approach to empathy is that he identified it as a force, a force in the same sense that gravity or electromagnetism are forces ... The prerequisite condition for the success of empathy is a kind of selfless compassion in the practitioner.

Calderwood goes on to suggest that a strictly scientific outlook can lead to a certain kind of fatalism. In the past some disabilities were seen to fall into this category. Sometimes this attitude became the official view and thus the outlook for the person with disability became bleak. But even if some, or perhaps all, aspects of a disability cannot be corrected or changed, then empathy – properly exercised – can lead to a full recognition and calm acceptance of the truth of the situation. Calderwood continues:

> But empathy, with its embedded compassion, does not direct us to abandon the handicapped person to a seemingly brutal and inescapable fate. Rather, it enables us to perceive just how the handicapped person copes now with his or her predicament, and how he or she may be helped to cope with it in the future. Empathy, properly deployed, might be described as 'practical destiny management' which, at worst, would be just making the best of a bad job, but at best could lead to a valid perception of the meaning, or point – indeed, the worth – of a person's destiny.

Given this effort to try to understand what it is like to be someone else, particularly someone so seemingly thwarted by circumstances beyond their control, it is not surprising that a great many children who passed through Camphill did change dramatically. Their disabilities were such that on the whole no major progress and certainly no cure could be achieved. But what did change was the children's behaviour. Frustration that had so often manifested as anger, despair and a complete disregard for others gradually diminished as the child felt acknowledged as a person – or to use Thomas's analogy, as the pianist and not the piano. And in this sense, of course, what unfolds in places like Camphill is only an exaggerated and extreme version of what is happening or can happen in all our lives, all the time. We grow and flourish to the extent that people believe in us and recognise our potential – first and foremost, of course, our own parents. Again I am reminded of Anne-Marie's tragic start in life.

Another thought that Thomas often expressed in his talks was related to the increasing number of children with severe disabilities in our midst. Rapid advances in medical knowledge and skill have been extraordinary and admirable but – as with the very old, as well as with children who previously would not have survived – we now have the task of caring for people who are fragile in the extreme. And this demands of us quite other skills and abilities. It is, suggested Thomas, a challenge for our compassion to catch up with our cleverness.

Compassion can, of course, take many forms. I remember a year or so later taking Thomas to see a Canadian documentary called *Warrendale* in London. I had already seen it on television and like many other people had been very shocked by its content. Warrendale was a residential home for severely disturbed children, all with traumatic backgrounds. Their tantrums, violence and anti-social behaviour were met with equally violent reactions from those caring for them. Confrontational therapy was their chosen approach.

I thought that Thomas would be as appalled as I was, but he had a very different reaction, the wisdom of which I have come to appreciate more and more. His view was that by far the most important therapy for these children was that somebody was bothering about them and that somebody cared. The fact that their actual techniques were maybe inappropriate, clumsy and even unhelpful was secondary to the fact that these people were trying to help, however inadequately they went about it. Thomas was not saying, of course, that one therapy is as good as another, but he was, I think, making a very important point about the primary importance of one's motives. It is one of the themes on which he elaborates in his book *Children In Need Of Special Care*, written three years after we made the film.

But it wasn't just the theories of Thomas Weihs and others that I came across in Aberdeen all those years ago, but people – the co-workers and the children in their care. In trying to describe them and my experiences that autumn I feel a huge responsibility. I am conscious, more than ever, of the inadequacy of words – or perhaps I mean my lack of skill in using them. The film crew and I felt so privileged to witness the daily life of the community, and in return – through the film we made – we were at least able to share with others glimpses of what we had seen and heard. But a film, unlike a book, is full of images as well as words; and there are pauses between all those words – wonderful, meaningful pauses. And images and pauses, in my experience, often speak more powerfully than words. Perhaps that's why I became a film-maker. And by images I mean more than pretty pictures: it is the children's expressions that I remember – their laughter and their tears; their bewilderment and their triumphs; one hand taking hold of another; a look that conveys love without the word 'love' ever needing to be mentioned; the peace at bedtime, when music and candlelight bring a certain harmony into the lives of little children who outwardly experience so much disharmony, so much frustration. The children, too, will surely have carried some of those beautiful images and memories with them into sleep – the flowers they picked in the garden that afternoon, the colourful pictures on their classroom walls, the homemade bread that nourished them, the kind and patient expressions on the faces of those who cared for them.

One image that I particularly remember is a beautiful coloured picture in the shape of an arc that the autistic boy, Peter, had drawn and which he brought to his termly clinic with Dr Weihs. Like many autistic people Peter had great skills, but in one narrowly focused direction. He loved colour, shapes and form. Thomas had this to say to his colleagues after Peter had left the session: 'This is typical of the pictures he has drawn so persistently. Very striking, very beautiful. And though we are not meant to fall in love with the pathology of the psychotic child, yet one can hardly avoid seeing in it what God otherwise puts on butterfly-wings.'

The final sequence of the film shows a celebration by the whole community of their Michaelmas festival. There was a play about Alexander the Great in which all the children took part, followed by a harvest meal. 'The rhythm of the year', I wrote in my commentary, 'with its seasons and festivals, the rhythm of each day, all this plays a vital part in the education of these children.' Then came a line from the interview I had recorded with Thomas Weihs: 'It does create in the child a subconscious feeling of his own worth, of his own place in the world; that he is not an accidental entity that could just as well not be, but he is part of a meaningful, complete whole.'

'Many will leave Camphill unable to read or write', I concluded. 'Some will never speak, or hear or see. But their life with each other teaches them much. Modern education is criticised by many for tending to think of itself more and more as a method of handing over knowledge and skill to the growing child and for ignoring the fact that children not only grow in knowledge and skill but also grow in maturity. And the maturing process will largely come about as the child learns to experience that he can extend help to another person, and that his behaviour is the basis for the survival and existence of the other.'

CHAPTER 8

Seeds for the Future

John is waving goodbye to me, but he's facing in the other direction. He's too shy, too complicated, to look my way, but very aware of my departure and very keen to express the same affection towards me that I feel towards him.

I am leaving Botton Village on the edge of the North Yorkshire Moors, having spent three weeks filming the second of my films about Camphill. It has been one of the most inspiring and enjoyable experiences of my life, the memory of which nourishes me still; and though I have visited Botton many times since then, including further filming, it is that special time during the autumn of 1967 that I remember most vividly and with such gratitude.

Botton was founded in 1955, and came about largely through the concern expressed by some parents whose children had been at the Camphill school in Scotland: 'What happens next?' At that time there were few options. Living at home was one, but parents won't be around forever. The sort of institutions that existed then were in bleak contrast to the quality of life and care with which these children had been surrounded.

From the start Karl König and his colleagues did not envisage that Botton, or any of the other Camphill Village communities that have sprung up in its wake all over the world, would be educational institutions. They were to be communities where adults with special needs, known as 'villagers', could live and work alongside houseparents and their helpers – known as co-workers – in dignity and freedom. As with the Camphill schools, there would be no wages; each person would contribute according to their ability. Above all, each villager would be accepted and respected like any other adult. Curative education and therapies belong to childhood. Now life itself, as it is for all of us, was to be the only and the great teacher. 'A full village life', I wrote in my commentary to the film, 'was the only medicine'.

Alistair is singing in his falsetto voice, as he works away in the garden. At noon he will switch to his other job, delivering the post to the seventeen households throughout the village and stopping for a gossip whenever possible. Alistair was the nephew of British Prime Minister Harold Macmillan, and it was the Macmillan family who helped König buy Camphill House in 1939.

Alistair Macmillan

Alistair was one of the first children to attend the Aberdeen school, and when the idea of a village community for adults later emerged, it was the Yorkshire estate of that same Macmillan family which became Botton Village.

Another John is also talking to whomever he can find, especially to visitors. He asks them endless questions, usually about their car, but is too excited to wait for the answers. His questions are really about wanting contact and then not letting you go. The dialogue makes no sense logically, but John is not interested in logic; he is interested in people and in making friends.

Nearby, Mary will have just finished cleaning the staircase of the house where she lives with her houseparents, their three children, two young co-workers and four other adults with special needs. It has taken her nearly the whole morning, but she does the job thoroughly and with great satisfaction. In the afternoon she will work on one of the farms. She likes the animals and will talk to them. She is less inclined to talk to other people. Many of the villagers have two different jobs, and it is this element of satisfaction and challenge rather than speed and efficiency that determines who does what.

Then there is Michael who wobbles his head or his false teeth, sometimes at the same time, and who, some forty years later, still remembers the names of my film crew, and really wants to know how and where they are. In thinking and writing about Botton Village now, I am there as vividly as ever. Perhaps a part of me never left in the first place. It all seems as close as yesterday.

I wonder if Johnnie has arrived yet at his workshop where they make beeswax candles. Long ago, for some mysterious reason, he decided that he must take 252 steps from his house to the workshop. If he arrives there having taken too few or too many steps he then goes back and does the walk again – and again! Fortunately there are no 'time and motion' experts at Botton, or Johnnie would be out on his ear.

Some of the villagers, on the other hand, are enormously productive. But that, too, can be a handicap of sorts. Neil works in the wood workshop making toys. He is enormously skilled and would work 24 hours a day if they let him. 'Obsessive, too precise', is how his work-master Alan Caas describes him. 'His work is a kind of disease. We benefit from it, but must be careful we don't exploit it.' Neil is severely autistic and never speaks. He has yet to meet his Julia – that paralysed girl at the Camphill School in Aberdeen whose helplessness called forth sympathy and finally speech from Paula. But Neil does go to the weekly social evening, though will never dance. A side of him, you sense, is longing to join in. Occasionally he steals a glance at other people, but mostly his face is turned away in an anxious frown.

The candle-maker, Johnnie, also never speaks, but he is certainly aware of others. 'A complete feeling-being' is how his work-master, Walter Brecker, described him to me during the filming. If people are sad or cross then Johnnie immediately picks it up, and his face darkens like thunder. And if the atmosphere is happy and relaxed, if people are laughing, then Johnnie walks around with a great grin on his face.

However, the majority of villagers at Botton, as I remember them from that first encounter, certainly did speak and were often extrovert in the extreme. 'What's your name?' 'Where do you live?' 'My name is Steven'. 'Is she your wife?' 'What colour is your car?' 'Will you come to our house for lunch?'

Characters who were 'larger than life' would be another way of describing my new friends – but men and women who, if living in our so-called normal world, would still tend to be shunned through embarrassment, prejudice or even fear; the same fear that prompted the boy Jem, in Harper Lee's wonderful novel *To Kill a Mockingbird*, to describe to his younger sister Scout, the narrator of the story, the man they called Boo, who lived next door but no one ever saw:

> Boo was about six and a half feet tall, judging from his tracks; he dined on raw squirrels and any cats he could catch, that's why his hands were blood-stained – if you ate an animal raw, you can never wash the blood off. There was a long jagged scar that ran across his face; what teeth he had were yellow and rotten; his eyes popped, and he drooled most of the time.

At the end of the book the children finally meet Boo – in fact he saves their lives; and it is a gentle but wounded human being who stands beside them. 'Atticus, he was real nice', Scout says to her father later that evening. 'Most people are, Scout, when you finally see them', he replies.

Everyone at Botton seemed to love us and to enjoy the whole crazy business of filming. I had the same delightful and highly professional crew who had worked with me in Aberdeen, so they were familiar with the eccentric, magical and profoundly humane atmosphere at Camphill. The cameraman, Charles Stewart, who had also shot my films for *World of a Child*, was an eccentric sort of genius himself and a pioneer in the technique of hand-

*Cameraman Charles Stewart and
assistant Ernest Vincze*

held camerawork, thus allowing us to film extremely naturalistic sequences in a relatively unobtrusive way. The rest of my team were also all wonderfully sensitive to the task we faced; and like me they, too, thoroughly enjoyed themselves.

But why am I writing in such detail about these experiences at Camphill? In my preface I promised to try to share what has helped and inspired me in my search for answers to the question: Where on earth is heaven? Like many people on such a quest, particularly those who have worked in places like Camphill, I have been enormously helped and enriched by my encounter with people who, for all sorts of reasons, are not quite able to be part of what we call the normal world. It is their transparency that has particularly touched me; they tend not to wear the masks behind which most of us hide. Like children, they don't beat about the bush and are disarmingly direct. One effect of such encounters is that one's own masks start to fall away. Honesty comes to the fore.

Perhaps the usual fear we have of lowering these masks is prompted by a sense that there is nothing much behind them. Another fear that haunts many people is that our lives, like the universe itself, have no meaning. Everything is mere chance. Questions about heaven are therefore pointless. Each life will end with death.

Very relevant to these fears is a powerful scene in Henrik Ibsen's play *Pier Gynt*, which opens with the hero kneeling on the ground in a forest glade, grubbing up wild onions. There he begins to imagine his own death:

> I'll creep beneath a fallen tree;
> Like the bear, I'll cover myself with leaves,
> And scratch in the bark, in great big letters:
> 'Here lies Pier Gynt, a decent chap,
> Who was Emperor of all the beasts' –
> Emperor?
> You absurd old humbug!
> You're not an Emperor, you're an onion!

Now, my dear Peter, I'm going to peel you,
However little you may enjoy it.

So he begins to peel an onion, each layer representing aspects of himself that he now rejects.

There's a most surprising lot of layers!
Are we never coming to the kernel?

Then comes the final shock, the terrible realisation:

There isn't one! To the innermost bit
It's nothing but layers, smaller and smaller.

My friends at Botton Village, however, confirmed for me that there is indeed something there – a kernel that it is often finer and purer than we could ever imagine. Nevertheless, as Thomas Weihs warned when confronted by Peter's artwork, we must not fall in love with the various pathologies behind disability. The conditions are in many ways a tragedy, and impose huge limitations on the people concerned.

One example was a young man I met who knew exact details of football scores going back over many years. Initially one can be rather in awe of such a facility, but in fact his mind was so clogged up with this useless information that he had problems knowing which day of the week it was, or how to tie his own shoelaces. Likewise the inability of some of the villagers I met – delightful as they were – to really empathise with another person's situation, and to realise, for example, when they were simply being boring, obsessional or irritating, creates a barrier of another sort behind which they can become self-absorbed and ultimately isolated within themselves.

Yet in other ways such lives can be seen as a kind of sacrifice, voluntary or otherwise, whereby through their lack of guile we are reminded of our own innocence and a certain purity that glimmers still in the shadow of our ego. I wonder if it was the recognition of this divine essence that we all share that prompted Charles de Gaulle, at the funeral of his daughter who was born with Down's Syndrome, to say, 'Now she is like the others.'

In my film, one of the house-mothers, Marianna Lehr, spoke of another aspect of the villagers' capacity to help and even heal us: 'Through those who cannot keep pace with the speed now ruling all over the world, there is a possibility given to reorientate oneself to their pace; we cannot speed on without them; we have to adjust our life to their life, and by that we gain a balance.' I've heard some mothers of babies and young children express the same thought; and if life allows it, they are often grateful for being forced to slow down and to live at a different and saner pace. Even some fathers are discovering a similar liberation.

The founding father and mother of Botton Village were Peter Roth and his English wife Kate. Peter studied medicine in Vienna and was one of the pioneering group who arrived in Scotland just before the outbreak of war. He eventually became a priest in The Christian Community, a religious movement founded by a group of young, disillusioned German theologians who were inspired by Steiner's lectures and writings on the Gospels, and in particular by his emphasis on the profound significance of Christ in human evolution. It was this conviction, centred around what he called 'the mystery of Golgotha', that finally caused Steiner's break with the theosophical movement in the early years of the 20th century, for it was not a vision they shared. In fact the two leading figures in theosophy at the time, Annie Besant and Charles Leadbeater, were grooming the young Indian boy, Krishnamurti as the reincarnated Christ – a label that he himself eventually rejected. After the break, Steiner spoke increasingly under the banner of what he called anthroposophy.

In the book *The Builders of Camphill*, Deborah Ravetz, herself a co-worker at Botton for thirteen years, writes of Peter Roth: 'Peter's life was Botton. Everything that happened to him before its inception, his sorrows and joys, prepared him for this great attempt to create a new kind of social structure.'

Peter and Kate Roth

Peter Roth had a wonderfully eccentric way of expressing himself. Unlike Thomas Weihs he was never completely at home in English and never quite lost his Viennese accent. Once when I was staying at Botton some years later Peter showed me to my room, explained the routine of the household and then mentioned that I was not to use the bathroom until after Monday. As it was Friday evening I was somewhat puzzled! However, I very soon realised that there was a rota in the mornings for Peter, his wife and the three villagers to use the bathroom. My turn was after Mandy.

In the film Peter spoke to me about Botton Village as a bridge, 'allowing the handicapped being and the world to communicate, and the world to hold such human beings without spitting them out or putting them into institutions or into some kind of humanitarian fridge.' And while we filmed the village's preparation for a Christmas play he also spoke about the importance they attached to acknowledging and celebrating the seasons and festivals: 'The more one lives with the seasons – at Christmas the light in the darkness, at Easter the resurrection – so do the seasons and the festivals become an accompaniment to life and not just a nuisance when it rains and a blessing when the sun shines.'

During the filming we spent time in most of the households, on the farms and in the workshops. Martha Frey, who ran the glass-engraving workshop, echoed what that Aberdeen co-worker had said about looking into a mirror when you live and work alongside people with extreme difficulties: 'Living with handicapped people makes you aware of how you are, and you find that you've got lots of prejudices regarding your own normality. You're not really so different, but their personalities are more outspoken, more pronounced.'

The work at Botton, it was emphasised, is not occupational therapy. The fact that what they do or make is valued and needed in the world is important for the self-confidence of the villagers. In the bakery at that time a blind man, Ben, was in charge of the ancient and temperamental oven. He called it Nellie, 'the hottest girl in Botton!' 'Never be afraid to take risks', was the advice Ben offered to us during the filming. I have yet to be as brave as Ben.

The ethos of working without wages seemed to come naturally to the Botton villagers and not, I believe, because they were simple-minded. In fact many of them are extremely intelligent, though not on the whole intellectual. 'Their attitude to work', said Peter Roth, 'is very much more to help others with their work, rather than through their work to earn their living … They are the pioneers', he went on, 'walking into the uncharted land.'

Above all, I sensed, it was the mutual tolerance among the villagers that so helped and inspired the co-workers at Botton, and continues to do so. Community living is not easy – these days many people increasingly experience how difficult it is to live side by side with one another; and the Camphill communities would, I suspect, have collapsed long ago if it hadn't been for the naturally unselfish and uncritical nature of most of those with special needs. I've heard the villagers described as the oil that lubricates the egos!

'Many of the villagers', I wrote towards the end of that first film I made about Botton, 'appear to outsiders as comparatively normal. But their normality is only able to come to the fore because they live in a community where their basic humanity is acknowledged. The handicapped mind or body that many have to carry through life is seen as a shell in which lives the individual and eternal being of each person.'

The year after Botton was founded, Anke Weihs wrote in the Michaelmas edition of the Camphill magazine, *The Cresset*:

> For many, the ideals and principles of the Village Community may seem remote and unworldly. Yet we know of no one who has been to Botton Village who has not been gripped by the immediacy of the social attempt being made there. The moment you enter the dale, you know you have entered a new province; its newness is already inscribed into the atmosphere, it casts a spell on you – not the spell of a cloister, the retreat, but the spell of the future. The future blows like a fresh wind down the dale, and you love the feel of it on your face...

In the same vein, König had said: 'The villages were not intended to be institutions for people with special needs; on the contrary the people with special needs made possible this effort to create new social forms.'

One of the last scenes in my film was what in the Camphill communities they call Bible Evening. On Saturdays each household has a special meal, reads a passage from the Bible and discusses it. And like all the other social occasions, and at many of the meetings, the villagers participate along with everyone else. Bible Evening is a tradition that goes back to the early pioneering days in Aberdeen when a group of refugees huddled together in a large and damp Scottish manse with no earthly possessions and little knowledge of the English language, but with a determination not just to start anew, but in a new way.

Quite by accident, if you believe in accidents, the reading on the particular evening that we filmed was from the Revelation of St John the Divine:

> And I saw a new heaven and a new earth: for the first heaven and the first earth were passed away; and there was no more sea.
> And I John saw the holy city, new Jerusalem, coming down from God out of heaven, prepared as a bride adorned for her husband.

Recently I have become even more aware of the significance of this particular passage, especially in relation to Jerusalem the place, the city around which so much anguish and violence continues to rage. My Jewish friends from Vienna chose to go west and not east. In saying this I am in no way passing judgement on those who settled in Israel – providing they make appropriate space for the Palestinians, either next door or ultimately, perhaps, together with them. Meanwhile all of us, including the Jews and the Palestinians, might benefit from taking far more seriously the idea that this 'new Jerusalem' is not in fact a geographical place, either in the Middle East or anywhere else, but rather a way of being together that will spring from an altogether different consciousness and sensibility.

The painter Stanley Spencer called his Berkshire village of Cookham, 'a holy suburb of heaven'. William Blake expressed a version of this idea in those celebrated lines:

> I will not cease from Mental Fight,
> Nor shall my Sword sleep in my hand,
> Till we have built Jerusalem,
> In England's green and pleasant land.

I am not suggesting that Botton Village is some new Jerusalem – a perfect system, or some magic formula and blueprint for the future. But what I liked about the community, above all, was that nobody felt superior to anyone else. And it does offer a glimpse, at least, of how we might start to think differently about how we live from day to day. One aspect of that is the relationship of work to wages. It becomes increasingly difficult, I find, to honestly say whose work is more essential, more important than anyone else's. How, therefore, do you decide an appropriate wage? At least we now have a minimum wage here in Britain, and fewer people fall completely through the net. But the disparity in terms of remuneration is still enormous. I've heard people suggest that at some time in the future – maybe in a hundred years, maybe less – people will look back on the wages system with the same incredulity and distaste with which we nowadays view slavery.

I don't believe, however, that a really fundamental change can or should be legislated or imposed, as was partly practised under communism, for example. In order for such a revolution to take place, it will need to be decided by each individual person, in their own way and at their own pace. In the Camphill communities there is an annual pot of money made up of grants for the disabled, income from products they grow or make in the workshops, and donations. Each person, each family, takes what they need in relation to the size of the pot. It sounds absurdly idealistic, but on the whole it works. It is, after all, how most families conduct their finances. At Botton the doctor is no richer than the young man milking the cows. One person may need more from that pot than another if, for example, they have a family and children. But everyone is, in my experience of Camphill over the years, richer in quite other ways. The gradual liberation from egotistical and acquisitive obsessions does, potentially at least, not only free us to explore and ponder deeper questions uncluttered by the baggage of materialism and the consumer-obsessed society that surrounds us, but also helps us to live according to our own deeper ideals – and not just to talk and write about them, as I am doing. Philip Toynbee, in his autobiographical journal, writes about 'clearing our clogged communications with God; clogged by too many possessions'.

On two occasions in my life, I almost took the step of joining the community in Botton myself. In the end my need to stay 'unattached' held sway. I have no idea whether I made the right decision. Perhaps 'right' and 'wrong' are not the appropriate words to use in such situations. What we need to learn and experience will probably come at us whatever route we take.

Meanwhile, it's important to recognise that the people in Botton Village are human and not saints. It would be unfair of me to paint them otherwise. The communal life I have described is not always easy. It is a huge challenge to live selflessly alongside so many people – fellow co-workers as well as villagers – whose foibles and failings have to be faced with understanding, and not with resentment or irritation.

At the close of my film, the Botton choir sang *The Song of Olaf Ästeson* conducted by a veteran co-worker and one-time Anglican priest Richard Poole. And over those last beautiful and haunting images of a Yorkshire Dale that was home to such an extraordinary collection of characters – people who had stirred my own inherent idealism so deeply, and whose faces and voices will remain with me always – I ran some words from my interview with Richard: 'The handicapped people, through their very being, through their nature act as a kind of shield – something of a protecting womb – in which seeds for the future can perhaps grow. In this sense, if our movement becomes anything in the future it actually will owe everything to the handicapped ... simply by virtue of their being, they allow a new future to come to birth.'

CHAPTER 9

No Ordinary Light

So far, the subjects of my films had been my own ideas, prompted consciously or otherwise by my search for what might make sense of life – for the words, in fact, carved on that green stick buried in the Zakaz forest near Tolstoy's home which, when discovered, could help us to bring about a world free of suffering and sorrow.

My next two projects were programmes that the BBC asked me to do. It's interesting to look back on my life and see how certain encounters that have become important to me seem to have crept up from behind, as it were, tapped me on the shoulder and said: 'Here I am!' And I suspect that tragedies, like blessings, also come our way unbidden if they are what we need to grow and learn. A friend of mine found an entry in her mother's diary, shortly before the old lady died, which read simply: 'Be friendly to your problems.'

Maybe from a wiser part of our being we are in fact the author, or at least the co-author, of our own destiny, in whatever form it unfolds. If so, rather than asking, as did some wit at odds with his life, 'Who wrote this lousy script?', we can try to identify with the prayer of the Trappist monk Thomas Merton: 'Let me want the life I've chosen.' However, in making such speculations I haven't forgotten the Anne-Maries of this world, and the possibility that some knocks in life are nothing to do with what we may have chosen for ourselves, or with our personal karma.

My first project after completing the two films about Camphill was to make a programme to mark the fiftieth anniversary of the collapse of the Habsburg Empire at the end of World War I. So there I was in Vienna, the city where some of my new friends in Aberdeen and Botton had grown up, and also where Rudolf Steiner had studied towards the end of the 19th century; a city that must, in its heyday, have had the sort of cosmopolitan buzz you can find nowadays in New York, and above all in London.

I worked on the film with the writer and journalist Edward Crankshaw, whose book, *The Fall of the House of Habsburg*, inspired us to approach him. Edward was a wise and gentle man, and the tale he tells is more than the history of the last decades of a great dynasty. The book portrays the break-up of the old European order, which gave way first to Hitler and then to Stalin; and the story coincides almost exactly with the sixty-eight year reign of the Emperor Franz Josef. Without concealing the magnitude of the emperor's errors, Crankshaw paints a compassionate portrait of a man bogged down in events that were increasingly beyond his control. All of us, to some degree, find ourselves caught up not only in our own personal karma, but also in what one might call world-karma – historical events that unfold around us, the roots of which are buried deep in our collective history.

'Vienna was never more beautiful than when it was dying' was a phrase I've always remembered from Crankshaw's commentary. He was referring to the extraordinary cultural flowering that took place above all in music and architecture, as well as in the intellectual debates nurtured by the rich cultural and ethnic mix of Vienna's population. And all this flourished despite the fact that the rising tide of nationalism throughout Europe was not only tearing the empire apart, but also sowing seeds for the far greater upheavals that engulfed the 20th century.

I travelled throughout what was once the Habsburg Empire – Czechoslovakia, Hungary, parts of Yugoslavia and northern Italy, and of course Austria itself. For me it was enormously interesting and helpful not only to immerse myself in this important period of history, but above all to experience and absorb through the landscape, buildings, paintings and music – and also archive film – this historically rich, beautiful and civilised part of the world. König's 'Middle Europe' was no longer just a concept for me; it became an experience. I was an English Romantic, albeit a very undistinguished one, already – like Byron and Shelley – seduced by Mediterranean sun and sea, and now – like Coleridge – also feasting on a culture and sensibility very different from my own, yet one in which I felt very much at home.

What I remember best from those travels through central Europe in 1968 were the few days we spent filming in Prague. It was the height of the Prague Spring. Under Alexander Dubček the Czechs and Slovaks were standing up to the USSR, and for a few brief months people felt free to say what they thought and felt, without fear of being locked up or worse. What interested me in particular about the many people we met and spoke to, including our young interpreter from state television, was that although they all wanted the Russians off their backs and the freedom to kick ideas around, there was no sense that they craved for a society modelled exclusively on western Europe and America. There was, at that time anyway, still an intense idealism; not perhaps as strong or as radical as that of Karl König and his colleagues in Scotland, but nevertheless a feeling that they had it in their power to create a fairer and freer life – initially in Czechoslovakia itself, but ultimately for all of us throughout the world.

A few months later the Russian tanks rumbled into Prague, as they had into Budapest twelve years earlier when, by strange coincidence, I was again near at hand – on a hitch-hiking trip in Europe and staying near the Hungarian border. Once again the aspirations of good and brave people were thwarted. But seeds were sown, and I have great faith in the potential of seeds, however long they take to germinate. In fact my next project was to bring me face to face with an idealism that was, in its way, every bit as profound and challenging as the words and deeds I experienced at Camphill, and as the hopes expressed by those courageous people on the streets of Prague and Budapest.

Mahatma Gandhi's poverty – a poverty embraced in total freedom – was not, as some people like to think, a political gimmick. For Gandhi it became simply impossible to indulge in any sort of luxury while people who had nothing were starving. It is a degree of sensitivity that Steiner spoke about on several occasions and which, in his opinion, would become more and more widespread as humanity evolved in the future. Cynics might say that we're heading in quite the opposite direction – what Thomas Hobbes, back in the 17th century, referred to in *Leviathan* as a war of all against all; and there is certainly plenty of evidence to support Hobbes's view. In my experience, however, there are many examples of people fumbling towards what Gandhi practised so single-mindedly, but their humble efforts are not on the whole news. Yesterday, however, I read in *The Guardian*, in their *Other Lives* obituary section, a woman's tribute to her postman father who spent the fifteen years of his retirement working tirelessly for asylum-seekers and political refugees. I'm sure there are many others like him.

If the life of Emperor Franz Joseph epitomised the end of an era, so Gandhi's life, I believe, points to the birth pangs of a new one. Of course neither Gandhi nor that retired postman were the first to experience such concern and distress at the suffering of others. The Buddha is one obvious example from history of this compassion in action. Likewise many of the initiatives inspired by the life and teachings of Jesus are sublime expressions of this same deep concern for the other person. The whole monastic tradition in Christianity and the charitable obligations that Muslims feel obliged to honour are further examples of our ability, and indeed our deep-seated wish, to transcend our instinctive egotism. It is, in a sense, a deepening of that sensibility we call empathy that I experienced so strongly in action at Camphill. Nor is it a sensibility that is possessed only by people with religious convictions or by those for whom a spiritual dimension to life is of the deepest interest and importance. In fact, if our motives for charitable work are too bound up with concerns about the so-called afterlife, particularly in terms of our own salvation, then the sacrifices that we make are not nearly so altruistic as we might like to imagine. As far as

I can understand, Gandhi had no such ulterior motives. He simply cared very deeply about his fellow human beings and tried to help – not only by freeing India from British rule, but above all by inspiring his fellow countrymen to work towards a fairer, more compassionate society.

Mohandas Karamchand Gandhi was born on October 2nd 1869. One hundred years later, among the many celebrations planned, was a BBC film to honour his life and work. This was to be my next task, and my first visit to India; and through it I was to meet a whole new group of people, both in Britain and in India, who were to have a profound effect on the way my thoughts and feelings were unfolding – above all in relation to the conviction I have long held about the importance of the here and now. I was interested, of course, in what might lie behind our sense-perceptible world, and have remained so. But my instinct has always been that what ultimately matters is how we live out our lives as human beings on earth, whatever might be hovering unseen in the background. And if gods and angels and demons do exist, albeit in forms and with names that need to speak more convincingly to our modern consciousness, they are, I believe – along with the souls of those no longer physically present – intimately connected with what goes on *here* and not with some separate existence elsewhere.

In the epilogue to his book *Gandhi: a Study in Revolution*, Geoffrey Ashe writes:

> To him God was 'there', and relevant every instant. But God was not a dispenser of laws or dogmas. He was a goal to strive towards … Everything Gandhi did was done by way of reasoned experiment, starting from what he could see and touch … To most religious believers, God exists and enjoins us to think and do certain things. To agnostics, he probably does not exist and is in any case an irrelevance. To Gandhi, he existed, but as the goal of a quest to be carried on in perfect freedom. Man should not live by the alleged presence or absence of the Absolute, as a given law of life like breathing, but by its possibility.

Ashe also suggests that Gandhi's uniqueness is revealed in the title of his autobiography, *The Story of my Experiments with Truth*. Much to Gandhi's discomfort he was increasingly exalted as Mahatma – Great Soul – a label that felt inappropriate for someone with his feet so firmly on the ground. 'He could speak the language of priests and mystics without entering deeply into the world of either', writes Ashe. 'Though he was open-minded about the supernatural, it had no place in his experience.' Gandhi's philosophy, if one can call it that, is for me best summed up in one of the few recordings he made in which he spoke as follows:

I do dimly perceive that while everything around me is ever-changing, ever dying there is underlying all that change a living power that is changeless, that holds all together; that creates, dissolves and recreates. For I can see that in the midst of death life persists; in the midst of untruth truth persists; in the midst of darkness light persists.

To produce a biography, whether in print or on film, is a very intimate task. One feels a great responsibility, particularly if the subject is no longer alive; one experiences, too, an increasing closeness to the person in question. During my research I read a great deal about Gandhi, spoke to many people, viewed hours of archive film and listened to those one or two recordings that still exist. Everything contributed to the portrait I was building up, but by far the most powerful experience was simply hearing Gandhi's voice; far more intimate, for example, than seeing images of him on film. And by 'voice', I don't mean the actual words, but rather the quality and tone of that voice. Traditionally people refer to the eyes as a window to the soul. In my experience the voice links one to something even deeper. I've had a similar reaction when listening to, and even filming people speaking in a language of which I have no knowledge whatsoever. Instead of waiting impatiently for a translation, I have enjoyed the encounters uncluttered by confusion over words and their meaning, and as an experience of what I'm tempted to call 'the being behind the mask'. For me, long after someone has died, the memory of their voice is far more powerful than any images I retain. Gandhi's voice, like all our voices, was in this sense his signature, and – like our fingerprints – was certainly like no other.

Gandhi grew up in a family that was neither illiterate nor notably cultured. As a youth, writes Ashe, 'he had shown no outward signs of any distinctive ideas, outstanding virtues, or special talents'. At the age of nineteen, on September 4th 1888, he left India to study law in England, in his eyes 'the land of philosophers and poets, the very centre of civilisation'. But over forty years later, during the early negotiations for Indian independence, a journalist asked

Mahatma Gandhi

Gandhi, as he disembarked at Southampton, what he thought of western civilisation. 'It would be very nice', he is said to have replied.

Much had happened in those intervening years, twenty-one of which were spent as a lawyer in South Africa. There he had gradually become the leader of the Indian community in their struggle against racial prejudice and unjust laws. It was in South Africa that he himself suffered his first political shock on being ejected from a 'Whites Only' train compartment.

Gandhi's philosophy of non-violence was inspired by reading Tolstoy's *The Kingdom of God is within You*, and they had a short correspondence in the year or so before Tolstoy's death in 1910. Much to the dismay and frustration of many of his colleagues in the freedom movement, Gandhi withdrew from anti-British campaigns whenever they turned even slightly violent. His increasing conviction that non-violence was the only right and effective way of confronting violence, injustice and evil was to influence not only millions of Indians in the struggles that lay ahead, but later Martin Luther King and the whole civil rights movement in America.

Gandhi returned to India from South Africa in 1915 at the age of forty-six. The campaign that he then waged was as much about addressing the injustices of the Indian social system as about bringing British rule to an end. Slowly he transformed the Congress Party from an intellectual minority into a mass movement. One of his particular concerns was to improve the conditions of the so-called 'untouchables' – those who were excluded from the Indian caste system altogether and upon whom were dumped all the dirtiest and most degrading jobs. He called them Harijans – Children of God – a term which has passed into Indian vocabulary, though it has not always been popular with the Children themselves. Nowadays they are known as Dalits, which comes from the Sanskrit word *dalita*, meaning 'oppressed'. Gandhi went so far as to say that if he had to be reborn, he would wish to be reborn as an untouchable, so as to share their suffering and to help in liberating them.

Gandhi himself was close enough to orthodox Hinduism to understand, if not to fully accept, the notion of karma and therefore caste – your circumstances in life being the consequence of deeds in previous lives. As outlined in the Baghavad Gita, caste was a four-tier system of ordering society: Scholar/Priest, Noble/Warrior, Merchant/Farmer – the caste to which Gandhi belonged – and Labourer. It was a functional scheme, ideally based on mutual self-respect, and not in fact so very different from, though maybe more explicit than, the social system that operated in all societies, including our own, until comparatively recently; in other words the notion of 'knowing one's place'.

Gandhi also campaigned unceasingly for Hindu–Muslim unity as Independence loomed, and with it the prospect of partition and the creation of an independent Pakistan. He did much for the status of women in Indian society, and above all believed passionately in the importance of revitalising Indian village life as an environment more appropriate for the dignity and fulfilment of each human being.

Gandhi was at the forefront in all these areas of social change, and set an example himself. His possessions were minimal; he practised as well as preached the dignity of manual labour. He did his own laundry and, back in South Africa, had cut his own hair – much to the amusement of his fellow barristers. In India he made the spinning wheel the symbol of self-sufficiency, and in relation to the millions of unemployed he wrote: 'I propose to utilise this spare time of the nation even as a hydraulic engineer utilises enormous waterfalls.' Gandhi also became the first caste Hindu to nurse a leper. And at the time of Partition, in an attempt to stop the terrible slaughter that was taking place all over India, he went to live with a Muslim family in Calcutta. Had he lived longer he intended to go and live in Pakistan to try to act as a bridge between the two communities.

His obsession with diet and hygiene were famous and had their comical side. During his visit to Britain for the Round Table Conference in 1932 he insisted on living in the East End of London among the poor, although the conference was taking place in Whitehall. At that time he was trying to live on a particularly austere diet, with goat's milk as his chief source of protein, so a goat was installed round the corner from the conference, at the Ritz. One colleague is said to have remarked: 'It's very expensive keeping Gandhi poor!'

But Gandhi never lost his sense of humour, however earnest or distressed he became. On that same visit to London he had tea at Buckingham Palace with George V and Queen Mary and was clothed as ever in his simple dhoti and sandals. Asked afterwards by a journalist whether he felt he was properly dressed for the occasion, he replied: 'There was no problem. The King was wearing quite enough for both of us!'

Among the helpful contacts I made in London before leaving for India was Satish Kumar (since 1973 the editor of the ecological magazine *Resurgence*). Kumar was a Jain monk in his youth, and was strongly influenced by Gandhi; through him I met some of those who had worked alongside Gandhi throughout the long struggle for Indian independence. One of these was the Quaker Donald Groom whom I interviewed for the film. He singled out as Gandhi's outstanding quality 'the extent to which he was interested in every single person, rich or poor, Indian or British'. Despite opposing the British system in India, Gandhi had no animosity towards the British themselves. Non-violence as practised by Gandhi was, said Groom, 'a concern for the welfare of the adversary as much as anything else'.

It was not only Tolstoy who had inspired Gandhi's faith in non-violence. He also knew Shelley's poem *The Mask of Anarchy*, written after the massacre of

English workers by government troops at Peterloo, Manchester in 1819. The poem is a passionate appeal to workers in their struggles against oppression:

With folded arms and steady eyes,
And little fear, and less surprise,
Look upon them as they slay
Till their rage has died away.

Then they will return with shame
To the place from which they came,
And blood thus shed will speak
In hot blushes on their cheek.

Gandhi's faith in the potential of each human being was what Groom emphasised to me most strongly. Even at the time of Partition, he said, when all sorts of terrible crimes were being committed, he never lost this faith. 'You have to love humanity in spite of itself', said Gandhi to a colleague at the time. When an American clergymen asked him what caused him the most concern he replied: 'The hardness of heart of the educated.'

In India itself I was fortunate to have as a travelling companion during part of my research trip Hallam Tennyson who, like Donald Groom, had worked in India after World War II, together with his wife Margot, on relief work in West Bengal. He had known Gandhi and was able to introduce me to many of his most interesting and inspiring followers. Tennyson had also written a book – *India's Walking Saint* – about Vinoba Bhave, the man whom many saw as Gandhi's spiritual successor and who walked literally thousands of miles all over India persuading rich landowners to donate one-sixth of their land to the poor. By the time we came to film, Vinoba was an old man and had taken a vow of silence. Tennyson now worked in radio drama for the BBC and was in India to make a parallel programme to mine for radio. He also worked with me on the script for my film.

In Delhi I also met Mark Tully for the first time; he had recently arrived from London. He and I were to make several films together in the years to come, both in India and later in Pakistan. At that time it still took about two days to get film equipment through customs, and that was with bribes. I remember Tully's Indian secretary who, in contrast to the sixties image of false eyelashes and painted toenails, sported a huge handle-bar moustache. His name was simply Ramachandran and he knew how to work wonders with the Indian babus, a network of obstructive bureaucrats.

Also in Delhi was Malcolm Muggeridge with another BBC film crew in tow. Part of his project for BBC Religious Programmes was to make his celebrated film on Mother Teresa that so touched audiences all over the world. I passed through Calcutta with my crew while Muggeridge and his team were at work. Again this was a meeting that would lead to a close friendship and some interesting work together, including a film with Stalin's daughter, Svetlana, and another with Alexander Solzhenitsyn.

Thus, it was a time of inspiring encounters and whole new areas of experience. To cap it all, early on my third morning in Delhi I had been woken by a telephone call from my boss, Gordon Watkins, to tell me that I had won an award from the British Film Academy (now BAFTA) for my documentary *In Need of Special Care*, about the Camphill School in Scotland.

It was on this first trip to India that I had what was for me an important experience regarding death. Despite my strong conviction that some form of immortality permeates all existence, I had always been extremely disturbed by any actual encounter with death, and in particular the ritual at funerals. It was that tightly closed box that upset me most of all, and my inability to get away from the idea that the person who had died was there inside their coffin. At that time I had never seen a human corpse. When my mother died, her body had been taken away by the time I returned from Scotland, and all that I ever saw was her coffin.

On my visit to Varanasi – the old Benares – on the banks of the river Ganges, I witnessed the burning of dead bodies that were not boxed away out of sight, and I was surprised at my reaction. True, the deceased were not people I had known, but nevertheless this experience was not something that I found in the least shocking or upsetting. The rituals were performed, as I remember, with great sensitivity and respect. But there was an honesty and openness about it all that made death somehow more acceptable and natural. It is somewhat of a cliché to refer to a corpse as a shell or a worn-out garment, but that is exactly how it felt to me.

Since then, on several occasions, I have sat with a person after their death, and in one case have been with someone as they crossed that threshold. Each time I have had the same powerful experience that after death the person I loved and cared about, though as real to me as ever, was no longer interwoven with a physical body. Thus my horror of coffins has gradually disappeared.

What I have not yet quite come to terms with are crematoriums. By the Ganges, all those years ago, the rituals unfolded while all around the busy life of the town and river continued uninterrupted. Death, if you like, was part of life. In a crematorium, unlike in a church where celebrations and rituals of all sorts take place, only death presides – and in a sanitised way that seems designed to protect us and thereby isolate us from the experience and the reality of what is actually taking place.

In telling the story of someone's life it is always interesting to observe the degree to which they move away from the traditions of their own background and assert their own individual identities. Some people, of course, don't make particularly dramatic changes. Likewise some of us resemble our parents physically; others not at all. In the case of figures like Gandhi you can see how, as they grow up, they often begin to express quite different values and aspirations from the family and the culture that has nurtured them.

Gandhi was born into a still very traditional society. At the age of thirteen he was married to a girl of his own age, chosen by his parents. At that time Hindu child marriage was quite normal. Gandhi, like Tolstoy, was no natural celibate, and eventually he and Kasturbai had four children. In the years ahead, however, Gandhi was to ponder deeply on the subject of sexuality and his own strong sensuality. His deliberations culminated, at the age of fifty-seven and in consultation with his wife, in a vow of chastity. Unlike Tolstoy, who made endless promises to himself that he never kept, Gandhi had an early experience of taking vows that he did keep and which obviously helped him to make further ones in the future. His mother expressed great misgivings about her young son going away to England. Only when he took a solemn oath not to touch meat, wine or women could she let him go. The young Gandhi, suggests Ashe in his biography, had no real convictions at the time regarding this oath, but he had very real convictions about keeping his word; and keep his word he did.

Gandhi's self-discipline was strengthened in the process, and in the years ahead he made great demands upon himself and, indeed, upon others. The poem *The Light of Asia* by Edwin Arnold tells how the Buddha forsook his wife and children to become a Sadhu, a holy beggar. Gandhi never considered such a step but was very aware, as described in that poem, of the liberation that is promised to the man who 'so constrains his passions that they die'. Unlike Tolstoy, however, Gandhi never felt that the sexual act was somehow degrading or wrong, and acknowledged its sublime role in the great mystery of procreation. But he was deeply

Mahatma Gandhi and his wife Kasturbai

influenced by the Hindu tradition of self-mastery and restraint, and of the goal of transcending one's purely selfish appetites in order to be of greater service to others.

Gandhi's ability to make this decision and others, and to stick by them, helped him increasingly to use fasting – if necessary to death – as a means of protest. His doctor, Shushila Nayar, spoke to me in the film about this most powerful of weapons: 'He believed that human beings are essentially good', she told me, 'and if you suffer yourself, you release the force of love which brings out the best in the other person.' Not everyone was transformed to that degree by Gandhi's acts of self-sacrifice, though in many instances he achieved his aim of curbing violence. Perhaps on a greater time scale he will prove to have been even more successful.

Apart from his numerous fasts, Gandhi spent a total of 249 days in jail while in South Africa, and 2089 days locked up in his own country. There was endless debate in India, and still is, as to whether he was a saint or a politician, despite the fact that at the conclusion of his autobiography he wrote: 'Those who say that religion has nothing to do with politics do not know what religion means.' Perhaps 'pragmatic improviser' describes Gandhi best of all: 'neither an Arcadian nor a Utopian', as Richard Lannoy, a distinguished writer on Gandhi, put it; but rather 'a relentless explorer of immediacy – immediate needs, immediate means, immediate ends.'

Asha Devi Aryanayakan

The meeting that I remember best of all and which touched me most deeply, during this first visit to India, was with a woman called Asha Devi Aryanayakan. She and her late husband pioneered the educational work that Gandhi had set in motion. In 1968 she was running a school at Sevegram in the very centre of India where Gandhi established his last ashram. The school was for the poorest children in the area. Learning in the early years was almost entirely through activity – growing their own food, making their own clothes. I asked Asha Devi, in typical and deliberately journalistic fashion, whether Gandhi was perhaps too idealistic and made demands on people beyond their capacity. Her response was wonderful, but I can only relate the words. Imagine, too, her smile, her warmth and gentleness, her deep sincerity. 'There is no limit to our capacity', she said. 'Aren't we supposed to have something of the divine in us? I think that was the secret of his hold on us – that he made the highest demands on us. We failed, as individuals, as a nation. But the very fact that he made the demands raised us a little.'

My memories of Sevegram are very special – the peace and simple beauty of the place; the uncluttered existence of all those who lived there. At dawn we filmed the community's daily routine of prayers, singing and spinning – a ritual as practical as it was holy. Maybe all that we do that is good and worthwhile, however simple, has this sacred quality but we fail to notice. I've always liked the idea of every meal as Holy Communion – a celebration of miracles.

It was at Sevegram that a wise old man, with whom I was discussing our potential as human beings to grow and change, said something that I have always remembered. And like many of the most profound insights, it is expressed very simply. 'In order to put new water into a bottle', he said, 'you have first to empty it.'

The Benedictine monk, Bede Griffiths – whose extraordinary life is described in *Beyond the Darkness* by Shirley du Boulay – spoke of how he found the other half of his soul in India; he lived there for nearly forty years. I wouldn't use quite the same words, but making that first of several films in India was for me, without a doubt, a very important new awakener – above all an encounter with people whose ancient and profound religious traditions still permeated every aspect of their culture.

But there was something else I met in India that transcends all cultures. I had had a similar experience in the Yorkshire dale that was home to Botton Village. Simplicity and serenity are the words that come to mind – a profound serenity in the way that people went about their daily lives. I'm speaking of rural India, in particular, and am very aware that in much of the country the pace of life was growing, and continues to grow ever more frenzied – as much as in Britain and elsewhere. At an oasis like Sevegram, however, I felt I witnessed, and was briefly part of, a way of life that once existed in all societies, and could exist again: one in which not just tradition, but a greater awareness of essentials permeates everything we do and how we do it; a life in which our technological skills can also play their part.

Cyrus Bharucha and John McGlashan

By now it was May and, although I like the heat, by ten o'clock in the morning it was too hot to continue filming. For the first time in my life I experienced real thirst: water, too, became sacred. For my cameraman, John McGlashan, and my assistant, Nicola Davis, as for me, it was their first time in India. As well as being a very talented and distinguished cameraman, John was a lay bishop in the Liberal Catholic Church, an offshoot of the theosophical movement, with its centre in Madras; so he and I had much to discuss, and many films later we are still discussing. The parents of sound recordist Dave Brinicombe had been Plymouth Brethren missionaries in South India. The camera assistant, Cyrus Bharucha, was a Parsee brought up in Bombay, yet for him too, with his relatively privileged and isolated city background, rural India was a revelation. For all of us Sevagram was, I think, the highlight of our trip; and we were in the very heart of that great country, in the place where Gandhi made his last home.

My brief for the film was not only to tell the story of Gandhi's life but also to explore to what extent his hopes and ideas lived on in India twenty years after his death. Gandhi had touched Indian life at so many levels – Hindu–Muslim unity, education, abolition of untouchablility and, above all, his belief in a decentralised village society free of exploitation and hatred. India's salvation lay not in becoming more like England, he believed, but in becoming more like India. For Gandhi, says Ashe in his biography, this implied reconstituting a simple life on a vast scale as the true expression of India's soul.

Besides Tolstoy, the beacons that Gandhi acknowledged in his life – his awakeners, if you like – were the *Bhagavad Gita*, which he came to appreciate through English friends while studying Law in London; the Sermon on the Mount, and finally a book called *Unto this Last* by the English art critic and social reformer John Ruskin. All Gandhi's experiments with community living, which started back in South Africa, along with his belief in the dignity of manual labour, were inspired by Ruskin's book. This particular aspect of his legacy interested me very much, especially after my experiences in Botton Village. Indeed there also seemed to me many parallels between Gandhi's Harijans, the untouchable outcasts of Indian society, and those people in western society, some of whom I had met at Botton, who are outcasts because they are too slow, too simple, too unacquisitive to cope with the pace of daily life.

Superficially the verdict on Gandhi's influence on Indian society then – in 1969, twenty years after his death – and even more so today, is discouraging. 'He is at best an icon, respected but not relevant', is how Rudrangshu Mukerherjee, editor of the *The Penguin Gandhi Reader*, has described him. After Independence, under its first Prime Minister Pandit Jawaharlal Nehru, India pursued a policy of centralised planning and industrialisation on a massive scale. However, by the time Nehru's grandson Rajiv Gandhi became Prime Minister in the eighties the government had come to realise that Gandhi was still relevant, and an act was passed aimed at reviving Panchayats, the village councils, by giving them more power and making the administrative structure less top-down.

Above all, as at Botton Village, seeds had been sown, and there are many who believe that in the future people both in India and beyond will look to Gandhi's ideas and example more and more, above all in relation to the dehumanising trends in modern society and the problems of sustainability. One such person was the radical economist Fritz Schumacher, whom I met in London before and after my trip to India, and interviewed for the film. He spoke to me of Gandhi as a fellow economist, which was a welcome change from the politician/saint debate: 'Gandhi always had in mind the human being, not an economic theory', he said. 'He never studied economics; he studied the human being.'

Schumacher, like Gandhi, recognised that you cannot expect people to stay in villages if all that goes on is low-grade agriculture, using methods that have scarcely changed since the time of the Buddha; hence the effort to revive local crafts and skills. 'But Gandhi was no fool', said Schumacher. 'For example, he was not against the wristwatch, but nor was he suggesting that wristwatches be made in every village. But life is not made up of wristwatches. Most of what we need for daily life can be grown or made on our own doorsteps.'

Gandhi also realised that in a country like India, which was rich in people but not in capital, what made sense was production by the masses and not mass-production. It was primarily for this insight that Schumacher acknowledged Gandhi as a fellow economist. His own celebrated book *Small is Beautiful* is subtitled 'a study of economics as if people mattered'. For Schumacher nothing made economic sense if it ignored the reality of the human being and saw people only in terms of producers and consumers.

During the filming we visited a number of Gandhian ashrams all over India – centres where basic skills of farming, carpentry, paper-making, pottery, weaving and health care were taught to the surrounding villagers. Traditionally an ashram is a place of retreat, like Emerson College had been for me. But like Emerson College, the Gandhian ashrams were not places to hide away from life, instead providing help and encouragement in facing life anew. Some people speak disparagingly of Botton Village as an escape – a peaceful and idyllic existence away from the rush and tumble of daily life. But escape is a complicated concept. Might not a stockbroker on Wall Street or a banker in the City of London also be escaping, in their case into an artificial world of gold and glitter? The only harmful escape is to ignore our daimon, our conscience.

On one occasion on our travels in India, in a remote part of the very impoverished state of Bihar, we experienced an amusing moment that forcefully conveyed a central aspect of Gandhi's philosophy. With the help of some Gandhian workers and with the added support of the British relief agency Oxfam, a group of Harijan families were building a village for themselves on donated land. I spoke to the Gandhian representative, and to the pink-faced, upper-class

John Hunt and Parisbhai

and cheery Oxfam volunteer, John Hunt, while in the background – and not just for the camera – the villagers wielded their pick axes and dug away in the midday sun. Gandhi would have been very pleased at such a scene, said Hunt – Harajans no longer marginalised and landless. 'And he would have been delighted to see us working together, an Englishman and an Indian', he said to his companion Parisbhai – a sort of Sancho Panza figure to John's Don Quixote. 'No,' said the faithful and grinning Gandhian, 'we should be digging too!'

Someone who *was* digging, despite his age, was the Reverend Dick Keithahn, an American missionary who had worked in India for over forty years, and whose early association with Gandhi led to him being twice deported by the British. We filmed Keithahn at work on a dam-building project in southern India in which the villagers themselves were again fully involved. At that time

Dick Keithahn

Gandhi's old Congress Party had lost control of two states to the Communists. I asked Keithahn for his reaction. 'Well, I always thank God for the Communists by my side', he replied. 'The rest of us, idealists, have stayed in our comfortable compounds with our good jobs and so on, and have neglected these people. But the Communist is bringing to our attention constantly the terrible conditions under which millions of people exist today.' He went on to describe how practically no government 'gets down to the very last, to the people who have not enough to eat, who have no land, who are being exploited'. His parting words, as he went back to his digging were: 'If we work constructively, non-violently, as Gandhi taught us, the Communist has no place. But I thank God, meanwhile, he is there to keep us alert.'

In the sixties Schumacher was responsible for the creation of the Intermediate Technology Development Group, and we saw examples of the application of appropriate technology in villages all over India. Donald Groom spoke to me about Gandhi's attitude to what we call progress, and about his recognition of the tremendous assets available to those who live in cities – business acumen, education, technology. But Gandhi was also very aware of the squalor and misery that huge cities generate, and of the difficulty for very many people of living a dignified and fulfilling life in such a setting. 'So Gandhi wanted all those assets available to the city, to the West, available to the villages', said Groom, 'and he felt that modern science could make that possible. Essentially, therefore, there was no conflict between the India of his dreams and the West.'

So is the verdict on Gandhi's legacy really so grim? It may depend on the timescale you judge it by. In *The Secret History of the World* Jonathan Black writes of Gandhi 'as a great embodiment of the new form of consciousness that the secret societies have been working throughout history to help evolve'. And in this respect he adds: 'The intention behind action can have a greater effect than the action itself.' I believe this very strongly, and it is why I have referred several times to the analogy of seeds being sown.

Meanwhile the real secret of Gandhi's hold over the largely illiterate population of India was, I believe, that he completely identified with them through the utter simplicity of his own life; and that this sacrifice, together with his honesty and moral courage, created an enormously powerful bond. Asha Devi spoke to me about 'his great love – a love that was not soft or sentimental, and which reached out to everyone; and the joy of life that he radiated.' Certainly the many photographs of Gandhi laughing confirm this observation. I would also single out his modesty; and, of course, his refusal to feather his own nest while others had neither feathers nor sometimes even a nest.

There is, however, an irony associated with the decline of village life caused by the mass migration to cities that resulted from Nehru's policy of industrialisation, for in these crowded and frequently squalid settings the caste system does slowly start to disintegrate. Cities are melting pots, whereas a strong element of conservatism often persists in the countryside – and not just in India. For me that doesn't negate Gandhi's dream of a decentralised society based on vibrant village life, but perhaps all cultures will need to go down this route to a more urban existence, if only to wake up in the process. Only then, in full consciousness rather than out of tradition, will we gradually create a saner way of life, not totally cut off from nature. As Donald Groom said, there doesn't have to be a conflict between the old ways and the new. There is good in both. As so often in life it is a question of balance. We have it in our imagination as well as in our power to forge an environment and a lifestyle that is truly appropriate for our humanity to flourish and evolve.

I will give Schumacher the final word on this subject of Gandhi's legacy – but not on Gandhi himself:

> The temptation, the glitter of the modern way of life, the western way of life is so great that you cannot expect Gandhi to be acclaimed as the major prophet once he had physically disappeared. We should not take it too seriously that twenty years since his death he is merely a symbol of something that was not followed. But the future lies with Gandhi. I hope they won't make a religion out of it, a dogma: 'Gandhi has said this, therefore it must be right.' But if good minds devote themselves to this they can draw the lines. To what extent, in what precise way is mechanisation a good thing? It's undoubtedly a good thing to take the strain out of things. It's undoubtedly a bad thing to reduce labour to a totally meaningless chore. But these are subtle points, and you can't expect Gandhi, who did many other things, to solve them all in detail.

In fact Gandhi himself, towards the end of his life, warned his followers to rid themselves of the habit of searching in his writings for textual authority: 'There is no such thing as Gandhism, and I do not want to leave any sect after me.'

On January 30th 1948, on the way to his daily prayer meeting, Gandhi was assassinated by a Hindu fanatic. His association with Muslims and his concern for them as much as for anyone else cost him his life. The day before he died he had written: 'Death is a true friend. It is only our ignorance that causes us grief.' Responding to the news of Gandhi's death, Albert Einstein declared: 'Generations to come will scarcely believe that such a man as this walked upon the earth.' Prime Minister Nehru spoke these words to the nation:

> Friends and comrades – The light has gone out of our lives and there is darkness everywhere and I do not quite know what to tell you and how to say it. Our beloved leader, Bapu as we called him, the father of our nation, is no more. Perhaps I am wrong to say that. Nevertheless, we will not see him again as we have seen him these many years. We will not run to him for advice and seek solace from him. And that is a terrible blow not to me only but to millions and millions in this country.
>
> The light has gone out, I said, and yet I was wrong. For the light that shone in this country was no ordinary light. The light that has illumined this country for these many years will illumine this country for many more years, and a thousand years later that light will still be seen in this country, and the world will see it and it will give solace to innumerable hearts … There is so much more to do. There was so much more for him to do.

Mahatma Gandhi

CHAPTER 10

Worms and Angels

After our death each one of us continues to exist for a while as a memory and perhaps even as an inspiration to others, though few people touch the lives of millions, as did Gandhi. And if Nehru was right, for one's light to still shine 'a thousand years later' would indeed be an extraordinary achievement, a great gift to humanity. But what happens to the individuality itself – to that essence which for seventy-eight years we knew as Mahatma Gandhi? Indeed what happens to any of us, whether we make our mark on history or not and yet like Gandhi have had hopes and dreams, successes and failures, loves and hates?

At the Atheist Alliance convention in Crystal City, Virginia in October 2007, the evolutionary biologist Richard Dawkins said this: 'I would like to see people encouraged to rejoice in the world in which they find themselves, the universe in which they have been born, to take full advantage of the tiny slice of eternity they have been granted.' Perhaps that's it; and not a bad sentiment in terms of helping us to focus on the here and now. But if, as Dawkins acknowledges, eternity is a reality, then perhaps we too, in the core of our being, share in that reality. If so, to speak of 'one tiny slice of eternity' is essentially misleading.

At this stage in my own life I was certainly enjoying my current 'slice', and for a while no longer experienced a conflict between what deeply interested me and what I was actually doing from day to day. There was still an idealism and energy at the BBC that corresponded to my own. I was thirty years old and feeling tremendously enriched by my time at Emerson College; also very inspired by what I had experienced in the Camphill communities, by what I had met in India, and by Gandhi's life in particular.

By now I had read a number of books on reincarnation. The whole theosophical movement was deeply influenced by Hinduism and much of its esoteric terminology is Indian in origin. These theosophists, initially in Berlin and then later all over Europe, including Britain, were the first people to take an interest in Steiner's esoteric teachings. Initially they tended to think that he, like their founder Madame Blavatsky, was the vehicle for what she had called the Masters; in other words that he was a medium. Steiner's books and lectures, however, were based on his own meditative research over many years, and grounded in the rigorous exercising of his intellectual faculties.

It was at the age of thirty-six, in 1897, that Steiner had moved from Weimar to Berlin, initially to work as editor on a literary magazine. Two years later he was invited to lecture at a Worker's Educational Institute on history and science. There he tried, for a while with great success, to tap into the idealism that had led many in his audience to Marxism, and to put this idealism into a wider perspective that went beyond a purely materialistic view of history. Ultimately, in the eyes of those behind the initiative, Steiner's 'political incorrectness' was unacceptable.

Steiner aged forty in 1901

Meanwhile, his urge to speak out on more occult matters was intensifying. At the end of his life, some twenty years later, he was to single out the law of karma and reincarnation as the most important subject he was trying to elucidate; he believed new insights into this law were needed, along with their communication in a form and language that resonated for modern consciousness.

The belief that an individual must undergo incarnation at certain intervals in order to make compensation for the past in a new life on earth, and to mature by encountering new experiences, can be traced back to ancient times. It is a teaching that does not simply imply an endless circle of birth, death and rebirth, but rather a spiral through which evolution – personal, earthly and cosmic – unfolds. There has always been, however, a certain fatalism in the East in relation to the idea of karma in particular; whereas in the West we have an instinctive sense that 'nothing is written', as T.E. Lawrence expressed it. 'We may be slaves to the past, but we are masters of the future' is a paradoxical and profound statement by Rudolf Steiner on this same subject.

Perhaps Benjamin Franklin's epitaph, composed by himself when a young apprentice printer, says it best of all:

The Body
Of
Benjamin Franklin
Printer
(like the cover of an old book
its contents torn out
and stript of its lettering and gilding)
Lies here
Food for worms.
But the work shall not be lost
For it will (as he believed) appear once more
In a new and more elegant Edition
Revised and improved
By
The Author.

As Nehru said in his broadcast on the death of Gandhi: 'There is so much more to do. There is so much more for him to do.'

But to talk about reincarnation, and indeed about anything that addresses the great mysteries of existence, at some point requires us to turn our attention inwards. Who is doing the talking? What is the real nature and make-up of a human being, and where do we belong in the scheme of things – assuming such a scheme exists?

In a recent interview with the cartoonist Gerald Scarfe, in response to a question about which living artist he most admired, he replied: 'Lucien Freud. He captures the fact that ultimately we are just lumps of meat.' It is a somewhat crude version of what we are all encouraged to believe these days – a view that I, along with very many other people, instinctively reject.

This question about the true nature of the human being is one Francis Edmunds returned to again and again in his lectures; and it is the question I also want to explore in this chapter – primarily through a book by Fritz Schumacher called *A Guide for the Perplexed*.

I stayed in touch with Schumacher after my interview with him about Gandhi. He lived quite near Forest Row in Sussex, a place that I often visited, as my brother and sister were now settled there through their involvement with the local Steiner School, Michael Hall. As an uncle I was also making my first close connection with children, as well as in my role as a godfather. This contact with the very young has remained an essential and enriching part of my life ever since.

Despite my travels and busy life in London, I also kept in touch with Emerson College – that English ashram which, like its Gandhian counterparts in India, was stimulating and inspiring all sorts of initiatives in the surrounding area. One such project that particularly attracted me, and which also interested Schumacher – who had close links with the Soil Association – was a farm managed by a delightful and gifted family, newly arrived in Sussex. Jimmy Anderson had already farmed in Scotland and Somerset, but with increasing misgivings about the direction agriculture was taking.

After a course at Emerson College Jimmy and his wife Pauline took on Busses Farm near East Grinstead. The method they adopted was a further development of what we nowadays call organic farming – which is, after all, only how people traditionally farmed before chemicals came on the scene. Biodynamic farming came about through a series of lectures that Rudolf Steiner gave in June 1924 at Koberwitz in Silesia to a group of farmers who already had concerns similar to those later expressed by the Andersons and many others.

In the Agricultural Course, as it is called, Steiner drew not only on his clairvoyant research, but also on his own peasant background. The biodynamic method respects the integrity of the farm as a complete, living organism and, as well as advocating a mixture of livestock, and the tradition of crop rotation, uses organic preparations in homeopathic dilutions in order to preserve and strengthen the inherent fertility and vitality of soil that has become increasingly depleted; thus the nutritive value of agricultural produce is also enhanced. And, through a deeper understanding of the relation between earth and cosmos, not only can the soil, plants and animals be healed, but also human life itself. The most propitious time to plant, for example, takes account of the planetary and other configurations in the vast spaces that surround us, and of the cosmic rhythms that underlie the seasons.

'Muck and magic' is the slightly dismissive slogan sometimes used to describe these kinds of initiatives. However in India and Egypt, for example, where the biodynamic method of agriculture is flourishing, and where there is still an instinctive connection to old traditions – where 'magic' is not yet a dirty word – such a slogan presents no problem whatsoever.

I, myself, spent many happy weekends at Busses Farm shovelling 'muck' and stirring preparations that were, I'm sure, full of 'magic'. For what, in fact, do we mean by the word 'magic'? 'Things that happen without our understanding' would be one answer. In which case most of life, from the microscopic to the distant heavens and everything in between, warrants that description.

It has always seemed to me strange that whereas most of us recognise without any problem that the sun is the source of our heat and light, and likewise acknowledge the gravitational forces that both sun and moon exert on our earth, many so-called educated people still tend to mock the belief that other influences might emanate from the planets and beyond. It is a subject that the mathematician Lawrence Edwards researched over many years with great diligence and wrote about in *The Field of Form*. His work suggests that a very real connection exists between rhythmic processes on earth and in the cosmos. In *Space and Counterspace* Nick Thomas describes how Edwards discovered that these rhythmic processes of moon and planets are mirrored throughout the winter in supposedly dormant leaf buds. Edwards had expected the shapes of the buds to remain static during the winter, but was surprised to find variations in size occurring within a roughly two-week cycle. 'As he looked into the matter further', writes Thomas,

> he found that different trees had slightly but distinctly different cycle lengths, and these correlated with the times between conjunctions and oppositions of the moon and a planet, so that for an oak, for example, this correlated closely with the conjunctions and oppositions with Mars.

Over nineteen years Edwards collected a large amount of data and discovered a method of analysis that confirmed the relationship of different trees to different planets.

This whole notion of our intricate relationship to the heavens is also examined in great detail by Richard Tarnas in *Cosmos and Psyche*, his book on astrology. In the early pages, in reminding us about that sense of the unity of all existence which we have almost completely lost, he writes how 'the achievement of human autonomy has been paid for by the experience of human alienation. How precious the former, how painful the latter'.

Tarnas goes on to describe how over thirty years of 'the most painstaking investigation and critical assessment' he became convinced that there exists 'a highly significant – indeed pervasive – correspondence between planetary movements and human affairs'. The evidence has suggested to him that it is not the planets themselves that cause various events or character traits, but rather that 'a consistently meaningful empirical correspondence exists between two sets of phenomena, astronomical and human, with the connecting principle most fruitfully approached as some form of archetypally informed synchronicity'.

One of the many correspondences that Tarnas explores in his book is the Uranus–Neptune alignment that took place between 1899 and 1918. This particular alignment is characterised, so Tarnas observes, by a widespread transformation of a culture's underlying vision, resulting in a general spiritual awakening, the emergence of new religious movements and philosophical perspectives, a rebirth of idealism and a major shift in people's artistic imagination. He mentions among previous such alignments the years 412 to 397 BC as the time of Socrates' most influential teaching in Athens; and the period 1472 to 1486 as the heart of the Italian Renaissance – this particular alignment also coinciding with the births of both Copernicus and Luther, 'the two men who initiated, respectively, the great cosmological and religious paradigm shifts that launched the modern era'.

In the alignment that took place from 1899 to 1918, Tarnas sees the characteristic influence of the Uranus–Neptune archetypal combination as 'dissolving boundaries and structures, merging that which was separate' and favouring 'the timeless over the temporal, the immaterial over the material, the infinite over the finite'. He finds this taking place in virtually every area of human activity, including art, literature, music and dance. In terms of a shift in cosmological vision he points to the work of Albert Einstein and all that stemmed from the implications of his theory of relativity. The beginning of the 20th century also coincided with the emergence of depth psychology in the work of Freud and Jung; likewise 'new philosophies that dissolved established assumptions and structures of belief' through figures such as William James in the United States, Henri Bergson in France, Alfred North Whitehead and Frederic Myers in England, Edmund Husserl in Germany and Richard Bucke in Canada. Finally, in the area that Tarnas calls 'esoteric philosophy and mystical spirituality', he draws attention to Rudolf Steiner's decision to 'go public' in presenting and advocating a spiritual science appropriate for modern consciousness.

Fritz Schumacher was profoundly aware of these major shifts taking place as the 20th century unfolded – his sister was married to the pioneering physicist Werner Heisenberg. Despite this he had a somewhat ambivalent attitude to Steiner's work and to anthroposophy. Partly, I suspect, he was wary of a certain cultish aura that can hover over the movement at times; and like many people he was suspicious of a seemingly close-knit circle of followers gathered round one charismatic teacher – a teacher who was no longer around to shake things up. Nevertheless he was clearly influenced by some of Steiner's basic research and observations.

Schumacher had come from Germany in 1930 as a Rhodes Scholar and from then on lived in Britain, and briefly in America. He spoke English more fluently and creatively than almost anyone I ever met. After the war he served as Economic Advisor with the British Control Commission in Germany, and then for twenty years was Economic Advisor to the National Coal Board. But he is best remembered for his concept of 'intermediate and appropriate technology' for developing countries, and his book *Small is Beautiful*.

E.F. Schumacher

Schumacher had read Steiner in English and was clearly interested in the ideas; but he told me that Steiner in German was too turgid and pedantic for him. I have heard other Germans express envy at the freedom translators have, though there are some who emphasise the importance and value of reading Steiner in the original. The difficulties that people have with the books – and also with the lectures, most of which are now in print – are not, I sense, simply to do with style. In fact Steiner frequently used the German language in a new and deliberately challenging way. It is more a matter of tone. At times his statements can, for example, come over as rather dogmatic; but for Steiner they were facts, not opinions. It is a major and very understandable hurdle for many people on first acquaintance with his work: How can someone be so certain about matters that are essentially so mysterious, beyond both our experience, and often our comprehension?

In the end it is, I suppose, a very personal and quite complicated matter – the way we respond to another person and their way of expressing things, particularly ideas and information of such a profound nature. In *A Guide for the Perplexed*, for example, which Schumacher wrote towards the end of his life, I find his attempt to describe what Steiner called 'the fourfold human being' in some ways more engaging and easier to grasp than Steiner's own descriptions in his two key books, *Theosophy* and *Occult Science: an Outline*. But perhaps 'easier' is a trap. How much am I really understanding? At least Schumacher's efforts are a helpful bridge – at times playful – and nobody can quarrel with that.

In his opening chapter, called 'On Philosophical Maps', Schumacher raises the key question: 'What am I supposed to do with my life?' He proposes the creation of a guidebook about how man is to live in the world. He suggests that we shall need to study:

1. 'The World'
2. 'Man' – equipment wherewith to meet 'the World'
3. his way of learning about the world; and
4. what it means to 'live' in this world.

Schumacher then cites as our task the need to look at the world and see it as a unity, to see it whole. The enlightened ones among our ancestors, he says, recognised what they called a great 'Chain of Being'; four kingdoms, as they used to be called – mineral, plant, animal and human. These traditional four levels of being can be looked at in descending or ascending order, depending on whether you view our origin as divine, in which case it has been a descent, or through the modern theory of evolution, in which case humanity has gradually ascended from inanimate matter.

Schumacher then proceeds to assemble an equation with some very basic algebra. In so doing he points out that the concept of 'life force' is no longer recognised by science, since no such life force has ever been found to exist, despite the fact that there is clearly a big difference between a dead plant and one that is alive. He calls this life force x, 'indicating something that is there to be noticed and studied, but cannot be explained'. The mineral level he calls m, and therefore the plant level becomes $m + x$.

'Animals can do things that are totally outside the range of possibilities of the typical, fully-developed plant', he then writes. These powers he labels y, associated with what we call consciousness. 'It is easy to recognise consciousness in a dog, a cat or a horse,' he adds, 'if only because they can be knocked unconscious, a condition similar to that of a plant.' The animal he therefore describes as $m + x + y$.

'Man has powers of life like the plant, powers of consciousness like the animal, and evidently something more: the mysterious power z', he continues. Schumacher quite rightly singles out our ability to be conscious of our consciousness as the defining feature of z; something able to say 'I' and to direct consciousness in accordance with its own purposes. We are self-aware and so can be written as $m + x + y + z$. But we must take care to remember, he warns, that such labelling is merely (to use a Buddhist phrase) 'a finger pointing to the moon'. The moon itself remains highly mysterious, as does the human being.

Although we have the ability – often only through scientific instruments – to observe these four levels of being, observation does not automatically result in understanding. Many people believe that the physical is all there is, and they bring this conviction to their research. Schumacher was among those who believe there is more, and maintained that only one of these four realms of existence – the mineral – is actually accessible to objective, scientific observation by means of our five senses, or through the instruments that are extensions of those senses.

One obvious limitation of Schumacher's otherwise clear and relatively simple algebraic equation: $m + x + y + z =$ human being, is that it fails to convey the dynamic and evolving configuration of these four elements – an interaction that is frequently far from harmonious. As Emerson said, 'The reason why the world lacks unity, and lies broken and in heaps, is because Man is disunited within himself.' In the case of those who, for one reason or another, are either mentally ill, brain damaged or in a coma, the phrase 'He's not all there' is an indication that we instinctively recognise this complex configuration that is the human being.

Schumacher concludes this chapter with another reminder: that until very recently the great majority of mankind has been unshakeably convinced that this chain of being extends upwards beyond man. In Christian tradition we enter here into the realm of what are called the angelic hierarchies, and are thus prompted to confront the notion that we are not only sustained by what we refer to as the lower kingdoms of nature – mineral, plant and animal – but also by a corresponding kingdom of angels, archangels, and so on, more highly evolved than us, which supports and sustains us in other ways and with which we are also interconnected.

However, I use the expression 'more highly evolved' with a certain hesitation, since the picture that has become increasingly meaningful for me is one of interdependence. We would, for example, be in serious trouble without the humble worm; also without the world of plants on which we depend to produce the oxygen we breathe. In some ways we seem to need these so-called lower realms of nature far more than they need us. And if there are realms of existence more evolved than us, then these angelic beings may, in some mysterious way, be dependant on us for their own further evolution, just as we are dependant on the world of nature for ours. If so, the implication behind the word 'interconnectedness' takes on even greater significance.

A question that has therefore increasingly interested me concerns the evolutionary potential of the human race – a question I discussed endlessly with Schumacher, and continue to do so with anyone else who is interested. I am less and less inclined to believe that this potential is simply to do with our so-called intelligence. Our brains are quite big enough already. Perhaps what Thomas Weihs suggested is a helpful clue – that our compassion needs to catch up with our cleverness. Meanwhile, in our complexity, both physical and psychological, we human beings may be 'higher' than plants and animals, but I don't actually feel either superior or inferior in relation to worms or angels. Perhaps humanity, like every other realm of creation, has its secret and significant task in relation to the whole.

What then were the formulations that Rudolf Steiner used in *his* attempts to describe the make-up of the human being? When he started to speak and write under the banner of what he called anthroposophy he initially retained much of the language used by oriental theosophists. He was never actually a member of the Theosophical Society, but it was in those circles that he first began to speak more openly about his spiritual research. Years later he referred to the early theosophists as 'homeless souls', who did not feel quite at home in the culture of their day. He, too, for all his learning and activity, could also be described in a similar way. Indeed many of us, at times, have the same feeling.

Theosophy has tended to remain a movement largely concerned with the human being's spiritual and moral nature, and with study, devotion and meditation at the centre of its activity. It is less concerned with the nuts and bolts of daily life. My own interest has always been with all dimensions of life – what is both 'seen' and 'unseen'.

Theosophy literally means the wisdom (*sophia*) of God (*theo*). By using the word anthroposophy Steiner was trying to emphasise that this wisdom could be reborn and indeed developed within the human being (*anthropos*). The gods were not being sidelined as such, but the responsibility for making things happen was increasingly ours. In a lecture he gave in 1920, Steiner emphasised the task ahead with these words: 'We can no longer wait passively, as if divine beings far away from us, without our aid, could affect human evolution.'

In speaking about the human being in *Theosophy* and *Occult Science*, Steiner uses the traditional language of body, soul and spirit as a starting point. He then goes on to describe the body as an interweaving of what he called the physical with the etheric – Schumacher's $m + x$. My picture of the etheric is of an invisible but living counterpart to the physical body that is present in everything we call 'alive'. Schumacher and others call it a 'life force'. Although not immune to emotional upheavals within the human psyche and their weakening and disorganising effect, this ether body remains intact whatever happens to the physical body – hence people's experience of a so-called phantom limb after the actual physical limb has been lost. At death, the departure of this etheric or life force brings about the decay and dissolution of the purely physical entity. But if composed of these two ingredients alone – physical and etheric – I would be as a plant; a living body, but no more.

Our soul is an expression of what Steiner also called the astral body –Schumacher's y. All desires, feelings and consciousness itself have their origin in this astral element. It is the very heart of what we experience as our inner life of sympathy and antipathy – without it the body would not be animated (*anima* is the Latin word for soul). But with $m + x + y$ alone, we remain as animals.

That final element z, that which makes us human ($m + x + y + z$), Steiner called the 'I' (*das Ich*) or ego (usually the former term is used nowadays, to distinguish from Freud's rather different use of 'ego'). Through the activity of the astral body we are conscious; through the 'I' we become conscious that we are conscious. It is the entity in us that is eternal, which transcends time and space. And it is this 'I' or human spirit – still an infant in evolutionary terms – which has the potential to transform the lower elements of physical, etheric and astral into new human capacities, and thus to transmute our instinctive nature into something higher.

The expression 'ghost in the machine' (originally coined by British philosopher Gilbert Ryle to parody René Descartes' mind–body dualism) is therefore misleading, not only because the body is not a machine but a complex and extraordinary configuration of living and dynamic forces, but also because the so-called 'ghost', as well as being my spiritual signature and the very essence of my eternal and evolving existence, is also intricately interwoven with that body in all its complexity. That body becomes an expression of my essence to the extent that I fully inhabit it, transforming what I bring from the past, what I have inherited genetically and what I have absorbed culturally. In this sense it becomes a sublime (or sometimes not quite so sublime) manifestation of who I am. In our waking life on earth the 'ghost' and the 'machine' are one; and likewise, to amend Emerson a little, the office where I work can increasingly be myself.

The Cartesian separation of mind and matter, resulting in this dualistic image of body and soul, is therefore extremely unhelpful; for if, as many have realised, mind and matter are ultimately as inseparable as are matter and energy in sub-atomic physics, then there is only one reality – a reality that Schumacher recognised clearly in the human being as three-quarters hidden; but hidden only if we 'look' rather than 'see'.

During sleep Steiner describes how the 'I' and astral body separate from the physical and etheric bodies, and thus what lies in the bed, alive but asleep, is indeed like a plant – but even then something more complex and sublime than Gerald Scarfe's lump of meat! We are simply 'not all there'. (I will return later to experiences of these higher aspects of our being during the night.) At death the etheric body, as well as the 'I' and astral body, leave the physical body altogether. Then indeed it is 'dust to dust'; but three-quarters of our being, those elements that Schumacher points out as inaccessible to objective, scientific observation, are not subject to the physical laws of decay; to other laws, maybe, but not to oblivion.

This potential we have to transmute into higher faculties what we inherit as a birthright from nature, is what esotericists such as Steiner say will gradually enable us to 'see' what at present is 'unseen'. In his *Guide* Schumacher defends with great clarity the reasonableness of at least contemplating such a latent capacity to know and experience more than we do at present. What is it, he asks, that enables us to know anything at all about the world around us? 'Every object, well contemplated, creates an organ of perception in us', wrote Goethe. In his book Schumacher points out that this is 'the Great Truth of *adaequatio* (adequateness), which defines knowledge as *adaequatio rei et intellectus*: the understanding of the knower must be *adequate* to the thing to be known'.

Having already outlined what he called the four levels of being, Schumacher goes on to indicate in his book that there is already some degree of correspondence between the structure of the human being and the structure of the world, as Francis Edmunds so often emphasised to us students at Emerson College. Here we are back with the ancient idea of the human being as microcosm of the macrocosm. Schumacher writes:

> Our five bodily senses make us 'adequate' to the lowest Level of Being – inanimate matter. But they can supply nothing more than masses of sense data, to 'make sense' of which we require abilities or capabilities of a different order. We may call them 'intellectual senses'. Without them, we should be unable to recognise form, pattern, regularity, harmony, rhythm and meaning, not to mention life, consciousness and self-awareness.

But whereas the bodily senses may be described as relatively passive – with all healthy people possessing a very similar endowment – Schumacher points out that there are significant differences in the power and reach of people's minds. As regards the intellectual senses therefore, it is quite unrealistic to try to define and delimit human capability, as if all human beings were much the same, like animals of the same species. As an example, Schumacher compares his inadequacy in relation to music to the genius of Beethoven; and the difference does not lie with the sense of hearing. For some, a symphony is as real as it was to the composer, he suggests, while for others it is nothing but a succession of more or less agreeable but altogether meaningless noises. For one person the mind is 'adequate' to the symphony, for the other not. He continues:

> The same applies throughout the whole range of possible and actual human experiences. For every one of us, only those facts and phenomena 'exist' for which we possess 'adaequatio', and as we are not entitled to assume that we are necessarily adequate to everything, at all times, and in whatever condition we may find ourselves, so we are not entitled to insist that something inaccessible to us has no existence at all and is nothing but a phantom of other people's imagination.

What Schumacher calls the Great Truth of 'adaequatio' therefore affirms that nothing can be perceived without an appropriate organ of perception, and that nothing can be understood without an appropriate organ of understanding. In other words everything in the world around us must correspond, as it were, with some faculty, sense or power within us; otherwise we remain unaware of its existence. For cognition at the physical level, our primary instruments are our five senses, reinforced and extended by a great array of ingenious apparatus. They register the visible world, but cannot register what Schumacher calls the 'inwardness' (and Gerard Manley Hopkins called the 'inscape') of things, and such fundamental invisible powers as life, consciousness and self-awareness. If we persuade ourselves, he warns, that the only 'data' worth having are those delivered by the five senses, and that a 'data processing unit' called the brain is there to deal with them, then we restrict our knowing to that level of being for which these instruments are 'adequate', and this means mainly to the level of inanimate matter.

Nor does Schumacher dismiss the role of faith in all this. Although greatly influenced by Buddhism he actually became a Roman Catholic towards the end of his life. 'Faith is not in conflict with reason', he wrote. 'Faith tells us what there is to understand; it purifies the heart, and so allows reason to profit from discussion; it enables reason to arrive at an understanding of God's revelation.' The Buddhists say that faith opens the eye of the heart. In his epistle to the Hebrews St Paul wrote: 'Faith is the substance of things hoped for and the evidence of things not seen.' Schumacher also quotes St. Augustine: 'Our whole business in this life is to restore to health the eye of the heart whereby God may be seen.'

A Guide for the Perplexed is a wonderfully wise and accessible book. Fritz Schumacher attached far more importance to it than to his better known work Small is Beautiful. In fact the word 'small' came to irritate him more and more, because what he really meant was that there is an appropriate size for everything and that may not always be small. I had dinner with him on the day that he received the first copy of his Guide from the publishers and he was clutching it lovingly. We were discussing a possible television series based on the book, but sadly he died very suddenly not many months later. I will leave you with one final quotation which epitomises both the wisdom and the wit of an extraordinary man: 'The modern world tends to be sceptical about everything that demands man's higher faculties. But it is not at all sceptical about scepticism, which demands hardly anything.'

Those words were written by someone who made sure that whenever possible, before leaving the house for London, Washington or New Delhi he made bread for his family; and who never ceased to emphasise the importance of the question: 'How much do I need?' rather than 'How much can I get?'

Helen Salter

Another person I met at this time, in my early thirties – an old lady called Helen Salter – was certainly not sceptical. On the contrary she radiated great optimism and energy despite her advanced age and immobility. To describe her as an old battle-axe would fail to convey both her warmth and her humour. But if she wanted to be visited, you didn't hesitate!

At one time Helen taught her own particular brand of psychology at adult educational evening classes in London and now lived in a small residential home in Sussex. Her room was cluttered with charts and diagrams from her teaching days, and it is one of these diagrams that I have always remembered as particularly helpful – one of those fingers pointing at the moon. The image is also very relevant to what I have been exploring in this chapter about the nature and make-up of the human being, and the complex configuration that makes us not only what we are, but also what we might become.

I met Helen through her interest in India, though she never actually managed to visit the country. It was an interest that developed late in her life and centred on her wish to build a bridge between Hinduism and the work of Rudolf Steiner. She had met an equally energetic and enthusiastic 'seeker' in London – an Indian called Major T. Ramachandra (we never discovered what the T stood for). He was a devoted follower of Gandhi and had initiated all sorts of social work in the slums of Delhi. I met him during my first trip to India and we stayed in touch for many years. Ramachandra became very interested in anthroposophy and through him, with constant prods from Helen Salter, all sorts of contacts were made and initiatives established. There are now biodynamic farms and Steiner Waldorf schools in various parts of India, as well as communities for children and adults with special needs.

But it is one of Helen's charts that I want to try to describe, because to my mind it conveys a crucial insight not only into an important aspect of our human make-up, but also into the phenomenon of death and into what is traditionally called the little death – namely sleep. It is one of only two diagrams in this book, and is, quite simply, a figure of eight.

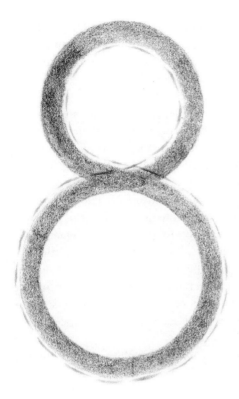

I would like you to imagine that the lower half of the diagram represents both our lifetime and also the period we spend awake each day. The upper part of the diagram is night time. It is also that interlude or pause between incarnations. The top half is deliberately smaller than the bottom half because we tend to spend about eight out of twenty-four hours asleep, a third of our day. (The question of time between incarnations I will return to later).

The dotted line represents our journey through the twenty-four hours of each day. It can also be imagined as the journey through one lifetime and on into the interlude that we spend digesting that lifetime – what some people, for obvious reasons, have called purgatory. The point at which this dotted line moves from the lower to the upper part of the diagram indicates the moment we fall asleep, and also the moment when we die. The dynamic of the diagram indicates rhythm; it also suggests that not only do we awake again each morning, but that likewise we return from a purely spiritual existence for a new incarnation – in both cases, one would hope, enriched and wiser.

One element of this existence between incarnations that Steiner describes is the experience of ourselves from the receiving end, as it were – both the pleasure and the pain we created for others. And it is largely out of this experience that we make the resolutions for our next incarnation. Above all, the picture that emerges from many esoteric writings and traditions is that the prime activity in this purely spiritual existence outside of time and space involves the working through of relationships, primarily with those whom we have been karmically connected. For it is through our relationships – and most often the difficult ones – that we actually learn and grow. A friend of mine remembers as a child anxiously asking her grandmother, who had been widowed twice, which husband she would be with in heaven. 'Neither, I hope', was her grandmother's reply. I wonder what's going on now!

In relation to all this, one of the most important aspects of Helen's diagram for me is that the dotted line in the lower half is on the outside, whereas it moves into the inside when above. It therefore illustrates how when awake, we experience everything as outside ourselves and as separate. We look outwards. In sleep we enter into quite another relationship with the world and with the surrounding universe – and even more so, I suspect, when we are no longer inhabiting a physical body. Then we look inwards. What was outside becomes our inner experience. In other words we become the object itself. We no longer experience our separateness. We become, in Steiner's words 'a macrocosmic being ... the universe becomes our organism'. This rhythm of expansion and contraction, in both smaller and larger cycles, is a subject that was to be greatly illuminated for me by a book on mediaeval mysticism that I will write about later.

In a celebrated article by the American philosopher Thomas Nagel, entitled 'What is it Like to be a Bat?' and published in the *Philosophical Review* in 1974, the author argues, as does Schumacher in his *Guide for the Perplexed*, that subjective experience eludes all objective scientific theories and experiments. And therefore, despite the fact that we can arrive at a scientific understanding of the brain and nervous system of a creature like a bat, since we possess a totally different way of orientating ourselves to our surroundings, it is impossible to actually imagine 'what it is like for a bat to be a bat'.

In his anthology *Western Philosphy*, John Cottingham writes on the subject of Nagel's article:

> Our own experience provides the basic material for our imagination, whose range is therefore limited. It will not help to try to imagine that one has webbing on one's arms, which enables one to fly around at dusk and dawn catching insects in one's mouth; that one has very poor vision, and perceives the surrounding world by a system of high frequency sound signals; and that one spends the day hanging upside down by one's feet in an attic. In so far as I can imagine this (which is not very far), it tells me only what it would be like for me to behave as a bat behaves. But that is not the question. I want to know what it is like for a *bat* to be a bat.

My point in mentioning Nagel's article is to share my sense that while occupying what is conveyed by the upper part of Helen's diagram, we do indeed have the capacity to experience what it's like to be a bat – or anything else which during the day we experience as separate and therefore different from us.

Nevertheless this total identification with the other is an extraordinarily difficult state to imagine, particularly from the perspective of our ordinary waking consciousness. We feel so very separate, and ever more so. I imagine what we call the lower kingdoms of nature don't experience these polarities of subject and object, waking and sleeping, life and death, to the same intensity that we do. It is probably somewhat of an exaggeration to compare humanity's waking life to 'solitary confinement'; yet the experience when asleep – and maybe, too, between incarnations – is, according to those initiated into these mysteries, or to people who have gone through a near-death experience, like a release from prison. Imagine being not a mere observer of the spring, of the apple blossom and primroses, but being the spring itself.

Our waking situation is meaningful, of that I feel sure. In such seeming isolation and loneliness we modern hermits certainly become aware of ourselves as separate individuals, but it is an evolutionary step that comes at a certain cost. In one sense consciousness cuts us off from reality in its fullest sense, but we wake up in the process. It is what I understand as leaving the herd, or standing on one's own two feet. It is what Jung identified as the process of individuation; and it was Jung's life and work that was to be the subject of my next major project for the BBC.

CHAPTER 11

Archaeologist of the Soul

The atmosphere in the department at the BBC where I had been working changed after the head, Gordon Watkins, who understood and indeed shared my idealism, stepped aside in 1970. Already there were hints of a certain shallowness and cynicism that was to pervade not just the BBC but television altogether in the years ahead. Not everyone liked the films I had made about Camphill. Some saw my work as rather too soft, not abrasive enough. To be idealistic was no longer in vogue. The sixties were over.

After *Gandhi's India* I worked on a four-part series called *What Sort Of World Do We Want?* My contribution was a film about current trends in education. The Open University was just beginning, and with it a boost for the notion of education as a lifelong process. In primary schools children were being encouraged to work on projects in small groups and away from the formality of a teacher facing rows of desks. Comprehensive schools were coming into existence, and efforts were being made to build bridges between schools and the communities they served. Not everyone welcomed the demise of grammar schools and selective education. In my film, the High Master of St Paul's School in London, John Howarth, expressed concern at what he and many others feared would be an inevitable watering down of educational standards in order to accommodate the many at the expense of an academic élite.

At another level this is a concern I've heard echoed in some esoteric circles, where traditionally the spiritual knowledge guarded by 'secret societies' was only passed on to a select few after a long process of initiation. Pupils underwent rigorous training in self-knowledge and purification – a rite of passage which could be compared, at a far more mundane level, to passing the old 11-plus examination, which determined whether you were clever enough to go on using your head as well as your hands.

In his book *Phases*, the Dutch psychiatrist Bernard Lievegoed calls the ancient centres of initiation 'the spiritual universities of antiquity'; they existed very early on in ancient Greece and continued into the modern era. But Lievegoed points out that although the content of the teaching was kept strictly secret, the results were manifest in the culture at large. By the end of the 19th century these teachings were starting to emerge into the daylight and became more widely available, and not just for the chosen few. Nowadays you can buy books on reincarnation and chakras at any airport bookstall, and I personally welcome this shift, despite the dangers and the superficiality of some of the offerings, and despite the understandable concern that some esotericists express. Steiner was among those who felt they had to break with the principle of secrecy because it was time to bring about a unity of worldly knowledge and spiritual knowledge – each path enriching the other.

The dictionary defines 'esoteric' as 'intended for and understood by only a small number of people with a specialised knowledge or interest'. It is usually associated with magic, astrology, the Kabbalah and alchemy. From the Enlightenment onwards, until a little over a hundred years ago, these practices – according to Nicholas Goodrick-Clarke in *The Western Esoteric Tradition* – were generally perceived as throwbacks to superstition and irrationalism, and rejected as 'a violation of reason'. 'The intellectual status of such topics was denigrated,' he continues, 'and they were kept in epistemological quarantine lest they cause a relapse from progressive rationalism.'

Yet for figures like Steiner, whose lives coincided with what Goodrick-Clarke describes as 'a period of sustained urban and industrial growth simultaneous with a decline of organised religion in the face of the challenges of secularism and science,' there was an eager and spiritually hungry audience. Occultism and esoteric societies flourished, attracting interest and debate on a scale not seen since the 16th century.

In the introduction to his book, Goodrick-Clarke goes on to point out that there are now specialist scholars who, rather than treating esotericism as a 'rejected form of knowledge', are working 'to document its significant influence on philosophical, scientific, and religious change'. He himself is Professor of Western Esotericism at the Universty of Exeter; there are two other dedicated chairs on the subject, at the Sorbonne and in Amsterdam. And in the United States there are graduate colleges such as Pacifica in Santa Barbara and The Californian Institute for Integral Studies (CIIS) in San Fransisco where these subjects can also be studied in depth.

Esotericism is thus not only being restored to a position of historical importance, but is being recognised as a particular form of spirituality – an undercurrent of wisdom – that has illumined and inspired western thought from late antiquity; and it continues to do so for increasing numbers of people.

As we mature as human beings, it certainly seems right that knowledge of every sort should be accessible to everyone who is interested and wants it, and not just to a spiritual or intellectual élite. What we choose to do with that knowledge is another question, and may be what will finally separate us in an evolutionary sense – as described in the Gospel of St. Matthew as the Last Judgement, when the shepherd divides the sheep from the goats. But even that may not be the end – a theme I explore in my final chapters; for in the end there is, perhaps, no end.

After that somewhat 'esoteric' digression I would like to say that I do understand what concerns the Howarths of this world in the here and now. I am far from happy with similar trends – often referred to as 'dumbing down' – in my own field of television. But at the end of the day I have sufficient trust in each person's potential to grow emotionally, intellectually and spiritually, to see this process of democratisation as progress, and not in the long run as a threat to the profound wisdom and insights that are there for all to discover. For this reason I am particularly fond of the statement: 'History is no longer written by kings, but by ordinary people doing extraordinary things.' I met many such people while making my film on education, and many more in the years that followed – all of whom reinforced my growing conviction that the true élite are those who live relatively humble and compassionate lives.

In my survey of various independent initiatives in education I filmed at a Montessori School in London where one or two handicapped or emotionally disturbed children were integrated into a class of so-called normal children, in the belief – as at Camphill – that they could sometimes help each other in ways unavailable to the teachers.

I also filmed some sequences at Michael Hall School in Sussex, and an interview with Francis Edmunds, in which he expressed concern – on behalf of many people working in education – at the trend towards an increasingly abstract and soulless curriculum. 'I look on adolescents as born idealists', he said to me. 'Now they can really enjoy a thought, an idea; but they want ideas that can become ideals for life. And if the ideas that they're nourished with are mainly utilitarian and rational, and evade the central issues of what a person is supposed to be in this world, then you get the sort of phenomena we have today. The revolt is not against the knowledge that is given, but it's a kind of inner grievance at what is being denied.' These days Edmunds' words seem more relevant than ever, as do many of the other issues I explored in the film – issues to which I returned later in my career.

Despite the worrying changes in the air at the BBC, the Corporation was still full of interesting, eccentric and highly creative people. No one, as yet, was glued to a computer screen, or on such short contracts that they dare not waste time kicking ideas around in case someone else stole them. Lively and stimulating conversations took place as we went in and out of each other's offices and, above all, in the BBC Club at lunchtime. It was there that I got to know the Head of Religious Programmes, the Reverend Oliver Hunkin. He didn't find the subjects I was exploring either strange or irrelevant. In other words he knew that there were many other people asking the questions I was asking, in one form or another. As a result of these lunchtime conversations I plotted to join Hunkin's department.

Around this time I wrote to Laurens van der Post, having much admired his travel books on Africa and the story of his encounter with the Kalahari bushmen. He clearly had a keen sense and appreciation of what I have called the spiritual dimension to life. I was particularly interested in his acknowledgement and appreciation of the innocence and purity that still exists hidden away in all of us – a theme that emerges very strongly in his writings, and which I wanted to explore on film.

I was invited to meet him late one afternoon at his penthouse flat in Chelsea. I no longer remember the details of our conversation, but what I do remember is that we talked for a very long time and that I was experiencing yet another important 'awakener'. Gradually it grew dark outside, but Laurens made no attempt to put on a light. Finally we were two silhouettes deep in conversation, and talking about Jung. I had read Jung's autobiography, and his ideas were already proving a helpful bridge for me into some of Steiner's more esoteric writings. I had no idea, however, that Laurens had known him and felt such a deep connection. It was through the psychotherapist and author, Ingaret Giffard, who studied under Jung and who became Laurens' second wife, that Laurens – on his return from the Far East after the war – met Jung in 1947.

By the end of that evening Laurens and I decided that I would approach the BBC, in the person of Oliver Hunkin, for a commission to make a series of three half-hour films on Jung's life and work. Hunkin immediately gave the project his blessing and within weeks we were underway. Nobody said, as I fear they might today: 'A good idea, but the audience wouldn't be interested in such an obscure subject.'

Carl Gustav Jung (1875–1961) wanted to study archaeology at university, but had no money to study anywhere except at neighbouring Basel, and in Basel there was no teacher of archaeology. It's interesting that he did in fact become an archaeologist of sorts, though his digging took place in what he called the psyche, the human soul. In his autobiography, *Memories, Dreams, Reflections*, he wrote that from the age of eleven 'my life has been permeated and held together by one idea and one goal: namely, to penetrate into the secret of the personality'. He called it 'my main business'.

Like Steiner, Jung had intense spiritual experiences as a child; in particular, powerful and symbolic dreams that he remembered all his life. He too lived among country people, though his father was a parson – 'a poor country parson' is how Jung described him in his autobiography. Clashes with his father over the subject of religion intensified as the boy Carl grew up. His father criticised him for thinking too much and for not simply believing. But for Jung the problem with faith was that it tends to forestall experience. At the time he was puzzled by what he called 'an impatient and anxious defensiveness' in his father whenever he tried to have a deep and serious conversation with him. 'Not until several years later', he wrote, 'did I come to understand that my poor father did not dare to think because he was consumed by inner doubts. He was taking refuge from himself and therefore insisted on blind faith.'

Finally there was tacit agreement between the young Carl and his father to avoid certain topics. The son was no longer reprimanded for cutting church and for not going to Communion any more. He writes of missing the organ and choral music, but not the religious community:

> The habitual churchgoers struck me as being far less of a community than the 'worldly folk'. The latter may have been less virtuous, but on the other hand they were nicer people, with natural emotions, more sociable and cheerful, warmer hearted and more sincere.

Jung was a scientist and explorer by nature, and someone – again like Steiner – who wanted to understand and experience the hidden and mysterious elements of life with the same clarity and precision that people examined and analysed the physical world. He was amazed that at university psychic phenomena were neither studied nor taken seriously. At the time he was still attending spiritual séances and he continued to take a deep interest in spiritualism for some years. For a while he dithered between the humanities and science as his area of study. Having finally opted for science he more or less drifted into medicine. It was only towards the end of his studies, when he read the phrase 'diseases of the personality' in a book on psychiatry, that his enthusiasm was stirred. For him this book – and in particular this phrase – was a major 'awakener', as geometry was for Steiner. In his autobiography Jung wrote: 'Here was the empirical field common to biological and spiritual facts which I had everywhere sought and nowhere found. Here at last was the place where the collision of nature and spirit became a reality.'

For me, Jung's life and work have been enormously helpful and important for a number of reasons. Although by now I was full of ideas and theories about life, like most other people my actual experience of life was largely determined by and confined to the role of a detached but caring onlooker who actually knew and understood very little. Maybe there is a certain wisdom in simply acknowledging that fact. In this respect I have been constantly touched by Jung's modesty, particularly towards the end of his life when, in the eyes of the world, he had achieved so much. 'I am an increasingly lonely

Carl Gustav Jung

old man', he said to Laurens van der Post, 'writing for other lonely old men.' And he concludes his autobiography with these words:

> This is old age, and a limitation. Yet there is so much that fills me: plants, animals, clouds, day and night, and the eternal in man. The more uncertain I have felt about myself, the more there has grown up in me a feeling of kinship with all things.

Jung's experience here reminds me of what I think Helen Salter was trying to convey in her diagram: namely that when no longer connected, or fully connected, with our physical body, in death or in sleep, or in the deeply reflective state of mind that Jung describes, we cease to feel separate from everything else, but rather experience that 'kinship with all things' that he felt so strongly in old age. Thus the boundary between the physical world and the so-called 'spiritual world' becomes a little more transparent.

We started our filming in the spring of 1971 in the village of Laufen, just above the Rhine Falls, where Jung spent his early childhood. He was born in 1875 in the village of Kesswil on the Swiss shore of Lake Constance, and was six months old when the family moved to Laufen. As a boy – and indeed throughout his life – he was in many ways happier when alone. In his autobiography he wrote of 'my delight in solitude'. He did have one particular and unusual companion at that time – a large stone on which he'd sit and play an imaginary game, which he describes as follows:

> I'm sitting on top of this stone and it is underneath. But the stone also could say 'I' and think: 'I am lying here on this slope and he is sitting on top of me.' The question then arose: 'Am I the one who is sitting on the stone, or am I the stone on which 'he' is sitting?' ... I could sit on it for hours, fascinated by the puzzle it set me.

Jung's powerful and symbolic dreams, some of which he only understood many years later, encouraged his tendency to brood and to withdraw into his inner world. Indeed it was he who was to coin the word 'introvert' some thirty years later. In moments of crisis, he wrote how

> it was strangely reassuring and calming to sit on my stone. Somehow it would free me of all my doubts. Whenever I thought that I was the stone, the conflict ceased. 'The stone has no uncertainties, no urge to communicate, and is eternally the same for thousands of years', I would think, 'while I am only a passing phenomenon which bursts into all kinds of emotions, like a flame that flares up quickly and then

goes out.' I was but the sum of my emotions, and the 'Other' in me was the timeless, imperishable stone.

We found an appropriate stone on which Laurens sat to tell this story. In documentaries the commentary is usually thrashed out later in the cutting-room – in this case in the stimulating and at times helpfully challenging company of film editor Les Newman. Statements to camera, however, are invariably delivered spontaneously and unscripted. Laurens felt uncomfortable talking directly to an impersonal camera, so throughout the filming I would tuck myself under the camera lens, and it was to me that he spoke. It felt a great privilege to be so intimately on the receiving end of his story-telling; and it was a technique we used again three years later, exploring the mythology of the bushmen in southern Africa.

Another striking feature of Jung's childhood, which in some ways grew out of his dialogue with the stone, was an increasing sense of being two different people; he called them his number One and number Two personalities: 'One of them was the schoolboy who could not grasp algebra and was far from sure of himself; the "other" was important, a high authority, a man not to be trifled with.' This 'other' person, he wrote, lived in the 18th century and wore buckled shoes: 'Often in those days I would write the date 1786 instead of 1886, and each time this happened I was overcome by an inexplicable nostalgia.' This experience of a number Two personality was to mature into the figure of someone Jung called Philemon, whom he eventually painted. In old age he wrote: 'I understood that there is something in me which can say things that I do not know.' For some this might conjure up the image of a guardian angel, or the daimon which James Hillman wrote about and which was such a reality for the ancient Greeks. Others might see in Jung's experience a hint of some previous incarnation. Whatever its nature, the figure of Philemon was to exert a powerful influence on him throughout his life. In his book *Jung and Steiner: the Birth of a New Psychology*, Gerhard Wehr draws attention to the similarity between the two boys in their 'certainty of a supersensible world' and their tendency to lead this almost double life.

In his autobiography Jung also writes about the 'sense of destiny' he already had as a young boy, and the conviction that he must do not what he, but what God wanted:

That gave me the strength to go my own way. Often I had the feeling that in all decisive matters I was no longer among men, but was alone with God. And when I was 'there', where I was no longer alone, I was outside time; I belonged to the centuries; and He who then gave answer was He who had always been, who had been before my birth.

Jung's relationship with his mother was warm and uncomplicated. 'You must read Goethe's *Faust* one of these days', she suddenly said to him one day – rather as my mother brought home for me that biography on Tolstoy. It was to be another of Jung's great 'awakeners'; the discovery of someone who took the devil seriously. 'At last I had found confirmation', he wrote, 'that there were or had been people who saw evil and its universal power, and – more important – the mysterious role it played in delivering man from darkness and suffering. To that extent Goethe became, in my eyes, a prophet.'

It is Faust, in Goethe's great epic, who utters the line: 'Two souls dwell, alas! within my breast'. Later Jung was to write: 'Neurosis is an inner cleavage ... the state of being at war with oneself.' He went on to suggest that what creates this situation is the sense we sometimes have that we consist of two people in opposition to one another. 'To be, or not to be?' asked Shakespeare. Hamlet clearly exists, but there also exists something in him that can decide whether Hamlet should go on existing. In Faust, egotism and personal ambition were at war with his idealism and a noble quest for knowledge.

We moved to Basel for the next phase of our filming, in which we described Jung's years at the Gymnasium (his secondary school) and then at university. Travelling all over Switzerland with Laurens was a most interesting and enjoyable experience. He was always sensitive to the needs and problems of a film crew, and at mealtimes a wonderfully entertaining raconteur. He knew many of the grand old 'Jungians' such as Barbara Hannah and Marie-Louise von Franz, whom we were also privileged to meet; and he was a great admirer of Switzerland itself – its efficiency and its decentralised democracy in which everyone is encouraged to have their say. Although as a visitor I, too, admire the country's order and cleanliness, I suspect that my inherent rebelliousness would turn me into an unwelcome and uncooperative citizen. Such trivial thoughts were not, I suspect, on the mind of the brilliant young pupil from the vicarage at Laufen.

Jung had written that the 'fog of his dilemma' had slowly lifted in his late teens, and that what he called his number One personality emerged more distinctly: 'School and city life took up my time, and my increased knowledge gradually permeated or repressed the world of intuitive premonitions.' Nevertheless, certain underlying problems remained: 'In science I missed the factor of meaning; in religion, that of empiricism.' He acknowledged that although science opened the doors to enormous quantities of knowledge, 'it provided genuine insights very sparingly'. Without the psyche he knew that we achieve neither knowledge nor insight: 'Yet nothing was ever said about the psyche.' It was the discovery of psychiatry – still in its infancy – that saved him.

On December 10th 1900, Jung took up his post as an assistant doctor at the Burghölzi mental asylum, which was also the psychiatric clinic of Zurich University. He wrote that he was pleased to leave Basel: 'the pressure of tradition was too much for me … Zurich relates to the world not by the intellect but by commerce. Yet here the air was free and I had always valued that.'

For six months he virtually locked himself away within the walls of the Burghölzi in order to get accustomed to the life and spirit of the asylum. Inspired by his mentor, the psychiatrist Eugen Bleuler, he too felt prompted to try and understand what was really going on in the minds of his patients. In the commentary Laurens described Jung's hunch that what passed for normality in life was often the force that had shattered the personalities of his patients.

The hospital still functions, and in one of the wards Laurens went on to speak these words: 'In the dreams and hallucinations of the patients Jung found increasingly a new world of meaning. To describe this injured and rejected area of the human spirit he used the word "complex" for the first time.' In one of my most treasured books, *Modern Man in Search of a Soul*, Jung elaborates on this concept. He begins by pointing out that the prototype of all analytical treatment is to be found in the religious institution of the Confessional:

> As soon as man was capable of conceiving the idea of sin he had recourse to psychic concealment – or, to put it in analytical language, repressions arose. Anything that is concealed is a secret. The maintenance of secrets acts like a psychic poison which alienates their possessor from the community.

In small doses, he suggests, this poison may be a priceless remedy, even an essential preliminary to the differentiation of the individual. However, a private secret, he warns, ultimately has a destructive effect. It resembles a burden of guilt that cuts us off from other people. And an unconscious secret is infinitely more harmful than a conscious one, for we are concealing it even from ourselves. Still on the subject of secrets, Jung writes in this same chapter:

> The emotion withheld is also something we conceal – something which we can hide even from ourselves – an art in which men particularly excel, while women, with very few exceptions, are by nature averse to doing such violence to their emotions.

His conclusion was that one form of neurosis is probably conditioned by the predominance of secrets, and another by the predominance of restrained emotions. 'To cherish secrets and to restrain emotions', he writes, 'are psychic misdemeanours for which nature finally visits us with sickness…'

It was at the Burghölzi that Jung first became aware of a most important yet in many ways obvious insight, that every human being has a story, and that derangement often arose when that story was denied or rejected; and that it was only in the discovery of this story that the patient could be healed. He wrote in his autobiography:

> The crucial thing is the story. For it alone shows the human background and the human suffering, and only at that point can the doctor's therapy begin to operate ... Through my work with the patients I realised that paranoid ideas and hallucinations contain a germ of meaning. A personality, a life history, a pattern of hopes and desires lie behind the psychosis. The fault is ours if we do not understand them.

He also adds that as early as 1909 he realised that he could not treat latent psychoses if he didn't understand their symbolism. It was then that he began to study mythology. 'The horizon of the human psyche', he wrote, 'embraces infinitely more than the limited purview of the doctor's consulting room.'

Jung's insights made me aware once again of how the tendencies and aberrations he encountered among his psychotic patients, like the extremes of behaviour I met in the Camphill communities among those generally described as having 'special needs', are present in all of us – only in less exaggerated, less pronounced form. And the importance that Jung attaches to a person's story does, of course, raise the question I have already touched upon, of when that story begins. In other words, do some of the problems we experience have their origins in previous incarnations? In which case those stories are likely to be very much more complex than we can grasp consciously; and they will certainly be longer. Perhaps we can draw comfort from the possibility that some of our difficulties are simply part of the collective growing pains of humanity itself. It is an area of experience that came to interest Jung increasingly, and which he called the Collective Unconscious.

'Freud was the first man of real importance I had encountered', wrote Jung in *Memories, Dreams, Reflections*. He first read Freud's *The Interpretation of Dreams* in 1900, but they didn't actually meet until 1907, in Vienna. What first interested Jung were Freud's insights into the repression mechanism within dreams, which corresponded to Jung's own experiments with word association. From the beginning of their relationship, however, Jung had strong reservations about Freud's conviction that the cause of repression was always related to a sexual trauma. 'I was familiar', he wrote, 'with numerous cases of neuroses in which the question of sexuality played a subordinate part.' Jung ultimately sensed that Freud's obsession with sexuality and his absolute rejection of any mystical or esoteric dimension to the human psyche was probably an indication of a repression mechanism within Freud himself; Jung referred to it as 'a flight from himself'.

Freud's other early disciple, Alfred Adler, became increasingly convinced that our troubles stemmed largely from what he called 'an urge to power', arising from a sense of inferiority. Jung wrote in *Modern Man in Search of a Soul*:

> It would be an unpardonable error to overlook the element of truth in both the Freudian and Adlerian viewpoints, but it would be no less unpardonable to take either of them as the sole truth. Both truths correspond to psychic realities ... It seems hardly necessary to add that I hold the truth of my own views to be equally relative, and regard myself also as the exponent of a certain predisposition.

Although Jung writes elsewhere of Freud's method of interpretation 'as resting upon reductive explanations which unfailingly lead backward and downward', in his autobiography he does also pay tribute to Freud in glowing terms, singling out his pioneering work in taking neurotic patients seriously. He compares him to an Old Testament prophet who undertook to overthrow false gods, 'to rip the veils away from a mass of dishonesties and hypocrisies, mercilessly exposing the rottenness of the contemporary psyche'. And he concludes his chapter on Freud by crediting him for not faltering, in the face of great unpopularity, in his discovery of 'an avenue to the unconscious'. By evaluating dreams as the most important source of information about unconscious processes 'he gave back to mankind a tool that had seemed irretrievably lost'. Nonetheless, in 1913 the two men parted ways. It was, according to Jung, Freud's obsession with his own authority that sealed the collapse of their relationship.

In *Feet of Clay* Anthony Storr suggests that Freudian psychoanalysis, like conventional Christianity, was for Jung another light that failed, another faith that had to be abandoned, which left him bereaved and rudderless. 'It was only after his final parting with Freud', writes Storr, 'that Jung was compelled to discover his own myth, even if he had to pass through a psychotic illness to do so.'

Initially Jung experienced what he called a period of inner uncertainty. He avoided all theoretical points of view and simply helped his patients to understand the dream images by themselves, without the application of rules and theories. He had married in 1903 and by now had a family. He wrote of the importance to him of normal life in the real world as a balance to his strange and often disturbing inner experiences. The demands made upon him as a doctor, husband and father 'proved to me again and again that I really existed'. He also wrote about his extreme loneliness and the painful gulf that he experienced between the external world and the interior world of images: 'I could not yet see that interaction of both worlds which I now understand. I saw only an irreconcilable contradiction between "inner" and "outer".'

What he called 'the land of the dead' became a powerful and at times overwhelming experience for Jung during these years. In *Memories, Dreams, Reflections*, he wrote:

> From that time on the dead have become ever more distinct for me as the voices of the Unanswered, Unresolved and Unredeemed; for since the questions and demands which my destiny required me to answer did not come to me from outside, they must have come from the inner world.

He describes these conversations as a kind of prelude to what he felt he had to communicate to the world about the unconscious. And he attached great importance to an almost methodical effort to understand and even classify every single image, so far as this was possible. So often we allow images to rise up, and maybe wonder about them, but that is all. 'We do not take the trouble to understand them,' he wrote, 'let alone draw ethical conclusions from them.'

Jung's sensitivity in relation to those whom we call 'dead' was very apparent during the famous interview with John Freeman for the BBC series *Face to Face*, from which I quoted earlier, and excerpts of which Laurens and I included in our series. At one point Freeman asked Jung whether he and Freud had analysed each other's dreams, which indeed they had. But when pressed by Freeman to reveal 'the significant features of Freud's dreams', Jung replied: 'That's rather indiscreet to ask. There is such a thing as a professional secret.' Freeman, however, persists: 'He's been dead these many years.' Jung pauses: 'Ah, yes – but these regards last longer than life. I prefer not to talk about it.'

For me that is one of the most touching and profound things that Jung ever uttered, and confirms my increasing sense of a deeper communion that exists, and continues to exist after our death, that transcends what we understand as normal communication.

In our film we concluded this period of Jung's life with a sequence shot in his old home in Seestrasse at Küsnacht, on the shores of the lake near Zurich. It was then occupied by his architect son, Franz, whom Laurens had known for some years. There we were given unique access to Jung's celebrated Red Book in which he had painted an extraordinary collection of images and mandalas. The creative activity had clearly helped him during those turbulent and lonely years after his break with Freud. Until now very few people had seen the Red Book, not even Laurens himself. Now suddenly before us were a sequence of striking and colourful paintings, including one of Philemon himself, of whom Jung was later to write:

Philemon and other figures of my fantasies brought home to me the crucial insight that there are things in the psyche which I do not produce, but which produce themselves and have their own life. Philemon represented a force which was not myself. In my fantasies I held conversations with him, and he said things which I had not consciously thought. For I observed clearly that it was he who spoke, not I. He said I treated thoughts as if I generated them myself, but in his view thoughts were like animals in the forest, or people in a room, or birds in the air, and added – 'If you should see people in a room, you would not think that you had made those people, or that you were responsible for them'. It was he who taught me psychic objectivity ...

'We all have our Philemons, whether we know it or not', said Laurens, as he gazed at Jung's powerful and beautiful paintings. 'Most people don't recognise it because we tend to find our Philemons in wise men and leaders in the world at large.' I am tempted to add that the choice seems very limited these days, but perhaps that will encourage us to trust our inner voice more often, and to take seriously Erich Fromm's conviction that each one of us has access to a wisdom that we all too easily repress.

As Laurens van der Post closed the Red Book he glanced somewhat nervously at Franz Jung. Had he said the right thing? Had he overstepped the mark? Our encounter with Franz was a reminder that it's not easy to be the son of a great man, particularly one who has been so honest about his shortcomings and his own descent into a chaotic and at times insane world. All was well, however – both for us and indeed for Jung himself. By the time his book *Psychological Types* was published in 1921 he was through his crisis. He no longer worked at the Burghölzi. He was on his own, but he stood erect. It was the world, said Laurens, that was now to become Jung's asylum.

CHAPTER 12

The Pattern of God

Jung's early book *Psychological Types* was in part an attempt to explain his break with Freud to himself and others. In it he also writes not only about the fundamental difference in character between the extrovert and the introvert, but about his observation of what he called the four functions within the human psyche and their interaction in each of us. He named 'thinking' and 'feeling' as the two 'rational' functions; and 'intuition' and 'sensation' as 'non-rational' and as relatively repressed in the unconscious. According to Jung we tend to have one function that is dominant (either rational or non-rational) closely supported by another (its opposite in rationality or non-rationality). Balance is the ideal, the objective. Likewise the extrovert, who tends to be at home in the world but may be not quite so comfortable with his inner world, needs to learn from the introvert, for whom introspection comes naturally but for whom the world can be a problem; and vice versa. My favourite joke about this somewhat complicated subject offers a definition of an extrovert mathematician as someone who looks at your shoes instead of at their own.

One can observe the potential clash between extrovert and introvert not only in personal relationships but also historically. The extrovert will want to change things outwardly and tends to be a person of action. The introvert is more reflective, more interested in inner transformation.

On the psychological front, Steiner, for his part, emphasised what he called 'the threefold nature of the human being': our capacities to think, to feel, and to act (in other words, to translate those thoughts and feelings into action). In his educational initiatives, in particular, he also drew attention to the traditional notion of the four temperaments – sanguine, choleric, phlegmatic and melancholic – and their interaction within the classroom. All these descriptions, however, are always in danger of sounding somewhat abstract, particularly the labels. It is why I warmed to the response of the Dalai Lama when he was once asked why there were different schools of Tibetan Buddhism. With his customary broad smile he replied: 'Because there are different sorts of people.'

I'm anyway not sure to what extent we can really change our temperaments, or do anything about them – though maybe through our relationships there is an opportunity to achieve some sort of balance. Instead of clashing, we can recognise and value the strengths and talents of the other; and so, by at least complementing one another, we may move towards that precious wholeness which Jung and others hold up as an ultimate goal.

Finally there is the problem of language in all such theories – words being 'the source of misunderstandings' according to the desert fox in Saint-Exupéry's tale of the Little Prince. As we filmed Laurens van der Post's long and detailed exposition on 'psychological types' in a corner of Jung's garden in Küsnacht, he concluded by quoting the French writer Anatole France on this subject of language: 'Human beings are forever killing one another over words, whereas if they had only understood what the words were trying to say, they would have embraced one another.'

To use the word soul is already a problem for some people, for whom it conjures up all sorts of religious beliefs and dogmas. It helps only slightly to do as Jung did and to use the Greek word *psyche*. 'To grant the substantiality of the soul or psyche is repugnant to the spirit of the age,' he wrote in *Modern Man in Search of a Soul*, 'for to do so would be heresy.' He was speaking largely with the scientific community in mind, but also as a man who, in all modesty, wanted very much to put his psychology on a scientific footing. Nevertheless he was well aware of how far we are from having anything like a comprehensive knowledge of the human psyche, 'that most challenging field of scientific enquiry'; hence the importance of granting validity, as he did, to a number of contradictory opinions such as those of Freud and Adler.

In the same chapter, Jung goes on to question, as did Schumacher, the modern attitude that dismisses the presumption of our forefathers that man has a soul,

and that the soul has substance, is of divine nature and is therefore immortal; and that there is a power inherent in it which builds up the body, supports its life, heals its ills and enables the soul to live independently of the body; and that beyond our empirical present there is a spiritual world from which the soul receives knowledge and spiritual things whose origins cannot be discovered in this visible world.

What Jung refers to here as 'soul' would, in Steiner's language, be 'spirit' – the soul for Steiner being the intermediary between spirit and matter.

But is it not just as fantastic, Jung continues, for modern human beings to assume that matter produces this realm of soul and spirit, that apes gave rise to human beings, and that the brain cells manufacture thoughts? The ultimate outcome of the contemporary approach, with all psychic happenings reduced to a kind of activity of the glands, is – he points out – a psychology without the psyche. He recognised, however, that a certain courage was going to be necessary in order to assume an autonomous psyche. 'We need not be alarmed at the unpopularity of such an undertaking, for to postulate mind is no more fantastic than to postulate matter', was how he reassured himself and others.

In terms of self-knowledge, Jung's concept of what he called 'the shadow' is undoubtedly a milestone. In our film, Laurens interviewed Jung's old colleague and collaborator, Professor Freddie Meier, who pointed out how we all tend to have people whom we dislike or who irritate us intensely. Very often, he suggested, such people display characteristics you have denied or repressed in yourself and which you then unconsciously project onto others. He compared the situation to the Dr Jekyll and Mr Hyde in each of us – a split which we need to recognise and come to terms with 'before we can make peace with the world; otherwise we always have a scapegoat somewhere'. Meier also spoke about the danger of this projection-mechanism on a mass scale, the most striking and dangerous example in recent history being the projection of the German shadow onto the Jews.

What is also absolutely central to the evolution of Jung's philosophy is the recognition of the process he called 'individuation' – a path that involves a high degree of consciousness and that removes us ever further from what he refers to as our original 'participation mystique' with each other and with nature: 'Every step forward means an act of tearing (ourselves) loose from that all-embracing, pristine unconsciousness which claims the bulk of mankind almost entirely.'

To move in this direction inevitably leads to a somewhat solitary existence for anyone who is what Jung called a modern person in search of their soul. And the mere fact of living in the present does not make someone modern, he wrote:

> He alone is modern who is fully 'conscious' of the present ... Indeed, he is completely modern only when he has come to the very edge of the world, leaving behind him all that has been discarded and outgrown, and acknowledging that he stands before a void out of which all things may grow ... An honest profession of modernity means voluntarily declaring bankruptcy, taking the vows of poverty and chastity in a new sense, and – what is still more painful – renouncing the halo which history bestows as a mark of its sanction.

Individuation could, in the language of Steiner and others, be described as a modern initiation process. Psychiatrist Anthony Storr described it as 'a kind of Pilgrim's Progress without a creed, aiming not at heaven, but at integration and wholeness'. It involves the gradual transcending of our egotistical inclinations until we reconcile our individualism with our common humanity. 'I could express the same concept with the words of St. Paul', wrote Jung. 'Now not I live, but the Christ lives in me.' He called this core of our being the self. For him it expressed the unity of the personality as a whole. He contrasted the self as the centre of psychic wholeness with the ego as the centre of consciousness. And he writes with great enthusiasm about the extent to which, in his experience, these discoveries, or this formulation, change a patient's standpoint and values, and how they can shift the centre of gravity of the personality. 'It is as though the ego were the earth', he continues, 'and it suddenly discovered that the sun (or the self) was the centre of the planetary orbits and of the earth's orbit as well.'

Many of these ideas I had been reading about – and now, in partnership with Laurens, was attempting to convey to a television audience – were initially not always easy for me to grasp in their entirety, or rather to make my own. However, I always felt that if an idea did become meaningful for me, the chances were that there would be other people who would also find it helpful. In other words my lack of expertise, rather than being a handicap, was what would help me to communicate more effectively as a film-maker. In this sense the reaction of the crew was always a good barometer. If they seemed more interested in where we were going for lunch than in the sequence we were filming, I knew we were in danger of going astray! In Switzerland I was

John McGlashan, Paul Kanwar, Chris King, Laurens van der Post, and author at Bollingen

working again with John McGlashan as cameraman; and he and his team were deeply involved in what we were doing – but that didn't prevent us all from enjoying the seductive comfort of our lakeside locations.

Jung's work with his patients was undoubtedly the focus of his life. 'About a third of my cases', he wrote, 'are suffering from no clinically definable neurosis, but from the senselessness and emptiness of their lives. It seems to me, however, that this can well be described as the general neurosis of our time.' Healing was only achieved, he felt, when his patients found meaning in their lives, their destinies and in their suffering. Central to this task was the attitude of the doctor himself. In his autobiography he wrote: 'The doctor is effective only when he himself is affected'; and he quotes the famous line: 'Only the wounded physician heals.'

Jung attached enormous importance to what he called 'the self-education of the educator' and was very aware of the danger for a doctor who 'cloaks himself in his authority'. He writes, too, of the danger of trying to pare down the meaning of a dream to fit some narrow doctrine, and about how easily we can be fooled by the manipulation of ideas. In his experience, however, the unconscious frequently has a way of 'strangling the physician in the coils of his own theory'. He likens dream interpretation to learning to read a text, and emphasised again and again the importance of acceptance:

> We cannot change anything unless we accept it. Condemnation does not liberate, it oppresses. I am the oppressor of the person I condemn, not his friend and fellow-sufferer ... If the doctor wishes to help a human being he must be able to accept him as he is. And he can do this in reality only when he has already seen and accepted himself as he is.

In this respect Jung also draws attention to the psychiatrist's tendency to label a patient 'confused', 'when he would do well to recognise the projection and admit his own confusion, for it is really his understanding that grows confused in face of the patient's strange behaviour'. He is also at pains to convey his determination never to try to convert a patient to anything, or exercise any compulsion: 'What matters most to me is that the patient should reach his own view of things.' Respect for a person's destiny is the very essence of this approach.

In his conversation with Laurens, Professor Meier used a phrase that became the title of the last in our series of three films; he spoke of 'the mystery that heals'. Even in the relatively straightforward case of a broken leg, he said, we do not really understand how healing takes place. We know what to do in order for it to happen, but the process itself remains a mystery. All we can do in all situations of healing, he added, whether physical or psychological 'is to render the patient open and make him accessible to those things that go on; we cannot make them take place, technically speaking … All we can do is prepare the ground for these processes to happen that are conducive to healing.' It is in the end, he said, a religious attitude that we have to establish.

Jung would undoubtedly agree with Meier, but for him and for those whom he calls 'moderns', a rediscovery of 'the life of the spirit' can no longer be achieved by faith alone which is, he acknowledges, 'in the truest sense a gift of grace'. From time immemorial, Jung observed, the human psyche has been shot through with religious feelings and ideas. But these intimations we now need to experience anew and in full consciousness. That was his message and that is the challenge; and the shirking of that challenge will make us ever more restless, neurotic and fundamentally at war with ourselves.

In 1920 Jung travelled to North Africa. In his autobiography he describes how, unconsciously, he wanted to find that part of his personality 'which had become invisible under the influence and the pressure of being European'. He goes on to describe how this predominantly rationalist European finds much that is alien to him and how he is inclined to pride himself on this without realising that 'this rationality is won at the expense of his vitality, and that the primitive part of his personality is consequently condemned to a more or less underground existence'.

Five years later he went with some American friends to visit the Pueblo Indians in New Mexico, and recounts a conversation with one of their Chiefs who remarks on how cruel Europeans look: 'They are always seeking something … they are always uneasy and restless … We don't know what they want. We do not understand them. We think they are mad.' When asked by Jung why he thought the whites are all mad, the Chief said it was because they say that they think with their heads. And to Jung's next question, 'What do you think with?' he pointed to his heart. Again I am reminded of the secret that the fox shared with the Little Prince: 'It is only with the heart that one can see rightly.'

The unshakeable conviction of this same Pueblo Indian that the sun is God ('Is not he who moves there our father?' he said, pointing to the sun) touched Jung deeply; so, too, the belief that their religion was of importance for the whole world, for without it the sun would no longer make its daily journey across the sky. 'Out of sheer envy', Jung writes, 'we are obliged to smile at the Indian's naivety and to plume ourselves on our cleverness; for otherwise we would discover how impoverished and down at heel we are.' That a ritual act can magically affect the sun, which to them is a god, is, in Jung's opinion, no less irrational than our own religious traditions. Man and God are intimately interlinked, and in our heart of hearts we know and have always known it.

Jung's visit to Kenya later that same year was to have an even more powerful effect on him. 'It was as if I were at this moment returning to the land of my youth', he wrote in *Memories, Dreams, Reflections*. He goes on to describe with great sensitivity his experience of the wild animals, the space, the silence – the world as it had always been, yet without human beings, and therefore no one present to know that this was the world.

It was there in Africa that what he calls 'the cosmic meaning of consciousness' became clear to him, and he writes: '"What nature leaves imperfect, the art perfects", say the alchemists. Man, I, in an invisible act of creation put the stamp of perfection on the world by giving it objective existence.' This act of creation, he points out, we usually ascribe to the Creator alone, and thus tend to view life somewhat like a machine, calculated down to the last detail and obeying predetermined rules. He calls such a picture 'a cheerless clockwork fantasy' in which there is no human drama, and no 'new day' leading to 'new shores'. It is, I suspect, what many people find so unsatisfactory in the stance of the Creationists. For Jung the notion of God doesn't have to be excluded, but the implication of his African experience is that there exists a dynamic relationship between humanity and God that is itself creative.

Jung thus arrived at the conviction that we are indispensable for the completion of Creation, for we alone have given the world its objective existence, 'without which, unheard, unseen, silently eating, giving birth, dying, heads nodding through hundreds of millions of years, it would have gone on in the profoundest night of non-being down to its unknown end'.

Jung's travels – he visited Egypt and Palestine in 1933 – also greatly enriched his awareness of what he came to call the 'collective unconscious'. Just as the human body has traces in it of its whole evolutionary past, so the psyche, he observed, seems to have access to 'the whole reservoir of human experience'. He discovered, for example, that certain archetypal dreams occurred in all cultures, and that their symbolic content seemed to transcend the everyday world of the dreamer. It was, he felt, an important clue to our common humanity, 'the foundation of what the ancients called the "sympathy of all things"'.

Jung was unsure whether this connection we seem to have to humanity's evolutionary past arises from a personal, as opposed to collective memory. If there is a personal element, then we have come by another route to the reality of reincarnation. His assistant during the last six years of his life, Aniela Jaffé, told me during our filming that Jung became increasingly interested in the subject of reincarnation, but was reluctant to pronounce on something outside his actual experience.

Dreams, on the other hand, were for him a constant source of insight. 'The evolutionary stages through which the human psyche has passed', he wrote in *Modern Man in Search of a Soul*, 'are more clearly discernable in the dream than in consciousness.' Jung was very open about the interpretation of dreams in general, admitting that in difficult cases 'I do not know where else to go for help.' He wrote a great deal about what he observed as the psyche's 'self-regulating system' – a law that he observed operating throughout nature and, indeed, at every level of existence. If things get out of balance, something will inevitably arise to restore that balance. The pendulum doesn't only swing in politics. Maybe we have dreams in which we are flying when life seems to be rubbing our noses in the dirt. Often, therefore, the content of our dreams is compensating for something one-sided in our conscious mind. Dreams can heal, or are telling us things that we should heed, and as such are an important window into the mysterious world of the unconscious.

For Steiner the content of a dream and the actual images were far less important than what he called the drama, the flow: 'whether there is anticipation, whether the anticipation leads to resolution, whether the anticipation leads to crisis'. For him this purely spiritual realm in which we live fully during sleep is not subject to earthly laws, but has quite other laws of its own: 'The "I" lives in a world in which moral laws have the same power and force as natural laws have here.' The dream can sometimes be a reflection, often a chaotic one, of this other dimension of existence. Depending on our inner maturity, dreams can also convey intimations not only of our whole spiritual biography, but also of our potential.

Jung's travels and his deep interest in the phenomenon of the collective unconscious prompted him to pursue a deeper study of what, in our film, Laurens van der Post called 'the neglected areas of history and philosophy'. In Jung's study, with rows of ancient texts in the background, Laurens described how this scholarly physician became ever more aware of how, for example, Christianity had maimed itself by cutting out the works of the Gnostics, who had tried to revitalise narrow dogma with their own living experience of religion. He recognised, too, that the despised alchemists were pioneers in his own field.

Jung in his library

Alchemy is commonly associated with the transformation of base metals into gold. But at a psychological level, with the human being as the base metal, it becomes a metaphor for spiritual growth and transformation. Through his extensive reading Jung eventually realised that the alchemists were talking in symbols, 'those old acquaintances of mine'. Only after he had familiarised himself with alchemy, did he become fully aware that the unconscious is a process; in his language, 'the psyche is transformed or developed by the relationship of the ego to the contents of the unconscious'. Only through a long and diligent study of these processes, together with his gradual understanding of alchemical symbolism, did Jung arrive at his concept of individuation. For him alchemy also gave him that all-important historical perspective. Grounded as it was in the natural philosophy of the Middle Ages, alchemy created a bridge into the past and into Gnosticism on the one hand, and into the future and to a modern psychology of the unconscious on the other.

One of the most interesting and privileged experiences we had during the filming was to visit the Tower that Jung built as a retreat for himself some twenty miles further down the lake from his home at Küsnacht. As we rowed silently towards it past a bed of reeds alive with dragonflies – we were filming a shot for the opening of this sequence – these words from Jung's autobiography came to mind:

> Gradually, through my scientific work, I was able to put my fantasies and the contents of the unconscious on a solid footing. Words and paper, however, did not seem real enough to me; something more was needed. I had to achieve a kind of representation in stone of my innermost thoughts and of the knowledge I had acquired. Or, to put it another way, I had to make a confession of faith in stone. That was the beginning of the 'Tower', the house which I built for myself at Bollingen.

As the water lapped against the side of our boat I thought, too, of my own strong attachment to water. I was brought up by the Thames and used constantly to be in or on the river. I also spent many holidays with my grandparents fishing the rivers and lochs of Scotland. Being by the lake near Zurich had a wonderfully calming effect on the task in hand, for filming – despite its somewhat glamorous image – can be hard work and hectic. The creation of his Tower was Jung's way of dealing with similar pressures in his own life.

The building is kept very private by the family and is not normally open to visitors. Jung started construction in 1923 and only completed the final addition in 1957, four years before his death. Laurens called Bollingen 'Jung's

Jung's Tower at Bollingen

Laurens van der Post at Bollingen

sanctuary', a place where he could exist 'outside of time'. He lived there very simply and usually alone. There was no telephone, running water or electricity. He chopped wood and cooked his own meals. 'These simple acts', Jung wrote, 'make man simple; and how difficult it is to be simple.' He often sailed alone on his beloved lake, and spent hours carving symbolic images in stone or simply playing with pebbles on the shore. Gradually he surrounded the place with young trees, which for him represented 'not only the beauty but also the thoughts of God'. Today they enclose his creation, making it almost invisible except from the lake itself.

In a smaller, adjoining tower Jung created an even more private space, 'a place of spiritual concentration'. Over the years he created paintings on the walls to express 'all those things which have carried me out of time into seclusion, out of the present into timelessness.' At Bollingen', he wrote, 'I am most deeply myself', and there he also seemed to have a heightened sense of his own ancestors: 'It is as if a silent, greater family, stretching down the centuries, were peopling the house.' Among these was his old friend Philemon, his number Two personality from childhood, 'who has always been and always will be'.

In her interview Aniela Jaffé spoke to us of how, towards the end of his life, Jung was happiest when silent, particularly at Bollingen: 'He felt a part of nature, part of the lake, part of the woods – and it gave him rest and gave him trust.' I know in my own life, as I've grown older, that I've appreciated silence more and more – though my family tease me this is only to do with my deafness! However I truly feel less inclined to volunteer opinions all the time, or enter into arguments – and not because I'm weary or uninterested (or very slightly deaf). I find myself increasingly treasuring the quiet space that each one of us periodically needs.

Aniela started to work for Jung in 1955, the year that his wife Emma died; and it was Aniela who was largely responsible for coaxing from him his *Memories, Dreams, Reflections*. He was, in her opinion, a deeply religious man; someone who felt himself to be a Christian, but who felt that Christianity needed renewal. 'Many people today can no longer simply believe', she said to us, 'They are not simple enough.'

As an example of what I think Aniela meant by this, I looked up something that Ray Monk wrote in his biography of the philosopher Ludwig Wittgenstein who, having experienced the full horrors of World War I, needed not only a religious faith but also a philosophy. 'That is to say,' writes Monk, 'he needed not only to believe in God – to pray to Him for strength and enlightenment; he needed to understand what it was that he was believing in.'

In his book about Jung and Steiner, Gerhard Wehr points out that Jung resolutely remained the psychiatrist and did not want to make theological statement or religious proclamations, but limited his research entirely to the material manifested in the psyches of his patients. This material expressed itself largely in pictures and symbols. Wehr's observation ignores, I believe, the wealth of inner experiences that Jung had himself. However, I do agree with him that in his writings Jung never attempted to present anything either to prove or disprove transcendental existence. It was not his style and, perhaps, not his task. Maybe he was also instinctively in sympathy with Emerson's statement: 'Of that ineffable essence which we call spirit, he that thinks most will say least.' Nevertheless Jung seems to have had no doubt about the existence of a supersensible reality, and has played a very significant role in helping perfectly rational people to become more open to it.

In *Feet of Clay* Anthony Storr writes that in his opinion the whole of Jung's later work can be read as an attempt to discover a substitute for the religious faith that he had lost. When asked by John Freeman in the interview for *Face to Face* in 1959 whether he still believed in God, there was one of those wonderful pauses that often say far more than any words can. Jung had already stated that as a child, like everyone else, he had attended church and that he had indeed believed in God. Eventually he gave this reply to Freeman: 'Now? Difficult to answer.' Another pause. 'I don't need to believe. I know.'

Such a response can, of course, sound somewhat presumptuous, even arrogant – though that is not at all how it came across. According to Aniela and Laurens, Jung felt extremely humble as an old man. This modesty comes across strongly in the last chapters of his autobiography. For example he quotes the Chinese sage Lao-Tzu – 'All are clear, I alone am clouded' – as expressing what he now felt at the end of his life. 'The archetype of the old man who has seen enough is eternally true', he wrote. 'At every level of intelligence this type appears, and its lineaments are always the same, whether it be an old peasant or a great philosopher like Lao-Tzu.'

For Jung the psyche remained as much a mystery as matter is for the physicist, explained Aniela. She saw one of the clear signs of his greatness in his willingness to admit when he came to the boundaries of his knowledge. 'For him life was a great mystery', she said. 'What we know and understand is only very little. But his longing for understanding was enormous. He was learning and trying to understand all his life. But he never hesitated to say "I don't know".' Back in 1926 Jung had written of himself: 'I am no philosopher but merely an empiricist. All difficult questions I try to decide from my experiences. If there is no experiential foundation I would rather leave a question unanswered.'

As an analyst herself, Aniela Jaffé could speak with experience when she stated that anything rising up from the unconscious is ambiguous; it's a paradox. The great danger of consciousness is its tendency to be one-sided. Jung's deep concern, she emphasised, was to see things from both sides. It was, above all, a search for balance. 'You cannot understand the world', she said, 'if you don't understand the paradox.'

Jung was sad that he was often not understood, she went on to tell us. And this, she felt, was not out of vanity. In fact, for a long time he resisted the setting up of a Jung Institute, hoping

Aniela Jaffé

that his ideas and research would seep into mainstream psychiatry without the label of his name. He was sad, too, because he feared for the future of mankind. 'We need more understanding of human nature', he said to John Freeman with great urgency in his voice, 'because the only real danger that exists is man himself. He is the real danger, and we are pitifully unaware of this. We know nothing of man – far too little.'

This observation was powerfully conveyed by Ronald Higgins in his book *The Seventh Enemy*. Six of our enemies are familiar ones – over-population, famine, shortage of resources, environmental degradation, nuclear abuse, and technology racing beyond our control. We ourselves are the seventh and the most lethal enemy of all. As well as political inertia, Higgins highlights what he calls individual blindness – the very area that so concerned Jung.

According to Aniela Jaffé, Jung felt that the only solution to our crisis was greater consciousness. Mass psychology was what he feared above all, she said, because the individual, as part of a mass, has no responsibility. This concern of Jung's not just for his individual patients, but for humanity as a whole, is also noted by Gerhard Wehr:

> We see that Jung's depth psychology is meant to be more than simply a diagnoses and therapy for individual mental illness. He diagnosed the present historical and cultural dilemma of the western world as a whole, and he wants to show the way out of this dangerous situation.

As Laurens van der Post wrote in his commentary, the world had indeed become Jung's asylum.

In our final sequence at Bollingen, amid the simple treasures that Jung had left behind and with the sound of the lake gently lapping on the shore, Laurens spoke these words:

> Jung's whole life had been a dialogue; a dialogue with his own unconscious; a dialogue with the whole history of man; and only here did he have the inner silence for the final dialogue. From Bollingen he wrote to me: 'I cannot define for you what God is, but I can tell you that my work has proved that the pattern of God exists in every man.'

The last sequence of all we filmed back at Jung's house at Küsnacht. To make things easier for Laurens I had arranged the two-week schedule so that he could tell Jung's story chronologically. Now, on our last afternoon, it was time to speak about his death. Throughout our shoot we had worked in beautiful spring sunshine, but suddenly the weather changed. As at the time of Jung's death, when lightning struck one of his favourite trees in the garden, a great storm suddenly arose. With the thunder rumbling in the background and as Laurens spoke his final words, a great flash of lightning nearly stopped him in his tracks. Was history repeating itself? Again I wondered: Had we got it all wrong and was someone trying to say so? Perhaps it was simply what Jung would have called synchronicity – a meaningful coincidence. We certainly felt a heightened awareness of his presence. It is a presence that has stayed with me as a wise companion ever since. 'Follow and trust that which has most meaning for you' was the advice that Jung once gave. I have tried to do just that.

Jung at Bollingen

CHAPTER 13

Tolstoy's Russia

Jung's emphasis on the importance of trying to understand and respect each person's story had deepened my interest in biography. Now I was about to explore a biography that magnifies questions which, in varying degrees of intensity, confront us all. Because it was a life in which the failures and the suffering were as monumental as the triumphs, it resonates with a particular poignancy. It is every person's life; an archetypal tale, but on a huge scale – intellectually, morally and socially.

My film about Tolstoy's life (1828–1910) was again for the Religious Programmes department at the BBC. At last I had managed to persuade someone – once more it was Oliver Hunkin – to let me loose on a subject so close to my heart. For logistical reasons the schedule had to overlap with my project on Jung, so I filmed in Russia in the spring of 1971 before the shoot in Switzerland. The contrast was extraordinary. From austerity, extreme bureaucracy and a chaotic infrastructure in the USSR I moved to Switzerland – a land of plenty, where everything was clean and worked efficiently. My Swiss hotel room boasted every facility – except a hidden microphone!

As I sat by the lake at Küsnacht, my plate piled high, I slowly transferred my attention from one extraordinary story to another; but it took a while. In Russia it had been uphill all the way. At that time it was the height – or perhaps depth is a better word – of the Brezhnev era. The authorities never quite trusted me. Was I, for example, trying to draw parallels between Tolstoy's problems with an authoritarian government, and the contemporary situation of that arch-dissident, Solzhenitsyn, who had not yet been deported from the Soviet Union? Did I want to film in Russia just to show how backward it was and how in the sixty years or so since Tolstoy's death so little had changed in the countryside, where peasants still ploughed with horses?

Visiting Russia that winter to make plans for the shoot, I was told I would have to work with a Russian film crew instead of bringing one from the BBC. Although not ideal, one important bonus emerged. The cameraman and I, though neither of us spoke each other's language, both knew enough German to communicate. Through Boris Pavlov, once he was satisfied that I wasn't a spy, I learned much of what lived in the hearts and minds of most ordinary Russians. In no way were they taken in by the endless propaganda; they simply endured a tyrannical and authoritarian regime as they had done under the Tsars. It was a situation vividly described by Laurens van der Post some seven years earlier in his book *Journey into Russia*.

The Novosti Press Agency, through whom our co-production was arranged, allocated me an interpreter and a production manager. Both were women and both were programmed to relay the party line and nothing else. As soon as I started to talk about anything other than the weather they rapidly changed into KGB robots. Thank heavens for Boris! I had gone to Russia full of curiosity, and far from enamoured by all that we worshipped on our side of the Iron Curtain. Then, as now, I enjoyed dialogue. How do we create a society in which individualism can flourish, but not at the expense of our neighbour, and of the weak in particular? I had been inspired by the idealism of Gandhi, and also by those pioneers at Camphill. I had read about the kibbutzim in Israel and had been impressed by Jung's formulation of what he called individuation. So what was working and what was not working in Russia? Can't we all learn from each other? My two female 'guards' would have none of it. Maybe, like Jung's father, they too were actually 'consumed by inner doubts' and were 'seeking refuge in blind faith'.

As consultants for the film I signed up Malcolm Muggeridge, for whom Tolstoy was a life-long hero, and the American writer and historian Theodore Roszak whom I had just met. I had come across Roszak's book *The Making of a Counter Culture* during my first visit to the States the previous year; now he was living in London and writing a sequel, *Where the Wasteland Ends*. What I so admired about his work was its serious study of what he identified as a counterculture without either tearing it to pieces on the one hand, or ignoring its more whacky extremes and adopting a starry-eyed and uncritical approach on the other.

In the preface to his book on the counterculture Roszak warns of 'a technocratic totalitarianism in which we shall find ourselves ingeniously adapted to an existence wholly estranged from everything that has ever made the life of man an interesting adventure'. He goes on to mention figures such as Herbert Marcuse, Allen Ginsberg and Alan Watts who all helped in their own way to question the conventional scientific worldview; and he suggests that a culture that subordinates or degrades visionary experience commits the sin of diminishing our very existence. He then writes:

> The primary project of our counter culture is to proclaim a new heaven and a new earth so vast, so marvellous that the inordinate claims of technical expertise must of necessity withdraw to a subordinate and marginal status in the lives of men.

It is a view that I feel sure Tolstoy would have whole-heartedly supported, though his solutions were far more radical and utopian than anything suggested by those gurus mentioned by Roszak. Tolstoy recognised, I believe, that the greatest challenge facing each person was not just this quest for self-knowledge and greater consciousness that Jung, Steiner and others all emphasised, but was also to find the courage and the will-power to act on that knowledge in putting one's own house in order – as Gandhi had tried to do so single-mindedly. It is relatively easy to preach; it's quite another thing to roll up your sleeves and do something, particularly if, as in Tolstoy's case, you don't have the support of those close to you. 'He is an artist', wrote his wife, 'and suddenly he becomes a shoemaker. It is plain insanity.'

Tolstoy's estate at Yasnaya Polyana, where he spent his early childhood and most of his adult life, was our main location. We were based ten miles away at a rather grim hotel in Tula, 130 miles south of Moscow. At the time this area was outside Intourist's jurisdiction and therefore closed to foreigners. Hence the hotel made no effort to impress. People slept in the corridors, and hot water was in short supply. The food reminded me of the inedible concoctions served up at my boarding school in the early post-war years.

However none of this really mattered because down the road was Yasnaya Polyana. The estate is a magical place. Although officially a museum, it still feels more like a home and you almost expect Tolstoy to come walking into

Yasnaya Polyana

the room at any moment. The house itself is surrounded by great bushes of lilac, and beyond is a forest of silver birch trees interspersed with paths leading into the distance. Six months earlier I had seen it all in the snow. I loved being there. For me it was a true pilgrimage, and the whole place seemed strangely familiar. Perhaps in life we are attracted not only to those of our contemporaries whose ideals correspond to our own, but also to allies long dead to whom we feel no less close.

In the opening commentary to the film, which I wrote with Theodore Roszak, we described how Count Leo Tolstoy, in the course of his eighty-two years, was a soldier, gambler, hunter, schoolmaster, devoted husband, domestic tyrant, novelist, shoemaker, biblical scholar, moralist and an enemy of the state who, by the time of his death, had become the conscience of the world. His fellow Russian, the writer Maxim Gorky said of him: 'I felt as long as he's alive, I'm not an orphan in the world.'

Though his mother died when he was two, Tolstoy himself was no orphan. A distant relative of his father, Aunt Tatyana, took care of the children – three older brothers and a younger sister. It was a happy childhood; joyful memories of a summer picnic are vividly evoked in his autobiography:

The coachmen stand in the shade of the trees. The light and shadow speckle their faces; kind, jolly, happy faces. Matryona the cowherd runs up in her shabby dress and says that she has waited long for us, and she is glad that we have arrived. I not only believe, but cannot help believing, that all the world is happy. Auntie is happy while asking Matryona with concern about her daughters, the dogs are happy … the hens, the roosters, the peasant children are happy, the horses are happy, and the calves, the fish in the pond, and the birds in the trees are happy.

The Russia into which Tolstoy was born was ruled by an autocratic Tsar and an aristocracy that still enjoyed a privileged status fast vanishing in the rest of Europe. This was the class to which Tolstoy belonged. The vast majority of people were still bound to a condition of serfdom in a Russia hardly touched by the liberal ideas and revolutionary currents of the 19th century. Most of the serfs were illiterate and lived in severe poverty. They could be bought and sold with the land, and flogged at their master's discretion.

In 1841, at the age of thirteen, Tolstoy went with his family to live in Kazan. Five years later, at the university of Kazan, he was reading avidly – Rousseau, Pushkin, Goethe – but he was a critical and restless student, and withdrew at the age of nineteen. The notebooks and diaries that he now began to keep reveal how haunted he was by a desire for self-perfection and by a nagging sense of moral failure:

With all my soul I wished to be good, but I was young, passionate and alone when I sought goodness. Every time I tried to express my most sincere desire, which was to be morally good, I met with contempt and ridicule; but as soon as I yielded to nasty passion I was praised and encouraged.

Leo Tolstoy aged twenty-one in 1849

He returned to Yasnaya Polyana for a while, but St Petersburg soon beckoned – 'Gambling, gypsies – I intend to stay here for ever.' In 1851, aged twenty-three, his brother Nikolai, an army cadet, persuaded him to return with him to the Caucasus where the Russian army, in league with the Cossacks, was involved in a protracted war against rebellious Caucasian hill tribes.

Life in the Causasus was a new and fascinating experience for the young Tolstoy. He came to admire the Cossacks he lived among for their freedom, rugged beauty and simple earthy philosophy: 'Ah, if only I could become a Cossack, steal horses, get drunk, sing songs, and, dead drunk, go climbing in at her window and spend the night without her asking why or who I am – then I could be happy.' For a while he imagined buying a hut, marrying a Cossack girl and settling down. But his diaries soon reflected the same despondency caused, he felt, by an application to the serious things of life too early. 'Gambling, sensuality and vanity', he wrote, 'are the three evil passions I have most to contend with.' His biographer, Ernest J. Simmons, writes a telling phrase in relation to the young Tolstoy's pangs of conscience: 'The law of his being had to be fulfilled.' A diary entry a few months later refers to

a great, a stupendous idea, to the realisation of which I feel capable of dedicating my whole life – the founding of a new religion corresponding to the development of mankind: the religion of Christ, but purged of all dogma and mysteriousness; a practical religion, not promising future bliss but realising bliss on earth.

Simmons also feels that Tolstoy, in his efforts towards self-perfection, was inclined to magnify his moral failings. That is probably what anyone's efforts tend to look like from the outside. Only each one of us knows, in our heart of hearts, how far we fall behind our ideals, of what we are potentially capable and how much more we could do.

Tolstoy finally decided to join the army, and also began writing his first novel, *Childhood*, based on the experiences of his early life. He was prompted to make the effort by a particularly strong feeling of guilt and self-reproach, while convalescing from a bout of venereal disease. The book was an immediate success and he went on to write *Boyhood*. In 1854 he was posted to the Crimea where Russia was at war with the English and French. Here he completed *Youth*, the last part of his autobiographical trilogy. Tolstoy then requested a transfer to the besieged city of Sebastopol where he experienced fighting at first hand. But the writer was by now living side by side with the soldier. Beginning as a patriotic tribute to the courage of the Russian soldier, Tolstoy's *Sebastopol Sketches* finished as a controversial and heavily censored revelation of the folly, hypocrisy and utter futility of war. 'The hero of my tale,' he wrote at the end of the second sketch, 'whom I love with all the power of my soul, whom I have tried to convey in all his beauty, who has always been, is, and will be beautiful – is truth.' A little earlier he had already begun to express concern at the absence in contemporary literature of what he thought should be its one aim – morality.

Tolstoy returned to St Petersburg from the Crimea a literary hero, but his own moral state continued to trouble him. Disgusted with his way of life he set off on a Grand Tour. In Paris, early in 1857, he witnessed a public execution in the Place de la Roquette:

> If a man were torn to pieces before my eyes, it would not be so repulsive as this dextrous and elegant machine with which in a flash a strong, clean, healthy man is killed. Human law – what a farce! The truth is that the State is a plot designed to exploit and corrupt its citizens. I shall never enter the service of any government anywhere.

I feel a particularly strong connection to Tolstoy's reaction to that public execution. I remember as a boy being deeply upset whenever a hanging was due to take place, and a horror of capital punishment has remained with me ever since; I even experienced it when Saddam Hussein was hanged. Violence prompted by anger of whatever sort, although horrible, is understandable. But cold-blooded and sanitised killing I find utterly chilling and repellent. To a lesser degree it was what I felt about canings at school, whether administered by the headmaster at my preparatory school or at public school by a prefect

– violence dished out without emotion of any sort. These ritual beatings – along with four pre-adolescent years of compulsory boxing – were, in my experience, far more barbaric than the more spontaneous conflicts that periodically blew up in those somewhat problematic all-male establishments.

———————•———————

That autumn, with the seeds of his pacifism and anarchism deeply planted, Tolstoy returned to Yasnaya Polyana. He was now well on the road that would lead to his epoch-making revolt against the whole organisation of modern society. There were three hundred and fifty male serfs and their families on his estate. He had long been concerned with their condition and had even offered them emancipation. Mistrustful of his motives, the serfs had rejected his proposal. But the problem that concerned him most of all was the illiteracy of the peasants. What use was it to write books that the vast majority of Russians could never read? Tolstoy was never satisfied with abstract thought. Ideas must be translated into action. Thus, in 1859, he opened a school at Yasnaya Polyana for the children of the village. In a Russia where serfs had no access to education whatsoever, it was a bold experiment.

The children were free to come and go as they pleased. Tolstoy rejected any form of compulsion in his teaching. There were no tests, no punishments, no rewards, no learning by heart. The fifty or so children chose their own subjects of study. Teaching, according to Tolstoy, could not be described as a method: it was a talent, an art. A pupil who imagines that the earth stands in water with fish in it, he declared, judges much more healthily than one who believes that the earth spins in space, but is not able to understand or explain the fact.

Despite his strong convictions about education Tolstoy never considered his school as some sort of prototype, and he admitted that the best school for a Russian village might be the worst possible model for a school elsewhere. However, his extremely radical position – described by Simmons as 'to the left of Rousseau' – represented a danger not only to the whole foundation of the educational system, but to the authority of the state itself. Children educated in this spirit would hardly grow up with the proper reverence for authority, since Tolstoy was

Leo Tolstoy aged thirty-four in 1862

placing the worth and well-being of the individual above the well-being of the state. Many years later he wrote of the school in a letter: 'It was all my life, it was my monastery, my church, in which I redeemed myself while being saved from all the anxieties, doubts, and temptations of life.'

Tolstoy's experiments with education were not dissimilar to those of the English educationalist A.S. Neill at his school, Summerhill, in Suffolk some hundred years later. I met Neill in 1970 while researching the film I made about current trends in education. He, too, made no rules about attending lessons. Children, he observed, are naturally curious and want to learn. Therefore, if the teachers are interesting – and interested in children as well as in their subjects – then the classes will be full. Sometimes, it seems, such extreme and radical initiatives are needed in all walks of life, not only to rock the boat but also to help restore a balance – in this case against the authoritarian and government-led regulations in education that are still very much with us.

To tell the story of Tolstoy's life, or of any life on film, without the use of actors, is always a challenge. Once you go that far back in time there is, for example, no one alive to interview. Instead one has to try and evoke a sense of the subject's presence through the buildings and the landscape that he or she inhabited. This can sometimes be more effective even than drama – closer to a book or the radio – since it leaves so much to the viewers' imagination: they are creatively involved.

I called the film *Tolstoy – from riches to rags*. As in other biographical films I had made, I also used a great many contemporary paintings; and thanks to the knowledge and skill of my film editor, Jonathan Gili, music became an especially important ingredient in the evocation of a truly extraordinary life. One of the most helpful of all these various windows into somebody's story, can, of course, be photographs. One exists of Sonya Bers, aged sixteen, taken two years before she became Countess Tolstoy. She was the daughter of a Moscow doctor and the families had known one

Sonya Bers aged sixteen

another for some years. Sonya had long held an exalted opinion of the great writer, Leo Tolstoy. Many times in the past he had contemplated and then fled from marriage. Only after months of agonised hesitation did he find the courage to propose to Sonya.

In September 1862, the thirty-four-year-old Tolstoy arrived at Yasnaya Polyana with his young bride; but already there were problems. On the eve of their marriage he had given her his private diaries to read. Later, in her own diary, Sonya wrote: 'All his past is so awful for me. He kisses me and I think – I'm not the first woman he has crushed to him in this way.'

Despite Sonya's misgivings, Tolstoy wrote of the happiness that marriage brought to both of them:

> I love her ... when I awake and find her looking at me tenderly. I love her when she says: 'Lyovochka', and then adds – 'Why are chimneys built so straight?' or 'Why do horses live so long?' I love her when she is a little girl in a yellow dress and shoves her chin forward and sticks out her tongue at me.

Sonya had never lived in the country before, but nevertheless she soon took responsibility for the home and estate. Tolstoy now found the time and the discipline for intensive literary effort. He finished *The Cossacks*, the story of his life in the Caucasus. But before him lay a far more ambitious work: 'I've never felt my mental and moral powers so free and ready for work, and the work is there in front of me. I've been completely taken up with a novel about the years 1810 to 1820.' At her desk each evening Sonya eagerly copied out her husband's nearly illegible manuscripts. Her sister Tanya had become the model for the heroine of the story. Like so many of the characters in *War and Peace*, Natasha Rostova was drawn from Tolstoy's own family. Their private lives were to provide a counterpoint to the great historical events of the Napoleonic wars.

Through two thousand pages Tolstoy struggled with the problems of individual freedom and historical necessity. Not since Homer's Iliad had any writer dealt with scenes of battle on so vast a scale. And yet Tolstoy never lost touch with the human realities of the men and women he created. With superb daring he used the defeat of Napoleon to mock the grand designs of conquerors. For Tolstoy the meaning of life could only be found in the triumph of the individual over personal adversity and suffering. Yet certain radical critics accused him of failing to portray the dark misery of the peasantry at that time, and for being blind to the faults of the privileged classes. In a letter to a fellow author he wrote: 'The aim of an artist is not to resolve a question irrefutably, but to compel one to love life in all its manifestations, and these are inexhaustible.'

In the six years it had taken to write *War and Peace* Sonya had borne Tolstoy four children and copied out his great work seven times. After the publication he was drawn again to the needs of peasant children. Having created the Russian national epic, he turned to the writing of an ABC book – a complete curriculum into which he claimed to have put more work and love than anything else. Once again his educational ideas were met with stern hostility by the state. His books were never officially used. He also wrote a number of stories for children, mainly adaptations of folk tales. 'I am still searching and searching', he wrote. 'It seems I have lost my way.' For a while he found himself balancing painfully between his art and his social responsibilities. The claims of real and imaginary people divided his heart. To whom did his talents belong?

In his next novel, *Anna Karenina*, all these doubts and uncertainties were to be reflected in the strongly autobiographical figure of Levin, whose passionate search for a just and honourable way of life revealed Tolstoy's growing alienation from the traditions of his class. Sonya was elated to see him return to his creative work and once again copied out the endlessly corrected manuscript. This novel was to establish Tolstoy among the supreme artists of the western world, and that world waited eagerly for his next offering. There were rumours of a sequel to *War and Peace*. But Tolstoy was occupied with other thoughts.

We travelled to the beautiful city of Kiev in the Ukraine to tell the next episode in Tolstoy's life. It was here, in 1879, that he made a pilgrimage to the magnificent Catacomb Monastery, searching to fill a need in his life far more urgent than the demands of his art. For several years he had been tortured by a sense of life's absurdity and of the meaninglessness of his own artistic achievements in the face of death. Not even the monks at Kiev could help Tolstoy through the crisis that now faced him. He wrote:

> When I thought of the fame my works would bring me, I would say to myself: 'Very well, you will be more famous than Gogol or Pushkin, or Shakespeare or Molière, or than all the writers in the world – and what of it?' And I would find no reply at all … I felt that what I had been standing on had collapsed and that I had nothing left under my feet. What I had lived for no longer existed and there was nothing left.

Tolstoy had already read extensively in science and philosophy, and now began a detailed investigation of religions – Buddhism, Hinduism and above all Christianity. He struggled to subordinate himself to the Russian Orthodox Church, striving to give his life a meaning which death could not destroy. Yet the established Church, philosophy, and science all failed to answer for him the basic questions of existence. His need of religion was great, but he could win his way to spiritual faith only through intellectual conviction. The limits of the intellect he accepted, but he wished to understand in such a way that everything inexplicable should present itself to him as being necessarily inexplicable and not as something he was under an arbitrary obligation to believe.

Tolstoy in his fifties

All his life Tolstoy had been searching for God, often in ways that evaded his own consciousness. 'Instead of sinning his way, like Dostoyevsky', writes his biographer Simmons, 'he had to reason his way to Him.' What now occurred was not a break with the past, but rather the intensification of a development that had been proceeding slowly ever since his youth. His fifteen years of happy marriage had not cured his underlying despair, but merely diverted it.

This painful episode in Tolstoy's life was summarised in *Confession*. He was now fifty-one years old and on the brink of a revolutionary change that was to take him far from his art and leave Sonya bewildered and deeply distressed. He wrote to a friend: 'This year I have struggled much, but the beauty of the world conquered me.'

For Tolstoy that beauty emerged from the everyday life around him. In the simple faith of peasants he found the resolution of his crisis. Despite their superstition and obedience to the authority of the Church, they displayed a brave acceptance of suffering and death. He went out onto the roads and spent many hours talking with peasants and pilgrims. From them he learned the nobility of labour and a simple life. And so these humble people of Russia gradually led him to a belief in God. But it was not the God whom theologians discuss that interested Tolstoy. What for him became meaningful was the existence of some higher power that manifested in the workings of reason and conscience. And through this experience Tolstoy became convinced that the existence of that power within him constituted a moral force for good which in turn gave a meaning and purpose to life that death could not defeat. Above all he came to see that true Christianity meant the absolute renunciation of violence, property and social privilege. This was the meaning – the essence, he felt, of Christ's teachings and example – which he emphasised in his translation of the Gospels. In the search for that source he had taught himself both Greek and Hebrew. But his Biblical translations were banned in Russia and first printed abroad.

Not only did Tolstoy rebuff and antagonise the established Church with his heretical interpretations of the scriptures, but he now placed his immense personal influence at the service of Russia's poor and excluded millions. He would become their voice, their champion. But pressure from his growing family was pushing Tolstoy in the opposite direction. In 1881 Sonya, now thirty-seven years old, persuaded him to buy a Moscow house so that the older children could have a city education and live in the style that she felt their social position deserved. She had borne Tolstoy ten children; seven now survived and an eighth was born that year.

Tolstoy believed increasingly that conventional education was harmful, because its aim was to fit men to rise above their fellow men. For Sonya life in Moscow came as a welcome relief from the monotony she experienced at Yasnaya Polyana. For Tolstoy it was intolerable. All day he would disappear, walking up to the Sparrow Hills on the outskirts of the city to saw and split wood with peasants. 'It's good for his health and cheers him up', Sonya wrote to her sister.

In his diary Tolstoy wrote, 'A month has passed, the most miserable in my life. They are all busy settling in – but when are they going to start living? Everything they do is done not in order to live, but because somebody else is doing it.'

For Tolstoy urban poverty was a new and appalling experience:

Scoundrels have banded together, robbing the people; they've assembled an army, elected judges to sanction their orgies and now they are feasting. There is nothing for the people to do but take advantage of other men's passions, and to get back what has been stolen from them.

In writings such as *What I Believe* and *What Then Must We Do?* Tolstoy now mercilessly castigated the idleness and self-indulgence of the rich. He didn't spare himself in these criticisms. Painfully aware of the glaring contrast between what he practised and the ideal of Christian humility he preached, he undertook to reform the entire pattern of his life. He became a vegetarian, gave up wine, tobacco and hunting. He began to cobble boots for his family and even made a pair for one of their old servants for her Feast Day.

He refused to let servants wait on him or clean his room or call him Count Tolstoy. Each morning he would rise early to empty his own slops and cut wood. In his diary he noted with delight that his younger children, at least, helped him with these chores. Again in a letter to her sister, Sonya wrote: 'He is a leader; he goes ahead of the crowd showing the way people should go. But I am the crowd … I cannot go faster, for I am held back by the crowd, and by my surroundings and my habits.'

Back at Yasnaya Polyana Tolstoy now took up ploughing for widowed peasants; and in his writings, most of which continued to be banned in Russia, he highlighted the ineffectiveness of the usual forms of charitable relief and the anomaly of the rich feeding the peasants with the food the peasants grew to feed the rich. 'The common people are hungry', he wrote, 'because we are too full.'

'I think that in many respects he has the answer for us,' said Malcolm Muggeridge in his interview for the film,

> because insofar as we seek wealth and power, whether individually or collectively, we enter upon servitude. We don't liberate ourselves; we make ourselves slaves … I think he thought, as such inspired people do, that men could literally and absolutely be virtuous and love truth. And he was not prepared, either in his personal life or in his views of society, to make any concessions whatsoever … I think we have to accept the fact that the great teachers and saints – perhaps it is what God means them to do – they confront us, as Jesus himself did, with absolute propositions which are not within our competence, within our reach. But it is insofar as we know about these propositions and reach after them that we live.

Muggeridge went on to speak about Tolstoy's increasing distrust of all forms of power and authority, and to suggest that what he and many other visionaries fail to realise, and what made Tolstoy's own life so tragic, is that although we need to grasp these great truths, in order to live in the world we have to accept the fact of human imperfection; and part of that imperfection is that authority and power have to exist. Even Jesus acknowledged that we have to render unto Caesar the things that are Caesar's. Tolstoy, said Muggeridge, wouldn't really admit that such imperfections were inevitable and this involved him, in his personal life, in great contradictions and suffering.

In his introduction to volume twenty of the centenary edition of Tolstoy's writings, the critic Gilbert Murray writes of how Tolstoy saw more clearly than others that the world was in need of repentance and a change of heart:

but meantime his own repentance is so strong a passion that he cannot see the truth for his tears. As Plato turned against poetry because he was too much of a poet, so Tolstoy turns against that sympathetic understanding of life which was the secret of his own art.

However, despite Tolstoy's low opinion of his own creative work, he had, for a number of years, been concentrating much of his literary effort on tales for the people in cheap editions. In just six years, more than twenty million copies were printed. His chief collaborator in this effort was V.G. Chertkov, a man destined to have increasing influence over Tolstoy's later years. I personally find these tales, along with some of his shorter stories such as *The Death of Ivan Ilych* and *Master and Man*, as inspiring as anything else he wrote. All great works of art, Tolstoy believed, are great because they are accessible and comprehensible to everyone. Art of this kind, he said, makes us realise to what extent we are all members of the human race and share the feelings of our common humanity. For this reason he was deeply allergic to any form of élitism or literary obscurity. To his close friend N.N. Strakkov he once declared: 'I do not understand or like poetry; it is a kind of riddle for which elucidation is always required.' Eccentric and dogmatic he may have been, but Tolstoy was certainly no literary snob.

Now, together with Chertkov, he planned to relinquish the copyright on his works. Sonya was totally opposed to the scheme. The books had become the family's major source of income. She threatened suicide over the issue. At last a compromise was reached which satisfied neither Tolstoy nor his wife. He renounced his copyright to all works written since 1881. They were for everyone and he wanted no reward. Sonya remained the custodian of all the earlier writings, including *War and Peace* and *Anna Karenina*. At the same time he divided his estate between Sonya and his nine surviving children, keeping nothing for himself – just as though he were dead.

In his next work *The Kingdom of God is within You*, Tolstoy carried Christian anarchism a stage further, condemning military conscription in one of the most powerful pacifist statements ever written. The Russian censor called it the most harmful book he had ever had occasion to ban. It was this book, however, that was to inspire and influence a young Indian lawyer in South Africa, M.K. Gandhi, who wrote to Tolstoy, calling him 'The Titan of Russia' and signing himself 'a humble follower of your doctrine'.

By accepting the literal meaning of non-resistance to evil with all its implications, much that had been obscure in the Gospels became plain to Tolstoy; for by not resisting the evil-doer, one will never do violence and therefore never do any act that is contrary to love. And it was love that Tolstoy felt was the real essence of Christianity. All who would fulfil this law must be prepared to abandon everything and endure all consequences. And that, of course, is exactly what Mahatma Gandhi did, transforming Tolstoy's pacifism into non-violent resistance on a mass scale.

With every passing year Tolstoy's international stature grew. The authorities of church and state denounced him, but dared not strike at him directly. Instead they persecuted his followers – 'the dark people', as Sonya called them. The victims included Chertkov, who was exiled for five years and spent them in England.

When Tolstoy did at last return to the novel it was with a social mission in mind. The Dukhobors were a pacifist sect living in the Caucasus and savagely persecuted by the Tsarist authorities. Through his influence they were finally given permission to emigrate to Canada. In order to finance their exodus Tolstoy decided to complete the novel *Resurrection*. He had been working on it for a long time, but rather half-heartedly. In his book *What is Art?* he had defined what he believed to be the role of art in society. If he was to write another novel, it would have to conform to his theories. But would he himself be able to live in accordance with what he preached to others? It was the old dilemma. 'Suddenly he wasn't so sure', writes Henri Troyat in another fine biography of Tolstoy:

> This lust for life, this love of nature, this need to expend his energies in the open air, or in bed, this childish desire to tell stories ... Was it moral? Was it necessary? At seventy Tolstoy the philosopher had begun to have suspicions of Tolstoy the author.

Nevertheless he did proceed. *Resurrection* tells of a nobleman, Prince Dimitri, who while serving on a jury recognises one of the defendants as a serving girl he had once seduced and abandoned. He decides to give up his title and wealth to follow her into Siberian exile. As social criticism it was Tolstoy's fiercest attack so far – a penetrating analysis of the corruption underlying the law courts, the prisons and the entire Russian social system of the time. Much was struck out by the censor. The tale is also, to my mind, a powerful example of the law of karma working itself out within one lifetime. We don't always have to wait for our next incarnation to try to right the wrongs we have committed.

Meanwhile Tolstoy's religious commitment made it impossible for him to endorse the radical ideologies of the day. He had read Karl Marx, but was repelled by his materialism. To a visitor he once said:

> Materialism is the most mystical of all teachings: fundamentally it places its whole faith in a mythical substance which creates everything out of itself, the foundation of everything. This is even more stupid than belief in the Trinity.

Against such provocations, it was only a matter of time before the authorities took action. On February 24th 1901, Tolstoy was excommunicated from the Russian Orthodox Church. 'In our days', the Holy Synod proclaimed, 'God has permitted a new false teacher to appear.' Only if Tolstoy repented could he return to the Church. He replied: 'I can no more return to that from which with such suffering I have escaped than a flying bird can re-enter the eggshell from which it has emerged.'

Because of censorship, the full text of Tolstoy's reply to the Synod was at the time published only in England. In it he admitted that he did not believe in everything that the Church believed, but insisted that he did believe in God, 'whom I understand as spirit, as love, as the source of all. I believe that He is in me and I in Him'. At the very centre of his faith he placed God's will that we should love one another and do to others as we would wish others to do to us. Above all he believed in the eventual establishment of the kingdom of God on earth, 'in which the discord, deception and violence that now rule will be replaced by free accord, by truth, and by brotherly love of one for another'.

As the story moved into the 20th century for the last ten years of Tolstoy's life, the advent of the movie-camera created a whole new source of material upon which to draw for my film. In the archives in Moscow I discovered some extraordinary footage, some of which had never been seen outside the Soviet Union. Family life at Yasnaya Polyana had always included a constant flow of friends and relatives; now, with Tolstoy having achieved the stature of a world personality, visitors from far and wide made the pilgrimage to see the great man, and many of them – social-reformers, journalists, students, artists, religious fanatics and cranks of every description – were filmed, along with Tolstoy himself.

His excommunication had also created a sensation, though not what the Synod had expected. Letters poured in from Russia and abroad, along with petitions signed by hundreds of people expressing support for Tolstoy. He himself was increasingly burdened by letters appealing for money or spiritual counsel, many from semi-literate peasants. He did his best to give them all his personal attention.

He was also working on some textbooks for children, including *The Teachings of Jesus Explained to Children*. The task reawakened his interest in pedagogy and he started evening classes for the village children. At first, fifteen of them came to the library, not this time to learn science, history and grammar; instead Tolstoy tried to teach religious and moral principles, using the simplest methods possible. Sonya was not impressed: 'Leo Nickolayevich has a new hobby', she said. 'He is droning away, teaching Christian truths to the children; they repeat after him like parrots. But they will turn into drunkards and thieves all the same!'

Russian village children around 1900

At the opening of *Anna Karenina* Tolstoy wrote, 'Happy families are all alike, but an unhappy family is unhappy in its own way.' In his own unhappy family the antagonisms of these final years reached bizarre extremes. Sonya, driven to distraction by suspicion and jealousy, convinced herself that the husband she had lived with for forty-five years was involved in a homosexual relationship with Chertkov. Meanwhile she herself had become obsessed with a strange and much younger man, the pianist Taneyev. She also found Tolstoy's spiritual strivings increasingly incomprehensible.

Tolstoy's family in 1892

Some years earlier Tolstoy had contemplated leaving Sonya and had even written her a letter:

> I have long been tormented by the incongruity between my life and my beliefs. To oblige you to change your way of life, your habits, which I taught you myself, was impossible; to leave you has also been impossible up to this time, for I thought that I should be depriving the children, while they were still young, of the influence, however small, which I might have over them, and should be causing you pain.

Now, some thirteen years later, Tolstoy could bear the situation no longer. Tormented by Sonya's irrational outbursts and threats of suicide he longed more and more for escape. The struggle between Sonya and Chertkov for control of his writings had grown ever more bitter. He planned a secret will in which his unpublished works, as well as his diaries and notebooks, should be made public property.

Since their marriage Tolstoy and his wife had allowed each other access to their diaries. Now Tolstoy began to keep *A Diary for Myself Alone*; even this Sonya found and read. The breaking point came when he awoke one night to find her searching for the secret will. He left a farewell letter and fled with his doctor before dawn. In it he

Leo Tolstoy and Sonya in 1910

expressed much the same thoughts as he had in the earlier letter – regret at causing her pain, and above all the intolerable situation he experienced in the home: 'I cannot go on living in the luxury by which I have always been surrounded'; and finally the wish to spend his last days alone and in silence: 'I thank you for the forty-eight years of honourable life you spent with me and I ask you to forgive all the wrongs I have done you, just as I forgive you, with all my heart, those you may have done to me.'

Tolstoy got as far as Astapovo, a remote country railway station. He had fallen ill on the train and rapidly developed pneumonia. The station master's hut became his sick room as there was neither a hospital nor a hotel nearby. His flight became immediate world news. Within a day a newsreel cameraman was on the scene to record Sonya's arrival. His elder children and

Chertkov were already at his bedside. The family and doctors persuaded a reluctant Sonya not to make her presence known. Tolstoy had sent a telegram to Yasnaya Polyana: 'Because my heart is so weak, a meeting with my wife would be fatal.' Actual film of these scenes was part of what I had unearthed in the Moscow archive. Without a doubt they are some of the most moving and poignant images I have ever assembled.

On November 7th 1910, four days after her arrival at Astapovo, Sonya wrote in her diary: 'Leo Nikolayevich died this morning. I was not allowed in until his last breath. I was not allowed to say goodbye to my husband. Cruel people.'

Until the end Tolstoy's hand could be seen moving across his bed covers as if still writing. He had murmured to his son, Sergei, 'I don't seem able to get to sleep. I am still composing. I am writing. Each thing flows smoothly into the next.'

Thousands of people assembled at Yasnaya Polyana for Tolstoy's funeral. Many thousands more might have come if the government had not forbidden the railways to supply extra trains. Two villagers led the procession. On their banner was written: 'Leo Nikolayevich, the memory of your kindness will not die among us orphaned peasants of Yasnaya Polyana.'

No priests were present at this first public funeral in Russia without religious rites. Tolstoy was buried at that place in the forest where, as a child, his brother had told him that a green stick was hidden – the Green Stick on which was carved the secret that would bring universal happiness to all mankind. That day all Russia and the world honoured Leo Tolstoy. How many knew the dream he had carried with him as he fled from home and family – the dream of finishing his life in a peasant hut, without fame or fortune?

To the very end many people, including his friend, the novelist Turgenev, and of course his wife, could not understand why Tolstoy had forfeited art in order to try to solve the riddles of existence. They did not seem to see that for Tolstoy the measure of true greatness was not what we achieve in a worldly sense, but the extent to which we wrestle with the task of becoming better human beings. Nor did they realise that the same magnificent qualities that made Tolstoy's art immortal – his sincerity and love of truth – were the very qualities that drove him on in his religious and social mission.

However, not everyone thought like Turgenev and Sonya, and it is not at all surprising that so many people flocked to his funeral on that bleak November day nearly one hundred years ago. For them he was not only a great artist, but above all a human being who had proved his freedom by changing his life radically in the pursuit of self-perfection. In this, perhaps, lay the secret of Tolstoy's literary magic. Tolstoy's finest characters – Pierre Bezukov and Prince Andrei in *War and Peace*, Ivan Ilych, Levin in *Anna Karenina*, and above all Prince Dimitri in *Resurrection* – were, like Tolstoy himself, all brought to the possibility of a new and nobler life through the anguish of self-revelation.

'Of course he was an irrational old man', said Muggeridge in his closing statement for the film,

> he was capable of great irrationality; and it's interesting and a proof of what goodness and truth glowed in him always that despite this I can't think of a single person who ever went to see him who didn't come away awed and uplifted. All sorts of worldly people used to go and see him, and there's not one example of someone coming away and saying: 'What a preposterous old humbug that man is.'

Not everyone would agree with Muggeridge. Maxim Gorky had increasing reservations, and in 1900 wrote to Chekhov:

> Tolstoy does not love men; no, he does not love them. The truth is that he judges them, cruelly and too severely. I do not like his idea of God. Is that a God? It is a part of Count Leo Tolstoy and not God, this God without whom men cannot live. He says he is an anarchist. To some extent, yes. But although he destroys some regulations, he dictates others in their place, no less harsh and burdensome for men. That is not anarchism, it is the authoritarianism of a provincial governor.

It's certainly fair to say that Tolstoy did have a tendency – like many other great idealists and social reformers – to love humanity more than individual human beings. But it was love, nonetheless.

Malcolm Muggeridge concluded his interview with these words:

> I don't think we can expect these truly sublime minds to conform to a pattern of logic. We can't expect to find in them the sort of consistency that we might look for in a lesser mind. Tolstoy was like the whole of creation. He contained everything. He was one of those truly great men who come into the world at long intervals, and we need them.

Leo Tolstoy may not have always succeeded in living up to the ideals he championed, but he certainly tried; and in that, I believe, lies his greatness. 'The true spiritual life', he said to a friend in old age, 'is liberated in man when he neither rejoices in his own happiness, nor suffers from his own suffering, but suffers and rejoices with others, and fuses with them into a common life.'

Chapter 14

In Defence of the Stork

By now, in my early thirties, my search for a little more insight into the relationship between heavenly and earthly existence had been hugely enriched in very different ways, particularly by my encounter with the lives of Tolstoy, Gandhi, Jung and Steiner. I had, of course, no absolutely clear answers, nor do I still – my gurus have been more challenging than that – but my questions had certainly deepened. I was also very fortunate that my work was still giving me a unique opportunity to pursue my quest. At times I may have appeared like Cervantes' lean and foolish knight, but the Sancho Panza in me was keeping my feet on the ground, as indeed were the journalistic demands of my profession.

So far my films for the BBC's Religious Programmes department had been about somewhat unorthodox subjects. The next one was to be even more so. I had stayed in touch with my friends at Camphill in Aberdeen and at Botton Village, and in particular with Thomas Weihs whom I used to meet on his visits to London. What I so appreciated about these conversations with him was that everything was up for debate; there were no certainties, despite the breadth and depth of the knowledge he had absorbed. Our own experiences were the ultimate focus in any discussion.

I had never forgotten Thomas's lectures in London on embryology that I attended while at Emerson College – lectures that explored the theme of our spiritual as well as our physical birth, and their interconnection. I therefore set about persuading both him and the BBC's Oliver Hunkin that a film could be made as a window into this subject of birth in its broadest sense. I use the word 'window' because I have always recognised that a film can only ever be that. Probably Thomas felt the same about the book that he wrote later on the same theme. Indeed all communicators must suffer from an awareness of how far they fail to do justice to the subjects about which they care most deeply. Certainly it is true of most of the films I have ever made. Yet I hope and believe that such windows have a value nonetheless.

I have always liked the definition of an icon as 'a window into heaven'. *In Defence of the Stork* was a very modestly executed icon, incorporating scientific and mythological images, as well as specially produced graphics of great beauty. It was filmed around a talk that Thomas gave in 1973 to his young seminar students at Camphill in Aberdeen. In his introduction he spoke to them as follows:

It is generally felt today that out of intellectual honesty we shouldn't tell children that it is the stork who brings their little brothers and sisters. It is, however, quite justified to ask oneself what did the mothers and grandmothers mean when they told this story. Did they believe it was true? Is it likely that grandmothers didn't know where children came from? Or is it likely that they wanted to deceive their children or grandchildren?

Thomas went on to suggest that our enquiry about a momentous subject like birth can go in two different directions. On the one hand we can ask: What is the mechanism of a particular occurrence? How does something come about? And those, he said, are very reasonable questions, particularly if we want or need to intervene, or to find out how we can alter a situation. But there is a very different enquiry possible, related to meaning; not How does it work? or How has it come about? but What does it mean? What is the significance?' 'I would like to try and show you', he said, 'a new meaning, a new significance of conception.'

Thomas continued by describing, very tentatively and imaginatively, a possible link between the description of the creation of the world in the first chapter of Genesis and the first phase of embryonic development, which spans about three weeks and which in most textbooks on embryology is subdivided into six stages during which the so-called embryonic sheath develops.

It is not easy to convey this section of his talk; it doesn't really lend itself to summary, for at times it was more in the nature of a meditation than a lecture. He did, however, describe in some detail certain scientific facts – the chaotic process, for example, that begins in the ovum at fertilisation; and how the nucleus breaks up and rearranges itself, leading to division. That division, he explained, is not only a division into cells – first into two, then four, eight, sixteen and so on, but is also a qualitative division. There are some cells that will develop into special organs – bone, liver, heart or muscles – while divided from them remains the germ cell, retaining its potential for recreation and never differentiating.

Thomas then started to read to the students from the first chapter of Genesis: 'In the beginning God created the heaven and the earth …' In the film, alongside medical diagrams of the fertilised ovum during those first twenty days or so, we used as illustrations some very beautiful medieval miniatures depicting the six days of Creation, painted in spherical shapes and with symbolic images extraordinarily reminiscent of the complex processes that take place within the mother's womb during the first six stages of embryonic development.

On the sixth day come those momentous words: 'So God created man in his own image, in the image of God created he him; male and female created he them'; meanwhile the first phase of embryonic development culminates at the sixth stage with the appearance of the embryonic disc – that minute entity which will become the human body.

Thomas went on to suggest that each one of us, during our first three weeks of life, goes through and relives the creation of the entire cosmos as described symbolically in Genesis: 'and only when we have recreated these great images of Creation do we step out into our own becoming, into our own body towards our birth.'

In fact it was the 19th-century German biologist, Ernst Haeckel, an enthusiastic adherent of Darwin's theories, who introduced the idea of evolution into embryology. In his book *Embryogenesis in Myth and Science*, Thomas Weihs describes how Haeckel took up some earlier theories of recapitulation and formulated the 'fundamental biogenic law': that ontogeny, which is the embryonic development of the individual, is a recapitulation of phylogeny, which is the evolution of the species as a whole.

In our film Thomas went on to speak about the description of a conception and birth that has played a tremendous part in the history of mankind over the past two thousand years. The birth of Jesus, he said, is described in a very strange way that seems profoundly contradictory. On the one had the Bible describes the fatherhood of Joseph and stresses the genealogy by citing all the ancestors of Joseph right back to Abraham. Yet at the same time it denies that Joseph is the father of Jesus, who is 'conceived by the Holy Spirit' and 'born of a virgin'. And the Holy Spirit, Thomas reminded us, appears on two other occasions in the story. At the baptism in the river Jordan it descends upon Jesus in the form of a white dove, so that Jesus leaves the Jordan as the bearer of the Christ. The third appearance is when the twelve apostles are gathered together at Pentecost, and through the inspiration of the Holy Spirit experience their own independence, dignity and power to communicate.

We might, suggested Thomas, consider that the description of the birth of Jesus is a description of human birth in its totality: that every human birth has these two aspects – the genetic, biological aspect carried by the hereditary streams of father and mother; and the other, the spiritual aspect, as symbolised by the Holy Spirit. We know, he said, that the word 'conception' has these two meanings – to conceive biologically, but also to conceive an idea mentally, spiritually.

He then pointed out how in our time we have tended to lose awareness of meaning, because our pursuit of the investigation of causes has become so infinitely successful and absorbing, allowing us to change and transform the world. But there is also another task, he suggested: namely to change and transform ourselves. And for that, he hoped, the spiritual aspect of conception – the story of the stork – will become meaningful again.

'Nobody ever believed,' he said, 'also no child ever believed, that this story was a causative, scientific explanation of birth.' What he then tried to convey in conclusion was that the legend of the stork, which features in many different cultures, was nothing less than a way of conveying the truth of our divine origin. In the story of the birth of Jesus, therefore, the innermost secret of each human birth is revealed, for every mother receives her child from the Holy Spirit – as symbolised by the dove, a white-winged bird like the stork. Every birth is thus a virgin birth if contemplated from a spiritual perspective.

In her book *A Short History of Myth*, Karen Armstrong writes: 'A myth was an event which, in some sense, had happened once, but which also happened all the time'. She goes on to point out that mythology 'points beyond history to what is timeless in human existence, helping us to get beyond the chaotic flux of random events, and glimpse the core of reality'.

For Thomas Weihs myth and science were not telling contradictory stories, but complementary ones. 'Myth is a fiction that gives us the truth' is something I wrote into my notebook many years ago. As a medical doctor and for several years a farmer, Thomas knew and valued the here and now. But he also knew that the fundamental truths of existence that sustain and inspire our daily life have periodically to be re-experienced and re-expressed in the light of our evolving consciousness. In the introduction to his book he wrote:

> What this book hopes to convey is that scientific theories, while divesting themselves of moral and ethical burdens and thus offering only tools, often open up new phenomena which can become the starting-points for fresh elucidations of ancient mythos or also initiate completely new symbolic and mythical insights. Thus science and mythos are not seen as contradictions, but as creative polarities, as male and female in nature.

Both Jung and Steiner shared the belief that myth and science are not pulling in opposite directions, giving us contradictory insights into reality. Plato himself spoke of mythos and logos as two ways of arriving at truth, each with their own sphere of competence.

For much of my life I have inclined towards myth and stories for nourishment and insight; though I remember very well the excitement, aged ten, of being given a chemistry set for Christmas. But not much happened after that – unlike my son, Thomas, who took delight in making explosions in the garden throughout his childhood. At school I liked history and literature, and later studied French and German. Only as my quest and questions deepened did I increasingly turn to science – or rather to a scientific mode of thinking – as a balance to my delight in the power of the imagination. Thomas Weihs's phrase 'creative polarities' is an excellent description of what I now feel about these two ways of knowing.

If, however, we allow these two paths to converge, problems of a new sort start to emerge. Both Jung and Steiner, although they never gave up on the empirical method, increasingly came up against the inadequacy of our everyday language to describe their experiences and research. Some contemporary biologists and physicists encounter the same difficulties. The phenomena themselves seem to demand a new way of thinking and therefore new words – almost a transcendental approach, hence Jung's frequent use of the word 'numinous'.

Some of what both men said and wrote does indeed hark back to ancient mythological insights, as well as evoking a picture of quite new ones. Jung's experience of the figure he called Philemon is a good example. Steiner spoke a great deal about the spiritual hierarchies as first described by Dionysius around 500 AD. These days cherubim and seraphim are occasionally sung about in church but nobody tends to give them much thought. However, if their existence was at one time acknowledged as the result of direct experience, then it would seem reasonable to assume that they exist in some form still. And if they, like us, are also evolving, then we shall not only need descriptions that speak helpfully and convincingly to our contemporary consciousness, but first and foremost actual experiences ourselves of what these entities or beings are in reality.

In *The Secret History of the World*, Jonathan Black writes: 'Esoteric philosophy calls for a rediscovery of the spiritual hierarchies ranged above us, and, intimately connected with that, a discovery of the divine capabilities ranged within us'. Perhaps that's the clue. These beings now exist, and maybe always did exist, as potential in each one of us. My ideals are certainly a reality, but the ultimate nature of that reality is a mystery – so why not call it an angel?

In Gerhard Wehr's book on Jung and Steiner, he writes that the traditional concept of reality became obsolete for Jung; it did not suffice any longer. He considered science's worldview to be as limited in its one-sidedness as western humanity itself. Clearly both Jung and Steiner were negotiating a threshold beyond which there is a need for a different way of knowing. In *Modern Man in Search of a Soul* Jung makes an interesting reference to this new way: 'Great innovations never come from above; they come invariably from below; just as trees never grow from the sky downward, but upward from the earth, however true it is that their seeds have fallen from above.' He goes on to point out that less sophisticated, less educated people are often the ones who are more open to unconscious forces within the human psyche. He calls them 'the much derided, silent folk of the land – those who are less infected with academic prejudices than great celebrities are wont to be'.

Wehr makes many other interesting and important points in his book not only about the similarities between Jung and Steiner, but also their differences. Whereas it was clearly the mission of both men to explore the world of the invisible, Jung undoubtedly preferred the intuitive approach. From Jung's standpoint, Steiner overvalued the rational function of thinking, though Steiner's understanding of thinking went way beyond mere brain activity. In fact, despite the powerful influence of intellectual giants such as Hegel, Steiner was enormously influenced by Goethe's emphasis on the importance of an intuitive experience of the intrinsic ideas underlying the phenomena of nature – in other words the 'archetypes'. For example, Goethe described what he called the *Urpflanze* – the archetypal essence of all plant life which can only be experienced through a more meditative approach. When Schiller objected that this was only 'an idea' Goethe replied that if so, it was an idea he perceived as tangible reality, a real driving force at work in nature. Knowledge acquired in this way relies on a certain openness that lives more strongly in our feminine sensibility, in contrast to our masculine instinct to dissect and analyse.

In his book *Goethe on Science*, Jeremy Naydler writes: 'Goethe was convinced that a contemplative observation of qualities and form in nature encountered directly, even naively, is sufficient basis for an awareness of the non-material formative forces and organisational principles which underlie them to arise.' This other dimension of existence, continues Naydler, cannot be penetrated by instruments that are sensitive only to what is material, nor by the abstract concepts that tend to accompany their use: 'This is why the human being, contemplating natural phenomena with alert senses and an open mind, is potentially a more powerful and exact instrument than any piece of specialized scientific equipment.'

One of the exercises that Steiner suggests to enhance this faculty to know experientially involves quietly contemplating the seed of a plant. Firstly we are encouraged to reflect for some time on what the eyes are seeing. Then can come the thought: 'Out of this seed, if planted in the soil, there will grow a plant of complex structure.' Visualise this plant in your imagination. 'What I am now picturing in my imagination', he continues, 'will later be drawn out of the seed by the forces of the earth and the light. If I had before me an artificial object which imitated the seed to such a deceptive degree that my eyes could not distinguish it from a real seed, no forces of the earth or light could call forth a plant from it.' As this starts to become an inner experience, thought and feeling unite in the realisation that:

all that will ultimately grow out of the seed is already secretly enfolded within it as the 'force' of the whole plant. In the artificial imitation of the seed no such force is present. And yet to my eyes both appear alike. The real seed therefore contains something invisible which is not present in the imitation ... This invisible something will presently transform itself into the visible plant which I shall have before me in shape and colour.

Hold onto the thought, says Steiner, that 'the invisible will become visible. If I could not think, then that which will become visible only later, could not already announce its presence to me.'

In an article on Goethe in *Resurgence* in the summer of 2006, the biologist Brian Goodwin, formerly professor of biology at the Open University and now scholar in residence at Schumacher College in Devon, writes:

In his studies, Goethe brought into the observation of natural form the heart and eye of a poet in allowing his intuition to speak to him about the transformations he saw taking place. He was highly attentive to the processes whereby leaves or anatomical structures came into being in a plant or animal embryo, and experienced them in their dynamic wholeness and relationships. In this and in his study of colour he became convinced that he was taking science in a significantly new direction.

This potentially new direction in science had its roots in the Romantic movement of the 18th and 19th centuries, of which Isaiah Berlin in *The Roots of Romanticism* writes: 'By the 1820s you find an outlook in which the state of mind, the motive, is more important than the consequence, the intention is more important than the effect.' He goes on to mention 'purity of heart, integrity, devotion, dedication' – sensibilities which these days we not only admire, but almost take for granted – as being first nurtured among those who followed in the footsteps of giants such as Goethe.

'In England', writes Goodwin, 'poets such as Blake, then Wordsworth, Coleridge, Keats and Shelley were part of this movement, developing their view of human nature in which thought and feeling are equal contributors to the expression of human knowledge and experience'. Thus the stork can become as real and important as the midwife – two sides of the same miracle.

Goodwin goes on to point out how the Romantic movement was a natural reaction to the scientific rationalism of the Enlightenment, which had developed from the work and writings of Galileo and Descartes in the 17th century, and which took the view that the only way of gaining reliable knowledge about nature was the objective method, systematically excluding feelings or subjective insight. 'By the 18th century', he writes, 'this method took on the characteristics of a specialised discipline that depended on a separation of the observer from what is observed so that personal qualities do not influence the knowledge gained from experiment.'

This method has, of course, been proved to work extremely well, particularly in the realm of Newtonian physics, and in the study of chemistry, electricity and magnetism. Without doubt, says Goodwin, science provides us with highly useful and reliable knowledge. The phenomenon of life itself, however, remains a very deep mystery. The problem, for example, with dissecting a dead mouse in order to understand it, is that it has ceased to be a mouse. As Mephistopheles, in Goethe's *Faust*, explains so clearly:

> He who seeks knowledge of living things
> First tried to drive out spirit's wings;
> In his hands the separate parts lie dead –
> Unjoined, alas, by spirit's living thread.

Goethe, however, was also aware of the danger of subjectivity when he wrote, 'The senses do not deceive; the judgement deceives.' It has taken nearly two hundred years for the scientific community to begin to catch up with Goethe, says Goodwin in his article: 'What he explored in his scientific studies was a method of observation that was holistic in two senses; the whole person is involved in the work; and the whole set of possibilities presented by the phenomena is understood as a totality.'

In considering the work of the two great pioneers Jung and Steiner, it is important to remember that Jung's depth psychology is primarily aimed at therapy. Jung was a doctor, and as such his mission was to heal. To do this effectively he knew that a greater understanding of the human being was necessary. Steiner's anthroposophy is in essence about knowledge – which is then applied to the tasks of daily life, including healing. It is also a knowledge that is strongly dependant on our capacity for self-knowledge and the enhancement of our latent capacities to know more, not just intuitively, but in full consciousness. And to arrive at knowledge in its fullest sense – in the light of what Schumacher called the great truth of 'adaequatio' – there must be a correspondence between our organ of perception and the object we are perceiving. 'How do you explain or describe colour to a blind person?' is the example often quoted to illustrate this point. If our task is, in Steiner's words, 'to awaken the spiritual in the human being to the spiritual in the universe', the implication is that we will gradually arrive at the most profound and sublime correspondence of all: 'So God created man in his own image, in the image of God created He him; male and female created He them.'

In comparing Steiner's and Jung's biographies, Wehr draws attention to the fact that destiny placed each man into a movement that prepared him for his ultimate life mission. For Steiner it was the Theosophical Society of H.P. Blavatsky and Annie Besant; for Jung, it was Freud's Psychoanalytic Association. These movements gave each man a platform from which he could announce the results of his research to interested individuals. Within a very short time Jung and Steiner were each given leading positions. Ultimately, however – having made their respective breaks – neither left any doubt about the provisional and unfinished character of their work. For this reason, writes Wehr, both Steiner and Jung emphatically distanced themselves from any dogmatic interpretation of their insights. Their teachings were not to be taken on authority; both men encouraged personal experience. Ultimately it is far better, and certainly healthier to arrive at one's own insights, however modest they may be. In one of his early publications the French writer, André Gide, exhorts a fictional disciple to burn all the books 'in the fire of his own experience'. And William Blake, that source of endless wisdom, wrote: 'No bird soars too high, if he soars with his own wings.'

What is very apparent in studying Jung and Steiner, however, is the different tone and style in which they spoke and wrote about their work. Jung is on the whole tentative and modest, particularly so in old age. From Steiner comes a certainty that for some people smacks of dogmatism, the very attitude he implored his followers to avoid. We are simply not used to people speaking in such precise detail about the great mysteries of existence – not least our own place in the scheme of things. But Steiner would say that he was speaking as a scientist. He had researched and verified his findings. We don't dismiss the work of an astrophysicist or a microbiologist simply because we are out of our depth. But their fellow scientists will, of course, ask awkward questions, and quite rightly so.

As yet in the anthroposophical movement – despite the fine work being done all over the world on farms, in hospitals and schools, and in people's own personal lives – there have not emerged, as far as I am aware, men and women who have sufficiently developed the faculties of which Steiner speaks to question or verify his research. Meanwhile for me, and I'm sure for many others, what I like to think of as simple common sense has helped me to keep an open mind. If Steiner does represent a significant shift in our human capacity to 'see' more, then in evolutionary terms it is still early days.

Towards the end of his life, in what he called his *Leading Thoughts*, Steiner again addressed the question of the limits to knowledge derived from sense impressions. He suggested that if we observe carefully how we become conscious of these limits, we would find in that consciousness the faculties to transcend them:

The fish swims up to the limits of the water. It must return because it lacks the physical organs to live outside this element. Man reaches the limit of the knowledge attainable by sense-perception: but he can recognise that on the way to this point powers of soul have risen in him – powers whereby the soul can live in an element that goes beyond the horizon of the senses.

In response to a similar statement by Steiner – 'The capacities by which we can attain insights into higher worlds lie dormant within each one of us' – Wehr makes this remark: 'This basic statement may certainly be correct, since it refers to the inherent human ability for inner development. But practical experience shows that only psychologically stable individuals should attempt this path.' This seems to me an extremely important observation and prompts me to repeat those lines by Edmund Spenser:

Once a man has missed the way
The further he doth go
The further he doth stray.

In his foreword to Wehr's book, the author and psychotherapist Robert Sardello goes even further by suggesting that without Jung, anthroposophy is in danger of becoming 'the dogmatic application of the ideas of a remarkable individual without inner understanding ... Steiner shows us much concerning the ways of the soul, but then there is the problem of living them. This can only be done by finding the way into the interior of the soul, which is Jung's forte.' Sardello is also critical of the fact that a lot of anthroposophical training goes on without any guidance in inner soul work, with no recognition of the importance of depth psychology, and almost no guidance in the meditative work recommended by Steiner (though this is now changing through the work of Arthur Zajonc and others). Sardello also emphasises that unless the endeavours of both Jung and Steiner are seen as quests rather than answers, 'each of these two very strong conceptions of the human future is bound to gather dogmatic disciples'.

In the very first page of his book, Wehr describes the problems that invariably arise both during the lifetime and then in the wake of a strong and charismatic teacher:

A circle of pupils as well as a group of opponents form. All too often, it is detrimental to the further development of the founder's original intentions when there is a group of uncritical admirers who swear by every word the 'master' has uttered – detrimental because others draw the wrong conclusions about the original achievement of the personality whose cause these people claim to represent.

In my experience there are many people who are trying to work creatively with Steiner's legacy, treating his statements not as instructions, but as the suggestions and indications they were meant to be. However there are some, inevitably, who remain dazzled by Steiner and have little interest in looking at anthroposophy in a wider context – a narrow-mindedness that sometimes gives the movement its cultish image.

Fully aware of this danger in his own field of work, Jung once wrote in a letter: 'It will be a task for my successors to systematically work up and clarify many of my thoughts that I only jotted down. Without such work there will be no progress in the science of analytical psychology.' And at a lecture Steiner gave in Vienna in 1922, three years before his death, he said: 'My hope is that more and more people who are able to build the necessary bridges will come forward from the circle of our friends.'

It will be clear from what I have written that I feel, as does Sardello, that a very important and helpful bridge needs to be built between the work of Jung and Steiner. In fact from Dallas in the USA Sardello has already helped pioneer a 'spiritual psychology' that aims to be a creative synthesis of depth psychology and anthroposophy, in which inner soul work is seen as a necessary preliminary to any kind of spiritual work. 'Preliminary', he writes, 'here is meant as something akin to doing warm-up exercises, as, for example, done by a musician. You can be a very advanced musician, but you cannot do away with finger exercises.'

There is one final point I want to mention in relation to the work of these two great 'scientists of the invisible'. I am often asked to what extent each man was aware of the other. Steiner died before Jung had really established himself after his break with Freud and therefore did not live long enough to see the really pioneering discoveries of analytical psychology. His few rather spiky remarks about psychoanalysis were aimed more in Freud's direction. Jung on the other hand was, I gather, suspicious of the almost religious aura which at that time hovered over Dornach, Steiner's base in Switzerland, and over the Anthroposophical Society that he left behind. I think he had a point, and the danger still exists – though the same kind of uncritical adulation can also be found in some Jungian circles. In Dornach, and in anthroposophical institutions and communities elsewhere, efforts are increasingly being made to change this somewhat sectarian image. Meanwhile Jung's ideas and his name have percolated into our culture to a far greater extent than Steiner's anthroposophy. Nevertheless, because of the advice and indications that Steiner gave to doctors, farmers and educationalists in particular, his influence is also being increasingly acknowledged and appreciated.

Perhaps in the end both men, with their own unique missions, like two vast liners at sea, needed to keep a certain distance from one another. Wehr suggests that the enigma of great figures in the history of the mind – if they are contemporaries – is that they are often able thoroughly and correctly to diagnose the times they live in, but fail to appreciate the significance of someone they may see as a competitor: 'It is not unusual', he writes, 'for personalities to live as if they had nothing in common, even though they might have complemented each other, could perhaps even have corrected and inspired each other in the pursuit of a common goal'.

It is also not uncommon for related ideas to lie hidden behind different terminologies. Signposts like 'ego', 'self', 'anima' and 'astral body' – and indeed 'stork' – are all in the end just fingers pointing at the moon; simply words, but words that can nevertheless be of help, some to you, some to me. But let's not lose sight of the moon itself as we stumble along the bumpy road, sometimes hand in hand, but finally and inevitably alone.

CHAPTER 15

No Language but a Cry

One way of keeping my head above water in my quest has been to re-immerse myself continually in what I recognise as my essential Englishness – pragmatism, an appreciation of understatement, and above all humour, especially in relation to the sort of profound questions I am addressing in this book. A nice example of such humour was a statement made by the late Archbishop of Canterbury, Robert Runcie, when he compared the Church to a swimming pool: 'All the splashing goes on at the shallow end.' It is the subject of religion that I want primarily to look at in this chapter – or at what John Betjeman called 'our search for God', in that letter he wrote to me when I was a young man searching for direction in my life.

One of Betjeman's favourite words was 'heavenly'. He'd use it about people he was particularly fond of. He certainly never used words like 'anima' or 'astral body', but nor would he be dismissive of people like me who find such signposts helpful. In his company I rested from philosophising and relished instead the more tentative insights that poetry can convey – intimations that were nonetheless meaningful and relevant to the questions I was asking. Everyday life was also constantly confirming, in small yet significant ways, the profound truths I had been exploring in India, Russia and in the German-speaking world on my own doorstep.

What some people call the divine was for Betjeman, and many like him, intimately interwoven with what we experience as daily life. In a film we made together in London called *Thank God it's Sunday*, he acknowledged, over a scene of early morning churchgoers, mostly elderly, mostly alone, the comfort that familiarity brings: 'Church remains the same', he wrote,

A reminiscence of the good old days
Our parents lived in and of Sunday roasts.
Church is a change from lonely sitting-rooms.
For rich or poor the aches of age come on.
Church is a chance once more of making friends
And meeting with the Eternal here on earth.

Working with John Betjeman on *Thank God it's Sunday* was, as ever, an enormously enjoyable and enriching experience, and we had a lot of laughs along the way. I filmed at a variety of locations that he and I had visited together, as well as scenes that just happened as we were passing. John then wrote his commentary in verse to the edited film, so that we were able to bring a great deal of spontaneity to both words and images.

It was England and summer, so the early morning sun soon disappeared:

Steady on just and unjust falls the rain
Across the soaking acres of the grass,
Over wet pavements and by dripping boughs
We pilgrims plod to the last shrine of all,
The best attended and the most revered
The Sacred altar of the Sunday press.
What's in? What's out? What's on? We ought to know
For if we don't we won't be thought informed.
Willingly we make offerings at the shrine.

We were in the Earl's Court Road. A newspaper kiosk had caught my eye – and then some road works. I knew what amused Betjeman, and also what infuriated him.

The newest feature of our Sunday streets
On double-time upon the Day of Rest
The deafening dawn chorus of the drills

We lingered in the parks, observed people queuing for the museums, imagined what others were having for lunch. By late afternoon we were in the West End. It was raining again. A demonstration was taking place against the war in Vietnam. This was 1973, and the march was in earnest:

London today has newer Evensongs
To usher Sunday out; and here they are
The priests processing with the acolytes.
The members have a dedicated look
Of those who think of others than themselves.
The grave churchwardens in their uniform
Pace on and on beside them and before.

The churchwardens Betjeman had spotted in the parade were the police escort. The chant: 'Take the tanks out of Prague – Turn them on Saigon'; and 'Workers of the world unite – One enemy – One fight.'

Hymns and responses are not quite the same
As those we know in church and chapel choir.
Banners are hardly Mother's Union type.
The Saints not mentioned in the Calendars
Of Rome or Canterbury, but concerned
With suffering and injustice to Mankind.
The newer Evensong is one of hope
And generosity and loving care –
Though some prefer the older service still …

The film ended, however, not in a church but on an old barge moored on the Battersea reach of the Thames, and with a guitar rather than an organ to play us out. Ralph McTell was singing *Mrs Adlam's Angels* – a song that very much captured another kind of mood among many young people at that time. The Beatles' interest in Transcendental Meditation was one manifestation of this new openness to spirituality, rather than to religion in a formal sense. McTell's song was a mixture of nostalgia and a sense that there is indeed more than meets the eye:

Sundays as a rule
Us kids went to Sunday school
And Mrs. Adlam said
Angels stood round our beds
Keeping us safe from dark
Right through till day began
And we used to lie awake
Just to try and see one;
Though we never saw one anywhere
We heard them singing softly in the air.

The second part of our film, about the exodus from London on Sundays, opened with Betjeman at Fenchurch Street Station buying a rail ticket to his beloved Southend. Later we went south to Sussex. The closing scene was of the last few overs of a village cricket match, while nearby a trail of cars, nose to tail, headed slowly back towards London; past a village church, past a couple on a peaceful evening walk with their noisy pet: 'Now we can take the dog out for a bark.' In the background I ran the sound of a small church congregation singing John Ellerton's beautiful hymn,

The day Thou gavest, Lord, is ended,
The darkness falls at Thy behest;
To Thee our morning hymns ascended,
Thy praise shall sanctify our rest.

The final image of the film, on an almost deserted Sussex beach, was an elderly man wandering alone – it could have been Betjeman himself:

At half past six
Some villagers will go to Evensong
For evening is a time when some of us
Are thinking of the evening of our lives
And of the vastness into which we go
Or nothingness, or of eternal bliss.
Whatever it is, for sure we've got to go
Alone, alone, and time will part us all;
And somehow, somewhere waits the love of God.
Sunday is sad, but Monday's so much worse
For those of us who haven't any hope.
Faith, hope and charity –
Oh, give me hope.

My last production for Religious Programmes was billed as 'Three weeks in the life of a Dorset village as it prepares for Christmas'. We called the series *Away in a Village*. It was filmed at Cerne Abbas in December 1972 and broadcast a year later in three episodes. I remember those three weeks as a very happy and enjoyable experience, thanks largely to the vicar, Hugh Mumford and his wife Margaret. Having travelled a great deal in the last few years, it was lovely to wallow in the pure Englishness of it all – but an Englishness that was not insensitive to the deeper mysteries of life.

One highlight was the Women's Institute production of a play they'd written called *The Three Queens*. Even Joseph had been axed from the cast! It was performed in the church on the Sunday before Christmas in place of the sermon. As the day approached it all became quite tense: at the dress rehearsal, when the producer bellowed at her Mary to 'put more roast-beef into it', I had to hide my giggles by disappearing to the back of the church, leaving my cameraman, John McGlashan, trying to keep his camera steady.

In a sermon that we did film, and in the fine tradition of a warm-up joke, the vicar related his somewhat complicated and obscure Old Testament text to a remark made by the founder of the Salvation Army, General Booth: 'I deal with the difficult parts in the Bible like I deal with a kipper; the bits I can't cope with, I leave on one side!'

Hugh Mumford epitomised all that John Betjeman so loved about the Church of England: he was tolerant, funny and kind, the sort of character that Betjeman light-heartedly celebrates in his poem *Blame the Vicar*:

When things go wrong it's rather tame
To find we are ourselves to blame,
It gets the trouble over quicker
To go and blame things on the Vicar.
The Vicar, after all, is paid
To keep us bright and undismayed.

And so it goes on – the Vicar never swears, he never drinks. He wears his collar the wrong way round, which obliges him to lend out his lawnmower and to sing in tune at Evensong.

For what's a Vicar really for
Except to cheer us up? What's more,
He shouldn't ever, ever tell
If there is such a place as Hell,
For if there is it's certain he
Will go to it as well as we ...

John Betjeman's verse autobiography, *Summoned by Bells*, is full of vicars. To celebrate his seventieth birthday in 1976, I made a film in which he narrated excerpts from the text. One scene describes an early experience of Evensong at the partly ruined church of St Ervan in Cornwall. 'Better come in and have a cup of tea', says the Rector after the Service:

He talked of poetry and Cornish saints;
He kept an apiary and a cow;
He asked me which church service I like best –
I told him Evensong ... 'And I suppose
You think religion's mostly singing hymns
And feeling warm and comfortable inside?'
And he was right: most certainly I did.

Summoned by Bells tells the story of Betjeman's childhood and student years. The Betjeman family had lived in London, in Highgate and later in Chelsea. From the start John was introspective:

An only child, deliciously apart,
Misunderstood and not like other boys,
Deep, dark and pitiful I saw myself
In my mind's mirror, every step I took
A fascinating study to the world.

His father had a small factory making luxury items for shops like Aspreys and Harrods.

> Following in Father's footsteps' was the theme
> Of all my early childhood ...
>   ... for myself,
> I knew as soon as I could read and write
> That I must be a poet. Even today,
> When all the way from Cambridge comes a wind
> To blow the lamps out every time they're lit,
> I know that I must light mine up again.

Guilt is one of the themes that recurs in Betjeman's autobiography – a guilt prompted by far more than having turned his back on the family business, as I myself had done. Jung had noted that very many of his middle-aged and older patients were suffering from the sort of guilt that periodically plagued Betjeman – people who had been deeply touched by Christianity but as a result tended to have a heightened awareness of their own inadequacies and with it the fear of 'such a place as Hell'. In the film I made about Jung's life, Laurens van der Post related something important that Jung had said on this subject: 'It is a great mistake to try and live one's life as an imitation of Christ's life. What is far more important and relevant is to strive to be as true to one's own destiny as Christ was to his.'

Cornwall featured a great deal in John Betjeman's childhood. The family holidayed every year on the north coast, at Trebetherick. In *Summoned by Bells* he vividly evokes a child's excitement at waking up on the first morning by the sea and running down to the beach before breakfast, 'monarch of miles of sand'. Already as a young boy he had a love of exploring, of looking at things and at architecture in particular:

> Dear lanes of Cornwall! With a one-inch map,
> A bicycle and well-worn Little Guide,
> Those were the years I used to ride for miles
> To far-off churches...
> In quest of mystical experience
> I knelt in darkness at St. Enedoc;
> I visited our Holy Well,
> Whereto the native Cornish still resort
> For cures for whooping-cough, and drop bent pins
> Into its peaty water ... Not a sign:
> No mystical experience was vouchsafed:

John Betjeman in Cornwall 1976

The maidenhair just trembled in the wind
And everything looked as it always looked …
But somewhere, somewhere underneath the dunes,
Somewhere among the cairns or in the caves
The Celtic Saints would come to me, the ledge
Of time we walk on, like a thin cliff-path
High in the mist, would show the precipice.

John Betjeman at Blisland Church

It's noticeable how often the word 'safe' crops up in *Summoned by Bells*. For me it is an indication of the vulnerability that made Betjeman such a wonderful poet and such a sensitive companion:

> Safe were those evenings of the pre-war world
> When firelight shone on green linoleum;
> I heard the church bells hollowing out the sky,
> Deep beyond deep, like never-ending stars,
> And turned to Archibald, my safe old bear,
> Whose woollen eyes looked sad or glad at me,
> Whose ample forehead I could wet with tears,
> Whose half-moon ears received my confidence,
> Who made me laugh, who never let me down.
> I used to wait for hours to see him move,
> Convinced that he could breathe...

And of his childhood home in Highgate:

> Safe, in a world of trains and buttered toast
> Where things inanimate could feel and think,
> Deeply I loved thee, 31 West Hill!

And finally, 'Safe Cornish holidays before the storm'. The storm was boarding school: first a Prep school in Oxford and then Marlborough College in Wiltshire, which he hated. Oxford came as a liberation:

> Privacy after years of public school;
> Dignity after years of none at all –
> First college rooms, a kingdom of my own:
> What words of mine can tell my gratitude?

One of the most amusing memories I have of working on *Summoned by Bells* is of filming in Oxford, at Betjeman's old college, Magdalen. It was a warm and sunny spring day, and the whole place was looking magnificent. We'd been shooting several takes of him walking round one of the quads that was draped in beautiful purple wisteria. Inevitably when you're filming people will come up and ask you questions. On that afternoon a group of American tourists descended on a hot and tired poet and asked him what we were doing. Politely and without the hint of a smile Betjeman replied, 'We're making a film about wisteria.' The Americans were quite happy with this, and went away to photograph the wisteria themselves. We were free to do yet another take.

Writing of his Oxford days Betjeman pays a special tribute to Maurice Bowra, the Warden of Wadham College. It was in his company that he learned to love the poetry of Alfred Tennyson, Thomas Hardy and Rudyard Kipling; from Bowra he learned, too, that wisdom was –

> Not memory tests (as I had long supposed)
> Not 'first-class brains' and swotting for exams,
> But humble love for what we sought and knew.

With equal love he describes his slow Sunday morning stroll

> ... by crumbling walls, and echoing lanes ...
> To worship at High Mass in Pusey House ...
> Some know for all their lives that Christ is God,
> Some start upon that arduous love affair
> In clouds of doubt and argument; and some
> (My closest friends) seem not to want His love –
> And why this is I wish to God I knew.
> As at the Dragon School, so still for me
> The steps to truth were made by sculptured stone,
> Stained glass and vestments, holy-water stoups,
> Incense and crossings of myself – the things
> That hearty middle-stumpers most despise
> As 'all the inessentials of the Faith.'

For John Betjeman, as for many people, religious ritual and the symbols that accompany that ritual were both helpful and meaningful. I, myself, have found them less so, though I did value and appreciate the routine of chapel and evening prayers at school. However I do understand and certainly respect this need that some people have to kneel, to sing and chant and, above all, to pray together. At times I still feel envious and even slightly guilty that I find communal prayer or group meditation so difficult.

That phrase of Betjeman's, 'all the inessentials of the faith', was an acknowledgement of a commonly held view these days that religion should manifest as deeds rather than ritual – a view that was summed up already in the 18th century by Thomas Paine with the words: 'The world is my country and my religion is to do good.' I am certainly in sympathy with that sentiment, and would even go as far as to say that without such an attitude any religious or philosophical search is on weak or even dangerous ground. Prompted by the opening line of the Lord's Prayer, Rudolf Steiner expressed in a verse somewhat the same sentiment as Thomas Paine, but without leaving out the notion of God: 'Thy kingdom expand itself in our deeds and in the conduct of our lives.'

Perhaps what is important, ultimately – whether in the company of others in a church, mosque, temple or synagogue, or simply in the privacy of one's own room or on some mountain top – is to acknowledge in true humility and as often as possible the mysterious and magnificent universe that we inhabit, and the creative wisdom we encounter wherever we look. And what we actually believe – whether expressed poetically, philosophically or simply on our knees – seems to me ultimately less significant than how we live our lives from day to day.

My rather simple summary of what I feel to be important still skirts around the thorny question of God. The scientist and author Lyall Watson once remarked that 'if the brain were so simple we could understand it, we would be so simple we couldn't.' It seems to me you could just as well substitute the word 'brain' for 'God'. For the Bulgarian mystic and spiritual teacher, Peter Deunov, the simple fact that human beings are capable of loving implied the existence of God.

John Betjeman's frequent references to 'the Management' tally with my own sense of gods rather than one supreme being. What is not generally known is that the word Elohim, translated as God in the first chapter of Genesis – 'In the beginning God made heaven and earth' – is in fact plural. The ususal rendering is therefore already a form of spiritual reductionism.

My main problem with the word 'God' however – particularly as expressed in the question: 'Do you believe in God?' – is the implication that there is one being, albeit infinitely wiser and better than us, who is somehow in charge. In fact I believe that this simplification in the use of the word 'God' is what increasingly puts people off religion. For me it might help if we stopped using the word 'he' – not that 'she' would be any better. Likewise, although Jesus was clearly a man and a Jew, when we refer to 'Christ' we are, I believe, touching on a cosmic reality that transcends all human categories of gender and race. Personally I am drawn to a thought expressed by the theologian Paul Tillich: 'God is Being itself, not a supreme transcendent Being.' In *The Shaking of the Foundations* Tillich writes: 'you must forget everything traditional that you have learned about God, perhaps even that word itself.'

John Robinson, in his controversial book *Honest to God*, published in 1963 while he was Bishop of Woolwich, doesn't go quite as far as Tillich, but he certainly questions the notion not only of a God 'up there', but also of one simply 'out there' in the everyday world around us; for suppose, he writes, 'such a Super-Being "out there" is really only a sophisticated version of the Old Man in the sky?'

Robinson quotes the German theologian and Lutheran pastor Dietrich Bonhoeffer's response to what seems for many as the increasing irrelevance and diminishing credibility of such a supreme entity. For Bonhoeffer, God

– despite being elbowed out of every other sphere – has 'a last secret place' in the private world of the individual's need.

What is increasingly evident in this theological debate, however, is that more and more people are left dissatisfied by revelation, of whatever sort, that seems fixed in stone. Cardinal Thomas Winning, in a television documentary in March 2001, said: 'We haven't the authority to change the message.' For me that is a devastating remark. Clearly, however, the appeal of 'certainty', not only among Christian and Muslim fundamentalists, but also among scientific fundamentalists like Richard Dawkins, is still very strong. Perhaps such intransigence from religious communities springs primarily from a certain insecurity and fear – fear not only of being marginalized, but of being obliterated altogether.

The Chief Rabbi in Britain, Jonathan Sacks, upset the orthodox Jewish Community with this sentence that was finally omitted from his courageous book, *Dignity of Difference*:

> God has spoken to Mankind in many languages, through Judaism to the Jews, Christianity to Christians, Islam to Muslims … no one creed has a monopoly of spiritual truth … In heaven there is truth; on earth there are truths. God is greater than religion. He is only partially comprehended by any faith.

Perhaps people's descriptions of the gods tend to tell us much more about them than about the gods. Yet Goethe believed that 'as the eye is formed by light to be the instrument by which light is perceived, so are Men formed by God to be the instruments which perceive God'. A hundred years earlier, however, another poet Alexander Pope wrote:

> Know then thyself, presume not God to scan;
> The proper study of mankind is man.

The quotation I like best on this subject, because it is funny as well as profound, is by the journalist John Diamond: 'I describe myself as a Jewish agnostic. I would say atheist, but I don't want to upset God!'

Karen Armstrong, in her book *The History of God* – described by one critic as 'the most fascinating and learned study of the biggest wild goose chase in history' – tackles all these questions and many more in thorough and illuminating detail. The chapters that particularly interest me are entitled 'The Death of God?' and 'Has God a Future?' Throughout history, Armstrong suggests, people have discarded a conception of God when it no longer works for them. Friedrich Nietzsche's pronouncement in 1882 that 'God is dead' signalled one such turning point. He realised, says Armstrong, that there had been a radical shift in the consciousness of the West that would make it increasingly difficult to believe in the phenomenon most people described as God.

Sigmund Freud, likewise, regarded belief in God as an illusion that mature men and women should lay aside. In her analysis of Freud's position, Armstrong writes:

> The idea of God was not a lie but a device of the unconscious which needed to be decoded by psychology. A personal God was nothing more than an exalted father figure: desire for such a deity sprang from infantile yearnings for a powerful, protective father, for justice and fairness and for life to go on forever. God is simply a projection of these desires, feared and worshipped by human beings out of an abiding sense of helplessness. Religion belonged to the infancy of the human race; it had been a necessary stage in the transition from childhood to maturity.

Armstrong goes on to point out that not all psychoanalysts agreed with Freud's view of God. Jung's God, for example, was similar to the God of the mystics, a psychological truth, subjectively experienced by each individual in the way described by Tillich.

For others the pain that this shift in consciousness caused is exemplified for Armstrong already back in the 19th century, in Tennyson's *In Memoriam*, which she calls the great Victorian poem of doubt. It was published nine years before the publication of Darwin's *On the Origin of Species*, but already the poet felt his faith crumbling and himself reduced to:

> An infant crying in the night;
> An infant crying for the light
> And with no language but a cry.

In more recent times, Karen Armstrong highlights, through the experience of European Jews, this increasing difficulty to believe in a personal God:

> If this God is omnipotent, he could have prevented the holocaust. If he was unable to stop it, he is impotent and useless; if he could have stopped it and chose not to, he is a monster. Jews are not the only people who believe the holocaust put an end to conventional theology.

In considering whether God does indeed have a future, Armstrong goes on to write about the French philosopher Jean-Paul Sartre – who spoke of the

'God-shaped hole' in human consciousness – and about the radical theologians of the sixties who enthusiastically welcomed Nietzsche's declaration that God was dead, thus freeing us from slavery to a tyrannical deity. For Armstrong herself 'the death of God represented the silence that was necessary before God could become meaningful again. All our old conceptions of divinity had to die, before theology could be reborn.'

Thus, during the second half of the 20th century there has, as Karen Armstrong points out, been a move away from the idea of a personal God who behaves like a larger version of us. She mentions Martin Buber who recognised, like many others, something potentially meaningful in the human experience of alienation; and Don Cupitt, Dean of Emmanuel College, Cambridge – dubbed 'the atheist priest' – who proposes a form of Christian Buddhism which puts religious experience before theology. She concludes her book by saying: 'Human beings cannot endure emptiness and desolation; they will fill the vacuum by creating a new focus of meaning.' But then she warns: 'The idols of fundamentalism are not good substitutes for God.' In other words beware of certainty.

John Betjeman himself was too honest and too intelligent to be seduced by certainty – religious or otherwise; honest enough to acknowledge, alongside his faith, his fragility and fear, and therefore to admit – as he watched that lone man on the beach at the end of our film – that he could only 'hope' that 'somehow, somewhere waits the love of God'. As a child, 'no mystical experience was vouchsafed' at that Cornish holy well. Instead he was sustained throughout his life, I suspect, by what Maurice Bowra taught him as an undergraduate at Oxford: that wisdom was 'humble love for what we sought and knew'.

I'm not sure what Betjeman would have made of a statement by the German scholar Manfred Schmidt-Brabant, a man much influenced by Steiner's work:

The religions must make themselves superfluous, it is sometimes said, not in order to get rid of religion, but so that all life becomes an altar, all human encounter becomes sacramental, all human existence is 'ecclesia spiritualis' – a holy gathering.

It's a thought that does, in fact, echo some of Betjeman's utterances, like the line in our film about 'meeting the eternal here on earth'; and indeed his reaction to those rather militant demonstrators marching through London in the seventies – 'the newer Evensong is one of hope, and generosity and loving care'. He liked Ralph McTell's picture of angels tangled up in Mrs. Adlam's hair. His encounter with the American tourists in Oxford may not have been exactly 'sacramental', but life for him was certainly an altar of sorts – an altar at which humour is, I believe, one of our sublime offerings. He certainly knew and endured the silence that may be necessary 'before God can become meaningful again'. What he was less inclined to do temperamentally was to ponder deeply and, in a sense philosophically, on what might be potentially meaningful in the human experience of alienation, though like most of us he experienced aspects of that alienation and suffered accordingly.

The relationship that many people have to religion these days was perceptively described by the present Archbishop of Canterbury, Rowan Williams, in a lecture at Leicester Cathedral in March 2009, in which he stated his belief that we are now living in a society that is neither secular nor deeply religious. 'I believe', he said, 'we are living in a country that is uncomfortably haunted by the memory of religion and doesn't quite know what to do with it.'

As we edge forward – if forward it is – our initial experience is often one of loss, alienation and loneliness, rather than liberation. Consciousness is, I sense, both the culprit and the key to our present predicament; and it is this subject of alienation and consciousness that I will attempt to address in the next chapter – prompted by my encounter with the mythology of the bushmen in southern Africa, in the company of Laurens van der Post.

John Betjeman at Trebetherick

CHAPTER 16

Free to Love

I have always regretted that I didn't travel to South Africa by ship, on the old Cunard Line to Cape Town, as Laurens van der Post suggested. Now the service no longer exists. Then, because of our absurd tendency to cram far too much into our lives, I found myself without enough time. Instead I went by plane and just saw a few clouds. Nevertheless once there, I was able to slow down and enjoy the magnificent sights and sounds of the African bush, and in the company of someone who knew it intimately.

Our task in the autumn of 1973 was to make a film about the mythology of the bushmen, a people about whom Laurens had written so lovingly in *Venture into the Interior*, *The Lost World of the Kalahari* and *Heart of the Hunter*. His own childhood was spent on a farm in the Transvaal and although he now lived in Britain, he returned at least once a year to breathe the African air and, incidentally, to help chip away at the pernicious system of apartheid.

Our film was for the long-running BBC2 series *The World About Us*. In those days there were many such regular and thoughtful series, very few of which have survived. *Yesterday's Witness* tapped into the memories of old people; *Man Alive* probed at the sharp end of contemporary life; *Omnibus* and *Arena* looked at the arts, *Horizon* and *Tomorrow's World* at science and technology, *Everyman* at religion and *Chronicle* at history and archaeology; *One Pair of Eyes* was a slot for interesting and often

Laurens Van der Post with bushman

eccentric people to explore a theme about which they cared passionately; and then there was *Forty Minutes*, a wonderful space for idiosyncratic and quirky documentaries that celebrated life in all its manifold garb. On top of all this was *The Tuesday Documentary* on BBC1 that attracted large audiences and which is a sad reminder that once upon a time the BBC respected to a far greater extent the intelligence of its television audience and their wish to be educated and informed as well as entertained.

In relating some of the bushman stories, Laurens wanted to show how for the bushmen – and indeed, once upon a time, for all of us – nature was like a mirror in which we learned to recognise aspects of our own make-up, both physical and psychological: a lesson that is, I believe, far from over. Above all, it was through the diversity of animal life and behaviour that these insights were experienced by the bushmen. Indeed we still talk about someone being as cunning as a fox, as wise as an owl, as strong as a lion or as obstinate as a mule. It is, in one way, an obvious example of the microcosm/macrocosm theme that I am exploring in this book – a theme that throws significant light on the polarity that exists between what we call 'heaven' and 'earth'. All that surrounds us, at whatever distance, exists also in each one of us. In his opening commentary to the film Laurens quotes the Elizabethan physician, Sir Thomas Browne: 'We carry with us the wonders we seek without: there is all Africa and her prodigies within us.' We called our film *All Africa Within Us*.

Our first base was a camp on the banks of the Limpopo river, near South Africa's border with Mozambique. Two rangers accompanied us to make sure we didn't get bitten, stung, squashed or eaten by the many the creatures that roared, crept, splashed and flew around us day and night. These creatures also watched us, some secretly, some – like the giraffes – with unashamed curiosity. A black mamba slithered silently past as we picnicked on the first day. Later I was told that after one bite you had about thirty seconds to say your goodbyes.

One story that Laurens related in the film, variations of which crop up in many cultures, is about the moon and the hare. In the early days of the earth's existence, the moon looked down and saw that human beings were afraid of dying. It then said to the hare, which was the fastest animal it could find: 'Go tell the people on earth that as I in dying am renewed again, so they in dying will be renewed again.' But the hare, being in too great a hurry, got the message wrong and told the people on earth that unlike the moon, which in dying is renewed again, they in dying would not be renewed again. And the moon was so angry at the hare for getting such a vital message wrong that it struck it on the lip to mark it forever with a split in order to show that it had borne false testimony.

There are endless bushman stories about the huge variety of animals we observed in that peaceful, far-away place at the northernmost corner of the

Kruger Park – stories inspired by an original sense of wonder we may often feel as children, and which Jung experienced so strongly on his visit to Kenya in 1925. There are stories, for example, about the elephant – stories that usually emphasise the danger of excessive size, and the importance of proportion; about the baboons, whose behaviour for the bushmen was a warning about our tendency to over-analyse and intellectualise our experiences; and about the hyena, with its sinister limp, who represented for them the dark, satanic forces in life. The bushmen had a phrase, 'the time of the hyena', which represented a moment in life when the human spirit is invaded by a sense of utter darkness and despair.

Above all, it was the lion that the bushmen held in awe. His formidable array of talents – power, courage, intelligence, tenacity and speed – are never abused. He kills only for food; and although devoted to family, he is ultimately the cat that walks alone. It was an intimation, said Laurens, of our potential to stand on our own two feet and not just be members of a herd, 'to live individually and not collectively'.

The stories that most interested Laurens, however, were those about Mantis, 'a mere stick insect' who presided over the bushmen's whole mythology. Perhaps it is not surprising that a people who were themselves so small in stature should have chosen a praying mantis as their God. 'The bushmen picked on him', said Laurens, as he lay sprawled on the ground at the feet, as it were, of one such bemused insect,

Laurens van der Post with a praying mantis

because he learned from nature that there was nothing so important as the small, and that it was only by giving the utmost reverence to what was apparently insignificant and defenceless that one achieved spiritually what was great and meaningful.

I was reminded of John Betjeman's life-long and touching affection for insects – the smaller the better; for like the bushmen, he knew that despite their size and seeming unimportance they mattered as much as any other living creature. He once wrote to his grandson David telling him why he liked spiders so much: 'They are very good mothers, they have eight legs and are wingless and defenceless. They enjoy jokes and if you talk to them they smile.'

In the early days of the world, according to the bushmen's mythology, it fell to Mantis to give every creature a name: 'Your name shall be Tortoise, and you shall be utterly tortoise to the end of your days.' Another story – a Hottentot legend that Laurens told us as we sat by a river early one morning, with the whole world waking up around us – was about their first great spirit, Heitsi-Eibib, who was killed again and again in the battle for life, but was always resurrected. The Hottentots recognised him as he returned in the reddest of dawns, bleeding from his victorious fight with the powers of darkness, so that all living things could have light on earth.

Towards the end of the film, and over images of old and solitary animals – an elephant, a wildebeest, a rhinoceros – Laurens spoke about Mantis's final message to human beings. In the mythology of the bushmen this humble stick insect taught them not only how best to live in the here and now, but also how to face death and beyond:

> I've always been deeply impressed how the animal towards the end of its life will separate itself from family and herd, not because it is forced to, as many believe, but as if out of some inner necessity – like the Hindu who traditionally in the last quarter of life feels compelled to take to the road alone in search of salvation.

Such a thought brings to mind Tolstoy's tragic yet heroic flight to separate himself from all that he was soon to leave behind. And for the Bushmen, continued Laurens, it was as if Mantis's command to live also as an individual had taught him that faced with death, the final reckoning, too, must be his own.

By now we had travelled several hundred miles west, to the southernmost region of the great Kalahari desert. Laurens called it 'Cinderella Earth' because, despite its arid yet beautiful appearance, it was home to an extraordinary variety of animal and plant life and, of course, to the bushmen themselves. And it was their wisdom and their simple way of life that had so touched him on the exploratory expeditions he made for the British government in the early years after World War II. He concluded his commentary with these words:

> At the end of the African day the first man brought back from nature an answer as full as it was clear. There is living meaning not only in the brief here and now, but also in death and beyond. Outwardly poor and himself rejected by our technological world, he walked rich in his own experience, certain of his significance in the scheme of things; and with a sense of belonging so close that he even spoke of the vultures who presided over his end as 'our sisters the vultures'.

These last words were spoken over a scene of those strangely sinister birds devouring an animal corpse, while in the background lurked a pack of hyenas, waiting restlessly for their turn:

> Unaided, out of his long alliance with nature, man had made of his spirit a fortress of light wherein he lived unafraid of the forces of darkness that the hyena represented; certain that no matter how fiercely they attacked him, the hyena would always retire, defeated again and leaving intact his vision of creation as a process not just of birth, procreation and death, but of life infinitely renewed and renewing.

I will write later about Laurens himself in old age, about our continuing friendship and work together, and about what was written after his death by the hyenas and vultures that plague us still.

Laurens Van der Post in the Kalahari desert

Laurens van der Post, it could be argued, had a somewhat idealised picture of the bushmen – a nostalgia, maybe, for humanity's seemingly innocent past when we lived in harmony with all that surrounds us and knew our place. Such a sentiment is similar to the nostalgia that many of us experience for our childhood and for those moments of intense happiness that Tolstoy wrote about so evocatively in his autobiographical novel *Childhood*, describing a family picnic when even the fish in the pond were happy.

Although I share this nostalgia to a certain extent, as witnessed by my feelings about rural India and about the daily routine in Botton Village, I am not someone who believes that something has gone terribly wrong, either in our own growing up, or in the evolution of the human race. At one stage, I imagine, we all lived like the bushmen that Laurens van der Post met and wrote about. We told similar stories, used the same sort of spears, and knew instinctively that there was more to life than meets the eye.

I don't want either to dismiss or to mock that phase of our evolution, any more than one would mock a baby because it cannot walk or a toddler unable to read or write. Yet whenever I reflect on our simple and primitive past, and the nostalgia that is increasingly and understandably felt for this so-called Golden Age, when human beings apparently lived at one with nature, I can't help thinking of an old radio programme from that wonderful series *Hancock's Half Hour*. Week after week the comedian Tony Hancock played out a tragic and hilarious character who epitomised all our sublime yet hopeless aspirations. In one particular episode Hancock decides to turn his back on the rat race and to go back to nature, to a simpler way of life. His plan is to go and live in nearby Cheam Woods, preferably in a cave. When he gets there he finds that his ridiculous and quirky side-kick, in the person of Kenneth Williams, has got there first and has set up home in a tree. Then it starts to rain; then come the coach-loads of tourists to gape at the Wild Man of the Woods – and so on! It isn't long before Hancock is back in his bedsit.

I tell this story because whenever I contemplate a scenario in which we all still lived in the equivalent of Cheam Woods, in harmony with the rabbits and squirrels and chestnut trees, I realise that in such a situation there would probably be no Tony Hancock. And terrible and destructive as our modern state of alienation is, I nevertheless feel that the world would somehow be a duller and sadder place without the likes of Hancock, Charlie Chaplin and Woody Allen. We human beings, whether we like it or not, are essentially restless and inquisitive creatures who, despite our many sublime creations, inevitably cause a certain amount of havoc and misery. But our ability to laugh at ourselves along the way may be one of our most precious and redeeming gifts. Humour is, after all, a great healer. Ideas tend to divide us; laughter unites us.

Meanwhile we can no more remain in a mystical and largely unconscious participation with nature and the divine than we can, like Peter Pan, cling on to our childhoods. We have to grow up and inevitably lose, in the process, our instinctive sense of awe and wonder. But in doing so we have the profoundly important potential to make choices, including – paradoxically – that of rekindling those original sensibilities with the same consciousness that initially undermines them; hence my optimism about gradually reconnecting with a simpler way of life as envisaged by Gandhi and Tolstoy, and as practised in the Camphill communities. In other words we have freedom, albeit at a very basic stage; but this freedom gives us the possibility to either make a mess of things, or to progress and evolve – for otherwise it is not real freedom.

Some people argue that there is no such thing as altruism and that selfless love is an illusion. (Perhaps the nearest that most of us get to displaying any real altruism is as a parent.) It's certainly true that what we call the Laws of Nature – as exemplified in the phrase 'survival of the fittest' – seem to point in that direction, though it seems reasonable to ask the question: Fit for what? Is our obsession with physical survival a distraction? Could it be that quite other seeds – in which consciousness plays a central role – have been sown in our evolving universe?

Consciousness, however – by its very nature – involves a separation from that of which we are conscious. The first stage is self-awareness – the capacity to stand back from oneself, and thus the birth of what seems like a double life. One sees this process very clearly in the growing child. The problem is how then to move on from a situation where this sense of separation isolates us in an ultimately unhelpful way from everything and everyone else; what we call, quite simply, selfishness. For without a real effort on our part, above all by developing compassion, we are in danger of becoming merely grown-up children, and far more lethal as a result; not just selfish, but rational and intelligent with it.

'It is the growth of consciousness which we must thank for the existence of problems; they are the dubious gift of civilisation', wrote Jung in *Modern Man in Search of a Soul*; hence the significance, he points out, of the description of that first act of consciousness – the eating from 'the tree of the knowledge of good and evil' – as a curse. The conscious sense of self, or ego as it is sometimes termed, is a double-edged sword if ever there was one, for what liberates us as individuals can then imprison us not just within our own skins, but within our own hearts and minds. This, then, brings me back to the subject of altruism and love.

We are sometimes told that God is love. Perhaps God, or the gods, are unable *not* to love. Is that what it means when we say that they dwell in heaven? We, on the other hand, are certainly capable of not loving. But was it really ever any different? How golden was that Golden Age? From what we know and understand of the bushmen, or the Indians of North and South America, or the Aborigines of Australia, they lived with an instinctive respect and reverence for the natural world around them. They knew, for example, as animals do, which plants were harmful and which plants would heal. On the whole they took from nature only what they needed to sustain their simple way of life. They fiercely protected their own kind. But can we call this love? It wasn't much fun if you stepped out of line, or if – one dark night – you suddenly bumped into a member of another tribe. I remember as a child when our pet canary Bing – named after Bing Crosby – flew out of the window one day and was immediately attacked by all the other birds, who clearly didn't like the colour yellow. It's a characteristic that we human beings are shedding only very slowly. In his book *River out of Eden*, Richard Dawkins writes: 'Nature is not cruel, only pitilessly indifferent.'

I sometimes wonder if our notion of a Golden Age is not nostalgia but premonition – a state of harmony to which we aspire and towards which we have to struggle through our own efforts. In his autobiography Jung wrote: 'As far as we can discern, the sole purpose of human existence is to kindle a light in the darkness of mere being.' He tried to convey his sense of this journey with that word 'individuation' – an exhortation to stand on our own two feet.

But how are we to resolve the dilemma of this emerging individuality, and the fragmentation and alienation that results – alienation from each other, from nature and from any sense of our divine origins? Certainly if, from our 'fallen' and isolated state, we do succeed, ever so gradually and of our own free will, to put the other person (and not just family or friend) before ourselves, then maybe a quite new form of love will come into existence – indeed is coming into existence. There is no obligation – only the stirrings of that mysterious entity we call conscience. But it is a love that can only arise from a position of separateness. And if such a process does have any reality, then it certainly starts to give meaning to that otherwise 'indifferent' universe. Dawkins, I suspect, would not agree. In that same book he goes on to describe what he calls 'one of the hardest lessons for humans to learn. We cannot admit that things might be neither good nor evil, neither cruel nor kind, but simply callous – indifferent to all suffering, lacking all purpose.' Fortunately not everyone shares this bleak outlook.

I've already referred to Gandhi as an example of someone who was unable to be at peace while others suffered. But there are, I feel certain, thousands if not millions of others who feel more or less the same and try, in their own tentative and humble way, to act and respond accordingly. Unlike Gandhi or Mother Teresa of Calcutta they don't on the whole make it into the news, but they are working away as best they can – neither saints nor sinners. In a beautiful essay entitled 'The Timeless World of the Play', featured as an introduction to the Penguin edition of his play *The Rose Tattoo*, Tennessee Williams writes: 'Men pity and love each other more deeply than they permit themselves to know.'

This isn't, therefore, just my own idealism projected onto the world; I have met many such people who truly care about others, and not only in countries like India. The nuns who looked after little Anne-Marie at that convent in Edinburgh loved the children in their care not just out of pity or because their religion demanded it. Mother Teresa once referred to a dying beggar on the streets of Calcutta as 'Christ in distressing disguise' – a label that could apply to all of us. But the love I am hinting at is not to do with just worshipping the so-called 'divine essence' in each person, but rather an acceptance of and compassion for our flawed and often bewildered state of being in the here and now. And we are able to recognise and empathise with such people because in truth we are all in the same boat. We live in a world that the rationalists and reductionists tell us has no meaning, and it hurts. It doesn't correspond to what we believe and know in our hearts.

The gradual disenchantment of nature and the universe since the Copernican revolution is one of the themes that Richard Tarnas explores at length in his widely acclaimed book *The Passion of the Western Mind*. The story he tells is of two-and-a-half thousand years of largely masculine thought and endeavour; a journey that has culminated in this seemingly soulless cul-de-sac in which, to use the words of the biologist Rupert Sheldrake, 'the heavens have become secularised and religion has lost its cosmology'. The way forward, in Tarnas's view, is closely connected with the redemptive role of the feminine sensibility and our capacity to look and listen more deeply; in other words a need for the more receptive, intuitive side of our nature to play a greater role in the future. The word 'disenchantment' in many ways sums up perfectly the essence of the modern world view. It is certainly what Dawkins, who has compared God to a computer virus, consciously encourages and promotes.

Yet Tarnas and those like him who sense, as I do, that there is purpose and meaning to life, recognise that this disenchantment is itself meaningful – or potentially so – and that huge gains have been achieved along the way. It has, for example, in many ways helped to wake us up and to bring us down to earth; for perhaps there are things that can only be learned and experienced through the consciousness we develop while on earth.

This sense that fallible human beings can create something that is both unique and meaningful is beautifully conveyed in Edwin Muir's poem 'One Foot in Eden':

One foot in Eden still, I stand
And look across the other land.
The world's great day is growing late,
Yet strange these fields that we have planted
So long with crops of love and hate ...
Evil and good stand thick around
In the fields of charity and sin
Where we shall lead our harvest in.

Muir goes on to point out that ' Blossoms of grief and charity / Bloom in these darkened fields alone ... Strange blessings never in Paradise / Fall from these beclouded skies.'

Yet the crucial question remains: Where do we go from here? What are these 'strange blessings' to which Muir refers? Our capacity to love seems to be the poet's answer, for only 'in these darkened fields' does grief give birth to charity. Of one thing I am clear; there can be no going back. We can never be bushmen again. In his autobiography Jung writes:

We do not know how far this process of coming to consciousness can extend, or where it will lead. It is a new element in the story of creation, and there are no parallels we can look to. We therefore cannot know what potentialities are inherent in it.

This challenge presented by our expulsion from paradise, the growth of consciousness, and our potential for compassion is explored with great profundity in the medieval story of Parzifal. As a boy he is isolated and protected from the world by his mother, hidden away in the depths of a forest. He knows and understands nature, but not the intrigues and conflicts of human beings. At the start of his journey, therefore, he is both pure but also naïve; in his innocence he could be compared to the bushmen.

In his book *Parzifal and the Stone from Heaven* Lindsay Clarke describes how, as the story unfolds, Parzifal is made aware of the extent to which he is 'a prisoner of his own ignorance', but then how 'the access of knowledge brings with it such pain and derangement that it seems as if consciousness is itself a kind of wound'. It is a wound, suggests Clarke, 'for which the only cure is greater consciousness'.

Parzifal was on a quest, the nature of which he was barely aware of at the start. Quest and question arise from the same source. The question that Parzifal was destined finally to ask had to be kindled by his compassion for the suffering of another – the wounded King Amfortas; and not out of mere curiosity or good manners, but out of empathy. To do that he had first to suffer himself, and in the process to lose all faith in

God. Only then was he ready, in full consciousness, to fulfil his destiny in relation to the mystery of the Grail and to assume his role as the new initiate king. The question that Parzifal finally asks is the same one that I believe we are all challenged to ask from that wilderness in which dwells the blinkered, solitary and self-conscious being that each one of us has become: 'Friend, what ails thee?'

T.S. Eliot, in those lines I quoted earlier from *Little Gidding*, acknowledges our need to go forward and to explore as Parzifal did, and as thousands of others in different ways have always done; and suggests that the end of that exploration, 'will be to arrive where we started / and know the place for the first time'. But what does this really mean? It certainly implies a greater degree of consciousness. Maybe the type of clairvoyance that Steiner developed, encouraging us to do the same, is simply bringing to consciousness what, in the past, we knew instinctively but unconsciously. If so, this process of separation and alienation as we grow up – both individually and collectively – and the freedom that ensues, enable us not only to re-experience our inter-connectedness consciously, but also to further human evolution through our own efforts.

Yet without nurturing our capacity to love, we could easily end up in a world of every man for himself, as already foreseen in that thought by Thomas Hobbes: 'the condition of man ... is a condition of war of everyone against everyone'. Conscious and clever, but ultimately isolated creatures, free to cause havoc – the possibility is there. Individuation is, indeed, a precarious path. We live on a knife-edge.

In the last few hundred years our awakening has been above all in relation to the physical world around us, and only gradually to the conditions of our less fortunate neighbours, or to the chaotic and damaged state of our own inner life. Now, it seems, we increasingly sense the need to activate other, still dormant faculties in order to understand the paradoxical nature of reality itself, aspects of which we have explored so successfully with the telescope and microscope. And perhaps the most paradoxical and mysterious entity of all in need of elucidation is that lonely onlooker: the human being. Whence comes our capacity to put another person first? What is the real meaning of love in a world where powerful forces still conspire so effectively to encourage our basic egotism?

A beetle is a beetle, and will always be so unless we interfere or bring about its extinction. A buttercup will go on being a buttercup year in, year out. 'Your name is tortoise', said Mantis, 'and you will be utterly tortoise to the end of your days.' Not so the human being; and it is above all in the realm of consciousness that evolution still seems to be at work. No new species – just restless, creative and often destructive human beings. So what's next? What are we challenged to become?

This further unfolding of the evolutionary process is most imaginatively conveyed in Paulo Coelho's book *The Alchemist* – the story of a boy, Santiago, whose dream leads him to undertake a great journey to the desert in search of treasure. Finally he returns to find the treasure on his own doorstep, buried at the foot of a sycamore tree. Towards the end of his quest he has a dialogue about love, first with the wind and then with the sun. The sun expresses regret that there was a sixth day of creation, for until then all creation understood that all was one:

> 'You are wise, because you observe everything from a distance', the boy said. 'But you don't know about love. If there hadn't been a sixth day, man would not exist; copper would always just be copper, and lead just lead.'

Santiago goes on to tell the sun that love is the force that transforms all creation and even 'the soul of the world' itself:

> 'Lead will play its role until the world has no further need of lead; and then lead will have to turn itself into gold. That's what alchemists do. They show that, when we strive to become better than we are, everything around us becomes better, too.'

What I want to convey, therefore, is that the growing self-awareness of this increasingly solitary onlooker that each of us has become, despite creating great sorrow and destruction in its wake, including the loss of a certain child-like innocence, is potentially positive and meaningful. This is because we cannot be selfless, cannot truly love in the sense I have been talking about, unless there is a self to do the loving. I cannot put myself into the shoes of another person unless I have first experienced my own self in all its seeming isolation and loneliness. Only then am I ready to ask the question that Parzifal took so long to formulate: 'Friend, what ails thee?'

The bushmen of the Kalahari experienced what Jung, as an old man, called 'a kinship with all things' – it was, indeed, a sort of Golden Age. But at that stage of our evolution we couldn't, I suspect, do otherwise. Now our consciousness has severed that instinctive sense of an interconnectedness with nature and with the 'gods' that live in nature. Yet as onlookers – as television viewers, travellers and readers of books – we are increasingly aware of the needs and the suffering of others, and not just of those from our own family or tribe; and that, I believe, is new. (See colour plate 1.)

If, therefore, we now manage to look forward and not back – but unlike Faust, avoid selling our soul to the devil on the way – and if we can gradually transcend our egotism, pay greater attention to our daemon and to our nobler and more idealistic instincts, we will perhaps not only one day 'know the place for the first time', but also give birth to something unique in the universe that maybe not even the gods possess. Both Steiner and Jung had this sense that the divine world, the hierarchies, depend on us human beings for their own further evolution. Jung goes so far as to suggest in *Memories, Dreams, Reflections* that 'if the Creator were conscious of Himself, He would not need conscious creatures'. In the diaries of Teilhard de Chardin, written during the last ten years of his life, we read: 'God is not dead – but HE CHANGES.'

In his book *Christianity as Mystical Fact* Rudolf Steiner uses a phrase 'the spellbound God'. It is a humbling and awe-inspiring thought. God is not dead, but perhaps the next move is up to us. Hence the silence that Karen Armstrong identifies – 'the silence that is necessary before God can become meaningful again'. Her thought, and that phrase from Steiner, give added meaning to those prophetic words in the Book of Revelation: 'And I saw a new heaven and a new earth: for the first heaven and the first earth were passed away...'. A new heaven, and not just a new earth, is the message that is so radical and profound; and herein lies my sense that the new heaven and the new earth may essentially be one.

But like all trials and quests, the journey will, I am sure, involve pain and sorrow, and will demand great courage and endurance. Nor do I think that the successful outcome is guaranteed. Parzifal was described as 'a brave man, slowly wise'. How long have we got? I have heard our task described as 'the redemption of the world'. Yet seemingly it is we who messed things up in the first place. Or was it? Is there something to the age old notion of a war in heaven? And are we somehow the battleground on which this war is being waged? Or, if we consider again those profound words: 'As above, so below', then perhaps we are not just the stage upon which this conflict unfolds, but rather each one of us lives out this battle between good and evil within ourselves.

Love in freedom is the goal; and what is central to that task is developing a maturity and sensitivity that prompts us to have compassion for everyone who suffers, as Parzival eventually felt for the wounded King Amfortas. It is a task in which we can only hope for the kind of help and inspiration that Gerard Manley Hopkins alludes to in his poem about the kingfisher:

> ... for Christ plays in ten thousand places,
> Lovely in limbs, and lovely in eyes not his
> To the Father through the features of men's faces.

Plate 1. *St Francis and the Leper* by Greg Tricker

Plate 2. *Christ in the Wilderness: The Scorpion* by Stanley Spencer

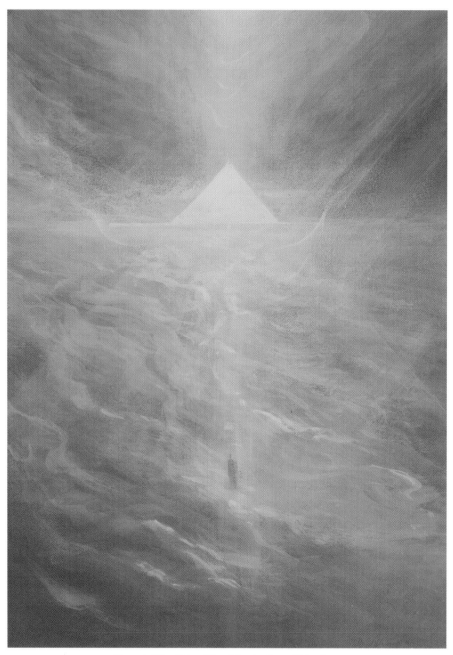

Plate 3. *The Other Wise Man* by David Newbatt

Plate 4. *Easter Saturday* by Ninette Sombart

Plate 5. *The Pilgrim Fool* by Cecil Collins

Plate 6. *The Sleeping Fool* by Cecil Collins (Tate Britain, London)

Plate 7. *The Wounded Angel* by Cecil Collins

Plate 8. *Meeting the Lady* by Greg Tricker

To Jonathan
With Love
from Peter
xxxxx

Plate 9. Gift from Peter Higham

Plate 10. *The Shepherds of Arcadia* by Nicolas Poussin (Musée du Louvre, Paris)
Photograph © RMN/ René-Gabriel Ojéda

CHAPTER 17

Midstream

I have called this chapter 'Midstream' because around this time in my life – halfway through my 'three score years and ten' – I did experience a crisis of sorts. It was nothing very dramatic, but simply a return of the feeling which, seven years earlier, had prompted me to leave the BBC and spend a year at Emerson College. Was I running away from my real task in life? I asked myself – someone always behind the camera watching other people doing the work; someone striding into interesting and important situations for a few months and then moving on to the next topic.

There was, I see now, a definite continuity to my work – a thread that wasn't always clear at the time. Occasionally I also experienced a certain loneliness brought on by a sense that I didn't quite belong anywhere. For example, some of those who shared my interest in esoteric subjects perceived me as rather worldly, perhaps too much so, whereas many of my television colleagues had an image of me spending a lot of time cross-legged on some mountain-top.

But I was no 'Gandhian' either, despite the impact made on me by my time in India. I enjoyed worldly things too much, yet not enough to prevent an undercurrent of guilt periodically surfacing. In trying to deal honestly with this guilt, I tell myself that we all have to balance our ideals with our appetites – though not as an excuse for slamming the door on change. Maybe tomorrow, or the next day, I will wake up as someone a little braver or better at practising what I preach and what I believe in.

I find it interesting that the phrase 'sitting on the fence' is a derogatory expression, whereas the idea of taking a middle path is recognised as a worthwhile and challenging task. I would like to think that it is the path rather than the fence I have sought throughout my life.

Despite all these ups and downs, however, I never lost my deep interest not only in the day-to-day world around me, but also in what might be going on behind the scenes, as it were – not just in my own life, but in the lives of everyone I was meeting. The idea that death might not be what is sometimes referred to as 'curtains' was still the theme that interested me most of all. In a play the curtains certainly come down, but the actors are still there, on the other side of that curtain – waiting, no doubt, for their agents to call them about their next part.

In 1975 I experienced a very poignant example of our continuing relationship with those who have died while directing a film about Admiral Yamamoto, the Japanese naval commander in World War II. I was now working under Richard Cawston in the BBC's Documentary department. Cawston was a distinguished film-maker himself, and his former film editor Harry Hastings was producing a series, scripted by the historian Correlli Barnet, called *The Commanders*.

Yamamoto was the architect of Japan's attack on the American fleet at their Hawaiian base in Pearl Harbour. As such he became, in the eyes of America in particular, villain number one until his assassination in 1943. In fact Yamamoto had been deeply opposed to the war, partly because, having spent time in America as Japanese Naval Attaché in the 1920s, he knew and indeed admired the country, and also knew that Japan would ultimately stand no chance against such a formidable power. However he was overruled by the army and so came up with a plan which he felt was their only chance of success: to launch a surprise and devastating blow to American sea power, and then negotiate a peace from a position of strength. The first part of his plan, despite being a tremendous gamble, worked perfectly – an undetected four-thousand-mile, eleven-day journey for six aircraft carriers, two battleships, three cruisers, nine destroyers and several tankers, all preceded by a fleet of twenty submarines. On December 7th 1941, 360 Japanese aircraft all but destroyed the American fleet in Pearl Harbour. Perhaps not surprisingly success went to the heads of the Japanese High Command and talk of peace was dismissed. America then did exactly what Yamamoto knew that they would do: they simply built another fleet.

Early in the conflict that followed, the Americans broke the Japanese code. One plan, as a blow to Japanese morale, was to 'take out' their hero Yamamoto, whose movements they could now follow in precise detail. They knew, too, that Yamamoto was a stickler for punctuality. He was also, as I discovered during my filming in Japan, a very fine and sensitive human being, and an accomplished poet.

Yamamoto had joined the navy in 1901 with 'a great desire to become a warrior'. Thirty-eight years later he was appointed Commander-in-Chief of the Japanese fleet. By then he was increasingly concerned at Japan's aggressive and expansionist policies, first in Manchuria and then in its invasion of China. In fact Japan was simply trying to compete with countries like Britain and France that had empires: she wanted one too. Yamamoto was also totally opposed to the treaty that Japan signed in 1940 with Germany and Italy, the so-called Triple Alliance. He became increasingly unpopular with the ruling élite and there were threats to his life. He considered retiring, but like most Japanese he had an unswerving loyalty to the Emperor – in their eyes God's representative on earth.

Yamamoto was a man who liked to live simply, in the countryside. It was there that he wrote his poetry and was surrounded by the many books he still wanted to read. He was, apparently, a devoted if somewhat silent father, but was lonely and unhappy in his marriage. In contrast to all this he was an almost fanatical gambler – he loved poker in particular. His attack on Pearl Harbour was the greatest gamble of his life.

I met and interviewed several of his old naval colleagues, some of whom had been trained as young officers in Britain and spoke good English: Japan had been our ally in World War I. Yamamoto's son, in particular, gave me great support in piecing together the story, as did the Japanese film crew with whom I worked.

On my way to Japan via Hawaii, I stopped in California to interview the man who was responsible for the plan to assassinate Yamamoto, and also the pilot, Thomas Lanphier, who was given the task of shooting down his plane. The Americans knew that Yamamoto was to visit a Japanese base on the Solomon Islands on a certain date and they also knew the precise time he was due to land. On April 18th 1943, at Henderson Field on the island of Guardal Canal, the following message was received: 'The peacock will be on time. Fan his tail.' Admiral Yamamoto had left Rabal to fly to Bougainville. A squadron of eighteen American planes took off on a four-hundred-mile flight, flying low enough to avoid radar – the first attempt in history to ambush an enemy Commander-in-Chief. The timing was perfect; Yamamoto's plane was shot down by Lanphier, and Japanese morale was, indeed, undermined by the death of their beloved admiral. The Americans were jubilant. It was only after the war that the truth about Yamamoto and his attitude to the conflict became publicly known.

This truth, of course, also became known to Thomas Lanphier, the man who had carried out the actual assassination. When I spoke to him there was no sense of regret, no haunting guilt. War is war, and people are killed. But what I did sense was that in some mysterious way Lanphier had developed an almost intimate relationship with this Japanese admiral whom he had never met and whose life he had ended. There was nothing sentimental in the way he talked, but he had clearly thought very deeply about the event and in particular about the man who was his victim: 'It gets to be kind of eerie as the years go by', he said to me. 'The personality of this particular man becomes more and more real to me; and the emotional excitement and outright indignation that led to a satisfaction when he was killed pales into the distance. We did assassinate this man; that may not be an explicitly correct term, but we assassinated him; we ambushed him, if you will – though his numbers were considerably superior to ours when we finally got to it. In any case, although I don't regret being a party to his death in that time, in that place and for those reasons, I must say I'm bemused as the years go by, and like to talk less and less about the actual fact of his being killed, and more and more about what an interesting man he was – and from his point of view a very correct one.'

It was clear from what Lanphier said, and even more from the pauses between his words, that a significant bond had grown up between him and his one-time enemy. It was karma on a world scale that had, as it were, brought these two individuals together. Whilst our personal karmas are inevitably interwoven with events and circumstances beyond our control, everything that matters is ultimately perhaps about relationships, however they come about – both from day to day and from lifetime to lifetime.

It is over thirty years since I made that film, and Lanphier is himself now on Yamamoto's side of the curtain. I have often wondered how those dramatic events will affect not only their individual destinies in the future, but also the actual relationship between these two souls – a relationship forged by such seemingly inauspicious circumstances.

––––––––––

From Japan I flew to the land where karma is a familiar word: I was back in India. Through my friendship with John Betjeman I had met his wife Penelope, and was very soon on the receiving end of her 'passion for India'.

Penelope Betjeman

The phrase became the title of the film that we made for the series *One Pair of Eyes*. Penelope's father, Lord Chetwode, was Commander-in-Chief of the Army in India from 1930 to 1935. As a young girl she had fallen in love with the subcontinent and had long planned to return on a regular basis once her children were grown up. Her special interest was in the hill temples of Himachal Pradesh, among the foothills of the Himalayas. She had already written a book, *Kulu: End of the Habitable World* – and it was to the Kulu Valley that we went to film.

There are two aspects of this project that are relevant to my theme, though there is much else I could write about our fascinating and at times hilarious journey. John Betjeman described Penelope as a true eccentric because she was convinced that she was perfectly normal and that everyone else was mad. We trekked for two weeks – my BBC crew headed by my old friend John McGlashan, and supported by three Indian porters, two mules, and a very disobedient donkey. Penelope and our Indian guide from the local tourist office, Narendra Sharma, rode on ponies; the rest of us were happy to walk.

A scene that people seem to remember more vividly than any other from all the films I ever made was Penelope crossing the river Sutlej on an inflated buffalo skin. It is, apparently, one of man's earliest ways of crossing a river. The ferryman lay sprawled across this weirdly shaped, balloon-like object, while Penelope – hardly an elf-like figure – lay diagonally on top of him. He then used his arms and legs as both paddles and rudder.

Penelope Betjeman crossing the Sutlej river

After many squawks and much giggling this extraordinary vessel was launched into the rapids, closely followed by Sharma on his own private buffalo. We'd rigged Penelope up with a radio-microphone, and mid-stream came that strident and plummy voice, so reminiscent of the British Raj: 'It would be awfully funny if we got a puncture.' In fact it wouldn't have been funny at all. Fortunately we were working in the days before Health and Safety Regulations, or else would probably never have been allowed to leave Delhi in the first place.

Penelope became a Roman Catholic early on in her married life, but it was her contact with India as a girl that first stirred her interest in religion. Reading about Hinduism, Buddhism and Sufism, she said, made her think: 'This is the cat's whiskers! Also I was delighted to find that Indians, unlike English people, weren't in the least embarrassed to talk about God.' These experiences prompted her to study the mystical tradition in Christianity and classical systems of meditation – all the wisdom that the dear old Church of England tends to bury under the flurry of Church fetes, Christmas carols and understatement.

Our journey in and around the Kulu Valley, at one point climbing to ten thousand feet to visit the temple at Chong, eventually led us to Manali. Already then in 1974 it was, despite its remoteness, a haven for western hippies; cannabis grew wild to a height of six or seven feet. In a beautiful and peaceful glade among the great deodar trees that surround Manali, Penelope talked to a group of young people about 'dropping out'. Like many men and women of her generation, for whom drugs were simply not available, she questioned the idea of so-called spiritual experience induced without any effort on the part of the searcher; to her it smacked of cheating. 'Gate-crashing heaven' was the phrase she used.

It was a good-natured encounter between Penelope and the hippies, but one in which no real shift took place on either side. Drugs were not part of my youth either, so I am hesitant to make strong judgements. I was aware at Emerson College that several of my fellow students, particularly from the United States, had been heavily into the drug scene. Like Carlos Castaneda in his book *A Separate Reality*, they spoke of experiences that had changed their lives; glimpses of reality that had prompted them to strive through their own efforts, primarily through meditation, to explore those deeper levels of existence.

For me a helpful guide to this realm of drug-induced experience is Aldous Huxley's *The Doors of Perception*, in which he describes how in Los Angeles 'one bright May morning' in 1953 he swallowed four-tenths of a gramme of mescalin dissolved in half a glass of water, sat down and waited for the results.

Despite the difficulty of putting such experiences into words, Huxley does manage to convey with great skill a glimpse, at least, of what happened over the next few hours: 'I was seeing what Adam had seen on the morning of his creation, the miracle, moment by moment, of naked existence.' For him a bunch of flowers became 'a bundle of minute, unique particles in which, by some unspeakable and yet self-evident paradox, was to be seen the divine source of all existence.'

Huxley goes on to describe how for him special relationships ceased to matter very much: 'The mind was primarily concerned, not with measures and locations, but with seeing and meaning ... And along with indifference to space there went an even completer indifference to time.' When asked by the person he called the investigator what he felt about time, all he would answer was: 'There seems to be plenty of it.' Exactly how much time seemed to him 'entirely irrelevant'. In this respect he writes of his experience as one of 'an indefinite duration or alternatively of a perpetual present ... Interest in time falls almost to zero.' It was above all, it seems, an experience in which everything, even the most mundane object 'was infinite in its significance'. A few lines earlier he writes of a 'sacramental vision of reality'.

One of Huxley's most interesting observations – one that is also very relevant to the notion I will be returning to, of a purely spiritual existence between incarnations as well as during sleep – concerns the experience of losing all sense of separateness, of becoming at one with the other. In Huxley's case the other was a chair, or rather the legs of that chair:

I spent several minutes, or was it several centuries? – not merely gazing at those bamboo legs, but actually being them – or rather being myself in them; or, to be still more accurate (for 'I' was not involved in the case, nor in a certain sense were 'they') being my Not-self in the Not-self which was the chair.

Huxley's most significant experience in relation to the main theme of my book – in particular to what I wrote in the last chapter concerning the redemptive power of love – concerns a diminishing of will, and especially an overwhelming lack of interest in other people. Although his visual impressions were greatly intensified – 'the eye recovers some of the perceptual innocence of childhood' – and his intellect remained unimpaired,

the will suffers a profound change for the worse. The mescalin taker sees no reason for doing anything in particular and finds most of the causes for which, at ordinary times, he was prepared to act and suffer, profoundly uninteresting. He can't be bothered with them, for the good reason that he has better things to think about.

For Huxley those 'better things' did not include other people. He then asks himself how one reconciles 'this cleansed perception ... with a proper concern for human relations, with the necessary chores and duties, to say nothing of charity and practical compassion'. In this question he recognises the age-old debate about the virtues of the 'actives' as opposed to the 'contemplatives', and that mescalin opens up the way of Mary Magdalen, the thoughtful and reflective companion of Jesus, but shuts the door on that of the busy and dutiful Martha: 'It gives access to contemplation – but to a contemplation that is incompatible with action and even with the will to action'. Yet for others, I'm told, mescalin has opened up huge and transforming vistas of our human potential to think, feel *and* act.

In that Himalayan glade, sheltered from the heat and briefly from the troubles of the world, Penelope was particularly interested in talking with a young man called Karl, who was brought up as a Roman Catholic in southern Germany. Why didn't the Church meet his needs and answer his questions? 'Countless persons desire self-transcendence and would be glad to find it in church', wrote Aldous Huxley in *The Doors of Perception*. 'But, alas, "the hungry sheep look up and are not fed". They take part in rites, they listen to sermons, they repeat prayers; but their thirst remains unassuaged.'

Penelope and Karl agreed that one problem was the pressure nowadays to take the mystery out of everything: to try to explain things in clear and simple language. Modern renderings of the Prayer Book and of the Gospels are a good example. It is the reason I like poetry – not the sort of poetry that Tolstoy referred to as needing elucidation, but the poetry that helps us transcend the everyday. For similar reasons Penelope loved her hill temples, not just because of their beautiful architecture, but also because they were home to seasonal festivals held in almost every village throughout Himachal Pradesh, the symbolism of which clearly gave meaning and nourishment to the entire community.

Temperamentally, however, I recognise that people tend to fall into one camp or the other: the so-called rationalists on the one hand – people who prefer to have things spelled out; and on the other hand, those for whom feelings and instincts are paramount. All the more reason, therefore, that we should talk to each other, and try to value and respect the many other routes up the mountain that complement our own search not just for knowledge, but for wisdom.

There is a scene at the end of my film with Penelope that illustrates this difficulty we sometimes have in understanding another person's point of view. While breakfast was being prepared on a peaceful hilltop, the ever polite and obliging tourist officer, Narindra Sharma, suddenly decided to challenge Penelope on the subject of progress. This was in response to her constant remarks about how the new roads would ruin the peace of the valley – just as Wordsworth had complained about the arrival of the railways in the Lake District a hundred years earlier. People's lives, suggested Sharma, will be improved 'by modern facilities'; roads, he pointed out, bring education and trade, not just noise and pollution. Penelope would have none of it, and turning her back on the gentle Sharma, she stoked the campfire and unintentionally enveloped him in smoke. Later she summed up her concern in the final words of her commentary: 'I must say that I worry very much what will happen when these Pahari people lose their faith. Respect for their gods certainly keeps them happy and law-abiding. But modern ideas are creeping up the valleys and will have the same destructive effect that they have elsewhere.'

Penelope's attitude highlights the same dilemma that concerned me in relation to the bushmen. Is not 'destructive' a misleading word? Modern ideas can certainly cause enormous disruption, but can also be liberating. Besides, disruption is not always a bad thing, particularly if, in the process, people can slowly arrive at a deeper understanding and appreciation of all those things that Penelope and other westerners so love and admire about the Kulu Valley. An understanding, in other words, that can in time be experienced more consciously not only by us outsiders, but also by the inhabitants themselves.

This journey to India, by way of Japan, had actually begun for me in the United States. I had visited the film archives in Washington and then stayed with my friends Ted and Betty Roszak in California. The early seventies were an exciting and lively time in Berkeley, across the Bay from San Francisco. Telegraph Avenue was plastered with enticing posters offering every sort of enlightenment and therapy. Almost everyone was interested in talking about anything, however improbable, somewhat as Penelope must have experienced as a young girl in India where no one was embarrassed to talk about God. It's what I still love about America – and California in particular.

The university campus at Berkeley had a freshness and vitality that was less apparent in Britain and the rest of Europe. On the pavements were New Age magicians and craftsmen of every sort, and in the bookshops a wealth of material that was harder to find in London except in Watkins bookshop off the Charing Cross Road. It was in one of the Berkeley bookshops that I happened to pick out 'by chance' an American publication of an early book by Steiner called *Eleven European Mystics*, later re-titled as *Mysticism at the Dawn of the Modern Age*.

My thirty-fifth birthday fell two weeks later while I was in Hawaii, filming at Pearl Harbour. I scheduled January 20th as a day off – a day to spend alone. However, like the melancholic donkey Eeyore in A.A. Milne's wonderful stories about Pooh Bear and his friends, I was not expecting any presents. By now I was aware of the idea that significant shifts often occur at seven-year intervals in our lives. At twenty-one I first came across the work of Rudolf Steiner; at twenty-eight, though still unconscious of the potential significance of the timing, I chose to break from the BBC to attend Emerson College; now, at thirty-five, I was half-consciously waiting to see what thunderbolt would come crashing into my life. Like Penelope Betjeman, when she called out to us as she was crossing the Sutlej river on her inflated buffalo skin, I too was in midstream – and was hoping that I wouldn't get a puncture.

I woke on the morning of my birthday to a clear sky and no thunderbolts. I drove to a remote beach and there started to read Steiner's essays on the mystics of the Middle Ages – and I have been re-reading them ever since. That original paperback is now falling to bits, but it's the copy I always return to. It was indeed a very special and unexpected present at that halfway stage in my life.

In his autobiography, the novelist and zoologist E.L. Grant Watson – whose work I was yet to discover – suggests that it is not mere chance that books present themselves to our notice when they do:

> Our individual capacity determines what can be read. No secrets can be betrayed, because no man who does not already possess the key can open the lock of another man's understanding. The lock and the key, though not one and the same thing, are intimately related.

Some books, I have found, belong to quite definite stages of my journey, whereas others become ever more significant as I grow older. 'Our skies change', writes Watson. 'Some stars fade, new stars rise, brilliant above the horizon; some grow brighter and remain.'

I once heard the milestone of becoming thirty-five years old described as follows: Imagine at birth you are given a sort of cosmic shove. Without any effort on your part during that first half of your life, the momentum from that shove will run down by mid-life. In other words you'll grind to a halt if you haven't created, or don't start to create, the resolve to keep growing and asking questions.

In his book *Phases*, the Dutch psychiatrist Bernard Lievegoed wrote about this stage in our lives as follows:

> Either the road goes downhill, together with the biological functions of the body and mind, or it leads into totally new territory in which quite different creative powers are awakened. These may make possible a second peak in the individual's powers of creation, the zenith of which lies in the second half of the fifties and may endure until far into the seventies ...

Some ten years later I explored the whole subject of the phases of life in *Seven Ages*, the television series with Ron Eyre that I mentioned in the preface.

Meanwhile, on my Hawaiian beach, I plunged into what for me was a whole new and extraordinarily helpful insight into areas of spirituality I had already been exploring for some years; it was helpful, too, in dealing with some of the on-going dilemmas I had been facing in own my life.

CHAPTER 18

Alone in the Desert

If there is indeed a spiritual dimension to life, how is it manifest in the world around us? In other words, where on earth is heaven? This was a question I had now been living with for some years. But questions yearn to be answered, and answers need to be translated into action. For me, at the age of thirty-five, although answers of a sort were gradually emerging, the nature of that action was often unclear. From time to time I felt that I would like to learn to be a gardener and live in a community. Camphill was an obvious choice, but I was still wary of a certain cosiness and even insularity that can arise when people spend most of their time with those who think like they do. And although I was drawn to new ways not just of looking at the world, but also of living in it, I was nevertheless not totally at odds with my very English upbringing and many of the traditions associated with it. Alongside this almost double life, I enjoyed my work enormously – particularly when I could express through my films the idealism that I felt so strongly and that I witnessed among so many of my fellow human beings.

Above all, in the people and the ideas I met or read about, I was looking for authenticity rather than rhetoric, experience rather than theory. It was spirituality, not religion, which interested me. I respond, therefore, to what Richard Geldard writes in his book on the spiritual teachings of Ralph Waldo Emerson: 'a paradox remains at the centre of the search for an authentic life. We have to break lovingly the vessels of our tradition to become one with the source of that tradition.'

Rudolf Steiner gave a series of lectures in Berlin in the autumn of 1900 in which he spoke about the struggles of eleven great explorers of the inner life to reconcile their individual strivings and insights with the religious orthodoxy of their day. Living during the four centuries that preceded the Renaissance they each, in their own way, anticipated the need many of us increasingly experience – whatever our faith or cultural tradition – to accept nothing second-hand. Authority and moral guidance, we feel, must be sought inwardly, and not dictated to us by mere tradition.

In his introduction to Steiner's book *Mysticism at the Dawn of the Modern Age*, which was based on those Berlin lectures, Paul Allen writes: 'to the medieval mind the word "reality" referred exclusively to spiritual, heavenly things'. From the 17th century onwards, horizons – both physical and mental – began to expand rapidly; and alongside this collective awakening, there developed an increasing sense of the importance of individual freedom. The transformation that was to take place affected every aspect of life – the way of looking at the world beneath our feet, at our fellow human beings and at what Allen calls the blue vault arching over our heads. He writes:

> From a conception of nature that saw the animate in everything
> – even in stones – new systems of classification, ways of analysis,
> of explanation, based more and more upon the evidence of the
> physical senses, and less and less upon folk-lore and tradition,
> came into being.

As one of the characters in Owen Barfield's autobiographical novel *Worlds Apart* says of the scientific revolution: 'it was an incalculable advance on anything that had gone before'; scientists finally gave up looking for spiritual and metaphysical causes 'and began looking to the phenomena to explain themselves'.

What particularly interested Steiner was a problem that had occupied him for decades and which confronts us ever more urgently – namely the impact of modern scientific thinking upon the experiences of our inner life and upon our religious sensibilities. Allen goes on to point out that in the conflict between reason and revelation which reached its climax in the 19th century, but which had its origins in much earlier times, Steiner saw the seed of a still greater conflict to come – one that would involve humanity in a struggle against the sub-human elements in modern technological development.

At a very mundane level – and like many other people – I increasingly come across situations in which I wonder who is actually in charge, a person or a computer. Likewise, what button do I have to press on my telephone to get through to an actual human being? In other words, how are we to live with modern technology in a way that prevents it undermining our essential humanity?

Steiner's message, however, has nothing to do with putting the clock back; nor, unlike some New Age groups, does he harbour nostalgia for some lost paradise. In his preface to the 1923 edition of his book on the eleven mystics, he is keen to emphasise that although the way of thinking that characterised medieval mysticism may be foreign to modern consciousness, what he calls 'the disposition of soul' which lived in this mode of enquiry still persists in thoughtful people today. He warns, however, against the tendency among those who incline towards mysticism to dwell on the past and to ignore the findings of natural science, so that 'they become strangers to what most occupies the present'. The spirit that existed among the mystics of the Middle Ages atrophied, so Steiner suggests, because it gradually lost its connection with inquiry. This, however, does not have to be so. For him this was confirmed by the deeper implications of Goethe's way of thinking. In this respect Steiner highlights in his book the life of the 15th-century churchman Cardinal Nicolas of Cusa as someone who, in his view, developed a way of thinking capable of incorporating the sort of knowledge that has come to us through our scientific discoveries.

The story that Steiner tells, however, begins some two hundred years earlier. In 1260 Johannes Eckhart, later known as Meister Eckhart, was born in the Thüringen village of Gotha in Germany. Around the age of fifteen he entered the Dominican monastery at Erfurt where he remained for nine years in preparation for the priesthood. His studies took him on to Cologne and later to Paris where he was deeply involved in the defence of Dominican teachings against Franciscan charges of heresy. Despite his considerable learning, Eckhart's interest and concern was, writes Allen, 'for the humble peasant, the shepherd from the mountains, the charcoal burner from the forest, rather than the scholar in the cloister'. With regard to his disputations with the Franciscans, Eckhart wrote years later: 'When I preached at Paris, I said – and I dare repeat it now – that with all their learning the men of Paris are not able to conceive that God is in the very least of creatures – even in a fly.'

Eckhart had been inspired above all by the great theologian Thomas Aquinas, whose work was an attempt to reconcile Christianity with the philosophical and scientific insights of Aristotle. Eckhart considered himself to be fully in harmony with the teachings of the Christian Church, but he wanted to bring new life to its content, to make it contemporary and relevant to the emerging sense of individual human freedom and autonomy.

I see Eckhart, therefore – along with the other figures featured in Steiner's book – as a pioneer of a whole new phase in the evolution of human consciousness. Reading about their struggles certainly helped me to understand better my own very modest ones, and to recognise that my need for inner confirmation of spiritual realities was not mere hubris or psychic gluttony. I became aware, too, that the spiritual experiences of others, although of enormous help, are in the end no substitute for one's own, however humble those experiences may be.

Thus *Mysticism at the Dawn of the Modern Age*, the book I began reading on my thirty-fifth birthday, gradually helped me to accept my own restlessness, and to cease feeling guilty about the rebelliousness I felt not only towards

Christianity, but also towards the common tendency to fix and institutionalise what needs to live and grow. Too often and too easily we set in stone the insights, experiences and intimations of others, thereby avoiding the far more challenging and essentially lonely task of doing the work ourselves.

What interested Eckhart was our human potential and, indeed, our imperative to experience revelation first-hand – what in religious terminology is called initiation; and initiation means confronting yourself – your demons as well as your daimon. And in relation to this task of standing on our own two feet, he wished to impress upon us the significance of Christ's words: 'It is expedient for you that I go away: for if I go not away, the Comforter will not come unto you.' The Comforter is what we also know as the Holy Ghost – that entity that can awaken in each one of us our full potential as human beings, as it did for the disciples at Pentecost. Eckhart used the following words to illumine Christ's statement about the necessity of his seeming departure: 'It is as if he said: you have taken too much joy in my present image, therefore the perfect joy of the Holy Ghost cannot be in you.'

Steiner then quotes an extraordinarily provocative statement by this courageous medieval churchman – courageous in that the Church was continually on the lookout for heretics – which shows that although Eckhart considered his God to be the same God of whom St Augustine and Thomas Aquinas spoke, yet their testimony of God was not his testimony:

> Some people want to look upon God with their eyes, as they look upon a cow, and want to love God as they love a cow. Thus they love God for the sake of external riches and of internal solace; but these people do not love God aright … foolish people deem that they should look upon God as though He stood there and they here. It is not thus. God and I are one in the act of knowing.

And in his treatise *Concerning Solitude*, Eckhart has this to say about his experience of the divine: 'Everything that understanding can grasp, and everything desire demands, is not God. Where understanding and desire have an end, there it is dark, there does God shine.' What is therefore central to Eckhart's message, and to the message of Steiner's whole book, is our capacity through inner work to gradually become united with God's essence in the very depths of our own being.

I have always loved the opening words of the 121st Psalm: 'I will lift up mine eyes unto the hills from whence cometh my help.' Yet more and more people seem to experience, like Eckhart, that this may no longer be the most helpful direction in which to look. The God to which David is referring may indeed be a reality, but, as Eckhart implies, that reality can increasingly be discovered and brought to life inwardly in each one of us.

'God has become man so that I might become God' is the statement for which Eckhart has probably become most famous. In other words, through self-knowledge in its very deepest sense we can experience the greatest of all correspondences: the interconnectedness of the divine spark in us with the divinity itself. But unlike our other human attributes – including our five senses, all of which are given – this divine spark has to be awoken through our own efforts. The implication behind Eckhart's words is that this awakening and transformation within myself also enables me to experience a rebirth of all that surrounds me. Through self-knowledge, writes Steiner, there arises 'a sun which illuminates something beyond the incidental individual personality of the beholder'. Gradually everything reveals itself to me in a fuller light.

I cannot honestly say, however, that my Hawaiian beach was suddenly transformed before my eyes. I swam in the sea, enjoyed my lunch, but for once ignored the obvious distractions and went back to my book. Yet over the years, as a result of reading this book in particular, I have felt an ever-deepening sense of my interconnectedness with everything that is seemingly separate from me. In relation to my fellow human beings it is best expressed by the word 'empathy' – a capacity that I, like most people, recognise and experience as being still very much in its infancy. My interconnectedness with nature is less complicated, less challenging. I know very well to what extent I depend, for example, on trees, water, bees and the sun for my physical existence. Gratitude and humility are very obvious and natural responses.

Meanwhile in another sense, and like everyone else, I experience myself as essentially alone. It's a puzzle and a paradox. Yet I realise that only in this state of inner isolation, as already explored in the chapter I called 'Free to Love', am I able to consciously appreciate and understand how I am absolutely *not* alone, nor indeed separate. It is not really such a strange idea. When, for example, I am deep in conversation with someone else – more interested in them than in myself – my self-consciousness all but disappears. Indeed, when absorbed by anything that is not me, I actually cease to be separate. It is no longer me looking at a flower, for the beauty and delicacy of the flower, and the joy I experience through that encounter, are one and the same thing. Our interaction with the other person presents the same possibility. 'Love begins with paying attention to others, with an act of gracious self-forgetting', writes the Irish poet and scholar John O'Donoghue in his *Anam Cara*.

What is initially a path of self-knowledge, therefore, can give birth not only to a deeper knowledge of the world, but also a kinship with that world and with all creation. Something can come alive in me that is more than my individual and isolated self – Steiner called it a sun – which reaches out to embrace everything of which my individuality is actually a part. One can recognise, therefore, in the journey of someone like Eckhart, the roots of Steiner's objection to Emmanuel Kant's view that we can never know 'the thing in itself', for it is precisely this spiritual essence in all that surrounds us that reveals itself to the spiritual essence within ourselves. On the one hand I am a thing among other things – trees, people, stars. I live in a body and through its organs perceive what lies outside my body. But I also live, or can live, another kind of life alongside my physical existence, which knows no such inner and outer. When I referred to the title of Ronald Duncan's autobiography *All Men are Islands* as both true and untrue, I was trying to acknowledge this paradox. Teilhard de Chardin, in his spiritual masterpiece *Le Milieu Divin*, describes what he sees as the essential aspiration of all mysticism: 'to be united (that is to become the other) while remaining oneself'.

In the introduction to *Mysticism at the Dawn of the Modern Age* Steiner writes:

> the destiny of the self is that only in its separation from the universe can it find contact with this universe. Man would not be man if as an 'I' he were not separated from everything else; but he would not be man in the highest sense if, as such a separated 'I', he did not enlarge himself out of himself to the all-I. Above all, it is characteristic of human nature that it should overcome a contradiction which originally lies within it.

Once again I am reminded of T.S. Eliot's words about the resolution of humanity's journey and exploration, and the prospect of returning to and knowing the place for the first time.

Steiner goes on to say, as he does in his book *The Philosophy of Freedom*, that human cognition is not some unimportant addition to the rest of the universal process, as if it were merely a repetition, in the form of ideas, of what exists externally. In understanding, something occurs which does not occur anywhere in the external world: 'the universal process confronts itself with its own spiritual nature. This universal process would be forever incomplete if this confrontation did not take place'. It is what Meister Eckhart must have meant when he wrote, 'God and I are one in the act of knowing.'

Steiner even goes so far as to say that if we call the highest which human beings can attain the 'divine', then this 'divine' does not exist as something external to be repeated as a mere image in the human spirit, but rather is awoken within us. To illustrate the point he quotes another of the mystics featured in his book, Angelus Silesius: 'I know that without me God cannot live for a moment; if I come to naught He must needs give up the ghost.' Such thoughts seem to echo what Jung was trying to express in his autobiography, in the chapter entitled 'Late Thoughts', where he calls the idea of creation, without any dynamic between the creator and his creatures, 'a cheerless clockwork fantasy'.

Steiner then suggests that for someone like Eckhart the relationship between God and his creation cannot be understood in images borrowed from our earthly existence: 'God cannot love His creation as one individual man loves another; God cannot have created the world as a master-builder constructs a house. All such thoughts disappear in the face of this inner vision.'

All this may seem, for some people, to be bordering on blasphemy – or certainly a severe case of hubris. It is therefore vital to be aware of the spirit in which such utterances were made, and indeed of the lives and achievements of those, like Eckhart, who arrived at such thoughts. All of them were first and foremost humble men who, for all their learning, gave priority in their lives to caring for their fellow human beings in the fullest sense. There was no aura of exclusivity about their inner work and spiritual ponderings. A belief in our potential as human beings is relevant for all humanity.

When Johannes Tauler was born in the city of Strasbourg in 1300, Meister Eckhart was forty years old. Tauler, too, joined the Dominican order and became one of the great preachers of his day, having been deeply influenced by the wisdom of Eckhart. What especially interested and touched me about Tauler was his transformation of Scholastic learning into Christian action – his concern, first and foremost, for the welfare of his fellow human beings in the here and now.

In 1339 Tauler left Strasbourg for a journey that was to have a profound influence on his life's work. On his travels he came into contact, particularly in Basel, with a group of mystics who called themselves 'Die Gottesfreunde' – the Friends of God. It was a time of great hardship for the common people, both physically and spiritually. A power struggle between rival rulers in Germany, resulting in a papal ban on the activities of the Church, together with years of abnormal and extreme weather conditions, convinced many that the world was about to come to an end. An earthquake reduced the city of Basel to a heap of ruins. 'Lacking spiritual consolation from the Church,' writes Paul Allen in his introduction, 'people sought the essential truths of life in their personal experience.' One outcome was people's increasing openness to one another and a compassion for their fellow human beings. It was in such an atmosphere that the Friends of God came into being. It was not a sect, for there was no dogma, no common form of religious devotion or practice, no common political outlook. The only desire the Friends of God shared, writes Allen, 'was to strengthen one another in their living relationship with God and the spiritual world.' Tauler's own relationship to Christianity was enormously enriched by his contact with these people. 'The theologians of Paris', he wrote, 'study great tomes and turn over many pages, but the Friends of God read the living Book where everything is life.'

During his seven years' absence from Strasbourg, Tauler became convinced that a layman has tasks to perform which are as spiritually important as those of the clergy. In a later sermon he acknowledged his respect for the way of life of the Friends of God:

> One can spin, another can make shoes, and all these are gifts of the Holy Ghost. I tell you, if I were not a priest, I would esteem it a great gift that I was able to make shoes, and I would try to make them so well that they would be a model to all.

I'm sure that both Tolstoy and Gandhi would approve of such a statement.

Tauler's writings, unlike those of Eckhart, are not so much spiritual and esoteric speculations as thoughts and feelings imbued with a down-to-earth common sense characteristic of the Reformation yet to come. Allen emphasises this point by quoting Tauler's desire 'to put out into the deep and let down the nets' into the world of study and meditation, while at the same time cautioning that 'such spiritual enjoyments are food for the soul, and are only to be taken for nourishment and support to help us in our active work'.

Steiner describes Tauler, and several other of the mystics featured in his book, as 'wanderers' for whom 'this blissful experience of rebirth', which Eckhart wrote and spoke about, had shown a new road down which they began to walk; for them the end of this road lay far ahead. Eckhart described the splendours of his vision; Tauler the difficulties of the road itself.

Like Eckhart, Tauler did not feel himself at odds with the Catholic Church, but he, too, needed to deepen his relationship with the great mysteries of existence through his own thoughts and experiences. For him what was meaningful was the notion of God 'as a Father who brings forth His only begotten Son in the soul, as truly as He brings Him forth in eternity, neither less, nor more'. And in this sense he was prompted to add:

> Herod, who drove away the Child and wanted to kill Him, is an image of the world, which still wants to kill this Child in the pious man, wherefore one should and must flee it if one wants to keep the Child alive within oneself, while the Child is the enlightened, believing soul of every man.

The implication behind Tauler's way of thought is the recognition that whereas natural science can examine and elucidate the development and evolution of living beings from the simplest to the most complex, right up to the human being himself – a development that lies complete before us – it is now up to us to take this development further. Our understanding enables us to recognise what has unfolded in nature through time; but also, through this same capacity to reflect and understand, there can come to birth in us what Tauler and others would call spirit. And this spirit has the potential to evolve from one stage to another, just as nature has evolved.

Tauler, however, was not just pondering on the great mysteries of existence. In 1348 Strasbourg was struck by the Black Death. All who could, fled the city, and soon only those who were suffering from the dreadful disease were left. Even relatives, nurses and physicians fled in fear; but not Tauler. He stayed to care for the sick, to comfort the dying and to bury the dead. And there he remained for the next thirteen years, in the service of others, until his death in 1361. And it was on his deathbed that he uttered those words I have already quoted, 'Eternity is the everlasting now.' This was also the man who wrote: 'the true and eternal word of God is spoken only in the desert, when man has left his own self and all things behind, and stands alone, deserted, and solitary'.

But for people like Tauler the desert does not necessarily refer to a physical place. Tauler did not isolate himself from his fellow human beings. His desert was an inner experience, a lonely place in another sense. But clearly for him and for many others it is a necessary space to visit from time to time on our long journey towards becoming more fully human.

I sometimes find such a space on long walks alone in the woods or by the sea. The atmosphere surrounding my thirty-fifth birthday became one such space in which I was able to quietly commune with my inner voice – the same voice which had first made itself known in the woods surrounding the film studios at Pinewood where I walked as a young man alone at lunchtime, and began a dialogue that has continued ever since.

I imagine that each of us, in our own way, has eventually to find that desert to which Tauler referred, whether by pottering about in a shed at the bottom of the garden, or spending Sunday sitting on a river bank, ostensibly trying to catch fish. Jung found it in the Tower he built by the lake at Bollingen. For some it comes via tears, and pain, and loneliness – and a silence in which we may gradually start to feel an overwhelming sense of hidden support and comfort.

For me Steiner's book on mysticism became such a source of comfort, and a powerful confirmation of ideas I had been feeling my way towards in the first half of my life. Above all, through what he writes about the life and quest of another of his subjects, Cardinal Nicolas of Cusa, I finally understood that mysticism is as much about being fully present and alert in this world, as it is about the pursuit of an inner journey into other dimensions of existence. Ever since reading Hermann Hesse's *Narziss and Goldmund* ten years earlier, the worldly route to what is called 'enlightenment' seemed to me as valid and challenging as the discipline and rigour of the cloister. The monk Narziss came to understand this very well in his appreciation of the hard and painful journey taken by his friend Goldmund.

Nicolas of Cusa is known as the last great philosopher of the Middle Ages. Born in 1401 at Cusa on the Moselle river, he became a mathematician and astronomer. He studied at the renowned University of Padua, then took a course in theology at Cologne. Steiner called him a precursor of Copernicus, for Cusa too believed that the earth was not fixed, but a moving heavenly body like others in the universe.

Nicolas lived through a time of enormous change, epitomised by the birth in 1452 of Leonardo de Vinci, who heralded the new spirit of investigation, universality, and freedom from traditions and conservatism that was to become known as the Renaissance. Nicolas had the courage to grasp the implications of that new age and its impact on the whole edifice of the Church, its power and its teachings. As Philip Ball reminds us in his book on Paracelsus, *The Devil's Doctor*, 'science' at that time was still the knowledge handed down by approved ancients such as Aristotle:

It spoke about natural phenomena in abstract and in strictly qualitative terms. It was to be learned and not questioned. The impiety of experimenters and magicians was that they dared to interrogate God's creation, to peer under stones, to look for answers where humankind was meant simply to accept what they found on the surface. For the thirteenth-century French philosopher William of Auvergne, magic was 'a passion for knowing unnecessary things'. It was in such an intellectual climate that 'curiosity' became considered a sin, 'a lust of the eyes' in St. Augustine's words.

Steiner draws attention in his book to a significant difference between Nicolas and figures like Eckhart and Tauler, both of whom sought to deepen their inner life primarily through the contents of their faith. Nicolas's spiritual journey impelled him to seek enlightenment by research into the things of this world, for he felt knowledge thus obtained would elucidate not only the external world, but also awaken insights into his own inner nature. But all three men worked under the shadow, if one can call it that, of Scholasticism which, for all its enormous achievements in the field of learning, insisted that the most profound insights can only be arrived at by faith and not by knowledge. Nicolas did not agree.

What Steiner singles out as Nicolas's most important concept for spiritual life, inspired by his ability to think scientifically, is something called 'learned ignorance'. It is a concept already hinted at in the lives of Eckhart and his followers. What we generally understand by knowledge is information about something that is experienced as outside of us, as separate. But if our own essence does in reality correspond to the essence in all that surrounds us, both visible and invisible, and if we recognise the fact, then we can no longer speak about knowledge in the ordinary sense, for we are no longer confronting something outside us. The observer and the observed are, in their innermost essence, one and the same thing; and thus we return again to that concept – though in different words – of the human being as a microcosm of the macrocosm. Steiner uses the word 'spirit' in trying to convey the identity of what in us is central to this experience:

> It [spirit] no longer knows, it only looks upon itself. It is not concerned with a 'knowing', but with a 'not-knowing' ... With his 'learned not-knowing', Nicolas of Cusa thus speaks of nothing but knowledge reborn as inner experience.

Nicolas himself wrote about how he came to this experience, having tried over many years to unite his thoughts about God and the world, about Christ and the Church. It happened on a voyage by sea from Greece; he called it 'an inspiration from on high ... the view in which God appeared to me as the highest unity of all contrasts'. It is not, of course, an original inspiration; yet in another sense such moments are indeed new and original for the person experiencing them. It is echoed, for example, in a particular school of Hindu philosophy, Advaita Vedanta, which teaches that the world is an expression of an all-encompassing unity – Brahman – from which all being originates, and to which it returns; a view in which the individual self and the universal self, Brahman, are one.

Steiner sums up Nicolas's position as that of someone standing before 'a fateful abyss' in human spiritual life. In temperament he was what we would now call a scientist, despite the fact that he was steeped in the teachings of the Church of that time. Teilhard de Chardin is an important contemporary example of someone facing that same predicament. To think scientifically, Steiner points out, has the effect – initially at least – of disrupting 'the innocent concord' in which we live with the world. We may still dimly feel a connection with the totality of the universe, but knowledge has the tendency to separate us from the whole, and indeed from everything which seemingly isn't us. Instead we create an inner world, a solitary world from which we confront all that surrounds us. It is a lonely, painful but necessary business, this growing up, as Jung so clearly understood in formulating the concept of individuation. Steiner, too, recognised its significance and the challenge it presented. How then do we reconnect through our own resources and efforts, without falling back on old and comforting certainties? How escape the solitude?

There are three roads upon which one can walk, suggests Steiner, if one has arrived where Nicolas of Cusa found himself. One is faith. The second is despair. The third route is what he calls 'the development of man's own deepest faculties. Confidence in the world must be one leader along this third road. Courage to follow this confidence, no matter where it leads, must be the other.'

Confidence in what life brings, and not just in one's own personal life, is one of the great gifts that this little book has given me. I haven't always had the courage to follow that confidence, but I'm grateful to men such as Nicolas, Tauler, and Eckhart for at least nurturing my innate sense that all will be well, and that harmony is at the root of all creation.

Theophrastus Paracelsus, another of Steiner's eleven European mystics, was born in 1493, thirty years after the death of Nicolas of Cusa. He was even more convinced that an honest encounter with the day-to-day world under our noses was the route to wisdom and enlightenment. He became, not surprisingly, another of my great heroes. In the years that followed – having now explored the biographies of several outstanding individuals in history – I increasingly focused my own work on the here and now, on the wisdom on my own doorstep, and on what at times we mistakenly think of as ordinary and even mundane. I felt tremendously enriched by what I managed to absorb from the wisdom of the past; I had basked in the insights and revelations of great and good people. Now it was up to me. What mattered increasingly was my own experience of life as it unfolded from day to day.

Paracelsus certainly had that courage to which Steiner referred; confidence, too, in his mission as a healer and in his quest for truth – but not just truth from old books. 'No one who can stand alone by himself should be the servant of another' was what today we would call his catchphrase. The physician must 'read the book of nature', he once said, and to do so he must 'walk over its pages'. That he certainly did, basing his work entirely on the results of his own observations, extensive travel and experience. 'From where do I obtain all my secrets, from what authors?' he once asked. 'It would be better if one asked how the animals have learned their skills. If nature can teach irrational animals, can it not much more teach men?'

Paracelsus also knew, points out Jonathan Black in *The Secret History of the World*, 'that consciousness was changing and that as the intellect developed humanity would lose the instinctive knowledge of herbs that heal – a knowledge that up till then it had shared with the higher animals'.

In his biography of Paracelsus, Philip Ball points out that in the 16th century you were lucky to reach fifty years of age. Old age tires the body by thirty-five, lamented Erasmus. Half the population did not live beyond the age of twenty. Ball writes:

> There were doctors and there was medicine, but there does not seem to have been a great deal of healing ... Man suffers, according to the

priests, because of sin, and for that there is only one remedy: God's grace, which is what they were here to dispense.

Paracelsus's courage was to break with the closed hierarchical structure of medieval thought and to explore and describe the natural world. In this knowledge and through his immersion in nature Paracelsus, like Nicolas of Cusa, recognised the foundation for all higher cognition. Like the mystics already mentioned, Paracelsus also eventually had the experience, in those precious moments of true enlightenment, that it was no longer he himself who was speaking but rather the primordial essence itself. 'And this which you must consider is something great', he wrote. 'There is nothing in Heaven and on earth which is not in man. And God, who is in Heaven, is in man.' Paracelsus therefore does not seek God or the spirit *in* nature; for him nature, as it appears to our senses, is immediately divine.

In his introduction to *Mysticism at the Dawn of the Modern Age*, Paul Allen also draws attention to what he calls the most far-reaching of Paracelsus's concepts, that of signatures: 'the idea that each single part of the microcosmic world of man corresponds with each single part of the macrocosmic world outside man'. Through careful observation extending over many years, Paracelsus concluded that mineral, plant and animal substances contain what he called 'active principles'. If a method of purification and intensification could be discovered enabling these substances to release their 'active principles', he believed the latter would be infinitely safer and more effective remedies than their crude and often dangerous originals. The solution and method was finally discovered two and a half centuries later by Samuel Hahnemann; he called it homeopathy.

'The life of a man cannot be separated from the life of the universe' became the essence of Paracelsus's message. But at times this message was delivered in frustration, anger and even despair. He believed – so Ball describes – that the heavens, once considered perfect and immutable, were in fact in a state of dynamic flux like the earth. 'Dynamic flux' is a phrase that well describes much of Paracelsus's own life. Yet in the midst of a particularly turbulent phase he wrote that 'the highest ground of medicine is love'.

Philip Ball concludes his biography of the 'Devil's Doctor' with information about what followed in Paracelsus's wake and the direction that medicine has taken since his death in 1541: 'And so the last of the magicians died, or were banished from science', he writes, 'and it became the business of sober professionals whose aspirations were typically modern and mundane.' He supposes, however, that Paracelsus would not have regretted this trend. Today's science, Ball believes, 'is precisely that "art" which Paracelsus, in his more lucid moments, wished to find'. We now have a medicine that works, he states, 'and a considerable understanding of the chemical composition of the macrocosm and the microcosm, and it has liberated us from the tyranny of the stars and put our fate in our own hands'. There are many people besides me – doctors included – who would not, I believe, accept that we now have a medicine that works in all cases, at all times. Nor do I believe that what emanates from the stars has to be seen as tyrannical. What is tyrannical is any form of fanatical dogmatism, whether religious or scientific.

Steiner sums up his interest in the figure of Paracelsus as someone who did not see in this so-called 'primordial essence of the world' something essentially complete; rather he had an intuitive sense of 'the divine in its becoming'. Is this, in Philip Ball's terms, lucid or not? For Paracelsus such an intuition indicated both an opportunity and a purpose for humanity in the process of an ever-unfolding creation. Paracelsus imagined our role as co-architects in this building of the universe: 'For nature brings forth nothing into the light of day which is complete as it stands; rather, man must complete it.'

Our self-creating activity through evolution is what Paracelsus calls alchemy: 'This completion is alchemy. Thus the alchemist is the baker when he bakes the bread, the vintager when he makes the wine, the weaver when he makes the cloth.' Paracelsus, the physician, can thus be understood as an alchemist in his field. 'He wants to investigate the laws of chemistry', writes Steiner, 'in order to work as an alchemist in his sense.' Steiner continues:

> One who does not look beyond such natural processes may be left cold by them as by things of a material and prosaic nature; one who at all costs wants to grasp the spirit with the senses will people these processes with all kinds of spiritual beings. But like Paracelsus, one who knows how to look at such processes in connection with the universe, which reveals its secret within man, accepts these processes as they present themselves to the senses; he does not first reinterpret them; for as the natural processes stand before us in their sensory reality, in their own way they reveal the mystery of existence.

If Paracelsus appears to us as someone with one foot in the past and one in the future, I sense that Philip Ball sees him as belonging more to the medieval world of superstition and magic, than to what we call the modern world; whereas Steiner sees him as one of the forerunners of something quite new – something which can incorporate and develop the ancient intimations about reality into a scientific approach. Steiner called this spiritual science. In this sense, perhaps, Paracelsus's day has yet to come.

Meanwhile, in considering the life and work of his tenth subject, Giordano Bruno, who was finally burnt at the stake for his beliefs, Steiner reminds us that by the 16th century human beings who thought for themselves were compelled to confront the world around them and in particular the vast star-filled spaces that towered over them, in a very different way. The scientific genius of Nicolas Copernicus, already anticipated by Nicolas of Cusa, demonstrated that the earth was not the centre of the universe; nor did the stars move in circles – the circle being the image of perfection. Humanity had instead to accept – for a while at least – that our home, the earth, was seemingly not unique, but just one among millions of other heavenly bodies. Likewise we were prompted to regard the phenomena of our earth as essentially no different from what existed in the rest of the universe. In other words our sensory world had expanded into furthest space. But where were the gods?

'In earlier centuries', writes Steiner, 'the meditating spirit of man had stood before another world of facts. Now it was given a new task.' The mystics featured in his book anticipated, each in their own way, what Bruno and his successors were now challenged to do – namely to discover within themselves and in nature itself those sublime mysteries that were previously projected outwards into the heavens. As the Franciscan, Angelus Silesius – the last of Steiner's subjects – once declared: 'Stop, whither are you running? Heaven is in you; if you seek God elsewhere you will forever miss Him.'

CHAPTER 19

Faith versus Reason

Elizabeth Ann
Said to her Nan:
'Please will you tell me how God began?
Somebody must have made him, So
Who could it be, 'cos I want to know?'

So begins A.A. Milne's 'Explained', in his much loved book *Now We Are Six*. The poem may not be in the same league as the writings featured in Steiner's *Mysticism at the Dawn of the Modern Age* but the important thing, it seems to me, is that we go on asking such questions. Eckhart and others spoke to their time; A.A. Milne, as far as I am aware, was no mystic, but he epitomised a particular sort of sensitivity and intelligence that speaks to our time – a time that I believe to be far more interesting and profound than is often acknowledged.

Milne goes on to describe Elizabeth Ann's 'wonderful plan' to run round the world till she found a man 'who knew exactly how God began'. She eventually returns home without an answer, and confronts her doll, Jennifer Jane, with the same question:

And Jane, who didn't much care for speaking,
Replied in her usual way by squeaking.
And what did it mean? Well, to be quite candid,
I don't know, but Elizabeth Ann did.
Elizabeth Ann said softly, 'Oh!
Thank you, Jennifer. Now I know.'

For me the poem is an imaginative, contemporary recognition of the inadequacy of words and indeed of theories altogether. What it also implies is that there are answers to our questions, but we need 'the ears to hear and the eyes to see'. Meanwhile, and quite rightly, we go on searching and coming up with answers that satisfy us for a while.

The need for humility in our quest was powerfully brought home to me through making a film with the astronomer Bernard Lovell in 1974, for the BBC series *One Pair of Eyes*. The executive producer, Malcolm Brown, had commissioned my film with Penelope Betjeman in India; now I was heading north to the great radio telescope at Jodrell Bank that Lovell pushed and pulled into existence in the early years after World War II.

In his introductory commentary to the film Lovell wrote:

> Not an ordinary telescope through which one sees the stars, but a huge steel reflector as big as the dome of St Paul's, suspended two hundred feet above the Cheshire Plain. It's driven with such precision that it can pin-point galaxies so remote in time and space that some of the radio waves received began their journey through space long before our earth came into existence.

Standing by a huge, tape-spewing computer, Lovell then delivered his opening statement to camera – a statement as courageous as it was profound, for a much respected and eminent scientist was about to question the infallibility of a purely scientific, rationalistic approach to reality:

> At this moment the telescope is receiving signals from a distant object in the universe; it's a quasar. In fact, at this moment this is the most distant object we know. The signals making the holes in this punched tape have been processed by a computer and they are an account of signals which have been travelling through space for about eight thousand million years. In other words we believe this quasar is at a distance of at least eight thousand million light years [light travels at three hundred million metres per second]. There are some who believe that holes in punched tape like this give us the only certain knowledge we can get about the birth and the early history of the entire cosmos. There are others who are not so certain that this scientific knowledge can be so unique and absolute. It was William Blake who wrote 'As a man is, so he sees.' In fact I am one of the doubters. What I see in these punched holes about the early history of the universe is a reconciliation and assimilation of what I observe and what I believe. And what I believe has been conditioned by many other influences in my life.

The full quotation from William Blake is: 'The tree which moves some to tears of joy, is in the eyes of others only a green thing which stands in the way. As a man is, so he sees.' Those final words, 'As a man is, so he sees', became the title of our film. In it Lovell set out to describe the many and varied influences on his beliefs. Over the years, incidentally, Lovell has surrounded his home with a wonderful collection of those 'green things' called trees, and possibly knows more about them than he does about the stars.

Lovell's dilemma is interesting to consider in the light of the challenges that faced Giordano Bruno and his successors from the 16th century onwards. The technology they developed enabled them to extend the sensory world into distant space, as well as into the microscopic world at their feet. And so, rather than speculating about some heavenly world – a realm that in some cases was clearly experienced, and not just imagined – we have increasingly searched in this sensory world for an understanding of existence. But an essential element of this existence, as I have tried to show, has proved to be as invisible as angels themselves, and therefore undetectable through our physical senses or our scientific instruments. Again as I've already suggested, perhaps the only instrument with the potential to detect reality in its fullest sense is the human being – if we are indeed a microcosm of the macrocosm. But without awakening that in us which corresponds to the great mysteries that still confront us, at whatever distance, we are faced by what Nicolas of Cusa faced all those centuries ago: a choice between despair, which can take many forms, and faith.

Many would say: 'What's wrong with faith?' It is clearly an honest and humble acknowledgement of our limitations as human beings, for which I have the utmost respect. Bernard Lovell is one of many fine people I've met who seemed reasonably content to keep his inner life in two seemingly separate compartments – faith and reason. Because I believe increasingly that what we think is far less important than how we behave, I am not at all bothered by the fact that many people, some of them highly intelligent, still tend to live this almost double life. If, on the other hand, what we think actually determines our future to a far greater extent than we realise, then perhaps I should be more concerned. For if knowledge, and above all self-knowledge – and not just knowledge for knowledge's sake – is an essential tool in creating a better world, then it is clearly very important that we explore the truths that underpin all existence, and our capacity to penetrate those truths.

As yet, it seems, the implications of 20th-century research into relativity and above all into the paradoxical nature of matter itself, as explored in quantum mechanics, have not radically influenced most people's everyday consciousness – though they have revolutionised physics itself. And so we continue to devise or go along with all sorts of theories about life with a mindset that hasn't yet shaken off the paradigm of the detached observer living in an essentially mechanistic universe. This activity and research is nevertheless carried out with great diligence, energy and goodwill – and in certain fields with huge success. For example, like millions of other people I have benefited from modern medical expertise, and am very grateful for it.

It is also important to recognise that a significant and very welcome consequence of this more earth-bound consciousness, which has become ever more apparent since the 16th century – in contrast to an obsession about some imagined afterlife – has been that our attention to the needs and problems of *this* world has increased enormously. In this sense I am fully in sympathy with the American poet Emily Dickinson when she wrote:

Faith is a fine invention
For gentlemen who see;
But microscopes are prudent
In an emergency!

What is crucial, however, is the interpretation we bring to the data revealed by those microscopes. Increasingly, perhaps, we require a new perspective if, for example, we want to move on from simplistic and reductive descriptions of our genesis, whether we imagine this as taking place in six days or with some Big Bang – both of which seem to me equally improbable.

We therefore need to study ourselves far more diligently – human beings as 'instruments' with the kind of potential which mystics throughout the ages have started to experience. 'We need more understanding of human nature' was what Jung so passionately believed and so urgently expressed to John Freeman in that interview for *Face to Face*.

In our film Bernard Lovell began by describing his life as being swayed between an idealistic search for truth and the demands of a materialistic world. Music and religion were the two great influences on his early life: his father was a lay preacher. Although Lovell finally chose to study physics rather than music, he continued to play the organ and was doing so still when we made the film. 'It was my passion for music,' he said, 'in particular organ music, which was the thread that held me to the Church at a time when the materialistic impact of science was eroding the fundamental beliefs inbred into me during my childhood.'

As a young man Lovell was deeply inspired by the life of Albert Schweitzer, a fellow organist who at the age of thirty, when already principal of a theological college, resigned his post in order to become a medical student so that he could work as a missionary in Africa. The other important influence on his early life was the philosopher A.N. Whitehead. At a time when science was making huge strides in our understanding about the nature of the atom on the one hand, and – through the telescope at Mount Wilson in the USA – about the nature and vastness of the universe on the other, Whitehead was writing: 'Have we any grounds for the belief that in some way things really are in those regions as our senses perceive those regions?' This problem about the nature of knowledge has, said Lovell, remained with him throughout his life: 'I am puzzled about the manner in which the individual himself influences the observations which he believes are telling him the truth about nature and the universe.'

Lovell went on to describe how his youthful idealism was gradually eroded by the events leading up to World War II – Italy's invasion of Abyssinia, the Spanish Civil War, Japan's aggressive expansion into Manchuria and then into China, and the inability of the League of Nations to settle the world's disputes by peaceful means. Eight months after the outbreak of war Lovell, along with many other young scientists, was recruited to develop the new and highly secret technique of radar for the defence of the country. At the age of twenty-six it was, he said, a complete change from what he had thought was science: 'This was science applied to a task, and a task involving the fate of nations.' In describing what he felt in those days, he wrote: 'Well, as a man is, so he sees. And as far as I and my young scientific colleagues were concerned, the civilised world seemed to be in mortal danger, and we were prepared to place our scientific skills at the service of the nation.' These skills eventually led to the development of a navigational and bombing aid that made possible the accurate targeting and devastation of many German cities including Hamburg, Leipzig and Dresden. 'My life and thought could never be the same', he wrote. 'I had been involved in using the immense powers of science for destruction.'

Bernard Lovell at Jodrell Bank

After the war Lovell returned to the science that had first attracted him – a search for pure knowledge, as defined by the scientific method. By 1948, at Manchester University, he had built a huge aerial to study the radio waves from space. There was only one problem – it was fixed to the ground. Four years later, after much persistence, the foundations were laid for a giant, steerable telescope. By 1957 the work at Jodrell Bank was almost complete, but the project had run into serious financial and political problems. They needed a miracle. That miracle came from behind the Iron Curtain. The Russians launched the world's first artificial satellite, the Sputnik. The West was staggered, not only by the scientific achievement but also by the realisation that its launching rocket, in another guise, was a Soviet intercontinental ballistic missile. Lovell's telescope was the only instrument in the world able to locate the rocket by radar. Overnight he became a hero and his project was saved.

From then on Lovell was able to continue his research work in relative peace. First the Moon and later Mars, hitherto an enigma to earth-bound astronomers, could now be studied in detail. Research of vital importance to our understanding of the origin of the solar system was becoming possible. But pure research accounted for only a small percentage of the billions of roubles and dollars being spent in those years. Rockets can carry either scientific instruments or nuclear bombs. Lovell was witnessing a classic demonstration of the interaction of scientific, commercial and military interests. It's a problem that in his opinion dogs science still.

In our film Lovell described his work at Jodrell Bank, and how initially very little was known about the origin of radio waves from the distant universe. The signals seemed to be coming from the space between stars and not from the stars or galaxies themselves. Then strange objects far outside our own galaxy were located. By 1959 one of these sources of radio waves was photographed – four and a half thousand million light years distant and receding from us at a speed of eighty thousand miles per second. In the search for ever more distant objects, the mysterious quasars were discovered. 'Sometimes', he said, 'it seems that the difficulty of interpretation increases the further we penetrate into time and space.'

This is a subject I have discussed with Lovell subsequently, and he has shared with me an increasing sense that at some point cosmology is in for 'a big shock'. Can we, for example, really assume that what we know and understand as the laws of physics are universally applicable, or that the speed of light is constant? My own simple analogy would be the assumption that because human beings grow roughly five or six feet during their first eighteen years of life, they will be about twelve feet tall by their mid-thirties.

Lovell's way of expressing his attitude to these great mysteries was to say that for him science is only one way of knowing. At the conclusion of our film he made this statement:

> Many may find it inconceivable that there might be limits to scientific knowledge. Well, as a man is, so he sees – and I am no more surprised or distressed at the limitation of science when faced with the great problem of creation than I am at the limitation of the spectroscope in describing the radiance of a sunset, or at the theory of counterpoint in describing the beauty of a fugue.

I don't consider, however, that it is scientifically out of bounds to ask what it is that lives in Lovell and, in varying degrees, in all of us that relates with such intensity to the beauty and wonder in nature, to art and music, and to the star-filled universe. In a conversation with Joan Bakewell for the BBC Radio series *Belief* (subsequently published in a book of the same title) the biologist Richard Dawkins came up with this response to the question: Where does beauty come from? 'Well, I think beauty ultimately has to come from the way the brain is set up.' He goes on to say what a 'devastatingly complicated mechanism' the brain is, how we're only just beginning to understand how it works, and how our response to something being beautiful must ultimately be explicable in terms of this understanding. 'When I am moved to tears as I can be by the slow movement of a Schubert quartet,' he says, 'it is not in any sense to demean the experience to say there is nothing going on other than activity in my neurones.'

I am far more convinced by something Emerson wrote in an essay on the 16th-century Swedish visionary Emanuel Swedenborg, in which he explores the need for both knowledge and holiness in the search for truth:

> The human mind stands ever in perplexity, demanding intellect, demanding sanctity. Without that balance, the human mind swings between these two desires in disturbing cycles. We recognize the face of intellect without sanctity and we recognize the face of sanctity without intellect. If sanctity is void of intellect it becomes dogma. There is no light in it. Light is the image of the intellect. If the intellect is exercised without sanctity, then the light is shown on nothing; it reveals nothingness.

Thus what Emerson writes is a plea for our intelligence to develop hand in hand with our religious sensibilities – not one without the other, nor in separate compartments.

Another 'man of science' whom I met at this time was the journalist John Davy, for sixteen years science correspondent of *The Observer*. He and I became trustees of Emerson College at the same time; John eventually went on to work there, later becoming vice principal, while continuing to work as a freelance journalist. In 1965 he was awarded an OBE for 'services to science'.

Everyone loved and respected John Davy, a man who always had time for whoever came knocking at his door. In the introduction to a collection of his articles, *Hope, Evolution and Change*, published after his sudden and early death in 1984, Owen Barfield wrote: 'Davy remained quietly convinced that the intellectual materialism characteristic of our age is a passing phase.' Modern science was perceived by him as a manifestation of this materialism in an age-long evolution of consciousness. In an interview – echoing an observation similar to one by Jung that I quoted earlier – Davy once remarked:

> It is odd that we should so easily accept the idea that for some thousands of years people had stupid, erroneous or superstitious ideas about the universe, and then, quite suddenly, from the 15th century onwards, the true facts suddenly begin to enter our heads.

Barfield goes on to point out how Davy perceived the evolutionary process as involving the severance of human consciousness from the spiritual world that underlies both nature and consciousness itself; but then, as I have already suggested, this same process presents us with the possibility of an eventual reunion with that world at a higher level. 'It is to the severance – the threshold between matter and spirit', writes Barfield, 'that we owe our self-consciousness, and thus our very existence as autonomous individual spirits.'

John Davy

One article that Davy wrote for *The Observer*, on April 15th 1979, is particularly relevant to my theme. In 'Life after Life', he reported on a meeting with the celebrated doctor Elizabeth Kübler-Ross, whose book *On Death and Dying* has helped and inspired very many people faced with that most challenging of all human ordeals. 'She describes her work', wrote Davy, 'with a kind of sober compassion, a blend of inner strength, objective judgement, and deep warmth for her patients that is unforgettable.' He goes on to point out that in our society, perhaps more than in any other in history, death is surrounded by uncertainties, and above all by taboos which seal patients and hospital staff alike into separate compartments of fear and silence. In the article he continued:

While I was with her I had to withdraw for an hour while she met a patient, a distraught young woman with two children. One had recently been diagnosed as having untreatable leukaemia, whereupon the father had hanged himself in the garage. There he was found by the second child. Her work is with people engulfed in a sea of pain.

Davy describes how Kübler-Ross, during the earlier phases of her work with the dying, began to realise that her patients were often undergoing unusual experiences: they would converse with invisible presences, and the next moment speak with complete lucidity to the doctor by the bed. Then one of her patients described an out-of-body experience of the kind now made familiar by Raymond Moody's book *Life after Life*. She eventually decided to brave the scepticism of colleagues, professional ostracism and the inevitable questions about her sanity, by speaking publicly of some personal experiences of her own. A former patient who had recently died appeared to her, thanking her for her care and encouraging her to keep on with the work.

'Her own experiences', wrote Davy, 'both personal and professional, have led her to the unshakable conviction that the body is the bearer of our existence during life, but not its cause, and that this existence continues when the body has been laid aside.' Many people have, of course, come to the same conclusions, and in the not too distant past it was the commonly held view. 'But our scientific culture is a very curious one, quite unlike any that have proceeded it', continued Davy:

> Within a comparatively short period, science has put into our hands quite unprecedented powers. This gives immense authority to the ideas, methods, and the people who have produced them. This authority easily hardens into doctrine. A basic proposition of molecular biology is quite unashamedly called 'the central dogma'. Thus a kind of assumption has come to permeate scientific culture, with almost tyrannous force, that most of what earlier cultures thought about the universe was primitive superstition.

In fact the many descriptions in recent years of near-death experiences closely resemble accounts from various older spiritual and religious traditions – as, for example, those contained in *The Tibetan Book of the Dead*. A purely materialistic conception of birth and death, Davy points out, is almost non-existent before our time, 'and even now does not seem to be held with total conviction by very many people'.

Davy goes on to cite a number of highly capable and creative people who over the centuries have claimed direct experience of other dimensions of existence – Swedenborg, Jung and Steiner among them. Both Jung and Steiner were, as already mentioned, highly critical of what Davy calls 'doctrinaire science', while vigorously upholding its essential and original striving, which they regarded as 'a kind of coming of age of the human spirit'.

'Science was born, not as a doctrine, but in defiance of doctrine, out of a spirit of resolutely independent inquiry.' This is the thought that speaks to me most strongly in Davy's article and echoes what had touched me so deeply in reading about those medieval mystics. It is because of this spirit of independent inquiry, Davy believed, that the medical and scientific community legitimately resists a simple acceptance of body-free existence, of an afterlife and of mere anecdotes of unusual experiences. 'Yet through fear of relapse into what are conceived as outgrown systems of belief', he writes, 'alternatives are offered which are themselves rooted in hypotheses which have fossilised into articles of faith.'

What is the scientific problem, asks Davy, in accepting that human beings can watch themselves being resuscitated from several feet above their own bodies? It is, he says, the conviction that consciousness is caused by brain processes. He then points out that in fact no agreed and coherent scientific accounts exist of how brains and minds function. 'There is far more mystery than certainty. So a reasonable humility is in order.' It is a subject I shall be returning to in more detail later in the book.

———————

One piece of John Davy's writing that has sadly never been published is what he called 'Screwtape Two'. Its inspiration is taken in part from C.S. Lewis's *The Screwtape Letters* in which, with great imagination, wit and insight Lewis attempted to expose some of the clandestine operations being directed 'from Below' by a high-ranking devil called Screwtape. The letters are addressed to his nephew, Wormwood, one of his agents in the field, and reveal some of the 'fiendish techniques' employed to lead human souls astray – in this case a man edging towards a deeper commitment to Christianity. Screwtape and Wormwood eventually lose the battle, but only after a spirited fight.

As the situation becomes more desperate for the agents of 'Our Father Below', Screwtape writes to his nephew:

> I see only one thing to do at the moment. Your patient has become humble; have you drawn his attention to the fact? All virtues are less formidable to us once the man is aware that he has them, but this is especially true of humility. Catch him at the moment when he is really poor in spirit and smuggle into his mind the gratifying reflection, 'By Jove! I'm being humble', and almost immediately pride – pride at his own humility – will appear. If he awakes to the danger and tries to smother this new form of pride, make him proud of his attempt – and so on, through as many stages as you please. But don't

try this for too long, for fear you awake his sense of humour and proportion, in which case he will merely laugh at you and go to bed.

C.S. Lewis's book is full of such penetrating insights into the frailty of the human condition. John Davy's update was written some forty years later and grew out of his work with a group of students at Emerson College studying Steiner's book *The Philosophy of Freedom*. Davy encouraged them to try to bring the thoughts to life themselves by writing their own version of the first seven chapters. 'Screwtape Two' was Davy's own attempt.

In commenting on Davy's text, Michael Burton, who has staged a number of performances based on 'Screwtape Two', writes of the importance and relevance that he attaches to *The Philosophy of Freedom* for understanding the modern world and our own place in it.

In our times two ideas rule our lives more than we are generally aware of, and the effects these ideas exert are with us everywhere: One is that we cannot know the world as it really is except through relying on scientific instruments that show a reality quite different from what our senses give us. The second idea is that human beings can never know the source of their own actions and therefore cannot be free. However, both these assertions can be challenged, and letting a devil be his own advocate is a very successful, as well as entertaining way to get us examining the basic assumptions present all around us and in our own thoughts and actions.

In the first letter in 'Screwtape Two', Screwtape's nephew Wormwood is reprimanded up front for allowing the soul in his charge to begin to think about freedom. Indeed, the main aim, he is reminded, is to prevent him thinking at all:

A life of unquestioning self-satisfaction is the surest – and for you the least strenuous – road to achieving our goal ... You say that you immediately pointed out to him all the ways in which he is not free: being human, he has to wake, sleep, eat, drink and perform all those organic functions which sustain his terrestrial existence. You told him he was a slave to nature. Of course he is – and he is used enough to it to realise that this is not what is bothering him. He accepts these limitations. Then you told him he was a product of his environment. This bothered him a good deal more. He has always vaguely thought of himself as 'independent' and 'non-conformist'. When you pointed out to him the degree to which he has been shaped by country, language, culture, class, family, education, friends and so on, he began to realise that a large part of who he is, is explicable as conditioning and habit. You showed him beyond all doubt that even a great artistic genius such as Goethe or Shakespeare has certainly been influenced by his upbringing and his environment, and you got him to start to accept that such a person may therefore be doing no more than working out their own life-traumas in all their creative work, and therefore not free at all.

Davy's Screwtape goes on to warn his nephew of the danger of people going beyond the thought that they are either free or unfree: 'Now he realises that he might be partly free – and you are in serious trouble.' One suggested tactic is to dangle in front of his victim at every possible moment the slogan 'You can't change human nature', and to continue to make him aware that his thoughts are as much conditioned as anything else. If he sees the weakness in this argument, then tell him his thoughts are nothing but brain processes. Screwtape continues:

> The trouble is that he has begun to realise that whereas he feels unfree in his organic needs and eating habits, he doesn't feel unfree when he thinks about these unfreedoms. He is beginning to wonder about thinking, about his own awareness of the problems of freedom. He doubts that cows or beetles worry about freedom. But he does. And he has begun to realise that he must investigate what it is in his own nature that asks questions about the world – and about freedom. This is extremely dangerous. At all costs he must be diverted from this line of enquiry. We have almost persuaded large numbers of his fellow souls that they're no more than animals or – even better – machines. He must not be allowed to become an exception.

The second letter opens by expressing Screwtape's concern at the path that the subject is taking, and his exasperation with his nephew for falling back on the excuse that he has 'tried everything':

> To begin with, you had every advantage on your side. Once he began to become interested in his own propensity to ask questions, he realised that these questions are prompted by a feeling of separateness from the world. (He doesn't have questions when he's asleep.) As we remarked in our previous communication, you should have prevented him from waking up at all.

Wormwood is reminded by his uncle of the success of the Research Department in devising many ingenious methods of ensuring that large numbers of the population are only capable of casual and superficial observations, even when in the waking state. The danger comes when people do actually begin to wake up, becoming aware of the outer world and starting to ask questions about it. It is then that they begin to feel 'separate'. Screwtape then adds:

> This was foreseen by our Controllers many centuries ago, and, as you are very well aware, preparations were made accordingly. You are too young to remember our victory celebrations in 1641 when one of our most effective field-workers persuaded his subject, René Descartes, to divide the entire universe into body and mind. You know how this enabled us to get a lot of very clever people to talk about themselves as 'detached observers', looking at the world without asking themselves where they were looking at it from.

The nephew is then told of two strategies, once the subject has got this far. One is to make the person so very aware of himself that he is easily persuaded that the world out there is his dream. It is a strategy, he is advised, that is particularly effective with those prone to intellectual speculation, who are usually more interested in their own thought processes than in what they choose to call the world. 'Universities are particularly fruitful territories for this ploy', he is told, 'as the majority of their professional inhabitants tend to live in a dream anyway.'

The alternative ploy is to persuade the person that there is a real world 'out there', but that because he is detached, he can't ever really understand it. The uncle then reminds his nephew of the Emmanuel Kant Memorial Day, in which he has often participated, and which celebrates the success of one of their distinguished colleagues in persuading 'this unfortunate philosopher' that he could never know 'the thing in itself', but only the pictures, the imaginations he made of the world in his own mind. Screwtape rejoices in the fact that their victim is 'soaked in the mental climate we have been able to develop out of this conviction', having absorbed a great deal of popular science which persuades him that the real world is actually quite different from how it appears to him. In other words, instead of trusting his own judgement and response to the phenomena that surround him, he has become diverted 'into speculating about what trees and birds are made of, about molecules and atoms and other realities which he makes pictures of but can never know'. Theories thus become realities, and finally dogmas.

Two alternatives are now open to Screwtape in order to consolidate a victory 'from below' rather than 'on high'. One is to reinforce the state of sleep from which the subject is still in danger of awakening:

See to it that he is fully occupied developing ingenious ways of manipulating the 'hidden realities' he is picturing. With luck, he can be effectively doped with enjoyment of his own technical ingenuity for the remainder of his terrestrial existence.

Here Screwtape adds that if successful with this ploy, the main task will then be to prevent the subject from waking up to the ecological mess he is making around him – something increasingly difficult to do. He acknowledges that a disturbing number of souls are waking up and asking questions about this situation. In other words, people are beginning to realise that the mess out there might have something to do with the mess inside themselves. An alternative, suggests the ever-cunning Screwtape,

again most effective with intellectuals and feeling-types rather than men of action, is to engender a mood of resignation, a general feeling of melancholia that he will always be separate from the world and never come to know it. Facing this situation, human souls respond in a variety of ways and one must be vigilant. At all costs, the response that the Opposition calls 'courage' is to be striven against, and if one is successful in this, melancholia can be extended into paranoia or self-destructive behaviour. The world is not only unknowable; it is basically impersonal and hostile.

This second letter, however, ends on an anxious note. Screwtape recognises from his nephew's reports that the subject persists in regarding 'himself', rather than the 'impersonal universe', as responsible for his dilemma:

He is saying to himself that his separateness arises as an experience when he wakes up in the morning and starts thinking. He is blaming himself for feeling separate from nature. He is talking about having a 'fundamental desire for knowledge' so that he can 'reunite' himself with nature. Worst of all, though, he is saying that he must look more deeply into himself to find out how the experience of being separate arises – and how he can resolve it. He is even hoping to find something to do with 'nature' (which we worked so hard to persuade him is an impersonal world 'out there') somewhere inside himself. If you can't get him to go to sleep again, or at least remain in a dream, he is going to make some very dangerous discoveries indeed.
P.S. If he goes on talking about 'Nature', stop him saying 'She'; only allow 'It'. Take a tip from an old devil!

In the five letters that follow we read how matters rapidly go from bad to worse. Screwtape's nephew fails, for example, to keep his subject solely absorbed in his laboratory and in museums, and away from actual plants; he therefore becomes increasingly aware that plants do indeed grow. Thus it becomes impossible to prevent him from realising that he begins to overcome his feeling of separateness from the world when he understands it. He feels more intimate with bicycles, explains the increasingly distraught Screwtape to his nephew, when he sees how they work, and with plants when he begins to understand how they grow. It is then that he notices that his knowledge comes from two directions: he makes observations, and he thinks about those observations. Thus he realises that when he finds the right thoughts, he understands his observations. In the act of observation he is receptive; the world comes to him. In thinking he is active; he has to work inwardly for his insights. 'As soon as he realised that thinking is something that doesn't happen unless he makes it happen,' writes Screwtape in letter number three, 'he began to get a glimpse of himself as a thinker, as a centre of what the Opposition calls 'spiritual activity'. Screwtape then bemoans the fact that their Enemy was responsible for that most treacherous deed of allowing some of His light to light up in the souls of His creatures.

For a while there is a slim hope that the senior Department of Temptation can successfully intervene – 'Temptation was operational before confusion' – pride, self-centredness and egotism being some of their usual procedures. It is the trap that C.S. Lewis describes so effectively in his original *Screwtape Letters*.

'You had him in your sights', writes Davy's increasingly desperate Screwtape in letter number four:

> You showed him that he is a miserably limited being, who can only be in one place at a time – so he can only make observations from his own point of view. And as he has to use an absurdly limited organisation, so he can't see things for which he hasn't got any senses.

It is then that Wormwood should have hammered home the idea that people only see the world through their sense organs and not as it is, 'so knowing means "processing sense data", but the things which are the sources of the sense data are therefore out of reach ... They are easily persuaded that there is no way out.'

The real disaster now experienced by Wormwood is being laughed at: 'Such are the treacherous ways of the Opposition', his uncle tells him. But it is too late. 'You need eyes to observe eyes', taunted their victim, 'Ha-ha-ha'. Far more serious, however, is Screwtape's recognition that his nephew has allowed his victim to continue to think about thinking and thus begin to realise that in this activity he is beyond subject and object, since they are both experiences produced by thinking. The fear is that he will soon start wondering whether thinking can't transcend the apparent inaccessibility of 'the thing in itself'. This letter ends on a note of panic: 'You have got to stop him!'

Yet the horrible truth is sinking in and Wormwood's career prospects are looking grim: 'Your subject has woken up, and you are paying the penalty. You will no longer be able to persuade him that the world is his dream. When human creatures dream, things just happen to them. When they wake up, they begin to make things happen.'

At this stage, Screwtape knows only too well that their victim has begun to realise that through thinking he can begin to transcend the limitations of his personality and to participate 'in the world of universal realities', whose forms he knows intuitively as concepts and whose substances he receives observationally as percepts. As he unites the two within his soul, writes John Davy through the gnarled hand of a defeated and humbled devil, he begins to participate again in the reality of nature from which he thought for a time he was separated. So, too, comes the realisation that it is not the universe that imposes limits to knowledge, but only his own nature, with its still limited capacities for observation and intuition. At the end of the fifth letter, Screwtape writes:

> The worst of it is that he is now beginning to wonder about the possibilities of going to work on his own nature so as to overcome some of its limitations, and thus extend his participation in reality. As you know, the Opposition regards this as essential future work for His Creatures. He wants to see them begin to participate, as transformers and transmuters of His Creation. He calls it Redemption. We call it bloody unfair deprivation of our rights to make some (or preferably all) of His Creation into our own.

In throwing light on their impending failure, Screwtape finally draws attention to that moment 'when the Opposition effected a change in His subjects so that they became capable of incorporating individually a disgusting paradox: a selfless self'.

One consequence of what Screwtape calls 'this treacherous manipulation' worked its ways through and surfaced 'in that dreadful and subversive movement which some subjects call Romanticism'. Artists began to be thought of as 'creative', whereas previously the universal had come to them – they called it being 'inspired'. Another great thorn in the flesh of Screwtape and his colleagues, that he just manages to spit out, are the words of 'one arch-Romantic' (Keats): 'I am certain of nothing but the holiness of the heart's affections and the truth of imagination.'

'Imagination is the start of the rot', concludes Screwtape in the sixth letter: 'That is when subjects begin to lift their hearts into their heads. This is what your subject has begun to do.' There is one last hope: 'Just possibly, you may be able to persuade him that what he is beginning to undertake is actually too difficult. He may have the desire, but has he the will?'

Apparently so; according to the now defeated Screwtape, the subject was already too interested in the journey itself; still worse, he was in good heart. But the final problem that confronted Screwtape and his nephew was something acknowledged as infinitely more profound: this human soul, writes Screwtape, 'could not be prevented from realising that he does have the power to resolve the questions he puts to himself, to meet his own destiny, because the Opposition's own emissary into our realms (to Whom we may never explicitly refer) successfully met His destiny one dreadful weekend some two thousand years ago'.

The Crucifixion, by Cecil Collins

CHAPTER 20

A Question of Balance

In the beginning
Adam blamed Eve.
Eve blamed the serpent.
The serpent hadn't a leg to stand on.
(Anon)

If only things were that simple! How about this instead?

Where does evil come from?
It comes
from man
always from man
only from man.

These words by the Polish writer Tadeusz Rozewicz are quoted by the Lithuanian poet and 1980 Nobel Prize winner Czeslaw Milosz at the opening of his poem *Unde Malum*. He took as his title St. Augustine's celebrated question: 'Whence evil?'

Alas, dear Tadeusz,
good nature and wicked man
are romantic inventions
you show us this way
the depth of your optimism.

so let man exterminate
his own species
the innocent sunrise will illuminate
a liberated flora and fauna

where oak forests reclaim
the post industrial wasteland
and the blood of a deer
torn asunder by a pack of wolves
is not seen by anyone
a hawk falls upon a hare
without witness
evil disappears from the world
and consciousness with it

Of course, dear Tadeusz,
evil (and good) comes from man.

I have an interesting collection of notes, this poem among them, under the heading of 'Evil'. My daughter, Ellie, around the age of ten, had a brief phase of being afraid of bedtime and spoke about 'lurky things'. It's not fashionable these days to believe in devils and demons, and in lurky things, though many people still have a vague sense that angels exist in some unknowable form. Indeed, despite the thick veneer of materialism that envelops us all, there is a surprisingly widespread belief in what, in the Judaeo-Christian world, we call God, and in what the Muslims call Allah. But what about devils? What about Screwtape? Are we human beings really the source of all that is evil in the world, as Tadeusz Rozewicz clearly believes?

Jung felt enormous gratitude to his mother for pointing him in the direction of Goethe's *Faust*. Here for Jung was a great and relatively contemporary mind that took the existence of evil seriously, and personified it in the person of Mephistopheles. C.S. Lewis clearly shared this vision. For them there is, indeed, a war in heaven. And if, as I suspect, what we call heaven and earth are essentially one, then that war is playing itself out in the here and now, and not somewhere else. As the shaman John Parry tells Will in Philip Pullman's *His Dark Materials*:

There are two great powers, and they've been fighting since time began. Every advance in human life, every scrap of knowledge and wisdom and decency we have has been torn by one side from the teeth of the other. Every little increase in human freedom has been fought over ferociously between those who want us to know more and be wiser and stronger, and those who want us to obey and be humble and submit.

Steiner spoke and wrote about the question of evil on many occasions. In his opinion and experience there are two very basic influences or polarities in human life, either of which, if taken to excess, can become dangerous and ultimately evil. Our challenge is therefore to hold the balance, to resist becoming one-sided. In this we are helped by a third great influence in human evolution, which for Steiner was the being of Christ.

One polarity in our nature individualises us. Our creativity and enthusiasm for life stem from this source, as does our self-awareness and urge for freedom, and the feeling of our own worth and importance. But taken to extremes it can blind us to the needs of our fellow human beings and undermine our engagement with the demands of daily life, encouraging us instead to escape into fantasies of one sort or another. It's a tendency that Aldous Huxley recognised in exaggerated form under the influence of mescalin.

Steiner frequently spoke of the being of Lucifer in this connection. In a lecture he gave in Hamburg in May 1910 he spoke about Lucifer as follows: 'All our greed, egotism, ambition, pride, vanity – all qualities connected with a sort of inflation of our ego, with a desire to be in the limelight – all this is the result of luciferic temptations.' Elsewhere Steiner goes so far as to say that the common trait of all evil is nothing other than egotism. Yet in another lecture, some eight years later, he said:

> It is simply not possible ... to reject all luciferic influences. If we did this our lives would grow shallow and unreal – we'd all become arch-philistines. It is the vitality and energy of the luciferic tendency in the human being that time and again provides us with the yeast to rise above pedantry and philistinism.

It is this philistinism that can emerge from the other polarity in our nature, the positive aspect of which ties us to the earth and keeps our feet on the ground. The earth, after all, is where we are, and where perhaps we can learn things that can be learned in no other way. But this polarity also, in its extreme form, has its dangers. Steiner speaks of a being he called Ahriman – a name that originates from Persian mythology. 'He is', writes Rudi Lissau in his introductory book on Rudolf Steiner, 'the calculating manipulator who tries, not to seduce like Lucifer, but to enslave individual man, to make him part of a collective, to let him forget his cosmic origins, to chain him to a lifeless earth.' We owe our rationality and earthly know-how to the influence of Ahriman, but it is an influence that has led us, among other things, to believe only in what can be weighed and measured, and to the experience of what Richard Tarnas, in *Cosmos and Pysche*, calls the 'disenchanted cosmos' – a view, in other words, that empowers the utilitarian mindset.

When, for example, we speak of the heart as a pump or the brain as a computer we are falling into the trap of thinking that our technological inventions can be remotely compared to the wonders of the living world.

This reductive tendency is, in essence, an unimaginative and lazy approach – a reluctance to stretch ourselves. Instead we drag everything down to a mechanical level and in so doing risk descending ourselves into the sub-human realm where technology is god.

I remember a lecture that John Davy once gave in which he drew attention to a modern trend that downgrades life at every level. Human beings, he said, are frequently treated as if they were animals, with their individual freedom and creativity undermined in the name of efficiency and order. Animals are treated like plants – chickens, pigs and even cattle that have no space to move around being one example. And finally the plant world itself – increasingly saturated with chemicals for short-term gain – is being dragged down into the realm of the mineral kingdom. When our cleverness flourishes at the expense of our humanity, we tip too far in all these directions, as exemplified by what I have already referred to as the potentially dehumanising effect of modern technology in our daily lives.

One suggestion that Steiner offered (and this was nearly a hundred years ago, when life was in many ways a great deal less complicated than it is nowadays) was on the one hand to draw on all that is positive in the ahrimanic realm – our analytical and objective intelligence, and our ability to stand back and judge things dispassionately – and to use these skills to counteract the excessive aspects of our luciferic nature. In other words to apply rigour and honesty to the process of self-knowledge, and through doing so arrive at a recognition of our potential for evil that arises from our passions, emotions and desires; or, put more generally, to widen our overall awareness and understanding by making our subjective life of feeling an object of scrutiny.

On the other hand we can likewise moderate our tendency to slide into a purely dry and intellectual interpretation of the world and our own place in it by bringing to the fore all that is creative and imaginative in our make-up. Everything that conspires to treat us as sheep or as a statistic should be sabotaged by our sense of self – and, indeed, by our sense of fun.

Thus, in Steiner's view, we oscillate between these two influences that can lead us in their extreme forms either to a kind of inner conceit, or to illusions about the external world. In this sense Lucifer and Ahriman are the yin and yang of our psychological make-up. Human life, like all life, unfolds in the tension between polarities. 'We experience our highest degree of freedom', writes Michael Kalisch in his introduction to a collection of Steiner's lectures published under the title *Evil*, 'not in a choice between one of two options, a good and a bad, as Kant believed, but in finding a balance … It may seem paradoxical to some, perhaps even blasphemous, but the mission of evil is to educate us to freedom.'

Kalisch goes on to suggest that since all life is continually evolving, evil can only be understood in the context of the evolution, not only of the human being, but also of the whole cosmos. He writes:

> Evil is not a static thing but a phenomenon of evolution; it appears, basically, when an organ or a stage of development arises in a temporally or spatially 'dislocated' fashion – at the wrong time or place, either too soon or too late.

The real danger that faces us, therefore, is not our actual encounter with these polarities that can lead us astray in one direction or the other, but that we encounter them without recognising what they are and what they represent. For some, like the writer Philip Toynbee, this recognition presented no problem: 'Ah, Mammon, if only God were as manifest as you are!'

In *The Secret History of the World*, Jonathan Black brings a fresh perspective to this subject by drawing attention to the work of the Russian novelist Fyodor Dostoyevsky through whom 'we encounter the paradoxical notion that those who confront this evil, supernatural dimension, even if they are thieves, prostitutes and murderers, are closer to heaven than those whose cosy world-view deliberately shuts out and denies it is there.'

Kalisch concludes his introduction by mentioning a further great mystery connected with evil that people have tended to lose sight of – the mystery of 'sacrifice'. Drawing on some of Steiner's more esoteric revelations, Kalisch puts forward the notion that evolution and development are not possible unless beings sacrifice themselves and so provide the foundation for the further development of other beings. Lucifer and Ahriman can therefore be seen in this light, yet without sentimentality. In another sense they are retarded beings; they have become rebels, spiritual delinquents, even.

It seems, therefore, that there may be cracks in the divine plan and that we are the victims of, as well as unconscious participants in the aberrations that unfold. In our eventual maturity, one task will be the redemption of such beings as Lucifer and Ahriman, just as we ourselves, from the Christian perspective, have been offered redemption through the incarnation of a god on earth. Indeed, it is through the mediating work of Christ, as an inspiration for us to become more fully human, that the potentially harmful influences of Lucifer and Ahriman can be absorbed and reconciled.

I am aware that we are getting deep into what General Booth might call 'kipper territory', the kipper being that smoked version of the elaborately-boned herring, detailed knowledge of whose anatomy is essential before attempting to eat it! The bits of anthroposophy that I can't quite cope with, like Booth with his kipper, I also tend to put on one side. But I have too much respect for Steiner to dismiss any of it as nonsense. I just simply live with the thoughts and insights, like those above, in recognition that something in me will, over time, need to grow to correspond to the revelation in question.

In his biography of Steiner, Gary Lachman likewise tries to keep an open mind. 'Ultimately', he writes, 'it's for the individual reader to decide what to make of Steiner's occult history. Depending on your point of view, you can accept it as truth, reject it as absurd, or, as the present writer finds most profitable, enjoy it for its sheer imaginative vitality, gleaning whatever insights from it you can.' Lachman's attitude, and I hope mine, is certainly what Steiner hoped for: that his research would not simply be believed, but rather – if well-founded – that it would act as an awakener for each person in his or her own time.

In his book *Occult Science* in particular, Steiner gives an extraordinary and complex description of what he calls cosmic evolution. And it is into this drama that Lucifer and Ahriman are interwoven, as is the whole unfolding of the Christian mystery. Perhaps it is helpful for some people, as Lachman suggests, to simply look upon this aspect of Steiner's work as his mythology – in the true and profound meaning of the word – a mythic revelation suited to contemporary consciousness. Because I am still digesting the material, and have been for over forty years, I am reluctant to expand on it further. I have not yet made the revelations sufficiently my own, though they have certainly become increasingly meaningful for me.

For those who have a problem with the idea of discarnate beings altogether, beings in the form of angels, archangels and demons – and for many years I was one such person – I can only say that for me the continuing reality and therefore presence of my relatives and friends who have died has helped me over that hurdle. If the essence of those I knew and loved does still exist, and not just as memory, then why not other beings – some benign, some malign – that are likewise invisible, mysterious and above all influential.

One hurdle that has not been a problem either for me or for many others, is the notion of the earth as Gaia, a living, self-regulating organism. The scientist James Lovelock, at the suggestion of the novelist William Golding, named it thus after the Greek goddess, Gaia. And if, like every other organism, the earth has a lifespan, then it too will one day die; so too – as we know already – the stars. But this doesn't have to mean that life itself ceases. Life manifests cyclically, and it evolves. Steiner's descriptions in *Occult Science*, therefore, of the earth and all that is connected with it – minerals, plants, animals and human beings – having had previous incarnations, and with further ones in the future, is not, in my opinion, remotely strange. Above all it confirms for me that there is meaning and purpose not only in my own individual existence, but also in all that surrounds me – devils included.

What also seems clear from all this – and above all from living with an awareness of these polarities that Steiner calls Lucifer and Ahriman – is that Czeslaw Milosz may not be absolutely correct when he writes: 'Of course, dear Tadeusz, / evil (and good) comes from man.' True, we are capable of causing appalling havoc and devastation both to the earth and among ourselves. And it is also true that human beings are responsible for many sublime creations and have performed deeds of great courage and sacrifice – and continue to do so. In all this, however, we are perhaps not alone. The arena of all these goings-on may indeed be the human soul, but other influences are at work. And here we can be helped or hindered. It's up to us. I've already compared the human condition to walking a tightrope. The challenge is to discriminate, honestly and consciously. Ultimately everything seems to be a question of balance.

A *Question of Balance* was the title of a film I made in Taiwan in 1977 for a series called *The Long Search*. In this case the balance we explored was between the teachings of Confucius on the one hand and what became Taoism on the other. The series of thirteen films was written and presented by the theatre producer, Ron Eyre, deliberately chosen by the executive producer, Peter Montagnon, because he was neither a theologian nor a paid-up member of any particular Church or faith. Ron spoke these words at the start of his journey:

> The long search is open to anybody. It doesn't have a tidy beginning, middle and end. You're on it the moment you start wondering where you were before you were born, where you'll go when you die and what you're on earth for in the meantime. If you knew the answers, you wouldn't ask the questions. But other people's answers should be worth collecting. And so should other people's questions. That's what we're going to try to do.

Ron Eyre

In the introduction that Ron wrote to his book *Ronald Eyre on the Long Search*, which grew out of the television series, he describes how a great deal of manoeuvring and diplomacy were involved in securing money, time and facilities 'for a great survey of the religions of the world – encyclopaedic, informative, clarificatory, authoritative'. The films themselves, we were all pleased to see, turned out to be, in Ron's words, 'exploratory, paradoxical and open-ended'. It was not our intention to follow in the tradition of Kenneth Clark in *Civilisation* (which Peter Montagnon had co-produced), or of Jacob Bronowski on science in that other prestigious BBC series at the time, *The Ascent of Man*. Ron was regarded and advertised as an Everyman figure, though it is hard for me to think of anyone more individual and less like anyone else I had ever met than Ron Eyre.

In the initial promotional material for the series we spoke of Ron as a 'bridge', but he was honest and realistic enough to declare: 'I'm no bridge. A bridge doesn't distort; I distort.' He was referring in particular to his Yorkshire, Methodist, male, and working-class background. But what he said does, of course, apply to everyone – we all have our particular baggage that clouds and influences our judgement and opinions. At least Ron recognised the fact, which is one step towards mitigating the dangers inherent in our subjectivity.

What we, the production team on *The Long Search*, all shared from the start was an interest in the word 'search'. Ron would often tell people, during the two and a half years that it took to make the series, that it was 'the long search' and not 'the big answer' we were exploring. It was partly why we felt it was important to leave 'religion' out of the title, for in Ron's view: 'the word "religion" appears to alarm, depress and send to sleep a large section of the British public'. It is in many ways a sad comment, and reflects as badly on religious institutions as it does on the supposedly sleeping public. However, I am convinced that many people are far more interested in such matters than is acknowledged either by the broadcasters or indeed sometimes by the viewers themselves. What matters, as in so many areas of life, is not so much what is being said or preached, but rather who is speaking the words. In this respect we three directors – Peter Montagnon, Mischa Scorer and I were helped enormously by the sensitivity, intelligence and wit of Ron Eyre himself, as well as by the many fine and thoughtful people we interviewed for the films.

Balance underpins Chinese religion and philosophy above all in the symbol of yin and yang which originally referred to the two sides of a hill: the yang was sunny, the yin in shadow. Yang has come to represent masculinity and action; yin, femininity and repose. For the Chinese these descriptions are neither good nor bad. However, a balance between the two is seen as healthy, whereas a prolonged imbalance which impedes the constant swaying of yin to yang and back again is unhealthy. Such imbalance is also, in Ron's words, doomed:

For just as yin is at its height, there appears in it the grain of yang, represented in the diagram by the tadpole-eye; and just as yang is at its height, there appears in it a grain of yin. Winter is born at the height of summer; summer, at the height of winter. In the 'eye', too, is a complete interplay of yin and yang, each with its eye that encloses in itself a further eye and a further eye, and onwards and onwards.

In a temple in Tainan, the old capital of Taiwan, we filmed a wall painting of an imaginary meeting between Lao Tzu and Confucius, the yin and yang of Chinese religion and philosophy. They both lived at that period of history which German philosopher Karl Jaspers has called the Axial Age, because it is perceived as pivotal to the spiritual development of humanity as a whole.

In the introduction to her book on the Axial Age, *The Great Transformation*, Karen Armstrong writes:

> From about 900 to 200 BCE, in four distinct regions, the great world traditions that have continued to nourish humanity came into being … During this period of intense creativity, spiritual and philosophical geniuses pioneered an entirely new kind of human experience.

This experience came to India through Hinduism and Buddhism; in Israel it came through the Old Testament prophets and what we have come to know as monotheism; in Greece there arose the philosophical rationalism that we associate above all with Socrates, Plato and Aristotle; and in China lived Confucius, born around 550 BC, and Lao Tzu, whose dates are less clear (the latest research suggests that he was an anonymous author – lao tzu simply means 'the old man' – writing in the middle of the third century BC).

In Armstrong's opinion 'we have never surpassed the insights of the Axial Age', and our turning to Confucius or Buddha for help is not just what she calls 'an exercise in spiritual archaeology'. The wisdom that originates from that time, which was later to inspire and express itself in Rabbinic Judaism, Christianity and Islam, can and does nourish and inform us still. But the prophets, mystics, philosophers and poets of that age were so advanced, she says, and their vision so radical, that later generations tended to dilute it. Thus there so often came about the kind of religiosity and dogma that the Axial reformers originally wanted to overturn. They didn't want believers, and they tended to have no interest in either doctrine or metaphysics. Armstrong continues:

> All the traditions that were developed during the Axial Age pushed forward the frontiers of human consciousness ... It was essential to question everything and to test any teaching empirically, against your personal experience ... What mattered was not what you believed but how you behaved. Religion was about doing things that changed you at a profound level.

In essence, therefore, it was a spirituality of empathy and compassion that was struggling to emerge during these troubled and often chaotic pre-Christian centuries. Each tradition was developing its own formulation of what Karen Armstrong calls 'The Golden Rule': 'Do not do to others what you would not have done to you.'

In the opinion of Huston Smith, the eminent American authority on the history of religion, 'Confucius was undoubtedly one of the world's greatest teachers.' Armstrong describes him as 'too blunt and honest to succeed in politics', and like other philosophers of the Axial Age someone who felt profoundly alienated from his time. Society was, to use Ron Eyre's phrase, 'splitting at the seams'. China was being torn apart by rival warlords and the collapse of old loyalties. The individual was emerging from group-consciousness to self-awareness, and was thus motivated more by self-interest than by social obligations. Greed was rampant; social anarchy and chaos loomed. It sounds familiar!

The solution that Confucius proposed was a return to the traditions and values of the past. However, his interpretation of some of these traditions was radically new. The focus of religion, for example, had been on heaven, and the appeasement of the gods and spirits who dwelt there. Confucius was more concerned with this world. What mattered was how we behaved here on earth, rather than dwelling on concerns about the afterlife. It must have been Confucius's legacy that prompted Teilhard de Chardin, on his travels in China, to observe 'an ever-present sense of the primacy of the tangible in relation to the invisible'.

Confucius was a worldly man 'whose humour and sense of proportion saved him from being a fanatic', writes Huston Smith in his classic book *The World's Religions*. Confucius knew that attitudes had to change, but a total reliance on our capacity to love one another, as advocated by some of his contemporaries, was to him essentially unrealistic. The shift that he advocated meant on the one hand keeping the force of tradition intact, while at the same time helping people to make clear decisions about the values they wanted to live by; a shift, in other words, to a conscious relationship with those same traditions. 'Moral ideals', writes Smith, 'were to be imparted by every conceivable means – temples, theatres, homes, toys, proverbs, schools, history, stories – until they became habits of the heart.'

'Human beings are by nature good' was the first sentence taught to every Chinese child for the next two thousand years. Confucius was convinced that although a society is composed of individuals, people can, through the power of suggestion, be prompted to behave in a socially responsible way – even, writes Huston Smith, 'when the law was not looking'. Confucius, like Gandhi and Tolstoy in our own time, and like many other great teachers over the centuries, believed unequivocally in our potential to be unselfish and capable of altruism and real empathy in our relationships with one another. He was therefore prompted to write:

> If there is righteousness in the heart, there will be beauty in the character.
> If there is beauty in the character, there will be harmony in the home. If
> there is harmony in the home, there will be order in the nation. If there
> be order in the nation, there will be peace in the world.

Confucius's teaching tends to be perceived more as an ethical code than a religion, though he never denied, for example, that the spirits of the dead exist, and advised treating them 'as if they were present'; his much quoted remark in this respect is 'He who offends the gods has no one to pray to.' Yet when someone once asked him about death, he replied: 'You do not yet understand life. How can you understand death?' Huston Smith sums up Confucius's attitude in the phrase: 'One world at a time'.

———————————

There was, however, another way of finding one's bearings in these great mysteries of life and death, heaven and earth:

> There is a being, wonderful, perfect;
> It existed before heaven and earth.
> How quiet it is!
> How spiritual it is!
> It stands alone and it does not change.
> It moves around and around,
> but does not on this account suffer.
> All life comes from it.
> It wraps everything with its love as in a garment,
> And yet it claims no honour, for it does not demand to be Lord.
> I do not know its name, and so I call it Tao, the Way,
> And I rejoice in its power.

So wrote Lao Tzu in his sublime work the *Tao Te Ching*, sometimes translated as *The Way and Its Power*. Huston Smith calls the work 'a testament to humanity's at-home-ness in the universe'. The *tao* itself has been described as too vast for reason to fathom; yet though ultimately transcendent, it is also immanent – permeating the universe and all that exists. Lao Tzu calls it 'the mother of the world'. The *tao* is also profoundly relevant to the way each human life unfolds.

The recommendations given by Lao Tzu revolve around the concept of *wu wei*, a phrase that translates literally as inaction, but in Taoism means something more like 'action which causes no friction either in our personal relationships or in relation to nature'. 'Actionless action' is another description – creative quietude, or action that goes with the grain of things. In some ways it reminds me of that concept of 'not-knowing' that Nicolas of Cusa struggled with – allowing knowing to flow into not-knowing, and thereby encouraging a higher form of cognition to awaken in us which is no longer mere knowledge of external things.

Central to Taoist thought and practice is the word *ch'i* which literally means breath, but is best understood as the vital energy that flows from the *tao* through each one of us. The movements and exercises performed in *t'ai-chi* are an attempt to remove blocks to this flow of *ch'i*; likewise the practise of acupuncture. In his book, Ron Eyre wrote: 'To practise *t'ai chi chuan* is to mirror, trace out, enact, embody, as the Chinese might say, nothing less than the movement of the universe.' I don't know enough about either Steiner's eurythmy, or the sacred dances initiated by Gurdjieff, to say how closely they mirror these ancient Chinese practises.

At that time all this activity was an important manifestation of people's awakening interest in subjective experiences and their inner journeys, in contrast to a Confucian emphasis on the sensible ordering of the outer world. Through meditation they could begin to experience, in Lao Tzu's words, 'the self as it was meant to be'. They saw not merely 'things perceived' but 'that by which we perceive ... To the mind that is still, the whole universe surrenders'.

At the conclusion of his chapter on Chinese religion and philosophy, Huston Smith writes:

Circling each other like yin and yang themselves, Taoism and Confucianism represent the two indigenous poles of the Chinese character. Confucius represents the classical, Lao Tzu the romantic. Confucius advocates calculated behaviour, Lao Tzu praises spontaneity and naturalness. Confucius's focus is on the human; Lao Tzu connects the human to what transcends it. As the Chinese themselves say, Confucius roams within society, Lao Tzu wanders beyond. Something in life reaches out in each of these directions, and Chinese civilization would have been poorer if either had not appeared.

Confucius and Lao Tzu, Narziss and Goldmund, Betjeman and Pevsner – I was learning about balance in all sorts of different and helpful ways on my journey towards a better understanding of that most profound polarity of all: heaven and earth.

Chapter 21

The Living Earth

In making a film one is constantly confronted, sometimes to an exaggerated degree, by the yins and yangs of daily life. We make elaborate plans, write treatments, book flights and hotels, arrange appointments – all in ways that Confucius would have approved. Then sometimes it rains, machines break down, and people forget promises or change their minds. So we have to adapt, think on our feet – or simply shrug our shoulders and, in the spirit of Lao Tzu, swim with the tide and go off to the pub for a drink!

Working in Taiwan in 1977 on *The Long Search* was certainly a challenge in this respect, but I had a fine team, and enormous help and support from our guide and interpreter Linda Wu. She spoke Cantonese, Mandarin and English, but Taiwan is a complex society and we needed the help of her two companions, one of whom spoke the local Taiwanese language, and the other a language called Hakka that originated in northern China.

Linda Wu and Ron Eyre

It was in 1544 that a Portuguese ship sighted the main island of Taiwan and called it *Ilha Formosa*, 'beautiful island', though it was the Dutch who established a commercial base there in the 17th century. Despite extensive industrialisation in the last fifty years, that beauty is still very much in evidence. In 1895, after the first Sino-Japanese war, Taiwan became a Japanese colony, reverting to Chinese sovereignty in 1945. It then became a refuge for the Republic of China's Nationalist government under Chiang Kai-shek in 1949 following the communist takeover of the mainland. Because of this influx of people from all over China, Taiwan was, and still is, a marvellous place to explore the richness of Chinese culture, religion and philosophy in all its diversity, unrestrained by communist ideology and regulations.

One spectacular sequence in our film is of a Taoist funeral. Ron Eyre took seven pages to describe it in his book, and we witnessed only two days of the forty-nine-day event. One of the rituals involved, in Ron's words,

> the support of the soul through its purgation, its release from imprisonment, its restoration to the upper world where it can rest before its journey to a pleasurable place, to which the family back on earth will have sent on ahead a spirit mansion with spirit furniture, spirit flowers in the garden, a spirit television set, a spirit car, a spirit telephone. This, in exquisite paper modelling and needing the strength of four men to control and lift, was carried down the path to the house ahead of us, placed in its own tented show-place where visitors could inspect it as, in the English tradition, visitors to a wedding inspect the presents and the wedding cake. After a few days it would be 'transformed' for use in the spirit-world by being burnt to ashes.

Taoism didn't emerge as a religion until around the second century AD. It was, in the view of some, a sort of home-grown Chinese response to the encroachment of foreign, missionary Buddhism. Our consultant for the programme, Dr Joseph Needham, suggested a useful comparison would be the idea of local Druids in England putting up organised resistance to St Augustine or the Celtic missionaries, pirating the shape of the liturgy, learning from their opponents' skill in church government, taking over a husk of Christian theology – all to preserve something authentically British for the future.

By institutionalising the traditional and universal practices of shamans, faith-healers, psychics and soothsayers, Taoist priests believed they were able – through elaborate and significant ritual – to bring to ordinary people a healing glimpse of cosmic realities. It is what the celebration of the Mass does for millions of others. It's easy to mock the naivety of that Taiwanese dolls' house and all the worldly clutter created for the departed soul, but the ceremony we filmed was clearly meaningful and helpful for the mourners, and maybe – who knows – in some mysterious way for the deceased also. 'That night', wrote the admiring theatre producer, Ron Eyre,

> I saw the Harrowing of Hell, the gates broken down, the locks forced and the dead brought to life again. And it was all achieved with a few sheets of tissue paper, a lath frame, a spot or two of glue, a trident, a chair on poles and a parasol, wielded by one visible protagonist, with five helpers and a chorus of auxiliaries.

Our visit to Taiwan also happened to coincide with the birthday of the earth god known as T'u-ti Kung. He is what we would call a nature spirit – a relatively senior one – and is honoured and respected in every community. There he has his shrine and his area, very much as a policeman has his station and his beat. In our chosen village we watched and filmed as people brought their gifts throughout the day – ham, tins of salmon, incense sticks, bottles of wine, kettles of tea. Once the offerings had been made, and presumably accepted, the food was retrieved and carried away.

T'u-ti Kung's task, it was explained to us, is to ward off mischievous or evil spirits and to be generally responsible for the welfare of the earth. Though he is a local official with limited jurisdiction, the Chinese whom we met regarded him as belonging to a vast celestial bureaucracy. The Jade Emperor presides, and deities can apparently rise to eminence or fall from favour. 'Their hauteur and prickliness', wrote Ron, 'need constant placation and sacrifice.'

One way to try to understand this celestial bureaucracy, to which T'u-ti Kung belongs, is to see it as a projection of our own society upon an imagined world of purely spiritual beings. Or is it, perhaps, the other way round? Do we arrange our earthly affairs as an unconscious, and at times clumsy, imitation of a supersensible realm in which hierarchy holds sway – but one that in no way denies the interdependence and value of all creation?

Responding to the festivities surrounding T'u-ti Kung's birthday in particular, as well as to other such rituals we witnessed in Taiwan, Ron formulated his reaction thus: 'Behind the quaintness I had a sense of something quite different going on. Here was a community saying, in its own way, "until you're right with the earth, nothing can prosper and there's nothing to celebrate".'

I sense that these days not only members of the Green Party would sympathise with such a sentiment. I suppose the stumbling block for some, in our so-called enlightened times, is the idea that invisible entities such as T'u ti Kung do actually exist and that they interpenetrate and indeed sustain the world revealed to our five senses.

In *The Doors of Perception* Aldous Huxley writes:

> Like the giraffe and the duck-billed platypus, the creatures inhabiting
> these remoter regions of the mind are exceedingly improbable.
> Nevertheless they exist, they are facts of observation; and as such,
> they cannot be ignored by anyone who is honestly trying to understand
> the world in which he lives.

I presume that those who are happy still to call themselves pagans would
have no problem with T'u-ti Kung and his realm. In fact one of my children's
most intelligent and sensitive friends is proud to be known by that much-
maligned label. The rest of us, I suspect, still have much to rediscover. A
respect for what is hidden is one of the main themes of this chapter.

The experience that we as a team all had at that birthday party in Taiwan
did raise for me yet again the whole question about the essential mystery of
physical life – and mystery it certainly is, as any honest scientist will admit.
Poets know it, too. T.S. Eliot expressed an aspect of this mystery – the life
that seems to permeate all existence, even a river, whether you call it a god or
not – in 'The Dry Salvages' from his *Four Quartets*:

> I do not know much about gods; but I think that the river
> Is a strong brown god – sullen, untamed and intractable,
> Patient to some degree, at first recognised as a frontier;
> Useful, untrustworthy, as a conveyor of commerce;
> Then only a problem confronting the builder of bridges.

Once the structural problem of building a bridge is solved 'the brown god
is almost forgotten / By the dwellers in cities' – writes Eliot. Yet the river
remains a reminder of what we choose to forget: ' Unhonoured, unpropitiated/
By worshippers of the machine, but waiting, watching and waiting.'

One way in which I try to make sense of nature spirits such as T'u-ti Kung –
if sense is the right word – is to contemplate more deeply this notion of the
earth's biosphere as a living organism in its own right. If this is so, then like all
living organisms it must have what Schumacher called a life force, and what
Steiner called the etheric. And it is within this life force in outer nature that
all cultures have, until comparatively recently, recognised the realm of what
are called nature spirits. In their diverse forms they are, if you like, the etheric
body of the earth and are interwoven with the four elements of earth, water,
air and fire. Another way to look upon them is as intermediaries between us
and nature, just as the angels are perceived as the intermediaries between us
and the divine realms out of which everything is born, sustained and renewed.

In this respect Steiner speaks about human beings as also having 'a certain mediating task in regard to nature and the beings inhabiting it'.

The eminent theosophist Charles Leadbeater, in a letter written after reading *Fairies at Work and at Play*, a book by a fellow theosophist, Geoffrey Hodson, about these elemental beings, wrote: 'Mr Hodson has caught most admirably the pre-eminently joyous tone of the life of the nature-spirits. They live so thoroughly in union with the divine intention; desire in them never seems to conflict with it, as it so often does with us.' In his introduction to that same book, E.L. Gardner elaborates on this theme of cooperation, suggesting that whereas our centre of consciousness is the mind, with these 'workers with nature' their centre is intuition:

> This shows itself throughout their activities, in their almost unconscious sense of cooperation with others at their own level, in their willing obedience to those members of their own kingdom who are of higher rank than themselves and in their direct sense of Nature's plan for growth in all kingdoms. This direct touch with the plan consists not in analytical knowledge, but in an unconscious recognition of its validity and a real delight in serving its purpose.

As yet I have avoided using words such as 'gnome' or 'fairy' for fear of pressing the wrong buttons, perhaps prompting you, the reader, to either skip to the next chapter or even abandon the book altogether. I myself have long puzzled about what it means when perfectly sane and sincere people speak or write about 'seeing' nature spirits. Perhaps it is that same 'seeing', rather than just 'looking', that Don Juan describes to Carlos Castaneda. I wonder, therefore, if 'experience' is a more appropriate word than 'see'.

One clue that I have found helpful is the realisation that I 'see' things in my dreams, when my eyes are very firmly closed. Even now, some four hours later, I can still just remember some images from last night's dreams. That, for me, is one important clue. The other is something that Gardner writes about in his introduction to *Fairies at Work and at Play*, a book in which Hodson recounts many detailed yet fleeting glimpses of this elemental world. Gardner draws attention to the theme of correspondences to which I have often referred. To investigate these seemingly hidden realms, he too suggests that we need to develop the organs of perception that correspond to what is being investigated.

According to some spiritual traditions this ancient faculty to see and experience more than meets the eye has of necessity been eclipsed by our intellectual development. Meanwhile, one could argue, the delight we experience in the beauty and delicacy of a flower is surely enough. Does it matter that we no longer sense that this flower, like we ourselves, has an etheric counterpart that gives it life and is intimately connected with these invisible entities at work in nature? Not an easy question to answer.

And why, I have also asked myself – if these hidden realms do exist – do people continue to describe and portray elemental and angelic beings in seemingly human form? Are these again simply projections of our own world onto something hugely mysterious? Perhaps we have no choice. I suppose the artist would answer: 'What else can I do but put wings on the back of a serene-looking human being when trying to convey the idea of an angel?' Clearly that sort of image has worked for a great many people, and for some it still does. Wings are a powerful symbol.

There were inspired efforts to convey this purely spiritual dimension of existence by the artist Cecil Collins, whose life and work I will be writing about later. So too, through the sensitive use of colour, does the artist Ninette Sombart communicate something of the profound mysteries surrounding the being of Christ (see colour plate 4). In music there is, and always has been, a real opportunity to express the inexpressible. As King Christian IV of Denmark, in Rose Tremain's novel *Music and Silence*, says of music: 'It is the human soul speaking without words.' To find such language – through sound, in images and sometimes even with words themselves – is a task that runs throughout our 'long search'.

I found Gardner helpful regarding these now traditional ways of portraying elemental beings – the gnomes who live largely underground, the undines in water, sylphs in the air and salamanders in fire. He acknowledges that none of these entities has a 'fixed solid body' as we understand the term, but rather that they take on the appearance that corresponds to the 'thought-form' that country people and children over the centuries have conjured up. In human terms we would express their reaction thus: 'If you think that I look like that, then that's what you'll see!' – a clue, perhaps, to how we recognise and make ourselves known to one another in a purely spiritual existence, and beyond one particular lifetime.

To a certain extent this process, whereby the power of thought and the imagination influence and even create what is perceived, takes place all the time. I am affected, for example, in varying degrees by what people think of me; and in that sense we can either strengthen or undermine another person. In our relationship to the elementals therefore, Gardner writes:

> No one who understands a little about the laws of thought … will be surprised that the fairies of tradition and the fairies observed clairvoyantly appear in the same garb – wings, wands, shining stars and all. The surprise would be if they were different. The elemental life rejoices to jump into a ready-made thought-form as much as an active child delights in dressing-up.

Gardner ends his introduction by mentioning what he considers as 'our human duty' to recognise and be grateful for the mutual interdependence that exists between us and these beings. However it is important, I feel, to try to put on one side what I call the Disney-inspired images of such entities, as well as the sentimentalised portrayals by certain Victorian illustrators; though perhaps the image matters less than the mistaken notion that these beings are somehow like us, only smaller.

Years ago I attended a lecture by an eminent German biologist and anthroposophist, Hermann Poppelbaum, on the subject of nature spirits. He, as I remember, looked somewhat like a gnome himself, which made the whole experience even more surreal. And although he spoke about quite extraordinary matters, the fact that he was clearly talking from his own experiences and not from theories, made his lecture very special. It is since then that I have always tried to keep an open mind about such things. What I particularly remember was Poppelbaum's message about gratitude. The elementals, he sensed, are somewhat sad at our lack of awareness – sad and puzzled. And what they can give us in abundance in return for our acknowledgement and gratitude, so Poppelbaum believed, is an enrichment of our imagination. But the situation is not all gloom. Apparently the gnomes find the colourful plastic replicas in people's gardens a source of great amusement. For me these objects are a poignant example of a loss that won't quite go away. We're too clever to believe in gnomes anymore, but we put false ones in their place – just in case!

In *The Fairies in Tradition and Literature*, K.M. Briggs writes: 'Encounters with the fairies are almost necessarily brief, for under ordinary circumstances men are supposed to see them only between one blink of the eye and the next.' It is a scholarly and insightful book in which she concludes by paying tribute to C.S. Lewis's Narnia books and above all to J.R.R. Tolkien's *The Hobbit* and its sequel *The Lord of the Rings*: 'Fairy lore in literature', she writes, 'has here reached its high water mark.' Yet she points out that even in these books,

> where the elves are in full power and activity, the end is one of diminishment and vanishing. After the fatal ring has been destroyed something of elfin power seemed to go with it, and the elves began to cross the sea to the Western Lands, and to leave the world increasingly to the dominance of men. In nearly all the fairy stories of this century that note is struck, the fairies are everywhere fugitive and in hiding.

But this is not, she writes, peculiar to this century. In the earliest mentions of fairies in literature they were already spoken of as departed or departing. Perhaps literature itself coincides with the gradual loss of our instinctive clairvoyance. Wisdom that was previously communicated through stories by word of mouth and lived in oral memory, had to be written down before those supernatural experiences were totally forgotten. Yet Katherine Briggs ends on a hopeful note of sorts. The tradition of fairies, she writes,

> burns up and flickers like a candle that is going out, and then perhaps for a time burns up again, but always the fairies are to be seen only between two twinklings of an eye; their gifts must be kept secret if they are to be enjoyed; they are, and always have been, the Hidden People.

In the autumn of 1923, eighteen months before his death, Steiner gave two very interesting and challenging lectures in Dornach – his base in Switzerland for the last eleven years of his life – on the subject of elemental beings in the plant and animal kingdoms. He, too, acknowledged that in our present phase of evolution we are not able to 'see' them, but adds: 'The fact that a thing is not perceptible does not mean, however, that it is not active in our world ... What they do can be very well seen, but not the doers themselves.' He describes how these nature spirits have 'their jurisdiction, their territory' in the elements of earth, water, air and fire: 'Just as the planet earth is our home in the universe, so these beings have their territory in one or another of the elements mentioned'.

Steiner also confirms what I suggested earlier: that the living cooperation of these nature spirits is the etheric or life body of the earth. He refers at one point to undines, the water spirits, as the chemists of the elemental world. There are many other extraordinary and detailed descriptions of these 'enchanted beings', of their tasks and aspirations, and of their potentiality in the evolution of the earth and cosmos. He speaks of their relationship to the elements and to the plants, as well as to the creatures with which they are especially connected – birds, fish, frogs and butterflies. Perhaps, then, it is the realisation – albeit largely unconscious – of this invisible activity that prompts the Chinese, in villages like the one where we filmed, to continue to pay tribute to T'u-ti Kung, and to the realm in which he works. Our harvest festivals are, I suppose, a somewhat vaguer attempt to do the same.

In the second of the two lectures, published in a volume entitled *Nature Spirits*, Steiner also speaks about the fact that not all these beings are 'benevolent'. What he calls our 'ordinary consciousness' is a protection here, for most of us would be unable to cope with such encounters at this stage of our development. It is one obvious danger arising from the use of powerful drugs – substances that bring down barriers artificially, before we are mature enough to withstand very frightening experiences. All mythical journeys of initiation tell of trials that test the courage and steadfastness of the pilgrim.

As Penelope Betjeman suggested to the young hippies in India, there are great risks involved in trying to gatecrash heaven.

Steiner also describes what he calls the phantoms and demons that we create through our misdeeds and that stay to haunt us. They, too, become part of this elemental world that surrounds us. What we think and do has, it seems, an effect far beyond our comprehension. And these phantoms connect themselves to the being whom Steiner called Ahriman, and as such become his messengers and servants – just as Wormwood was Screwtape's servant. Ahriman possesses, according to Steiner, 'an intelligence far superior to that of mankind'. It is in this context that he warns against mediumship – a trance-like state that replaces consciousness. Through such channels, malign and mischievous elements from other realms of existence 'trespass into the world we inhabit between birth and death'. He acknowledges that spiritual revelations of sorts are occasionally transmitted at séances, as I witnessed as a boy through my mother's interest in spiritualism – though I experienced increasing unease about the authenticity of the contacts we seemed to be making. What Steiner calls 'the deceptive and highly hallucinatory element in everything connected with mediumistic consciousness' is underlined by the fact that those who contact these beings tend to have no understanding of their real nature. Sincere as my mother and her friends were, this was certainly so in our case.

In the light of what Steiner says in these two lectures about elemental beings, I have a sense that what we call 'the kingdoms of nature' can be understood as the visible signature of a vast supersensible reality which, at this stage of our evolution, we only fully experience after our death. Animals, plants and even minerals are, as it were, the manifestations of entities that don't incarnate as fully as we human beings, and whose essential nature – what we ourselves experience individually as the 'I' or ego – we only encounter when we live in an altogether different dimension of reality. There these entities or archetypes are, in Steiner's words, 'our companions between death and a new birth'. As such they never die because they are never born. Our own essence likewise, although it does incarnate by becoming more closely interwoven with our physical body, is also immortal – not subject to the laws of death and decay.

On earth, therefore, what we call body, soul and spirit – physical and etheric, astral and ego – have, in the kingdoms of nature, a different configuration at each level of complexity. The animal differs from us in that the ego of each species does not incarnate into the physical organism. Grant Watson, in an essay called 'The Wisdom of the Wild' from his anthology *The Leaves Return,* describes how birds such as plovers and starlings, flying in flocks, do not follow a leader, yet they all turn at the same instant of time. 'They behave', he writes, 'as though each separate bird were an organ of a larger living unit.'

Only the physical and etheric are manifest in the plant; and the physical alone is present in minerals – hence the expression 'dead matter'. But according to this picture there is much more to a lump of gold, for example, than what glitters before our eyes. Many people are discovering – or rather rediscovering – that crystals can have a power and resonance that defy their seemingly lifeless state. Likewise something that appears as mundane as water seems to be capable of retaining memory of substances that are no longer physically traceable in the water itself, hence the efficacy of homeopathic medicines. Water is increasingly recognised as having a distinct life of its own, as conveyed by Theodor Schwenk in his book *Sensitive Chaos*, and more recently by John Wilkes in *Flowforms: the Rhythmic Power of Water*.

Thus through my travels and my reading – and as I continued to ask the sort of questions that John Davy's Screwtape was so keen for us not to ask – it became ever clearer to me that there are indeed many more things in heaven and earth than we, like Horatio, might dream of. Maybe, for example, it is after death and in collaboration with the entities that stand both above and below us that we shed our isolation and, like those starlings, become instead part of the living dynamic that underpins the whole of creation; citizens not of a clockwork universe, but of an arena of creative activity that makes possible not only life on earth, but also what the poet Dante described as 'the love that moves the sun and other stars'. And perhaps the experience of my childhood friend, Doyky, was somehow connected with these invisible realities; but I wasn't thinking about such things aged five. If I had been, I probably wouldn't have been aware of him. I wouldn't have 'seen' him.

CHAPTER 22

Orthodox and Unorthodox

In his introduction to *The Long Search* Ron Eyre made clear that it was not only people's answers that interested us, but also their questions. In this sense the word 'search' was crucial. In the films I directed for the series, in Taiwan, Romania and California, there were certainly plenty of questions. And in learning to experience and respect what other people believed and what was meaningful for them, as well as what puzzled them, my own quest was greatly enriched and deepened.

Initially at least, Chinese culture was one of the most difficult for us, as outsiders, to penetrate. What I have discovered on all my travels, however, is that once you meet and get to know individual people, these seeming barriers quickly start to fall away through the experience of our common humanity. Our similarities, in other words, are far more evident than our differences, as had already become apparent to me in Russia, India and Japan – and now through my glimpse into the great civilisation of China.

One of the last sequences we filmed in Taiwan was of the Lin family celebrating the spring festival, Ch'ing Ming. At a time when new life is emerging from the ground, the Chinese traditionally remember the dead, their ancestors. Graves are visited and swept, and offerings of food and wine are made. To the accompaniment of firecrackers, the family unpretentiously performed all these rituals, honouring twenty generations of Lin ancestors, as well as the small stone that marked the presence of their local T'u-ti Kung, the earth god. We also noticed how particular care was taken to make an offering to what are called the hungry ghosts. 'For every contented spirit that enjoys generations of respect from its family', wrote Ron, 'there are many lonely ghosts without food, attention, respect; and, neglected, they can become resentful ... Small offerings of food are left to absorb their malice.' Quaint, one might think, and yet if there is indeed some sort of psychic existence before birth and beyond death, such awareness and sensitivity must be as significant as it is in our relationships here on earth – particularly towards those who have, for one reason or another, fallen through the net.

The previous spring we had filmed a very different festival in which the solemnity of death on Good Friday is followed by the celebration of rebirth and resurrection on Easter Sunday. For our 'long search' we chose Romania as the place to explore the Christian Orthodox tradition, despite the fact that in 1975 the country was still part of the communist bloc and firmly under the control of President Ceausescu. Since almost four-fifths of the population were Orthodox Christians, however, the government was sensible enough to avoid ideological persecution and to recognise that, for the time being at least, religion rather than communism created a cohesive society.

Romania had just celebrated one hundred years as an independent state. Its borders had only been stable since 1947, when the communists came to power under Russian protection. But Ceausescu's policy was above all to make Romania Romanian and less a satellite of Russia, much as their national hero, Stephen the Great, had kept the Turks at bay in the 15th century. Ceausescu's attitude to religion was pragmatic rather than tolerant – Baptists and Lutherans had a very much more difficult time than Orthodox Christians; and if you wanted to get on in society, particularly in government or as a teacher, you would certainly avoid being seen in any sort of church. However the authorities were clearly proud enough of their flexibility – in contrast to the policies of their giant neighbour to the north – to allow us the freedom to film.

There are about a hundred and fifty million Orthodox Christians in the world, as far apart as Finland and Japan, but mostly in Eastern Europe – Bulgaria, Greece, Romania and Russia. They claim two thousand years of unbroken Christianity: in their eyes the Roman Catholics in 1054 AD were the first to break rank – the first Protestants. For them the Pope in Rome has no divine right to supremacy over the Christian Church. The titular head of the eastern Orthodox Church is known as 'the first among equals' and the laity as 'a royal priesthood'. There is a deep respect for the idea that God's truth is revealed through 'the conscience of the Church' and through 'the consensus of its members'. For them the living icon of the faith, as it was founded and meant to be, is a bishop among his people – following in the footsteps of Christ's apostles.

We met and filmed one such bishop, one of the most remarkable and impressive people I have ever met – a truly holy man. Bishop Justinian epitomised for me that paradoxical phrase that so stuck in the throat of John Davy's Screwtape – 'a selfless self'. In the Orthodox tradition a parish priest is encouraged to marry, bring up a family and to be generally rooted in the community. A bishop, on the other hand, is celibate; Justinian was a monk for thirty-three years – 'able to travel light' is how Ron described him. But Ron was somewhat less comfortable with Justinian than I was: 'It's alright when icons stay within the frames', he said in his commentary, 'but when they move at you it's quite worrying.' And later in the same sequence:

The trouble between Bishop Justinian and me, if you can call it that, was that I asked questions, thinking that I knew about Christianity but had in some sense got beyond it, and he treated me as a pre-Christian, a western pagan – somebody for whom Christianity had yet to happen. He may well have been right.

Bishop Justinian

Justinian spoke to us about what he saw as the coming eclipse of the Christian Church, its reduction to its elements, its purgation, its resurrection in a new shape. It was, wrote Ron in his book, 'a prospect he appeared to walk towards with equanimity, trust and something like merriment'. On another occasion Justinian expressed the thought that the Christians made a great mistake when they turned Jesus into a religion. I was reminded of Emerson's own problem with the Church, while he was still a Unitarian minister, over the practice of Communion. His assertion that Jesus had never intended to ritualise the Last Supper not surprisingly caused great consternation at the time. Emerson's hope was to make Communion less a matter of ritual and more a spontaneous commemoration of one's faith.

Teilhard de Chardin expressed similar concerns when he wrote in *Science and Christ* that Christians needed to 'rethink' their religion – what he later called 'a new mysticism'. Ursula King interprets the development of Teilhard's understanding of Christianity as less and less 'a particular set of doctrines', but rather 'a catalyst for the development of modern spirituality', and love as 'a creative force in the evolutionary process itself'. The great historical religions, including Christianity, were – so Ursula King goes on to point out in *Towards a New Mysticism* – originally linked to a dualistic worldview that is now fast breaking up. There is, however, what she identifies as 'a disenchantment with science because of the reductionist and pragmatic narrowness frequently associated with scientific practice'. In her view spirituality must, more than ever before, be understood and practised in relation to the central concerns of society. For scientists like Teilhard, she suggests, 'the future lies in a new synthesis of the rational and the mystical, in a truly integral vision which can animate all areas of human endeavour'. In *Christianity and Evolution* Teilhard writes of a new 'mysticism of evolution', as opposed to an earlier 'mysticism of evasion'. He believed too that as our capacity and inclination for self-reflection was growing, so 'the mystical temperature' of mankind was correspondingly rising. I sensed a similar awareness in Bishop Justinian, not only through conversations we had with him, but simply in his presence.

In his massive work *The Ever-Present Origin*, the Swiss cultural philosopher Jean Gebser also wrote of what he called 'a more intensified Christianity' that was emerging as humanity came through its current 'three-day period of descent into hell'. Gebser shared with Steiner a sense of Christ's renewed activity in the world, not as some 'Second Coming' in the physical sense, but as a presence for those – whether so-called Christians or not – who suffered, or who were sensitive to the sufferings of others.

In Romania, just before Easter, we visited one of the country's two theological institutes for the training of priests, in the Transylvanian town of Sibiu. At that time there were nine hundred students. Ron spoke to three of them. 'Which is more important', he asked them, 'to be in a church and say the liturgy, or to go round the village, discover who needs help and bring it?' The students were adamant that both things are equally important. For them, at least, religion and social obligations to one's fellow human beings were inseparable. Asked about tradition versus reformation, one of them expressed the strong conviction that the Christian church has the capacity to renew itself from within and thus will never die. He meant, I believe, that although the Orthodox church, in particular, is steeped in tradition, the wisdom and insights that lie behind those traditions can and need to be constantly re-experienced and thus renewed.

On our visits to various churches, we were particularly impressed by the powerful way that the liturgy unfolds in an Orthodox service. To an outsider it comes across as a dramatic and mysterious dialogue between the priest and his congregation. The climax – the consecration of the bread and wine – takes place in the sanctuary behind a screen with closed doors – 'as if to say', wrote Ron, 'there are things you can't hear, can't see, can't understand'. Later, as an experienced theatre director, he compared it to staging a murder in a play, which can be far more dramatic if it takes place just off stage, out of sight. Our imagination is both stimulated and challenged. This experience of the liturgy certainly stirred in me an understanding of a ritual that previously I always found difficult to relate to.

For Holy Week we travelled up to Moldavia, in the north east of the country. In the villages each family had a horse and cart, and a sledge for winter. Almost every household kept a cow, pig and chickens. The people made a lot of their own clothes and furniture. And almost everyone went to church. It was a powerful reminder of our medieval roots.

Remus Rus, Bishop Justinian and Ron Eyre

We filmed at several of the famous Moldavian churches, painted inside and out like gigantic picture books. As well as being impressed by their great beauty, we were interested to see on the walls, among the familiar scenes from the Old and New Testaments, the images of Plato, Aristotle and Pythagoras. Our guide, Remus Rus, explained to us that in the Orthodox tradition these personalities are also recognised, each in their own way, as preparing for the coming of Christ.

Andrew Welburn explores the subject in *The Beginnings of Christianity*, where he writes not only about the Greek philosophers in this connection, but also the earlier cultures of Persia and Egypt. Thus the legend of the Three Kings, the three wise men from the East, takes on special significance for Welburn:

> The Iranian sages carrying their gifts into the heart of Judea embody the truth that Christianity came not only as the fulfilment of the spirit and the hopes of ancient Judaism, but also in fulfilment of the wisdom of oriental religion, more especially the ancient wisdom of Zarathustra.

What emerges from Welburn's research is almost universal anticipation throughout the ancient world of the incarnation of Christ. In the Zoroastrian tradition this being was known as Ahura Mazda, the god of light, the sun god. It is an extraordinary narrative that Welburn weaves, taking in the subject of compassion as exemplified by the Buddha, the individual moral consciousness that developed among the Israelites, the rational thought and art of the Greeks, and the unique role played by the Essenes – an ascetic sect with whom Jesus was almost certainly in contact. And casting his net even wider and further back in time, Welburn writes about the Bhagavad Gita in relation to the Epistles of St Paul. It is, in other words, a synthesis on a mighty scale. The overall message of Welburn's book prompts one to contemplate Christ's mission and deed as a truly cosmic intervention in the evolution of humanity. This is also, I suspect, what prompted Bishop Justinian to speak of the mistake in turning Jesus into a religion.

Christ's incarnation at the baptism of Jesus, uniting with the pure and humble man of Nazareth, was – as many have always sensed – a deed intended not only to unite humanity but also to awaken in each of us, as it did in Jesus, what can transcend our individual egos and thereby all that separates us by way of race, colour, gender and creed; what St Paul called: 'Not I, but Christ in me.' Perhaps not surprisingly one of the thoughts that Andrew Welburn leaves us with at the end of his enthralling book is the suggestion that 'we stand at the very beginning of Christianity, not near its end'. Easter in Romania, despite all its traditions, did not for me contradict such a thought.

Moldavia, with its painted churches, is also the land of the great monasteries and convents. At the time of our filming there were over two thousand Orthodox monks and nuns scattered in well over a hundred houses. It's a custom in the monasteries that the abbot – not a servant or one of the novices – serves the visitors at mealtime. He will only eat when his guests have finished. We certainly enjoyed some wonderful hospitality not only in huge and beautiful refectories, but also in many humble homes; and throughout Romania we met some extraordinary, kind and thoughtful people. Among them were monks, nuns and parish priests who, alongside their neighbours, farmed their land, tended their orchards, mended their carts and dug their ditches. As Ron wrote:

> If the clergy had made strong alliances with the rulers, any of the rulers – the Turks, the Austro-Hungarians, the monarchy – the communist regime might have found it easier to unseat them when it came to power with atheistic intentions. But an alliance between clergy and people is harder to crack.

In Romania people seemed to attend Confession less frequently than Roman Catholics do, often only once a year during this period before Easter. And if they did, then wherever possible they went to a monk. Spring-cleaning was thus as much an inner as an outer activity. We saw plenty of evidence of both, with rugs hung out on every fence and balcony, and queues of people at the nearby monastery.

The tremendous climax of the festival comes in those first few minutes after midnight, when the sorrow of Good Friday and the silence of Saturday give way to Easter Sunday – from death to resurrection. The church has been in total darkness. Then one frail light is carried from the altar by the priest through the centre door of the screen and out to the people. And so the light starts to spread as each person's candle receives light from the next. It is a powerful reminder of our inter-connectedness. 'You can learn things from a child, from an old man. You can receive light from anybody.' Those words were Ron Eyre's response. It is what Bishop Justinian meant, I believe, when he said to us: 'If we knew the truth of it, every day is Easter.'

The third film I made for *The Long Search* was in California, and was the only one in the series, apart from the concluding episode, *Loose Ends*, which didn't focus on any one particular religion or teaching. People do, of course, search in many ways, not least those who call themselves scientists. For some scientists, like Bernard Lovell, their religion coexists harmoniously with their scientific research. For others, like Richard Dawkins, religion is a dangerous anathema and nothing to do with a genuine search for knowledge and understanding.

Our film in California, however, was not just about science. We called it *West meets East*, because much of what we looked at was an interaction between what is termed the western mindset on the one hand and the traditions and practices from China, India and Tibet on the other. It was, above all, about people trying to be aware and benefit from the many ways to what is called enlightenment. The film could have been made in a number of places, but our decision to make it in the Bay Area of San Francisco meant that among other things it emerged as a good contrast and balance to the film that my colleague, Mischa Scorer, made in Indianapolis – *Protestant Spirit USA*. There he and Ron Eyre witnessed how many of the descendants of those 'protesters' against the dogmatism of the Roman Catholic Church over four hundred years ago had themselves become as hard-line fundamentalist as those they originally opposed.

In his opening commentary Ron introduced our Californian film with these words: 'The culture we live in is scientific, pushy and in love with its machines. Up through the nooks and crannies of this culture there creeps something that's been called the counterculture.' It was Theodore Roszak who originally coined that word, and I asked him to be our consultant. 'A state of confusion, mixed with a raw hunger for transcendence' was how another commentator described the mood among many young people at that time, and not just the students on the campus at Berkeley.

By way of an introduction to this theme of a counterculture we filmed Roszak (whom we knew as Ted) being interviewed by Michael Toms for New Dimensions, a community-supported public radio station in San Francisco. Ted spoke about what he perceived as 'a great religious appetite' reaching out in many directions that are not traditionally religious in character. A great deal of this went under the heading of therapy, parapsychology and consciousness research. 'What they're trying to do', he said, 'is to salvage something out of the spiritual traditions of the past and bring it into their lives as a living and daily reality.' He went on to acknowledge the many 'false starts', the tendency at times towards superficiality and the inevitable 'follies along the way'. But he concluded the interview with these important words: 'It's one thing to mock the many inadequate ways people seek to meet that need, it's quite another thing to mock the need.'

Theodore Roszak and Ron Eyre

Sat Santokh Singh was born a Jewish boy in New York and was a veteran of the peace and civil rights movements. When we met him he had been a Sikh for several years and lived with his wife and children, together with fifteen like-minded companions, in downtown San Francisco. The group ran a house-painting business, and some of them also taught meditation, yoga and reflexology. Their day started at 4.30 in the morning with two hours of yoga exercises, chanting, meditation and prayer. They were a cheerful and friendly community, and not remotely self-righteous.

Sat Santokh's journey was similar to many who have thoroughly immersed themselves, perhaps over-immersed themselves, in the so-called good things of life – in his case the glamour and excitement that surrounded the rock-and-roll scene. He told Ron how finally one night, unable to sleep and with a full moon eying him through the window, he realised 'there was nothing further for me to gain in my search for psychedelics'. No longer did he want the ups and downs of drug-induced experiences. What mattered, he finally decided, was the quality of his life from day to day, from moment to moment. And with this came the realisation that he needed to find a spiritual discipline and a teacher. Many young Americans have felt attracted to Sikh discipline and the Sikh message: that there is one God who transcends all barriers; that a person should work in the world and earn his keep; and that he should share what he has with others.

Sat Santokh Singh and friends with Ron Eyre

Ron asked Ted Roszak why he thought so many westerners were turning east. His response was that while the Christian tradition is as various and rich as any religious tradition, most people tend to think of it is as church on Sundays, catechism, Sunday school, and as a doctrine and system of belief. To someone who feels an outsider, he said, there seems to be very little experience involved – apart from experience that manifests as 'a fervour of believing'. What is significant about the oriental religions in particular, he suggested, is that they all have something to do with experiencing religion rather than just talking about it.

Experiencing, rather than simply believing, was certainly the path followed by Dr Kenneth Pelletier. During the seventies he moved from the practice of Zen meditation to techniques brought to the West from Tibet. Perhaps, in the end, it doesn't matter so much whether we look east or more deeply into our own traditions. What does matter is that through having real and profound experiences of spiritual potential, not just in ourselves, but in the whole of creation, we will find a faith again, and one that satisfies our reason as well as our instincts; a journey, in other words, that is forwards, not backwards.

Ron Eyre and Ken Pelletier

Pelletier's meditative discipline was, if you like, his foot in the past. But he was also a thoroughly modern man – well educated, intelligent and sensitive; and, as a doctor, he worked with all the clarity that characterises modern consciousness. He worked, too, with some complicated and very modern machinery. Biofeedback has been called the yoga of the West. In his commentary Ron explained it thus:

> Seen from one point of view, biofeedback happens to us all the time without machinery. Usually, when we blush, we know we are blushing. But there are other reactions, less obvious; variations in the body waves; skin and muscle tension. All of them tell a story. The machinery allows us to observe in ourselves what would otherwise be hidden. It isn't a medicine. It doesn't in itself change your situation; it reflects your situation and from there, by paying attention, you can perhaps help yourself.

Pelletier explained to us how with a migraine headache, for example, which is an abnormal distribution of blood flow, you could learn how to alter the blood flow to other parts of your body and thereby alleviate the problem. And it was Pelletier, through his contact with an Indian cardiologist at a conference, who alerted us to the true meaning of the word 'guru'. It literally means 'teacher', but can be ascribed temporarily to any other person who reminds you of a higher aspect of yourself. What it does, he said, is to allow you to look at your life as a series of lessons. Every person, every event, experience, illness – even those biofeedback instruments – are potential teachers in that sense. 'Anything', wrote Ron, 'that comes as a reminder that, puffed up as we already are, there is more to us than we know: and that knowing it, we will gain our proper modest size.' Some time later he scribbled this note to me:

> I've started to realise that, for me at least, when I have a question, the person who helps me most is the one who is full of questions too. The guru at his most powerful has always, in my experience, turned out to be a question mark.

One such guru whom we filmed – someone with as many questions as answers – was the psychologist Dr Gay Luce. Originally she worked on the study of growth in children. Now she was interested in growth in the aged, and had created a group called Sage. 'What we're doing', she said, 'is antidoting all the things that the culture has done to make them feel unwanted, rigid, stereotyped and isolated – cut off from each other.' People come to her sessions, she said, because of hope: 'It's the hope of new possibilities; the realisation that something hasn't happened; they haven't been all they could be in their lives; that there's still more to come.'

Ron asked Gay whether they talked about dying. She responded by describing how, rather than advice or theories, she had introduced simple meditation, and that through these experiences people had begun to realise that 'the universe is a safe place'. They had learned to accept that ageing and death are part of life and that what was happening to them was 'OK'. 'It's not that something else should be happening', she said. 'When people get to that place the terror begins to dissipate a little bit – slowly – because in our culture the medical profession says to us that until we reach a certain age we shouldn't die. We've got that beat into us so hard that we fight the whole process, which means we have to fight our lives.'

She went on to remind us that every time we make some change in our lives – divorce, new job, whatever – we go through a little form of dying. It reminds me of another thoughtful insight into the subject of death that calls it simply 'Letting go'. Our whole life can thus be seen, in part, as a lesson in learning to let go.

Gay Luce concluded by saying that in her opinion there is no such thing as real health without some spiritual development. 'We're not disconnected from the actual reality of the universe and whatever laws those are', she said. 'No matter what our culture tells us, we cannot disconnect ourselves. That's what we're part of, whether you call it God or not.'

Another area of searching that we looked at in California came under the heading of what Ted Roszak called 'demystification' – the modest efforts by a vanguard of people to reclaim in their lives a human quality and a human scale that is increasingly under threat. 'It's an attempt to bring the city – in fact the whole culture – down to a scale that you can manage', said Ted. 'And that's quite an achievement in a society where we are so dependant on various kinds of authorities, experts, professionals.'

What these people did was sometimes as simple as learning to grow their own vegetables – an activity and skill long neglected in urban America. In a less affluent part of the Bay Area we visited a house in which various experiments in urban self-sufficiency were demonstrated, including solar heating and the recycling of human waste – initiatives that thirty years ago were only just beginning to be taken seriously.

At the Briar Patch Cooperative Auto Shop, people were learning to repair and service their own cars. 'Cars stand at the neurosis point of industrial society', wrote Ron. 'They give you the freedom to overtake your neighbour and to escape the city, but – as your gasket blows – they remind you that you are powerless.' The climax of this section of the film was a hilarious scene, in someone's Palo Alto backyard, of Ron learning to milk a goat:

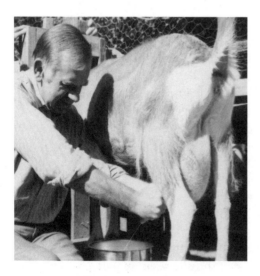

It's amazing to me that two generations ago my grandfather would do what I'm trying to do as a natural part of his daily work. And here am I, all fingers and thumbs, having a piece of encounter-therapy with a nanny-goat which leaves me poised between embarrassed clowning and a sort of remorse that something so simple for my grandfather should be so difficult for me.

Ron's encounter-therapy

A particularly significant encounter for Ron, and one that also involved some goat-milking-type laughter, was with the philosopher and writer Jacob Needleman, whom we met – along with many other enterprising and thoughtful people – through Ted Roszak. As Ron walked with Needleman by the Pacific Ocean just south of San Francisco, they discussed Matthew Arnold's poem 'Dover Beach', written over a hundred and fifty years ago. One stanza compares the ebb of the sea with the end of religion – describing the 'melancholy, long, withdrawing roar' of the sea of faith. Ron asked him about his view of the state of the tide. Had the sea of faith withdrawn for ever? Was it on the turn? Needleman's answer was both positive and negative: 'The positive side is that it's a rejection of old clichés, a rejection of frozen dogmas ... so the positive side is the search. The negative side is the finding ... It's the searching that is so exciting about California; and the thing that makes it look so suspicious is how people go from one thing to another. It has this negative side, but behind it is this positive thing – "I want something that works, that really means something".'

Needleman went on to warn of the danger of people devising their own tailor-made religions: 'Then it can be rather shallow, and not very hopeful ... Man is most alive when he is in question, when the security is taken away from him', he said. 'In other words, it's in weakness there's strength. If we can stay weak and keep open, keep moving around and come to the point where we just give up and know that what we are doing, where we are going is hopeless, really hopeless, and not grab on to something else and try to build a structure out of it, then we reach a state which in the traditions of the West is called despair. Another word for despair, in this sense, is deep openness. When you're in despair, when you come to the end of the rope, only then can help come.'

At another location Needleman continued this theme, speaking with passion about how we tend to settle for too little. By changing a few things in ourselves, he suggested, we start to assume we've achieved some kind of wholeness: 'I may even start a new community on the basis of that ... but it's such a tiny piece of the whole thing.' In response to such thoughts, Ron wrote in the last chapter of his book:

> I do not wish to make the whole of *The Long Search* seem to be a journey towards Jacob Needleman in San Francisco (for who knows what nonsense he may be up to when he is not talking enormous sense to me?), but it so happens that we had one day a long conversation during which we did seem to be pushing at something quite sharp and nervy.

This conversation began with a question to Needleman about change. 'If, as seems the case', asked Ron, 'we are under constant pressure from teachers and teachings to change, to be born again, to realise our Buddha-nature, to be made alive in Christ, to crack the small self and understand our identity with the large self, what is the first step to take, the basic beginner's move?' Needleman then asked Ron what made him want to change. Was it just change for change's sake? Was it simply to be happy? Probably not.

What Needleman then suggested as a first step was to look inside oneself and try to be clear who it was that wanted to understand and to change. In other words to try to look at oneself as an outsider, in much the same way that Steiner suggested as a preliminary exercise on the path to a regular practice of meditation. It's a step, Needleman told Ron, that is often missing in religions both old and new: 'They start a little too high', he said. ' They start with us as though we already know what we want, as though we're ready to make our commitments. But we are not. We are much below that.' A really practical mysticism, he suggested – one that could really bring about change – needs to start with studying ourselves as we are. It is a rung of the ladder that he felt was often missed out.

At this moment in the conversation we had to reload the camera. Needleman then returned to the question from a slightly different angle: 'To be available for change, you have to make room, I think. This is what you get if you read or approach the great teachings in a state of need rather than a state of curiosity. In a state of need you are not just interested in getting information; you are willing to set something aside, to give something up … What are you willing to pay for this change? … That question, when it comes back to you, is a measure of

Jacob Needleman

your sincerity. It's a measure of your seriousness. And perhaps you see that you are not all that serious: "I just wanted to know what you were thinking, Buddha. I didn't want you actually to do anything to me". And the Buddha will say, perhaps: "Well, all right. That's fine. Goodbye".'

You can see from these brief descriptions of just some of our challenging encounters why Ron was prompted to write at the very end of his book: 'The Long Search has radically altered my ignorance.' In California there remained one more subject that was to contribute to our state of both confusion and exhilaration. It was preceded by a conversation Ron had with Ted Roszak on the subject: 'Is God dead and did science kill him?' To this question Ted replied: 'I think the only way you get rid of one god is by replacing that god with another god'. He went on to suggest that in our increasingly secular society our religious faith has simply gone over into another area of life. 'I suspect', he said, 'that we now address progress, growth, affluence, industrial power with all the emotional enthusiasm that once characterised our religious faith.' Ted then pointed out, however, that many scientists these days on the fringe of the scientific community had begun to doubt whether our science is an adequate description of reality, 'Whether it's an adequate god', he added.

One such scientist is Fritjof Capra, author of *The Tao of Physics*. Ron talked with him as they walked along the top of the two-mile-long linear accelerator at Stanford University. 'I suppose you could call it one of the holy places of modern science', wrote Ron. 'Things called particles hurtle the length of this great cathedral nave at near the speed of light, come into collision and from the debris scientists, the observers, search for clues to the nature of reality'. Nowadays, at the even more complex establishment at Cern, in Switzerland, similar techniques are being used to seek for those same clues.

Ron Eyre and Fritjof Capra at Stanford

In his writings Capra has, among other things, tried to relate some of the insights of modern physics to what are called in the religious traditions 'mystical insights'. He has, for example, compared the universe of the modern physicist to that experienced by eastern mystics – a universe engaged in a continuous cosmic dance, like the dance of the god Shiva, reflecting a reality behind the world of ordinary sense-perception.

Capra began by explaining to us that there is something called 'old physics' and something called 'new physics', and that by using the latest machinery this new physics is undermining, one by one, the assumptions on which the old physics, science itself and all this machinery has been built. 'It sounds', wrote Ron, 'very much like sitting on the branch of a tree and sawing it off.'

Capra told us how these 20th-century developments in physics were shocking to physicists at the time. 'The world view of classical Newtonian physics', he said, 'was essentially a mechanistic view, where the world was seen as consisting of a multitude of different objects working together in some kind of huge machine. And furthermore this machine can be observed and understood objectively – that is without ever mentioning the human observer: totally separated from the human observer. Furthermore it is made of several basic building blocks – the atoms – which in turn consist of some fundamental material substance.' This description sounded to me like some giant Lego set. He went on to explain that the prevailing approach to understanding things was to take them apart (like Lego) and study their components. And if you don't understand those, take them apart, and so on – ad infinitum. This Newtonian world view had a very extreme and important influence on all the other sciences and on society in general, he told us. The natural sciences, as well as the humanities, modelled themselves on classical Newtonian physics.

Ron then asked whether, since God was clearly not available for scrutiny under a microscope, he became increasingly irrelevant? Capra's response was that although God was indeed perceived as 'outside', for a long time he was seen – and still is by many – as providing the fundamental laws according to which everything moved.

'What changes in our thinking and in our society may happen because of this revolution in physics?' was Ron's next question. 'The impact will be considerable' was Capra's reply. 'The new physics', he said, 'the world view of 20th-century physics, is not mechanistic but rather can be called an organic view, or a holistic, ecological view. The world is no longer seen as being made of a multitude of objects ... The world and the universe of the modern physicist is an on-going and ultimately indivisible process. This process shows patterns – the patterns are molecules, atoms, particles – but the patterns cannot be understood as isolated physical entities. The only way to understand them is through their interconnectedness to the whole. So the universe is fundamentally inter-related, and every part of it can only be understood through its relation and connection to the whole.' At this point we were reminded of the words of the distinguished 20th-century astronomer, James Jeans: 'The universe begins to look more like a great thought than a great machine.'

We went to California as a place to glimpse what the gods of the 21st century might be like, and to sense in what direction 'the long search' might continue in an increasingly mechanised and materialistic world. We concluded that despite the modest and valiant efforts of a few people to reclaim some control over their lives, along with a sense of meaning, the prevailing 'religion' both there and increasingly everywhere else was undoubtedly science – and for the most part the Newtonian model. It may not, as Ted Roszak suggested, be an altogether adequate god, but it clearly has a pretty firm hold. However, the search for knowledge is a noble pursuit and maybe, as Needleman and others recognise, that search simply needs to go deeper. Clearly what Capra described as the new physics is challenging scientists to do just that.

On the university campus at Berkeley, Ron met another scientist, Geoffrey Chew, chairman of the physics department. 'In the religion of science (if you'll stomach the phrase)', wrote Ron, 'he'd be high priest, and one of the grandest.' Ron asked Professor Chew whether he was demoralised by the fact that the new discoveries in physics were rocking the solid foundations that underpinned his science. His reply was: 'Not at all … To find that the concepts which I had accepted through my whole life are, in fact, not reliable adds to the excitement.' What did demoralise him was the thought that he was not going to live long enough to see the next step. (I don't remember if we asked him whether he believed in reincarnation, which, if a reality, might offer him yet more excitement in the future – though perhaps not necessarily as a physicist.)

Ron did ask Chew what he thought that next step might be. 'If I were going to guess at a path which will take us out of our present set of paradoxes', he replied, 'I would say that it is the realisation of the importance of approximation. Scientists like to believe that they are dealing with absolute truth. They know they're not. There's a strange contradiction in their behaviour.' He then spoke about the problem of language: 'The acceptance of approximation as an inevitable basic limitation is very closely connected with the need for finding a new language.' He explained that the language we still use is understandably based on the notion of objectivity: 'If we get a totally new language, then the notion of truth will have a totally new meaning.' And this, he told us later, can be summed up as the need for a new way of knowing.

Before making this film I had already read a book called *Supernature* by the biologist Lyall Watson, which made quite a stir at the time of its publication in 1973. At the very opening of his introduction Watson echoes exactly what Chew admitted to us: 'Science no longer holds any absolute truths. Even the discipline of physics, whose laws once went unchallenged, has had to submit to the indignity of the uncertainty principle.' He then goes on to say that in this 'climate of disbelief' we have begun to doubt even fundamental propositions, 'and the old distinction between natural and supernatural has become meaningless'.

It is a realisation that already seven hundred years ago was clearly in the mind of the Persian poet Hafiz, in some lines imaginatively rendered by Daniel Ladinsky in his collection *I Heard God Laughing*.

> Pulling out the chair
> Beneath your mind
> And watching you fall upon God –
> What else is there
> For Hafiz to do
> That is any fun in this world!

CHAPTER 23

The Everlasting Now

There is a hole in the wall of the conservatory where I sit and write, through which come what for me are two very different miracles. One is the stem of a vine from which every year grows a magnificent crop of delicious and very beautiful grapes. The other miracle is the cable that connects my computer to the internet, enabling me to tap into seemingly endless information, as well as to store thousands of words through which I try to express my thoughts and feelings – my own humble grapes.

Beside me, in the shade of the vine, are piles of books, all of which have, in their own ways, helped me in my efforts to understand not only these two contrasting miracles – the vine and the computer – but, above all, that mysterious word 'heaven', and what people mean by a spiritual world, or a supersensible existence outside of time. Many of the books point to what the physicist Geoffrey Chew called 'a new way of knowing'. Yet I would hesitate to label my search either scientific, philosophical or religious, for it seems to me that the urge to know and understand underpins all quests, under whatever banner we huddle.

In the prologue to his book *The Age of Wonder: How the Romantic Generation Discovered the Beauty and Terror of Science*, Richard Holmes writes:

> Romanticism as a cultural force is generally regarded as intensely hostile to science, its ideal of subjectivity eternally opposed to that of scientific objectivity. But I do not believe that was always the case, or that the terms are so mutually exclusive. The notion of wonder seems to be something that once united them, and can still do so.

It's certainly true that the moon, for example, need lose none of its magic because we can now see it in great detail through a telescope, or analyse its rocks in a laboratory. A buttercup can be something we simply classify, take for granted and even trample on; or it can be an annual miracle to be honoured and appreciated for its beauty and complexity, as well as to be understood anatomically. In this sense our imagination seems to me as valid a tool for understanding as our intellect. How sad and revealing it is that people nowadays say: 'It's just your imagination.'

One book rich in imagination, with all the profound simplicity of some of Tolstoy's tales, is *The Five People You Meet in Heaven* by the American writer Mitch Albom. There he writes of a sad and disappointed man called Eddie who feels trapped in a meaningless life at a seaside amusement park. 'The Head of Maintenance' is his title, though the kids know him as 'the Ride Man at Ruby Pier'. The dull routine of his work accentuates his feelings of loneliness and regret. Then, on his eighty-third birthday, Eddie dies in a tragic accident, trying to save a little girl from a collapsing roller coaster.

Eddie awakens in the 'afterlife' where he discovers that heaven is not the lush and serene Garden of Eden we are led to expect, but a place where your earthly life is explained to you by five people who shared it with you: some closely, others as seeming strangers. One of Eddie's encounters is with the captain who was his commanding officer in the army and who died fighting in the Philippines during World War II. It prompts Eddie to relive experiences as a soldier – some traumatic, some heroic. The book is full of meaningful flashbacks that, in their turn, prompt other important memories.

During his conversation with the captain, the hillside on which they are talking suddenly reverts to its barren and shattered state, and Eddie realises that this is the place where the captain was blown to pieces by a land mine. Eddie then witnesses the full horror of that moment: this, he realises, is the captain's burial ground. 'No funeral. No coffin. Just his shattered skeleton and the muddy earth', writes Albom.

> 'You've been waiting here all this time?' Eddie whispered.
>
> 'Time' the Captain said, 'is not what you think.' He sat down next to Eddie. 'Dying? Not the end of everything. We think it is. But what happens on earth is only the beginning.'
>
> Eddie looked lost.
>
> 'I figure it's like in the Bible, the Adam and Eve deal?' the Captain said. 'Adam's first night on earth? When he lays down to sleep? He thinks it's all over, right? He doesn't know what sleep is. His eyes are closing and he thinks he's leaving this world, right?'
>
> 'Only he isn't. He wakes up the next morning and he has a fresh new world to work with, but he has something else, too. He has his yesterday.'
>
> The Captain grinned. 'The way I see it; that's what we're getting here, Soldier. That's what heaven is. You get to make sense of your yesterdays.'

To make sense of my yesterdays, and to share what might be worth sharing from that process is one of the aims of this book. But unlike the captain I'm still alive; so maybe the heaven Mitch Albom has written about is not actually confined to what people call the 'afterlife', but is instead a state of being in which reflection rather than action is the primary activity. In that sense I can see that sleep – and even more so the pause between incarnations – may be particularly appropriate and conducive for such reflection. However, our need and wish for a space in which to take stock of our lives clearly doesn't have to be confined to a possible existence outside of time and can take place at any moment.

I have endless notes about 'time' and 'eternity' scribbled down over the years, and the main purpose of this chapter is to explore this mysterious subject as it relates to the questions I address in this book. 'Time was invented by nature so that everything doesn't happen at once' is one light-hearted entry in my notebook. On the same page is something I noticed on a plaque in Westminster Abbey: 'Here lies that which is mortal of Isaac Newton.'

What emerge again and again from these notes of mine are versions of the thought I have already expressed in preceding chapters: only that which is eternal in us can comprehend eternity. That clearly rules out the brain which, despite being a magnificent and awe-inspiring phenomenon enabling us to function as physical beings in a physical world, is as mortal as the rest of our body. The activity of thinking can certainly bring us to the realisation that there may well be an existence outside of time and space, but the brain itself is an inappropriate organ through which to actually experience that eternal dimension.

Indeed, there is no real evidence that our brains produce any thoughts at all, whether about eternity or what time to get up in the morning. Certainly when the brain is damaged our ability to cope, either mentally or physically, can be severely impaired; but that in no way proves that our thoughts originate there. For this reason, despite the general assumption that it is our brain that does the thinking, consciousness itself remains a mystery, not only to laymen like me but to neuroscientists and psychologists alike. Yet consciousness is the very basis of our perception of the world and of our formulation of science itself.

There are, of course, plenty of theories surrounding the mind–brain dilemma, but those who would have us believe that the human being consists solely of flesh and bones, all of which are transitory and perishable, are – it seems – on increasingly flimsy ground, for reasons that I will continue to explore in the pages that follow. Equally misleading is the idea that our brain and whole nervous system function like some very complex computer. It is we who have invented such machines which, for all their ingenuity, conspicuously lack the element that led to their creation in the first place:

namely imagination. Computers are certainly clever, as are their inventors, but they are not in themselves inherently creative. In that sense my vine is an infinitely more miraculous and complex structure than my computer, for it is a living entity depending for its existence on an interaction with its whole environment of light and warmth, and for its nutrition from what is also alive – the soil itself. How far the vine's environment extends is still a mystery; but there are those like me who believe, as did our ancestors, that the source of the vine's very structure and existence may be located far out in space, among the world of the stars.

I am genuinely puzzled that people who are perfectly aware of the situation I have described – people who will no doubt be puzzled that I am puzzled – can assume that natural selection and random mutations, albeit over huge periods of time, can explain my vine; whereas it is perfectly clear that the computer didn't one day drop from the trees, but that some very able people designed and made it. In saying this I am not advocating some simplistic creationist theory whereby God, once upon a time, created a vine – along with millions of other plants and animals. Clearly evolution is a reality: but 'evolution from what?' is the really interesting question. It is also worth remembering that my computer is still incapable of producing another computer. The writer and broadcaster Malcolm Muggeridge once wrote: 'You can leave two computers in a room by themselves without the slightest anxiety!'

If, therefore, my brain is not in itself the source of my thoughts and ideas, but rather the organ, the filter through which this activity can express itself, what then is the actual nature and source of this activity that we call the mind and which, on the whole, we tend simply to take for granted? And what is its relationship to time? Is this, perhaps, what some would call the human spirit; an entity that constantly interacts with the creative thoughts that animate the cosmos itself – thoughts that stem from a reality some would call God? Indeed, is the human spirit dynamic evidence of that reality itself?

One book that I often return to when struggling to understand the mind–brain dilemma and the mystery of time is an anthology edited by David Lorimer called *Thinking Beyond the Brain*, which grew out of a series of conferences organised by the Scientific and Medical Network. Various contributors to the book address the mystery of consciousness, challenging the notion that we are nothing but a pack of neurons that will eventually reveal their secrets in the laboratory. Instead, they ask – as I have been asking – whether our conscious mind, and with it our self-awareness, stem from some dimension beyond material investigation. How, too, are we to account for parapsychological phenomena in which consciousness seems to defy the boundaries of time and space?

In one contribution, Professor David Fontana, who for many years has studied the relationship between western and eastern psychological systems, together with methods for deepening and expanding consciousness, acknowledges that the term 'beyond the brain', 'presupposes that psychological events are not bounded by the neuro-physiological processes that take place inside the cerebellum'. He declares that he is not unhappy to accept 'this dualistic hypothesis' since human beings do not experience themselves as brain but as mind. This mind, he points out, is something that is only really accessible to the person who experiences it, whereas the brain is a physical organ 'in the public domain' and only directly observable to others. For this reason, he argues, it is reasonable to suppose that 'the whole of our psychological life takes place beyond the brain, and cannot be understood by any examination of the brain'.

At the conclusion of his article, Fontana mentions the goal in the Tibetan Buddhist tradition of maintaining consciousness even in dreamless sleep – a state that he equates with deep meditation – and he emphasises that such practices involve a methodology very different from that of western science: 'They are concerned with a knowing rather than a knowing about,' he writes, 'direct knowledge based upon personal experience, rather than indirect knowledge based upon the experience of others.' This is exactly what interested Steiner about those European mystics of the Middle Ages such as Eckhart, Tauler and Paracelsus.

Finally Fontana describes how in the East there is always a certain amount of amusement at the idea that western psychologists base their work upon the examination of the minds and behaviour of others rather than their own. Not surprisingly he concludes by quoting those words carved above the portal of the Oracle of Apollo at Delphi, 'Know Thyself', suggesting they could serve as watchwords for all scientists.

In another contribution to *Thinking Beyond the Brain*, Peter Fenwick, the distinguished neurosurgeon and psychiatrist, highlights the importance of what he calls 'post-modern science', a movement that started in the sixties inspired by the work of Thomas Kuhn. 'He was', writes Fenwick, 'the first to describe science as being culture bound.' William Blake, some two hundred years earlier, made almost the same point with those words: 'As a man is, so he sees.' In other words, a person's or indeed a culture's overall mindset or world view determines not only the questions they ask but also the answers that satisfy them. Fenwick points out that science, conducted within cultures in which soul and spirit are experienced as primary, is as valid as one which investigates matter alone. And evolution, it seems, is at work not only in nature but in these realms of the mind as well.

Thomas Kuhn introduced the phrase 'paradigm shift' in his book *The Structure of Scientific Revolutions* to describe turning points in human consciousness – shifts in what we had previously taken for granted in making judgements about the world and our own place in it. The transition that began in the 15th century, from a Church-dominated culture to what we know as the scientific revolution, was one obvious example. Another would be that period around 500 BC – the Axial Age – about which Karen Armstrong has written so insightfully. Kuhn clearly believed that we have been entering a similar period of change in recent years, one manifestation of which Theodore Roszak labelled the counterculture. The phrase 'New Age', although it increasingly conjures up a somewhat flaky image, is a recognition of these same stirrings.

Meanwhile, however, the reductionism and materialism that have characterised modern science, particularly since the beginning of the 19th century, are still very much with us, and are – it has to be said – highly successful in enabling us to manipulate and seemingly control forces and phenomena that previously controlled us. Our technology is undoubtedly a triumph – my computer being an obvious example – though how we apply this technology is proving quite another challenge.

Our understanding of life itself, for example, has not always been enriched by this powerful, yet narrow mindset – least of all the understanding of our own complex make-up, of which consciousness and the actual origin of life itself are the most mysterious and elusive of all. As the physicist Fritjof Capra explained to Ron Eyre on our 'long search' in California, in the theories and conclusions that we make about the world and about life itself, we are always in danger of making fundamental errors if we fail to acknowledge the observer's role and influence, coloured as we are by all the cultural baggage and prejudices we carry with us. As Albert Einstein once said: 'You cannot solve a problem with the same mindset that caused the problem in the first place.'

One aspect of our current mindset, as explored by Otto Scharmer in his book *Theory U*, is our failure to recognise that many of the problems we face arise from being bogged down by what he calls 'systematic blind spots in our thinking'. Scharmer suggests that there are two sorts of learning: learning from the past, and 'learning from the future as it emerges'; and that experiences from the past aren't always helpful in dealing with current issues. Our challenge, he writes, 'is to tune in and act from one's highest future potential – the future that depends on us to bring it into being.' What he calls our blind spots stem from not being fully aware and in touch with 'the inner place' from which attention and intention originate. He writes, therefore, about the need to invent another type of telescope, 'not one that helps us to observe only what is far out – the moons of Jupiter – but one that enables us to observe the observer's blind spot by bending the beam back upon its source: the "self" that is performing the scientific activity.' Perhaps that same telescope will also help us to discover that elusive entity referred to by some scientists as 'the god particle'.

'How can we act from the future that is seeking to emerge?' is the essence of Scharmer's message. To what degree, therefore, are we prepared to discard past habits, to be open to challenging our basic assumptions about the nature of time and space, and to listen to and trust our own inner and authentic voice? 'For it is only through this listening', writes Peter Senge in his introduction to Scharmer's book, 'that we will unlock our collective capacity to create the world anew.'

For me one of the most interesting and exciting contributions to *Thinking Beyond the Brain* addresses the very important subject of time – and if ever a radical shift was needed in our understanding of life's great mysteries, it is, I believe, in relation to the phenomenon of time. In his essay 'Beyond Space and Time', psychiatrist Dr Andrew Powell first describes some of his thoughts and observations on working with patients in group meditation sessions, guided fantasy and past-life therapy; he then concludes that these and many other clinical examples all clearly point to one thing: 'When we move beyond the constraints of sense perception and the bounds of physical space-time, we enter a domain in which all time is now and all space is here.' Meditation is, in other words, one way of freeing ourselves from time.

Rudolf Steiner said something similar in a lecture he gave in Nuremberg in 1918 on the subject of our communication with those who have died. He spoke about the moments before falling asleep as particularly appropriate for putting questions to those with whom we were close. The moment of waking in the morning is when answers can come back to us if we are sufficiently attentive and open to this form of communication. But what I find especially interesting is his next sentence in which he points out that such moments, which for us seem to be separated by many hours, are really 'simultaneous'; or, in Powell's words 'a domain in which all time is now'.

In the same lecture, published in an anthology called *Staying Connected*, Steiner emphasises the mystery of time with these words:

> Spiritually, what is past has not really vanished but is still there. In physical life people have this conception only in regard to space. If you stand in front of a tree and then go away and come back later to look at it, the tree has not disappeared; it is still there. The same is true for time in the spiritual world. If you experience something at one moment, it has passed away in the next as far as physical consciousness is concerned; spiritually conceived, however, it has not passed away. You can look back at it just as you looked back at the tree.

These insights into the nature of time stem in Steiner's case from research into what he called the Akashic record: many of his pronouncements, like 'man can penetrate to the eternal origin of things', originate from his claim that after many years of inner work it is possible very gradually and tentatively to tap into a permanent record of all that has unfolded through time. 'Spiritual archaeology' is a phrase that comes to mind; my more prosaic image is of a psychic memory-stick with unlimited storage.

Such a claim can easily sound as though we're entering the world of science-fiction rather than anything remotely scientific; yet, like so much of what Steiner unearthed, confirmation of sorts is slowly emerging through the cracks in our over-rational and often blinkered culture. As Gary Lachman points out in *The Secret History of Consciousness*, it is significant that Steiner's research was not carried out in a trance-like state, but in full consciousness and thus with 'the clarity of mind' that could observe phenomena accurately. 'One result of this', writes Lachman, 'is that Steiner's accounts have a precision unlike other reports of the Akashic record.' He is referring in particular to Madame Blavatsky's somewhat haphazard utterances at the end of the 19th century.

Lachman also draws attention to the fact that Steiner's insights are reminiscent of an idea expressed by the distinguished French philosopher Henri Bergson that 'the past still exists' and is potentially 'present to consciousness'. All we have to do, said Bergson, is 'to withdraw a veil'. In Marcel Proust's novel *Remembrance of Things Past*, it is the narrator's action of dipping the little Madeleine cake into his tea that removes the veil; and suddenly in flood detailed memories of his whole childhood. It's significant, too, that in old age memories of one's childhood and early life start to become as vivid, if not more so, than those of yesterday – as though time itself is telescoping. Jung's theory of the collective unconscious – that we can have 'access to the whole reservoir of human experience' – points in this same direction, though with the added implication of access to a time that precedes our current lifespan.

In an article entitled 'The Rediscovery of the Akashic Field' in *Network Review*, the journal of the Scientific and Medical Network (Winter 2005), the Hungarian philosopher Ervin Laszlo writes:

> The idea that there is something in the universe that connects and correlates is not a discovery but a rediscovery. As an intuitive insight it has been present in all the great cosmologies, most explicitly in Hindu cosmology. There it was known as Akasha, the most fundamental of the five elements of the cosmos – the others being *vata* (air), *agni* (fire), *ap* (water), and *prithivi* (earth). Akasha embraces the properties of all five elements; it is the womb from which everything has emerged and into which everything will ultimately re-descend.

By way of introduction to his article, Laszlo – who for years has been working on a re-visioning of science-based findings in physics, biology and consciousness research – points out that those he calls 'cutting-edge scientists' are coming to a remarkable insight: 'the universe is not a world of separate things and events, of external spectators and an impersonal spectacle'. Unlike the disenchanted world of classical physics, he writes, it is not even material. In a subsequent article on this subject in *Network Review* (Summer 2007) Laszlo writes:

> Phenomena occur in all the principal domains of experience and observation that cannot be adequately explained in reference to the established concepts and theories of the physical, biological, and psychological sciences. The phenomena consist of a form of coherence that could only come about if the elements of a system were non-locally connected – i.e. if they were mutually 'entangled'.

For Laszlo this indicates a law that transcends time and space, and relates closely to the ancient concept of Akasha as 'the enduring memory of the universe'. Laszlo is therefore taking the bold step of acknowledging a force or field which is as much a part of the universe as electromagnetic, gravitational, and nuclear fields, and which he believes connects organisms and minds in the biosphere, and particles, stars, and galaxies throughout the universe – at whatever distance, and simultaneously.

In another contribution to Lorimer's anthology, Stanislav Grof also writes about this interconnectedness of all things, drawing on his many years of experience as a psychiatrist and as one of the founders and chief theorists of transpersonal psychology. This movement is deeply influenced by the work of Jung, and in particular by Jung's theory of the collective unconscious. Transpersonal experiences are defined as those in which our sense of identity expands beyond the personal to encompass wider aspects of existence. Such experiences clearly violate some of the most basic assumptions of mechanistic science, says Grof, again implying the arbitrary nature of all physical boundaries:

> Many transpersonal experiences involve events from the microcosm and the macrocosm, realms that cannot normally be reached by unaided human senses, or from historical periods that precede the origin of the solar system, formation of planet earth, appearance of living organisms, development of the nervous system, and emergence of Homo Sapiens.

Grof's research into 'non-ordinary states of consciousness' reveals an extraordinary paradox concerning the nature of the human being. It clearly shows, he says, that in a mysterious and unexplained way each of us contains information about the entire universe and the whole of existence, and that as a seemingly insignificant biological entity I have potential access to everything. If true, the internet and all those impressive websites pale into insignificance. The implication, it seems, is that if we can make this ability conscious, there would be no need for computers, telephones, etc. We ourselves are the only instruments necessary. Perhaps the rapid growth in what's called communication technology is a material and ultimately limited manifestation of this psychic faculty that we already possess, and which seeks to evolve and become more conscious.

Much of Grof's own work has been conducted with the use of hallucinogenic drugs and through what he calls holotropic breathwork; others work with hypnosis. During my time as a young director at TWW in Wales I met a healer called Arnold Bloxham who played me tapes he had recorded of people under hypnosis speaking in languages of which they had no previous knowledge. In Steiner's research into the Akashic record there is, however, one very fundamental difference to the work done by Bloxham, Grof and others. Over many years Steiner developed a way of accessing this great reservoir of human history and experience in full consciousness, bringing to it all the clarity, sound judgement and capacity to discriminate that we strive to develop in our interaction with the physical world around us. If such disciplined work is by-passed there is an obvious danger of chaotic and even dangerous results, though I know that in the wise and sensitive hands of someone like Stan Grof every effort is made to protect and help patients.

———————•-•-•———————

In his essay 'Beyond Space and Time', from which I have already quoted, psychiatrist Andrew Powell points out – by way of an historical perspective on the subject of time and space – that Newton's laws of motion and gravitation, together with the mind–body dualism of Descartes, led to a science of material realism that profoundly shaped how we think about the nature of reality. Powell continues:

> We conceive of an enduring physical universe out there, a stage on which we live our lives and make our exit. The physical realm is held to be the primary one and consciousness is seen as a miraculous by-product of evolutionary biology. Anyone holding the view that we are eternal souls in physical bodies has been obliged to hypothesise another parallel but non-physical world in which the soul resides.

This, Powell continues, has led to all kinds of problems such as where heaven is actually located and why what he calls 'energy transfer' has never been shown to take place between the two worlds. On the other hand, the science of 'material realism' has advanced apace, its world firmly bounded by the five senses. But just when it begins to look like game, set and match to material realism, states Powell,

> physicists discover quantum theory, which tells a different story. The wave–particle experiment breaks with three hundred years of certainty. Depending on the way the experimenter sets up the light experiment, particles become waves and waves particles. We find we have two realities with equal validity. If two, why not twenty? If three dimensions, why not four?

Powell goes on to point out, as did Capra in our film in California, that electrons are no longer thought of as particles spinning around the nucleus of the atom like a miniature solar system:

> Instead the electron is smeared throughout all of space as a probability wave, which only collapses into its space-time location when a conscious observer makes a measurement. Nor can the velocity and position of the electron be known at the same time, for this is a world of uncertainties. There is only a statistical probability that the electron will appear where you expect it to be. It may just materialize hundreds, thousands or even millions of miles away, and when it does so, it takes zero time to get there.

Powell's bewildering conclusion, like that of Laszlo, is that both space and time are bypassed and that such experiments reveal 'the breath-taking interconnectedness of the cosmos'. He then quotes the physicist David Bohm:

> Ultimately, the entire universe (with all its particles, including those constituting human beings, their laboratories, observing instruments, etc) has to be understood as a single undivided whole, in which analysis into separately and independently existent parts has no fundamental status.

It is an extraordinary thesis which Bohm explores in great depth in *Wholeness and the Implicate Order*, but no less extraordinary and challenging than this final statement by Andrew Powell himself:

> We have to conclude that the old-style Newtonian universe is an illusion, for there is no such thing as an external world 'out there' that exists apart from consciousness. Everything is mind. We are not part of the universe, we are the universe.

The word 'mind' can, of course, be rendered in other terms – words such as energy, spirit, brahman, and the tao, even wakefulness and, of course, God. All such terms offer a bridge to those who come from a different direction or out of different traditions. In fact one of the contributors to Lorimer's anthology, Professor Ravi Ravindra, does have his roots elsewhere, deep in the spiritual wisdom and traditions of India. He now lives and works in Canada where he teaches and writes about physics, philosophy and religion. *The Yoga of Christ* is the title of one of his books; and more recently *Science and the Sacred*. I've heard Ravindra speak at a conference in England, and for me he was an embodiment of the wisdom that can be expressed, not in words alone, when all that is best from East and West unites in one person.

Ravindra starts his essay by recalling something that his two-year-old daughter said quite casually to him one winter's night as they lay huddled together in the snow gazing up at the stars. 'Daddy, before I was born, I was a star in the sky.' In another experience, a Zen master offers him a spontaneous gift in return for what the master said was a deed in a previous life. These two affirmations of other dimensions, of other lives, prompt Ravindra to question how sensible it is to constrict our view of reality to what can be understood by what he calls 'the narrow aperture of the rational mind'. He reminds us that religious traditions universally affirm that the person is not identical with the body but that (as I've discussed in previous chapters) each of us has an innermost core, a spiritual entity which not only does not die but which, in a sense, is also never born. But this is not our precious 'personality', nor does it have anything to do with that drawer full of certificates testifying to our worldly achievements, skills and knowledge.

This thought leads Ravindra to lay bare the egotism that can so often underlie our hope of and belief in some sort of afterlife. This so-called 'everlasting life' is, he suggests, in so many cases envisaged as 'a quantitative extension in time', prompted by a fear of losing one's personal ego. 'Because I am self-occupied', he writes,

> I regard myself as the centre of the universe and, in my ego-centred imagination, I believe that the whole universe would collapse if I were to cease existing in the form I know. I project my fear of the loss of the known onto the unknown and I devise whole systems of consolation which would vouchsafe an everlasting life for me. The wish for continuity, the tendency to repeat myself and the inertia of a psychological momentum prevent my transformation …

To the extent, therefore, that we fail to awaken this sense for the cosmic dimension of our being, suggests Ravindra, so we also fail to realise that 'eternity is a quality of being, rather than extension of temporality'. To live in eternity – to escape the tyranny of time – another dimension of consciousness is needed. Once we have awoken to that reality we are able to dwell both in time and in eternity. In his *Tractatus Logico-Philosophicus*, Ludwig Wittgenstein wrote: 'If we take eternity to mean not infinite temporal duration but timelessness, then eternal life belongs to those who live in the present' – a nice, simple statement from someone who was not famous for making things easy, either for us or for himself. It is, of course, exactly what Johannes Tauler said some six hundred years earlier: 'Eternity is the everlasting now.' Tennessee Williams, in his foreword to *The Rose Tattoo*, writes: 'Snatching the eternal out of the desperately fleeting is the great magic trick of human existence.'

Living fully into the moment is, of course, what children do quite naturally. It is why our childhoods seem to have had an almost eternal quality – the summer holidays went on for centuries, in contrast to the experience we have as we get older of ten years passing by in an instant.

A whole book on this subject, *The Power of Now*, has been written by Eckhart Tolle, and judging by its popularity it has clearly been of help to many people. 'Whatever the present moment contains', he writes, 'accept it as if you had chosen it. Always work with it, not against it. Make it your friend and ally, not your enemy. This will miraculously transform your whole life.' Such a statement echoes the profound prayer by Thomas Merton that I quoted earlier: 'May I want the life I've chosen.'

Tolle goes on to warn of the danger of being trapped in time, 'the compulsion to live almost exclusively through memory and anticipation'. As a result we tend to live 'with an endless preoccupation with past and future', and therefore fail to appreciate the significance of 'now'. 'There was never a time when your life was not now, nor will there ever be', he writes. Asking the question: How long is now? is another way of approaching this same thought. As Tolle implies, you could argue that it is always 'now', so 'now' actually lasts for ever. Our unease, anxiety and stress, all of them forms of fear, are caused, so Tolle believes, by 'too much future, not enough presence'. Likewise our feelings of guilt, regret and sadness are caused by too much past and again not enough presence, a failure to live fully into each moment.

As far as we know it is only human beings among living creatures who, in the words of Percy Bysshe Shelley in his poem 'To a Skylark', '…look before and after; And pine for what is not …' Hence the liberation experienced by Aldous Huxley under the influence of mescalin, when time seemed to him 'entirely irrelevant'.

Meditation itself has been described as the activity of being fully present. Tolle quotes the great 12th-century Sufi mystic and poet, Rumi: 'Past and future veil God from our sight; burn up both of them with fire.' In this sense I find the word 'being', as in 'human being' or 'angelic being', very helpful because it implies neither 'was' nor 'will be', but 'is'.

Another poet who clearly thought deeply about the subject of time and eternity was T.S. Eliot. In 'The Dry Salvages' from *Four Quartets* he wrote:

Men's curiosity searches past and future
And clings to that dimension. But to apprehend
The point of intersection of the timeless
With time, is an occupation for the saint –
No occupation either, but something given
And taken, in a lifetime's death in love,
Ardour and selflessness and self-surrender.

On this same theme Ravi Ravindra writes: 'As long as we remain confined to our ordinary consciousness, we experience and move only in time, having only vague and occasional hints of eternity.' I'm not sure that Ravindra is completely correct in this statement; nor, for that matter, do I believe that the understanding to which Eliot is pointing is for the saint alone.

I have a hunch that all of us, albeit unawares, have a constant experience of eternity through the very fact that we are conscious of living in time; for we couldn't experience time unless there was something in us that is outside of time to do the experiencing. If we – like, I suspect, the animals – lived solely in time, without any ability to observe the fact, we would be unconscious of time, and only dimly aware of an inner clock in relation to our need for food and sleep.

In our conscious lives we may indeed have only 'vague and occasional hints of eternity', but whenever we experience time, we are, I believe, transcending it in the very act of that experience. It is why, I imagine, those older patients of Jung prompted him to conclude that life behaves as if it's going on forever. Of course, the part of us living in time and space knows perfectly well, as did Jung's patients, that our shell – along with all its psychological clutter – is transitory and mortal. Our bodies clearly live in time, and age in the process. But the faculty in us that enables us to come to such a realisation is not, perhaps, subject to those same laws. In my mind I can transport myself back to an hour ago, or to yesterday – or even to when I was ten years old. And if this ability is nurtured and strengthened, I can start to imagine how access to what we think of as the past can, in fact, be detailed and instantaneous. We are living in 'the everlasting now'. Indeed, by using my imagination, rather than memory, I can even have an existence a month from now.

And yet, it seems, we need this precious time, this 'now', in which to learn and grow. It is what I sense T.S. Eliot meant when he wrote in 'Burnt Norton' that only through time is time conquered.

CHAPTER 24

Ancient and Modern

For the writer and broadcaster Malcolm Muggeridge heaven was very definitely somewhere else. As he became older and ever more committed to Christianity, he increasingly dismissed as an 'absurdity' (one of his favourite words) people's aspirations to build some sort of paradise here on earth or, in the words of Otto Scharmer, 'to create the world anew'. Eventually, at the age of seventy-nine – together with his wife Kitty – he was received into the Roman Catholic Church. In a sermon he preached in the chapel of Hertford College, Oxford in 1968 he spoke these words: 'This has been the century of the kingdom of heaven on earth; many and varied have been its prophets and its guises.' He went on to cite 'the American Way of Life', 'The Welfare State', and 'the New Civilisation' created by Stalin as examples:

> But what has come to pass, I fear, is better described as the kingdom of hell on earth, soon, I should suppose, to pass into oblivion, its piled-up radioactive dust one more monument to the folly of man when he supposes that his destiny is in his own hands.

Utopianism, he then noted with pleasure, was decidedly on the wane – 'though some dons and half-baked students continue to traffic in it'. It's a typical Muggeridge exaggeration – ignoring all the fine yet subtle shifts that have taken place in people's sensibilities during the last hundred years or so, yet spoken with all the wit and skill that made him such a successful and celebrated figure.

I want to write in some detail about Malcolm Muggeridge, with whom I worked on a number of films, not because his thoughts and ideas influenced me to the same extent as those of others I have mentioned – in fact some of his views were in direct opposition to my own – but because he exemplified very clearly for me something to which I have already referred: the relative insignificance of what people think compared to how they actually live their lives. Malcolm was a wonderfully friendly and kind person, and someone who also made me laugh a lot. But his views on life, as he got older, became increasingly eccentric and doctrinaire. Yet despite his pronouncements on its gloomy fate, he enjoyed and cared very deeply about this world of which he so despaired. Perhaps at work below the surface was a projection onto life of an unconscious dissatisfaction and disappointment with himself – an unresolved conflict with his own inner voice.

Author with Malcolm Muggeridge

Malcolm's views were hugely influenced, I believe, by his experience as a young journalist on the *Manchester Guardian* in the thirties when he reported at first hand on the upheavals taking place in the Soviet Union. In the documentary *Winter in Moscow* that he made for the BBC in 1969 he wrote:

> The England I turned my back on in 1932 was a dismal place. Old Jerusalem was falling down and no New one building. From the Manchester Guardian office, resounding with Liberalism's dying platitudes, I gazed disconsolately out upon the ravages of what the politicians called an economic blizzard. It seemed evident beyond any shadow of doubt that capitalism, as Marx had foretold, was now irretrievably moribund and doomed – offering its captive workers no hope.

Born in 1903, Malcolm had been strongly influenced by his socialist father to whom he was deeply attached. One of his earliest memories as a child was of 'my father and his cronies plotting the overthrow of the capitalist system in the drawing-room of our suburban house in South Croydon'. And so, like the more militant of those 'captive workers' – and, indeed, many left-wing intellectuals – Malcolm turned his attention to the triumphant proletariat in the USSR. 'This was the Marxist paradise', he wrote, 'which I was now to report for the blameless readers of the *Manchester Guardian*.' In fact he and Kitty went to Russia with the intention of staying there. They sold all their possessions deemed bourgeois, including Malcolm's dinner jacket and Kitty's only long dress.

When the idealistic young journalist then witnessed the appalling situation in the Ukraine – widespread famine brought about by the enforced collectivisation of agriculture, and the brutal liquidation of the land-owning peasants – he was deeply shocked and disillusioned. An almost greater shock was his newspaper's reluctance to give prominence to his reports since they didn't correspond with the paper's liberal views. He wasn't helped by the fact that celebrated 'political pilgrims' such as Bernard Shaw and the socialist icons Sidney and Beatrice Webb (she was Kitty Muggeridge's aunt) were determined to see nothing but good in all they were shown.

Pravda means truth in Russian, but the 'pravda' served up to them bore no relation to reality. Those three months in the USSR dramatically changed Malcolm's life and way of looking at the world. His articles made him an outcast among western intelligentsia, and his lone spiritual journey began – a journey that could be described in the same words that Steiner used about Nietzsche: 'The disappointment which his idealism had caused him drove him into a hostile mood toward all idealism.' This was certainly true of Muggeridge: his antipathy to communism never swayed him towards capitalism. Talking to me later about that crucial time he spent in the Soviet Union Malcolm said:

> The general feeling was that, if you reacted strongly against a communist regime, you must therefore be equally strongly in favour of a capitalist way of life; but I didn't see any occasion to alter any judgement I'd made. Strangely enough, when I came to know George Orwell, in a sense we had this feeling in common, because he too, through his experiences in the Spanish Civil War in Catalonia, was bitterly critical of how the communists behaved there, but it didn't make him find the Franco regime any more palatable. Partisanship is expected of us all today; I had none.

In the first volume of his autobiography, which he called *Chronicles of Wasted Time*, Malcolm wrote:

> Truth is very beautiful, more so than justice which easily puts on a false face. In my lifetime the world has overflowed with bloodshed and

explosions whose dust has never had time to settle before others have erupted; all in purportedly just causes. The quest for justice continues and the weapons of hatred pile up; but truth was an early casualty. The lies on behalf of which our wars have been fought and our peace treaties concluded! The lies of revolution and counter-revolution! The lies of advertising, of news, of salesmanship, of politics! The lies of the priest in his pulpit, the professor at his podium, the journalist at his typewriter! It is truth that has died, not God!

I first met Malcolm Muggeridge in India in 1969 when I was making my film on Gandhi and Muggeridge was filming Mother Teresa in Calcutta – both projects for the BBC. We stayed in touch and three years later I filmed an interview with him for the film I was making about our mutual hero, Leo Tolstoy. Then in 1980 my new boss in the BBC Documentary department, Christopher Ralling, suggested that I work with Malcolm – considered by many one of the wittiest and most elegant writers of his time – on an autobiographical series drawing on some of the excellent films about his life and career that he had already made in the sixties with a number of very talented directors. My task was to fill in the gaps and to weave it all together, sometimes talking with him on camera about his thoughts on his earlier thoughts. In the foreword to the anthology based on the series, put together by my assistant Jane Bywaters together with Christopher Ralling, Malcolm wrote:

Muggeridge, by Trog

It was the strangest of situations. I as myself, looking at another self on the screen, and appraising this other self's performance … Could it really be me – this attitudinising, opinionated alter ego or 'doppelganger'? Clearly yes, and then again, clearly no.

The result of our efforts was a series of eight programmes that we called *Muggeridge – Ancient and Modern*. 'I'd much rather be a hymn than a him' was his reaction to the title. The cartoonist Wally Fawkes (Trog) brilliantly captured Malcolm's so-called ordeal.

During the war Muggeridge worked as an Intelligence Officer for M16 (recruited at the suggestion of his friend Graham Greene), serving in

Mozambique, North Africa and finally Paris. In 1945 he joined the *Daily Telegraph* and was soon sent to Washington as their foreign correspondent; five years on he became the paper's deputy editor. After two more years he was appointed editor of *Punch*, but gradually work for the new medium of television began to take over – initially as an interviewer on *Panorama*. In the years that followed, although he became a television celebrity whom people either loved or hated – and in the days when the word 'celebrity' still implied a certain maturity and stature – his attitude to the medium that fed him became ever more ambivalent. By the time I filmed a conversation with him in the old *Panorama* studio at Lime Grove he was deeply suspicious of people's addiction to television: 'In those early days of *Panorama* in the 1950s', he said, 'it used to call itself "A Window on the World", but it's always strange to me that these studios have no windows. They're completely and utterly cut off, isolated from the world, and I feel that they are places of fantasy not connected with life.' As justification for his prodigious television output in a medium he increasingly despised, he once compared himself to a pianist in a brothel playing Mozart. By the time I knew him there was no trace of a television set at his Sussex cottage. He was fond of telling people that he'd had his aerials removed: 'a very simple operation – it doesn't hurt in any way – and you'll feel infinitely better for it'.

In his biography of Malcolm Muggeridge, his friend Richard Ingrams wrote:

> The frustration of any biographer is that unless he is a Boswell he cannot recapture the quality of talk. Most of Malcolm's was gossip … His tone was generally disparaging, but at the same time affectionate. He seldom bore a grudge and seemed baffled when others took offence. What gave his conversation its special flavour was its gleefully apocalyptic tone. Everything and everyone was going to pot. The Prime Minister – Macmillan, Wilson, Thatcher – was 'pretty well washed up'. The Monarchy would not last my lifetime. The Press was irrevocably doomed. But nothing in this catalogue was a cause for gloom and anxiety. It was all made to seem extraordinarily funny.

In those few lines Ingrams captures perfectly the paradoxical nature of the man. To be with him was always fun and uplifting. He enjoyed filming and was very easy to work with. Yet what he said – particularly as he got older – was certainly laden with doom and gloom. But the humorist, the satirist was never far below the surface. Whenever I arrived to see him at his Sussex home it wasn't God that he initially wanted to talk about, but who was doing what to whom at the BBC – the juicier the story, the better.

When Malcolm heard that a 'Malcolm Muggeridge' had been installed at Madame Tussaud's in London he wrote:

> I feel very frightened indeed, and more than that, exceedingly sorry that I ever agreed to become a waxwork, for I have been told since, if the public grow weary of your presence, or if Tussaud's get offended with you, they melt you down, and build up a more popular fellow out of your dripping.

And on a slightly more serious note:

> Without a god, men have to be gods themselves, and fabricate their own immortality, as they have in wax in London's Madame Tussaud's Exhibition, a place of images. In the beginning was the image, and the image became wax and dwelt among us, full of absurdity.

Malcolm's conviction that this world was essentially insignificant compared to the heaven to which we go at death was a subject about which we argued constantly, but always good-humouredly; yet it became increasingly difficult to have a real discussion with him. At times I felt that humour, much as I love a joke, was a shield behind which he hid. Somewhere there was a disappointed man concealed behind that constant flow of magnificently chosen words. 'A purveyor of news' was how he described himself in the introduction to an anthology of his diary extracts – news being 'the ultimate fantasy of the age'. Yet the other label he chose – 'a vendor of words' – was coined by another of his great heroes, St Augustine.

The best way to respond to the sermons of St Mugg, as he became known, was simply to lie back and be entertained. In this sense he was wonderful company and was much loved by those of us who were privileged to know him. I spent many happy days with him and his wife Kitty at their home in Robertsbridge, and on trips to Paris, London and Berlin for the television autobiography. At Park Cottage there were simple vegetarian lunches, with cold meat and cans of beer on hand for less saintly visitors, followed by long walks whatever the weather. The garden was increasingly overrun by scruffy-looking chickens that Malcolm rescued from a local broiler house. Having taken their frustration out on each other, they had almost no feathers; but there they found a heaven of sorts to end their days. Yet the apparent serenity in this little Garden of Eden was in some ways deceptive. The journalist Harold Evans said of Muggeridge: 'Malcolm may float like a butterfly but he stings like a bee.'

In the introduction to his biography, Richard Ingrams writes about Malcolm's inability to listen to, let alone accept, other viewpoints: 'Malcolm had formulated his own view of his life in his two volumes of memoirs and it was difficult if not impossible to get him to modify any of his views by confronting him with evidence.' Such rigidity does, of course, often come with age – particularly, I imagine, if you have experienced a great deal and thought deeply about those experiences. Laurens van der Post had much the same tendency, but not, in my experience, John Betjeman, who became ever more open, unsure and humble as he grew older, and consequently quite silent: not gloomy, but content merely to look and listen.

Early on in his broadcasting career, in February 1957, Muggeridge interviewed the philosopher and peace campaigner Bertrand Russell on the radio, for the BBC's World Service. The subject was: 'Is the notion of progress an illusion?' Needless to say Muggeridge thought that it was. Russell suggested that if it was an illusion, which he didn't think his interviewer really believed, 'one might as well take to drink and sink into the gutter'. It was the meaning of this word 'progress' over which they clashed. Muggeridge called it 'an arrogant idea' and said that for him what made human beings humane and kind was humility. Russell, citing the eradication of slavery, improvements in health -care and the spread of education, stated that caring for people's material well-being does not in itself have to undermine spiritual values, but nor should we be content with spiritual values that ignore the rest of the world.

Like so many encounters in which two or more people seem unable or unwilling to really listen to each other, the discussion went nowhere. My own sympathies, on reading the transcript, are far more with Russell, though I understand Muggeridge's argument – that our true fulfilment and happiness will be achieved through inner rather than outer transformation. But that inner transformation is, I believe, inseparable from an involvement in trying to make the world itself a better and fairer place for everyone, materially as well as spiritually.

At one point Malcolm challenged Russell to judge the relative stature and worth of two men – Henry Ford and St Francis of Assisi – both of whom genuinely believed they were serving their fellow human beings. Malcolm, not surprisingly, chose St Francis. Russell then pointed to the cruelty, intolerance and endless religious wars that arose in the wake of figures like St Francis. Malcolm would have none of it, returning again to the word 'progress': 'I would say that what progress really means, as I see it', he said, 'is the creation of a kingdom of heaven on earth, of perfect conditions on earth, and I believe that to be complete baloney, a complete fallacy. Whereas the other idea is the idea of human beings who can conceive a kingdom of heaven in heaven – a much finer, more wonderful, more productive idea than the idea of a kingdom of heaven on earth which was Ford's idea.'

For me one of the early and at the time surprising glimpses into a more reflective and sensitive Malcolm Muggeridge was a film he made in 1965 called *Pilgrims to Lourdes*, most sensitively directed by Mike Tuchner. Despite his image as a witty and abrasive journalist and his subsequent emphasis on the significance of the next world as opposed to this one, it was clear from this film that he did have a deep compassion for his fellow human beings in the here and now, particularly those whose lives – like those poor chickens – had been in some ways thwarted. In his commentary he wrote:

> It's easy to ridicule acceptance of the magical qualities of this place and of the waters of the spring people drink and bathe in. One can look with a sceptical eye at the rather unconvincing display of crutches allegedly cast aside by cripples who've been miraculously cured. I find no such inclination myself. It seems to me in all sincerity, and even humility, that these Lourdes pilgrims – mostly very humble lowly people – may have had a clearer and even more practical vision than other traffickers in hope in our time, like psychiatrists and advertisers, and travellers to the moon.

Malcolm then asked himself that inevitable but difficult question when confronted by such suffering: 'Whether these maimed, stunted lives should be protracted, and, in the case of congenital defects, ever begun? Can these poor souls, one asks oneself, sometimes in outward appearance barely human, really wish to go on living?' His response was very similar to my own when I encountered the work at Camphill for children and adults 'in need of special care':

> The scientific answer, of course, is emphatically no. In a broiler house, there's no place for such poor specimens. They are, to use a particularly odious expression, useless mouths. But then, our world is not a broiler house, though alas, as we've seen, it can easily be made one.

If, however, the Christian view is correct, Malcolm continued, and mankind is indeed one family – and here I would acknowledge a similar conviction held by many millions who don't call themselves Christians –

> then these twisted, tangled bodies have a rightful place in the human family as any others, even when they can scarcely utter their insistence that life has been to them a precious gift, and they duly offer thanks to their Maker for it. I, as it happens, believe them more readily than I do the pronouncements of experts on population and eugenics. It can be argued, it seems to me, that no lives are worth living, or that all lives are worth living, but not that some lives are worth living and others not.

It is not difficult to see why Malcolm Muggeridge, some three years later, was so moved and inspired when he met and interviewed Mother Teresa in London. He then went to see for himself her work for the destitute and dying – people whom she and her Sisters rescued from the streets of Calcutta. *Something Beautiful for God* was the title of the film Muggeridge then made. It was a powerful example of what the medium he increasingly criticised could achieve. As a result of his programme and his subsequent book of the same title, this devout and humble Albanian nun became world-famous, and ten years later was awarded the Nobel Peace Prize. Never able to keep a straight face for long, Malcolm wrote: 'Strange to think Mother Teresa wins a Peace Prize provided by the inventor of dynamite.' This ability to laugh at what we otherwise take very seriously – including above all ourselves – is, I believe, a deeply significant human attribute. 'Humour is the only thing about which the English are completely serious' was one of my favourite pronouncements by the Sage of Robertsbridge, as Muggeridge became known as he grew older.

Humour bubbled away below the surface in another superb film – *Twilight of Empire* – that Muggeridge made in India with the director Kevin Billington. In one sequence he returned to the Christian College in Kerala where he had gone to teach in 1924 after leaving Cambridge. There an old professor who remembered him reminded Malcolm of a remark he had made after presiding over a lecture on Shakespeare by a visiting professor. 'If I go to heaven', Malcolm had said, 'which I very much doubt, I shall ask of God one favour. And that is to send Shakespeare down to earth again, and make him sit a Madras University examination in Shakespeare, just for the fun of seeing him fail.' His old colleague agreed with him that Shakespeare would indeed fail. With his irreverent streak firing on all cylinders, Malcolm then added, 'The question is: whether God would pass an examination in theology? What do you think about that? It's an awkward question!'

Another of Malcolm's remarks that I love emerged from a conversation he had in Jerusalem where, in 1967, he was attending the military parade to mark the Israeli take-over of the whole city – the first time for many centuries that a Jewish army had been in charge in Jerusalem. 'On such an occasion', he wrote, 'the Wailing Wall was a place one instinctively made for. The Rabbis were out in force, all wailing away. "Why wail now?" I asked a man in a white cap standing near me. "Oughtn't they to be throwing their fur hats in the air?" "There's always plenty to wail about", he answered sternly. "So there is, so there is", I agreed'.

Being such a witty and intelligent satirist, you would think that Malcolm's job at *Punch* would have suited him perfectly; not so. He complained:

The great difficulty of the job was that you wanted to satirise what's going on in the world and the people who run the affairs of the world, but discover that they are intrinsically more absurd than anything you can invent. You try, for instance, to be funny about the BBC, which is a pretty easy target, and discover that the BBC is liable to satirise itself – witness a Third Programme talk on the place of the potato in English folklore.

Malcolm was certainly not enthusiastic when looking back on his time as editor of *Punch*, but then he did seem to have a need to mock everything with which he had been closely connected.

Malcolm Muggeridge

By the time I met him, already in his mid-sixties, another and more puritanical Malcolm was emerging. What he seemed unable to accept or even contemplate, however, was that the views he now held, together with his abstemious lifestyle, probably only came about because – like St Augustine, Tolstoy and many others before him – he had actually woken up and learnt a thing or two precisely by going astray. His thundering against the decadence and self-indulgence of our time seemed to betray something in him that was not totally at peace with his own colourful past. If so, it would explain his inability to be more tolerant of the weaknesses in others and more relaxed about the temptations that lie in wait for all of us – temptations which he experienced to the full, and which, as catalysts in our lives, should perhaps even be celebrated. 'To condemn one's past is a most enticing way of praising one's present state', wrote Philip Toynbee in *Part of a Journey*. A month earlier he had written in the same journal:

although those long years of energetic sinning were often so painful to myself and others I can't honestly say that I'm 'ashamed' of them. The person I see back there seems, from here, to have been acting as he had to act, and seems to have been bringing me, however clumsily and blindly, to my present state of at least lesser blindness and partially-changed desires.

In 1976 Malcolm made an important series of six films for Canadian television – *A Third Testament* – and wrote a book with the same title to accompany the series. He chose six men whose lives and work had deeply influenced his own quest for truth: St Augustine, whose *Confessions* he hailed as the first great autobiography; the 17th-century French mathematician and scientist Blaise Pascal; William Blake, passionate believer in the power of the imagination; the Danish eccentric Søren Kierkegaard, champion of the individual over the crowd; Leo Tolstoy who through his beautifully lucid commentaries on the New Testament and the account of his conversion in *Confession*, along with many of his short stories, gave generations of Russians access to Christianity at a time when bibles were banned and most churches closed; and finally the Lutheran pastor and distinguished theologian Dietrich Bonhoeffer who made the momentous decision to join the conspiracy to kill Adolf Hitler, even though he recognised that to do so might be a mortal sin. 'In other words', wrote Malcolm, 'he considered that delivering Germany from the Nazi regime was more important even than saving his own soul.' Bonhoeffer was executed by hanging on April 8th 1945 at the age of thirty-nine for his involvement in the failed plot.

Writing later about Bonhoeffer, during a visit we made to Berlin in 1980 while filming *Ancient and Modern* and while Germany was still divided by the Iron Curtain, Malcolm gave full vent to the pessimism that he increasingly felt about the direction in which the world was going:

> Standing on the Berlin Wall I tried to imagine what would have been Bonhoeffer's feelings if, instead of being martyred, he had lived on into post-war divided Germany. Eastwards, I could see the familiar scene of desolation and oppression … Westwards, the other sort of desolation and oppression, equally familiar, the gleaming neon and glass, the exhortations to spend and to consume … The pursuit of power versus the pursuit of happiness, black-and-white television versus colour, the clenched fist versus the raised phallus, guns before butter and butter before guns. And in between, the no-man's land or limbo of

Muggeridge and author at Berlin Wall in 1980

vigilant sentries on watchtowers, dogs and land mines and armed patrols. Was there anything here to risk eternal damnation for, or for that matter to live for? The strip-tease joints and the garish posters announcing the mighty achievements of the triumphant German proletariat, equally fantasy. Plastic flesh and fraudulent statistics – where's the difference? Perhaps, after all, the limbo is the place, lurking among the land mines.

Limbo is the state in which Malcolm, I suspect, increasingly saw himself. In many ways it's a courageous position. One of his favourite sayings, whispered to him by a sympathetic stranger at a time when he was under attack and increasingly isolated for his outspoken views, was 'Only dead fish swim with the tide.'

The situation in Berlin and elsewhere in Europe has changed of course – at least outwardly – since Malcolm wrote those words. But below the surface the same extremes, expressed by the words 'power' and 'affluence', continue to threaten us, perhaps more dangerously now because they are often subtly concealed, usually in the guise of that ambivalent word 'progress'. In saying this I realise that I am starting to sound like the gloomy side of Muggeridge himself, but I wouldn't be writing about him so extensively if I didn't respect his analysis – albeit exaggerated – of some of the dangers we face.

After making the autobiographical series *Ancient and Modern*, my work with Malcolm continued as a result of some correspondence he showed me with Svetlana Alliluyeva, the daughter of Joseph Stalin. She had first written to him in 1967, after her defection to the USA at the age of forty-one, to thank him for his book *Jesus Rediscovered*. It was in that same year that her sensational book *20 Letters to a Friend* was published in the West. Svetlana had been secretly baptised a Christian while still living in the USSR. There she had been married twice, and had to leave the children of these two marriages behind when she left.

After a gap of almost twelve years, during which time Svetlana had married an American, become a mother again at the age of forty-five, and then divorced, Malcolm received another letter in which she wrote:

Dear Mr. Muggeridge – Sometime if you are interested to listen to one of the most funny stories of our time – my paradoxical life – I will be glad to tell you more. It is a saga, an irony, a satire and a tragedy all in one. I'm glad I have survived it all and am still an optimist. But I do laugh a lot at myself, and if I lose that blessed capacity my end will come fast.

In 1981 I went to see Svetlana at her home in Princetown and persuaded her to accept Malcolm's invitation to visit him in Sussex. The film we made of that visit we called *A Week with Svetlana*.

It was, indeed, a saga that she told us – not least the bizarre circumstances surrounding her father's death, which at first no one dared to either acknowledge or announce in case he suddenly came back to life. This and many other stories and reflections during that week were interspersed with energetic walks, a shopping trip with Kitty, quiet evenings listening to music and gardening duty with her host.

Malcolm and Kitty Muggeridge, with Svetlana Alliluyeva (standing) at Park Cottage

Svetlana spoke to us on one occasion of the communist government as 'a little group of terrorists at the top', her father included. What she seemed unable to accept was that Stalin was any worse than the others. The daughter in her was perhaps understandably not able or not willing to go as far as to class him as a monster, despite her fear of him as a child and their growing alienation when she became an adult. Nevertheless, she and Malcolm were in complete agreement about Dostoevsky's genius, in his novel *The Devils*, in recognising and depicting the reality of an inner evil that can take possession of a human being. Svetlana's amused reaction to the book's alternative title in English, *The Possessed*, was prompted by the implication that an acknowledgement of the Devil is also an acknowledgement of God – a stumbling block, she thought, for many intellectuals.

Equally relevant to my theme was Svetlana's description of how many people in the USSR, herself included, found faith in some sort of transcendent reality as a reaction to 'the godless and terrible life'. And millions, she reminded us, never lost their faith in the first place, despite decades of propaganda and persecution. The thought with which Svetlana left Malcolm, at the end of their final long walk together, was a quotation from St Augustine, which had clearly been of help to her over the years: 'Trust the past to the mercy of God; the present to his love; the future to his providence.'

The last film I made with Malcolm, a year later, was created around an interview he did with the celebrated Russian writer Alexander Solzhenitsyn when he came to London to receive the Templeton Prize. At that time Solzhenitsyn was still in exile in the USA and Brezhnev in power at the Kremlin; he finally returned to Russia in 1994, in the wake of Mikhail Gorbachev's reforms.

Malcolm couldn't resist asking Solzhenitsyn whether, in his hideaway in Vermont, he had been living 'the great American dream'. Clearly he hoped that Solzhenitsyn would say something disparaging about that dream, echoing his own disillusionment with what he saw as a worldwide American-led descent into decadence; but Solzhenitsyn would only express his gratitude for being able to work in peace for twelve hours a day, without the fear of a knock at the door.

They spoke together about many things – the prophetic wisdom of Fyodor Dostoevsky, life in the Gulag, 'Marxist acrobatics', the danger of socialism in a Christian guise, the threat of nuclear war and the situation in the Soviet Union at that time. Solzhenitsyn time and again expressed his optimism about the future, comparing the dark shadow of communism all over the world to an eclipse of the sun, confirming his faith that the shadow would slowly pass across the earth and clear. Communism's only victory was the victory of power, he said, yet it had failed to destroy the Christian faith.

But he expressed concern, too: a concern that if the western world did not rediscover a moral and spiritual force, then Christian civilisation might well disintegrate. Solzhenitsyn added that the lessons mankind has to learn would take many centuries. In his view the situation was not, as Malcolm had suggested, hopeless. 'Thank God', he said, 'and I mean "Thank God", the situation is never hopeless.' The notion of Christendom may indeed disappear, he went on to say, but not Christ. Solzhenitsyn then expressed the thought that in the future we may well see many other forms of Christianity on earth, thus echoing what Bishop Justinian said to us in Romania, and also what the Jesuit scientist Teilhard de Chardin so often expressed.

Towards the end of his life (he died in 1990) Malcolm increasingly shared Solzhenitsyn's view that our suffering stemmed primarily from what that great and courageous Russian called 'the loss of a sense of a moral order in the universe'. For Malcolm the answer was inextricably connected with 'the everlasting truth of Jesus' revelation'. In his book *A Twentieth Century Testimony* he wrote about

> an extraordinary illumination that comes flooding in on one's being,
> an extraordinary awareness of quite exceptional poignancy and force;
> a knowledge past knowing, a hope past hoping. Call it faith, which
> swallows up all the little intricacies of doubt and factual fidgeting. Call

it being reborn, a new creature arising out of the dust and grubbiness of worldly living, like a butterfly out of its chrysalis. Whatever it may be called, it came to pass in Galilee. A new dimension was added to our mortal existence; a new freedom, not for a tiny élite, not based on institutions or propositions, but burgeoning in each human heart and needing only to be allowed to grow.

In the same book Malcolm wrote: 'I can say with complete truthfulness that everything I have learned in my seventy-five years in this world, everything that has truly enhanced and enlightened my existence, has been through affliction and not through happiness, whether pursued or attained.'

In this sense Malcolm must, in some ways, have gone on learning until the end, for his last years were far from happy. 'Alas', wrote his friend Richard Ingrams, 'as he grew older serenity was replaced more and more by feelings of frustration … Journalists no longer called him up seeking his opinion on every subject under the sun.' The public began to forget about him. Slowly his mind deteriorated and those around him were made to suffer too. Someone described him as 'retreating into old age and slamming the door'. Even his precious sense of humour seemed to forsake him – one example being his outbursts against the film *The Life of Brian*, in which he seemed to mistake satire for blasphemy.

Yet there were glimmers still of the Muggeridge who had entertained, infuriated and inspired so many people for so long. 'Being in my seventies', he wrote, 'I fall into a category which I understand is widely used in hospitals. They put on medical cards of people my age, and over, the magic letters N.T.B.R, which means "not to be resuscitated". I can't wait.'

CHAPTER 25

The True Wilderness

During the late seventies I continued to travel a great deal and, despite Malcolm Muggeridge's gloomy view of the state of the world and the absurdity of presuming it could be otherwise, my own faith in the essential wisdom and goodness underlying all existence was constantly affirmed by many interesting and inspiring encounters with people who were striving, often in modest ways, to make real the words of the Lord's Prayer: 'Thy kingdom come … on earth as it is in heaven.' However, I am not so naïve or blinkered as not to recognise that all is far from harmonious in the world at large and in many of my fellow human beings, myself included. Our egotism and underlying selfishness – whether personal or national – are, it seems to me, usually at the root of all our problems. And yet it is that very experience of being an individual and not part of a herd that is potentially our most precious gift – the key to our maturity as human beings. It is the two-edged sword to which I have already referred.

A boost to my optimism came in 1978 through another visit to India, the country that had first inspired me ten years earlier. This time I was working with the BBC correspondent Mark Tully, on a film about Morarji Desai, the idealistic eighty-two-year-old Prime Minister. Desai succeeded Indira Gandhi after her eleven years of increasingly authoritarian rule – a period that culminated in a state of emergency when she imprisoned many of her opponents, including Desai himself. He spent eighteen months in solitary confinement, and Mark himself was expelled from the country for a similar period.

Mark spent the first ten years of his life in India – his father was a Calcutta-based businessman. He describes how their English nanny's main task was to keep the children away from the servants, from the natives – in other words to prevent them, in the language of the British Raj, from 'going jungly'. She clearly did a poor job, for after his education at Marlborough College, and Cambridge University where he read History and Theology, and a brief spell in which he considered a career in the Church, Mark found himself back in India and has lived there ever since. He was for many years the BBC's much respected South-Asia correspondent based in Delhi, speaks fluent Hindi and loves the people and their country with a passion that goes way beyond that of an ordinary journalist.

Mark has always shared my admiration for Mahatma Gandhi, and the work that continued in his wake. We were therefore both extremely encouraged when his devoted disciple, Morarji Desai, finally became Prime Minister. During the long years of India's struggle for independence, Desai was imprisoned by the British for seven years. After Independence he became Chief Minister of Bombay State, until Prime Minister Nehru called him to Delhi as Finance Minister. They had a complicated relationship – Nehru's vision for India, involving large-scale industrialisation, was not what Gandhi had hoped for. Desai eventually became deputy to Nehru's daughter Indira Gandhi (no relation to the Mahatma) when she became Prime Minister, but later they fell out and he found himself in prison once again.

Indian Prime Minister Morarji Desai and Mark Tully

Almost inevitably Morarji Desai was best known outside India for the fact that he drank his own urine – a therapy that he actually discovered through a book by an Englishman. He wasn't in the least embarrassed by Mark's questions on the subject: 'I have a principle in life', he said, 'that I shouldn't do anything about which I am ashamed to speak about.' He was also a vegetarian, ate no cooked food and had taken a vow of celibacy at thirty in the age-old belief that such abstinence strengthens one both physically and mentally. Like his hero Gandhi, and like Gandhi's hero Tolstoy, he strove to be as self-sufficient as possible: even as Prime Minister of India he made his own bed, did his own packing and began each day at 5 am with two hours of meditation and yoga. Many of Desai's beliefs and practices belonged to the ancient traditions of Hindu mysticism, but to some they seemed strange, if not outrageous in the modern world of politics and government. 'To me', wrote Mark in his commentary, 'he is a symbol of how little we in the West really understand India.'

At the time we made the film, India was still being criticised by many for dragging its heels and falling behind the so-called Asian Tigers like Japan, Singapore, Taiwan and South Korea. Mark Tully never shared this view, and was fond of reminding people of the story of 'The Tortoise and the Hare'. Time seems to be proving him right, and in addition India's slow but steady advance has not on the whole been at the expense of its spiritual and cultural traditions. Desai, and Gandhi before him, recognised nevertheless that some of those traditions, in particular untouchability, urgently needed not just reform but to be abandoned altogether.

During the filming we travelled with Desai to the State of Orissa where he visited a remote area inhabited largely by tribal people who were excluded from the caste system altogether, and were therefore constantly exploited. It was and still is a major challenge in India, and in many other developing countries, to somehow ensure that increased wealth and prosperity benefit the very poorest and most marginalised people in society. Back in his Bombay days as Chief Minister, Desai had done a great deal to encourage cooperatives, as well as small-scale technology at the village level, in order to stem the tide of migration from the countryside to the cities – an exodus which creates squalor and poverty on a far greater scale. Another Gandhian-inspired initiative we looked at were a number of rural universities where the students are encouraged to interact with the local villages in the hope that, once qualified, they will stay connected with the needs and problems of rural India, rather than seeking well-paid jobs in the cities or overseas.

While we were in Orissa we escaped for an afternoon to the coast where Mark had spent holidays as a child. One of my most vivid and lasting memories of him is of this hardly sylph-like figure splashing about in the waves and singing hymns. For nearly an hour the little boy that still lived in him, alongside the vicar he never became, were blissfully united in the waters of the Bay of Bengal.

Back in Desai's office in Delhi, Mark talked with him about India's giant neighbour to the north, China. Did India have lessons to learn from that direction? Desai's response was that under a totalitarian regime, in which compulsion operates, no permanent change tends to come about in people's hearts and minds. Mark then dangled in front of him the 'Bread before Freedom' slogan. Desai strongly rejected the notion, and dismissed as patronising a remark once made by the eminent British Socialist Aneurin Bevan that 'democracy was a luxury for the poor'. 'Democracy is more essential for the poor than for the rich', he said. 'The rich can fend for themselves, but the poor can become weaker and weaker, and more and more afraid.' Desai went on to express his confidence in the good sense of the Indian people – that they would always reject dictatorship and that democracy would survive. It certainly does seem that India has clung on to the democratic institutions that the British left behind; also her formidable and efficient army has never once threatened a coup.

Desai also spoke to Mark about his admiration for the British Commonwealth, which he called a unique institution with unique possibilities. It was not deliberately arrived at, he said, but was the result of an empire and the break-up of that empire. He compared it to a family in which people share their pleasure and pain, and try to help one another. Mark asked him whether he thought the more privileged members of that family sufficiently shared the pain of those still struggling. 'Everybody is in need of support in one way or another', was Desai's reply. He drew attention to the word 'commonwealth', but acknowledged that the sharing implied by such a word will not come tomorrow: 'We need to work towards it.'

At the office of the *Times of India*, Mark talked to the editor, his old friend, Giralel Jain, who was one of many among the educated élite in India who had great reservations about Desai and all he stood for. But he was, as Mark reminded him, at least free to say so. Jain pointed out how unsettling western science and technology inevitably were for all agrarian civilisations, for in their wake came the attitude of questioning everything: 'not accepting anything given, much less God-given'. Nothing is sacred, nothing taken for granted. For Jain and others like him it was dangerous to simply idealise the past. He dismissed Gandhi's notion, which Desai shared, of a basically rural and decentralised India in which technology and education are introduced and developed at a village level – an approach that the economist Fritz Schumacher had also advocated for all developing countries, as a way to ensure that the whole population benefits from increased prosperity. As I had experienced ten years earlier, this approach is not a rejection of the benefits that science and technology can bring, but rather a way of ensuring that life continues on a human scale. Nor does it have to exclude the obvious benefits of questioning everything. Some traditions are clearly wise, helpful and appropriate still; others quite clearly are not.

Mark concluded our film by asking Desai how he reconciled his very important position with his Gandhian views, since Gandhi himself refused to take office at the time of Independence, preferring to live and work among the people in order to bring about change from the grassroots. Desai's answer was that it is ultimately government which affects people's lives, and that unless the government acts morally and rejects corruption, is seen to be truthful and practises non-violence, then society will not change. 'It's only by personal example that you can show people the way', he said, 'not by telling them what to do.'

To some, concluded Mark in his commentary, Desai was seen as a selfish and obstinate old man, 'the embodiment of India's most chronic disease, its preoccupation with the past. To others he is the only man with the moral stature and wisdom to prevent the country collapsing into chaos and then dictatorship. Time will tell'. Well, despite various ups and downs, democracy has survived in India and the country seems to be going from strength to strength. Mrs Gandhi was returned to power in 1980, her international status enhanced by her acceptance of political defeat at the polls. Perhaps Morarji Desai was the right man at the right time.

Still working in the lively and creative atmosphere of the BBC's Documentary department I went on to make two films about British diplomats overseas. *Our Man in Caracas* was about a cheerful and enterprising ambassador called Jock Taylor. In Lusaka the High Commission was headed by an equally energetic and unstuffy diplomat called Leonard Allinson. Both films opened up for me not only the complexities and at times the tedium of diplomatic life far from home (it was a profession I had once briefly considered myself) but also the contrasting atmosphere of Venezuela, where fostering trade was the diplomats' prime objective, and Zambia, where the political problems in neighbouring Southern Rhodesia – soon to become Zimbabwe – were still very much to the fore and therefore almost daily on Allinson's plate.

Most importantly of all I was again meeting many new people of different nationalities and from very different backgrounds, whose hopes, struggles and preoccupations were all, in their very diverse ways, absolutely relevant to my interest in what I think of as the hidden thread working through all our lives: in the life of our Zambian driver, whose parents gave him the name Hitler, and who was one of the gentlest people I ever met; in the life of the diplomat's wife who had no job and longed for a quiet party-free evening at home with a boiled egg; and in the life of the white farmer who thought of himself as first and foremost Zambian, whatever was happening politically.

I have come across the tendency among some people to speak about those who are 'on a spiritual path', thus implying that others are not. I am very disturbed by this notion, for I firmly believe that if there is a spiritual, as well as physical, evolutionary process at work, then absolutely everyone is part of it. I can see that some people are more conscious of this process and more interested in the idea than others, but that doesn't mean that their destinies are somehow more meaningful and important. Spiritual élitism is a dangerous trap.

As I have travelled all over the world and into other people's lives – fortunately for more than just a day, as filming takes time – I have asked myself constantly what it is that lives just below the surface of consciousness, prompting us to do one thing and not the other: to worry, feel guilty, laugh, make horrible mistakes or behave with great nobility and courage. How, in other words, is each person's relationship with their inner voice, with their daimon, playing itself out from day to day?

Like all of us I am hugely grateful to the many thoughtful and creative people throughout history who have addressed these questions with great insight and sensitivity. I also feel very privileged to have encountered and been able to reflect on such a variety of contemporary situations myself, and I am eternally grateful to my profession for giving me so many opportunities to meet my fellow human beings.

In 1982, shortly after Svetlana's visit to Malcolm Muggeridge, I made another film with Mark Tully – *From Our Delhi Correspondent* – to coincide with a major Indian exhibition in London. For Mark, having been the BBC's India-based correspondent for ten years, it was also an opportunity to take stock, to find out and to report on what Indians thought of their country and its prospects. After some lively scenes in his office and a quick drink and chat with some Indian journalists at the Press Club – 'my favourite pub in Delhi'– Mark, with BBC crew in tow, flew to the state of Gujarat to report initially on a by-election, and then to travel further afield. Gujarat was and still is one of the most progressive states in India, famous for its businessmen and industrialists. It is also the state where Gandhi was born and grew up.

Mark Tully and cameraman Derek Banks

We visited impressive examples of India's industrialisation and space programme. Indeed, one reason for Nehru's belief in the importance of India developing its own technology was the danger he foresaw of a scientific imperialism replacing political imperialism. We also met a passionate promoter of the highly successful cooperative movement, Dr Kurien, who – like Desai and Gandhi – had enormous faith in the potential of the people themselves. True development, he said, is development of people, and it is they themselves who must therefore be involved: 'Cooperatives are where people do things for themselves.' Echoing Fritz Schumacher's comments in my film some twelve years earlier, he then added that in his opinion one of India's greatest assets is its people. In his eyes, the middlemen and the government bureaucrats, the babus as they're called, were the ones who should be bypassed – something that the cooperative movement was doing successfully.

Mark also talked to another dynamic pioneer in this field of helping the poor to help themselves. Ella Bhat had started a bank for women in which pitifully small and yet hugely meaningful sums of money could be borrowed or deposited. It was a similar initiative to the Grameen Bank in Bangladesh, founded around the same time by Muhammad Yunus, for which he was awarded the Nobel Peace Prize in 2006. Poverty may not yet be history, but the vision and courage of such pioneers shows us how one day it could be. Ella Bhat spoke of Gandhi's faith in women and in the role they, in particular, could play in improving the lives of the poor and in the transformation of society altogether. Like so many people we met, she was deeply grateful to Gandhi for the confidence and courage he had inspired among the very humblest in society.

Mark Tully concluded the film with a reminder that these millions of people who had so little materially were only able to take initiatives and to influence their government because they lived in a democracy; he ended with these words:

> Critics of India point out its all too obvious failings – poverty, corruption, population explosion, and bureaucratic inefficiency. What they fail to respect is that India has the courage to acknowledge its failures and to discuss remedies openly. Surely in this must lie hope for the future of the world's largest democracy – a future which concerns all democrats everywhere.

I continued to see a great deal of John Betjeman between these travels, sometimes in Cornwall and more often spending quiet evenings at the home in Chelsea where he now lived with his friend Elizabeth Cavendish. Remembering his love of insects I brought him back a huge spider from

Venezuela, safely at rest in a perspex paperweight. John had been knighted in 1969, and in 1972 – at the age of sixty-six – was made Poet Laureate. In his early seventies, with the onset of Parkinson's disease, he became increasingly frail, and problems with his balance gradually made him dependant on a wheelchair. But he still liked to get about, and his interest in life and people was undiminished. For this reason, among others, I proposed that we make a television series about his life, drawing extensively – as I had done with Malcolm Muggeridge's biography – on the tremendous wealth of archive material that existed at the BBC and elsewhere.

During the filming I took him back to Berkshire where he had lived with his wife Penelope and where their children grew up, also to some of his favourite haunts in London and, of course, to his beloved Cornwall. Another essential ingredient that seemed appropriate in looking back at Betjeman's life was to film some informal conversations with several of his close friends, as well as with Penelope, and with his daughter Candida Lycett Green – who has subsequently edited her father's letters and prose writings so lovingly. John Osborne, Barry Humphries, John Piper, Osbert Lancaster and John Sparrow all made entertaining and illuminating contributions, as did his publisher Jock Murray and the composer Jim Parker, who had skilfully set some of John's poems to music in a series of delightful recordings.

Another encounter was with Betjeman's close friend Harry Williams – at one time Fellow and Lecturer in Theology at Trinity College, Cambridge, and for eleven years Dean of Chapel. By now Harry was an Anglican monk in the Community of the Resurrection at Mirfield in Yorkshire, but a monk who still much enjoyed the good life, including regular trips to Chelsea and the company

John Betjeman and Harry Williams

of John Betjeman, Elizabeth Cavendish and their close circle of friends. We in turn certainly enjoyed Harry's visits. And like John, he was not afraid to show his vulnerability and to share his doubts – he called his autobiography *Some Day I'll Find You*. During the filming he and John spent a lot of time talking not about theology but about laughter, and particularly about the importance of laughing at religious pretensions. Harry expressed his admiration for Betjeman's poetry because it was notably free of such pretension, and he acknowledged that John, more than anyone else, had taught him 'that in order to say something real and perhaps even profound you have to be simple'. Sophistication, he said, was in his experience invariably bogus.

Author with John Betjeman and John and Myfanwy Piper at Harefield Church in Middlesex

The artist John Piper, in answer to my question about Betjeman's influence on *his* life, paid the poet a rather different sort of compliment: 'He taught me how to be nostalgic without being sentimental.' Piper went on to say that Betjeman, with whom he had edited many of the early Shell Guides, also helped him not to feel guilty about liking old churches – churches that he went on to celebrate in his art with such skill and sensitivity.

Harry Williams's most acclaimed book was a collection of his sermons entitled *The True Wilderness*. He himself had suffered a number of crises in his life, not least in the process of coming to terms with his homosexuality. In the introduction to this book he wrote:

Human life is very largely a wilderness, a dry land where no water is. Riches are the artificial grass and plastic flowers with which we try to cover up the stony ground and persuade ourselves that we live in a watered garden. Death is the realistic acceptance of our wilderness for what it is, a refusal to cover it up with simulated appearances of life. Once we thus accept our wilderness and no longer try to hide it from ourselves, there follows the miracle of resurrection. The desert becomes verdant. The stony ground itself brings forth rich pastures.

In the actual sermon on this theme, Harry acknowledged that unlike the experience of Christ, who after his baptism spent forty days and forty nights in the desert, most people's wilderness is experienced inwardly. I presume he meant that Christ experienced both – an inner as well as an outer desert (see colour plate 2, *Christ in the Wilderness* by Stanley Spencer). Our wilderness Harry described as 'inner isolation' and 'an absence of contact':

> It's a sense of being alone, boringly alone, or saddeningly alone, or terrifyingly alone. Often we try to relieve it – understandably enough, God knows – by chatter, or gin, or religion, or sex, or possibly a combination of all four. The trouble is that these purple hearts can work their magic only for a very limited time, leaving us after one short hour or two exactly where we were before.

In essence Harry Williams was confirming in his own way the view that I have frequently expressed in this book that our wilderness experience is a necessary stage in the process of becoming mature human beings. In one way it echoes some of the basic ideas behind existentialism, which emphasises above all the importance of personal responsibility, freedom and self-reliance, and which – despite its somewhat nihilistic image – for me celebrates the courage and passion of those prepared to stand alone in defiance of conformity, and in the face of uncertainty. For many such people religious belief is seen as an act of cowardice – Albert Camus called it 'philosophical suicide'. For them Christianity and religion in general are perceived as expressions of the herd instinct and personal weakness. For the French philosopher Jean-Paul Sartre, the heart of existentialism was not gloom or hopelessness, but a renewed confidence in the significance and worth of the human being.

For Harry Williams, behind each and all of the temptations that meet us in the wilderness lies the Devil's most deadly weapon, the arch-temptation to disbelieve in what we might become. Yet our self-doubt is not unconnected to what took place

The Resurrection, by Cecil Collins

in the desert of Judea two thousand years ago. 'Here, as always', wrote Harry, 'we see in His life the meaning of our own.' Indeed, perhaps only when we have individually experienced the anguish that prompts the question: 'God, why hast thou forsaken me?' will we know and understand the answer, and grow accordingly.

'What do you think, John?' I asked Betjeman at one point during our conversation with Harry Williams. 'I can't think', he replied. It reminded me of a line in his autobiography *Summoned by Bells* about his very early connection to poetry: 'My urge was to encase in rhythm and rhyme / The things I saw and felt (I could not think)...' Nevertheless John knew exactly what Harry and I were talking about. He just preferred to listen.

The last scenes I filmed for the series *Time with Betjeman* were at Trebetherick in Cornwall, on the cliffs overlooking the Camel estuary and the Atlantic Ocean, and finally in the garden of John's cottage, Treen. Here he talked about his father whom he'd feared as a child. 'He was a nice man', he said. 'I'm beginning to see that now, too late. But I expect that in eternity he knows that I'm fond of him.'

John Betjeman with author on Greenaway in Cornwall

John spoke to me, too, about poetry: 'It makes life worth living', and his fascination with television commercials and advertising slogans, and also about the buildings he loved: 'not ones that are so old that they're considered archaeology. Then they're boring.' And inevitably there were thoughts about what he called 'The Management': 'I hope The Management is benevolent and in charge of us', he said. 'Hope rather than believe?' I asked him. 'Yes', he replied, 'certainly. Hope's my chief virtue.' I'm sure John knew from Greek mythology that along with all the evils that plague humanity, hope was the one blessing that escaped from Pandora's box. And maybe it was not only Pandora's curiosity that brought about this situation, but also Zeus himself who knew that without hope we mortals would not be able to keep going.

It was on that final afternoon of our work together, in response to my question about whether he had any regrets – what he'd done, or hadn't done – that John Betjeman came up with the line that everyone still seems to remember: 'Not enough sex.' Using the theme of time passing, advertisers even incorporated the scene into a television commercial for watches! I've no idea whether John really meant what he said, but I do know that he said it deliberately to change the mood after a serious discussion about death and eternity. He had that very English habit of not letting things get too serious for too long, and I knew by the twinkle in his eye that something mischievous was coming before he even spoke.

Throughout the filming of the series there were moments when, in contrast to his jokes and his sharp and witty descriptions of his loves and hates, he would slip into reverie and silence – he was somewhere else – and would sometimes then say things that were especially deep and thoughtful. Once or twice I have had similar experiences with small children at bedtime when they are no longer fully awake and yet still not quite asleep: it's then, on this threshold, that they too can sometimes come out with statements of great profundity. At one point in our conversation John was gazing out to sea, happy and peaceful, and I wasn't rushing in to fill the silence. Then came these words: 'I think there is something beyond death – and it's all the time.' 'What do you mean "all the time"?' I asked him. 'I think it's eternity', he replied. 'Eternity is around us all the time.'

CHAPTER 26

The Holy Fool

John Betjeman had the blissful experience of eternity being around us all the time. Malcolm Muggeridge was convinced that such serenity came only after death. The artist Cecil Collins was preoccupied with the notion of a lost paradise – a state of being which we knew once and longed to find again. 'The true purpose of art', he once wrote, 'is to remember the paradise we have forgotten.' Past, present and future – three different perspectives on the theme of heaven and earth from this trio of thoughtful and sensitive men, all trying to make sense of their experiences of being alive and their intimations of immortality.

I met Cecil Collins in 1972 at the Hamet Gallery in London, at a retrospective exhibition of his work. The meeting was at the suggestion of a BBC colleague, Mark Kidel, who thought Collins would be 'up my street'. He was absolutely right, and Cecil, together with his wife Elisabeth, soon became close friends with whom I spent much time. For all his asceticism and seeming unworldliness, Cecil was very fond of certain things in the here and now – especially his food. In particular he came to love a favourite restaurant of mine in Fulham called The Hungry Horse which specialised in traditional English dishes like roast beef and Yorkshire pudding, kedgeree and, best of all, that most eccentric of puddings – spotted dick and custard. Much of it was what is termed 'school food', but there it was cooked to perfection.

Author with Cecil Collins

Cecil Collins is often referred to as a visionary painter and has been described as the most important English metaphysical artist since William Blake. He once wrote: 'Art is the illusion by which we can understand Reality.' In the words of his biographer William Anderson:

> He has managed at times to offend both the conventionally religious and the conventionally non-religious. I think the reason he has given offence is much the same in both cases: his work infiltrates thoughts and feelings into these people's awareness that disturb their settled prejudices.

The poet Kathleen Raine described her response to the work of Cecil Collins as 'entering a world infinitely familiar; a sense of homecoming'. But she acknowledged in this same essay, *Cecil Collins: Painter of Paradise*, that there are always those who say, 'I am afraid I don't understand these paintings, can you explain them to me?' Her reply:

> To explain to those who need such explanation is probably impossible; one can but say, they are. This is in fact what Cecil himself said to a hostile critic who complained to him that the landscape and figures he painted didn't exist. 'They exist now', was the artist's reply.

I'm reminded of a parent's reply to the child's question: 'Does Father Christmas really exist?' 'Yes', is the answer, 'if you believe in him.'

There are echoes in this playfulness of what the 20th-century French scholar Henri Corbin called the *mundus imaginalis*. For Corbin, Professor of Islamic Religion at the Sorbonne, this 'imaginal world' was not only the world of the soul, but also of the dead. Like so many of the people about whom I have been writing, Corbin upheld the primacy of the invisible, of spirit, and believed that imagination was a route to knowledge as well as to creativity. Christopher Bamford, in the introduction to Corbin's *The Voyage and the Messenger*, writes of him as 'a Knight of the Invisible'. It is a title that suits my dear, eccentric friend Cecil just as well.

Cecil Collins's parents were Cornish, but he was born over the Tamar at Plymouth in 1908. 'I think the health of a nation is dependent on the quality of its childhood', Cecil once said. His own, as he vividly remembered it, was full of wonder and magic. At the back of the house was a real forest – or so it seemed to the boy who many years later wrote:

> It wasn't a forest by grand standards but it was a forest to me. It was a wood actually, and it was there that I learned, I suppose, the language

of stones and grass and trees and clouds … It was moments like this, I think, that came together and formed a kind of unconscious certainty that what we normally see is a very contracted and superficial view.

Holidays were spent back in Cornwall at the mouth of the Fal estuary, where both sets of grandparents lived. These two great river estuaries in south-west England, the Fal and the Tamar, also made a powerful impression on the young boy.

Cecil's mother was an imaginative and sensitive woman; his father, to whom he was also very close, was an engineer. But in the depression after World War I Harry Collins found himself having to earn a living as a labourer on the roads, and his only child had to leave school at fifteen. Cecil was apprenticed to a motor-engineering firm but hated it and soon left. Within a year, through a seemingly chance encounter, he was at the Plymouth School of Art doing what he'd loved to do since earliest childhood. It was also at this time that he discovered what he considered to be the prime influence in his art, namely music. Without any music lessons he began to play the piano, developing a considerable skill at improvisation.

In 1927, the year that his father suddenly died, Cecil won a scholarship to the Royal College of Art in London. It was there, in the following year, that he met a fellow student, Elisabeth Ramsden. Towards the end of her life Elisabeth wrote about the young exhibitionist who three years later was to become her husband: 'After making a good painting, he used to limp – it was the sign. He walked everywhere limping, and everybody said, "Ah, he must have done a good painting!".' His genius and his eccentricity were already apparent at this time – so, too, his deep and thoughtful nature. Anderson notes in his biography that the Royal College gave Collins exactly what he needed at that time: 'serious training; friendship with talented fellow students; contact with well-established artists; and, above all, the experience of being part of the cultural life of a great capital city.' Yet from an early age Cecil believed that in essence 'art is not about art'. Here already was a man destined to follow a solitary path. Throughout his life he was to suffer at times from a deep loneliness in what he called 'this land of unbelief and fear'.

Years later, in an essay entitled 'Why does art today lack inspiration?' Cecil wrote about the subject of loneliness – not his own, but the loneliness and sense of alienation that so many people feel in a society where there is so little to remind us 'of a destiny that transcends our small personal life'. Already as a young student, it seems, he was coming to the view that the task of the artist is to hold up a mirror to what he called 'the Divine Reality' and so to remind people of what they perpetually forget, just as for some the church bell is a reminder still.

For a short while Collins's professional loneliness was interrupted by the sudden appearance of the surrealist movement. At Herbert Read's invitation, Collins's work was shown at the International Surrealist Exhibition in London in 1936. Here artists like Salvador Dali were affirming Cecil's own belief in the primacy of the imagination, striving to portray other dimensions of existence and feeling. Cecil described the atmosphere as 'very intoxicating' after the shallowness and aridity of the contemporary art world that he first experienced on leaving college. 'Art for art's sake' is how he described it years later to his friend the publisher Brian Keeble: 'a kind of weekend pleasure trip into hedonism'. But Cecil's reservations about surrealism came to the surface already when Read, in his speech at the opening of the exhibition, spoke of the event as the dawn of a new age. William Anderson imagines Cecil's silent response: 'No, it isn't. It's the sunset.'

Looking back on the whole phenomenon of surrealism in his conversation with Keeble (published in *The Vision of the Fool and Other Writings*) Cecil spoke about his recognition in hindsight that the movement embodied 'the last remnants of the Romantic movement gone to seed'. He acknowledged the vital role that the Romantics had played 'in protecting the human soul' through the darkest periods of rationalism in the 19th century. But in the surrealist movement he discerned not a rebirth, but a final dispersal of that energy. 'I don't believe in surrealism', he later wrote, 'precisely because I do believe in a surreality, universal and eternal, above and beyond the world of the intellect and the senses; but not beyond the reach of the humility and hunger of the human heart.' And in that conversation with Keeble about the surrealists he said: 'They congealed themselves into formulas, clichés. They had a kind of psychic furniture they moved about in their pictures. It was really easy to paint a surrealist picture. You just put a boiled egg on top of a railway station, that sort of thing. It was really quite easy.'

His fellow artist Julian Trevelyan was to write of his friend in this period: 'Collins, whom I knew well, had far too much of a personal religious mysticism to make him a good surrealist. He has always been a cat that walks by himself, prophetic, poetic, visionary.' And another artist, his friend John Lane, wrote that although Cecil Collins may have borrowed aspects of the surrealist's distinctive language, he remained at root a traditionalist, 'closer in spirit to the ancient tradition of sacred art'. In the introduction to his republication of Cecil's essay *The Vision of the Fool*, Brian Keeble wrote:

The lancing of the boil of the putrid psyche of the modern world was, in Collins's view, surrealism's cathartic achievement. But his enthusiasm for its achievement did not prevent him from recognising that 'Surrealism is over. Its work done.'

One consequence of such a stand, noted Keeble, was that Collins would have to 'hawk his wares as chance decides in a society from which he is in exile'.

In fact Cecil Collins, rather like Malcolm Muggeridge – a latecomer to self-imposed exile – enjoyed life immensely despite his pessimistic diagnosis of the state of the world. Eventually he immersed himself thoroughly in many aspects of society – the cinema, music and teaching being just some examples. Yet for over forty years he and his wife shared the fate of many artists – and not just artists – who are not prepared to compromise their vision: the struggle to survive financially. But they had many friends and admirers, and a small but loyal group of collectors. Cecil's students loved and respected him; he had great energy and enthusiasm, and a wonderful sense of humour; above all he could laugh at himself – the most precious gift of all. His somewhat seedy appearance was an obvious target, with his rather shabby and ill-fitting coat, his ancient and battered trilby hat and his patched shirts. On several occasions I heard him liken himself to 'a Lebanese date-trader'. He also clearly identified himself with the image of the Fool, which became an increasingly familiar figure in many of his paintings.

It was actually a drawing by his wife Elisabeth, in 1939, of a wounded Fool lying on the ground with a spear piercing his heart, being mocked by a group of people looking at him over a wall, that first stirred Cecil's imagination. A colleague responded enthusiastically to the drawing and told them about the importance of the Fool in European art and folklore. This information, together with the atmosphere of his wife's drawing, acted as a catalyst for the young and thoughtful artist. Later he was to write of the Fool:

> I believe that there is in life, and in the human psyche, a certain quality, an inviolate eternal innocence, and this quality I call the Fool. It is a continuous wisdom and compassion that heals with magic and fun. It is the joy of the original Adam in men.

For Cecil the Fool also became the symbol of 'the lost ones of this world'.

He held a successful one-man exhibition at the Bloomsbury Gallery in 1935 (among the artists and critics who came to the exhibition were Eric Gill, Henry Moore and Herbert Read) but by that time Cecil and Elisabeth had left London – initially for life in a remote corner of the Chilterns. In his biography William Anderson emphasises the significance of this decision to move out of London, for it meant that without distractions Cecil had time to explore the imaginative world increasingly opening up for him among the silence of the beech woods and in the company of his very special wife. He made full use of the opportunity, producing a large body of work drawn from his own intuitive nature. Anderson writes how this period provided:

one of the most essential groundings for a young artist: the conviction that he can produce good and original work. Such a conviction is vital to the self-confidence of an artist: up to a point recognition by others is quite secondary because it is from this self-confidence that an artist will continue to trust his particular vision of the truth. It is also this self-confidence that enables him to endure the ups and downs of fashion in the world of art that may, one year, take him up and for the next decade ignore him entirely.

During this time, near Penn in Buckinghamshire, Cecil worked on a huge canvas, nine foot by six foot, originally called *The Holy War* and now known as *The Fall of Lucifer*. It was an attempt, among other things, to address the legend that describes the arrival of egotism in human evolution. Anderson suggests that it also represented stirrings of the Lucifer within himself, wanting to claim the visions he'd been given as his own, thus bringing him fame and power.

A former curator at the Tate Gallery, Judith Collins, who selected and catalogued the major retrospective exhibition of Collins's work at the Tate in 1989 – the year in which Cecil died – sees this painting of Lucifer as marking the arrival of his maturity as an artist; that was in 1933, when he was twenty-five years old. Above all, the painting heralded with great intensity and clarity the major theme of so much of his subsequent work: namely our expulsion from paradise.

Meanwhile, during the early years of their marriage, and like so many wives of great (and often not so great) men, Elisabeth was sublimating her own creativity as an artist to cope with life in a tiny cottage without water and electricity and with only a very meagre income. From a practical point of view it was certainly an expulsion from paradise, for Elisabeth had grown up in a large and comfortable home in Yorkshire.

Cecil and Elisabeth Collins in 1936

Cecil himself, when not painting, was reading the esoteric writings of the German mystics Jacob Boehme and Meister Eckhart, and the poetical works of Thomas Traherne, whose experience of God came through a delight in the created world around him. This echoed Cecil's own increasing appreciation of innocence and simplicity – so long as it wasn't him having to keep body if not soul together!

Life in Buckinghamshire was not entirely solitary in these years. Cecil had a lively relationship with their neighbour Eric Gill who, as a devout Catholic, had problems with Cecil's thoughts about the nature of God. Yet despite their differences, Cecil later wrote of Gill as having 'more understanding of the desperate position of the creative mind in our time than most people in England ... one of the few great men of conviction'. Through Gill, Cecil met the painter and poet David Jones who was to become a lifelong friend. He later spoke to Brian Keeble of David Jones as 'a very great artist, but of a dying culture'. Cecil acknowledged a shared 'sacramental dimension', but expressed the hope that a Hindu, or anyone else, even a person belonging to no religion at all could come into contact with his work 'and find the eternal world is mirrored there ... Whereas the images in David's work are combined correctly within the context of a single religious perspective'.

Collins went on to speak of the quality of twilight in Jones's work, 'a beautiful twilight', whereas in his work the predominant striving was to introduce a mood of dawn: 'I feel a sense of very great adventure working in something that is growing and not closed and finished.' The conversation with Keeble prompted Collins to express his strong reservations about orthodox religion altogether, particularly when allied with nationalism, which 'clings to a kind of tribal view of culture'. For Collins the time of tribal gods was over: 'this is a period of no god'. But for him this meant forging a new relationship to the divine that transcends old boundaries and that is inevitably a personal and lonely journey.

Another visitor to the cottage in Buckinghamshire was the American artist Mark Tobey, director of the Art Studio set up by Leonard and Dorothy Elmhirst on their estate at Dartington Hall. It was this friendship with Tobey, who was a member of the Baha'i faith, that prompted them to move to Dartington in 1936 and also encouraged Collins's interest in eastern thought and religion. The potter Bernard Leach and the poet and translator Arthur Waley also became friends at this time. The artist John Piper, on a lecturing visit to Dartington in 1943, was very struck by Collins's recent creation *The Pilgrim Fool* and insisted on taking it to London to show to Kenneth Clark, then director of the National Gallery. In the same year John Rothenstein, who had been a fellow student at the Royal College and whose father Sir William Rothenstein was its principal, purchased *The Sleeping Fool* for the Contemporary Arts Society. In 1951 the painting was accepted by the Tate Gallery; John Rothenstein – by then director of the Tate – remained a life-long supporter and friend to Collins. And so, despite that lonely path, there was a small and distinguished group of people – Kenneth Clark and Stephen Spender among them – who were beginning to notice and collect his work. (See colour plates 5 and 6, *The Pilgrim Fool* and *The Sleeping Fool*.)

Around this time Cecil had an experience in the magnificent grounds of Dartington Hall that was to powerfully reinforce many of the feelings about the nature of reality that he'd had since childhood. He described it years later in a BBC radio interview:

One April afternoon there'd been a shower … and the sun was just sinking behind the woods, and the light was shining on this bush, and it had drops of rain on the leaves, and the light was shining through them. They were like diamonds. And on top was a thrush singing. I suddenly saw that this bush was the shape of the song of the bird.

Such a moment of illumination seems to point to what Jacob Boehme called 'the signature of all things'. John Lane has written of this capacity we all have 'to see through the veil of appearances'. For Collins, he believed, 'an understanding of the interrelatedness of all phenomena is the vital root of his teaching and his art'.

In writing about this phase of Collins's life, which in many ways was the nearest Cecil came to finding his lost paradise on earth, William Anderson draws attention to what was undoubtedly another important experience while at Dartington. Until now Cecil had been somewhat combative and argumentative. He liked a good verbal punch-up, but increasingly came away feeling wounded, realising he had wasted valuable energy. Gradually he saw that he was projecting his own inner tensions onto others and that basically the problem stemmed from a conflict between his heart and his intellect. 'His heart had led him in the direction of mystical interests and the visionary subjects of his art', wrote Anderson, 'while his intellect was always criticising and analysing what his heart loved.' Slowly Cecil came to see that what he really valued in himself was his childlike art, and he told Anderson of his recognition that the true purpose of his keen analytical mind was to defend his heart, not to betray it.

In the early years of the war, Cecil was offered a job at Dartington and so discovered his gift for teaching – an activity that in the years to come was to become for him a necessary complement to his own creative work. Then from 1943 until their move to London in 1970, Cecil and Elisabeth were based largely in Cambridge. In 1947 his essay *The Vision of the Fool* was published, confirming his considerable ability to work with words as well as with paint; it was a unique and unusual gift. As a film-maker who has always worked with a combination of words, images and music, I know only too well how difficult it is to rely on words alone, particularly in trying to communicate intimations from a realm for which we have so few words anyway. Yet despite Cecil's frequent urge to write, and indeed to talk, he made it perfectly clear where his final loyalty lay: 'When the Image speaks in silence, words cease.'

At the opening of *The Vision of the Fool*, Cecil does indeed apologise 'for the numerous imperfections of writing with which this essay is strewn'. From then on all reticence ceases:

> Modern society rejects the Fool because of his faith in the essential holiness of life itself; contemporary society has mutilated the holiness of life by concentrating upon almost everything else but that, and by its neglect of the very means by which the sense of the holiness of existence is developed, namely Religion and Art.

He goes on to characterise our time as 'ruining the leisure of the soul'. Painting is neglected because people have no time to look, to become receptive, to reflect and absorb, 'no leisure to form a connection, a communion with the painting. And it not only applies to painting; we have no leisure to form a communion with life itself'. Everywhere he sees the triumph of what he calls 'the enemies of the imagination, the despisers of the spirit, the philistines'. Formal religion is likewise attacked: 'We have lived to see the Church become the corpse of Christianity.' He refers to the machine age as being responsible for 'the crucifixion of the poetic imagination', making it – along with art and religion – a heresy. For Cecil, the Fool was the symbol of that heresy. From my own experience of the Camphill communities, I recognise that society is often fearful or embarrassed by the 'fools' in its midst, and so will either ignore them or hide them away.

But Cecil was also a realist. He knew that the sensitivity he yearned for – this 'poetic imagination' – is only born when we are ready for it, when we are so hungry that we realise we are starving and empty. Only then do we recognise the true nature and substance of what we are hungry for. His essay ends on what is essentially an optimistic note:

> The saint, the artist, the poet, and the Fool, are one. They are the eternal virginity of spirit, which in the dark winter of the world, continually proclaims the existence of a new life, gives faithful promise of the spring of an invisible kingdom, and the coming of light.

In all Cecil Collins's work, therefore, it is not surprising that there is a constant hint of redemption – the same redemption that Cervantes celebrated in *Don Quixote* and that Rose Tremain conveys so sensitively in her novel *Restoration*, describing the journey of the 'holy fool' Merivel.

A Fool Praying, by Cecil Collins

The Fool was also, as Anderson rightly points out, a projection of Cecil's own nature: his wit and love of puns, his sense of fun and his passion for cocking snooks; it was what made him such wonderful, as well as inspiring company. At Dartington there hangs a picture he created with pen and wash in 1940 called *Fool picking his nose in front of a Bishop*. Cecil's many utterances on, as well as images of, this treasured theme of the Fool are also reminders of the long tradition in all societies of the Holy Fool – someone who is, in Cecil's words, 'in a state of creative vulnerability and openness'; someone who not only symbolises but also embodies a primordial innocence and is therefore easily destroyed by the world. His painting *Christ before the Judge* is a powerful depiction of this vulnerability before the cold and soulless forces that can so easily penetrate our lives. The picture is what Kathleen Raine called 'a strong and terrible image' of the contrast between paradise and the fallen world. Above all Cecil believed that the Fool is primarily concerned with 'the transformation of consciousness which comes about through direct perception'; also, most importantly, he is interested in awakening the Fool in each one of us.

Christ before the Judge, by Cecil Collins

In 1951 Cecil started to teach at the Central School of Art in London, though his home was still in Cambridge. From the beginning, apparently, he declaimed his radical ideas loud and clear: 'If painting is merely a process and nothing but an arrangement of colours, forms and textures for their own sake, then the artist becomes a mere manufacturer of visual confectionery.' The aim of Cecil's teaching, writes Anderson, 'is to lead his students into an existential discovery of the nature of creativity. To him creativity is concerned with revealing something and therefore the starting point is the student, not the painting.' At times he got the students to go through a series of movements or listen to music, so that they came to a stillness within themselves.

One of his students from those early days at the Central School was the artist Robin Baring, who has continued to plough a lonely but enlightened furrow ever since. Another former student is the highly gifted Saied Dai who has written of Collins:

> His influence came at the right time and I was ripe enough to benefit. I had wound myself up into a tight ball at art school by becoming involved in hard, pragmatic, investigative and analytical drawing. Cecil's classes taught me to let go; it was the antithesis of everything I had learned. In that sense his influence was enormous. It was as though I had been breathing in for years, and he helped me to breathe out; and I am still breathing out.

Head of a Woman, by Cecil Collins

Not everyone, however, appreciated – then or now – what Cecil Collins was striving for. At an exhibition in 1956 at the Leicester Galleries, John Berger – whom Anderson describes as 'the pope of left-wing art criticism' – dismissed Collins as 'an entirely introspective artist'. Cecil, however, was undeterred and through his growing interest in what Jung called the *anima* – the feminine and more inward side of a man's nature – pursued the line of introspection even further. His wife Elisabeth had for many years been both his muse and his model, and there are many fine paintings that capture the beauty, serenity and receptivity that Cecil so revered in the feminine archetype.

In 1963 Cecil was invited to speak to a body called The Centre for Spiritual and Psychological Studies. Founded by an extraordinarily intuitive and gifted woman called Alison Barnard, it aimed to bring together artists, writers, philosophers, scientists and followers of various Christian, Islamic and eastern paths and sects. One regular speaker was the remarkable Russian Orthodox bishop, Anthony Bloom. Other contributors included Laurens van der Post, the neurosurgeon and psychiatrist Peter Fenwick, the celebrated artist Thetis Blacker, and Edward Robinson, director of the Alistair Hardy Religious Experience Unit in Oxford (now at Lampeter University in Wales). The Centre, as we called it, had no formal membership and virtually no financial backing. Through my friendship with Cecil and Elisabeth, I attended many of their gatherings over the years and was eventually on Alison's council. What I liked so much about the set-up was that besides enabling me to meet an extraordinary range of interesting people, it all took place under no particular banner. That seems to me a most healthy situation, given our tendency to latch on to one particular guru or teaching and thereby often ignore all the other potentially enriching perspectives that exist.

In 1970 Cecil and Elisabeth moved from Cambridge to Chelsea, into the top half of a house owned by their friend Kathleen Raine. Their arrival in London enabled Cecil to accept an invitation to teach evening classes at the City Literary Institute, alongside his work at the Central School. It was his first experience of adult education and his classes were hugely popular. Over the next seventeen years many talented and creative people were enormously helped and inspired, several becoming teachers themselves in the style of their eccentric and always challenging master.

One former pupil, Stella Astor, has described in her little book *Angels* how Cecil kept them on their toes, reminding them constantly that true creativity is about the transformation of consciousness. The classes were full of surprises; students had sometimes to draw with their eyes closed and using both hands. 'Cecil Collins had a very clear understanding of the potency of the imagination', Stella writes, 'and the role it plays in creativity ...' Another pupil, Nomi Rowe, in the introduction to her anthology *In Celebration of Cecil Collins*, mentions the sensation of 'coming home' that is often described by Cecil's adult students. 'For me', she writes, 'it was the feeling of freedom, of a re-connection to childhood delight in an adventure into the unknown which overlaid all other impressions.'

In the year following the move to London, Cecil had an exhibition at the Arthur Tooth Gallery. One visitor, the psychologist James Hillman, was prompted to write in his 'avant-propos' to the catalogue about the capacity of Collins's paintings 'to move places in the psyche that we rarely sense'. He went on to say: 'There is a debt we owe those who see that which mostly we cannot see, who must reproduce what is intensely complex and intensely restrained, who make no concession to what we each want ... They are the initiators.'

Around this time Cecil met a young curator at the Tate Gallery, Richard Morphet, who was later to become keeper of the modern collections, as well as a great friend and supporter of the artist. By now the Tate owned six major works by Collins; of one of these, *Hymn to Death* acquired in 1961, Morphet wrote that 'it envisages death as a moment of transfiguration, and parallels Collins's belief that in the very gravity of the problems of the modern world – a kind of breakdown corresponding to the death of a system – lies the potential for a new consciousness which can transform existence.'

Cecil Collins, a pilgrim without a Church, was now confronted with an extremely difficult artistic challenge. The Dean of Chichester, Walter Hussey, commissioned him to paint an altar front for the Chapel of St Clement in Chichester Cathedral. It was a brave decision to choose a man not famous for his orthodox views and who some six years later, in the conversation with Keeble, was to say:

Religion is born as a vision and ends as a cliché – a set of reflex actions and formulas. First you have the revelation and then you have it rationalised into dogma and theology, which crystallises. And remember dogma and theology are peculiarly male preoccupations, of finding security in justification and definition. The soul of man, which is much more feminine, finds no need for definition and no need for justification. The soul is essentially concerned with relationships with the divine.

At first Cecil was unwilling to accept the commission: for how create a sacred work of art, without imposing his own personal views of the deity, to which the worshippers and visitors could and would respond? One of his favourite sayings was: 'You become what you contemplate.' His resolution was to turn to the ancient symbol of the sunburst – the disc of the sun, portrayed as a human face and radiating shafts of light. The sun had already featured in a number of his paintings as the symbol of a new age. Later he wrote: 'I was moved to paint an image of God that would unite all men.'

Nevertheless to label Cecil Collins a religious painter would, I believe, be wrong. He was essentially a painter of the sacred. Kathleen Raine writes about sacred art as mediating the spiritual visions and intuitions of humanity, whereas religious art tends to illustrate the symbols of some cult. In her 1979 essay on Cecil Collins she writes:

In the course of time the cult images become external copies of copies; spiritual art never copies copies but returns always to the source, to the Imagination, that holy land where abide the originals of which the cult-images are remote copies.

Cecil's *Icon of Divine Light* at Chichester is acknowledged by most people as a fine, worthy and above all original creation in one of England's great cathedrals. On the frame of the altar are carved the words from The Revelation of St John: 'Behold, I make all things new.'

For those like Cecil who rock the boat and try in their own modest way to make things new, there are inevitably turbulent moments. As his biographer William Anderson observes, when an artist or writer sets himself against the barely questioned climate of opinion of his time 'he walks among dragons'. Some of these dragons were on Cecil's own doorstep, in the art establishment itself. (I had begun to experience a milder version of this trend at the BBC.)

At the Central School there were those who were disturbed by Cecil's promotion of a metaphysical view of art and life. They turned to the Rule Book about retirement at sixty-five as an excuse not to renew his contract. Cecil, however, was no fool when it came to a fight. He enlisted the support of a formidable group of supporters and in the end he won. 'However unpleasant and depressing it was at times,' writes Anderson, 'it forced the hermit crab in him out of his borrowed shell of diffidence and seclusion, and taught him the use of his claws.'

By now Cecil was represented by the prestigious Anthony d'Offay Gallery, and in 1979 – at the age of seventy-one – he was awarded the MBE. It was in that same year that Kathleen Raine wrote her tribute to the artist, Cecil Collins: Painter of Paradise. She describes his world as:

> the interior country of the human imagination, where rivers and mountains and stars, sun and moon and seas, trees and birds, exist not as natural objects but as imaginative experiences. It is a world of correspondences, not arbitrary but intrinsic; for in the Paradisal state meaning and being are indivisible, are the same thing.

The inhabitants of this world she compares to spiritual beings who clothe themselves 'not in bodily garments but in the joyous adornments and regalia of their inner states – crowns, wands, robes, fantastic shoes not made for walking this earth'. The aspects they assume, writes Raine, are whatever we imagine, 'incarnating our fantasies as naturally as an exotic bird adorns itself in its plumage'. In this context she mentions Swedenborg's accounts of the spirit world, and how the discarnate spirits imagine into existence gardens, landscapes, houses, and change their appearances at a thought; for in the inner worlds, she reminds us, appearances correspond to thoughts, 'so are the heavens and hells created'.

In 1978, Stephen Cross made a film with Cecil for the Arts Council called The Eye of the Heart. In an address that Cecil once gave, he referred to an ancient idea in the spiritual tradition of the Sufis that in all our hearts there is an eye, and when this eye is shut we are asleep. It echoes St Augustine's words: 'Our whole business in this life is to restore to health the eye of the heart whereby God may be seen.' Stephen Cross explored this theme most sensitively and imaginatively through Collins's visionary paintings.

Five years later I was responsible for a new series of *One Pair of Eyes* at the BBC. The team I was allocated included director Christopher Sykes whom I then steered in the direction of Cecil Collins. In the resulting film there are some revealing scenes of Cecil at work – both painting alone, and teaching at the Central. He was also filmed visiting his altar painting at Chichester, and attending a retrospective exhibition of his work at the Plymouth Arts Centre. In the catalogue for that exhibition John Lane wrote: 'All Cecil's figures of the soul, not only his Fools but his Angels, walk inviolate in their own innocence; their very vulnerability makes them seemingly almost invulnerable.' In the same film Cecil reiterated certain of his key beliefs: 'An angel says unite, wake up or perish' – 'The artist enables people to experience what they cannot see themselves' – 'It is not necessary to understand in order to create; it's necessary to create in order to understand' – 'Each one of us is haunted by the memory of a lost paradise'.

Collins's vision of a lost paradise has parallels in all the ancient cultures. In every case there is a memory and also a mourning for the state of being from which our immortal souls arose. In Europe it is a tradition that took on new life in the Renaissance with the recovery of Plato's work. But there is another myth that has emerged strongly in the last few hundred years which is not about loss but about progress. This modern myth reverses the story, and portrays the idea of humanity's slow emergence from ignorance and barbarity to the creation of a paradise here on earth, where our evolving intelligence and reason will gradually solve all our problems. In this myth there is no such thing as a soul, immortal or otherwise. In this scenario we are determined, as I described in Chapter One, solely by genetic inheritance and by our environment.

In the chapter entitled 'Two Paradigms of History', in *Cosmos and Psyche*, Richard Tarnas addresses these two world views. The myth of progress has much to support it, particularly in terms of our ever-increasing scientific knowledge and technological skills. But these advances, as we are learning only too well, have come at a certain environmental and human cost that provides the ammunition for the other argument. We have, therefore, two seemingly antithetical myths: that of Progress, and that of the Fall – a myth that is prompted by what Tarnas calls 'the tragic narrative of humanity's gradual but radical fall and separation from an original state of oneness with nature and an encompassing spiritual dimension of being'. Tarnas sees these opposing myths as constituting the underlying argument of our time: 'Whither humanity? Upward or Downward? ... Is history ultimately a narrative of progress or of tragedy?'

In my chapter entitled 'Free to Love' I have tried to explain why I think that in some ways both these myths, loss and progress, are true – paradoxical as that may seem. The loss of which Cecil was so aware is real enough, and the sense of tragedy therefore quite understandable. Yet the potential for progress as a result of that loss is also very real – a progress in which we ourselves can reconnect consciously to the reality of soul and spirit as well as body, and to the fuller reality out of which we are born and sustained.

In the last few years of Cecil Collins's life, the recognition that he so deserved was increasingly apparent, culminating in the retrospective at the Tate in 1989. A year earlier he was elected a Royal Academician, and in that same year I attended a service at the Church of St Michael and All Saints in Basingstoke for the consecration of the huge West Window which Cecil had designed, working with his friend the stained-glass artist Patrick Reyntiens. On that occasion he spoke about angels – those intermediaries whom he called 'the winged thoughts of the divine mind'. They feature in the window itself and indeed throughout his art. At other times he called them images of what is highest in us. 'We need to rediscover our friendship with the divine world' was the essence of his message to that congregation. For Cecil, 'angels exist to help transform our consciousness, to open our awareness – and contemplation of their beauty purifies us'.

Angel Paying Homage to Christ, by Cecil Collins

One of Cecil's most striking paintings, *The Wounded Angel*, depicts an angel that has returned to paradise and is lying wounded on the ground. 'Bruised and broken in its combat with the mortal world' is how Kathleen Raine described it (see colour

plate 7 *The Wounded Angel*). Another painting, *Fool and Angel entering a City*, is described by Judith Collins, in her essay for the 1989 Tate Gallery catalogue, as conveying the possibility of an Angel accompanying a Fool on his pilgrimage 'because the Fool, with his innocence and purity of spirit, is willing to listen to its voice'. Her perceptive conclusion is that it takes a Fool to recognise an Angel. In a letter on the subject of teachers, Emerson wrote 'all giving and receiving is reciprocal; you entertain angels unawares, but they cannot impart more or higher things than you are in a state to receive'.

In Cecil's early work angels often appear more as cosmic powers, dancing with the sun and moon, rather than in their traditional role as messengers and mediators. Kathleen Raine draws attention to the fact that since the Renaissance there have been virtually no serious attempts to depict angelic beings in the Christian West. For her the only parallel to Cecil's creations are the angels invoked in Rilke's poetry, and to a certain extent the archetypes envisaged by Jung. More recently Anthony Gormley has created a very conspicuous and arresting sculpture, *Angel of the North*, on the hills near Newcastle. Some of the paintings by Greg Tricker – on the lives of St Francis of Assisi, Kaspar Hauser, Anne Frank and St Bernadette – also have a truly angelic and innocent quality (see colour plate 8 *Meeting the Lady* by Greg Tricker). And I also have to admit to being strangely moved by the beings Steven Spielberg created in his film *Close Encounters of the Third Kind*. In his book *In the Belly of the Beast*, however, Sevak Gulbenkian draws attention to films like *Independence Day*, which go some way to meeting our thirst for knowledge of other worlds, but which he sees as ultimately unsatisfactory:

> what they offer is only a materialistic substitute. We are not alone in the universe, they tell us ... However, although they may look a bit different, the beings we share creation with are in essence just like us ... The effect of such messages is that they lock us into a spatial, material conception of other worlds and beings. The idea of purely spiritual dimensions is buried under the weight of this materialistic view.

One of Steiner's followers, the Russian painter Margarita Voloschin, wrote in an early draft of her autobiography, *The Green Snake*:

> How can I paint an angel or an archangel, when I have never seen one? I thought. I don't know how they look. I wanted to have a clear vision before me, which I could then paint. It was a transfer of naturalism into another realm. I wished to confront the spiritual world with the same passive attitude that a naturalistic painter maintains towards nature. I was not conscious that the hierarchical beings, who

are active within and around us, are able to reveal themselves just through the intuitive activity of painting.

In an article for the journal *New View* (Winter 2006/7) entitled 'I Believe in Angels', Richard Bunzl suggests that we will not progress beyond a simple pictorial understanding of angels unless we begin to experience in our thoughts, feelings and aspirations 'an enduring reality over and above our physical bodies'. Without a recognition of this purely spiritual dimension and activity within ourselves, he continues, 'we will not gain the foothold necessary for us to understand the concept of beings which are entirely non-physical'.

In a lecture Steiner gave in Paris on May 25th 1914, he attempted to convey his clairvoyant experience of the angelic realm with these words: 'We identify the angels and archangels not by their appearance, but by the mildness that flows into us from the angels, and the strength and power that flow into our feeling and will from the archangels, if we allow it.'

Both Cecil and Elisabeth Collins would often ask me about Steiner, knowing of my interest in his work and touched by the films I'd made about the Camphill communities in particular. Like many thoughtful and sensitive people I've met – Betjeman, Muggeridge and Laurens van der Post among them – they sensed that Steiner was, indeed, 'on the side of the angels', but his anthroposophy was not a particularly helpful window for them. The books I gave or lent them went largely unread. Likewise, Cecil consciously avoided reading Jung, hinting that such an analytical approach was in danger of prejudging experience. This was clearly not the world from which he drew his inspiration. 'God is like art', he once said. 'He can't be proved, only experienced.' Nevertheless I maintain that a serious pondering on the wise and philosophical insights of others, from whatever source, can be an experience in itself and not just an intellectual exercise or descent into abstractions.

Meanwhile the faculty we call imagination, so treasured by Collins and by William Blake and the Romantics – although increasingly in danger of being sidelined in our head-bound culture – has its dangers too; for to rely on imagination alone can produce results as one-sided as any excess of rationality. Perhaps it is again a question of balance, and we should simply celebrate our differences, while at the same time try to heal our one-sidedness by remaining open to the insights of those who seem to come at life from another direction.

The visionary work of William Blake was clearly an important influence on Collins, as he still is on so many others who strive to see not just with, but through the eye. But Cecil had his reservations, and wasn't always happy at being associated with the artist whom he called the Beethoven of painting.

He felt it was no accident that Blake and Beethoven both lived at the same time, both in fierce reaction to 18th-century rationalism. The great surge in Romanticism that they unleashed, however, was, in Collins's opinion, based on conflict – a conflict with the age in which they lived and, in the case of Blake in particular, an unresolved conflict within himself: a mirror, suggests Collin, of what is referred to in the Kabala and elsewhere as a 'war in heaven'. Blake was, therefore – in Cecil's eyes – a very aggressive artist, 'saved only by the greatness of his last works'. There was none of the peace and serenity that he so admired in Buddhist art or in the art of Byzantium – a serenity that was the signature of so much of his own work.

In another film – one that Cecil made at the age of eighty with the poet Peter Levi, for a Channel Four series produced by Harry Marshall entitled *Art, Faith and Vision* – he again spoke of his nostalgia for 'that direct perception we had as children'. In the film Cecil described the whole of his art as 'a return to the originals'. And it was not, he insisted, an art of self-expression but one of service: 'You can't give people anything – only awaken what they already know.'

Yet despite his seeming nostalgia for some Golden Age, Cecil Collins essentially looked forward. 'My face is set towards the dawn', he once said. The same was true of his wife Elisabeth, as Bryan Robertson perceptively observed in the introduction he wrote to the catalogue of her exhibition at the Albermarle Gallery in 1989, which coincided with Cecil's retrospective at the Tate: 'The very nature of a return to anything at all is overlaid by so many complexities, not the least being hindsight, that the action of return is far more of a venture into the future than any conceivable retreat into the past.'

Elisabeth and Cecil Collins

In his conversation with Brian Keeble in 1979, Cecil referred to what he called 'a strange sense of expectancy' that was in the air. He spoke of a civilisation that despite its brilliant achievements showed all the signs of exhaustion. And it was in art, he believed, rather than in science that the true picture of our culture could be discerned. 'There is about modern art', he said, 'a staleness; and at the same time there is also a sense of something trying to be born … The image that is arising now is an image of universality.' And he related this universality to the increasing recognition that spirituality does not depend on religion, but that religion does depend on spirituality. 'We've discovered', he said, 'that everyone is in the presence of God. There are those who know it and those who don't know it … We've got nothing left but the process of exploration through disillusionment and development of spiritual sensibility.'

Cecil went on to tell Keeble that he no longer felt lonely and that the world had radically changed since he was a student. 'The books we used to read under the table, mystical or metaphysical books, are now read openly everywhere … One is no longer laughed at when mentioning God.' In all this, however, he was still aware of the danger of the masculine tendency towards abstraction. As an example he mentioned what he saw as Kandinsky's delusion in thinking that you could manifest supernatural reality in abstract form. For Cecil, divine reality called out to be recognised 'in the wholeness of human experience, in nature and in man himself'.

'Old men ought to be explorers', wrote T.S. Eliot in 'East Coker'. That is certainly what Cecil Collins continued to be both outwardly and inwardly, even from his wheelchair, as he was pushed among the crowds at the Tate Gallery during that final exhibition, surrounded by one hundred and forty-seven of his finest works and by a great many more of his friends and admirers. Among them was the composer John Taverner who was later to write in his dedication for the catalogue of a 1994 exhibition of Collins's work at the Anthony d'Offay Gallery:

> Cecil's unique iconographical vision – 'the way of symbols along forgotten tracks on which we remember the youth of the world' – touched me very deeply. And it was not only the 'artist', but also the man whom I loved, with his unique brand of humour.

Taverner went on to quote the Russian poet Blok's definition of the artist: 'One who by some fatality independent of his own volition, sees not only the foreground of the world but that which is hidden behind it.' And it was the conviction of another poet, his friend Kathleen Raine, that sacred art – whatever its roots and its character – 'is always a witness to the spiritual reality inherent in our very nature'.

In the foreword to the catalogue for that 1989 Tate exhibition, the gallery's director Nicholas Serota wrote: 'Cecil Collins, now aged eighty-one, has consistently and with dedication pursued a singular path through six decades of 20th-century British Art.' On this pilgrimage, both in his art and his writings, Collins's quest for a lost paradise grew paradoxically into a vision of the future – an intimation of a spiritual maturity for humanity that was within our grasp.

Cecil Collins died on June 4th of that year. Elisabeth was to live another eleven years, during which time her own art flourished and three of her paintings were acquired by the Tate. I took her on several jaunts to Paris and back to Cambridge and Dartington. We had many enjoyable meals at the Chelsea Arts Club and a party there to celebrate her ninetieth birthday. A remark by Nietzsche, 'Forget not the hero in the soul', was one of her favourite sayings in these last years of her life. Sometimes when I telephoned to see how she was, she would say that 'bits are falling off'. And in these occasional moments of gloom, when she was feeling down in the dumps, she would say that her angel had probably gone on holiday. In fact both she and Cecil knew very well that it is not the angels who leave us, but we who move away from them. They are always there, ready to comfort and inspire, but we must be sufficiently open and sensitive to their presence for a communion to take place: Cecil might say 'sufficiently foolish'.

Ron Eyre, Elisabeth Collins, and author

Two Fools Dancing, by Cecil Collins

CHAPTER 27

Seven Ages

On a recent visit to Botton Village, the Camphill community in Yorkshire where I periodically long to be, I met up with one of the older villagers and asked about his mother, whom he had often mentioned to me. With a wonderfully serene smile on his face he told me that she was now 'in the heavenly worlds'. In that moment, through Midgeley Reeve's simple and sincere faith, I felt as much assured of the reality of what we call 'heaven' as by anything I had ever heard or read.

A great deal of what I still wish to relate is about my encounter with so-called ordinary people – adults and children – and about their contribution to my understanding and response to the questions that underpin this book. On the subject of ordinary people, a friend of mine was once asked in all seriousness at an Oxford University garden party: 'Are you somebody, or are you somebody's wife?' My own wife now teaches at Oxford, and although I have settled happily into the role of being 'somebody's husband' at such gatherings, I have become ever more convinced that everybody is 'somebody' – that every life is of significance and value.

In writing about my early years I used the word 'awakeners' to describe the various signposts, ideas and insights that helped me find my way in life. That process has continued, but as I have grown older, it has been the simple goodness that I've met in daily life that has been an equally important awakener. The distinguished television reporter Kate Adie, who has seen much in her life, called her autobiography *The Kindness of Strangers*. The phenomenon she acknowledges isn't written and talked about as much as aggression and violence, yet I believe it is far more widespread than its opposite.

Characters like Midgeley at Botton, and countless other kind and gentle people I have met and sometimes filmed are, in my experience, all a part of the unfolding of our human story. This awareness is touchingly captured in John Betjeman's poem 'The Hon. Sec.' written on the death of the secretary of his local golf club in Cornwall. In the poem Betjeman remembers the simple things the man loved: on the golf course itself, 'the stream at the eleventh

... the pale sea-pinks'; and in his own garden, 'where the robin waited ... his lilies of the valley'; and 'the flip of cards on winter eves...

> The Times would never have the space
> For Ned's discreet achievements;
> The public prints are not the place
> For intimate bereavements.

> A gentle guest, a willing host,
> Affection deeply planted –
> It's strange that those we miss the most
> Are those we take for granted.

On the morning of May 19th 1984, John Betjeman died at his cottage in Cornwall. Within a few hours I was there to say a goodbye of sorts. Several years earlier, along with others, I had taken turns to sit with Cecil Harwood during the three days between his death and funeral. Harwood was the man whose lectures at Emerson College and elsewhere so inspired me as a young man. John Betjeman's friendship was an even greater influence, and I felt it important to be with him in silence for a while, to say so and to thank him. At the undertakers in Wadebridge they agreed to keep the coffin open for a day or so, and thus I was gradually able to come to the experience that the body – that familiar and much-loved figure lying in the coffin – was no longer the person I had known, and yet that John himself was very present. I hope and believe that such quiet moments of reflection are helpful not only for us in coming to terms with what has happened, but also for the person who has died to do the same.

As Betjeman had grown older, and so also many of those he knew, he had often used that phrase: 'Is he (or she) still with us?' My silent answer, whatever the circumstances, has always been: 'Yes, in a way, most definitely so.' And in John Betjeman's case, for example, I don't just mean as a fond memory, or in photographs and on film, or in bronze at St Pancras Station, but 'Yes' out of my sense that a physical parting is not the end of a relationship and that we are present for each other wherever love exists.

John's funeral took place at St Enodoc, the remote and ancient little church amid the sand dunes of the Camel estuary, where my wife Jackie and I had been married almost exactly three years earlier. Six of us had to carry the coffin over half a mile through a ferocious Atlantic gale, arriving at the church – so someone said – looking like a gang of Cornish wreckers. It was as though nature itself acknowledged that the life which was now complete had been, despite Betjeman's somewhat cosy and cuddly image, a powerful and radical one.

Sir John Betjeman's funeral, by Joan Cockett

John Betjeman's biographer, Bevis Hillier, wrote in the epilogue of his third volume: 'If England stays much the same, it will be delightedly recognised in Betjeman's poems; if ruined, it will survive in them.' I would only add that through the medium of television in particular, Betjeman's enthusiasm and passion – a passion that was often prompted by anger as much as by devotion – stirred in very many people an appreciation not only of what surrounds us as heritage, but also what lives in us as potential to become ever more sensitive to the trials and tribulations of others.

At about this time I made the move from the BBC in London to Bristol. Since my marriage I had been living in Berkshire and commuting to London, but now, with a small child, I wanted to be around at bedtime and not stuck in a traffic jam on the motorway. In Bristol I would be able to walk to my office or the cutting-room. Before leaving London I made a film tribute to John Betjeman, and also directed a film for a series called *The Italians* about a delightful and impressive publisher called Giovanna Mazzocchi. It was another helpful reminder that there is much to learn from people who haven't necessarily got their heads buried in sacred texts, or even profess any particular religion or spiritual discipline, but who simply live out the ups and downs of their daily lives with good humour, a kind heart and a concern for others.

On arrival in Bristol, until my own ideas could find their way into the system, I was asked by my new head of department, John Shearer, to produce a series of films with Alan Whicker about British people who'd settled in the USA. *Living with Uncle Sam* ended up as a series of ten one-hour programmes, which involved travelling all over the States interviewing and filming over fifty very different people – including a cowboy in Colorado, a New York businessman, a professional poker-player in Las Vegas, a White House adviser, the actress Joan Collins and a policeman in Los Angeles. We were on location for ten weeks, constantly on the move. It gave us, and I hope the audience, a unique window – through the eyes and experiences of fellow Brits – into a country that in one sense is very familiar and yet in other ways is totally foreign.

In my experience the USA, although far from being 'a heaven on earth', is home to a great many people who feel passionately that it still could be. There is an idealism, energy and enthusiasm that I always find inspiring, despite the tendency at times for these virtues to slip into naïvety, insularity and various forms of fundamentalism. Through their films in particular, the Americans are also better than anyone else at criticising the false gods that so many of them – and we who follow in their wake – are inclined to worship these days.

For a long time I have sensed that the world is increasingly polarising in almost every area of life, nowhere more so than in the United States. There, all that is creative, energetic and compassionate stands alongside and in stark contrast to everything that threatens our very humanity. Americans live in what, for two-thirds of the world, appears to be an affluent and technological paradise. Yet a certain soullessness that hangs over a way of life so absorbed by material things, can and often does have the effect of calling forth a yearning for what is truly paradise – what heaven on earth might really mean.

This contradiction in the American psyche is highlighted for me in the way that Emerson's famous essay *Self-Reliance* was gradually appropriated by many to support and even justify the doctrine of American individualism as so often expressed in outright selfishness. Emerson's real message was that our independence – in its true sense – is a discovery of an authentic voice that rises above the limitations of personality and becomes a spiritual liberation. Thus grows the urge to unite, rather than stand divided one against the other. In *The Spiritual Teachings of Ralph Waldo Emerson* Richard Geldard writes:

> Emerson saw that in an America, only sixty years old when this essay [*Self-Reliance*] was written, there was a possibility that the growth and character of the nation could be characterized by sublime principles if only the individual could escape from the prisons of conformity and materialism to seek a truer freedom.

Recently I came across another now distant, but nevertheless pertinent, observation about America, made in the middle of the 19th century by the French politician and writer Alexis de Tocqueville. Despite his admiration for the United States as a country committed to liberty and equality – in contrast to a European society still constricted by aristocratic privilege – he feared that the virtues he valued could be threatened by 'the tyranny of the majority'. And like so many other observations about America, past and present, what he wrote applies increasingly to the rest of us, since we are all – for better and for worse – ultimately affected by the trends originating in what is still, in many ways, the New World. In *Democracy in America*, Tocqueville wrote:

> I seek to trace the novel features under which despotism may appear in the world. The first thing that strikes the observation is an innumerable multitude of men, all equal and alike, incessantly endeavouring to procure the petty and paltry pleasures with which they glut their lives. Each of them, living apart, is as a stranger to the fate of all the rest; his children and his private friends constitute to him the whole of mankind. As for the rest of his fellow citizens, he is close to them, but does not see them; he touches them, but he does not feel them; he exists only in himself and for himself alone … Above this race of men stands an immense and tutelary power, which takes upon itself alone to secure their gratifications and to watch over their fate. That power is absolute, minute, regular, provident, and mild. It would be like the authority of a parent if, like that authority, its object was to prepare men for manhood; but it seeks, on the contrary, to keep them in perpetual childhood; it is well content that the people should rejoice, provided they think of nothing but rejoicing.

In the American Declaration of Independence, the inclusion of the phrase 'and the pursuit of happiness', following the right to 'life' and 'liberty', was something to which Malcolm Muggeridge often drew attention as evidence of a fundamentally flawed start for that new and potentially great nation. I came across a more subtle and insightful analysis of this word 'happy' in an address given to graduates at University College, Utrecht in June 2006 by the Dutch businessman and cultural impresario John van Praag. The title of his talk was: 'Can you be happy in the 21st century?' In his conclusion he said to the audience:

> if you realise that everything, including all the problems you will encounter along the way in your lives, that everything, without exception, is there not to make you happy, but to make you conscious, then you will be happy.

For some time I had wanted to work again with Ron Eyre. In his company I was both happy and conscious of being happy! Despite his successful career as a theatre and now opera director, he was still, like me, on 'the long search' – asking awkward questions about life, God and everything else. The idea we came up with was to make a series of seven films loosely based on Jacques's celebrated speech in *As You Like It*; 'All the world's a stage / And all the men and women merely players'.

The seven ages that make up one lifetime, as described by Shakespeare and as paraphrased by Ron Eyre, are: 'puking infants, dawdling children, crazed adolescents, reckless soldiery, pompous officials, grandads with whistling teeth, and finally dribbling senility' – all of them, incidentally, male and placed by Shakespeare into the mouth of someone who, as a confirmed misanthrope, would be inclined to see life that way. At the opening of the series Ron made this statement:

> Our line-up is different. First the magicians – watch any four-year-old. Then the age of certainty – the world at ten. Next the fledglings leaving the nest. Fourth, the go-getters – the pushy thirties. Fifth, the big question mark – the mid-life crisis. You catch your second wind and the sixth age comes – the swinging sixties. Last, the brave remnant – the over-eighties.

We acknowledged, of course, that not everybody swings at sixty or pushes at thirty, but we had to start somewhere; in Ron's words, 'with a good, thumping generalization!'

I worked on *Seven Ages* with another producer, Michael Croucher. We agreed that I should direct the two programmes about childhood, the one that explored the trials and opportunities of mid-life, and the final episode on old age. Michael directed the other three. The whole series was filmed by a very talented cameraman, Mike Fox, who had worked with Whicker and me in the States; our research assistant Deborah Hill was responsible for finding many of the wonderful characters we singled out to film.

A Chinese proverb describes life as 'twenty years for learning, twenty years for fighting and twenty years for attaining wisdom'. In his book *Phases*, the Dutch psychiatrist and educationalist Bernard Lievegoed introduces the subject by imagining life as the unfolding of three quite distinct threads. The biological aspect can be described as one of ascendancy and decline; then there is the psychological aspect that manifests in our thoughts, feelings and deeds; the third thread is the spiritual aspect, for which Lievegoed uses Jung's term 'individuation' – the process of becoming an individual who controls their own destiny and who ceases to be a slave to either their biological or psychological nature.

Lievegoed pays particular tribute to the German philosopher Romano Guardini and his book *The Periods of Life* in which Guardini writes:

> The child is in the world not merely in order that he may become adult, but also, and primarily, in order that he may himself be a child and, as a child, a part of mankind ... Every phase exists for the benefit of the whole and for the benefit of every other phase; if it is damaged, both the whole and every individual phase suffer.

We filmed the opening sequence of the first programme at the Maternity Hospital in Bristol; and it was to Bristol that we returned for the final programme on old age. In trying to describe those miraculous first nine months of life in the mother's womb, Ron highlighted familiar and yet nonetheless extraordinary details – like the fact that our first phase of existence is spent under water, that we're fed through our stomachs, and that although we scarcely move we have the heart beat of an Olympic sprinter going for gold. 'And we're not afraid of the dark', he added. 'What a piece of work is a baby.'

Ellie

'But what's it really like to be a baby?' he asked. We can't remember, and all the literature on the subject has been written by adults: 'Obvious but worth pondering', he wrote. 'There are baby-haters, like the Duchess in Alice of Wonderland, King Herod, and Evelyn Waugh; and baby-worshippers like many of the rest of us. But the silent witness throughout is the baby.'

With no babies to interview, all we could do was watch and wonder, and try to imagine how the world appeared to them. My own one-year-old daughter, Ellie – seated on the grass and with Ron beside her – was transfixed by the wind in the trees. 'It will be another year before she knows the word for tree and the word for wind', said Ron, 'so what is this nameless event she's lost in on an afternoon in Bristol she will never remember?' He then made another observation – obvious yet deeply thought-provoking: 'How did most of us look two years ago? Much the same. But Ellie hadn't even started.'

Meanwhile, her three-year-old brother Thomas – Ron's godson – took him on an imaginary journey to Bath with the kitchen chairs as a train and

Thomas and Ron

accompanied by half a dozen of his make-believe friends. Ron's encounters with the infants in the local primary school were no less bizarre. One little boy described in detail his dreams about tigers. 'I dream about prams', said the little girl beside them: *Prams and Tigers* became the title of the film. Another little girl, eager for attention, shared with Ron the startling secret that her mother put her babies in the oven. 'Then they're fried', she said. 'Mummy ate them, but I didn't.' 'What do you do?' asked Ron in his commentary, 'Ring the police? Smile indulgently? Or just drop the subject as Susanna did, once she knew she'd hit the target?'

'After a spell in nursery school', Ron concluded, 'and "spell" is the word, I started to feel like a Roman invader pushing through Britain around 50 BC. The four year olds were the Celts; I was the Imperial power. They had the woods and the magic and the mistletoe.' Fantasy, so Lievegoed and others believe, is actually the foundation of creativity in later life – hence the concern among many at the increasing pressure on very young children to develop intellectually at the expense of play.

Perhaps the most memorable scene in this film, certainly when pondering the mystery of life and death, was Ron's conversation with five-year-old Maudie, the younger daughter of Michael Croucher. It started with a discussion about the recent death of her sister Alice's gerbil. It was quickly established that there was 'a gerbil heaven' and 'a human being heaven'. Ron then asked her who we meet in heaven. 'Angels, fairies, God', was the quietly confident reply. 'Tell me about God', he waded in. Much surprised, Maudie replied: 'Don't you know who God is?' Ron was suitably abashed. 'He's the person who made the world', she continued. 'But there wasn't a beginning or an end of the world.' Another nice paradox to ponder, but it didn't seem to be a paradox for Maudie. 'Is he a man?' asked Ron. 'He's a spirit. He's a good spirit. If you die you can go up to heaven and talk to him', she told him. Ron then asked another 'grown-up' question, wondering how God had time to talk to everyone. 'It's very simple', replied the serene and un-phased Maudie. 'He just says the same thing to all of us. He's saying it all the time.' She went on to tell Ron some basics about reincarnation. Her own wish was to return as a swan; and while she was waiting, she'd settled for Saturday morning ballet classes – the closing scene of our film. 'We're magic swans', the fluttering teacher tells the children, 'and we're going to help a prince – a prince who's in great distress.'

'But Maudie isn't stupid', wrote Ron, as Tchaikovsky did his stuff in the background and the little girls fluttered with their teacher:

> She knows make-believe when she sees it. I'm the one who's bewitched by her childhood, its originality, its guile, its daring, and would like it to stay as it is. She's already negotiating to trade it in for something she thinks she'll enjoy much more – a say in the world, staying up late, a prince of her own.

Slugs and Spice was the title we chose for the second film – the world of ten-year-olds, filmed in Ron Eyre's native Yorkshire. After observing and talking with a lively group of children at the Grassington Primary School, he wrote:

> Speaking as a ten-year-old – by that I mean knowing exactly what I think even if it's wrong – I'd say we all carry around with us a medley of ages alongside the one which corresponds to our birth certificate. Some rare spirits – geniuses, clowns, simpletons – keep the quality of three year olds. All school prefects, all politicians, all heads of all departments, all kinds of inspectors do what they do effectively with the bit of them that is ten or eleven.

We filmed a variety of delightful children both at school and in their homes – all with lively ideas about the various phases of life, and all confirming in their different ways Ron's conclusion that 'this is the age when packs run, teams play, gangs roam, followers follow and leaders lead'.

When we moved from the countryside into Bradford and met Asian families, other themes emerged. We visited a group of Muslim children who, every day after school, spend an hour or so at their local mosque studying the Koran. Their home lives seemed to be altogether more structured than most of the other children we met, but some of them were already suffering because of their perceived difference. Ten-year-old Afsheen, a gentle, articulate and intelligent little girl, told Ron about her hopes of one day becoming a doctor, but also about the hurt she experienced almost daily at being taunted as a 'darky'.

In Afsheen's class at school we had also filmed an angelic-looking little boy called Craig who sang in the Cathedral choir. Later, while Afsheen was in her mosque, we filmed in Bradford Cathedral where Craig and his fellow choristers gave a sublime rendering of the anthem *Give us the wings of faith,*

O Lord by Ernest Bullock. Ron's commentary, however – in the form of a prayer – introduced a very necessary note of discord:

> Lord Jesus – a Jew, to the Muslims a prophet, to the Christians the Son of God – You were born nearer to Pakistan than to Bradford. Your pigmentation is likely to have been closer to Afsheen's than to Craig's. Don't come back just yet, till we've sorted things out a bit better.

This film ended with a sequence at a children's disco – ten-year-olds starting to act and behave as though they were sixteen. 'From the moment you learn to stand upright', wrote Ron, 'forces are at work to make you keel over. I suppose death is the one we all know about, but there are hoards of others in different disguises to watch out for before that.'

Puberty was clearly that next hurdle, and beyond that adolescence. In his book *Phases*, Lievegoed sums up the central problem of adolescence in the form of three questions: Who am I? What do I want? What am I capable of? He then writes:

> The individual who has failed to ask these questions in this phase of life, even if only by realising that he suffers from not knowing the answers, has failed to lay the foundations for the awakening of his psychological being, so that he runs the risk in the important middle phase of life of finding himself stuck at the passionately vital stage, an eternal adolescent who in his appreciation of values remains dependant on what the world thinks of him, or who, on account of his own insecurity, continues to kick against the world.

In programmes three and four Michael Croucher and Ron Eyre explored the years between fifteen and thirty-five. *A Girl Called Dick* was filmed in London, and *Bossy Wee Things* in Glasgow. They dealt with the theme of 'awakeners' in many forms, and of taking that plunge into work, career and relationships. Then came programme five, *A Few Pills and a Good Brisk Walk*, and the question of whether life does, in some ways, begin at forty. For some can 'breakdown' lead to 'breakthrough'? In Dante's *Divine Comedy*, he begins the story with these words:

> Midway life's journey I was made aware
> That I had strayed into a dark forest,
> And the right path appeared not anywhere.

Faust was only thirty-five years old when he made his pact with Mephistopheles, feeling that he had arrived at a dead end. In her analysis of this phase that we associate with mid-life crisis, the German psychologist Martha Moers draws an analogy with puberty which, as Lievegoed points out and which Ron Eyre also indicated, is preceded by a period of assurance, abruptly terminated by the discovery that we know neither ourselves nor life. With it can often come the thought: 'If only I knew what I was really put into this world to do.'

Lievegoed sees the beginning of the forties as a kind of fork in the road leading to the rest of our lives. We either start to go downhill psychologically, alongside our gradual physical decline, or we move into a totally new phase, 'in which quite different powers are awakened'. In this respect I have always liked the poem 'Stopping by Woods on a Snowy Evening' by Robert Frost, in which he seems to warn against comfortable options if we start to run out of steam and are tempted to settle for less. He concludes the poem with these words:

> The woods are lovely, dark, and deep,
> But I have promises to keep,
> And miles to go before I sleep,
> And miles to go before I sleep.

Such promises are often buried very deep, yet they gnaw away as conscience and surface from time to time as seemingly spontaneous decisions to do this, go there, change that; promises that perhaps we have made to ourselves after digesting our failures and shortcomings in past incarnations; promises prompted by gratitude or guilt in relation to another person.

For me, in my forties, finally turning my back on the idea of communal living in a place like Camphill was not, I think, a decision that was either right or wrong. Our promises can unfold in many different ways. What mattered now was what I did instead. If I went on directing films, what sort of films were they to be? The 'lovely woods' that Robert Frost writes about could, for me, have been the easy option of making films that attracted large audiences and popular acclaim, rather than digging my heels in and persevering, for most of the time, with less glamorous but more thoughtful and challenging subjects – an area of television I felt was increasingly neglected.

And now, at the age of forty-three, after years of being a so-called 'carefree bachelor', my life had changed significantly. I had a young family to care for – and the joy of two children who loved stories, games and fantasy as much as I did. Although I wouldn't describe marriage and fatherhood as carefree – any more than being single is actually carefree – for me it has been the happiest, most enriching experience of my life. At the same time I was often on the road again with a film crew and presenter in tow, enjoying all the creative interaction that filming involves. At this midway point in my life, I was able to survey not only my own journey so far but, through my children,

The author's wife Jackie and their children

the extraordinary journey we all make from birth to death, from waking up to the world to slowly falling asleep again.

We made our programme on the subject of mid-life in the Midlands. At the Birmingham Settlement, among their many charitable activities, they ran a mid-life crisis centre. The director of the Settlement, Peter Houghton – himself experiencing many of the questions raised by those seeking help – spoke to us about some of the most common problems the centre encountered: people feeling stuck in a dead-end job, or faced with redundancy or early retirement; stale relationships; and women, in particular, suffering from the empty-nest syndrome. Above all, he said, underlying all this was invariably the problem of meaning: What is the point of my life? It was the question that even the great and successful Leo Tolstoy struggled with in mid-life, and with such intensity. For Lievegoed the problem is summed up by the question: 'What is my real task?' Houghton's own solution in relation to meaning was simply to say: 'I don't know … I'm glad I've got something to do … I may, after all, not be able to change the world, but at least I'll do what I can.'

At the Settlement we also met a man called Harry, a redundant machine-tool maker, who had come to terms with taking on the household duties while his wife went out to work. It hadn't been easy, but he seemed cheerful, and was certainly proud of his new cooking skills. Another person – on the other side of Birmingham – clearly fulfilled by a dramatic change in direction, was the Reverend Peter Hammersley, who in an earlier phase in his life, in the SAS, had sought what Jacques described as 'the bubble reputation even in the cannon's mouth'. This was followed by a stint in industry, but if as a businessman he had acquired the 'fair round belly' that Jacques attributes to middle age, it had certainly disappeared during his life as a clergyman – a career that, in retrospect, both he and his wife could recognise as an inevitability: one of those 'promises' perhaps.

It's sometimes good, however, to have one's theories turned on their head. Our encounter with Pearl Bryan, mother of seven daughters, married to motor mechanic Ken, and originally from Jamaica, did just that. She worked three nights a week on a hospital ward for severely disabled adults. Being a vegetarian she also cultivated her own allotment; and it was there, as they dug away together, that Ron told her about the theme of our film and asked her whether she'd had a mid-life crisis. 'I'm too busy. Too much to do', was her calm and cheerful reply.

One more encounter, before the most dramatic and revealing sequence of all, was with Jane Thomas. Aged forty-five she had just taken up the piano – a somewhat hesitant rendering of 'The Blue Danube' wafted from her red brick villa in Worcester as a prelude to the interview. A few years earlier Jane had also started her own business – *Hang Ups* – making up-market curtains. Much of her conversation with Ron centred on the subject of her son Archie, who had died at the age of sixteen. 'What did he teach you about age?' Ron asked her. Her reply: 'That it doesn't matter how long or short you live – what matters is how you live.' She went on to tell Ron how she and her husband felt that Archie's life was truly fulfilled and was not a life cut short. He had been diagnosed with a brain tumour at the age of three and was not expected to live more than a few months. 'He taught us, too', she said, 'not to waste a minute'.

On the day of our visit to Jane's curtain workshop it was, coincidentally, the fortieth birthday of two of her helpers. One of them spoke of 'the quality of life' as becoming increasingly important to her, replacing 'the appeal of material things'. 'Time for me' – 'What do I want to do with the rest?' – 'Time to take stock', were some of the other sentiments expressed. And Jane's final message to us: 'If you haven't come to terms with yourself by the time you're forty-five, you're in trouble.'

Gillian Limb was certainly in trouble, although by the time we met her the storm had subsided: she was training to be a counsellor and was feeling sufficiently strong to describe her breakdown. She told Ron how she came from a church family, 'a family of copers'. 'I tried unknowingly to emulate that', she said. 'It was natural to try and give to others, and not to think of myself.' Gillian was married and had two children. As she approached her forties she became depressed: 'Who am I? Where am I in all this?' She described how increasingly she felt that she wasn't being true to the person she really was. Her husband tried to help. 'He very much encouraged me to find my own space and to do my own thing. It's just that somehow I didn't feel free to do that. I felt very inadequate beside him. He was the expert. He was the one who did things well. He related well to people. He had the answers. I didn't feel I was good enough.'

Gillian became increasingly ill. 'Physically I shrank to nothing ... But there was a little bit of me that I knew was worth hanging on to ... The rest I had to let go.' Ron responded by saying that the picture reminded him of a child in the womb. 'Yes, I became very much like a child again', she said. 'I curled up and just wanted warmth. I felt very cold.'

After various drug-centred treatments in hospital, Gillian found her way to a remarkable nursing home called Park Attwood near Kidderminster. The clinic integrates orthodox and complementary medicine, and works with some of the pioneering research done early in the early years of the 20th century by a Dutch doctor, Ita Wegman, in collaboration with Rudolf Steiner. At Park Attwood they eventually allowed Gillian to truly let go, gently nursing her through the crisis.

Among the therapies made available was painting, not to discover hidden talent, but to uncover and work through overwhelming emotions. 'I was shaking', said Gillian. 'It was the only time I stopped shaking.' At first she was encouraged to work with the calming colour of blue. Then came red, and anger broke through. 'I hadn't been able to express anger for many years.' She was asked to paint fire, as if she was fire itself.

At this point Ron asked the therapist, Pat Thompson, with Gillian beside him, whether she had sympathy with someone listening to Gillian's story who might say: 'Well, she could have got through all this with a few pills and a good brisk walk.' Pat replied by saying that it depended on how a person wanted to meet their crisis. 'Sometimes people decide: Well, maybe there's more to me than a kind of surface that can just be put back together with chewing gum and bayonet wire.' She went on to say that people coming to a place like Park Attwood tend to want to look at the totality of their lives, at their biographies and at all the things that have led to this point. Where and what is the meaning in it all? 'And these are the people', she said, 'who aren't going to be satisfied with a few pills and a good brisk walk.'

Ron then asked Gillian's doctor, James Dyson, whether he thought she'd had any other option. Had she displayed bravery or just submitted to what had to be? 'I think she went the way she had to go', he replied. 'She resisted to a certain extent, or perhaps I should say that those parts of her – which also belong to all of us – that needed security put up a fairly strong fight. Certainly in the earlier years when I was in contact with her before the full throes of the breakdown she was very successfully managing to hang on to the image of herself that she wanted. And at that stage I didn't feel it was my job to

Ron Eyre and Gillian Limb

disillusion her; I didn't make any judgement about the course that things would take. I simply tried my best as a doctor and as a counsellor to try and help her maintain her identity and dignity, and help her to cope.'

Ron went on to ask whether we were right to locate the forties as a time of turbulence for a lot of people. 'I think on the whole it's fair', said Dyson, 'though many people can hit that problem at a much earlier stage of life, and many people can put it off. It doesn't have to happen at a certain age.' 'What is the problem?' Ron asked. 'I think the problem of mid-life', he replied, 'has to do with finding the way of working out of one's own real inner resources, one's own inner being, irrespective of what one's upbringing has taught, irrespective of what the conventions and customs that surround one have projected onto one as expectations; and, of course, that can include expectations coming to one from one's marital partner, from one's children, from one's work situation.' Dyson described this journey as initially not one of clarity or of light, but of darkness: 'It's then a question of whether the person will find the courage and the inner possibility to confront that darkness, or will they hang on to the known securities?'

In their last conversation together, Gillian told Ron that what she'd learned above all over the past five years was that it's alright not to cope: 'If I can't cope, I'm actually still OK.' He then asked her a very interesting question which prompted from Gillian a simple and yet at the same time enormously profound reply. 'If you are clinging on', he said, 'and are made to release your grip, that's one thing. But if you say you are enabled to give up, that suggests that somebody is giving you the feeling that something or somebody is going to catch you. Nobody will ever let go of anything they're clinging on to unless they are given the assurance of being caught. Now what's catching you?' There was no hesitation in her reply. 'Me, actually. At the bottom, in that pit, there was still a spark of me that was worth hanging onto and that was of value and had the potential to be rekindled and live again.'

In the chapter entitled 'The Stages of Life', in *Modern Man in Search of a Soul*, Jung describes how he came to distinguish between what he called a psychology of the morning of life and a psychology of its afternoon. The life of a young person is characterised by an urge to go out into the world, to achieve something, and perhaps to change that world. If a neurosis develops at this stage, so Jung observed, it can usually be traced to a hesitation or shrinking back from this necessity. The life of an older person, on the other hand, is distinguished by a contraction of those forces, and by a confrontation with what has and has not been achieved. Neurosis arises if a person clings on to a youthful attitude which is no longer appropriate. 'Just as the youthful neurotic is afraid of life', wrote Jung, 'so the older one shrinks back from death.' In fact Jung went so far as to suggest that there was something 'psychically hygienic' in discovering in death a goal towards which one can strive, 'and that shrinking away from it is something unhealthy and abnormal which robs the second half of life of its purpose'.

The 19th-century art critic and social reformer, John Ruskin, in his *Fors Clavigera* (Letters to the Workmen and Labourers of Great Britain), looks at the subject of death with even greater profundity:

Youth is properly a forming time, that in which a man makes himself, or is made, what he is to be. Then comes the time of labor, when, having become the best he can be, he does the best he can do. Then the time of death, which, in happy lives, is very short; but always a time. The ceasing to breathe is only the end of death.

A Different Kind of Adventure was the title of our seventh and last film in the series *Seven Ages*. (Michael Croucher and Ron had made episode six – *It's not Fat, it's Muscle* – about what they called 'the swinging sixties' in and around Newcastle.) Our title came from a thought expressed to us by an eighty-six-year-old woman, Kathleen Dodd, who lived in a Quaker home for the elderly, Avenue House in Bristol. 'A different kind of adventure, but not one I would choose', she said, without a trace of self-pity. 'But here it is and it's got to be lived.' Barely able to move, she spoke to us of her wish to still give something back to life, not just to take. She had brought up a large family, some of whom she had adopted. She described how, having more time now, the things she'd read or reread had more intensity; the whole of life had more meaning. Ron asked her if she thought that time was a bit of an illusion. 'There's no such thing as time', she replied, and then recited these lines, which I believe were her own:

I see before, I see behind
According to the nature of my mind.
I am. I was. I will be.
All these I see.

It is not time that changes
But change in me.

Bernard Lievegoed writes in his book about the wisdom of old age as revealing itself in 'a timeless world of values'. As an old man, Goethe described the phases of life in these terms: the child is a realist, the young man an idealist, the man a sceptic, the old man a mystic. Jung, however, was increasingly concerned that what lives in old people is no longer valued, no longer listened to by others. 'Where is the wisdom of our old people – where are their precious secrets and their visions?' he wrote.

I wish Jung could have met Margaret McNeill, another of the residents at Avenue House. Ron suggested to her that in each age there's a hazard, something we could get wrong. What would she warn us about old age? Where might we get it wrong? 'To think that old age is easy, serene and lovely', was her reply. 'It can be', she continued, 'but it would be very wrong to assume that is the whole picture.' She spoke to us about the obvious problems of sight and hearing and mobility – also of pain. Then there was, both for her and for many others, 'the feeling that you've had it. Your life is over and have you lived it rightly? Would you have done things differently if you could have it again? These things are sometimes saddening', she said.

Miss McNeill used to teach and, if not one of Goethe's mystics, she was certainly wise. She also wrote poetry, and she read us one about a blackbird. She had told us how sometimes when she was feeling low this blackbird would come and perch on the bird-table outside her window. 'It seems to me', she said, 'that he's come to restore my confidence in some way. I've never answered this question "Was it coincidence?" and I don't want an answer.'

Was it coincidence that the blackbird came?
Or could I know that God would do the same for me,
As long ago he did for those whose need was great?
So great, perhaps, they thought they could not wait.
God sent his sign. Could this be mine?
Gently towards accustomed perch he flew.
He did not tell me 'I have come for you'.
Perhaps he did not know.

Another resident, ninety-three-year-old Mrs Diamond, who had been widowed for thirty years, had lost all three of her children at birth. Ron asked her if time had healed. 'Perhaps it takes off the sharpness', was her reply. Like so many other old people we met on our travels, there was no hint of self-pity. She quoted that remark by Kingsley Amis: 'You're old when younger people raise their voices to tell you things you know already. You're also old when you let them.' At coffee break in the communal lounge at Avenue House, Kitty Richards played the piano, forcing everyone to raise their voices. 'Being ninety-seven,' said Ron in his commentary, 'she knows she played better fifty years ago. Being ninety-seven she doesn't care.'

After coffee we watched some silent, grainy, scratched and often out of focus home-movies shot over fifty years ago by one of the few male residents, Mr Mills. Ron compared it to a séance, 'calling up milky images of the long-since grown and the long-since dead'. Glancing at the wise and gentle man beside him, Ron then added: 'I guarantee that the internal movies that Mr Mills runs through his head are in better shape, better shot, and with real colour and real sound.'

Near to the magnificent Clifton Suspension Bridge lived the celebrated architect, eighty-seven-year-old Berthold Lubetkin. We accompanied him to the local casino where he was a regular visitor. Asked by Ron, 'Have you ever said to yourself I'm too old for this game?' he replied with a chuckle, 'I only listen to what I want to hear. It's a form of self-defence.'

Berthold Lubetkin and Ron Eyre

At the casino he spoke to us about randomness, on which roulette is based. His theory was that there are components within this randomness which are repeated from time to time. 'They do occur in a certain periodicity', he told us. 'That, I think, is fascinating, because it opens up the possibility, the notion of whether randomness is random at all; whether there is an order in disorder. I find it infinitely absorbing to watch.' In fact he didn't only watch, and frequently arrived home wealthier than when he left.

The Reverend Albert Thomas Humphrey

'The thing that interests Lubetkin least about Lubetkin is his age', observed Ron. It was certainly also true about our last subject, a one-hundred-year-old clergyman known to everyone as Humph. The Reverend Albert Thomas Humphrey, born in 1886, was a widower and lived with his daughter in the countryside south of Bristol. He told us the story of his interview prior to ordination at a time when priests and bishops still tended to come from the gentry, the upper classes. In response to Humph's reply about his somewhat humble family background, the bishop had said condescendingly: 'Quite a lot of people who come for ordination these days have been in trade.' Humph told us that he longed to say to him, but didn't dare: 'You are in the service of someone who was in trade – a carpenter of Nazareth.'

'Does the idea of death scare you?' Ron asked him. 'No', he replied. 'My wife died just over five years ago. She's buried in the churchyard, but I never think of her as there. I constantly feel that, in a different sense, she's here.' He then spoke about the experience of influences, thoughts and inspirations that sometimes seemed to come from her, 'as if she's conscious that my life on earth is going on, and I've got this job still to do'.

In response to the question: 'What about Heaven?' came his somewhat startled reply: 'We've got to wait and see. I don't think we're supposed to know; except that there is a kind of life that one can apprehend and see which has an eternal quality.'

The last sequence of the film, and of the whole series, was of the Reverend Humphrey, on December 27th 1986, baptising his great-grandson. With that the seven ages had come full circle. These were Ron Eyre's concluding words:

'Second childishness and mere oblivion' takes the infant 'muling and puking' in his arms and tells him that there's little he can do for him except hold him, let him watch what pleases him, be there when he's overwhelmed by things that fail to please. And even then Humph won't last for ever. The toughest lesson that any of us babies of any age have to learn, I think, is that the safe arms we feel beneath us aren't all that safe. And, if we're going to survive, we must discover others – or learn to walk.

CHAPTER 28

Laughter and Tears

In an article in *The Guardian* (April 2006), the journalist Peter Preston wrote: 'I know that God is compassionate, wise and merciful, and mighty when raised to wrath, because I have been told so many times. But I do not know whether he has a sense of humour, because there is scant textual evidence to hint as much'.

Preston describes this picture of God as one of his troubles with religion, 'my struggle at the hurdle of acceptance. Not many jokes'. I share his concern, and not only in relation to religion. There is always plenty of talk about our precious intelligence, but humour, it seems to me, is something absolutely central to what it means to be human, and as such is intimately connected with the mystery of consciousness and self-knowledge. Moreover, without humour we are in danger of becoming not only too intense, but worryingly disconnected from the human condition. Life is serious, admits Preston, 'but not that serious'. The first indications that my own very small children were not just cuddly puppies, but actually human, were the smiles and above all the giggles I was able to call forth.

Peter Preston, having searched in vain in the Old and New Testaments – 'Maybe Abraham managed a grin when his ninety-year-old wife bore him Isaac … Maybe the parting of the Red Sea had its lighter side, unless you were an Egyptian' – concludes his article with that same phrase: 'Not many jokes'. He then adds a short sentence that in its own way points very clearly to a theme I have often raised. 'And so', he says, 'we have to write them for ourselves.'

At the risk of doing what Preston warns against in talking about humour – 'sounding as pretentious as a researcher carrying a clipboard and pencil' – I would like to suggest once again that it might be our task, as humanity evolves, to bring into being and foster what has previously not existed, humour being one example. As well as helping to keep us cheerful, humour can also prevent us from getting too big for our boots – especially in our ability to laugh at ourselves. In my own life the element of laughter has not only been an essential and welcome ingredient, but has also prompted me to make several films with people for whom humour is absolutely central to their work.

Beryl Cook was a self-taught artist, famous for her larger-than-life characters, usually women with a good earthy sense of humour. She was an avid collector, not of antiques, but of junk; she also took a keen interest in the graffiti plastered all over the walls of Plymouth. Filming her at work, in a programme called *I have no Message* for the series *One Pair of Eyes*, she admitted that her people were huge simply because she was bad at painting backgrounds. A lot of these backgrounds were pubs which she very much enjoyed visiting, despite her apparent difficulty in painting them and her shyness at talking to the people in them.

The cartoonist and writer Posy Simmonds was another artist with whom I worked, shortly after my move to the BBC in Bristol. *Tresoddit for Easter* was a film about an imaginary fishing village in Cornwall featured in Posy's long-running strip cartoon for *The Guardian*. Tresoddit was loosely based on Padstow where she had a cottage, and was the place where her cartoon characters George and Wendy Weber and their children escaped to from London. The problem was that everybody else was doing the same thing. Our tendency to destroy what we love became the theme of the programme, with Posy supplying not only the drawings but also the voices, both of the tourists and of the Cornish locals. The film was also about escape and our search for some sort of earthly paradise – a theme I was to explore in greater depth five years later in a film with the Nigerian novelist and poet Ben Okri.

Posy Simmonds with the Weber family in Cornwall

Alan Bennett in Dinner at Noon

Still wearing my humorous hat, I made a film with Alan Bennett at a smart hotel in Harrogate: 'a setting where you see people trying to behave', he wrote, 'which is always more interesting than them just behaving'. He described how for him hotels and restaurants used to be 'theatres of humiliation, and the business of eating in public every bit as fraught with risk and shame as taking one's clothes off'. Interspersed with the touching and often hilarious scenes that unfolded in *Dinner at Noon* were memories of Alan's own parents' embarrassment in such situations; also their efforts to come to terms with the menu once Bennett himself had moved up in the world. 'My Mam would say the dread words: "Do you do a poached egg on toast?" Then there was the ordeal of the wine list: 'We've found an alcoholic drink that we like', said his mother. 'It's called Bitter Lemon'.

There was also an autobiographical element in the film we made together four years later at the Leeds City Art Gallery. Alan Bennett has a strong interest in art, though he remembers as a boy coming to the gallery from the reference library next door simply because he wanted a break. 'I got to know

Alan Bennettt and crew in Leeds City Art Gallery

the pictures by accident', he said, 'by osmosis almost; I just absorbed them.' In *Portrait or Bust* we filmed him wandering through room after room, looking at the paintings, and looking at people looking at paintings. My very skilled cameraman Mike Fox and sound-recordist Keith Rodgerson were able to capture, as they had done in Harrogate, some wonderfully intimate moments of the visitors' reactions to the art on display.

In his youth Alan Bennett, like Mark Tully, for a while considered a career in the Church; but he ended up, again like Mark – and like John Betjeman and Malcolm Muggeridge – holding up a mirror, with compassion, wit and insight, to the joys, sorrows, and absurdities of life in the here and now. I hope and believe that heaven, whatever and wherever it is, is likewise not totally solemn.

The boldest plunge I took into the realm of comedy was the film I directed in 1989, in collaboration with Martin Duncan, for the two-hundredth anniversary of the French Revolution, featuring the National Theatre of Brent. In fact the company consisted of just two

Patrick Barlow and Jim Broadbent as Louis XVI and Marie Antoinette

people, and that's where the joke starts. Patrick Barlow is the genius behind their many productions, mostly performed for the theatre. He is the writer and the main performer – portraying an impossibly pompous, egotistical and humourless figure called Desmond Olivier Dingle. At that time his partner – though stooge would be a more accurate description – was the actor Jim Broadbent. Simply called Wallace, Desmond allocated him all the small and unimportant parts, including of course any female roles.

Revolution was made in the style of a documentary, with Desmond as presenter and Wallace virtually sidelined. Periodically, however, the two of them would act out what Desmond called 'helpful scenes' – Danton and Robespierre having an argument in a café, the storming of the Bastille, Louis and Marie Antoinette's flight to Varennes, the Death of Marat – all filmed in and around Paris with the minimum of props and costumes. The final summing-up sequence was shot at the Moulin Rouge, though Wallace was too engrossed by the show to make much of a contribution.

The whole drama, if one can call it that, was performed with the utmost seriousness – yet clearly on a shoestring budget, and with a script that skilfully appeared to match. Above all it was very funny, while at the same time managing to convey the essence of that very complex series of events. At times the film was also strangely touching, particularly Jim Broadbent's portrayal of Marie Antoinette on the night before her execution. Crouched in a cell, a rather gawky Englishman in a cheap grey suit and wearing a bonnet, was able to convey through his utter sincerity the poignancy of such a tragic situation. Much to the bewilderment and amused tolerance of the French who witnessed us at work, the mad English had managed to both laugh at, and yet also pay tribute to, an iconic moment in French history.

On my return from the fun and games in Paris I persuaded the BBC to let me make a three-part series to celebrate the fiftieth anniversary of the Camphill movement – half a century since that small group of refugees from Vienna had arrived in Scotland in 1939. I will describe several of the encounters in some detail because, as with my two earlier films *In Need of Special Care*, they have greatly influenced my thoughts about that polarity we describe as heaven and earth.

I had stayed in touch with my friends at the school in Aberdeen and at Botton Village in Yorkshire, and those locations became my starting point. But I wanted to show how the work of Camphill had not only developed but also expanded all over the world during those fifty years. How, too, the ideals of living in a community without wages, pension and privacy were becoming increasingly difficult for many people; and how more and more government regulations and endless form-filling were making the task even harder for those who did still want to live in this way.

The children and adults I filmed in the sixties had not only grown up or grown older, but had also moved countries and even continents. Christof Andeas Lindenberg – the music therapist and housefather at the Aberdeen school – had moved to America in 1982 and has since founded a training course for music therapists at Beaver Run, a Camphill school in Pennsylvania. John Byrde was another of the co-workers I had filmed in Aberdeen. He was now married and living in a Camphill community called St Prex, near Lausanne in Switzerland, where they look after both children and adults with special needs. With his wife Heide he was now a houseparent, as well as still working as a teacher. Like all Camphill co-workers he received no wage and there was no going on and off duty. When I asked him how he coped, he made a remark that he's been teased about ever since: 'Well, there's coffee and there's cigarettes!'

On the subject of money, Camphill has always acknowledged that people have needs, but often very different needs – depending on size of family, age, and so on. They also recognise that people like and want to work, bringing a great variety of skills all of which are valued. But the two things – work and money – are kept quite separate in their communities. John, therefore, doesn't benefit financially from being a teacher with many years' experience, but he clearly benefits in quite other ways. He spoke to me with great devotion about the children with whom he lives and works, and how he and his colleagues strive to make contact with that in the person that is

John Byrde

not handicapped. They call it the being behind the mask, but it is no easy task. He described how when working with an individual child there is, even after ten years or so, often no outer sign of progress: 'He can't walk, can't speak, can't feed himself – no more than he could ten years earlier.' Yet the parents, he said, and particularly friends of the family who meet the child much less often, will describe how the child has grown inwardly, 'how the actual personality of the child comes shining through'.

John's approach to his work was echoed by another teacher at St Prex, Claire-Lise Batoudor, who reminded me of what most of us simply take for granted in life – walking, eating, speaking; what some have called 'the miracle of normality'. 'And when you have children who have to battle daily for every little thing,' she said, 'you can only be full of compassion, wonder and devotion.'

John Byrde also described how the children have the capacity to bring out both the best and worst in us; how they challenge us to confront what he called 'the darker, more instinctive side in one's nature'. Since this, our second meeting, John has gone on to help found a Camphill community in Romania where I gather the need for cigarettes and coffee has been even greater.

Another co-worker at St Prex, Tho Ha Vinh, originally from Vietnam, spoke to me about the difficulty that people everywhere increasingly experience in living together. He then described how in Camphill they found 'an incredible social strength' through living together children and adults with special needs. 'In our world', he said, 'we tend to give value to people, to judge people from the point of view of efficiency, productivity, social status and things like that. When you live together with the handicapped person you have to forget that, and you have to try and meet the human being.'

Tho went on to describe how when only the co-workers are together it could be quite difficult socially, with each person expressing their own opinions, desires and ideas. What brought them together, he acknowledged, was the presence of those with special needs, because of their basic selflessness. 'They also have this incredible faculty for gratitude', he said.

'They not only accept what we try to give them, but accept it with gratitude. And gratitude is a quality that is so tremendously missing in our time.'

These thoughts were echoed in my second programme in the series by a housemother at Botton Village, Almut ffrench, who doubted whether communities like Camphill could actually work at all without the gifts that those 'in need of special care' bring to communal life. 'There is a certain pride in each one of us', she said, 'which is broken down by the directness and the warmth of the handicapped person.' She also spoke about the social benefits of bringing up her own children in such a community: 'They appreciate that a handicapped person is a human being, and has strengths and weaknesses like everyone else.'

The founder of Camphill, Karl König, had an image of Camphill as 'a candle on a hill' – a symbol of the fragile yet visionary nature of the idealistic community he was founding; and in those grim days before and during the war Camphill must certainly have been a light in the darkness. I called this new series of films *Candle on the Hill*, and a book edited by Cornelius Pietzner – a Camphill co-worker in the USA – was published with the same title.

Another encounter from 1967 that I now followed up was with Peter, the autistic boy whose painting had so touched Thomas Weihs, and whose attention had been so transfixed by puppets, enabling him to watch and listen without having to confront another human being directly. Peter was now thirty-five years old and living in a mental hospital near his home in Cheshire. In his early twenties he'd been for a trial visit to Botton Village but was too disturbed and unpredictable to cope with a largely unsupervised way of life. Like many autistic and psychotic people he had great ability in certain areas – in Peter's case it was art. His mother, Olive Higham, whom we filmed visiting him in hospital, told us that he knew all his colours before the age of three. The pictures she showed us – intricate patterns using an enormous and subtle range of colours – were extraordinary and very beautiful, each one meticulously and indeed obsessively executed. One picture was entirely in orange; Peter told us himself that there were over fifty shades of orange, and I have no doubt he was right. *Fifty Shades of Orange* became the title of this particular programme. During our visit Peter's mother tried to coax him to draw for us, but for Peter this had to be preceded by what he called 'the ritual' – a kind of hypnotic state, lasting up to ten minutes, before releasing a very precise sound. Much of our precious film stock was used up waiting for the moment. Later he sent me the result (see colour plate 9).

For the same programme I went to see Peter's old teacher, Christoph Rascher, who was now living and working at Lehenhof, one of four Camphill communities near Lake Constance in southern Germany, and one of over eighty worldwide. 'I've never met a person who has such an acute sense of colour', he said to me, and described how you could show Peter a certain green leaf, for example, and the next day, from memory alone, he could reproduce that exact colour. 'In fact he lives so much in his sense impressions', said Christoph, 'that he has to guard himself against the onrush of the world, and withdraw into the oddities of his behaviour.'

Christoph told me that he had often wondered how it would be to meet Peter again – he hadn't seen him for fifteen years. 'I know he wouldn't come rushing towards me saying: "Christoph, here you are at last." Perhaps he would stand looking out of the window and not take any notice of me. Yet he would know exactly who was there, but wouldn't be able to cope with the situation and would have to withdraw. I wondered then, if one would gently remind him of certain situations which we had gone through together, whether this gentle smile would break out and he would say: "Yes, I remember how we were together and what we did together."'

He then spoke to me very movingly about one of the questions one carries as a special needs teacher: In what way to help a person like Peter 'out of this cage of autism', if one is then unable to follow it up and find a place for him in the world? 'Perhaps he had to go back into this cage', he said. 'You can even call it a cell, like a monk.' He then imagined Peter saying, if Peter could allow himself to talk: 'That's my world, and please don't come too near, and don't break it up. That's how I can live, and if there's too much interference I can't stand it.'

Christoph Rascher also told me about Peter's almost suicidal acts as a child, but also about his, Christoph's, conviction that essentially 'Peter loved life', despite it being at times almost unbearable for him. This conviction – 'He still loves life' – was made dramatically apparent to Christoph while on a climbing trip to the Cairngorns in Scotland when they were caught in a storm near one of the summits. The wind was tremendously strong, and Peter had a rope tied round his waist. Then suddenly he started to pray. 'Let me go on living', Peter said. 'Please God, I don't want to be blown down this mountain. I want to go on living.'

While we were at Lehenhof, Christoph Rascher was rehearsing a play Karl König had written for Easter. The setting was Imperial Rome; it was Good Friday, and soldiers were in the process of rounding up various misfits in society for exile to a remote island. At the start of the play each character – the epileptic, the leper, the blind man – is absorbed in his own tragedy, seeing his handicap as a cruel blow of fate. In casting the play, Christoph was following König's advice and avoiding any sort of type-casting among the adults in their community; someone with epilepsy, for example, would play a different role altogether in the production.

Gradually, as the story unfolds, the victims come to accept not only their disabilities but also each other, a theme that goes right to the heart of

Camphill. 'By the time the soldiers arrive,' said Christoph, 'they have not only come to an acceptance of their fate, but also that this desert island will not be a desert island if this brotherhood that has come about persists.'

'For me', he continued, 'the play does not only apply to people with handicaps, but to anybody.' He described how we repeatedly meet situations in life when something seems to come at us from outside: 'It has nothing to do with me, you think, and you revolt against it.' But as in the play, suggested Christoph, you can come to an acceptance that destiny is part of who you are. 'That's what people used to call serenity', he said; and then added: 'We have accepted that actually every person is handicapped in a way, that we all have shortcomings; we are not perfect human beings. And I think it's important for us that handicaps are not seen as things which other people have. Rather we realise that each of these handicaps that other people have in a very pronounced way, we can find in ourselves.'

In the second film of the series I followed up two more people who had featured in my earlier programme. One was Christine Everard, who had visited Botton Village on a work camp and stayed to join the community as a young co-worker. She was now married and also living at Lehenhof in southern Germany as a housemother, and with a family of her own. Her husband, Henry Everard – also from England – ran one of the farms. 'I wouldn't like to make Camphill sound like some sort of utopia where we're blissfully happy all the time', she said. 'Most of the time I really enjoy it, but having this extended family, there are times when you think "Let's just clear off", especially at mealtimes!'

Speaking about the special needs adults in her care, Christine drew attention to an observation often expressed by visitors to one of the Camphill Village communities – 'Just why are they here?' The sanity of daily life, and normality rather than madness, is what strikes one so forcefully on first acquaintance. 'But when one knows them and their case histories better,' she said, 'one can understand that yes, maybe some of them could manage outside, but under what sort of conditions would they be living? It's not easy, if you're a bit different, to live in normal surroundings. And I think our villagers work so well here because they're not under any sort of pressure.'

It could be argued – and I don't mean this in any critical sense – that many of the co-workers in Camphill likewise need this protective umbrella in order to live and function creatively in the world. Steiner spoke about many of his followers as 'homeless souls'. I sense that many people these days increasingly have the experience of being at odds with contemporary life – its shallowness, excessive consumerism, and competitiveness. A hundred years ago a number of people inspired by Tolstoy's ideals, and equally estranged from their contemporaries, set up utopian communities in which, for example, land ownership was forbidden. Tolstoy was not on the whole in favour of such initiatives, seeing them as the first step in the direction of a Church. To his friend Butkovich he said:

> To stand aloof, to shut oneself up in a monastery, surrounded by such angels as oneself, amounts to creating a hothouse and those conditions in which it will be easy to be good oneself, but no one else will be warm. Live in the world and be good – that is what is needed.

This observation by Tolstoy sums up very well one of the reasons I never took the plunge and joined a Camphill community myself. But I also recognise that in my inability to make such a courageous and revolutionary step, my own attachment to what is mine and mine alone was an important and inhibiting factor.

Ralph Waldo Emerson, too, kept his distance from the various communities that were forming in 19th-century America, but was sought after by them as a teacher and supporter. Richard Geldard, in his book on Emerson, calls the contemporary equivalents of these communities 'monasteries without the trappings of religion'; and their students 'the monks and nuns of an invisible Order ... Most are simply places where people of like mind gather to bring some semblance of discipline to spiritual study and practice.'

In this connection – in a lecture Steiner gave in Oslo on October 5th 1913 (now printed in a volume called *The Fifth Gospel*) – he spoke about Jesus' early connection with the Essenes, an ascetic community living apart from the world around them. Steiner describes a clairvoyant picture he had of Jesus' overwhelming experience of demonic beings in flight from the purity of such a community. Through their way of life, he says, the Essenes protected themselves from such harmful influences, 'in order that they themselves may live in blessedness'. But the demons don't simply disappear; they enter into the world at large. It was experiences like this, Steiner suggests, that prompted in Jesus the increasing awareness that his mission was for the whole of humanity and not just for an isolated minority.

In *Memories, Dreams, Reflections*, in the chapter called 'Late Thoughts', Jung writes very interestingly about the challenges associated with his concept of individuation, and with great understanding for those who hold back and cling to some group identity. He refers to what he calls 'the secret society' as an intermediary stage on the way to individuation:

> The individual is still relying on a collective organisation to effect his differentiation for him; that is, he has not yet recognised that it is really the individual's task to differentiate himself from all the

others and stand on his own feet. All collective identities, such as membership in organisations, support of 'isms', and so on, interfere with the fulfilment of this task.

Jung goes on to say that although these collective identities can be viewed as 'crutches for the lame ... beds for the lazy, nurseries for the irresponsible', they can be equally understood as 'shelters for the poor and weak, a home port for the ship-wrecked, the bosom of a family for orphans, a land of promise for disillusioned vagrants and weary pilgrims ... and a mother providing nourishment and growth.' He therefore believed that it would be wrong to regard what he calls 'this intermediary stage' as a trap; 'on the contrary', he writes, 'for a long time to come it will represent the only possible form of existence for the individual, who nowadays seems more than ever threatened by anonymity. Collective organisation is still so essential today that many consider it, with some justification, to be a final goal.'

Jung doesn't mention the word 'pioneer' in his list of those who seek support and companionship in collective initiatives and so ignores, I believe, the possibility that exists for individuals in communities such as Camphill – providing those communities are sufficiently open and undogmatic – to develop as independent and free human beings in the close, mutually supporting company of other people. The 'weary pilgrim' can continue his task as a pilgrim, but in the knowledge that he is not alone and that he remains involved in the welfare of others and not just in his own salvation.

There was nothing weary about the 'pilgrim' Mike Fuller, a young gardener I met at Botton Village during the filming. The attraction for him of joining Camphill, he told me, was primarily because he would not be paid. He'd been a successful self-employed landscape gardener in the smart suburbs of London. But he described how the more he got involved in the work, the less he got involved in the actual plants: 'I was more interested in the money. I would look at somebody's garden and they would ask me what I thought of it; and I would look at that border and say £50, and that bit over there is £100; and I would forget that there were nice roses in the garden.' For Mike the situation got worse and worse, culminating in a dream in which pound notes and turf were all rolled up together. 'Enough,' he said to himself, 'I can't keep working for money. I want to do something that's real.'

One of the many 'real' things that Mike Fuller did by going to Botton, some four years after I met him, was to marry Suzanna who was working there as a nurse in the household that cared for some of the older people in the community. Suzanna was two years old when I first filmed at Botton in 1967. Her mother, Gerda Blok, was in charge of the dolls workshop, and she and her husband Piet were also houseparents. Shirley le Duc was one of the villagers in their care, and gradually began to look after Suzanna when her parents were busy. She did the job wonderfully and it clearly gave her a great sense of her own worth.

Some years later Shirley chose to leave Botton. I went with Suzanna to visit her in Scarborough where she lived alone in a Council flat with a small dog and a canary, and with a conspicuously empty fridge. She'd been married briefly, but insisted she wasn't lonely. She had a home help, and went to a

Suzanna Blok and Shirley le Duc

day centre twice a week. She'd had trouble with some local boys throwing bricks through her windows, but was very sure that she'd made the right decision in leaving Botton, saying that she was 'glad to live like a normal person'.

'I had a very unfair childhood', she said to us. 'My parents put me in a nut-house. There's nothing wrong upstairs, as you can see. I've never been a violent person, never harmed anyone. I've spent half my life in a loony-bin.' Suzanna asked her if that was the reason she left Botton. Again Shirley used this word 'normal': 'I want to live a normal life. You only live once. Once you're under the ground, you're under the ground. That's it. You don't come back, unless you come back to haunt people, and I don't want to do that.'

Later I asked Suzanna for her reaction to Shirley's situation. 'After Botton', she said, 'it seems to me a rather empty life, but Shirley seems happy – happy to have her own front door, as she says. That, for her, means more. I think she's alright, really.' Was she putting a brave face on it? I suggested. 'A lot of the time', replied Suzanna. 'But I think what underlies it – that she wants to be independent – is something very important.'

Before I left the BBC in London I had made a film for the series *One Pair of Eyes* called *An Independent Life*. That, too, was about a person with special needs choosing to live, and in his case also to work, in the local community. 'At my birth they accidentally pinched my brain with some forceps', said Simon Trehearne at the opening of the programme. 'It was nobody's fault, and I found learning as a child rather difficult – especially at lessons – and I had to go to a special school.'

The style of the series was that each person presented and narrated their own story, as both Bernard Lovell and Penelope Betjeman had done in the films I made with them for *One Pair of Eyes*. Simon took on the challenge enthusiastically and with great skill. I filmed him at the small furniture factory where he worked; his job was to look after the boiler, as well as to keep the place clean and to fetch sandwiches for everyone at lunchtime from the local café.

At the age of eighteen Simon had left home and gone to live in a small Camphill hostel in Stourbridge with Mark and Rosalind Gartner, who helped and encouraged the residents to find jobs locally, and when ready to step out and live on their own. Simon had clearly been determined from a young age to stand on his own feet and not be over-protected or 'stifled', as he put it, by his parents. He now shared a house with his friend Max who had a job in the local park. Simon cooked, Max washed up, and together they did the shopping. And both of them had the support and help of Camphill in the background if problems arose.

There is an increasing trend these days towards what is called 'integration', though many people are concerned that it isn't always an appropriate route for some of the most fragile and vulnerable children and adults. In Simon's case, however – as with Shirley – it was clearly what he wanted. In Switzerland I had filmed a Camphill initiative similar to the Stourbridge project, in the village adjoining the St Prex community. There six 'compagnons' lived with a housemother, Elisabeth Wider, above a newsagent and gift shop which they helped her to run; they also did odd jobs like window-cleaning around the village. 'They want to integrate into normal life', she said, 'but the problem is that they are not accepted socially'. This remark highlights the problem of what is termed 'care in the community'. Although such set-ups are on the whole generously funded – two or three vulnerable adults living together, with visiting social workers to help with their practical needs – critics will say that there is in fact neither 'care' nor 'community' in the real sense of those words. Instead these tender and wounded people are invariably lonely, and also without work. 'Simply closing down institutions is not enough', said the Camphill co-worker at St Prex, Tho Ha Vinh. 'Real integration is only possible when we are willing to live together with them an absolutely normal social life'. In the village of St Prex efforts were being made to do just that. 'In the evening they have a cosy home where they are accepted', said Elisabeth. 'Weekends we go out and we do things with them, and that is what gives them the security that they would not find if they lived alone'.

Likewise, the help and support that Camphill has given to people like Simon Trehearne is an attempt to acknowledge the idealism that stands behind the notion of integration, while at the same time ensuring that they don't end up in a physical and social ghetto. Simon was keen to demonstrate in our film that people like him *could* lead independent lives, and to encourage others to do the same. Much of the programme dwelt on Simon's attempts to

Simon Trehearne

help his friend Alisdair who, since his mother's death, had lived on his own. But unlike Simon, Alisdair had never been allowed or encouraged either by his parents, or by a set-up like Camphill, to do things for himself. Thus, in his forties, he was living in a flat that was not only chaotic, but bordering on squalid. 'I'm sure that his problems can be sorted out', said Simon at the conclusion of the film, 'if I find the right people to help me. Anyway everybody has a problem at some stage in their life. Everybody in this world has got a handicap in some way or other, and we all need support. An independent life is much more than being independent.'

My glimpse into Simon's life brought home to me strongly the truth of that statement about ordinary people doing extraordinary things. In saying those words about independence – 'an independent life is much more than being independent', and above all in trying to live by them, Simon was, it seems, drawing instinctively on the same wisdom that inspired John Donne, over four hundred years earlier, to write the line I have already quoted: 'No man is an Island, entire of itself.' Yet nor does such a thought contradict for me what Johannes Tauler wrote even longer ago: 'The true and eternal word of God is spoken only in the desert, when man has left his own self and all things behind, and stands alone, deserted and solitary.'

Ideally, I suppose, we should strive to find a balance: a time for contemplation, and a time to work with and for others. The story of Mary and Martha in the life of Jesus highlights the polarity of these two ways of being. Our instinct to side with Martha, who is always busy getting on with the work that needs to be done, is understandable. But Jesus defends Mary in her life of contemplation and prayer as being just as worthy of admiration. Philip Toynbee, in his wonderfully honest journal, admits to being 'incompetent' in both these areas of life, yet says:

> perhaps there is a third way, which is to share this moral and spiritual incompetence with others, and encourage them not to lose hope by keeping one's own hope alight in the murky confusion of repeated doubt and failure.

Most people's temperaments tend to steer them in one particular direction or another. Some are more reflective by nature, whereas others thrive on action, on making things happen. Then there are those whose strong feeling life will determine the path they take. What is clear, I believe – whatever route we take – is our need for each other, so touchingly acknowledged by Toynbee.

For me this balance between inner and outer, and our interdependence along the way, is captured with great charm in the stories of A.A. Milne. Those animal characters he created in the Hundred Acre Wood seem to have got it pretty right in that each one lives alone – in Jung's language 'individuated' – but they are in and out of each other's lives in a wonderfully haphazard yet supportive way, each one balancing out and complementing the strengths and weaknesses of the other. Pooh Bear, the extrovert, needs his faithful companion, Piglet, to share in his adventures; and Piglet, the introvert, is anyway too scared to be on his own for long. Eeyore, the melancholic donkey, and Owl, the intellectual, are both contemplatives of a sort, but need others to whom they can either moan or show off.

Christopher Robin – whose toys they are – is, I suppose, their god of sorts. But eventually he, like our gods, has seemingly to move away. At the end of the final story, with schooldays looming, Milne describes with great tenderness Christopher Robin's attempt to say goodbye to the companions of his childhood.

'Pooh, promise you won't forget about me, ever.
Not even when I'm a hundred.'
Pooh thought for a little.
'How old shall I be then?'
'Ninety-nine.'
Pooh nodded.
'I promise,' he said.

Christopher Robin and Pooh by E.H. Shepard

CHAPTER 29

The Emperor's Clothes

Camphill pioneered a new and in many ways still unique approach to those with special needs. In fact the founder Karl König believed – or rather hoped – that if one day the world was a different and kinder place, then communities like Camphill would no longer be needed. Those were the words I wrote at the end of *Candle on the Hill*, my tribute to a network of people who had awoken in me so many helpful and inspiring insights. Meanwhile, I concluded, in a world that many see as in too great a hurry and too clever for its own good, those who have some kind of 'special need' present all of us, it seems, with the chance and the challenge to slow down, to think again.

'Not much sign of that happening', some might say. Such idealism is, I know, increasingly dismissed as naïve by many of those who determine what we read, watch, and listen to these days. Even at the BBC, by the late eighties, respect for the audience's intelligence and sensitivity was eroding, and with it came the view that people were not interested in more thoughtful and reflective programmes. In fact, in my experience, it was the people in charge, not the audience, who were turning their backs on the kind of projects that I and many of my colleagues had tried to nurture over many years.

In 1990 I therefore decided to leave the BBC; at that time staff in their fifties like me were anyway being encouraged to take early retirement. Instead I would work as a freelance producer/director. I joined forces with my old colleague and friend from *The Long Search*, Mischa Scorer – one of the most talented documentary film-makers of our generation – and then had ten very happy and productive years in a small independent film company in Bristol. Most importantly this enabled me to go on exploring, through my work – as well as quietly on my own – those deeper questions I had been pondering throughout my life.

One question that continued to occupy my thoughts, and does so still, concerned the possible bridge between the 'seen' and the 'unseen' – not a question that is much debated at present, either in print or in conversation. The current materialistic orthodoxies seem to hold sway – at least on the surface. Yet when I read, for example, certain pronouncements by the scientific establishment, whether concerning the universe or a frog, I often find myself imagining that one day, perhaps one day soon, we'll wake up and realise – like the innocent and honest little girl in Hans Christian Andersen's fairy tale – that the Emperor is wearing no clothes. By that I don't mean to dismiss the extraordinary skill and dedication with which scientists work, nor the detailed understanding of the physical world, in particular, that continues to emerge. But somehow, somewhere, we seem to be missing the point – or rather not seeing the wood for the trees.

I take some comfort from the fact that I am not alone in noticing that the Emperor, if not totally naked, is somewhat scantily clad. Thomas Weihs's emphasis on the difference between our understanding of how things work, on the one hand, and what they might mean on the other, is a help in mitigating the unease I feel about our blinkered view of the world.

During the Middle Ages intellectual life in the West was characterised by rigidity and other-worldliness and by the authority of a Church that essentially blocked further revelation. This was followed by the Reformation and Renaissance, and in their wake the Scientific Revolution, the Enlightenment and the so-called Age of Reason. In their beginnings all of these movements from the fifteenth century onwards promised liberation and change, but all were in danger of themselves becoming dogmatic and creating a new orthodoxy. There is a view that science in particular has become a new religion with a modern priesthood of men in white coats.

There is, however, a distinct change in the air. A paradigm shift of the kind that Thomas Kuhn identified is slowly but surely taking place. Scientists like those I wrote about in Chapter 23, and not just scientists, are starting to look at the world differently, and at the role their own consciousness plays in the assumptions and conclusions we make about that world. The new frontiers will, I believe, be characterised by a major shift in the way we understand ourselves.

In all the great Mystery schools of antiquity self-knowledge was recognised as the source of all knowledge; for, at the end of the day, we ourselves – and not our telescopes, computers and microscopes – are the instruments capable of probing deeper aspects of reality. The technology can help of course; but what finally matters is the interpretation we bring to scientific data. And even more important, perhaps, are the questions we ask in the first place. How do things work? What do they mean? Perhaps these two questions are finally inseparable if we are really going to understand ourselves and all that surrounds us. We can travel to the moon in rockets, or in our imaginations; but to truly understand the moon – or my buttercup – we shall have to work harder on the instrument of inquiry itself: namely ourselves. And in our search for life out there in the universe we also need to be clearer about what we mean by life.

One man for whom these questions were of great interest was the twentieth-century English biologist E.L. Grant Watson, who spent a number of years as a field zoologist in Australia, a country in which several of his novels are set. In his book *The Mystery of Physical Life* he challenges Darwinian orthodoxy, raising profound and unanswered questions about the origin and the evolution of life itself. Watson was a man who never seemed to lose the wonder we often experience in early childhood, as his many fine books on the phenomena of nature bear witness – books like *Enigmas of Natural History, Animals in Splendour,* and *Nature Abounding.*

In the introduction to *The Mystery of Physical Life* Watson writes about how his scientific, psychological and philosophical studies carried him 'into realms of speculation but did not in any way decrease the wonder; for, behind the ever-changing forms of living things was the mystery of existence'. This mystery, he felt, along with his own experiences in the field, demanded an explanation; but, as the distinguished homeopathic doctor Ralph Twentyman writes in the foreword, 'no such explanation was forthcoming from conventional wisdom'. Watson's emerging and almost heretical view of the nature of reality – questioning not only what those around him were questioning, but also what almost everyone else was taking for granted – has to be understood against what he calls 'the tremendous faith modern men have in anything that bears the label "scientific"'. This faith has been slowly eroding in the intervening years, as the one-sided and often destructive effects of much that is done in the name of science sink in.

The paradoxical implications that lie behind 20th-century discoveries in physics with its redemption of subjectivity and its recognition of the interconnectedness of what had previously been regarded as separate, are starting to influence not just biology and chemistry, but also philosophy, psychology, and even theology. All these influences are nudging us towards a realisation that instead of new thoughts of the same kind added to old ones, we need – as Twentyman and others are suggesting – a change in our way of thinking.

Watson recognised, for example, that although we know a great deal about cell division and the building of tissue, what actually causes growth – as well as healing – remains a mystery. It was this mystery that increasingly occupied him throughout his life. He recognised, too, that many of the discoveries of modern science were, in his opinion 'still held within a framework of enlightened rationalism that confined them in a state of psychic paralysis'.

In his autobiography *But To What Purpose?* Watson writes about returning to Cambridge as a graduate with his young family. Reading in the university library he became 'ever more sceptical of the validity of the mechanistic interpretation of Nature which is implicit and often explicit in the accepted classical theories of evolution'. He always remembered the advice he received while an undergraduate at Cambridge from the Professor of Zoology, Adam Sedgewick: 'Forget the theories: concentrate on the facts.' Increasingly he recognised the inadequacy of the laboratory – in contrast to observation in a natural environment – as a setting for studying the natural world. He acknowledged that laboratory experiments have their place, but felt that such experiments are often invalidated if they assume that the lives of animals and plants can be regarded in their entirety in terms of physics and chemistry. 'The invisible counterpart', he writes, 'which, ever more convincingly, appeared to me to form the essential portion of the organism, was seldom taken into account.' He goes on to describe how removing a creature from its natural environment 'always does a certain violence to its essential nature'.

In his foreword to *The Mystery of Physical Life*, Twentyman also points out that not only Darwin, but also Marx and Freud 'had cast a dark shadow over three fundamental sciences: biology, sociology and psychology'. Their materialism, he writes, their mechanistic interpretation of things – justifiable up to a point in dealing with the inorganic world and above all with technology – 'has invaded our understanding of life itself, social affairs and the soul'.

Some twenty years later there are signs, however, that this dark shadow to which Twentyman refers is starting to lift. The thoughts expressed in David Lorimer's anthology *Beyond the Brain*, discussed in Chapter 23, are encouraging examples. Another is a book written by Denis Noble, Emeritus Professor of Cardiovascular Physiology at Oxford University, called *The Music of Life*. In essence it is a response to the increasing trend to break living systems down into their smallest components – into individual genes and molecules – in order to understand life.

Noble acknowledges that this work over the past fifty years or so has been an impressive achievement, but he also points out that 'the answers that we arrive at reflect the process of investigation that we follow'. Humpty Dumpty has been smashed into billions of fragments. Can we put him together again? he asks. 'At each level of the organism', writes Noble, 'its various components are embedded in an integrated network or system. Each system has its own logic. It is not possible to understand that logic merely by investigating the properties of the system's components.' What he advocates is a return to what is called 'systems biology': 'ways of thinking about integration that are as rigorous as our reductionist procedures, but different'. Noble compares this systems-level view of life to music. Where then is the score and who was the composer? he asks. His central question, therefore, throughout the book is: 'Where, if anywhere, is the program of life?'

The popular view is that the instructions for the development of each living organism lie in its genes. The theme of Noble's book is that there is no such program. The genome – the so-called 'book of life' or blueprint – he sees as a 'database' for the transmission of successful organisms, rather than a program that 'creates them'. Noble likens the delusion that DNA causes life to the idea that a CD 'caused' his sublime experience of listening to a piece of music by Schubert. 'The human genome is in some ways a little like a CD', he writes. 'It carries digital information.' Another way I've heard DNA described is as an architect's plan. It's an instruction, but behind it stands the intention. Likewise there is an organisational principle in every living organism. In the seed lives the intention to become a flower.

The subtitle of Denis Noble's book is *Biology Beyond Genes*. To understand life, he argues, we have to recognise it as a process, a web of connections in which gene, organ, system, body and environment all interact. Although such a view leaves many questions still unanswered, it is a huge stride from the mechanistic approach that has dominated mainstream biology for so long. 'I gave the title *The Music of Life* to this book', writes Noble, 'because music is also a process not a thing. And it has to be appreciated as a whole.' How refreshing it is that eminent scientists are taking other levels of experience seriously, not just as relaxation, but as important windows into their search for understanding.

Paul Davies – Professor of Natural Philosophy at Macquarie University, Sydney – points to a similar breakthrough in the preface he has written to an anthology called *The Re-Emergence of Emergence*. The theory of emergence seems to be another attempt to counteract, and indeed to replace reductionist philosophy. In describing the theory Davies writes:

> Roughly speaking it recognises that in physical systems the whole is often more than the sum of its parts. That is to say, at each level of complexity, new and often surprising qualities emerge that cannot, at least in any straightforward manner, be attributed to known properties of the constituents. In some cases, the emergent quality simply makes no sense when applied to the parts. Thus water may be described as wet, but it would be meaningless to ask whether a molecule of H_2O is wet.

Davies goes on to explain how at the time the theory of emergence was first adopted in Britain a hundred years ago, particularly in the realm of chemistry and biology, many biologists were what was known as vitalists: 'adhering to the notion that living organisms possessed some form of additional essence that animated them'. Orthodox physicists would have none of this. Organisms were seen merely as highly complex machines: 'their novel behaviour', writes Davies, 'being ultimately explicable in terms of basic physical laws operating at the molecular level.'

Emergencists, apparently, took a middle road, dismissing the notion of vital essences, but also rejecting the idea that living organisms could be explained or understood by analysing the mechanics of their components. For them there was profound significance in the fact that something was alive, even if no individual atom in that organism is itself alive. Davies continues:

> Emergence in biology would open the way to biological laws that supplement the laws of physics, perhaps enabling scientists to pin down exactly what it is that distinguishes living matter from non-living matter. The greatest impact would surely be in the field of consciousness studies, where the mind–body problem could be solved by appealing to mental causation as a legitimate category augmenting, but not reducible to, physical causation.

Such a step, suggests Davies, would enable scientists to take consciousness seriously as a fundamental property of the universe, and not as an irrelevant and incidental mental state, seen merely as a by-product of brain activity.

What a pity that Grant Watson didn't live long enough (he died in 1970) to witness not just the re-emergence of the emergence theory, but the arrival of many other books and essays along the same lines, by thoughtful and open-minded scientists all over the world. For me, an enormously helpful window into this wealth of exciting and revolutionary material has been through the Scientific and Medical Network – a body tolerant enough to allow a non-scientist like myself to be a member. The declared aims of the Network are:

> To challenge the adequacy of scientific materialism as an exclusive basis for knowledge and values; provide a safe forum for the critical and open-minded discussion of ideas that go beyond reductionist science; integrate intuitive insights with rational analysis; encourage respect for Earth and Community which emphasises a spiritual and holistic approach.

It's not surprising that someone with such a mind as Grant Watson was eventually drawn to the work of Jung, and indeed to Steiner. In his book, *The Mystery of Physical Life*, he quotes a celebrated remark by Jung: 'Science stops at the frontiers of logic, but nature does not – she thrives on ground as yet untrodden by theory.'

Both Jung and Steiner were deeply influenced by Goethe who, in his approach to nature, cultivated not the mystical path of old, nor the total separation of the observer from the observed as advocated by modern science, but rather a conscious participation that he called 'the creating of exact imaginative fantasy' – sometimes translated as 'exact sensory imagination'. Another of Goethe's descriptions, 'delicate empiricism', likewise points to this enrichment and expansion of consciousness whereby we can start to experience what he called a 'hidden something' in the object which corresponds to a 'hidden something' in the subject – the subject being ourselves. In other words we can train our imaginative faculties to become instruments of a conscious and exact cognition. Such an activity is closely related to the notion of 'correspondences' to which I have often referred and which is summed up in that phrase of William Blake's 'As a man is, so he sees.' In fact Goethe went even further, saying that only what you love can fully reveal itself to you.

In *The Mystery of Physical Life* Grant Watson writes:

> I have tried in my experience as a field-naturalist to look at the instinctive behaviour of animals, and have felt within the regions of my awareness for a corresponding relatedness, believing that only in so far as this relatedness with the object can be felt, can I achieve understanding, as opposed to mere knowledge. I have become aware of what C.G. Jung has called 'the noumenal reality which embraces the whole situation', which includes the observer and the observed.

Watson eventually underwent Jungian analysis, but only after initial resistance to the idea. Later he actually met Jung, by which time his views had changed radically, so that in his autobiography he was able to write of analysis as 'the instrument in the grasp of man for his possible, immediate redemption'. But he then added that he didn't look upon it as 'a permanent and everlasting panacea, but as the instrument of our time'. Both Jung and Steiner attached great importance to making subjective feelings an object of scrutiny.

Like Jung himself, Grant Watson was very inspired by reading Goethe's *Faust*, and it was the nature and reality of evil that particularly interested him. It prompted what he describes in his autobiography as a life-long task: the laying bare of the 'shadow' or negative side of life. 'To get out, even a little way, from the ruts of compulsion', he writes, 'it has been essential for me to understand something about the "Shadow", that side of life which we all naturally wish to hide and cover up.' The essence of the task, he realised, was to start to sift 'the potential evil in myself', otherwise – like most other people – he was simply projecting his own unconscious guilt on to everyone else.

Another angle on this task of looking at oneself with the utmost honesty was conveyed in a letter to Laurens van der Post by his friend the distinguished psychiatrist Alan McGlashan: 'The depth of darkness into which you can descend, and still live', he wrote, 'is an exact measure, I believe, of the height to which you can aspire to reach.'

In *The Mystery of Physical Life* Watson also writes about meeting Jung at Küsnacht in April 1960, when they discussed possible ways of looking for the origins of the patterns in plant and animal behaviour, and in the metamorphosis of growth. Jung apparently dismissed the Darwinian idea of evolution through chance and natural selection alone, as being too simple to account for the contradictions in the ways of what he called 'the Elfin Goddess of Life'. It is a view increasingly expressed, even among many biologists, who recognise that although natural selection clearly operates within a particular species, it doesn't fully explain the great transitions that have taken place in nature as a whole, nor the origin of life itself. Darwin describes in wonderful detail how organisms adapt and evolve, and how those that are unfit are eliminated – but not how they arose in the first place.

A huge amount has been written about Darwin recently, prompted by two anniversaries, the 200th of his birth, and the 150th since the publication of *On the Origin of Species*. Most of what has appeared has been largely uncritical, but in an article for the magazine *Resurgence* (Jan/Feb 2009) the biologist Brian Goodwin suggests that some of the assumptions on which Darwin's ideas about evolution are founded 'have now become new superstitions and dogmas that are not enlightening, but enslaving and limiting'. Goodwin goes on to point out that science has moved on significantly since 1859 'in recognising how theories reflect their historical context, and need to be continually re-evaluated – and Darwin's ideas are no exception'.

As a man of his time, Darwin accepted that science was about observation, measurement and quantities. 'Qualities such as health, beauty and integrity', writes Goodwin, 'were not part of the scientific toolkit'. The transformation of Darwin's theory of evolution into 'a liberating vision for the 21st century' is Goodwin's plea. 'Quantities tell us about the properties of the parts', he writes; 'qualities tell us about the condition of the whole ... They cannot be separated from our study of nature without losing something essential ... What we need is a science of qualities and quantities.'

At the conclusion of *The Descent of Man*, written twelve years after *On the Origin of Species*, Darwin asserts that despite our 'noble qualities' and our 'god-like intellect', despite 'all these exalted powers – Man still bears in his bodily frame the indelible stamp of his lowly origin'. And if, indeed, our bodily frame is all that we study and take seriously, then it's easy to see why Richard Dawkins and his like uphold Darwin's observations as virtual proof that no creative principle is at work in the evolutionary process. Yet in fairness to Darwin it should be noted that in the same book, *The Descent of Man*, he writes: 'Important as the struggle for existence has been and even still is, yet as far as the highest part of our nature is concerned there are other agencies more important.' If, however, we confine our gaze to what the physical senses reveal, without acknowledging and nurturing what is not physical in our surroundings and in our own make-up – what Darwin called these 'other agencies' – we will only see evidence of those lowly origins. The human genome, for example, indicates that there is surprisingly little difference between a human being and a banana; even less so between a human being and a chimpanzee. Yet there is clearly a huge difference – a difference that is not going to be understood until we look with new eyes, and until we work out of the kind of science advocated by Brian Goodwin. Only then, perhaps, will we begin to understand the true nature of our common ancestry.

At their meeting in Switzerland, Jung and Watson both edged in this direction, discussing two alternatives to the Darwinian theory, which might account for the unfolding of life on earth, in all its wonder and complexity. In *The Mystery of Physical Life* Watson writes:

> Either there is an emergent impulse which manifests in a developing consciousness linked with an increasing complication in form, something akin to the entelechy of Aristotle and the vitalism of some modern schools; or else there has been, and, continues to be, a descent of the Spirit, as believed by the Gnostics and some of the early Christians.

E. L. Grant Watson

The first possibility was the one explored in our own time by the Jesuit palaeontologist Teilhard de Chardin, and is even implicit in Richard Dawkins's notion of cultural genes that he called 'memes' – as outlined in his book *The Selfish Gene*. The problem with that theory, as I see it, was already summed up over two thousand years ago in the saying by Parmenides I have already quoted: 'Nothing can come out of nothing.'

Watson sums up the second possibility that he discussed with Jung as a gradual incarnation of the Logos: 'In the beginning was the Word, and the Word was with God, and the Word was God.' In this scenario the Logos or Word, which contains all potentialities, only gradually becomes incarnate. 'Jung did not commit himself to either of these alternatives', writes Watson, 'nor did he deny either.' Apparently he did challenge the word Logos, but when Watson suggested that the archetypes in the unconscious were objective spiritual realities, Jung agreed. He warned, however, against using the terminology of the Church – words like Logos – unless you are prepared to abandon any claim to scientific reasoning. 'You can't put new wine into old bottles', Jung said. 'If you try to do so you will have a hundred thousand scientists against you, and you will be alone.'

Watson's whole book, nevertheless, is a courageous exploration, in the face of scientific scepticism, of the idea that plants, animals, and humanity itself present different expressions of such an incarnation. And it's interesting to bear in mind in this debate that although the physical characteristics of an organism (the colour of eyes, hair, skin, and so on in the case of the human being) are determined genetically, the origin of form remains one of the major unanswered questions of biology.

In his book Watson goes on to point out that philosophers from Plato to Hegel assumed that all natural objects are the expression of thought. Life is not a by-product of matter. Spirit is primary. Not only theologians and philosophers have thought this way. Watson quotes the German naturalist, Heinrich Steffens, who suggested that animals are 'fixed ideas incarnate', thereby implying that the formative idea behind incarnation has become, in Watson's words, 'rounded off and fixed within the limitations of the species. It has, as it were, been jettisoned from the onward moving stream of evolution.'

Such thoughts correspond in many ways to a crucial aspect of Steiner's research and suggestions, explored in depth by a biologist I mentioned previously, Hermann Poppelbaum. In *Man and Animal* Poppelbaum describes the human being not as some chance descendant from the animal kingdom, but rather – in his archetypal form – as the *ancestor* not just of animals, but of all living things; what he calls 'the centre of gravity in the kingdoms of nature'. In his autobiography Grant Watson expresses a similar thought: 'Man is an archetype and from him the apes have been devolved.' Or, in Gary Lachman's words, in summarising Steiner's teachings on this subject: 'Apes and other animals are not the "raw material" out of which homo sapiens emerged, but are instead evolutionary cul-de-sacs stemming off from the main branch of human development.' Philip Toynbee, in his journal, refers to 'the frozen self-containment of those lovely creatures, the swan and the puma'.

Poppelbaum elaborates further on this unusual, and indeed scientifically heretical theory:

Man, not the final product of evolution, but from primordial times
its hidden source ... The human soul, no longer a further and more
highly developed animal soul, but the harmonious and uncorrupted
archetype in which the animal soul is contained as a part ... The
human spirit no longer the reflex of the nervous system, but the
microcosmic reflection of the Divine ... The whole man the key to
the physical and spiritual universe.

Poppelbaum then adds that our morality, as it evolves in earthly life, can be
imagined as 'the seed of a cosmic future'.

The debate, or perhaps I should say feud, between the so-called
evolutionists on the one hand, and the creationists on the other, rages on –
and will, I suspect, continue to do so for many years. Some of those inclined
towards the creationist camp have adopted the label 'intelligent design', which
conveniently avoids the word 'God', but by implication rejects the idea that
random mutation and natural selection alone can account for the created
world as we know it. But there are other hypotheses, like the one suggested
by Poppelbaum and Watson – one which echoes, consciously or otherwise,
what Plato wrote in the *Timaeus* concerning the process of devolution from
the human archetype. This hypothesis steers us along an unfashionable but
far more challenging middle road, in which a certain truth is recognised in
both the creationist's and the evolutionist's viewpoints.

In an article in *The Guardian* (January 6th 2009) Thomas Crowley,
Professor of Geosciences at the University of Edinburgh, responded to
the outcry prompted by the suggestion that creationism should be taught
in secondary school science courses by pointing out that things are not as
clear-cut as we tend to think, and that there are at least two definitions of
creationism. 'A hard definition', he wrote, 'is that the earth is about 6,000
years old and that God created man and all the other creatures as in the Book
of Genesis. This definition is out of line with virtually all scientific evidence
and cannot fit in a science course.' Crowley then describes a softer definition,
and one not so easily dismissed:

Although science can state a great deal about what followed after
the big bang, it cannot in fact explain how 'something' (the energy of
the universe compressed into a volume the size of a golf ball) arose
from nothing beforehand. ... This yawning logical gap leaves open
the possibility that something else may be going on.'

His conclusion is that as long as science cannot explain how the universe
evolved from nothing, scientists should not be in such a hurry to write off a
more subtle, 'softer' version of creationism.

In relation to this debate, the biologist Rupert Sheldrake has spoken to me of the creative capacity that he sees as *inherent* in all living things, thereby implying – for me, at least – that what was previously understood as outside of us and somehow in control, now exists (and perhaps always existed) in creation itself. Aristotle used the Greek word *entelekheia* to describe a state of being in which something is actively working to be itself.

In the preface to his courageous book *A New Science of Life*, which the editor of the scientific journal *Nature* savaged as 'the best candidate for burning there has been for many years', Sheldrake writes:

> Most biologists take it for granted that living organisms are nothing but complex machines, governed only by the known laws of physics and chemistry. I myself used to share this point of view. But over a period of several years I came to see that such an assumption is difficult to justify. For when so little is actually understood, there is an open possibility that at least some of the phenomena of life depend on laws or factors as yet unrecognised by the physical sciences.

It is some of these unrecognised 'laws or factors' that Sheldrake goes on to explore in his book, and has continued to explore in his work despite the scientific Inquisition to which he has often been subjected. For example, in his theory of morphic resonance, he suggests that the laws of nature are really more like habits: 'a plant takes up the form characteristic of its species because past members of the species took up that form; and an animal acts instinctively in a particular manner because similar animals behaved like that previously.' This hypothesis challenges the mechanistic theory 'that everything in the universe can be explained from the bottom up, as it were, in terms of the properties of atoms, or indeed of any hypothetical ultimate particles'. It also suggests that in an evolving universe, and therefore in nature itself, there are no fixed laws as such, but rather an eternal dynamic and interplay between habit and creativity.

However, as a scientist with no claims to be clairvoyant, Sheldrake makes an important and understandable point about morphic resonance when he writes: 'This hypothesis is concerned with the repetition of forms and patterns of organisation; the question of the origin of these forms and patterns lies outside its scope.' This question of origins, it could be argued, lies outside everyone's scope, particularly as it implies the dimension of time which, although very real to us, may be ultimately misleading. Steiner does attempt to convey a picture of origins – but only so far back, and still within the framework of time – in his book *Occult Science*. Some would say it is a task for the imagination rather than the intellect, and that knowledge of such mysteries is beyond either our abilities or our comprehension.

For reasons already stated, I do not believe in such limitations. Why should humanity's long search grind to a halt with us? There must have been numerous instances throughout history when we – or, if you prefer, our ancestors – were faced with what seemed insurmountable barriers to further knowledge and understanding. It is this aspect of Richard Dawkins's message with which I am in complete sympathy. But the way forward may not just be either greater intelligence, or a synthesis of intellect and imagination, but rather a metamorphosis of those faculties into a new way of knowing altogether.

In one way this human journey of discovery is continually mirrored in the unfolding of our individual lives. At the age of seven I was not only ignorant of many of the things I now know, but more importantly was completely incapable, at that stage of my development, of grasping those facts and insights. At seventy I know a little more, but in no way do I feel 'That's it!' Just as I have learned a little each day, each month, each year of my life, so I trust that I will continue to grow and mature through many lifetimes. And there will, I hope, always be courageous people like the alchemist in A.A. Milne's poem of that name, who are prepared to go on exploring, often alone and frequently mocked or persecuted, even if the proof – the repeatable and therefore verifiable experiment – initially eludes them:

The Alchemist, by E.H. Shepard

There lives an old man at the top of the street,
And the end of his beard reaches down to his feet,
And he's just the one person I'm longing to meet,
I think that he sounds so exciting;
For he talks all the day to his tortoiseshell cat,
And he asks about this, and explains about that,
And at night he puts on a big wide-awake hat
And sits in the writing room, writing.

He has worked all his life (and he's terribly old)
At a wonderful spell which says, 'Lo, and behold!
Your nursery fender is gold!' – and it's gold!
(Or the tongs, or the rod for the curtain);
But somehow he hasn't got hold of it quite,
Or the liquid you pour on first isn't right,
So that's why he works at it night after night
Till he knows he can do it for certain.

I have found some very helpful clues to this whole subject of what we call 'the natural world', evolution and our own place in it, tucked away in one of Rudolf Steiner's very early books, *Christianity as Mystical Fact*. The book itself attempts to show how the ground from which Christianity arose was prepared in the Mystery schools of pre-Christian times. Steiner does, however, already in the preface declare his conviction that a modern form of mysticism will only develop from methods acquired through natural science, and therefore by implication in full consciousness. He advocates here, as he continued to do throughout his life, that the supersensible realm can and should be investigated with the same diligence that scientists use to investigate the sense-perceptible world. But in doing so, he warns of the prejudice against a spiritual dimension to existence that so many people carry, 'confused as they are by their exclusive observation of physical phenomena'. The importance of impartiality is what he emphasises, whatever one happens to be investigating:

An eye would be a bad eye if, from its own point of view, it did not assert the unconditional reality of its perceptions. The eye is right as far as it goes, and is not deprived of its due by the eye of the spirit. The latter only allows us to see the things of the sense in a higher light. Nothing seen by the eye of sense is denied, but a new brightness radiates from what is seen.

It is this experience of seeing things 'in a higher light' that Steiner describes in relation to the path of initiation in the ancient Mysteries – in Greece, in particular. The candidate for initiation was gradually led to an experience of what was called 'the hidden god', who can never be found through the senses alone. Neither our reason nor our imagination can truly grasp the divine, he was told. 'God lies spellbound in the world and you need his own power to find him. You must awaken that power in yourself.' These are the words that Steiner uses to evoke the profound ritual of initiation. 'Where is God?' he continues:

> This was the question asked by the soul of the mystic. God is not existence, but nature exists. And in nature he must be discovered. There he has found an enchanted grave. It was in a higher sense that the mystic understood the words, 'God is love.' For God has exalted that love to its climax; he has sacrificed himself in infinite love; he has poured himself out, dismembered himself in the manifold things of nature. Things in nature live and he does not live in them. He rests in them. He lives in the human being. And we can experience the life of God in ourselves. If we are to come to knowledge of God, we must release this knowledge creatively in ourselves.

It is this experience that Meister Eckhart and others throughout the Middle Ages were arriving at out of their own efforts – and a very different picture from the 'lowly origin' to which Darwin referred.

Steiner goes on to describe how, for the mystic, there is in the soul 'a sacred place' where this spellbound divinity may be set free. He calls the soul the mother, who through her interaction with nature can give birth to the divine. 'Out of the marriage of the soul with nature, the divine is born', he writes. 'No longer a "hidden", but a manifest divinity.' In other words, only through life on earth can this profound event take place; Steiner calls it 'the spirit in the human being released from enchantment, the offspring of the spellbound God'. This is not God himself, but rather a revelation of him: 'The Father remains at rest in the unseen; the Son is born to man out of his own soul.' Steiner concludes this extraordinary picture with these words:

> The uninitiated person has no experience of the Father of this offspring, for the Father slumbers under a spell. The Son appears to be born of a virgin, the soul having seemingly given birth to him without impregnation. All her other children are conceived by the sense-world. Their father can be seen and touched, for he has material existence. The divine offspring alone is begotten of the eternal, hidden Father – God himself.

In his autobiography Grant Watson acknowledges that there is no 'scientific evidence' for many of Rudolf Steiner's statements, 'but his sweep of thought and imagination was bold, and often so vigorous as to carry my native scepticism well off the ground of its ordinary mundane activities'. Steiner's response – and Goethe's too – would be, I believe, that these statements are verifiable as and when we develop the organs of perception that correspond to the realm we are investigating; but that unlike our other, naturally-endowed senses, our expanding consciousness and these new faculties have to be nurtured by our own efforts, primarily through meditation; but nurtured hand in hand with an ever deepening morality, if we are to avoid the pitfalls of spiritual egotism, and slipping into all sorts of delusions regarding a personal hotline to God. In this respect what impressed Watson were three particular words that Steiner emphasised as indicating windows into a greater sensitivity towards life and other people. One was *appreciation* – becoming ever more aware of the multitude of things that prompted and warranted admiration. Then came *gratitude*, and out of gratitude grows a feeling of *reverence*. Watson quotes the opening of the Lord's Prayer, 'Hallowed be thy Name': 'Hallowed through appreciation, through gratitude, through reverence', he writes. 'This is an idea which I find increasingly solid and useful.'

Meanwhile Steiner maintained that if we simply live with his ideas and insights as hypotheses we will eventually find that the pattern they make is a consistent one, and indeed – according to Watson – offers the most rational explanation of the cosmos. However, in his anthology of Steiner's writings and lectures, *The Essential Steiner*, the philosopher Robert McDermott acknowledges on page one of his introduction that Steiner's claims 'to privileged knowledge immediately, and rightly, render his writings suspect'. He adds that it is neither surprising nor unfortunate that occult or esoteric thinkers are subject to special scrutiny. Steiner himself welcomed such scrutiny, insisting that his claims ought not to be accepted as a matter of belief. 'He referred to his teachings as spiritual science', writes McDermott, 'precisely because he practised and advocated a phenomenological, or empirical, approach to the spiritual world.'

Nevertheless, Watson had reservations about aspects of Steiner's work and his anthroposophy. 'All that he says about the Hierarchies of the Angels leaves me outside its range', he writes. That seems a reasonable way of reacting, which is not totally dismissive and corresponds to what I've called my 'kipper territory' – putting on one side what we cannot cope with. But Watson then goes further:

I feel puzzled and uncertain and refuse to take the attitude of so many of Rudolf Steiner's followers, that all he says must be true. Even if it were true for him, I argue, it is not true for me, unless it rings with my own experience.

I don't actually think that Steiner – who, as McDermott points out, saw himself first and foremost as a scientist and spiritual researcher – would be troubled by that thought; nor indeed by the one that Watson adds to it:

> In the way of discovery and belief a man must not hurry one step in advance of personal experience. Ideologies can easily be formed. Their bonds not so easily escaped from. Surely we live in an age when ideologies, any kind of ideologies, are our greatest danger.

A similar concern about ideologies is expressed by Jonathan Black in a section on 'sources and bibliography' at the end of *The Secret History of the World*. Black refers to Steiner as 'a colossal figure in arcane circles ... He has done more than any other teacher to illumine the difficult and paradoxical world of esoteric philosophy', but Black then indicates his reservations with these words: 'I think a problem with Steiner is that he is such a great figure that people who follow in his footsteps find it hard to think freely and independently. Steiner's shadow can inhibit originality.' This has, of course, been a challenge facing the followers of any great figure since time immemorial. It is a danger that was clearly articulated by Krishnamurti in an address called 'Truth is a Pathless Land' that he gave in 1929 when he dissolved the Order of the Star which had been created around him:

> I maintain that Truth is a pathless land, and you cannot approach it by any path whatsoever, by any religion, by any sect ... A belief is purely an individual matter, and you cannot and must not organise it. If you do, it becomes dead, crystallised; it becomes a creed, a sect, a religion, to be imposed on others ... You are all depending for your spirituality on someone else, for your happiness on someone else, for your enlightenment on someone else ... When I say look within yourselves for the enlightenment, for the glory, for the purification, and for the uncorruptibility of the self, not one of you is willing to do it. There may be a few, but very, very few. So why have an organisation?

With Jung's legacy this tendency towards fossilisation had been less of a problem, partly because of the numerous splits that have taken place since his death in the school of psychology he inspired. Although such quarrelling is a puzzle to outsiders (surely these people are on the same side?) it does prevent an orthodoxy establishing itself. Jung was also very conscious of people's tendency to turn important insights and intimations into some sort of new religion, and was therefore deliberately tentative in many of his pronouncements.

What for some people is a stumbling block in relating to Steiner is the claim of his followers that he not only went further than Jung, but that he belonged in that long line of what esotericists recognise as initiates – people who can, to a considerable degree, 'see' as well as 'look'. In his book *Meditation as a Contemplative Inquiry*, Arthur Zajonc sums up Steiner's detailed presentation of his supersensible experiences as 'an extraordinary example of a modern, scientifically orientated, and philosophically trained contemplative who is writing and speaking directly out of his meditative experience'. However, the presence of an 'initiate' in an age that seems to be increasingly encouraging us to think and experience for ourselves, presents a paradox. At the very least, I believe – wherever we are on our journey – we owe Steiner, and teachers like him, the sort of respect and gratitude that holds us back from being mere followers. In *Thus Spake Zarathustra* Friedrich Nietzsche writes: 'One ill repays one's teacher by remaining only his student.'

After Steiner's death in 1925 there was for many years a split in the anthroposophical movement – a split that has now healed. At one level one can look back and see that division as stemming from what we quite simply call 'personality clashes'. At another level there are those who see such conflicts, which continue to surface from time to time, as having deep and significant karmic roots. Without dismissing the more esoteric explanation, I tend to see the problem as very often a matter of temperament (though temperament itself may be something we bring from the past) – a division between those who want to work quietly and diligently with Steiner's legacy, and those who feel the urge to take the ideas out into the world and interact with others. I personally believe both paths, inner and outer, are necessary and important, and in no way contradictory. What matters is that people recognise the validity of those in a different camp; that the extrovert values and appreciates the introvert, and vice versa. Although a peacemaker by nature and therefore someone who welcomes the healing of splits wherever possible, I also recognise that healthy debate and even divisions can be valuable in preventing dogmatic orthodoxy establishing itself when people unite for the wrong reasons, whether prompted by fear, loneliness or ignorance.

First Goetheanum

Second Goetheanum

Jung understood very well our need to be alone sometimes, as part of the process of learning to stand on our own two feet. At Bollingen he built his tower where he could commune in peace with what he sensed as the eternal aspect of his being. Steiner, it seems, didn't need an actual place for himself alone in order to have that inner dialogue. He too, however, created a building, the Goetheanum in Switzerland – first in wood and then, after a fire in 1923, in concrete. It was, and still is, a place for anyone to come in search of spiritual renewal and the company of like-minded people.

Rudolf Steiner in 1914

Had Steiner lived to the same sort of age as Jung, he too might have needed to escape at times and lead a more tranquil existence. Jung was eighty-five when he died; Steiner was only sixty-four, worn out by the demands made on him by his followers and victim of an unexplained illness. Perhaps he might also have worked harder at persuading those followers to stand on their own feet, and to abandon or modify some of the labels that he himself introduced in the early days – not least, maybe, the word 'anthroposophy' itself. For in the end he was only doing – albeit with great dedication and in an appropriately contemporary way – what philosophers, mystics, scientists and artists have done throughout history: namely contributing to the long tradition of human enquiry. As will be perfectly clear from what I've written, I am one of those who believe Steiner's work represents a profound turning-point in that quest; but I am concerned that by giving it a special name – anthroposophy – Steiner's contribution tends to become isolated from everything else that is taking place as men and women all over the world pray, think, and use their imaginations as they have always done. Nor do people, and particularly young and thoughtful people, want labels any more; they belong instinctively to their time and not to any ideology or 'ism'. To call oneself an 'anthroposophist', therefore, I find increasingly problematic.

I may, of course, be quite wrong in my reaction. I can see that for some of Steiner's followers it is helpful and reasonable to think of anthroposophy as a new branch of science – hence the expression 'spiritual science' – which involves research into the human being and the natural world not only as they manifest physically, but also in terms of soul and spirit; and, most importantly, a science in which life is recognised as an interweaving of these three elements which at present we still tend to study under the separate disciplines of science, psychology and religion. In this sense the label 'anthroposophy' (as opposed to 'anthroposophist') is perhaps, for the time being, both appropriate and justified.

It is clear, however, that many people – including even some who call themselves anthroposophists – have a difficulty with the tone of some of Steiner's communications, whatever name you give them. In his autobiography Grant Watson writes of his problem with 'this cloak of virtue and commanding goodness and all-knowingness', saying that he preferred what he called 'the cleaner, franker atmosphere which surrounds Dr Jung's writings'. Jung was certainly able to communicate and inspire in a way that leaves us free to go on exploring. Some of Steiner's pronouncements, on the other hand, can have the opposite and almost paralysing effect. Rupert Sheldrake has on several occasions described to me his difficulty in reading Steiner simply because the material comes over as 'too dogmatic'. Philip Toynbee, in his autobiographical journal *Part of a Journey* wrote:

> I can get no help at all from the occult. Perhaps there do exist intermediate orders of reality between Earth and Heaven. Yet when I try to read Steiner or Gurdjieff I am immediately irritated by their purple gateways, green-clad guides and magic runes. Such super-confidence in the way they map out these areas for us!

I can understand such reactions, though I suspect Toynbee had read very little of either Gurdjieff or Steiner – voices that were simply not on his wavelength. For me, however, the content and the general thrust of Steiner's teachings has been so powerful, convincing, and helpful that I have never been put off by what for some is a rather dry and old-fashioned style – particularly in some of the printed lectures. In fact the most helpful glimpse I have had into what Steiner must have been like as a communicator emerges from the talks he gave between 1922 and 1924 at the request of the workmen at the Goetheanum – carpenters, plumbers and painters – later published in seven volumes with cheerful titles like *From Crystals to Crocodiles* and *From Comets to Cocaine*. His spontaneous and lively responses to their very real and penetrating questions are noticeably free of the rather more formal and solemn tone of his lectures to members of the Anthroposophical Society. There are also some good jokes that he was clearly happy to share with these men who had that common sense and lack of prejudice that can exist quite naturally among people who are not over-educated. With them, therefore, Steiner had absolutely no inhibitions about calling a spiritual spade a spiritual spade.

In the chaotic years following the end of the World War I Steiner was also involved in some very practical efforts to address social problems; and above all he was working with ideas that aimed to transform the role of government in human affairs. Once again he found himself talking to large audiences of ordinary working people, as he had done at the turn of the century when he lectured at the Workers' Educational Institute in Berlin.

One of his main concerns was the state's tendency to have its fingers in too many pies. In his opinion, shared by many others both then and now, the role of government should be confined to protecting its citizens from internal and external threat; to making sure that none of those citizens fall through the net in terms of basic welfare; and to upholding the independence of the judiciary. In education, he believed teachers and parents should determine what is taught, not politicians. The government's role is merely to make sure that every child has access to that education. Likewise industry and commerce should not be the business of the government – other than in a certain regulatory role.

In formulating his ideas Steiner would sometimes speak about giving the old ideals of the French Revolution – *liberté, egalité, fraternité* – a new, more detailed and clearer realism, rather than seeing them as some magic package for solving all our problems under one simplistic banner. He advocated, therefore, 'freedom' in the cultural and religious sphere; 'equality' before the law; and cooperation and enterprise – 'fraternity' – in the economic sphere, with greater emphasis on associations of producers and consumers. He was also concerned that an individual's capacity for work should not be degraded to the level of a commodity. Nor, indeed, that money itself should be treated as a commodity, whereby money can be made from money.

This threefold nature of society mirrored and corresponded to what Steiner perceived as the threefold nature of the human being. His efforts here were not ultimately taken further, owing in part to a combination of mistrust among trade union officials, the self-interest of entrepreneurs, and the unwillingness of politicians themselves to consider anything radically new. Steiner also finally recognised that the timing was simply not right and he withdrew from that area of work. Given the current financial turmoil, it seems that those three strands – all of which have quite distinct qualities – remain hopelessly and unhelpfully entangled.

Returning to the subject of Steiner's style in general, I think it's important to be aware of the cultural atmosphere in which he found himself in those early years of the 20th century. Communication between people at every level of society was much more formal than it is today – hence the surprising freshness of Steiner's interaction with those workmen. Also, as well as having to increasingly distance himself from the theosophical movement, he had to fight his corner from many other directions – in particular from the scientific and philosophical communities, as well as from the Roman Catholic Church. Jung faced similar challenges some years later, particularly because, like Steiner, he wanted his ideas to come over as scientifically respectable – 'hence his reluctance to make more public the extent of his use of astrology', writes Tarnas in *Cosmos and Psyche*: 'In the context of 20th-century beliefs and the dominance of scientific thinking, he had already pressed the boundaries of intellectual discourse about as far as could be sustained.'

This sense of being cornered was one of the reasons, I suppose, why Steiner came over at times – unintentionally, I'm sure – as trying to sell anthroposophy like a soap powder; what advertisers call 'a hard sell'. Anthroposophy washes whiter! But according to the many accounts I've read by people who knew and worked with Steiner, he was not a crude proselytiser, but a gentle, sensitive and kind man who gave himself fully to whoever came for help and advice. Another reminiscence of the Russian artist Andrei Belyi is very revealing in this respect:

> In his kindness, the demands he made upon himself were unending. 'Compassion has its limits', Mariya Yakovlevna said to him. But he replied: 'No, compassion has no limits.' Of love he said: 'It is a giving faculty. The more one gives, the more one has to give.'

Steiner also struggled, as do all seers, to find the appropriate and most helpful words to describe experiences and realms of existence for which, for very understandable reasons, we have as yet so few. Gary Lachman sums up his understanding of Steiner's life and work, simply yet profoundly, as 'an attempt to get human beings to recognise who they really are'.

Grant Watson was clearly someone who benefited from this attempt to which Lachman refers, as he did from Jung's pioneering work in studying the human psyche. In the title to his thoughtful and challenging book, Watson chose the word 'mystery' in relation to physical life. I have barely mentioned his many beautiful and perceptive descriptions of the physical world, which he spent so many hours and years contemplating. The Australian poet and critic, Dorothy Green, in the anthology of Watson's writings that she edited, wrote:

> In his image of the transformation of the butterfly through a series of violent deaths from larva to imago, Watson leaves open the possibility that we may be living through a period of stupendous breakdown which seems like death and destruction to those experiencing it, but which may also be the precursor to some unimaginable development of the human spirit.

Through his observations, research, and ponderings Watson ultimately came to believe that there is what he called 'a discarnate universe of thought':

> In life we are in the presence of something which transcends material form. Life leads us into the region of what has been vaguely named spirit; by thinking about life, rather than about things, we enter into the spiritual world.

Yet so often, it seems, the physical sciences – whether dissecting the atom or peering into the majestic infinity of space – come face to face with this 'spiritual world' but are unable or unwilling to recognise it as such: in their eyes the Emperor is fully clothed. It is a blindness that is even more powerfully expressed in the opening lines of St John's Gospel: 'He was in the world, and the world was made by Him, and the world knew Him not.'

Instead many people, no longer just scientists, still tend to resort to abstractions – the kind of language that explains very clearly the mechanisms of our own making, but struggles to explain life itself. Watson, and many others like him, maintained that if we are courageous and honest enough to assume that there is an invisible yet objective environment which manifests itself as the objects our senses perceive, we could find facts to support it. But he knew only too well, as an artist as well as a scientist, how difficult it is to convey such mysteries. He had gleaned much from both Jung and Steiner, but I sense that his real hero was Goethe 'who did not dogmatise so freely about the supersensible as did Steiner'. Poor old Steiner, in trouble again! But as a fellow Englishman I, too, am often drawn to intimations rather than pronouncements, to Betjeman rather than Pevsner. 'If there must be prophets', wrote Watson in his autobiography, 'let them be poets who speak in images.'

So out of respect for a courageous and imaginative pioneer in the movement to reconcile science and spirituality, I will give the final word in this chapter to a poet, Walt Whitman, who wrote in 'Song of Myself', in his anthology *Leaves of Grass*: 'I hear and behold God in every object, yet understand God not in the least.'

Chapter 30

Light in the Darkness

'Blooming Christmas here again', says Raymond Briggs's wonderful portrayal of Father Christmas. And so it continues: 'Blooming snow ...Blooming chimneys ... Blooming feet frozen'. But things do eventually improve, once the presents are delivered: 'Nothing like a good bath ... Nice clean socks ... Good drop of ale ... Lovely grub'; and all this despite 'Blooming awful tie from Aunt Elsie' and 'Horrible socks from cousin Violet'.

For some time I had wanted to make a film on the subject of Christmas which, for an increasing number of people – including, it seems, Father Christmas himself – is approached in a spirit of dread rather than celebration; dread, above all, of those many pressures and obligations, both social and commercial. No wonder people eat and drink too much.

Yet in our hearts we know that somehow it should be different. Christmas – not just as a Christian festival, but as a celebration of the return of light into our lives as the days start to get longer again – cries out to be acknowledged as the annual culmination of our inner life of reflection and hope. Instead it is increasingly a ritual in which we indulge all that is acquisitive and escapist in our natures, in the form of excessive consumption and too many possessions. Thus it becomes a disturbing reminder of what we mistakenly worship.

So it came about that in 1992, as one of my early projects as a freelance director, I made *Another Christmas* for the BBC series *Everyman* – a long-running and much respected strand from the Religious Programmes department, a strand which now no longer exists.

My proposal, and other projects that followed, also stemmed from my urge to continue exploring and testing in the here and now some of the profound ideas that had preoccupied me for decades. I was fifty-four years old, and by now more or less at peace with the Narziss and Goldmund – the spiritual and the worldly – within myself. But I still had many questions in relation to the themes that run through this book, the answers to which I continued to feel lay concealed not only in my ever-growing pile of books and in what I had absorbed from giants such as Tolstoy, Gandhi, Jung and Steiner, but also in the lives of my fellow human beings, if I listened attentively enough. For although my own philosophy of life was emerging more clearly, I felt it was important to go on learning more about the many different ways that other people make sense of their lives, even if the philosophy that some of them adopt is articulated as a rejection of any sense of meaning or purpose to life. In other words I wanted to better appreciate and truly respect the uniqueness and validity of every human journey. And so, for the next ten years or so, I was to meet an extraordinary range of new and interesting people from all over Europe and as far away as Pakistan, all of whom, in their different ways, enriched my own quest and made important contributions to this book's conclusions.

For some of us the festival of Christmas is still a supreme moment when earth and heaven become one through the birth of the child Jesus; and maybe this union is there at the birth of every child – an event which we repeatedly and rightly experience as a miracle full of potential. And so, within ten miles of where I lived in Gloucestershire, I filmed a number of very different people, all striving in their own way to celebrate Christmas in a meaningful way.

Eric Pycroft was a retired Anglican priest who in appearance was not unlike Raymond Briggs's glorious creation. He too liked his grub, but there the similarities ended. Twice a week, in a converted cowshed at the bottom of his garden, he met with a small group of people for an hour or so – largely in silence. 'If you are to hear the word of God', he said, 'you have to listen. If your pattern of prayer is always one of talking, of telling God what he ought to be doing about his world, and so on – well, how do you hear? And there is a well-established tradition of learning to be silent, of letting go of all the ideas, concepts, images – all of that – and then you discover something; you discover that within yourself there is a profound silence which begins to inform your whole life and the way you live.'

Eric spoke to me later about what he saw as three ways of expressing one's relationship to God. One is primarily expressed in terms of working in the community and in helping people directly. The second is primarily through worship. Lastly there is what Eric called 'the inner way'. He acknowledged that ideally all three of these elements should play their part. 'But what I want to emphasise,' he said, 'is that this contemplative dimension needs to be present.'

I have tended to be drawn to people who fall into the first category – those who 'worship' by serving others. It is why I was so touched by the legend of The Other Wise Man, whose gifts for the infant Jesus he gradually gave away to those in need. It was this same gesture of compassion that so impressed me about the nuns who looked after children like Anne-Marie. Gandhi seems to me one of the most striking modern examples of this altruism in action – though in relation to Eric Pycroft's point about the 'contemplative dimension', it's interesting that Gandhi, prompted perhaps by his Hindu background and tradition, kept totally silent for one day every week.

One of the people sharing the silence of Eric Pycroft's cowshed was the artist Oliver Heywood. He spoke to me later about what Christmas represented for him: 'an extraordinary mystery of the universal becoming manifest within the individual', exemplified to a sublime degree in the birth and life of Jesus. He also pointed out that it's probably no coincidence that the date on which we celebrate Christmas coincides more or less with the winter solstice in the northern hemisphere, after which the sun begins to get warmer, darkness recedes and the days gradually lengthen. This moment has been celebrated since far back in time; Heywood described it as an indication of the potentiality for new life – what he called 'the seed that lives in each one of us, ready to be warmed into new life'. (It was, incidentally, Oliver Heywood's son, Pip, who edited with great skill and sensitivity this film and many of my other productions in the years ahead.)

I also included in *Another Christmas* a modest yet very sincere example of this wish and need to serve, to put the other person first, and not only at Christmas; it's an instinct that most people experience in varying degrees, if only in relation to their own families. Marjorie Leaney was one of the Meals on Wheels drivers on duty near us, delivering the special Christmas dinners. One of her customers, Bill Neaves – a retired forester – had been widowed for three years and was clearly very lonely. 'It's far more important that we have a word with him', said Marjorie, 'it's more important to him to have a chat than to have the meal, quite honestly.' Bill was also treated to a glass of sherry and a Christmas card from the drivers. With great enthusiasm and delight he told Marjorie about the jay he'd seen that morning in his garden, and I was reminded of Margaret McNeill's blackbird at the Quaker home in Bristol – 'Was it coincidence that the blackbird came?'

When Eric Pycroft talked to me about Christmas, he drew attention to what for him was profoundly significant about the two groups of people who first came into the presence of the infant Jesus. The first group were simple shepherds; the second, the three wise men: 'So you have at his birth', he said, 'an emphasis on simplicity and wisdom, and both of those are qualities which we need to recover. And I suppose you could say that the celebration of Christmas each year as it comes, gives us a fresh focus, a new opportunity – if we want to take it – to be stopped again in our tracks and to look and say: "Well, where is the simplicity, and where is the wisdom in the way that I am living?"'

To help convey what I felt was an essential aspect of the Christmas story I was drawn again to a community of young adults 'in need of special care'. Here simplicity in its most endearing form permeated much of their daily life – a small farm, a large and productive vegetable garden, and several workshops where they made simple and beautiful objects from wood, clay and wool.

Friedrich Roder

The Paradise Community takes its name from the hamlet where it is situated, on the edge of Painswick. In my experience the name is absolutely appropriate, though it would be wrong to over-sentimentalise the sometimes bizarre and even anti-social behaviour of some of the residents. The founders, Friedrich and Eli Roder, had experience in Camphill and have been deeply helped and inspired by many of Steiner's thoughts about human development and the aberrations that can occur.

Friedrich spoke with great warmth about the thirty or so young people in his care who, in his experience – because of what he called 'their special nature' – often had an enhanced capacity to feel and experience profound truths, 'having access to deeper layers of meaning which may be difficult for people who are purely intellectually orientated'. Referring to Christmas and to the nativity play they were rehearsing, he said that he wanted them initially to experience the mood, the story and the mystery – because in his view it is experience that leads to real understanding.

The play that we filmed at the Paradise Community, in rehearsal and then in performance, was the second in a trilogy of medieval plays that were rediscovered in the 19th century in a German-speaking enclave in Hungary. Friedrich Roder described to me a very touching and profound moment at the end of the first play when the angel drives Adam and Eve out of paradise, but comforts them with the knowledge that he will recall them again in a far-distant future. For Friedrich this event encapsulates the truth of humanity's spiritual history: 'Expulsion from paradise, entering into the physical, material world – into the materialism in which we live today – but then there is this promise that an angel, as it were, will call us back into a new state of paradise, into a new connection with spiritual realities.'

The first play is thus about humanity's suffering due to our expulsion from paradise, but it ends on this note of hope. The second play, the one they were performing, was the nativity play and is based on the story told in the Gospel of St Luke about the visit of the shepherds. It is a play, so Friedrich felt, about a deep, inner experience of compassion, of love. It tells of a child born in a stable, but also points to something that can come to birth inside each human heart.

The third play, based on the Gospel of St Matthew, has a very different mood. Central to the story is the figure of King Herod, and through him the forces of evil that also surround the sublime event in Bethlehem. But there is another presence – the power of wisdom, as represented by the Three Kings. They symbolise the possibility of true insight and understanding that can endure and ultimately help to defeat the evil in the world.

At that December afternoon rehearsal – still so present in my memory – while Jasmine, Martin and Sophie became for a while characters from a distant age, Friedrich Roder spoke to me about the two polarities of love and wisdom, as described by Luke and Matthew. He saw them as the potential living in every human being, from which can develop a harmonious future for mankind.

The final scene of my film was another conversation with Eric Pycroft – not this time in his cowshed, but in the local pub. Puffing away at his pipe, with a pint of beer in the other hand, he reminded me more than ever of Father Christmas – once the ordeal with chimneys, weather and reindeer was over!

'I wouldn't want to dampen down anyone's enthusiasm at all', he said, 'or the need to celebrate in the midst of winter, and to have a great feast if you like.' It

Eric Pycroft

was an appropriate statement, given the setting. He went on to say that what he felt to be so often missing was the central meaning of Christmas: 'We ought almost, as it were, to take our shoes off lest we trample on the meaning.'

Clearly he felt that meaning was being trampled on, not only by the secularised world, but also to a degree by the Church itself, which he saw as constantly in need of reformation, to counteract its tendency to become 'fossilised in the past' or 'over-influenced by contemporary society'. In Eric's opinion the Church is not always sufficiently open to people's deepest needs:

'It's offering them a kind of shell,' he said, 'instead of a centre; and I think there are many people seeking the centre.' And the meaning of Christmas that was evading us, he felt, was deeply connected with the Latin word *mysterium*, which means not a mystery – like some sort of puzzle which, if you were clever enough and worked long enough, you could solve – but rather 'the disclosure of something that's hidden, something that's already there. It's telling us something about ourselves which we can't see because we've got our blinkers on. We need to be able to see with what I would call the eye of the heart.'

To see with our eyes we need light. To see with the heart we need to be enlightened, thereby achieving insight. The clues are everywhere in the language we use from day to day. In the year that my film about Christmas was broadcast, an important book was published in America called *Catching the Light*, subtitled 'the entwined history of light and mind'. In it the author, Arthur Zajonc, Professor of Physics at Amherst College in Massachusetts – and someone with whom I have had deep and helpful conversations in recent years – explores the profound connection between the outer light of nature and the inner light of the human spirit. He calls his book 'a biography of that invisible companion who accompanies us inwardly as much as it does outwardly – light'. One reviewer of the book, Theodore van Vliet, sums up the essence of the story that Zajonc sets out to tell: 'Once light was worshipped as the presence of divinity in the world. This perception paled in time to a sense that divine forces lay behind and were speaking to us through sun, moon and stars, through lightning, rainbow and aurora'. But such sensitivity has gradually faded, except in the consciousness of poets and mystics. 'Meanwhile', writes van Vliet, 'natural science, enamoured of matter and the measurable, has set up its own idols to replace the gods.'

But light, it seems, defies such reductionism. Arthur Zajonc describes in his book what he calls Project Eureka in which he and a colleague have designed and constructed a scientific exhibit – a carefully fabricated box inside of which one can view a space filled with light from a powerful projector. Yet when there is no object in the box we see only darkness. Only when an object is inserted into the box do we see anything. 'Light itself is always invisible', writes Arthur. 'We see only things, only objects, not light.'

He writes, too, about what he calls the 'inner light', prompted in part by examples of people cured of blindness but who initially are unable to make sense of what they see. Vision, it seems, requires far more than a functioning physical organ. 'Besides an outer light and eye', Arthur points out, 'sight requires an "inner light", one whose luminance complements the familiar outer light and transforms raw sensation into meaningful perception. The light of the mind must flow into and marry with the light of nature to bring forth a world.'

Arthur Zajonc

Indeed it was Plato's view that two lights – an inner and an outer – come together as mediator between the human being and what Arthur calls 'a dark, cavernous external world'. But how will we see light tomorrow? asks Arthur at the end of his fascinating and scholarly survey of our whole cultural and scientific relationship with the phenomenon of light – from the Bhagavad Gita to Albert Einstein – and all that has been both learned and forgotten along the way. 'First, it will require the modest recognition', he writes, 'that we are all only partly sighted creatures, and so know only a part of nature.' He recognises, too, that 'the habits of our culture' and 'the dogmas of our education' constrain our sight, as they have always done. At present atoms have become 'immortal gods' and photons 'their stern messengers', but light remains as fundamentally mysterious as ever.

In the introduction to his *Theory of Colour*, Goethe wrote these lines:

Were the eye not of the sun,
How could we behold the light?
If God's might and ours were not as one,
How could His work enchant our sight?

Arthur Zajonc believes that during the last three centuries or so – with the notable exception of figures such as Goethe – the artistic and religious dimensions of light have been kept strictly separate from its scientific study. 'I feel the time has come', he writes, 'to welcome them back, and to craft a fuller image of light than any one discipline can offer.'

In recent years he has, among other things, been involved in a series of dialogues with the Dalai Lama, together with four other physicists and a historian. Their discussions on the philosophical implications of current thought in quantum physics in relation to Buddhism have now been published under the title *The New Physics and Cosmology*, and are another important contribution to our understanding of that most challenging question of all, the nature of reality. And reality, as more and more people are sensing, undoubtedly consists of 'more than meets the eye'. Any understanding, however, will be determined as ever by the questions we ask, as well as by the answers we are willing to accept.

'Seeing light', writes Arthur at the end of *Catching the Light*, 'is a metaphor for seeing the invisible in the visible, for detecting the fragile imaginal garment that holds our planet and all existence together. Once we have learned to see light, surely everything else will follow.'

As a healer, Elaine Heller works constantly with the invisible. She was one of the subjects in my next project – a series of ten films in which I talked to ten very different and thoughtful people about their inner journeys. One of Elaine's ambitions, she told me, was to work more closely with the medical profession, helping to show doctors 'that reality doesn't stop at the physical'. The essence of what she did with her patients, she explained, was to try to put them in touch with their own spirituality and with a sense for what they are really meant to be doing with their lives. In terms of her own life and the journey that had led her to healing, she spoke about the experience of reconnecting with who she really was.

We also talked about the healing experience of pain. 'If, for example, you cut yourself', she said, 'it hurts; but that means the body is sending a lot of energy there to rebuild the damage.' If you accept the pain, she went on, then this activity taking place will change the wound from a cut to a scab, and so begin the healing. Elaine feels that likewise we can heal the mind or spirit if we allow ourselves to be drawn into a process and not fight against it.

A turning point in Elaine's inner journey came at the age of twenty-eight – often a significant time in a person's life, influenced on the one hand, so some believe, by the unfolding of the seven-year rhythm that I had gradually become aware of in my own life. In astrological circles one's late twenties also roughly coincides with a major rite of passage known as the first Saturn Return: the planet Saturn takes approximately twenty-nine and a half years to orbit the sun. When it returns to the exact degree along the ecliptic that it occupied at the time of a person's birth, this is referred to as their Saturn Return. To many astrologers this first return marks the true beginning of adulthood.

Elaine was having a successful and heady time in the London of the sixties when she saw a poster at an Underground station saying 'Do you want to know more?' For her the answer was obvious; and so began an exploration through Buddhism, Sufism, t'ai-chi, theosophy and yoga. As with so many healers, her ability was spotted by another healer. For Elaine it was a total surprise – one that was to be followed by many years of rigorous training.

For me one of the most interesting and helpful things that Elaine said was to do with spiritual experiences altogether. This was a piece of advice that her first teacher passed on to her: 'First hear the note, and then learn its name.' With this thought in mind Elaine told me that she very seldom spoke about her spiritual experiences for fear of preventing people from having their own, and thus arriving at what was truly meaningful for them. 'I think free will is something we should take incredibly seriously', she said. 'In their own time a person will come to the experiences they need. And as a healer, I know if I try to fix people I'm not healing.'

The series Inner Journeys was commissioned in 1993 by HTV in Bristol, the company that had taken over from my first employer TWW some thirty years earlier. Thanks to the sensitivity and trust of the executive producer, Steve Matthews, I and my thoughtful and energetic research assistant Annie Wilson were completely free to select whoever we wanted, with no pressure to feature celebrities. One potential danger of dwelling too much on those who, like Gandhi and Tolstoy, stride ahead of the crowd, is that you can feel very small and inadequate in comparison, and that their example can have an almost inhibiting effect on your own humble efforts. The people we filmed for *Inner Journeys* were on the whole part of the crowd – yet nonetheless special because of it. And although they all came over as very grounded individuals, at times they also felt as fragile and bewildered as we all sometimes feel – none more so than Val Pommier.

Val and her artist husband, Jean Noel, were wardens of a Quaker meeting house in Bristol. The Quakers – along with people like Eric Pycroft in his cowshed – have great respect for silence. 'People gather in silence and wait in silence', said Val. 'I think "waiting" is the word I would use about a Quaker meeting. It's a moment of expectancy, a moment when anything is possible.'

I asked her what she felt Quakers were waiting for. She was understandably hesitant about putting an answer into words. People clearly attend a Quaker meeting for all sorts of reasons, and come with all sorts of ideas and thoughts. 'I suppose', she said, 'if I can use an image, it's a bit like shaking up a glass jar with some muddy water in it. And as you put it back down and let it settle, then the mud all goes to the bottom and the water becomes clear. So there's a waiting for that clarity, which some people would call the spirit of God; others might call it the inner light – all sorts of words. But it's waiting for that moment when we see things or hear things that we wouldn't perhaps have seen or heard before.'

Val went on to speak to me about George Fox, the founder of The Religious Society of Friends, usually known as Quakers, and his conviction that every individual could be in touch with what people call God. We don't need a priest to mediate. 'If we wait and we're quiet', she said, 'out of that quietness we can hear again what he would have termed the voice of God'. In the 17th century, it was a very radical way of thinking and Quakers were forbidden to meet together. Today not all Quakers would call themselves Christian, but the movement grew out of the Christian tradition.

I then asked Val about that phrase 'the voice of God', sensing that she had difficulties with it. She admitted being 'in a state of rebellion – the word "God" has so many different meanings for different people'. She was happier with the term 'creative energy' – something that was evident to her in looking out into the universe. She then added: 'I have a childhood vision of God, and I want to rebel against that at the moment.'

She then told me a little about her upbringing in a strict Baptist family and how as a child the Church was an important part of her life, to which she went willingly. 'I had this image of God up there in his heaven,' she said, 'and he was a man, both benevolent and judgemental. It was very clear to me that things were either black or white. I was either a sinner or I was saved. I would either go to heaven or to hell. And I'm not quite sure when that started to worry me.'

Val went on to describe how she prayed daily, read the Bible – learning passages off by heart; but alongside all this was 'a sense that God was watching me … As a little girl I was very careful how I behaved … I would do my homework and be quiet in school because that's what God would want me to do.' But although in Val's mind God was there to help, he was also there to judge. This thought became an increasing burden for her: 'And I was very, very scared of the picture of hell.' Another problem was the realisation that as a Christian her life should be 'full of joy', yet inside she experienced fear, sadness and a loneliness about which she spoke to no one, not even to her parents: 'I wanted to show them the good side, and not let them down.'

As Val grew up she became increasingly preoccupied with the question of predestination and free will, and very frightened at the idea that her life might in some way be planned out for her. Although at college she met people who were asking the same questions and sharing the same doubts, she continued to go to a Baptist church throughout those three years. Then training as a teacher, she felt more and more challenged by members of the Christian fellowship to which she belonged, and uncomfortable at the idea that 'it was our job to convert the rest of the world'.

Thus it was that Val began to realise 'each of us has something to offer that mustn't be denied by anybody else, and that our own experience is really, really important'. Then came a significant turning point: her sister, for whom she had great respect, took her to a Quaker meeting in Oxford. Back in Coventry she hunted out the local Quakers and started to attend their meetings. 'And I guess that was the first time I'd ever really made a step on my own to do something.'

At Quaker meetings anyone present is welcome to speak, sing or say a prayer. Sometimes the whole hour will be silent. Val remembered one of those early meetings, when a man stood up and began to weep as he spoke. 'I can remember feeling at home', she said, 'and thinking maybe this is a place where I can come, just as I am. I don't have to pretend, and if I'm sad or upset maybe I can bring that here.' At another meeting another man stood up and quoted an American Indian proverb: 'Don't judge a man till you've walked a mile in his moccasins.' 'That was really meaningful to me', she said, 'because I really wanted to be somewhere where I wouldn't be judged.'

I then asked Val whether she'd come to terms with the question of predestination, and whether she was now happier and had found her purpose. 'Not completely', she replied. Sometimes she awoke in the night, frightened

Val Pommier

at the idea that something has been predestined for her. At one level she did now seem to accept that at any given moment we have a choice, and that drawing on the 'creative energy' that some people call God we have the capacity to create our own lives, but it took a long time for her to accept the idea: 'It was actually very frightening for me, because it meant daring to want something for myself, and I hadn't ever dared to want because again I felt I had to know what God wanted for me. And I suppose I started to experiment with the idea that maybe what He wanted for me was what I wanted for me; and that was a very liberating thought.'

Am I right in seeing Val Pommier's inner journey as one of learning about acceptance? I asked her. 'Yes,' she said, 'it's about acceptance of myself and about allowing to come to the surface what is already there.' She then told me a French proverb that they had pinned up in their kitchen, 'La seule verité c'est de s'aimer' ('The only truth is to love'). It's actually not easy to translate, she explained, because the French verb 's'aimer' means both to love oneself and to love other people. 'They're synonymous', she said, 'there's no separation'.

Towards the end of our conversation it emerged that Val had experienced just as many problems with the notion of a devil as she'd had about God. But that too was easing as she'd gradually come to understand both God and the devil 'not as something separate but part of the same whole'. She then used that favourite word of mine – paradox. 'We live in a world that seems to be dualistic', she said. 'Either/Or. Black/White. But it isn't like that at all.'

And so for Val words like 'God' and 'devil' now no longer conveyed to her the meanings they once had. This insight was enriched by her study of acupuncture, and the Chinese concept of *yin* and *yang* – in the symbol of one rests the seed of the other, and *vice versa*. Heaven and hell had both, in their way, become 'places of shelter' for her, she told me. She spoke of heaven as being in the light, but also spoke of going down into what she called her own deep cave, 'where there have been a lot of really good truths to be found'. She talked, too, of trying to embrace the whole of herself, 'the bits that are deep down of which I'm frightened, as well as the bits that I know about and can celebrate'.

Although Val Pommier trained as an acupuncturist, and despite the illuminations that gradually came her way, she didn't feel confident enough to practise. 'I still hadn't let go of wanting to be perfect.' But then a healer whom she was seeing said to her one day: 'Just let go of what you think you ought to be doing and do what comes naturally.' And what came naturally was listening to other people. 'And so I allowed myself the privilege, perhaps for the first time in my life, of not doing what I'd been trained to do, but doing what instinctively came naturally to me, and not trying to be perfect – just being as good as I could be.'

When we made the film, Val was seeing about ten people a week, 'sharing their inner journeys', and training to be a full-time counsellor. I mentioned to her those famous words 'Only a wounded physician heals' that had so resonated for Jung. 'Sometimes I've questioned myself', she said. 'With all the pain in my life, how dare I sit with other people? But I'm encouraged to be there because of my wound.'

Our final words were about George Fox, whose courage and honesty over three hundred years ago have helped so many people ever since. 'He was prepared to stand up for what he believed was his own personal experience,' said Val, 'rather than accepting the experience of somebody else.'

CHAPTER 31

Inner Journeys

If the inner journey, as experienced by Val Pommier, is in part a confrontation with our own inhibitions, guilt, and fears – in other words a struggle with our inner demons, but also a struggle that can lead to a gradual discovery of individual potential – then what is it that the outer world has to teach us along the way? What is the significance of being what we call 'on earth'?

For Aonghus Gordon, another subject in my series *Inner Journeys*, our earth in all its variety, complexity and wonder was the essential tool that he used in his work as an educator, helping troubled adolescents to connect to a world with which they were at odds – and thus to their own potential.

Working alongside practising craftsmen – in leather, wood, stone, wool, glass and metal – and caring for animals on the farm, as well as harvesting and cooking, the students learned not only practical skills but also grew in maturity as their self-confidence and self-esteem were nourished. 'They experience too', said Aonghus, 'a kind of reunification with the living world around them.' But it doesn't stop there. 'Outer activity', he continued, 'becomes in the young person a kind of inner capacity to work on themselves, even though they might not do it consciously ... These threshold experiences are very important in adolescence.'

Aonghus Gordon began his work in 1986 at Ruskin Mill near Nailsworth in Gloucestershire. It was a derelict building that his father bought, inspired by a vision of transforming the old industrial mills of the Stroud valleys into 'pearls of cultural renewal'. But then his father suddenly died when Aonghus was twelve years old.

As a teenager Aonghus became deeply involved in a meditation group, and then spent a number of years travelling, particularly in Greece and Egypt. His experience of hitch-hiking, he told me, taught him an important lesson. At one level there was never any guarantee that he would get from A to B as planned. But what he found was that if he simply relaxed and put his trust in fate, he would reach his destination. In life we are, in one sense, never actually in control, he said, 'but one's inner attitude invariably carries the day'.

The Ruskin Mill Educational Trust is, in Aonghus Gordon's words, 'inspired by the work of Rudolf Steiner, William Morris and John Ruskin'. It has since expanded to Stourbridge in the West Midlands where, at the Glasshouse College, the craft traditions of glasswork have been revived, along with blacksmithing and charcoal-making. And at Freeman College in Sheffield – a converted pewter factory – they are building on the town's rich metal-working heritage, as well as developing drama work started in Stourbridge.

Aonghus's students clearly benefit from what would, I am sure, enrich us all – a closer connection with the natural world from which we feed, clothe and house ourselves; a connection, too, with the correspondences that live in us, for we also all contain mineral, plant and animal substances and qualities. In addition, of course, we possess that most precious and profound ability to recognise the fact.

At thirty-eight, Aonghus was one of the youngest of our subjects in the series. Diana Lodge, at eighty-six, was by far the oldest. Her outer journey began in a Welsh village in 1906. She married a poet, son of the distinguished physicist and spiritualist Oliver Lodge, and was a self-taught and accomplished artist. At the age of sixty-one she became a Roman Catholic, but her inner journey and its struggles began many years earlier.

The first milestone was when her four-year-old son suddenly developed severe diabetes, was rushed into hospital in a coma, and was given only a fifty-fifty chance of surviving. 'What can you do, as a mother?' she said to me. 'You throw yourself on your knees.' That was the start of Diana's discovery of the importance of prayer. Shortly afterwards a friend lent her a book called *The Seven Storey Mountain*, the autobiography of the Trappist monk Thomas Merton. 'He grabbed at life with both hands', she said. 'It made a tremendous impression on me, reading that book.'

For a while Diana was involved in a religious movement that originated in Indonesia called Subud. But at their weekly ritual called the *Latihan*, when people's ecstatic experiences often caused them to make a great deal of noise as the 'spirit' possessed them, Diana realised increasingly that all she wanted to do was quietly pray. A turning point came during a visit to Paris when she wandered by chance into a Catholic church at St Germain des Prés and was struck by the fact that people there were really praying – and not just the token ten-second kneel that is so often performed by visitors on arrival in a church. In describing the experience she used almost the same words as Val Pommier in relation to the Quakers: 'I realised this is where I belong.'

The writings of Teilhard de Chardin, who helped open my eyes as a young man, also now became increasingly important for her. By the time we met she had become what is called a Benedictine Oblate at nearby Prinknash Abbey in Gloucestershire, following their guidelines *ora et labora* – work and pray – but staying in the world.

I asked Diana if she felt she was able to express her faith in her art. 'Yes, it's the love, I suppose.' She told me about painting a picture of a beautiful white cathedral in Puerto Rico once, and suddenly saying out loud 'I love you'. 'I realised I was speaking to God in a way,' she said, 'so if I paint a thing I love, although it isn't a so-called spiritual picture, it's really God showing himself through a daisy or something like that.'

Our final conversation was about her routine – a daily walk whatever the weather – and her efforts to pray at regular moments during the day. She compared confession to having a bath, and spoke of the importance for her of saying 'I'm sorry'. But there was nothing self-righteous or fanatical about Diana Lodge, whatever we were discussing. She radiated great warmth and gentleness, and we laughed a lot. Her concluding words were prompted by the title of the poet John Masefield's autobiography *So Long to Learn*. 'I feel like that', she said. 'It's taken me so long. Maybe that's why I've had to have a long life, because I'm so slow. God has given me a chance to try to catch up with the things that some people know when they're quite young.'

In making *The Long Search*, *Seven Ages* and then *Inner Journeys*, I felt enormously privileged to have access to the very heart of people's lives – their hopes and fears, and how they dealt with the challenges and disappointments that came their way. One common thread that kept emerging from this tapestry of stories was particularly apparent among those who started to tap into the mystical traditions of one or other of the great world religions. At this level of experience the differences between us, and the labels we give those differences, start to fall away.

There are many ways to sum up the insights that these ten people shared. I was often reminded, for example, of those words by Gerard Manley Hopkins, 'What I do is me, for that I came', for what I perceived as another thread was everyone's recognition of the importance of listening to, and trusting, their inner voice. Yet another experience that all our subjects shared, whatever wisdom they tuned into, was the inevitable encounter with trials and tribulations along the way – mountains to climb, dragons to slay, pain and sorrow to endure.

Some of the most stimulating and enriching encounters I have had – not just working on these particular films – have been with people whose quests and questions are forever resurfacing: pilgrims who resist the temptation to settle for easy, comfortable and satisfying answers along the way. Ron Eyre was one such courageous individual; so, too – in very different ways – were Thomas Weihs and John Betjeman. For many, like Diana Lodge, this journey takes them through many different experiences and teachings. Another example of this healthy restlessness was the path taken by one more of our subjects for *Inner Journeys*, Leonard Sleath.

With his wife Willa, Leonard was warden of the Chalice Well Trust at Glastonbury – a place of pilgrimage and healing. 'People don't always know what they're searching for', said Leonard, 'but somehow they're drawn to a place like this.' Willa then added, 'I think Glastonbury is a very confusing place, but it's also a very necessary place in the scheme of things; and it's very personal. People come for all sorts of reasons – illness, bereavement; something gives them a shove. Very often, I have to say, you find that women come up into the garden and men stay outside in the car with the dog! Then the women go back down and say, "Oh, do come in" … and actually the men often have a much richer experience than the women, but initially there's quite a lot of resistance to something unknown, to something mysterious, to something that isn't rational.'

The inner journey of Leonard Sleath took him from the Bank of England to a Gurdjieff community, then into the probation service, and for four years to the Findhorn Community in Scotland. On the way there were encounters with the teachings of a number of 'wise men'. 'Leonard, why do you keep changing your religion?' people often asked him. His reply: 'Well, actually I've never really had one.' As a child he loved church music, but never learned much about Christianity. He did have a feeling of 'something different' that separated him from his family, 'a sense of something missing'.

During his time in the RAF he remembered discussions about Aldous Huxley, Bertrand Russell and others, but said that this didn't affect his decision to join the Bank of England where he worked for twelve years. He used the word 'schizophrenic' to describe that time: 'By day I was a city gent, and the rest of the time I was on the search.' He took up yoga and became interested in the teachings of the 19th-century Indian saint, Paranhansa Ramakrishna, who drew not only on the wisdom in Hinduism, but also on Christianity and Islam.

For a while Leonard became involved in the work of Gurdjieff, who also attempted to build bridges – in his case between Sufi and Christian beliefs in particular, as well as teachings from India and Tibet. Much of what went on, he told me, was to do with 'Westerners getting through a lot of their stuff' – coming to terms with the reality and the aggression of western life, 'and the fact that we don't really choose very much in our lives; we think we do.' Gurdjieff tried to address the stupidity of unconscious suffering, and the resentment and misery that it causes. 'It's alright suffering', said Leonard, 'provided you make use of it and become more conscious, more aware.' But he found the Gurdjieff work 'too serious, too humourless', having experienced 'the lightness of the path of yoga'.

At the age of thirty and already married to Willa, Leonard Sleath left the bank and joined J.G. Bennett's community at Coombe Springs where he encountered what Diana Lodge also sampled, the Indonesian movement called Subud. 'I thought this was marvellous', he said, 'an ecstatic state with no need of alcohol or drugs … A process that involved a great deal of letting go.'

Gradually, however, Leonard became aware that what he called 'the spiritual life' was not something that had to be practised in the serenity of some monastic institution. At Coombe Springs he had already worked in an adjoining therapeutic community for maladjusted teenage boys, but now wanted a more private life for his growing family. So began his twenty years as a probation officer.

Leonard described one aspect of the years that followed as 'getting out of my head and into my heart'. He found that Jung's work helped to clarify for him his relationship to what he called 'a softer part of myself'. 'All the Semitic faiths – Christianity, Judaism and Islam – are basically patriarchal faiths', he said. 'They relate very well to the masculine, God the Father stuff, but don't in my view relate sufficiently to the feminine, the female part of creation.'

At the age of fifty-two Leonard Sleath felt the need to change direction once again, and he left the probation service. He and his wife then joined the Findhorn community in northern Scotland – 'the cutting edge of the New Age'. It was, he said, the spiritual equivalent of a couple who sell up everything, give up their jobs, buy a yacht and sail around the world.

The Findhorn community is best known for its founders' acknowledgment of the existence and importance of nature spirits. A working relationship with these entities is not just a matter of producing larger cabbages – although they certainly do this too. The move also meant for Leonard and Willa the challenge of living in a community with other people again, and not falling back on old patterns. 'You cannot approach the spiritual life and develop in it', he said, 'if you retain all the facets of your previous personality, with all your desires and wants, likes and dislikes. You have to keep shedding.'

At one point in our conversation Willa referred to herself and Leonard as 'spiritual gypsies'. By the time I met them they had a new teacher in their lives, Sai Baba, and were making regular visits to his ashram in India. 'The most peaceful place on earth', said Leonard. 'I couldn't live there all the time, not yet. Maybe I never will.' Willa then volunteered the thought that for her India is not ultimately separate and somewhere else: 'India's inside me, and inside you, and inside Leonard. East and West are in all of us.'

Back in Glastonbury, it was tempting at times to see Leonard Sleath as accumulating rather than shedding, yet I admired tremendously his restless and courageous search. I asked him finally about his and many other people's need for a guru figure. 'I'm reassured by the fact that there are people in human form who are further ahead than I am', was his reply. 'When I'm in the ashram I've absolutely no doubt that God exists.'

'And when you're walking in Glastonbury High Street', I asked him, 'do you also have that same conviction that God exists? Or do you need to be in India?' 'It's not so easy in ordinary life', he replied. 'It's difficult to retain that sense, that flavour. It's much easier if everything around you exudes it and shares in it. That's what the Hindus call *satsang* – good company.'

Good company was what I certainly experienced in making this series of films. Another subject was Girish Patel who gave yoga classes in Stroud with all the sensitivity and skill you would expect from someone of his background. The first five years of his life were spent in Kenya and then India, after which he grew up in England, in the Midlands. Although his family were Hindus, Girish as a child was fascinated by the image of Christ, and it was to Christ he began to pray. In keeping with Hinduism's all-embracing tolerance, his parents accepted their son's attraction to Christianity. It was not until university, through an interest in yoga, that Girish connected with the traditions of his Indian background – but still today he has a small picture of Christ on his shrine beside the image of Krishna.

Girish and his wife Sharon ran a small business cooking and selling Indian food in Stroud market. Previously he worked for three years as an administrator for Oxfam. His greatest challenge, he told me, was trying to live simply amid the bustle and pressures of modern life. What helped him was his daily routine of yoga and meditation, and a weekly gathering with friends to chant and sing.

Another person whom we filmed also had a somewhat unusual relationship with her religious tradition. Alix Pirani's inner journey had taken her into, out of and back into Judaism. At a conference at Dartington, on the theme of 'Religion beyond Belief', Alix said in the lecture we filmed that this theme was almost irrelevant to Jews because they're not really expected to believe in a creed as such. 'Judaism is not a religion, but a way of life', she stated.

Alix Pirani, writer and psychotherapist, was living at the time on her own in Bath. She was divorced, with four grown-up children. Her grandparents on both sides were Jewish immigrants from eastern Europe. Alix was born and grew up in London. Religion for her family 'wasn't very strong, much more a social thing … three days a year Judaism', she told me. Despite this she took herself off to Hebrew classes – unusual and unnecessary for a Jewish girl – and around the age of sixteen became very orthodox, much to the consternation of her parents.

At Cambridge, however, where Alix Pirani read English, the works of T.S. Eliot and William Blake in particular began to undermine her Judaism. 'I needed to get at some kind of truth', she said, 'and had an instinctive feeling that I was living a lie … After all, you can't be very inspired by D.H. Lawrence and at the same time be with a religion that is very puritanical about sex.' But it wasn't only English literature that rocked her faith. 'If you're going to be very orthodox you had to think: "Yes, the world was made in seven days." Well, for goodness sake, one can't stay in Cambridge very long and believe that!'

In Bristol Alix took me to an orthodox synagogue where the layout, with its separation of the sexes – men downstairs, women upstairs – symbolised the aspect of Judaism that she still found hard to take. 'It's partly that separation, but partly what it represents in terms of attitudes to women.' Being relegated to a virtual spectator often leads, she said, to a sense that what's going on down there isn't the same as what's going on up here. In her lecture she'd spoken of Jewish women as 'victims of victims', but apparently in the early centuries of the synagogue women were much more active, and are now starting to reclaim that position.

Alix went on to tell me about what she described as 'thirty years in the wilderness', largely brought about by the emotional differences between herself and her physicist husband, 'a dogmatic atheist'. Given that his expertise was in relativity and the work of Albert Einstein – in itself 'something very equivalent to a spiritual search' – she was always surprised that they couldn't build a bridge.

During this period, around the age of thirty-five, she developed heart trouble and depression, 'what I would now see as a mid-life crisis … "Heart trouble" means heart trouble'. She began to write a novel, 'a book about the lost Judaism, and then it slowly all began to come out – what was really amiss – and that brought me out of my depression'. She then trained as a psychotherapist.

Alix Pirani's way back into Judaism came about through her crisis, as well as through the liberal movements that had been gathering pace – and in their wake the appearance of women rabbis. She also discovered Jewish mysticism and the Kabbala – 'a wonderful coming back … The Kabbalistic Tree of Life … Now here was a Jewish tradition I could respect'. And she confirmed my sense that through immersion in the mystical traditions of one's faith a bond quite naturally develops with all other faiths, and indeed with all human striving that respects the contemplative dimension so valued by Eric Pycroft and his friends in that Gloucestershire cowshed.

Alix was now attending what was called a progressive synagogue – no balcony, no separation of men and women. 'I like the simplicity of it', she said. 'Originally that's what synagogues were like, and some of them still are – just rooms, sometimes in people's houses … A place of learning, originally; then it became a place of prayer.' I asked her whether she would like to be a rabbi. The idea had crossed her mind, but she decided against it: 'I'm too alternative'. She then added: 'A lot of women therapists are actually being rabbis or priests, which they weren't able to be under the old system. And of course many of them, I think, do quite a lot of what one would call spiritual work through therapy.'

Finally I asked about her plans. 'Surviving depression', she replied, 'the depression of getting old; that sits on me quite a bit. Were I in a Jewish community I would be looked after in my old age; or were I with my family … It's the lot of many people.'

She spoke then of the spiritual dimension of existence: 'That's where gods come from. You have to produce something to keep you company – somebody, some person.' 'Are they real?' I asked her. 'What's reality?' was her response. 'Are they real? I think there are moments when emotionally they're very real to me. You know, if I feel particularly lonely and distressed, and can somehow visualise a being which may be a goddess or god or whatever, who's in there with me, that's very real to me … I'm in a process which is much longer than my life, and I have to trust that process and trust myself to feel my place in it … It's hard, but it has become much easier as I get older. It's a question of giving up the wish to control everything and a wish to have everything go my way.'

This same experience of ceasing to want to control every aspect of one's life was echoed by the writer Lindsay Clarke, whose inner journey received a severe jolt when his first wife left him for someone else. After an initial reaction of extreme rage and black despair came the realisation that it was a hopeless struggle: 'There was no way I was going to be able to impose my will upon the situation.' He described to me how, after a long sleep and then a walk, he had the feeling that he inhabited a completely different world, 'a much greater sense of ease, of belonging, of participating in life, rather than trying to bully life into being what one wanted it to be'.

Lindsay Clarke identified listening as a child to Grimm's fairy tales as the start of his inner journey: 'The wisdom of generations formulated these stories, and they provide one of the best handbooks that we have to this rather complicated software that we come issued with.' In response to my mention of the doubt expressed by some modern parents about the violent and frightening content of many of the stories, he referred to them as 'an education in fear … learning how to cope with fear and seeing it as part of a process'. Children don't actually take the stories literally, he believed. 'Literalism tends to be a limitation of the adult mind.' He saw them rather 'as nourishment for [children's] own imaginative life; thereby they are provided with images and metaphors by which they give shape to the pattern of their own experiences, as they try to make sense of the world around them'. The stories are also about journeys. 'All good stories are', he said.

The only child of working-class parents, Lindsay Clarke grew up in Yorkshire, 'absolutely sure from a very early age that I lived in a world where I was surrounded by love, and got the confidence that came from that knowledge.' He went to a grammar school and then read English at Cambridge, 'a good way of training to become a writer'; but he found instead that he was being trained to be a literary critic. 'I was learning to discover exactly what was

Lindsay Clarke

wrong with all the authors that I most loved and revered, and the end of this process was a complete loss of confidence in the belief that I could ever be a writer myself.'

It took Lindsay twenty years to recover that confidence. Meanwhile, he went to Africa with his young wife. It was there, he said, that his real education began: 'I had gone there as an over-educated, rather arrogant young man, assuming that I had a great deal to teach these people, and it wasn't very long before I began to realise that there was a great deal that I had to learn – much more to learn in fact than I had to teach.'

There followed 'a prolonged period of exploration into religious traditions', while working as a teacher in Norfolk. Through the writings of Jung he became interested in the figure of the Fool, 'having woken up to how much of a fool I had been, and the feeling to be starting afresh, to being an absolute beginner again – and so being an innocent fool in that sense'. In the Tarot pack, the fool who is naïve at the start of his journey passes through the major cycles of experience as depicted in the other cards, and ends up as the wise fool – 'a fool only in the sense that he now knows how much he doesn't know'.

Through Jung's interest in the *I Ching*, Lindsay began exploring the language and vocabulary of alchemy, which furnished him with the principle metaphors for his novel *The Chymical Wedding*, which won him the 1989 Whitbread Prize for fiction. This 'chymical wedding' is one of the central metaphors of alchemy, he explained to me. It's to do with the marriage of sulphur and mercury, or of sun and moon, or male and female – all of which were regarded by the alchemists as opposite but complementary forces underpinning the structure of matter and the order of life. 'And much of the time', he said, 'as we know from our own experience, these elements are at war with one another – the male and female – being ill at ease with one another, pulling and tugging, nagging and each trying to get from the other what is desired. The goal of alchemy was to bring these divergent, apparently contradictory, hostile forces, into creative relation one with another. And of course this is the way new life gets made, when the male and the female come together in harmony and work creatively together – a new life gets engendered from them. This we can see obviously at work in the natural processes around us. What may be less obvious, but is equally powerful, is how this process can take place internally within the life of an individual, and on a wider scale within the life of a community. It's the essential process of renewal.'

In the light of these observations I asked Lindsay whether he thought that men these days had a tougher time than women on this inner journey (he now lives in Somerset with his second wife, Phoebe, a potter). 'It's not that men have a tougher time than women', he replied, 'it's just that the official view of reality is, by and large, pretty much determined by what men have regarded as the tolerable, workable, viable way of ordering and seeing the world. And as things change, as it becomes apparent that there are inadequacies in that view of the world, men may have a tougher time than women letting go of some of their own prejudices and assumptions about the way things are.' Despite being aware that he was now on delicate ground with statements about gender, he did add that biologically and temperamentally women seem to have a more natural degree of access to what is stirring in all areas of life. 'It's more their time that's coming.'

We went on to talk about imagination – a word that crops up again and again among the people I tend to admire and respect. For Lindsay Clarke, like many other creative people – including the struggling poet Winnie the Pooh – ideas often come when on walks, not while sitting at his desk staring at a blank sheet of paper. 'I allow my inner thoughts to roam as my feet are roaming.' And did he feel that they were, in the end, his ideas? 'No, by no means. I feel that they're my version of ideas which feel to be in the air; although the work, when it's finished, is my relationship to those ideas … In fact a large part of my work is trying to get out of my own way.'

Lindsay and I talked about many other things on that summer day. Although I can date it, in other ways it seems to me quite outside of time. We discussed *yin* and *yang*, and awakening the Sleeping Beauty within oneself; then there was that old favourite, the evolution of consciousness; also our willingness to take risks; and finally some thoughts on the legend of the Grail, about which he has also written. We went for a walk ourselves, and we watched Phoebe at work in her pottery. My favourite of all his utterances during our filming was, without doubt: 'Imagination is the hotline into meaning.'

'So is the imagination really your religion?' I asked him finally. 'I suppose it is,' he replied, 'and I suppose writing is my yoga. That's the way I try to discipline myself, because not belonging to a particular faith has its freedom, but it also means that one doesn't have the benefit of working within the disciplines that a particular faith requires of one. But writing itself is a pretty massive discipline – to get to the end of a book, once you've actually started writing the first page.' It's a thought that has certainly resonated for me during the last three years.

As a practising Sufi, Robert Burton – also living in a Somerset village – knew all about discipline. The discipline of meditation had nourished his spiritual path from an early age. He remembered, as a small child, sitting for hours by a pond, 'interludes that had a very special feeling which I'm quite sure now, in retrospect, one would call meditation'.

Robert's father was a Buddhist, but had no objection to his son being baptised at the age of ten so that he could sing in the church choir. 'It was when I came into my teens', he told me, 'that some of the Buddhist ideas started to rub off on me.' He described it as 'something that made sense to me', whereas Christianity was difficult to understand. 'The ideas of Christianity now make sense to me', he said, 'but that's only as a result of having gone through Buddhist practice.'

The requirement to believe in something, which is absent from Buddhism, was the stumbling block for Robert in relation to religions like Christianity. 'The Buddha said: "Look at life. What do you see? What is your experience of life?" His whole teaching stems from that', Robert explained. 'It's what I would regard as something consistent with a scientific outlook. You start by observation, and there's no requirement to believe anything. You just have to test hypotheses and see if you find that they're true. It was that aspect that appealed to me.'

Robert Burton was an information technology training officer for Somerset County Council. He met his wife Latifa through a common interest in Buddhism. It was a second marriage for both of them. We spoke together about Buddhism's emphasis on mindfulness: 'being mindful all the time of one's own actions and the effect they have on other people … and seeing through all that to what it is that's causing suffering'.

We also talked about the intellect – its strengths and its limitations – and the shift that can take place in our understanding through meditation. The concepts of reincarnation and karma are also central to Buddhist understanding. 'If you want to know your past', Robert suggested, 'look at what you're experiencing today, now. It's the result of what's gone on for you before. And if you want to know your future, also look at how you're living now, because that will influence it.' Buddhists, however, don't have to believe in reincarnation. 'Buddhism tends to focus more on rebirth as a process that you can see happening in your everyday life', Robert explained, 'so that's not a belief; rebirth is something you can observe – the rebirth of a thought, the rebirth of an emotion.'

I then asked them both where God fits into all this. Robert replied by saying that this subject was one of the most misunderstood things about Buddhism. Although Buddha never introduced the concept of God, because his teaching is essentially a practice – a journey of inner development – it leads to a growing awareness; 'and from that growing awareness', said Robert, 'awareness of what we call God develops'.

But this was not the end of the story of Robert Burton's inner journey. Like his wife Latifa, he now had a different name – Subhan. Although Buddhist practice had remained central to their lives, they had begun to seek 'companionship in our practice' and 'something more devotional'. Eventually they joined a local Sufi group. What appealed to them was not only the company of like-minded people, but also Sufism's emphasis on the unity of all religions. Along with various esoteric contemplative practices, the most important of which is a type of private 'prayer of the heart' known as *dhikr*, the Sufis consider service to society and to their fellow human beings as the supreme form of worship.

Although Sufism is associated with Islam, in essence its origins stretch much further back, and it too – like the Kabbala – has much in common with the mystical traditions in other faiths, including those of Christianity; hence the sense of unity that attracted Robert and his wife. Their particular group belonged to the Sufi Order of the West. They met together regularly, and their rituals involved dance and chanting. 'It's really about getting out of the head and into the body ... We're learning through the dances to experience what other people experience when they practise their own faith ... What is in the heart of the Muslim, chanting to Allah, is the same as that in the heart of the Christian praising God through Jesus, or in the Hindu dances honouring Rama and Krishna.'

'Stagnation is the danger', said Latifa towards the end of our conversation. When I observed that they both seemed very fulfilled and asked whether their inner journey was over, Robert replied: 'It feels as if it's just beginning.' His response was characteristic of all the encounters I experienced in making the series, not least the final one with Canon Peter Spink – a journey that for me was to resonate most powerfully of all.

Inner Journeys, *from left to right, Alix Pirani, Elaine Heller, Girish Patel,
Lindsay Clarke, Annie Wilson, Peter Spink, author, Diana Lodge, Leonard Sleath,
Robert Burton, Aonghus Gordon, Val Pommier*

CHAPTER 32

In Search of Arcadia

A manor house in Somerset was the location of the last of my films for the series *Inner Journeys*. It was the home of the Omega Order, founded by Peter Spink – at one time a missionary in India, and later a canon at Coventry Cathedral. It was a contemplative, ecumenical community for men and women who were, in Peter's words, 'seeking wider horizons, but who also wanted to hold onto their Christian faith'. He has written several books about the growing awareness of the essential unity underlying all faiths, and about the need that many people have for an experiential relationship with God. At the opening of his book *Beyond Belief* he quotes the 6th-century mystic Dionysius: 'God is neither perceptible to our senses nor conceived by our intellects, but He is sensible to the heart.'

Peter Spink described his Omega initiative as springing out of the pastoral situation during his nine years at Coventry Cathedral. 'I became increasingly aware', he said, 'that there was some change taking place within the religious consciousness of the congregation – not just the congregation for which I was responsible. And it seemed to me that this reflected a change perhaps taking place throughout the whole of the western Church. My description of this change, my way of looking at it, is that this was a change from devotionalism – that is, devotion to the God out there – to an awareness of the God within. And that this awareness of the God within required – if I can put it this way – a new kind of spiritual discipline by which this awareness could grow and develop.'

I suggested that for many people this experience he was describing made the Church irrelevant. His view was that although such a reaction is understandable, it is not necessary. He spoke of the notion of the indwelling Christ – the Christ within – which was central to the teachings of St Paul. He also recognised in this new consciousness something of what the mystics in all the great religious traditions had experienced and tried to express over the centuries. He called it an awareness of 'beyond Easter'. 'So many of us who call ourselves Christians get lodged in the area before Easter', he said, 'before the Crucifixion, before the Resurrection. It's the movement from the Jesus of the Gospels to the Christ who fills all things.'

At this point I asked him to tell me about his own pilgrimage. As a small boy he had attended Sunday School reluctantly, sent there by a non church-going family. Around the age of seventeen, however, 'something very dramatic happened – a conversion experience. I was brought face to face with the Jesus of the Gospels.' But he went on to describe his position in the years that followed as 'ambivalent'. 'I loved Jesus, to use the language that was real to me at that stage', he said, 'but somehow I was smothered by the framework into which the particular tradition that I belonged had placed me.' He spoke of 'not breathing very easily', yet was sufficiently loyal to his perception at that time to become a missionary in India.

Peter then described how he began to feel increasingly stifled in the ecclesiastical framework to which he belonged. The Bible was interpreted in a very rigid kind of way, and there was no awareness of what he called 'this great cosmic dimension'. Having learned Hindi and Urdu he was sent out to the villages to preach the Gospel, but came face to face with questions he felt unable to answer. 'I was expected to believe that all Muslims and Hindus – indeed all non-Christians – were on the road to hell.' Despite the very real charitable work being done by the missionaries who propounded this kind of Gospel, Peter came to the point where he could no longer accept the situation. He lost his faith, yet nevertheless continued to go through the motions of being a missionary, 'but inside me I was dying'.

The climax came on a visit to a village when he quoted to a Muslim teacher the passage from the gospel of St John: 'God so loved the world that He gave His only begotten Son, that whosoever believeth in Him should not perish, but have everlasting life.' For this man such words were blasphemy and he spat in Peter Spink's face. Peter left the village with the thought that this person had simply rejected the Gospel, 'but unconsciously something began to work in me. Had he heard what I thought I was communicating? Did words adequately convey the Gospel? What indeed was wrapped up in this apparent confrontation?' So began a journey back, step-by-step, 'a long painful journey', to a rediscovery of 'the glorious freedom of the Gospel of Christ', and with it came the decision, despite all his reservations, to become an Anglican priest.

However, despite his time at theological college and then becoming a parish priest, Peter Spink's doubts lingered on. He spoke about once again being made 'to fit into a box ... until the day came when I felt "Up with this I can no longer put!" This is not the Gospel that frees. This is something that restricts.'

Peter was now in his early thirties and married. Then something that he called 'rather extraordinary' happened in his life. It was a striking example of what can often occur in times of crisis when someone – maybe a complete stranger – comes into one's life and says something or does something that clarifies the path ahead. In the 14th century Johannes Tauler experienced such a moment in his encounter with someone simply called the Friend of God. Perhaps all of us have such a friend, waiting in the wings, if we are open and sensitive enough to recognise them.

Peter had been asked by his bishop to represent him at a conference on the island of Iona – a conference on the theme of the 'cosmic Christ'. He described sitting at the back during the lectures, and on one occasion had felt the need 'to defend the faith', and accused the speaker of preaching heresy. It was the only time he spoke at the conference, yet he felt that something was happening to him at a very deep level. Then, on the last day, one of the speakers walked towards him at the end of her lecture and he heard himself saying, 'When can we talk?' She smiled and said 'When you are ready.' Then again he heard himself saying 'I'm ready now.' They then talked and walked together for two or three hours. He described the encounter as one in which he was gently forced to confront all the motivations that had underpinned his life so far: 'Why I was a priest. Why I was at the conference. Why I was an actor – because she saw me as an actor – dressed up in these robes. I was then given some encouraging help on how I could become, I suppose, what I can only describe as a real person. I was given some disciplines of meditation.'

'I was impressed very much by this individual', he continued, 'because she told me nothing about herself, gave no labels, didn't profess to be an authority on the spiritual life, but was someone clearly acting as a mirror in which I began to see myself in a new light.' Peter called the meeting a turning point, and found that born within him was 'a new desire for reality'. Devastated at first, he began to feel, in the context of this new self-awareness, 'that some seeds of hope were sown'. He was given a very simple meditative discipline that he could practise daily 'which began to show me myself – not in a way that I couldn't cope with … rather the vision of a possibility of becoming real'.

I asked Peter what had been happening since then. 'It's been an on-going process now for about fifteen years', he replied. 'For me meditation is very important. It's still a struggle – as much of a struggle now as it was in the early days … Finding what I understand to be the still centre; standing back from the emotions; standing back from the intellect; and allowing myself to be still in the presence of God is not easy. It's tough.'

I suggested that in that silence there must be many voices clamouring to be heard, hence the importance of discrimination. 'I'm certainly not listening for voices', he replied, 'not listening for divine intervention' (though I hadn't meant voices in the literal sense). 'Normally I have a symbol that I can hold onto,' he continued, 'and for me the concept of light is very important, so I will be aware of light within the heart. I'm not very good at imagining things. I can't imagine light, but hold onto the concept of light as being what I conceive as the core of my being. For me it's the source of hope – a source of vision throughout everyday life.'

And did he still sense that at times he was playing a role, I asked – or had he shed that? 'I think I have to play roles – all of us have to play many roles. What is important for me now is that I know when I'm playing a role, and I know why I'm playing that role, and that I can separate it from what I trust is the real me, the essential me.'

----●----

What also came out of the Iona conference for Peter Spink was his discovery of the work of Teilhard de Chardin, the man who, on his return from a four month expedition in Mongolia, wrote: 'I am a pilgrim of the future on my way back from a journey made entirely in the past.' Like Jung on his return from Africa, Teilhard increasingly felt that despite the enriching experience of his travels in China and India, answers to life's greatest mysteries – answers that might satisfy and inspire modern consciousness – had to be sought elsewhere. He wrote of a voice that whispered, 'Now, my brothers of the West, it is your turn.' In *Letters from a Traveller* he continues:

> Our turn. Yes, sleep on, ancient Asia; your people are as weary as your soil is ravaged. By now your night has fallen and the light has passed into other hands. But it was you who kindled this light, you who gave it to us. Have no fear: we shall not allow it to die … So long, too, as a few wise men still have your life (your own life – not a life we would seek to impose on you) in safe-keeping, it is not extinguished. Tomorrow perhaps it will shine once more over your ravaged plateaux.

These thoughts of Teilhard were often expressed in terms of what he called 'the road of the East' and 'the road of the West'. For him the East became synonymous with the past. 'It stands', writes Ursula King in *Towards a New Mysticism*, 'for a stage of man's religious quest which once existed to a greater or lesser degree in all religions.' She associates it with passivity, asceticism and 'an excessive other-worldliness'; but as the scholar Joseph Needham has pointed out, it is misleading to associate Teilhard's pronouncements on other-worldliness exclusively with the East. For him it represented a universal and outdated spirituality that failed to comprehend the evolutionary pattern in both nature and spirit. 'Although distinct from the temporal', writes Ursula King, 'the spiritual is not sharply separated from it but grows out and beyond it.' The next stage in Teilhard's view was, she says 'a clearer perception of the importance of temporal realities.' But this new 'road of the West' was not to be identified with Christianity alone. In *Activation of Energy* he called it 'a hitherto unknown form of religion' which would contain a mixture of both eastern and western elements. Elsewhere he described it as 'a new mysticism of convergence'; and in *Science and Christ* he wrote of 'a religion of action'.

Peter Spink spoke to me of the enormous vistas that Teilhard's work opened up for him: 'a man with tremendous vision of the Christ who fills all things, a Christ who is within the whole evolutionary process and not encapsulated within the ecclesiastical system'. Peter's respect was enhanced by the fact that Teilhard was prepared to humble himself and remain silent. 'For many years the Church put him into the wilderness. They sent him to China because his writings were presumed to be heretical ... It was only after his death in 1955 that his work was published.'

The enigmatic Gurdjieff, with his search for 'the hidden wisdom' in remote parts of Asia, was another of Peter Spink's heroes, but for quite other reasons. Pamela Travers, the author of *Mary Poppins*, told Peter that Gurdjieff had told her before he died that she was to be 'the sole transmitter of my teaching when I'm gone'. But she knew that he had said the same thing to at least twelve other people, 'and that authenticates Gurdjieff for me', said Peter, 'because he sought to smash cult at every point, even the cult that he knew would follow his death'. I responded by saying that from what I knew he hadn't been very successful. 'No, indeed', said Peter, 'cult always follows dynamic. I'm afraid that there'll be an Omega cult when I've gone. I tell the community that they're to smash it as soon as they can and destroy my writings. Cult always follows dynamic, organisation follows organism. It's inevitable.' With those words Peter echoed my own ambivalent attitude about splits that occur in religious, philosophical even scientific circles, and my question about whether the benefit of undermining a potentially deadening orthodoxy outweighs the pain and animosity that can result from such divisions.

The last person we spoke about, whose portrait hung at Winford Manor alongside one of Teilhard, was Pope John XXIII, who summoned the second Vatican council in the sixties. 'It's very difficult for people who've been born since then', said Peter, 'to realise the tremendous impact he had, not only on the Roman Catholic Church, but on the whole of Christendom and beyond, when he threw open the doors and windows of the Church and said that he was going to call an ecumenical council for the whole world. Now the ecclesiastical authorities in Rome quickly cut that down to size, but his openness to the whole of humanity, his love that encompassed all people, has been a tremendous inspiration to me personally.'

Before founding the Omega order, Peter had spent several more years at Coventry Cathedral, 'learning to be still; learning to reverence my body as a temple of the holy spirit; learning to accept myself, and to know that within the totality of my being the glorious Christ, who ascended far above all heavens that he might fill all things, was struggling to come to birth.'

Peter described the difficulties, at times traumatic, of shifting from his conditioned awareness and obedience 'to the God out there', to what he called New Testament religion. 'I had tremendous guilt problems to get rid of … that God was somehow in the background of my life like a resident policeman.' And as a parish priest he had to learn the lesson that not everyone could respond to this presentation of the Gospel. A fellow priest described him as racing round the cathedral, with the tremendous enthusiasm of a convert, telling everyone they had to be quiet and still, and that they had to learn to find the inner Christ. 'I had to step back', he said, 'and realise that within the Church there are those for whom one aspect of God is real, and for others another aspect of God.'

But for Peter himself, as Eric Pycroft also experienced, it became increasingly important 'to be quiet and still' and 'not to bombard God with hymns and prayers … This perpetual activity in our services seems to me to be keeping God at bay', he said. 'However, there's nothing more terrifying to some congregations than saying "Let us be silent for five minutes". One can sense the fear, because we need to be taught how to use silence; how to create space that isn't a vacuum.'

When I filmed at Winford Manor there were ten so-called Companions, as well as a number of long-term guests. Many others came for a day, weekend, month or even a year. 'People can come for a variety of reasons', Peter told me. 'It can be anything from an emotional problem to someone who's really searching spiritually and for guidance.' Many had become disillusioned with

the Church, had travelled and, like many of the young people who also came to Winford, had been awakened spiritually through contact with Buddhism, Islam or Hinduism. 'They've reached the stage where they want to relate to the Christian faith intuitively', he said 'but they can't do it in terms of a package deal. They need to be recognised as already on a spiritual path … In their own way and at their own speed they can again become related to what the Church is all about.'

I had already filmed the community receiving Communion, eating lunch together and quietly enjoying the calm and beauty of the place. Before my final conversation with Peter I filmed them

Peter Spink

not praying, not talking, but dancing

together – hand in hand, in a large circle. 'The dances that we use are mostly contemplative', said Peter. 'That is, they help people come to a place of inner stillness and thus ease the way into silence. It's very easy after doing what we call the Meditation Dance to go into stillness. Certain movements of the body produce stillness.'

I asked him whether, in this stillness, he still experienced moments of crisis in his faith. 'Throughout the whole of my life', he replied, 'all through my spiritual pilgrimage, the battle I've had to fight is to conceive of myself as being of any significance at all in the divine plan and purpose, of having any meaning. I've always been aware, in varying degrees, that there is a plan and a purpose – this tremendous dynamic of history. My struggle has been to see that I have any significance in relation to that.'

I was impressed by Peter's modesty, his humility – yet puzzled that he didn't sense there might perhaps be a plan, a purpose to his own life. It prompted me to ask whether the notion of an afterlife had meaning for him. His reply expressed very beautifully what I myself have increasingly come to believe: 'The afterlife has meaning for me only insofar as the present moment has meaning. I can conceive of the present moment as being a moment of eternity, a moment relating to eternity.' Beyond that, he said, for him it was 'mere speculation'. There I would disagree, for although I have had no clairvoyant experiences myself, I am prepared to trust those I respect who speak from more than mere speculation – those, in other words, who seem to belong to that long line of initiates whose insights have, in the past, nourished and inspired the world's great religions. I trust such teachers as I would a nuclear physicist who explained to me, in words that I could understand, about a subject of which I have very little actual knowledge but which he or she had spent a lifetime studying.

While still on this subject of an afterlife Peter talked to me about what he called 'the imagery of the New Testament' and the fact that he didn't dissent from that imagery. 'But I personally cannot project myself beyond death', he continued, 'other than as reflected in the present moment. If there is a reality now, then that reality is eternal, and I am part of that eternal reality.'

An awareness of those who have died, and of my mother in particular, has been an important element in my conscious life for a long time. These people are for me quite definitely a part of what Peter Spink called 'that eternal reality'. Inevitably, as one gets older oneself, more and more of one's family and friends enter that state of being – what my friend Midgely at Botton Village called 'the heavenly worlds'. It's a realm of existence with which we are, I believe, intimately connected all the time, and especially while our bodies rest during the night; though perhaps 'recover' is a more appropriate word than 'rest', for our soul life of desires and passions takes its toll – as, I imagine, does consciousness itself.

On December 16th 1996, Laurens van der Post died two days after his ninetieth birthday. He, too, now became one of my many friends on what is sometimes called 'the other side'. During the following year I produced a film tribute called *Voice from the Bundu* in which I interviewed his daughter Lucia van der Post and granddaughter Emma Crichton-Miller, as well as several of his close friends. Ten years earlier I had made a film to celebrate his 80th birthday in which he talked to me about his long and adventurous life.

Laurens van der Post, by Jane Bown

Five years after Laurens died, an official biography by J.D.G. Jones was published. Jones called it *Storyteller: the many lives of Laurens van der Post*. It was a provocative title given the book's slant. I am often asked about Laurens, John Betjeman, Malcolm Muggeridge, and others: What were they like to work with? What went on once the camera was switched off? I have tried to convey, as far as is relevant to this book, something of what it was like to spend time with such interesting and thoughtful people. Laurens was one of those with whom I worked who became a friend. Like most public figures he had quite a number of critics, as well as many loyal admirers – and for the admirers, Jones's biography raised a lot of awkward questions, some of which still linger on.

Laurens was born in South Africa, the thirteenth of fifteen children. He turned his back on university to go into journalism, and by the age of twenty-one was in London. In 1929 he wrote his first novel *In a Province* – one of his early initiatives in the fight against colour prejudice and what was to become the South African government's policy of apartheid. During the thirties and already married, he tried to combine writing with farming in Gloucestershire. In World War II he was a prisoner of the Japanese for three and a half years. The film *Merry Christmas Mr. Lawrence* was based on his book *The Seed and the Sower*, which described aspects of that experience in powerful and disturbing detail.

After the war, which for Laurens involved two extra years in the Far East working for Lord Mountbatten as mediator between the Dutch and Indonesians, the British government commissioned him to spend three years exploring the Bundu – remote and unknown areas of central and southern Africa. 'The parable of life as a journey, both an inward and outward journey, is told beautifully in *Venture to the Interior*', his daughter Lucia said to me in our film tribute. The books that followed – *The Lost World of the Kalahari* and *Heart of the Hunter* – consolidated his reputation.

Laurens had met Jung through his second wife, the psychotherapist and author Ingaret Giffard. 'Laurens was not in any sense a Jungian', said his friend Christopher Booker in the same film. 'He knew him as a friend. Jung was surrounded by a lot of very po-faced devotees who regarded him as a sort of God on earth, and there was Laurens who didn't ...' Booker went on to point out that Jung himself didn't solve the entire problem of human existence: 'What he did do was to provide some extraordinary insights into the way we all work. Now you have really to go through that and come out the other side.'

I, myself, am not quite as sure as Christopher Booker that Laurens did completely come out the other side. When I made those first films with him, I constantly had to try to filter out or tone down his tendency to place Jung on what I considered to be an unhelpfully tall pedestal. I recognised, perhaps, the tendency in myself and others to do the same in relation to Steiner; and I understand very well how our uncritical adulation of a person or cause can have a very alienating effect – particularly for those coming to such ideas for the first time.

However, it wasn't so much this aspect of Laurens's character that Jones laid bare, but rather his tendency to exaggerate a story to the point where it actually became untrue, often in the process elevating the importance of his own role in some event, whether in the war, politics or the field of conservation. I experienced a very mild version of this tendency when we were filming in the Kalahari desert and had a spot of bother with some lions. The following day Laurens related the incident to someone else, by which time the danger had become magnified beyond all recognition. Yet this tinkering with the truth must have been largely unconscious, since I who knew what had actually happened was there beside him – silent, but inwardly open-mouthed.

When talking with his granddaughter Emma about his increasing tendency in old age not to listen to alternative opinions, she drew attention to another aspect of this 'poetic licence' he so often employed. 'The other side of the capacity of telling stories', she said, 'is a kind of forcefulness of myth-making which won't brook contradiction. So he will have formed for himself an idea of a situation and it will have become so powerful a story that any alternative opinion is given no room. The story just sweeps over it.'

It's important at this stage to restate that Laurens van der Post was, in my experience, a most considerate and easy person to work with. He enjoyed being part of a team, and was always generous in his acknowledgement of other people's efforts. He was, however, somewhat weak on humour, and certainly didn't like to be teased – as happened once when we were on location in Africa. Quite a crisis developed when, after a hard day's work and in need of some relaxation, the delightful and talented cameraman Paul Bellinger played a game in which he gave us all nicknames. Laurens was none too pleased at being called a boy scout and decided we weren't taking 'the African experience' seriously enough. Perhaps this difficulty he had with laughing at himself was why *Private Eye* was constantly having a go at him, 'that South African Rasputin, van der Pump'; and on another occasion, in a parody of our series on Jung, it called him 'Laurens van der Post Office Tower Hamlets'.

The roots of these contradictions and flaws in Laurens's character are only explored briefly by Jones, and not with any great depth or sympathy. He does address what he calls Laurens's 'obsessive need to fantasise', including the invention of a family history 'to fit and illustrate his aspirations', but these observations are never balanced by any real acknowledgement of how much Laurens's writings meant to so many people at a time when the idea of a spiritual dimension to life was being increasingly elbowed out from every direction.

When Jones came to talk to me while researching the book, I trusted him sufficiently to share some of my reservations, as well as my enormous admiration and respect for what Laurens had achieved and for what he had championed. Jones largely ignored what I and others said that was positive. Instead he rather cruelly suggests in the book that Laurens simply had the wit, charm and literary skills 'to persuade the world that his inventions were real'. What is therefore unfair and dishonest about the biography is that everything that was fine and upright about Laurens's life and work, like the moral and practical support he gave to conservationists such as Robin Page and Ian Player, was largely side-lined to make way for what was clearly intended as a demolition job. No one's life is whiter than white, but very few people are complete villains either. 'Like most of us,' said Laurens's daughter Lucia, 'he did have trouble admitting to his shadow side. He was incredibly sensitive to criticism. He hated it. He really did feel obliged to be as wonderful as he wanted to be; and I think this is a problem we all of us have – admitting that there are areas in which we are less than perfect.'

'He taught me to trust the spirit in myself and guard it', said his granddaughter Emma. 'We live in an age', added Christopher Booker, 'when there are very few genuine wise old men. Laurens was, in many ways, a wise old bird – speaking for the spiritual dimension in all of us.'

'And he was a very complex man,' admitted Lucia, 'and very much more vulnerable than most people know. He told me a story once, and with such sadness. He always knew that his father didn't really like him. And I think that hurt remained with him for the rest of his life. He wanted love terribly. He needed admiration and he needed love. And I think that was the source of it.'

Towards the end of Laurens's life, the French writer Jean-Marc Pottiez compiled a book from a series of conversations that he had with Laurens. It was called *A Walk with a White Bushman*, which for me is a misleading title in that Laurens's ability to empathise so strongly with the bushmen came, I believe, from the very fact that he – like most of us – was very far removed from that primitive and in many ways blessed state in which the bushmen lived. Thus he was all the more aware of what we have lost and how one-sided we have become. Laurens was no bushman, but he had a strong sense and appreciation of that pure and childlike essence that still exists not just among a few people in the Kalahari desert, but in all of us – waiting to be reawoken at a more conscious level.

As he grew older many people increasingly looked upon Laurens van der Post as some sort of mystic, and therefore, depending on your understanding of that term, as either a wise and inspiring influence on people like Prince Charles, or a muddle-headed idealist who had somehow lost the plot. Jones quotes two dictionary definitions of the word mystic. The first: 'a person who seeks by contemplation and self-surrender to obtain union with God'; and the second: 'one who believes in the possibility of the spiritual apprehension of knowledge inaccessible to the intellect.' Jones then sticks the knife in, and imagines another definition. 'A third possibility', he writes, 'is that Laurens in his later books was so impenetrable that many of his admirers, unable to unravel their precise meaning, saw them as the work of a mystic.'

At the conclusion of Pottiez's book, Jean-Marc asks Laurens what he meant when, at the end of *Yet Being Someone Other*, he wrote that there was a 'Pentecostal spirit' blowing through the world. Laurens had already expressed the view to Pottiez that we are all, both individually and collectively, compelled increasingly to look within ourselves. There was nothing impenetrable about his reply to Pottiez's question, if you read the words carefully:

> Yes, it is one of the signs, and like all fateful signs is apocalyptic as well as redemptive. I think you never get a thrust into the human spirit which is not also accompanied by a thrust into the world without. This introverted thrust of nations and people I am talking about is accompanied by this extrovert thrust into outer space. And as we go farther into space and look down onto the earth, we will see it whole, not fragmented as it appears from here. We have now a universal goal, both within and without, in which everybody can participate and unite. This, I feel, in the end, will contribute decisively to a united view of human diversities designed not for conflict and fragmentation on earth, but to enrich our meaning in a common preparation for our journey to the stars.

The year after I made the series *Inner Journeys*, I directed the first of three films that were primarily about outer journeys – not to the stars, but here on the ground; one across Pakistan with Mark Tully, another in Spain with Michael Portillo, and then one from London to the Peloponnese in Greece with Ben Okri – all by rail: a bit like *One Pair of Eyes* on wheels! To separate inner from outer, however, is somewhat misleading, as the two are invariably intertwined.

Mark Tully

What so often motivates our outer journeys, I suspect, has its origins in what is stirring in relation to the deeper promises we've made to ourselves.

Enquiring about the train arrival times at the ticket office in Karachi, where our journey in Pakistan began, Mark was given various details, followed by the inevitable, *Inshallah* ('God willing'). 'In an Islamic country', he reminded us in his commentary, 'nothing is believed to happen without God's help.' Not such a quaint idea, I believe – especially if you adapt the words to include the idea of fate, karma, or simply the notion that we are not as completely in charge of our lives as we sometimes like to think. Working on the series *Great Railway Journeys* was a challenging exercise in accepting this fact, as well as bringing me in touch with many new and interesting people and places; and above all it enriched my thoughts on this theme of life as a journey.

The climax of our twelve hundred mile journey from Karachi to Peshawar – with a detour via the Bolan Pass to Quetta – was a thrilling ride in a small steam train through the Khyber Pass to the Afghan border. But my most lasting memory of Pakistan is something outwardly far less spectacular, but inwardly perhaps of much greater significance. I was constantly impressed by the way almost everyone stops what they are doing at regular intervals throughout the day to say their prayers. A railwayman, at whose signal box we were shooting a sequence, gave us permission to film him doing just that. It may not always have been the quality of prayer that Diana Lodge experienced in her Paris church, but I was impressed that so many people, especially in rural areas, exercised that discipline wherever they happened to be. Prayers apart, regular acknowledgement that there is something greater and wiser than us must surely be healthy.

In Spain, Michael Portillo's journey was from Granada in the south to his father's roots in the beautiful city of Salamanca. It was a touching tribute by a son to his poet father, Louis Gabriel Portillo – an idealist and a teacher of Law

Michael Portillo

who found himself on the wrong side in the Spanish Civil War, became a refugee in Britain and couldn't set foot in his native country until after Franco's death some twenty years later.

As we approached Salamanca at the end of our journey, Michael described the city not only as his father's scholastic *alma mater*, but as his spiritual home, 'the place he longed to be in those decades of exile. And I have no doubt that when he died, his spirit did return there.'

Later, alone in the city at night, Michael spoke very movingly about his father's last farewell to Salamanca, by which time the old man's mind was starting to wander. It was a farewell to life itself. 'Thinking back', he said in conclusion, 'it was better for my father to live in exile than under the yoke of fascism. But what a sacrifice – to walk away from your language and career and country and family. It puts firmly into context the setbacks that the rest of us sometimes suffer. They are as nothing.' In fact Michael had just recently lost his bid to lead the Conservative Party, and was soon to leave politics altogether.

Enriching and inspiring as these experience were in Spain and Pakistan, the railway journey that had a special relevance to this book – to the quest for meaning in our lives, and the questions we ask along the way – was the one I made in 1995 with the Nigerian poet and novelist Ben Okri. I had been very impressed by the originality and above all the authenticity of his acceptance speech in 1991, when he won the Booker Prize for his novel *The Famished Road*. However, when I approached him about making a film for *Great Railway Journeys*, his first reaction was 'Why?' and 'Where to?' I was now even more impressed – impressed that he hadn't simply jumped at the suggestion as an opportunity to be in the limelight and on television. A week or so later he came back to me with an idea for a theme, based on his initial reaction to the proposal. Why do we travel? he asked. Why are we so restless? What are we looking for? Is travel a quest or an escape? I was reminded of Don Quixote's idealism, and his eccentric yet chivalrous journey, prompted by far more than mere curiosity.

Together Ben and I then hammered out a treatment that took some time for the BBC to accept. Were we being too highbrow? Would we be making too great a demand on the audience's intelligence? Such was the attitude increasingly permeating the corridors of power at the corporation. Fortunately the executive producer of the series, David Taylor, was a thoughtful and supportive ally.

The journey we eventually worked out and filmed was from London to Arcadia – a remote and unspoilt region of the Peloponnese in Greece, made famous by the poets Ovid and Virgil over two thousand years ago. Since then Arcadia has become synonymous with rural tranquillity, simplicity and ancient virtues – a Golden Age which was, according to a popular Greek proverb, 'before the creation of the moon'. This notion of some terrestrial paradise, a sort of lost Garden of Eden, has inspired writers, composers and artists for centuries. Ben called it 'a cry for peace'. As we observed the faces of anxious travellers at the old Eurostar terminal at Waterloo Station, he spoke these words: 'Anxiety and stress. Anxiety and stress. What are we looking for? Where are we going? Problems. Partings. Restlessness. Have we lost something? Can we find it again? These questions bother me. Don't they bother you?'

Those faces – the first of many powerful and beautiful images in the film – were captured by Mike Robinson, who had also been my cameraman on the programme with Michael Portillo. My equally perceptive assistant producer, Rachael Heaton-Armstrong, helped me to find the many and varied characters who, along the way, would illuminate our theme from every sort of angle.

Ben's first conversation was at the Gare du Nord in Paris with the driver of our train, Jean-Luc Romain – 'a man', wrote Ben, 'who spends most of his working life with trees, roads and houses hurtling towards him at nearly 200 miles per hour. I wonder what his sense of reality is like?' Eurostar had kindly agreed to lay on a driver whose passion was gardening, and it was to his garden in the suburbs of Paris that he invited us. In the film the encounter was presented as though it all happened by chance – such are the tricks we get up to.

Jean-Luc's beautiful creation was an example, Ben suggested, of how many people create their own modest Arcadias in the form of a simple garden amidst the noise and pollution of the modern age. 'Because of the impact of technology in all our lives', said Jean-Luc, surrounded by his dahlias and geraniums, 'we need to return to our origins, to nature. We need space to work the earth, to rediscover our roots and to find some peace'. Ben then asked him whether he thought that it was possible to combine modern life with a glimpse, at least, of paradise. 'Yes', said his wife, 'we need it – if we want to survive, yes.'

From a little Arcadia we moved on to a large one. For the French kings, Versailles was a sort of terrestrial paradise, but not for Marie Antoinette, the wife of Louis XVI. 'One king's paradise', wrote Ben, 'was another queen's prison.' And so, a mile or so from the palace, she created L'Hameau – a little hamlet with its own farm, pond and mill; it was her own idea of Arcadia, modelled on the Austrian countryside of her childhood. Here she changed into the clothes of a shepherdess, so the legend goes; but the buildings themselves are only a façade, like a stage set – as sad and empty as the queen's attempt to live a different and more authentic kind of life.

Our main reason for stopping off in Paris, however, was to see not only one of the greatest and most enigmatic paintings in the world, but also one of the most important icons of the Arcadian legend. On Tuesdays the Louvre is closed, and that was when the director, Pierre Rosenberg – a passionate expert on the French painter Nicolas Poussin – was able to guide Ben through the labyrinth of Poussin's painting of the *The Shepherds of Arcadia* and their mysterious encounter with a tomb (see colour plate 10). Rosenberg called it a sad story, 'a story Poussin is able to tell with his brushes and not with words'. On the tomb is written *Et in Arcadia ego* ('I too am in Arcadia'), and the figures are studying the inscription. 'What does it mean?' he asked. 'It means that in Arcadia, even in paradise, even when everyone is happy, death is present. So these four people are discovering the existence of death.'

Rosenberg told Ben that in another version of the picture, also painted in the 17th century, by the Italian Guercino, two startled shepherds have come across a skull. In Poussin's first version of the scene there was also a skull. These pictures represent what Rosenberg called a brutal encounter with

Ben Okri outside the Louvre

death. In the version at the Louvre, Rosenberg said, 'it is more a meditation. It is not a dead person. With Poussin that is always his greatness. He's not only a man of events; he's a man of thinking, of contemplation.'

'Listening to Pierre Rosenberg speak with such feeling about Poussin's painting', wrote Ben, 'made me wonder whether he too had some private place of enchantment.' 'Where would you say your Arcadia lies?' he then asked him. 'The Louvre on a Tuesday' was Rosenberg's immediate answer, the day when the museum was closed to the public and he could enjoy it on his own. He went on to suggest that museums are, in a certain way, Arcadias in our time. 'People come here to forget the troubles of everyday life. They come here because they know that contact with great masterpieces is a way for them to be enriched by this contact. There's a certain morality in museums.' He acknowledged, too, the educational task, and indeed simply the pleasure that museums can give people. He also spoke of the responsibility that those in charge of museums felt, and his awareness that people are not only expecting to see great works of art, but 'are expecting something more, and we have to try to find out what it is exactly. Arcadia is a good answer.'

On the train from Paris to Switzerland Ben entered into conversation with some American tourists and told them about the theme of our journey. One of them responded by saying that when travelling around she'd often thought 'this would be a good place to be'. Yet she always ended up feeling that her home was the place where she felt most at peace, 'and if I can be at peace with myself that's what is most important … Travelling teaches one that the grass is not always greener on the other side'.

Travelling, whether inwardly or outwardly, is, on the other hand, a very basic instinct in everyone who is even remotely curious about the world and our own place in it. In Goethe's great epic *Faust*, there is a scene in Part Two in which Faust, now old and blind, goes on an inner journey through the cultural and spiritual phases of human evolution, and for a brief moment, seduced by the Arcadian childhood of mankind, is tempted to cease his restless striving.

Our next stop was the Goetheanum in the village of Dornach, near Basel – the huge and striking building designed by Steiner and dedicated to Goethe, and the headquarters of the Anthroposophical Society. Ben called it 'as bold in its shape as Goethe's work as poet and scientist'. Here, every few years, over a period of five days, the whole of *Faust* is performed. In Part One, Faust finally makes his pact with the devil, Mephistopheles, so overwhelming is his quest for knowledge. Ben talked to the actor and director Georg Davas about Goethe's message – that essentially we have to move on and grow up, however tempting the Arcadian state of innocence may be, and however dangerous the way ahead. As *we* moved on, travelling through the Alps towards Italy, Ben spoke these words:

> Journeys are full of surprises. Isn't it strange that on our way to Arcadia we encounter Goethe's Faust, and through it are reminded that materialism – the dirt and stuff of life – is actually an essential part of our growth, our spiritual growth. We also need, like Faust, to roll up our sleeves and get our hands dirty, and somehow live with life's awkward compromises and squeeze out from them some sort of redemption. Rather than slaying the dragon of materialism, we should be getting into its skin, suggested Goethe's disciple Rudolf Steiner. Think of what could be done with all that fire and energy if directed wisely towards the great problems of our personal lives and our troubled age. So perhaps what Goethe is whispering to us is that our restless striving is the clay out of which we have to shape the wonderful possibility that God created in his own image.

These thoughts about 'the dirt and stuff of life' echo what the Jesuit scientist Teilhard de Chardin wrote in his essay 'The Spiritual Power of Matter' in *Hymn of the Universe*, where he communicates both his reverence for the material world and his constant awareness of spirit. For Teilhard, with his vision of creation as an evolutionary process, the existence of matter is the necessary precondition for the appearance on earth of spirit. He calls it 'the matrix of spirit' – in other words not the source of life, but that which supports its emergence.

'Son of man', wrote Teilhard, 'bathe yourself in the ocean of matter; plunge into it where it is deepest and most violent; struggle in its currents and drink of its waters. For it cradled you long ago in your preconscious existence; and it is the ocean that will raise you up to God.' And in his 'Hymn to Matter', in the same book, Teilhard writes with even greater passion:

> Blessed be you, harsh matter, barren soil, stubborn rock: you who yield only to violence, you who force us to work if we would eat ... Blessed be you, mortal matter: you who will one day undergo the process of dissolution within us and will thereby take us forcibly into the very heart of that which exists ... I bless you, matter, and you I acclaim: not as the pontiffs of science or the moralizing preachers depict you, debased, disfigured – a mass of brute forces and base appetites – but as you reveal yourself to me today, in your totality and your true nature.

Back on our train to Arcadia and before reaching Brindisi in southern Italy and the boat that would take us to Greece, we stopped in Venice – a magnificent testament to humanity's ability to shape 'blessed matter' into forms that are both sublime and functional. There Ben talked to the professor of English and American literature, Rossella Zorzi, herself a native of the city. They discussed Venice's Arcadian quality – the beauty, the water, and no motor cars. 'Not pastoral', she said, 'but very human ... You talk to people in the street ... a more old-fashioned world.' She spoke of the peace of the place when there were fewer tourists around, and the way that writers who come there are often helped to find their voice again.

In response to Ben's question about her own private Arcadia, Rossella chose the Palazzo Barbaro, and its relationship to the writings of Henry James, 'the transformation of this beautiful place into words by James'. He stayed there for a time and described it in *The Wings of the Dove* and in some of his essays. 'It still exists,' she said, 'faded, still as it was – not redecorated, not flashy.' She spoke of her Arcadia as 'a pause from the horrors of the world, which I feel are very strong today'. And as long as we still believe in the power of art and literature, she concluded, there is an opportunity for everyone to have small Arcadias of their own.

'A city of water that mirrors the heavens – but also paradoxically has something of the decaying grandeur of humanity. Is that why Venice haunts us?' asked Ben as we left the city and headed south. On the train we had another of those wonderful encounters that turn all theories on their head. Ben – in full philosophical mode – suggested to a young American backpacker that we're all searching for something. 'What is your search about?' Ben asked him. 'Gee', he said, 'I don't know. I just want to have fun.'

A little later, through our delightful interpreter Alessandro Nigro, Ben asked two young Italian children in our compartment what their idea of paradise on earth would be. 'A country only with children', was the reply, accompanied by lots of laughter. 'And your parents?' asked Ben. 'There would be one country for children and another country for parents', he was told.

Before catching the overnight boat from Brindisi to Patras, Ben paid his respects at the statue to Virgil, sadly covered with ugly graffiti – 'surely he deserves better than this'. Ben called him one of the greatest poets who ever lived, the man who wrote: *omnia vincit amor* (love conquers all). Although Virgil never visited Arcadia, it was he above all who inspired the whole Arcadian legend. 'I hope', said Ben, 'that in some way he's with us as an invisible guide.'

On deck at dawn the next morning Ben came across the Greek writer and philosopher Emilios Bourantinos. It was, in fact, another of my schemes, made to look like chance, though as with all the other interviewees I had kept them entirely apart until we started to film. As the boat headed towards the Ionian Islands, Emilios shared with Ben his sense that all travelling is an attempt to reclaim our oneness with the world. 'We lost it', he said, 'when we began objectifying the world and intellectualising it. When we did that, we lost our ability to be in total contact with the world, and that's what we're trying to regain by journeying, whether physically, as I am doing now, or otherwise.'

Ben then asked Emilios whether he thought this loss was perhaps necessary, in order that our oneness with the world could be experienced at a higher level. It is, of course, the thought that lies behind those lines of T.S. Eliot about returning to where we started and knowing the place for the first time. Emilios agreed. 'Absolutely! Eve had to bite the apple in the Garden of Eden.' He then told Ben a story about a student studying the Kabbala who asks his teacher: 'Why is the world in such a mess if God – the all-knowing, all good – created it?' The teacher replies that God had to learn his lesson as well. He had to make mistakes. Ben responded by mentioning 'a very mysterious and very beautiful thought' expressed by the German poet Rilke, that it is only through us human beings that God learns.

Ben then told Emilios that most of the people he'd talked to on our journey to Arcadia had spoken of travelling as either an escape or a quest, but when he'd asked what they were questing for they hadn't been able to say. 'They don't know what they're looking for,' he said, 'but they're looking for something, and they'll know it when they find it. Do you feel this is an intrinsic part of travelling?'

'Oh, yes', replied Emilios. 'If you really knew what you were looking for, you would not be travelling; you would stop where you are. You don't need to travel if you really know.' This sense that the truth is staring us in the face, right under our very noses as it were, was one of the thoughts expressed by

Ron Eyre at the end of *The Long Search*; but he also recognised that the journeys he'd been privileged to make had helped him to realise it.

Likewise, Saint-Exupéry's little prince had to leave his planet and travel to our earth in order to understand his relationship with the troublesome and temperamental rose that he loved so much. There, in the desert, the fox teaches him about taming and responsibility, and that one only understands what one has tamed: 'It is the time you have wasted for your rose that makes your rose so important … You become responsible, forever, for what you have tamed'. It was a lesson that could only be learnt through a truly momentous voyage.

During Ben's conversation with Emilios we passed the island of Ithaca, which is why I had got them both out of bed at 6am! It was the place from which Odysseus had set off to fight in the Trojan Wars; the struggles and obstacles of his twenty-year journey home are the subject of Homer's *Odyssey*. A modern Greek poet, Cavafy, took this prolonged return to Ithaca as a metaphor for the journey of life. Ben discovered that Emilios shared his passion for Cavafy's poem 'Ithaca', and read him these lines:

Always keep Ithaca in your mind.
To arrive there is your ultimate goal.
But do not hurry the voyage at all.
It is better to let it last for long years;
and even to anchor at the isle when you are old,
rich with all that you have gained on the way,
not expecting that Ithaca will offer you riches.

Ithaca has given you the beautiful voyage.
Without her you would never have taken the road.
But she has nothing more to give you.

And if you find her poor, Ithaca has not defrauded you.
With the great wisdom you have gained, with so much experience,
you must surely have understood by then what Ithacas mean.

Back on a train again, we travelled from Patras to Corinth, to begin the final journey into Arcadia itself. But before Corinth we stopped at a little taverna by the sea (where I tried unsuccessfully to teach Ben to swim!) The taverna was run by Mary Kelly and her Greek husband, Elias. She told Ben that she'd left Ireland simply to see the world, but with no intention of leaving her homeland for good. 'I was looking for somewhere where I could feel more myself', she said. She now had three children and seemed blissfully happy. 'It's my husband', she went on, 'it's he that makes it idyllic for me. He just lives his life as it comes; never worries about tomorrow and never cries about yesterday. And that's something new for me, and something really good for me.'

'Another private Arcadia', observed Ben in his commentary. 'One that is found in a relationship.' And before leaving the taverna I introduced him to another character whom Rachael and I had uncovered on our recce several months earlier. Nigel Fisk-Solomons was an Englishman with an intriguing story, an artist who'd settled in Greece and had a Greek wife. Like Mary, he seemed to have found his fulfilment away from his homeland. Ben asked him why he left in the first place. He'd lived in Cheltenham, and worked as an undertaker, 'to support my vice which is painting'. But every day, as he put bodies into coffins, he'd thought, 'It's one day closer to me being inside a coffin.' Finally, offered a chance to sail with a friend in his boat to Ibiza, and after an initial hesitation, he said to himself: 'What the hell!' – chucked in his job, gave his flat to his brother, sold his possessions, set sail – and has never looked back. The encounter left Ben with this thought: 'Nigel is the only person we've met who, like the shepherds in Poussin's painting, seems to have actually encountered the enigmatic inscription *Et in Arcadia ego*. Even in life there is death. Even in happiness there is death. Wouldn't it be magnificent if we could learn to be more inspired by death.'

Nigel Fisk-Solomons and Ben Okri

The last stage of our journey was visually the most spectacular of all. 'Increasingly away from the stress of cities', wrote Ben, 'travelling by train has become for me a kind of moving oasis. A little red and blue oasis would now take me up into the mountains of Arcadia.' The train had only three carriages, and for a while we parked ourselves in the rear, in what would have been the driver's compartment had we been travelling in the opposite direction. 'Sitting in the back of this train', said Ben in a spontaneous and inspired soliloquy, as he pretended to be the assistant train driver, 'you see not a landscape that is approaching, but receding. It is, in some ways, a regrettable way of travelling. You don't greet things, you say goodbye to things.' At this point, a beautiful and spectacular viaduct disappears into the distance. 'You think about bridges that you've just crossed', he added.

Gradually Ben warmed to the experience. 'I actually quite like this kind of looking', he continued: 'Always one lives through life with one's eyes facing forward, so things come at you and then they go behind you. And when they go behind you it's as if they disappear, they vanish, they don't exist anymore. Whereas like this they always exist.'

I was reminded of my interest in time, and the idea that it too – the whole of the past – never actually disappears. This experience of travelling into the future but facing backwards, not forwards, then prompted another thought from Ben – of life being like a chain, a sort of relay system 'whereby each one of us just passes on the baton of our lives to the next generation, and that way we keep something alive that is greater than us. Maybe what we keep alive are the hidden dreams of a forgotten divinity.' He then added: 'Maybe these dreams are the divinities themselves.'

Before Ben got off the train at a little station in the heart of the Arcadian wilderness, he stuck a pin in the notion of a neat, happy ending to our quest. 'I'm very ill at ease with arrivals', he said. 'Or if you do arrive, you should continue to keep postponing your destination, keep extending your dream. Because when you arrive, what do you do?'

'You will see me get off in Arcadia', he concluded, 'but you won't see me arrive there, because I've postponed my Arcadia to somewhere else, and I'm going to be doing that till the end of my days.' In saying this Ben had well and truly taken to heart what Cavafy had written about the journey to Ithaca. Perhaps it is healthier to concentrate not on the destination, but on the next stage of our journey. We all have a goal, an Arcadian dream – some of us more consciously than others. We long, too, for answers to those great questions: Why am I here? Who am I? What does it all mean?

It would be nice to imagine, as did Tolstoy as a child, that there is a secret carved on a green stick and buried in a forest that answers all these riddles. In fact it is probably only through the journey itself, if we are courageous enough to keep going, that the secret is gradually revealed.

CHAPTER 33

Time to Learn

The famous American hairdresser Vidal Sassoon had his own television show for a while – a mixture of beauty hints, dietary information and popular psychology. In one programme, as the theme music surged up to announce the commercial break, Sassoon had just enough time to say: 'Don't go away. We'll be back with a marvellous new diet, and then a quick look at incest.'

Neil Postman relates this incident in his book *The Disappearance of Childhood*, and his theme – the trivialising and corrupting influence of television – is further developed in his equally insightful and important book *Amusing Ourselves to Death*. 'The problem', he writes, 'is not that television presents us with entertaining subject matter, but that all subject matter is presented as entertaining.' In his view – he was writing about television in the USA thirty years ago – 'We are a people on the verge of amusing ourselves to death.' He refers to Americans as the best entertained and quite likely the least well-informed people in the western world; and he quotes the celebrated television presenter Bill Moyers's concern that 'we Americans seem to know everything about the last twenty four hours, but very little of the last six centuries or the last sixty years'.

Postman himself goes so far as to say that the problem is not what we watch but *that* we watch. Increasingly the style and content of television in America – with its hundreds of channels – is becoming the norm everywhere; not even the BBC is immune, and in its rush to adjust to the so-called digital age seems to have dismembered itself in the process, and somehow lost its soul along the way. Picture quality may have improved, and output increased, but the range has narrowed. None of this is helped by the fact that our screens are increasingly dominated by people called 'celebrities' who are, as they say in Texas, 'all hat and no cattle!'

In the Hetherington Memorial Lecture delivered in November 2008 the distinguished writer and broadcaster Joan Bakewell spoke of the 'insidious falling away of moral integrity' that has crept into broadcasting generally. And in an article in *The Guardian* (July 7th 2007) entitled 'A Great Turn-Off', the media journalist Janine Gibson wrote of British television as 'unrecognisably degraded' and permeated by a 'corrosive cynicism'. She quotes the television executive Michael Grade's description of the once respected medium as having 'a casual contempt for the viewer'. Another executive, at Channel Four Television, recently defended the company (in its use of 'fruity language') as 'a champion of pushing the boundaries'. It's a pity that other boundaries of real significance aren't explored more often.

In an article in *The Guardian* (May 11th 2009) on the demise of cultural programming on the main terrestrial channels, the BBC's creative director Alan Yentob said: 'It tells us we're in different times'. In my opinion it is the negligence and lack of vision on the part of those who call the tune in broadcasting that is to some extent responsible for these 'different times'.

Postman in his foreword to *Amusing Ourselves to Death* writes about George Orwell's fear, expressed in *1984*, that we will be overcome by externally imposed oppression. He points out that in Aldous Huxley's equally chilling *Brave New World*, however, no Big Brother is required to deprive people of their autonomy, maturity and history. As Huxley saw it, people will come to love their oppression and to adore the technologies that undo their capacities to think. Postman writes that:

> Orwell feared those who would deprive us of information, Huxley feared those who would give us so much that we would be reduced to passivity and egoism. Orwell feared the truth would be concealed from us. Huxley feared the truth would be drowned in a sea of irrelevance.

I mention this partly because Postman's book on the erosion and disappearance of childhood is very relevant to one of the main themes I will be exploring in this chapter, but also because his gloomy analysis of television has a bearing on the obstacles I was increasingly meeting in my own career, and in my attempts to explore deeper issues through documentary films.

The last film I produced for the BBC was plastered all over with the contempt for the viewer to which Michael Grade referred. In 2002 I was contracted to make a programme with Michael Portillo about Queen Elizabeth I for the series *Great Britons*. But by this time the ethos was such that a telephone number had to be superimposed in the top corner of the picture almost throughout the programme so that people could call in at any moment to vote for Elizabeth as against Brunel, Churchill or John Lennon as the greatest Briton ever. The implication behind this farce was that nobody will watch a boring old documentary unless there is some gimmick to jazz it up.

Until now I had tried to make programmes about people and subjects that interested and inspired me, and which I believed would be of interest, and perhaps an inspiration, to others. Many of my films were quite simply tributes of one sort or another; but what was increasingly required were programmes with a sensational slant, and above all ones that didn't challenge what was perceived as the shrinking attention-span of the audience. 'A Quick Look at Incest' would have no shortage of backers.

Certainly, programmes about sensational or distressing subjects have their place, but if – along with the news itself – they tend to dominate the schedules, elbowing out coverage of the many positive and courageous initiatives that are taking place at every level of society and in every culture, they will invariably have the effect of reinforcing people's sense that the world is a terrible and depressing place, and getting worse by the day. There are, of course, many worrying and dangerous trends politically, socially and economically, and these should undoubtedly be reported – as they are with particular skill and sensitivity by *Channel Four News*. There are also still, from time to time, thoughtful and superbly made documentaries and dramas, but they are increasingly thin on the ground. The shallowness of so much else that is now on offer has fortunately not entirely overtaken radio.

The trend to 'dumb down' is based, I presume, on the assumption that people would simply not be interested in anything more challenging. I believe this is totally misguided. People are, at heart, neither stupid nor insensitive, and it is this recognition that should underpin a commitment to public service broadcasting in particular. Indeed, the licence fee is only justified if a substantial number of programmes are made that would not otherwise be made, and in a climate that is free of both commercial and government pressure and influence.

One example of the more thoughtful disposition that I believe lives increasingly in many men and women today, and which is related to the area that particularly interests me, is that despite the recent publishing success of anti-God books and their spin-offs on television, more and more people seem to be searching for something deeper and more meaningful in their lives. And especially, it seems, there is hunger for something that points to a spiritual dimension to existence that is not necessarily expressed either in the language of mainstream science or of traditional religion; something, in other words, that tries to synthesise and transcend both these ways of seeing. It's why, I imagine, Philip Pullman's *His Dark Materials* trilogy has been so successful, with its talk of interpenetrating universes, witches, a Republic of Heaven, talking animals, and dark matter.

Pullman, despite his claims to be just a story-teller, is clearly interested in the new frontiers that confront physicists, as well as in people's sense that there are beings and forces behind the sense-perceptible world, and that these realms are as much in evolutionary turmoil as the world we inhabit consciously from day to day. The idea of a war in heaven is made startlingly real and contemporary, but in the story Pullman tells, it is a war against God in which the angels are on the side of humanity.

My only problem with Pullman's trilogy is that, along with other modern sagas like *Star Wars* and the *Harry Potter* series, it is largely technological gadgets rather than the potential in human beings themselves that enable their heroes to travel into other worlds or into other dimensions of reality. These heroes and heroines do, however, often display great courage, and that – it could be argued – is perhaps our finest potentiality of all. The huge interest in these books and films is certainly another indication of the appetite there is for stories that break through the barriers of what we call 'reality', touching on some very profound areas of metaphysics. Pullman's use of the word 'Dust', for example, as 'only a name for what happens when matter begins to understand itself' echoes certain thoughts of Teilhard de Chardin.

'There is a correspondence between the microcosm and the macrocosm', a mad old Professor in *Northern Lights* tells Lyra, the child heroine of *His Dark Materials*. But Pullman has already written that 'even in the depths of his madness a little common sense still flickered'. And so the Regius Professor of Cosmology at the University of Gloucester continues: 'The stars are alive, child. Did you know that? Everything out there is alive, and there are grand purposes abroad! The universe is full of intentions, you know. Everything happens for a purpose.'

This may all sound far-fetched to some, but how about this paragraph written by *The Guardian*'s science correspondent, Ian Sample, in an article (May 15th 2007) entitled: 'A ghostly halo that could unlock the dark secret of the universe':

> Scientists know there is more to the universe than they can see because the small percentage of the visible universe – stars, planets and clouds of gas and dust – moves as if acted upon by gravitational forces seeming to come from nowhere.

The article is about a possible new clue to the invisible and hypothetical substance called dark matter which astronomers believe accounts for eighty per cent of the mass of the universe, stretching out to form what Sample calls 'a celestial skeleton around which galaxies form'. If you start to juggle with care a few words like energy and infinity with the familiar language of the great religions, it doesn't take much imagination to start building bridges from contemporary science to insights and intimations that have long existed about the mysteries that underpin all existence – though the danger also exists of trivialising both science and spirituality in the process.

Someone steeped in those mysteries is Rowan Williams, the current Archbishop of Canterbury. In writing about the National Theatre production of *His Dark Materials*, Williams has no problem in recognising that the God who is the arch-villain in Pullman's trilogy, and who is finally destroyed, is not the God of Rowan Williams's religion. In the story Pullman calls him the Authority; he is not the Creator. 'There may have been a creator', says the African King Ogunwe in *The Amber Spyglass*, 'or there may not: we don't know. All we know is that at some point the Authority took charge, and since then, angels have rebelled, and human beings have struggled against him too.'

At the conclusion of his article, Rowan Williams mentions the phrase 'purification by atheism', which he takes to mean that faith needs to be reminded regularly of the gods in which it should not believe. He writes that in his opinion Philip Pullman and his stage adapter Nicholas Wright have done this very effectively for the believer. 'I hope too', he adds, 'that for the non-believing spectator, the question may somehow be raised of what exactly the God is in whom they don't believe.'

It's a good question for people like the evangelical atheist Richard Dawkins, whose book *The God Delusion* has created such waves. My own feeling about this cleverly written diatribe from Dawkins is that he has produced a fundamentally dishonest book. Some of the gods he demolishes do indeed deserve such treatment, as do their fanatical and narrow-minded followers. But in language that is often cruel and insensitive, Dawkins puts everyone who has a sense that there are forces and influences greater than us into the same boat. 'I decry supernaturalism in all its forms', he writes. For him anything that is not capable of being analysed physically is not eligible for scientific investigation and therefore outside the domain of objective knowledge. Yet much to the embarrassment of many in the scientific community, he is increasingly perceived to be as rigid a fundamentalist in his sphere of work as the religious fundamentalists he quite rightly exposes.

There is also a strange confusion in what Dawkins has written about the so-called 'selfish gene': on the one hand he acknowledges that although our biological nature sets us apart and therefore in competition with one another, we have the potential and, in very many cases, the urge to transcend our genetic destiny and our inherent selfishness, and to become more altruistic. 'Let us understand', he writes in *The Selfish Gene*, 'what our own selfish genes are up to, because we may then at least have the chance to upset their designs, something which no other species has ever aspired to.'

What he fails to acknowledge, however – and here lies the confusion – is that the aspirations we have to evolve in the way he advocates, appear to be unconnected with our physical, biological make-up, and belong therefore under the heading of that word he so decries – 'supernaturalism', a word which, along with 'God' and 'spirituality', are out of bounds in his vocabulary.

I can understand that as a scientist Dawkins experiences extreme irritation that everything which is still deeply mysterious – the phenomenon of life itself being the greatest mystery of all – tends to be automatically shuffled off by many into a religious pigeonhole. He calls this the 'God of the gaps' – the gaps being the holes in our knowledge. Those who say that there are things we not only don't know, but can never know, is for Dawkins like a red rag to a scientific bull, and understandably so. But to arrive at the right answers to life's mysteries we must ask the right questions – a fact understood very well by a man whom I have already quoted many times, Ralph Waldo Emerson. 'Undoubtedly', he wrote in *Nature*, 'we have no questions to ask which are unanswerable.'

What Dawkins and his like fail to recognise, however, is that to comprehend the mysteries still confronting us we will need to grow not just intellectually, but in wisdom. Cleverness – the rationalistic and analytical way of knowing – is not enough: it's not the only way of knowing. In any case, the scientific and psychological data itself, as Professor Chew at Berkeley and others have indicated, seems to demand a new way of knowing. What we call science will need to develop in depth and vision in order to truly understand the universe and our place in it. And what we recognise as the religious sensibility is, I am sure, an essential ingredient in arriving at that wisdom. It is, after all, an attitude of openness and humility, without which the truth remains inaccessible. It's what every good scientist, as well as artist, acknowledges constantly. We have two very helpful words to describe these windows into the source of all wisdom and creativity: imagination and inspiration.

The wisdom we strive towards will gradually help us to recognise, perhaps, that God is not some sort of separate person in the way that we experience each other in daily life; indeed that the word 'God', partly because of its previous connotations, may not always be the most helpful word to use. That doesn't mean, however, that past intimations about the divine are nonsense or misguided, but rather that they reflect a state of consciousness that attempted and attempts still, as best it can, to make sense of and articulate a sublime truth; an acknowledgement, in other words, of the intelligence that clearly pervades the entire universe, and which is very hard to explain by chance alone.

Yet to challenge the existence not only of God, but of the human soul itself, is the mission of militant atheists such as Richard Dawkins and Christopher Hitchins, as philosopher Jeremy Naydler suggests in an article for the journal *New View* (Autumn 2007). Naydler describes Dawkins as writing 'with a kind of demonic energy', but accuses him of not having the patience to enter into meaningful dialogue with religion, or with the religious mentality:

> While he is often incisive and willing to sustain a line of rational argument if he feels he is on a winning streak, he also tends to dismiss the more recalcitrant and deeper questions of religion with a passing caustic remark. He is a master of sarcasm, ridicule and mockery.

Ultimately what Dawkins seems unable to recognise, either in himself or in the world around him – and despite his basic optimism about our human potential – is an underlying and supersensible reality that inspires and nourishes not only our capacity to reason, but also our ability to have emotions and intuitions, and to glimpse a sense of meaning in our lives and in the life of the universe. But 'meaning' is another word that Dawkins hates. Perhaps, at the end of the day, it is simply a whiff of arrogance on his part: 'No one can be cleverer than us scientists, and therefore it must all have happened by chance.' Yet this ignores the fact that although the people who built the microscope that Dawkins uses, or the car that he drives, are indeed extremely clever, we human beings are infinitely more complex and miraculous than any machine – and we certainly didn't make ourselves. Surely it is reasonable to suppose, therefore, that there must have been intelligence and creativity at work in that particular task, however long it took to evolve, and that this intelligence may be the source of our own growing ability to think, imagine and create.

In a recent anthroposophical journal Andrew Wolpert offered another interesting perspective on Dawkins's obsession, suggesting that the compelling motive to prove that God does not exist 'actually betokens an unconscious yearning to connect with this ineffable thing'. He compares Dawkins to a child who deliberately challenges the authority of parents, 'not to irritate them, not from a superior position of insight, but deeply out of a longing to have the authority confirmed, to feel the safety of the boundary that is reaffirmed in the loving and reassuring response to the challenge'.

I have long been interested in the parallels between child development and the evolution of consciousness to which Wolpert refers. These processes also seem to me very relevant to our changing image of heaven. In 1993, in order to continue making films about such subjects, I formed a small non profit-making company called *Hermes Films*. One of my first commissions was to make a promotional film for the Steiner Schools Fellowship that we called *Time to Learn*. I filmed at four schools – in rural Herefordshire, a city school in Aberdeen, at Kings Langley on the outskirts of London, and finally at Michael Hall in Sussex, the school I had first visited exactly forty years earlier. At the time there were twenty-five Rudolf Steiner (Waldorf) Schools in Britain and over five hundred worldwide. They have their own curriculum, but bridges of various sorts are made to state examinations. Timing – what is taught when – is an all-important consideration.

In a story called *William the Conspirator*, Richmal Crompton's famous character William has this to say in anticipation of a bad history report:

> What's the good of us usin' up all our brains at school so's we'll have none left when we're grown up an' have to earn our livins? I'd rather

keep mine fresh by not usin' it till I'm
grown up an' need it. I think that's why
grown-ups are so stupid, 'cause they've
used up all their brains over Latin an'
History an' such like when they were at
school, an' haven'nt got any left.

In essence, William's rather extreme view
sums up very well one aspect of the Waldorf
approach to early learning. In Steiner's view
the forces that unfold as intellect are initially
at work in building up the human body. If,
therefore, these latent intellectual faculties
in a child are awoken and stimulated
too early, it will in the long term have a
weakening effect on the physical organism
itself. Referring to the very early years in a
child's life in a series of lectures that he gave
in 1923 at Ilkley in Yorkshire on the theme of

Just William

education (published as *A Modern Art of Education*), Steiner said, 'Herein
lies truly the mystery of human evolution: All that is of the nature of soul
and spirit at one stage of life becomes physical – manifests itself physically
in later life.'

A considerable amount of research in Europe and the USA indicates that
intellectual pressure on very young children does not necessarily lead to high
achievement in later years, and can even have a damaging effect in terms
of their overall stability and self-confidence, and their well-being generally.
Along with a number of other thoughtful educationalists such as Froebel
and Pestalozzi, and the French psychologist Piaget, Steiner also recognised
childhood as having quite distinct phases. His conviction was based on
research into what he called the incarnating human individuality, the ego or I
– a process that takes place not just at conception or birth, but which unfolds
during three seven-year stages. Wrong or harmful input at an inappropriate
time could, in his view, cause major problems later in life. In fact our very
maturity as adult human beings can be undermined if these phases are not
acknowledged and respected, particularly in the early years of a child's life.

One of Neil Postman's main themes in *The Disappearance of Childhood*
is how 'grown-ups', as William calls them, are increasingly imposing their
mindset on children, especially through television, and are thereby eroding
the precious years in which awe and wonder, fantasy and imagination quite
naturally unfold. If we really want children to grow up into adults who are
creative and imaginative, as well as intelligent, then it would seem sensible

to nurture these very special gifts. Parents in particular, in their concern to prepare their children for a competitive world in which exams, university and ultimately the job market are what counts, often contribute to the pressures that the young increasingly experience. 'Expelled from the garden of childhood' is the metaphor that Postman coins to describe this alarming trend – a trend in which five-year-olds are now being threatened with tests before they even start school.

'Education is a journey not a race' is how one Waldorf teacher described their approach. For the opening sequence of *Time to Learn* I filmed in the kindergarten at Michael Hall where the emphasis was on creative play, imagination and rhythm. There is no formal learning until the children enter Class One around the age of six or seven – a tradition in mainstream education that is still normal in parts of Europe. There is, however, a definite structure to the day and to the week. Monday, for example, was the day for painting; Friday for baking. The teacher, Sally Lange, compared herself to a sort of second mother. The children helped her with the washing-up after break, cleaning the floor, polishing the table. She left them to play on their own.

There were tears and tantrums, like anywhere else, and I don't want to write about Waldorf education in the language of a promotional leaflet. However, I have to say that in the scenes I filmed, Sally did seem to be achieving her aim of creating a sort of second home for the children, with a busy, creative but essentially peaceful atmosphere in which reverence for life permeated everything. There was a daily prayer, and a 'ring-time' when they sat in a circle and sang traditional folk songs. The morning session ended with a story, the same one every day for a week, because of the children's instinctive love of repetition; and she told it, rather than read it. 'These fairy stories have a very deep meaning', Sally told me, 'and you can work on that when you learn them by heart.' I told her about a quotation of Einstein's that I had read recently: 'If you want your children to be intelligent, read them fairy tales. If you want them to be more intelligent, read them more fairy tales.' Lindsay Clarke, in our conversations together, referred to such tales as 'nourishment for the child's imaginative life'. I've also heard them described as 'dramas of the soul' – every character in a fairytale representing an aspect of our own make-up.

In *The Wisdom of Fairy Tales*, Rudolf Meyer writes of how these characters can lead us to discover 'the treasures in our own soul', for through them we become instinctively aware 'of the sorrows of life and the guidance of destiny'; aware, too, of the importance of faithfulness and morality, and that only through adversity are the prince and princess in each one of us finally united.

Still absorbed by this theme of early education, a year later I made a film for the BBC called *Clouds of Glory* in which I explored the concerns of a group

CLOUDS
OF
GLORY

A FILM
BY JONATHAN STEDALL

of parents in Brighton about what they and others perceive as the erosion of childhood. Some of the scenes were shot in the kindergarten of the Brighton Waldorf School. There, one of the helpers, Janice Britz – herself trained as a state nursery teacher – described to me a recent moment in the playground when some four-year-olds turned over a brick and discovered a nest of ants. Even she was amazed at their fascination and absorption with the scene, and at their ability to simply watch in wonder. At the back of her mind was the training she had received: 'Ask the children how many legs an ant has. Where is its thorax?' But she kept silent. Experience rather than knowledge seemed to her more appropriate for children to whom the world is still essentially a magical place. 'When they study biology later', she added, 'and start looking at the ant's thorax and things like that, they will have had the real experience of what ants are.'

Most of the parents and teachers with whom I spoke while making these two films – *Clouds of Glory* and *Time to Learn* – felt that children benefit from this gentle start and from being spared a premature confrontation with more abstract concepts. When ready, they take to their lessons with a freshness and eagerness to learn that is often not so apparent among children who have been at it longer. They are nourished, so the adults believe, by being allowed to adjust to the world at their own pace, in their own time. 'Each child has their own path to tread', said one of the teachers at Brighton, Thais Bishop. The unique gifts and qualities with which children are born need time and space to unfold – a process that can all too easily be undermined or even thwarted by an obsession with targets and competition. Of course children do gradually have to learn the ways of the world and to grow up. Nobody in the Waldorf School movement or anywhere else is denying that, or the wisdom and good intentions behind much that exists in the National Curriculum.

I know with my own children, both of whom attended Waldorf kindergartens – though in my son's case he preferred to be at home much of the time simply doing his own thing – that neither of them, despite drawing and painting endlessly, and knowing the letters of the alphabet from an early age, showed any inclination to read or write until they were about six, though we would never have put any obstacle in their way had they wished to do so. They simply enjoyed being read to, and above all listening to made-up stories. But if we are to be true to the notion of children adjusting to the world at their own pace then we have to recognise that some children do want to learn to read and write from quite an early age. Here there can be a certain rigidity in Waldorf education which becomes even more apparent as the children grow older and don't necessarily conform to some idealised pattern. They are, for example – whether we like it or not – simply more sophisticated, more worldly, than they were in 1919 when Rudolf Steiner launched the first Waldorf school in Stuttgart. We can and should do things to counteract the more extreme consequences of this trend, but we cannot turn a blind eye to the fact that what Steiner called the incarnating process is taking place more rapidly. Puberty, for example, is now often two or three years earlier than it was fifty years ago – though psychological maturity may still conform to traditional patterns, despite the seeming worldliness of many teenagers. This is all the more reason, the Waldorf teachers believe, for a curriculum that corresponds to what is taking place inwardly in the growing child, and not to what sort of clothes or jewellery they may be wearing. But as a generalisation it would be fair to say that children are, for better or worse, more awake to the world at a younger age.

Certainly, by the time my daughter moved into Class One at a Waldorf school she was ready to take off in terms of learning, and experienced enormous frustration at the slowness of the pace – so much so that after two terms she refused to continue at the school and from then on fitted happily into the state system. I'm sure she benefited from the absence of pressure, both from us and from her kindergarten, in those very early years, but I'm sad that at her Waldorf school, at that time, there wasn't sufficient flexiblility to accommodate a bright child who was eager to learn and no longer wanted to be treated like an infant.

Much the same thing happened to my son, though he stayed on until he was ten. From an early age he'd been interested in how things work and in building all sorts of contraptions. At school he became increasingly frustrated that his questions weren't answered, or by being told that he'd learn about that subject in three years' time. The budding scientist in him was neither acknowledged nor encouraged, and he too became bored.

This lack of flexibility on the part of some teachers is indicative, I feel, of a much deeper problem within the whole anthroposophical movement. Much of what Steiner communicated, usually as lectures, is in the form of suggestions. He, too, like all scientists could only probe so far. And here lies a danger; for if these suggestions – whether on the subject of education, agriculture, art or medicine – are taken literally and uncritically, they all too easily become dogmas. And anyway no system or theory – however profound the insights behind it – can be effective unless the teachers, farmers, doctors or artists make it their own and imbue it with their individual creativity and imagination.

People of all persuasions frequently use the phrase: 'Helping children to achieve their potential'. No one argues with that notion: it is a fine ideal, particularly if you imagine that our potential might be both magnificent and limitless. And, if translated to a world scale, this ideal makes what might seem naïve optimism on my part about a heaven on earth into something perfectly reasonable. What the world might become, like the child itself, has no limits. But it will finally depend on us, which is why education is so important and why I am dwelling on it at some length. There is an idealism that lives quite naturally in the young – alongside, it has to be said, all that is essentially self-centred and that divides us one from another. It is therefore essential that those finer qualities which exist in every child are nurtured, encouraged and allowed to unfold, otherwise nothing will really change in the world at large.

A global initiative called the *Alliance for Childhood* has come into being to help uphold these ideals. On their website the declared intention is to promote 'policies and practices that support children's healthy development, love of learning and joy in living', bringing to light 'both the promise and the vulnerability of childhood'. One aim is to raise public awareness of 'the importance of play and its current endangered status'; another – in the recognition that computers are reshaping children's lives both at home and at school – is to 'consider the potential harm, as well as the promised benefits of this change'.

In his book *Set Free Childhood*, Martin Large explores the impact of this early exposure to computers and television, and what concerned parents can try to do about it. In highlighting the seriousness that he and many others see in these trends, he writes: 'the needs of young children and the demands of the electronic media are on a collision course'; at present he sees children and childhood as the losers. Sally Lange at Michael Hall spoke to me about the increasing recognition – not just by Neil Postman – of the harmful effects that television can have. 'When children come for an interview', she said, 'I can tell whether they're television-watchers or not. It comes out most strongly in the way they play. Their concentration is not so good.'

There is, however, a danger that I readily acknowledge of ignoring children's simple resilience to what is harmful, as well as over-romanticising the innocence and purity of childhood – similar to the tendency I discussed earlier of being over-reverential towards our Stone Age ancestors. I too have read *Lord of the Flies*. In the scenario that I am imagining, we adults – despite all our failings and inadequacies – have a crucial role to play. We have been children ourselves and have gained as well as lost something along the way. Some people – though not William Golding – believe that children, like Rousseau's noble savage, are naturally good and that it is the world that corrupts them. But one of the kindergarten teachers at Brighton, Jose Alwyn, expressed the important thought that children cannot be described as either good or bad. 'However, they are open', she said, 'wide open to whatever surrounds them. The challenge is for *us* to be good.'

Despite the disappointment my wife and I experienced with our own children's time at a Waldorf school, I was very impressed with most of what I saw and experienced in Brighton and at the schools that I visited for the filming of *Time to Learn*. The Hereford Waldorf School has, since it was founded by Greta Rushbrooke in 1983, always valued the input of parents, both at a practical level as well as creatively. This has undoubtedly been a healthy influence on the atmosphere that permeates the school. Like a number of teachers in the Waldorf School movement, the Class One teacher, David Donaldson, came from the state system where he had taught English at a comprehensive school. It was the curriculum, he said, 'and the very thorough, satisfying and comprehensive view of child development' that attracted him to Waldorf education. Ideally he would now stay with the same group of children for eight years, taking them through what is called the Main Lesson for the first half of every morning. It is in this Main Lesson, taught in blocks of three or four weeks, that the curriculum unfolds – all the key subjects, from simple beginnings to the standards expected of any fourteen-year-old. 'It's a challenge', said David, 'but it is also one of its attractions. As a teacher you can never get stale.' But here lies one of the dangers, for if the class teacher is unable – at every stage – to meet the children's needs as they mature over those eight years, then frustrations and problems can develop.

In Class Three at the Kings Langley school we filmed the children drawing pictures of David and Goliath, having just been told the story in their religion lesson. Earlier in the year their teacher, Margaret Morgan, had given these eight- and nine-year-olds a four week Main Lesson on farming. It was time, she said, for children to come to grips with the world, to tackle the nuts and bolts of life – but still with the emphasis on doing things, rather than abstract knowledge. Their building Main Lesson was still to come, in which they would learn the whole process of getting permission, choosing and clearing a site, digging foundations, mixing cement and laying bricks. Part of their project was also to do maintenance work on the Wendy House that the previous class had built and which now had problems with its roof. There was a lovely scene in my film of some small children squashed into it, complaining about its size as well as the leaky roof.

In Aberdeen one of the Class Teachers, Bill Milne, had joined the Waldorf school after seventeen years as a history teacher in the state system. His experience there had been of dedicated teachers increasingly forced to teach in a certain way, with assessment taking over and a methodology that resulted in children glued to work sheets. 'You had to devise questions which were absolutely objective', he said, 'and the only way you can do that is by asking purely factual ones – dates, the names of kings etc.' He said in the end he felt that instead of being a teacher, he was becoming 'more of a classroom manager'.

I have always found the teaching of history in Waldorf schools particularly interesting. A real effort is made to give children the sense of a story unfolding, in many ways parallel to their own development towards maturity. An Ofsted report in July 2007 noted that although children between the ages of seven and eleven 'often know something about selected periods or events – for example, children in Victorian times, Henry VIII and his wives, or the Aztecs – they are weak at linking this information to form an overall narrative'. The report emphasised this point by saying that although taught in depth, 'major events such as the two World Wars and the holocaust are not set in a broader context'.

In the more recent Cambridge review of Primary education (February 2009) there is strong criticism of an over-emphasis on the skills of reading, writing and mathematics at the expense of other subjects. In the opinion of the seventy or so academics behind the report, who over three years consulted thousands of children, parents and teachers across the country, this one-sidedness limits children's enjoyment of school and risks severely compromising their natural curiousity, imagination and love of learning. National testing at the age of eleven has meant that schools focus on short-term learning at the cost of children's long-term development.

I spoke a great deal to one teacher at Kings Langley, Helen Weatherhead, who also came to Waldorf education from the state system and, like David Donaldson, was initially attracted by the curriculum: 'There was nothing that hadn't been thought out, nothing haphazard.' (I recently met the twelve year old granddaughter of a friend, who told me she'd been learning about Freud at her comprehensive, which sounds to me not only inappropriate but haphazard in the extreme.) Helen had been telling her class of ten-year-olds a Spanish folktale whose theme of resurrection and transformation showed, in her view, 'how loyalty and love can transform people', and therefore felt appropriate for

Easter. One of her aims in the religion lessons, she said, was 'to foster in the children a mood of reverence and respect for all living things, for the whole earth'. She went on to tell me how they try to give children the confidence to recognise their own individuality, 'to become individuals in their own right', an aim that I imagine no educator would quarrel with. 'Of course they have to have information', she said. 'They have to learn to think … but along with that you also have to educate the head through the heart, and educate their feelings. Because if you can do that, then they can transcend their own opinions and their own ideas, and can sympathise with other people. Even if they don't agree, they can understand other people's ideas.' This sort of education, she felt, can provide the basis for community, 'and that is what a classroom is, a class of mixed-ability children. It's like a microcosm of society, and I can't really think of a better preparation for life than that.'

Waldorf schools have a reputation for encouraging the arts, and certainly the art and craft work in all the schools I visited was impressive. The intention, however, is that art not only permeates all the work done in the classrooms, but that every subject is taught artistically – in other words creatively and imaginatively. A good example of this creativity was the scene I filmed at Kings Langley with the physics teacher, Nicholas Ridley – himself a former pupil. Just back from a surveying exercise with Class Ten (sixteen-year-olds), I asked him what characterised the teaching of science in a Waldorf school. With a great deal of excited activity going on in the background, he began by explaining that GCSE coursework is a major element in many subjects, including physics. He liked coursework, alongside the Waldorf curriculum, because it gives the opportunity to do lots of experimental work, 'and particularly because it gives the opportunity to observe keenly and accurately. And this business of observing is something we've done much more of in the younger classes. Observation, as accurately as possible, has been the accent; not so much interpretation. You can't do that usefully until you're certain of what you've seen or done.' In this respect he mentioned the pupils' ability to see what might be wrong in a situation, what they could do about it, and thereby notice when something unexpected happened.

Nicholas also spoke of coursework as an opportunity to bring all the observation encouraged earlier to some kind of development in which the dimension for interpretation could then be added. 'It brings the thing full circle', he added, 'and that's science; at least that's my idea of science – adding interpretation to the observation, and then drawing conclusions. This, to my mind, is education as opposed to training. That's the difference. I'm not suggesting that other schools don't have the same approach. But it's very much the underlying intention here.'

The final scenes of *Time to Learn* were shot back at Michael Hall, where the film began. It was midsummer, and staff, pupils and parents were celebrating the festival of St John. A Shakespeare play was performed by Class Twelve in the evening, preceded by a pageant in which the younger children, class by class, presented a scene connected to what they had been studying over the past year. Thus, for that audience in the June sunshine, fragments of the whole Waldorf curriculum unfolded before their eyes – a curriculum based on a recognition of the significance of the evolution of human consciousness in history. And this great story was mirrored not only through the children as actors, but also through each one of them as individual embodiments of that same evolutionary process as it repeats itself in the childhood of every new life.

The date on which all this took place was no arbitrary Saturday near the end of term. In all Waldorf schools, as in the Camphill communities, much importance is attached to rhythm – the rhythm of the day, the week and the year – and therefore to celebration of the festivals. Teachers also feel that such occasions help the children, albeit subconsciously, to keep a sensitive connection with the earth, the seasons, and with the themes of death and rebirth which run through all the great religious traditions. At the heart of such awareness lies the greatest mystery of all – the miracle of life itself.

Amid the colourful festivities on that summer afternoon, not only children and adults were present, but also babies and infants in prams – and they too deserve a mention under the heading of miracles. We have no memory of those first two or three years of life, and cannot really imagine them either. Yet this must be the time when what takes place around us affects us most deeply of all. In the same lecture that Steiner gave in Ilkley in 1923 he referred to the child in those first three years of life as 'one great sense-organ', saying that everything is learned through imitation. He also suggested that the child is not only sensitive to the physical influences of its surroundings, but also to subtle moral influences and to people's thoughts. And it is during these three years that the greatest miracles of all take place – we learn to stand upright and to walk, and we start to speak. Then comes the moment when our capacity to think and become self-aware prompts us to use the word 'I'. It's a journey beautifully described by Tennyson in his 'In Memoriam':

> The baby new to earth and sky,
> What time his tender palm is prest
> Against the circle of the breast,
> Has never thought that 'this is I'.
> But as he grows he gathers much
> And learns the use of 'I' and 'me',
> And finds 'I am not what I see,
> And other than the things I touch.

At this stage conscious memory now begins. Some people see it as a re-enactment, in every human life, of what is described in the Old Testament as the Fall – the experience that I and the world are no longer one. Yet intimations of that paradisal state of oneness rather than separation can stay with us for some time. Jung, at the opening of his autobiography, wrote about what he sensed to be his earliest memory:

> I am lying in a pram, in the shadow of a tree. It is a fine, warm summer day, the sky blue, and golden sunlight darting through green leaves. The hood of the pram has been left up. I have just awakened to the glorious beauty of the day, and have a sense of indescribable well-being ... Everything is wholly wonderful, colourful and splendid.

Memories of such a blissful state of consciousness are, perhaps, most powerfully conveyed by William Wordsworth in his celebrated ode 'Intimations of Immortality' from 'Recollections of Early Childhood':

> There was a time when meadow, grove and stream,
> The earth, and every common sight,
> To me did seem
> Apparelled in celestial light,
> The glory and the freshness of a dream.
> It is not now as it hath been of yore;
>   Turn where so'er I may,
>   By night or day,
> The things which I have seen I now can see no more.

In the next verse he writes of rainbow, rose, the stars at night: 'But yet I know, where'er I go / That there hath passed away a glory from the earth.' A little later come those most celebrated lines of all:

> Our birth is but a sleep and a forgetting:
> The Soul that rises with us, our life's Star,
> Hath had elsewhere its setting,
> And cometh from afar;
> Not in entire forgetfulness,
> And not in utter nakedness,
> But trailing clouds of glory do we come
> From God, who is our home:
> Heaven lies about us in our infancy.

These lines leave me not so much with the question I have already addressed in earlier chapters, of why we have to forget this heaven that lies about us in our infancy, but rather whether we can again experience such serenity during our lifetime, and not only, perhaps, after our death.

My own favourite evocation of very early childhood is by Dylan Thomas in his 'Poem in October', and was the subject of one of the films I made for TWW with Gwyn Thomas in 1961, at the start of my career. 'It was my thirtieth year to heaven' – so begins an early morning birthday walk at Laugherne, as Dylan sets off alone on a familiar path up the hill:

> And I saw in the turning so clearly a child's
> Forgotten mornings when he walked with his mother
>   Through the parables
>   Of sunlight
> And the legends of the green chapels.
>
> And the twice told fields of infancy
> That his tears burned my cheeks and his heart moved in mine.
> These were the woods the river and sea
>   Where a boy
>   In the listening
> Summertide of the dead whispered the truth of his joy
> To the trees and the stones and the fish in the tide.

Leo Tolstoy in his *Recollections* wrote some less familiar but equally evocative lines towards the end of his life. There he tells of his two earliest memories: the first, of being tightly bound in swaddling clothes and his screams of protest; the other, a happier one, was bath-time in a large wooden tub. He then writes:

> It is strange and frightening to realise that from my birth and up to the age of three – when I was being fed at the breast, when I was weaned, when I first began to crawl about, to walk, and to speak – I cannot find a single recollection except those two, however much I search my memory. When did I begin to be? When did I begin to live? And why is it pleasant to imagine myself as I then was, but frightening – as it used to be to me and as it still is to many people – to imagine entering a similar condition at death, where there will be no recollections expressible in words?

Tolstoy goes on to marvel at what is learned and achieved in those first few years of life:

From a five-year-old boy to me is only a step, from a newborn babe to a five-year-old boy there is an immense distance, from an embryo to a newborn babe there is an enormous chasm, while between non-existence and an embryo there is not merely a chasm but incomprehensibility.

He then reflects on the apparent rhythm between what he calls 'subjection' to space and time, and our 'liberation' from them.

It is a response to Tolstoy's use of the words 'non-existence' and 'incomprehensibility' that I feel is the ultimate challenge that I face in writing this book. In my concluding chapters, however, I am not, I hope, going to fall into the trap of suddenly trying to make everything 'comprehensible'. I have warned against certainty far too often to do that. I shall stick to my intimations, but at the same time continue to affirm my sense that there are no actual limits to knowledge – even though, at each new horizon, another one seems to appear. I feel on firmer ground in dismissing the notion of 'non-existence'. We are, I believe, present all the time but in different guises. Nor is there somewhere else, but there is something else – a dimension seemingly hidden, but intimately interwoven with what we experience as the here and now, and with the world that we can see and touch. And the existence of these visible and invisible dimensions of reality, and my own awareness of them, prompts me to ponder the life-affirming question: Why is there something rather than nothing?

CHAPTER 34

Our Ancestors Were Us

To commemorate the fiftieth anniversary of Indian independence in 1997, Mark Tully and I persuaded the commissioning editor for news and current affairs at Channel Four, David Lloyd, to let us film portraits of ten very different people from all over India and from every level of society. Although the series was essentially about India, many of the issues raised were of universal interest and importance, and the aspirations expressed by some of the subjects were very relevant to my own increasing conviction that humanity is edging towards a saner and more humane world, despite the many problems that still confront us. The journey was also to take me back, once again, to a country where belief in karma and reincarnation still permeates every aspect of its life and culture. The idea that an eternal essence in each one of us matures and evolves through many lifetimes will be the main focus of this chapter.

Laboni Jana was twenty-six years old, with a first-class degree in economics. She worked for an NGO – The Child in Need Institute – on the edge of Calcutta, an organisation primarily concerned with health care for poor mothers and their babies in the surrounding Bengali villages. Most of Laboni's contemporaries were working in banks and multinationals. 'I love to be with the people', she said. 'The pay is not so good, but the satisfaction I get from the work is a big compensation.'

In that simple statement Laboni was already turning her back not only on the increasing enticements to make as much money for oneself as possible, but also on tradition and the rigid interpretation of caste. Destiny – what we do with our lives and how we conduct ourselves – can be in our hands, and doesn't have to be determined by our family and upbringing, nor even by the values that superficially seem to characterise our time.

Another of our subjects in *Faces of India* was a Muslim shopkeeper and sweet-maker, living with his extended family in old Delhi. He blamed the politicians for the riots that periodically erupt between Hindus, Muslims and Sikhs, accusing them of 'creating trouble in order to stay in power'. Allaudin's close friend, Murari Lal, who shares his passion for pigeon-racing, is a Hindu and came with us on a buying spree to the bird market. Allaudin's daily life

– like the lives of most people who don't make it into the top ten of some competition or other, or don't blow up aeroplanes, or stab someone because they are a different colour or call their god by a different name – will never make the news; but his friendship with Murari Lal, and the millions of friendships like it, are what I feel we should also be reporting and celebrating every day across the airwaves.

A maharaja and an army major also featured in our series, as did the successful industrialist, Rahul Bajaj, whose company manufactures scooters on a massive scale on the outskirts of Poona, a town that was once a stronghold of the British Raj. 'My grandfather, grandmother, my father and mother were all in British jails during our freedom struggle', he told us.

Still struggling with an aspect of the colonial legacy was District Commissioner Vandita Sharma. As a civil servant she worked in a vast bureaucracy inherited from the British, and which she and others are still trying to transform. Mark expressed surprise that there had been no wholesale reform of the system over the past fifty years. 'We have assimilated democracy into administration, which was not there at the time of the British', was the reply of this charming and hard-working government official. In colonial days the DC's role was that of a ruler; government was a controlling body. 'We are no longer here to control our people', she said, 'we are here to serve the people.'

One example of someone who was certainly benefiting from the government's concern for *all* its citizens was Laduri Bhai. An illiterate tribal woman, she was head of her local village council because the parliament in Delhi had recently decided that a third of all *panchyats* must be made up of women. 'She is the first head of this *panchyat* man enough to take an oath to neither pay nor receive bribes in connection with her work', said Mark in his commentary.

'We have to struggle because we're not educated', Laduri Bhai told us. 'We don't always know what our rights are, what the government should be doing for our village and for us women. And if we don't know what our rights are, we won't get them.' There was inevitably a lot of paperwork requiring her signature and it was her very supportive husband who had taught her to sign her name.

At a meeting of the women in the village that we filmed, the subject of drunkenness among men came up yet again. 'Alcohol is available here in plenty', she told them, 'but we've no proper drinking water. Is this right? You're always complaining that your husbands beat you up when they're drunk. If we all stand together this can be stopped. If only one woman complains she gets thrashed.' Such a meeting, said Mark, would have been unthinkable before voluntary organisations came here and encouraged women to stand up for themselves. Laduri Bhai admitted that there would still be many problems ahead: 'It's up to me to use the knowledge I now have.'

'Laduri Bhai's confidence may be justified', concluded Mark. 'India's leaders are realising that unless women become involved in every aspect of life, the prosperous and just nation that India set out to create fifty years ago will never be established.' He added that many now believe that the future of India lies with its women. It's a thought that I would extend far beyond the boundaries of India.

My enthusiastic and energetic assistant producer, Gillian Wright, who is Mark's partner and has lived in India for many years, found an equally interesting but somewhat sadder example of someone living near the bottom of the pile. Budh Ram was a *Dalit* – a member of a group once known as untouchables, the outcasts of Hindu society. He now had a plot of land himself, but it wasn't large enough to feed him and his family. 'It's still a struggle to get our "rosi roti", our daily bread', he told us. 'We're very poor.' This gap between the rich and the poor, so Mark believes, is the greatest failure of Indian democracy. When he then asked Budh Ram what his hopes were for the next fifty years, he replied: 'What can I say? Only God knows what will happen in the future.'

Recently, some ten years after we filmed the series, Mark revisited Budh Ram and wrote about the meeting in his book *India's Unending Journey*. There had been a few changes for the better, yet now in his early seventies Budh Ram still had to work for others as an agricultural labourer in order to survive. His staple foods remained rice and dhal – 'an improvement from the days when we used to pick out the grain from the dung dropped by the bullocks on the threshing floor, wash it and eat it', he said.

In his book Mark expresses doubt about what is called 'the trickle down effect' – wealth generated at the top finding its way into the pockets of the poorest. Recently I saw a documentary about Mumbai – part of a BBC series, this time marking the sixtieth anniversary of India's and Pakistan's independence. This film, celebrating the new wealth among the super-rich, was much applauded but I was appalled – in particular by a sequence in which a wealthy lawyer was happily filmed outside her luxury apartment haggling with a hunch-backed beggar over how much she wanted to be paid for a pile of her old newspapers which he would then sell at the recycling depot.

Mark goes on to point out in his book that a real distribution of wealth to the very poorest hasn't even taken place in a rich country like the United States, let alone India. Rishad Lawyer, another of our subjects, was actually educated in the States, and had returned to India to join the new economic revolution as a young advertising executive in Mumbai – the commercial capital of India, and now the cultural capital of consumerism. While he was supervising the shoot of a television commercial for a luxury refrigerator, Mark asked him whether he wasn't helping to build up resentment among the vast majority of Indians for whom such an object was way beyond their means. Rishad admitted that in many of the villages there still isn't electricity to run such gadgets; they, therefore, wouldn't even see the commercials. 'I don't know if resentment is the right word', he continued. 'It's a very religious country. People believe that if they are born into something, by the law of karma, that is where they are meant to be. One of the charms of India is acceptance.'

I don't wish to give the impression that Rishad was some slick, insensitive yuppie. One of his charms was his openness to Mark's concerns and criticism. He was not defensive, and expressed quite honestly his own perception of the law of karma – a perception that was shared by the Hindu priest who was the last subject in our series. The location was the temple at Chidambaram, unique among South Indian temples, with shrines dedicated to two of the great Hindu gods – Shiva and Vishnu. But although Hindus worship many gods, they say that all are manifestations of the one God – aspects of a single principle and the one reality. Hinduism has its trinity, too: Brahma – the creator; Vishnu – the preserver; and Shiva – the destroyer. What Shiva – together with his terrifying wife Kali – destroys, so Hindus believe, is the finite, to make way for the infinite. This deed can therefore be seen as a manifestation of the cyclical process underlying all existence – a perception that is at the heart of Hinduism.

Raja was one of three hundred hereditary priests at Chidambaram. 'We were born in the priestly community', he said, 'so we are born priests'. Pilgrims passed through the temple at Chidambaram throughout the day, and much of the time the atmosphere was more like a busy railway station than a holy place of worship: it was noisy and at times even quite disturbing. The main purpose is to have a *darshan*, a sight of what we would call the idols. For Hindus, Raja explained, these are powerful aids to worship, 'reminding them of the awe and mystery of God'.

Some twenty years earlier, in the first episode of *The Long Search*, Ron Eyre – bewildered and overwhelmed amid the sights and sounds of Varanasi, the holy city of Benares – asked his guide, the local tourist officer, about these many gods, replicas of which were on sale at every street corner. Did people really worship a god in the shape of an elephant called Ganesh? The delightful and unperturbed Mr Sharma explained that these gods were all symbols, merely pointers. 'Suppose I want to point at something', he said, 'how long should I keep my finger pointing like this? As long as you have not seen the object. As soon as you see the object, I take my finger away.' Ron then asked him whether some people never understand what you're pointing at, and spend their whole lives looking at the finger. 'For them, God is not in a hurry', was Sharma's cheerful reply.

One of Raja's tasks at Chidambaram, along with his fellow priests, was to conduct the daily awakening ceremony of the gods, and at night to return them on palanquins to their bedchamber. Some of the actual rituals that we witnessed and filmed during the day provoked great frenzy among the pilgrims. In our terms they appeared to be quite out of themselves, similar perhaps to the ecstatic state that Diana Lodge described taking place in the Subud ceremony of Latihan.

In *Letters from a Traveller*, Teilhard de Chardin wrote of his disappointment with Hinduism and of 'the numbing and deadening effect of a religion obsessed by material forms and ritualism'. However I suspect the subdued celebration of Matins in an English village church would be equally bewildering to a Hindu pilgrim. Teilhard spent three months in India in 1935, on an expedition led by the German scientist Helmut de Terra who wrote how the fakirs 'squatting beneath the broad branches of mango trees, their naked torsos smeared with ash, and their long matted hair piled turban-like atop their ascetic faces' reminded Teilhard 'of the human bondage caused by religious fanaticism'. The aspect of Hinduism that emphasises an ultimate cosmic unity, similar to his own ideas, seems not to have touched Teilhard, and nor did the religious fervour of the people themselves.

For similar reasons to those expressed by Teilhard, the scenes and rituals in the temple at Chidambaram were for me the most difficult side of Indian life to identify with. There was, for example, none of the serenity I associate with mosques, churches or synagogues. I admit to this reaction with a certain shame, since I believe in the importance of trying to understand and empathise with each person's way of relating to some transcendent presence in their lives. For Mark and Gillian on the other hand, both of whom have lived in India for many years, the visit to Chidambaram was the highlight of our six-week journey. Mark explained in his commentary that Hinduism does, in fact, vary greatly from person to person: 'Many devout Hindus never go near a temple and don't bother with ritual. There's no Church to tell you what to believe.' He went on to say how Hinduism is an enormously accommodating and tolerant religion – a characteristic he very much admires and which, to a lesser extent, has parallels with the Church of England to which he – like John Betjeman, and for similar reasons – is deeply devoted.

Mark pursues this theme of tolerance in greater detail in *India's Unending Journey*. Above all it is India's 'genius for absorption and adaption' that he singles out for praise, along with her people's ability to recognise opposites, to marry the sensual with the sacred, to find a balance between the acceptance of fate and free will, and finally their healthy instinct to treat all forms of certainty with great suspicion.

There are, of course, certain dangers inherent in a belief in karma and reincarnation. One error would be failing to recognise that our karma is not always personal. We come into life trailing not only our own private baggage, but also the karma of the nationality into which we are born, and of the human race altogether. The karmic consequences of the slave trade, for example, are with us still, and will be for years to come. And if misunderstood, the idea of karma can also, as has often happened in the East in particular, lead to a fatalism and therefore to a very conservative and static society in which the poor and the weak are perceived as having warranted the circumstances in which they find themselves. Thus they are trapped in a situation that seemingly cannot be altered during this particular lifetime (not only will they not get a fridge, but the implication is that they don't even deserve one). Such an attitude leads to the rigidity of a caste system – 'the rich man in his castle, the poor man at the gate'– in which there is little flexibility to explore areas of life unconnected with our birth and upbringing. Many people I know are fond of saying, 'Go on! Do it! After all, you only live once.' The words may not be quite accurate, but the sentiment behind them is in many ways healthy.

On the other hand, the idea of karma and reincarnation, if we live with it creatively and imaginatively, can encourage us to accept personal responsibility for the circumstances of our lives rather than always blaming others, our upbringing, or some abstract notion of fate. And even if there are people who have harmed or thwarted us in one way or another, as soon as we know and understand just a little about their lives, and why they are perhaps as they are, then the word 'blame' starts to fall away.

In sayings like 'As a man sows, so he reaps', we are perfectly familiar in the West with the law of cause and effect, and indeed experience it from day to day – and not just subconsciously from one lifetime to the next. But that thought of reaping what we sow can also imply a rather depressing inevitability about what unfolds for us. I've already quoted Rudolf Steiner's statement, 'We are slaves of the past, but masters of the future', which for me gives a very clear and helpful indication of the challenges involved in negotiating a path between past and future. While acknowledging that we cannot shirk the consequences of what we've done – in other words simply press the delete button on the bits of our life we regret – it reminds us that we are free at any moment to redeem the situation and to start to put things right. Thus karma means dealing with and working through unfinished business, and largely through a web of relationships through which we learn and grow. And maybe sometimes, as Jung once suggested, we meet our destiny on the road we take to avoid it. Acceptance of this fact was most movingly conveyed by Oscar Wilde in *De Profundis*, the autobiographical essay he wrote in prison:

> I forget that every little action of the common day makes or unmakes character, and that therefore what one has done in the secret chamber one has some day to cry aloud on the housetops. I ceased to be Lord over myself. I was no longer the captain of my soul, and did not know

it ... what lies before me is my past. I have got to make myself look on
that with different eyes. This I cannot do by ignoring it, or slighting
it, or praising it, or denying it. It is only to be done fully by accepting
it as an inevitable part of the evolution of my life and character: by
bowing my head to everything that I have suffered ...

The belief in reincarnation – and that the law of cause and effect is at work
over many lifetimes – is something that still seems to divide people quite
strongly. For me it has always made sense, seemed quite obvious, and belongs
to that whole cyclical picture of creation that Hinduism in particular teaches.
In the *Bhagavad Gita* the god Krishna tells Prince Arjuna before his great
battle: 'Many are my past lives and yours, Arjuna.'

In Laurens van der Post's conversations with Jean-Marc Pottiez for the
book *A Walk with a White Bushman*, the question of an afterlife and the
subject of reincarnation came up. Laurens was characteristically open about
the idea, being neither firmly for or against:

I have an immense respect for the boundary walls of human awareness.
I know these walls are finite, but at the same time I know they are
not opaque. There is a very strange light coming through them. But
most of all there are strange events that come over these walls that
I cannot explain and that I cannot ignore. I just accept them and
they prove to me how great the area of unknowing is outside, and
how important it is for our own increase not to reject it but just to
allow the sense of mystery and wonder it evokes to preside over one's
imagination. There is a dynamic reality beyond the here and now.

I remember as a ten-year-old boy having to learn and recite Alfred
Tennyson's poem 'The Brook':

I come from haunts of coot and hern
I make a sudden sally
And sparkle out among the fern
To bicker down a valley.

And after every third verse comes the refrain:

For men may come and men may go
But I go on for ever.

In recent years I have often thought about that poem, and how to explain to the
brook that although its perception about human beings is very understandable,

it isn't absolutely correct! Clearly we each disappear physically every seventy years or so, but – as must by now be perfectly clear – I do believe that in another sense we, too, 'go on forever'.

One Chapter in a Longer Story is the title of one of my most recent films, and is a quotation that for me is a very profound yet simple way of trying to convey the idea that we live many lives on earth, returning cyclically, as we do every morning from sleep, and as do the seasons every year or the full moon every month. And yet, unlike the plants and animals, we are still changing, growing, evolving with each new incarnation. A cow produces a cow and we are deeply grateful for the fact; from a daisy comes another beautiful daisy. But I am only a copy of my mother and father in the sense that I am a human being, and not an animal or a flower. In most other ways I am uniquely myself and ever more so, as is everyone else. One way to put this is that each person is gradually becoming a unique species in their own right. But, as I've already suggested, only by transcending the inevitable egotism that arises on such a journey will we slowly experience our full evolutionary potential, and what it means to become truly human.

The 'longer story' quotation came from a speech therapist called Leonard Roach who worked at St Christopher's School in Bristol for children with severe learning difficulties. They asked me to make a promotional film about their work that I later showed to the Director of Programmes at HTV, Sandra Jones. She was sensitive and intelligent enough to watch and listen to it with the eyes and ears of the sort of viewer who is increasingly neglected these days. She then asked me to incorporate into the film a little more of the philosophy that lay behind the work at St Christopher's before broadcasting the programme on television.

St Christopher's has always been strongly influenced by the educational philosophy of Rudolf Steiner, including the importance he attached to the spiritual law of karma and reincarnation. In filming the new interviews for the HTV film I was hoping, as always, for people to express ideas like these in their own words. Leonard Roach was quite a shy man – or perhaps a better description is someone understandably hesitant about pronouncing on such mysteries, and about imposing his views or intimations on the great television public. Only when I gently prodded him did he volunteer, very tentatively, that the lives of these brave and disadvantaged children – and indeed all our lives – might be 'just one chapter in a longer story'. Leonard spoke, too, about how this idea of our life as being just one of many, might help us to accept that there may be wisdom in the present situation, and even a good reason for it. He called it 'God's secret – we're not allowed to see it'. In Karen Blixen's memoir *Out of Africa* she writes: 'God made the world round so that we would never be able to see too far down the road.'

The fact that nothing happens in life that is without meaning doesn't, as I understand it, have to imply that everything is preordained. There is a tendency among those for whom the ideas of reincarnation and karma are meaningful to attribute, and even excuse, whatever happens as 'karmic'. In a letter Rudolf Steiner wrote in 1905 he says very clearly that accidents unrelated to either personal or world karma can and do happen. He was writing to a friend, Günther Wagner, one of the founders of the German Theosophical Society, whose wife Anna had just died:

> It is easy to interpret everything that is linked to our destiny as a karmic debt. But that is not always the case. True though it is that karma is a real and all-embracing law, it is equally true that karmic blows can insert themselves into the chain of our relationships simply as primal cause. Blows of fate that strike us are not always the result of past events; often they are new entries in our book of life that will only find their recompense in the future.

In other words, for example, the circumstances of Anne-Marie's early childhood – prior to being sent to the convent – may have been nothing to do with what she had or hadn't done in earlier incarnations. What is clear, however – whether you believe in reincarnation or not – is that the situation in which she found herself will continue to have repercussions far into the future.

The same thought applies to those children at St Christopher's; yet whatever the circumstances behind their seemingly thwarted lives – karmic or otherwise – I feel sure that they, like an increasing number of vulnerable people all over the world, benefit from being acknowledged as individuals in their own right, irrespective of disability or circumstance. I could certainly see that this recognition by Leonard and his colleagues of what they would call the eternal essence in each of us was of enormous significance in helping the children we met and filmed to live in the world without being totally overwhelmed by frustration and dispair.

In a promotional film I made a few years earlier about the Paradise Community in Gloucestershire, and its work with vulnerable young adults, the founder, Friedrich Roder, spoke very movingly about his feeling that nothing is ever lost, either individually or collectively, whatever the circumstances of a life. Everyone, he believes, makes a contribution to what he called the general stream of evolution, as well as participating in their own unfolding destiny. He spoke these words over a scene of a young disabled woman slowly and with great difficulty loading and then unloading her wheelbarrow full of compost in the vegetable garden at Paradise House. 'We can often do things very easily', he said, 'because we have the appropriate skills and faculties.

A handicapped person has to make an enormous effort to do maybe just a fraction of what we can do. But this effort is not lost. It appears to me as if the effort which is made turns back onto the person who makes this effort as a positive source of power.' He then added that if we live with the idea that every human being will have the opportunity of creating a new life – another incarnation – one could imagine how these efforts might bear fruit.

In 1904, just before his death, Theodore Herzl – the founder of modern political Zionism – wrote his last letter to a friend, saying: 'Don't do anything foolish while I'm dead.' If reincarnation is a reality, then a crucial and reasonable question might be: 'What happens in between?'

In a film I made about the life of Florence Nightingale, the writer and presenter Phillippa Stewart – standing beside the great lady's grave at East Wellow in Hampshire – told a story related by Miss Nightingale's niece who, at her aunt's bedside, had been discussing friends who had recently died, adding that 'they were now at rest'. Florence Nightingale, apparently, pulled herself upright from the pillow and said with the utmost conviction: 'Oh, no. Not at rest. I'm sure it's an immense activity.' Perhaps part of that activity is doing what Mitch Albom's character, Eddie, was told in heaven by his former commanding officer: 'Making sense of our yesterdays.'

The more conventional view, as articulated by Florence Nightingale's niece, was conveyed in a *Guardian* report of Boris Yeltsin's funeral by the journalist Luke Harding. He described how before the coffin was lowered into the ground, his widow, Nania, came forward to say farewell, smoothing back his grey hair and kissing him fondly. 'His daughters then flinched', wrote Harding, 'as an artillery battery outside the cemetery's walls fired off three salvoes. Russia's national anthem sounded and Yeltsin sank into his final resting place.' No activity; just rest.

It is not quite clear what those who say 'May he rest in peace' actually envisage beyond that. A final resting place for the body of Boris Yeltsin it undoubtedly was; but whether he is now at rest is another matter, for what of the spirit, if you are prepared to contemplate such an entity, that inhabits the body? A spirit that perhaps even has a role in that body's creation; certainly cares for it; often takes it for granted; will occasionally abuse it; will probably sometimes be proud of it; perhaps will even sometimes marvel at its complexity and the way that it carries on working – heart beating, blood circulating, digestion functioning, lungs inhaling and exhaling – all without any seeming input from its caretaker.

Another picture of the so-called afterlife that still haunts many people is the notion of a Day of Judgement, which likewise seems to preclude any further dynamic after death, let alone the thought of reincarnation. In the trilogy of films I made about Westminster Abbey with Alan Bennett, we touched on a version of this scenario. As Alan wandered round the darkened Abbey after Evensong, with an organist quietly at practice, he quoted the 18th-century essayist Joseph Addison who called the Abbey 'this great magazine of mortality' and who is buried in the Lady Chapel. Addison wrote:

> When I see kings lying by those who deposed them, rival wits placed side by side, or the holy men that divided the world with their contests and disputes, I reflect with sorrow and astonishment on the little competitions, factions and debates of mankind. And when I read the several dates of the tombs of some that died yesterday and some six hundred years ago, I consider that great day when we shall all of us be contemporaries and make our appearance together.

Maybe that appearance, if not exactly all together, happens more often than we realise consciously, and is not just in 'heaven', but here on earth through many lifetimes. If so, it's extraordinary to contemplate that we ourselves are not only our own ancestors, but also that it is we, not just our grandchildren, who will inherit the miracles and the mess that we have created and left behind. I find it a sobering but also strangely inspiring thought that our individual journeys stretch far back in time, and will continue to unfold far into the future. We've each been many people, played many parts – both male and female. Emerson once wrote: 'There is no history – only biography.'

In his autobiography, *Memories, Dreams, Reflections*, Jung wrote as an old man about memory, about what had remained important to him, and about the people whose names seem to have been 'entered in the scrolls of my destiny from the beginning, so that encountering them was at the same time a kind of recollection'. However, in the chapter 'On Life after Death', Jung quite rightly warns about the danger of speculation in such matters:

> Cut off the intermediary world of mythic imagination, and the mind falls prey to doctrinaire rigidities. On the other hand, too much traffic with these germs of myth is dangerous for weak and suggestible minds, for they are led to mistake vague intimations for substantial knowledge, and to hypostatise mere phantasms.

Jung goes on to acknowledge that the conception that many people form of the hereafter 'is largely made up of wishful thinking and prejudices'. It is usually pictured as 'a pleasant place', he writes.

> That does not seem so obvious to me. I hardly think that after death we shall be spirited to some lovely flowering meadow ... The world into which we enter after death will be grand and terrible, like God

and like all of nature that we know. Granted that what I experienced in my 1944 visions – liberation from the burden of the body, and perception of meaning – gave me the deepest bliss.

In the same chapter he does suggest that 'in my case it must have been primarily a passionate urge towards understanding which brought about my birth. For that is the strongest element in my nature'. But he goes on to say:

> I know no answer to the question of whether the karma which I live is the outcome of my past lives, or whether it is not rather the achievement of my ancestors, whose heritage comes together in me … I could well imagine that I might have lived in former centuries and there encountered questions I was not yet able to answer; that I had to be born again because I had not fulfilled the task that was given to me. When I die, my deeds will follow along with me – that is how I imagine it. I will bring with me what I have done. In the meantime it is important to ensure that I do not stand at the end with empty hands. Buddha, too, seems to have had this thought when he tried to keep his disciples from wasting time on useless speculation.

Steiner wrote and said a great deal about reincarnation and karma, including over eighty lectures in 1924, the year before he died. These are published in English in eight volumes under the title *Karmic Relationships*. In fact he considered that bringing to the modern world an awareness of this whole profound dimension to existence was one of his most important tasks. If we are prepared to seriously contemplate his claim – potentially on behalf of us all – that he could 'see' into the supersensible world, it was not, in Jung's words, 'speculation' – and certainly not 'useless'. Nor was it simply based on the traditional teachings of Hinduism and Buddhism, but rather on his research into the mysterious realm known, in Sanskrit, as *Akasha* – a psychic record or imprint of all that has ever been thought or accomplished, which I wrote about in Chapter Twenty-Three.

To what extent, then, do all these insights throw light on what Florence Nightingale called 'an immense activity'? Such activity does, of course, presuppose a purely spiritual existence – one outside of time and space – that is very hard for us to envisage. Yet if we think and imagine with our intellect alone we are bound to feel at sea, for our mortal brain on its own – as already discussed – is simply not able to comprehend these immortal and eternal dimensions of existence. Its job, which it does magnificently, is to enable us to cope with physical existence in the here and now. Thus, in asking questions like 'where on earth is heaven?' we are trapped, it seeems, by what Professor Ravi Ravindra called 'the narrow aperture of the rational mind'. If, however, we consider that we may be more than just physical bodies – and not just after death, but also already during our lifetime – and that we continually partake in a parallel existence outside of time, then the picture changes radically. For Jung, too, this psychic existence was an absolute reality, both in his own experience and in the experience of his patients – 'only ignorance denies these facts'.

At the end of Chapter Nine I attempted to convey, as far as I am prepared or able to, something of the experience that I sense we undergo between incarnations – gleaned in part from the meditative research done by Steiner, and indeed from my own humble ponderings, and flashes of what Nicolas of Cusa called 'learned ignorance'. Steiner hints, for example – in utterances that are hard to pin down with our purely rational minds – that after death we eventually participate in the creativity that underpins all existence, not least the creativity that manifests as our own physical existence. Our bodies are miracles that are neither simply produced by our genes – a misunderstanding that Denis Noble addresses in *The Music of Life* – nor are they miracles that come off some cosmic conveyor belt. Steiner's picture further suggests a creativity that sustains not only life on earth as we know it, but the whole universe – a universe that is not some inanimate entity, but a living and evolving organism which, like us, is in need of constant nourishment and inspiration. It is quite simply an extension of the Gaia hypothesis into farthest space.

Helen Salter's diagram (see page 133) and the dynamic rhythm that it conveys between 'waking' and 'sleeping', and between what we call 'life' and 'death', has greatly helped me to imagine – with that bit of myself which can at moments transcend the everyday – a state of being in which I am no longer a spectator looking out at the world in all its beauty and complexity, but that I become that world – the leaf, the bird, the sunlight, and indeed the other person. T.S. Eliot hints at such an experience in 'The Dry Salvages', when he writes:

> … music heard so deeply
> That it is not heard at all, but you are the music
> While the music lasts.

The microcosm that is me becomes the macrocosm that is also me. Out of this experience, perhaps – together with confronting my past life – come the resolutions for a future incarnation. We may not remember them as such, but the intention remains. It is a process, I believe, that repeats itself in miniature every night while we sleep.

In *The Water Babies*, Charles Kingsley writes of Tom, the boy chimney sweep who runs away and is drowned in a river, as being 'washed clean by the sea'. The story that unfolds is, in fact, an imagination of life after death

– of making sense of our yesterdays; it's a book that, if stripped of some of its Victorian sentimentality, offers a simple yet profound glimpse into the laws of karma and reincarnation.

It is meaningful, I am sure, that at this point in our evolution we don't remember our experiences between incarnations consciously. It doesn't mean, however, that we are unaffected by them, but rather, like Mole and Ratty in *Wind in the Willows* when they experienced the god Pan, we also need 'instant oblivion … the gift of forgetfulness' so that we can not only 'be happy and light-hearted as before', but also awaken to our sense of self through the isolation and loneliness that consciousness brings. Our past incarnations may not be accessible to our brain-centred memory, yet the signature of those incarnations is, I suspect, revealed in what we are like individually as human beings now, in this moment of time.

The notion, therefore, that 'you only live once' certainly focuses attention on the present, and on both the need and the potential to transform it. As the fourth wise man instinctively felt and eventually came to understand, our tasks are in the here and now. If there is a heaven, it is to be created here on earth. Only in coping with the trials and tribulations that we face from day to day do we develop the spiritual muscles to build that heaven.

One aspect of memory that has long intrigued me is our lack of conscious recognition of those with whom we have been closely connected in previous lives. Maybe the strong and instinctive sympathy – and indeed antipathy – that we feel for certain people in our current lives is a clue. They are somehow familiar because we have already shared much. It is clearly what Jung sensed in that quotation from his autobiography, 'encountering them was at the same time a kind of recollection'.

I have already written about the idea of comparing continuity from one incarnation to the next to the role of actors in a play. In between they rest – in the case of several actors I know, longer than they like! Then comes another play, another part. And if they're in a repertory company, they'll be with the same people, also now playing different parts. Having worked in Rep myself, I know about the comradeship that can develop – a bond that isn't fooled by costumes, wigs and false moustaches. We knew and recognised each other as real people, not by the parts we played. Likewise, in life – if we are sufficiently awake – we have the growing ability to see through the masks and disguises, and to recognise the authenticity and true identity of the other person.

Reflecting on my relationship with my children, who are now in their twenties, has also helped me come to terms with the possibility that we've known certain people in many different guises. Although there is a continuity that is very real – for I do, of course, have clear memories of them at different ages – I also have to admit that I am now in the company of two people who are very different from ten or more years ago. Already it feels as though I've met several different incarnations of the same person within one lifetime. At times I even find myself mourning that little boy and girl who, in one sense, no longer exist. Yet the bond I made with them in their infancy is a huge influence on the bond that I have with them now, twenty years later – a bond and a blessing.

When I spoke to Elisabeth Collins once about my mother, whom she never met, and about the tragedy surrounding her death, Elisabeth said simply, 'I'm sure she'll reoccur.' It's a beautiful way of conveying what I understand by reincarnation. We all reoccur – every morning, and every new incarnation; but not, I believe, as some repetition of our all too mortal, disposable, and transient selves, clinging onto an egotistical longing for immortality.

In a lecture that Steiner gave in Torquay in August 1924, published in volume eight of *Karmic Relationships*, he said 'it is the inner, deep-rooted impulses of the soul and not external similarity of thought and outlook that are carried over from one earthly life into another'. He comes at the subject from a slightly different angle in the early pages of his book *Christianity as a Mystical Fact*, where he mentions what he calls 'spiritual ancestry'. If I can write, he points out, it is because I learned to write. No one who has a pen in his hand for the first time can sit down and write. Likewise what we refer to as 'the stamp of genius' is not a miracle out of the blue, but is a manifestation of what has already been learned. The talent and abilities someone displays in life – whether genius or not – have been forged in previous incarnations; though elsewhere Steiner indicates that actual skills do not necessarily repeat themselves. Genius, too, can take many forms. In fact invariably we have the urge to learn something new – hence the significance of alternating between a male and a female body. What reoccurs, as suggested in the quotation above, is the evolving maturity and sensitivity of the individuality concerned.

On this cyclical journey we search out those with whom we have already been closely connected, through whom we can continue to learn; those, too, whom we can help; and above all those with whom we have a deep and long-standing bond of love. We marvel, quite rightly, at the salmon's ability to find its way back to the river where it was hatched; likewise the immense journeys made by migrating birds and even butterflies. Maybe the time and place in which we each find ourselves in life is an example of that same, subconscious homing instinct.

For me some of Steiner's most interesting insights into this whole subject are contained in a series of lectures he gave in Hamburg in 1910, published under the title *Manifestations of Karma*. In them he addresses, among other things, the karma of our relationship with the animal kingdom and the sacrifice on their part so that we can continue to evolve. As I discussed in Chapter Twenty-Nine, their incarnation and evolution ahead of the human race allowed us to hold back. They have now become trapped as premature and one-sided expressions of that human archetype. Far into the future their redemption will be our task and responsibility. It is an extraordinary insight that throws light on the humbling experience that a bird can build a nest instinctively, without being taught, while we are initially so helpless in comparison, having at first to learn the very simplest of things. Yet the very fact that we are not so narrowly specialised allows us to create – in the form of ideas, art, and constructions – things that have never existed before. We, too, are creatures, but we are also creators.

The karma of illness is perhaps the most profound and complex of all the subjects Steiner speaks about in these lectures. To connect with his ideas requires an understanding, or at least an intimation, that the configuration of body, soul and spirit is an absolute reality, and not just a New Age cliché; and that the polarities in our human make-up, that Steiner called luciferic and ahrimanic, are harmful influences both psychologically and physically if not held in balance by the human ego or I – the evolving essence in each of us which is both supersensible and eternal. Steiner refers, for example, to the tendency in the human organism towards sclerosis and hardening as an ahrimanic influence, whereas all that manifests as fever and inflammation is associated with luciferic influences. And everything about these insights points to the fact that how we live, both outwardly and inwardly, leaves its mark – not just tomorrow or next week, but in future incarnations. In their book *Anthroposophical Medicine*, Dr Michael Evans and Iain Rodger write:

> Awareness of this karmic element in our development opens up the possibility of finding a meaning underlying major events in our lives, such as illness. It becomes possible to see illnesses as more than unfortunate accidents – to see them instead as challenges which are both opportunities for, and catalysts of, personal development.

In the introduction to their book, the authors state quite clearly that the aim of anthroposophical medicine is to stimulate the natural healing forces in the patient. This doesn't mean that allopathic drugs or surgery are not sometimes appropriate, helpful, and indeed life-saving. But in the chapter entitled 'The Use of Medicines', for example, they write:

> The main cause of most infections is the patient's susceptibility to them, rather than the mere presence of the bacteria or virus. While the use of antibiotics shortens the period of infection by killing the offending bacteria, it does nothing for the patient's susceptibility to infection.

I recently came across a leader in *The Guardian* entitled 'In Praise of Placebos'. This word 'placebo' is often used to dismiss the effect of certain medicines, particularly those of a more subtle kind. The article reads:

> From the Latin for 'I shall please', the term placebo was applied to hired mourners in the 14th century who were paid to weep for the dead. Ever since, the temptation has been to treat placebos as impostors, second-rate versions of the real thing.

The writer of the article goes on to report that Dan Ariely, author of a study of placebos at Duke University in the USA, shows that the placebo is also a demonstration of the body's ability to heal itself: 'Sick humans secrete substances you can't buy over the counter.'

In those Hamburg lectures of 1910, Steiner singles out two basic aspects of the healing process, over and above our own potential to do the work ourselves through the forces we develop by overcoming an actual illness or psychological crisis. One aspect concerns the kingdoms of nature that surround us, all of which have correspondences within the actual human being. Natural substances have the capacity to heal because unlike their counterpart in us, which has become negatively entangled in the complex evolution of humanity through the presence of retarded and potentially destructive angelic forces, they are unpolluted. 'That which exists in the world in its purity', said Steiner, 'is the external cure for the corresponding substance in its damaged state'.

Somewhere in the world of nature in which we delight, he continued, is hidden the right healing substance for every illness to which we may succumb. The fact that the substances in homeopathic and anthroposophical medicine are often so diluted during the potentising process that they are no longer measurable in no way lessens the argument, because the process itself actually increases the potency of the medicines in question. It is the invisible and non-material forces within those substances, interacting with the corresponding elements in us that can bring about healing. And it is these non-material aspects of our make-up that Steiner called the etheric and astral bodies – the very constituents that make us living, ensouled members of creation.

The other significant and profound aspect of healing that Steiner mentions is what he calls 'the transmuted power of love', a belief expressed by Paracelsus four hundred years earlier with the words: 'The highest ground of medicine is love.' In the lecture Steiner gave on May 27th 1910 – also included in *Manifestations of Karma* – he made this simple and arresting statement: 'Love is the medicine we give to the other ... The earth's mission is to weave love into everything.'

In that same lecture he spoke – with a certain hesitation, given the profundity of what he wanted to communicate – about the world of matter and substance, and the human soul. Every single substance, he said, be it gold, silver or anything else, is the condensation of one fundamental substance 'which is no longer matter ... Every substance upon the earth is condensed light'. The physicist David Bohm said much the same thing when he referred to matter as 'frozen light'. And Peter Spink, in talking to me about his inner journey, had said: 'I can't imagine light, but hold onto the concept of light as being what I conceive as the core of my being.' Steiner continued his lecture with these words:

> In as much as man is a material being, he is composed of light ... And every single stirring of the soul, wherever it occurs, is love modified in one way or another ... love and light are the two elements, the two components, which permeate all earthly existence: love as the soul constituent of earthly being, light as the outer material constituent of earthly being.

It seems to me deeply significant that the near-death experience is frequently described in terms of these two words, light and love – an intimation, perhaps, of a return to our origins, and to the source of all existence. Thus what Steiner said about healing falls into place through a recognition of our interconnectedness with the world around us:

> We either draw the remedies out of our surroundings, out of the condensed light, or out of our own soul by the healing act of love ... If the disturbance is in the realm of love, we can help by applying the power of love ourselves; and if the disturbance is in the realm of light, we can help by trying to find that light in the universe which will dissolve the darkness within us.

The implication of Steiner's words suggests a healing task on a mighty scale, and not just one for doctors. And if there is indeed truth in what he tried to convey, it is clear why we might need more than one lifetime to even make a start on what calls out to be done.

CHAPTER 35

Dying and Becoming

There's a story I was told recently about a Zen abbot on his deathbed, surrounded by his adoring disciples. 'Master, don't leave us', says one of them. The somewhat bewildered abbot replies, 'But where would I go?'

A major theme of this book, and indeed a thread running throughout my life, has been the question about the possibility, and if so the nature, of a 'spiritual world', particularly in relation to what we call 'life after death' – a place that the Zen abbot clearly imagines as not being somewhere else. But does all this matter? Is pondering and speculation about eternity and infinity relevant to most people's lives? Are we simply too busy, or too lazy, to bother? Or do we, as the hundred-year-old Reverend Humphrey said in response to Ron Eyre's question 'What about Heaven?', simply have to wait and see?

In his story *Master and Man*, Leo Tolstoy writes of a humble peasant, Nikita, whose previously tyrannical and selfish master, on a night-time journey through a snowstorm, freezes to death while saving his servant's life by lying on top of him. Tolstoy, on somewhat the same note as Humphrey, concludes his tale with Nikita's own death some twenty years later with these words: 'Whether he is better or worse off there where he awoke after his death, whether he was disappointed or found there what he expected, we shall all soon learn.' And there Tolstoy leaves it.

For some people, particularly those who are in the eyes of the world prosperous and successful, life is often too seductive for them to bother about the mystery of death and similar enigmas. I don't believe, however, that worldly advantages have to be an obstacle to thinking and acting thoughtfully and even philosophically, though they can sometimes make it harder. Wealth can either insulate us from other people, or be an enabler. In Tolstoy's case, it was those very advantages and privileges, together with his powerful conscience, that prompted him to search and to go on searching throughout his long life. Perhaps the greatest obstacle of all is certainty – another form of laziness which cuts us off from further exploration. Only the closed mind is certain. But the saddest condition of all, I often feel, is apathy.

Anyway, whatever our shortcomings, why speculate about our potential faculties to know and experience more, when we have such miraculous and efficient ones already? Many of the people I love and admire don't spend a great deal of time thinking about reincarnation and karma, or whether angels really exist. Only perhaps when a close friend or relation dies, do some people's thoughts turn to questions about heaven, and whether there is any meaning to life.

I realise, too, that people like me, who do think a great deal about such matters, are the fortunate few to whom life has given the opportunity to sometimes pause and reflect. Also, having clocked up three score years and ten, my attention now no longer revolves around the daily problem of getting to work, feeding and educating children, or – as is the case for very many people all over the world – simply struggling to stay alive. You don't, on the whole, write poetry on an empty stomach, let alone gaze at the night sky and wonder what it's all about. Nor, on the other hand, do you automatically become a better human being just because you ask the sort of questions I've been asking.

Meanwhile life goes on, whether we are rich or poor, thinkers or doers. Most people live out the ups and downs of their daily lives with courage and good humour. Some of the finest people I have met – like Pearl, who was 'too busy' to have a mid-life crisis – do just that. And however impoverished or humdrum some people's lives may seem to be, I believe passionately that every single person is living out a story that is of significance, however thwarted their journey may be. In this sense I can't emphasise enough the importance I attach to alleviating poverty and ignorance in the world, alongside a more sensitive and diligent stewardship of the world itself. 'Earth is our gracious host', said Satish Kumar during his thoughtful documentary film about Dartmoor, 'but are we gracious guests in return?'

My interest in today, and not just yesterday or tomorrow, is also why I have been so touched by the lives of Gandhi and Tolstoy in particular, and by the work carried out in the Camphill schools and villages; touched, too, by Henry van Dyke's story of *The Other Wise Man*. It is also why I value simple human kindness above all else. For despite my interest in what, to some, might seem both abstract and remote, I am primarily concerned with the 'here and now'. But I believe the present can and needs to be illumined and further transformed by a conscious connection with spiritual realities that 'we know in our bones', thereby informing and enriching our efforts to make the world a better place. Steiner spoke of this ability we all have, by paying greater attention to what unfolds in our lives, to awaken something within us that would otherwise remain dormant: 'We begin, as it were, to read between the lines of life.'

Emerson, whom I have also often quoted, clearly spoke out of this ability to tap into deeper truths. *In Writing in the Time of War* he wrote:

everything that moves or breathes … every fragment of force … every spark of life … is equally sacred … for, in the humblest atoms and the most brilliant star, in the lowest insect and the finest intelligence, there is the radiant smile and thrill of the same Absolute.

One definition in the dictionary of the word 'absolute' reads: 'a principle regarded as universally valid'. One problem in trying to write about a subject like heaven is that the words one uses tend to mean different things to different people. It's difficult, therefore, to come up with anything that could be regarded as 'universally valid'. In a letter that Tolstoy sent to a religious fanatic who strongly rebuked him for the beliefs he had forcefully expressed – beliefs which contradicted her own, and were therefore in her eyes heretical – he wrote:

I am eighty years old and I am still searching for truth … Every man in the depths of his soul has something he alone comprehends, namely his attitude towards God. And this sphere is sacred. We must not attempt to invade it or to imagine that we know all that lies hidden in its depth.

One reaction I have to Tolstoy's response is the recognition of how difficult it is, perhaps even impossible, to share those sacred and innermost thoughts and feelings with anyone else. And yet we try to do so all the time. I have certainly been nourished and inspired over the years by reading and listening to the wise ponderings of others. I am far more hesitant about holding forth myself, and yet this is what I too have finally done.

Above all, through the story of my own journey, I have tried to explore my sense that what awaits us after death is not as mysterious, remote and unfamiliar as people imagine, for we live in that realm every night while our bodies rest. Thus we are united with those close to us who have died, not just when we ourselves finally die, but potentially every night. For over forty years now I have lived without my mother in the daytime of my life. But during that time I have been asleep for approximately fourteen years – asleep to time and space, and therefore, I imagine, to the cycle of dying and becoming; it is an amazing and comforting thought. And in the same way that sleep is as much a part of our earthly existence as our waking life, so what we call 'life after death' is, I believe, an experience that is likewise intimately interwoven with what continues to unfold on earth.

The world we inhabit in sleep, when not fully connected to our physical bodies, or after death when that connection is totally severed, is therefore not somewhere else – not a different world to the one we experience daily through our physical senses; it's just that we no longer confront it as onlookers. Our waking consciousness separates us from all that surrounds us, and for a purpose. In sleep and after death we enter into whatever we previously surveyed. And there we discover the invisible and eternal element that corresponds to the invisible and eternal element in each of us, inspiring our own creativity and inherent wisdom; in so doing we recharge what I think of as our 'spiritual batteries'. And it is this interconnection with all creation that we can also start to experience in our conscious, waking life through meditation, and which at a certain stage becomes what Steiner called 'clairvoyant perception'. The implication of that potential, through such inner activity, is that the boundary between what we call 'life' and 'death' gradually disappears. There is only one world, but we need more than our eyes to see it.

I am therefore neither a materialist, in the sense of someone who only takes seriously what is accessible to the five senses and can be weighed and measured, nor someone drawn to any religion or cult that promotes the idea of a heaven as somewhere else and that is basically unknowable. What I do believe in is a spiritual dimension to existence that transcends time and space and which permeates everything, including ourselves. And what appears to be dispersed throughout the whole of creation is perhaps, in some mysterious and miraculous way, also contained in each one of us. If so, it therefore follows that the extent to which we know and understand ourselves will determine our experience and understanding of every aspect of reality, both visible and invisible.

King Lear's daughter, Regan, says of her father, 'Tis the infirmity of his age: yet he hath ever but slenderly known himself.' Such an admonition could just as well be applied to Regan herself – or, indeed, to all of us. Self-knowledge on the scale suggested is a huge and on-going task, and yet another reason for recognising why we might need many, many lifetimes.

Yet who am I? I ask myself. Who really stands behind that person looking back at me in the mirror? And what is it that gives continuity to my existence? What is this essence that I am challenged to recognise, nurture and gradually transform – an essence that endures? Clearly not my physical body; nor, I suspect, much of what people perceive as my personality, largely made up as it is of transient and ephemeral elements related to my race, gender, culture and environment.

There are, I believe – if we are sufficiently awake – many clues to this question, not least in the language we use from day to day. I don't say, for example, 'my brain thinks'. 'I' think – though I would certainly have trouble doing so if my brain were damaged. Likewise, as Thomas Weihs pointed out to his students, I don't fully identify with my emotions or soul-life. I can be ashamed of my feelings. And, as I've suggested a number of times, this experience of my own evolving sense of identity and individuality grows, and only grows, through the experience of being seemingly separate from everything and everyone else – including from my own body and soul.

In this sense, the notion of objectivity fostered by, and so central to what we call science, is perhaps of real significance not primarily because of the discoveries we have made through science – some of which may eventually prove deeply misleading – but because of the stimulation this activity of objectifying the world gives to our awakening self-awareness. I am me, and that over there is that. The experience that enables me to make such a statement has prompted me, slowly and over many years, to realise that I do in fact have what one might call a supersensible existence, not just after my death, but in the present – in what Johannes Tauler called 'the everlasting now'.

A very early and significant indication of the importance in human evolution of our potential to become individually independent and self-aware appears in the Old Testament, in the book of Exodus, when God appears to Moses in the burning bush:

> And Moses said unto God, Behold, when I come unto the children of Israel, and shall say unto them, the God of your fathers hath sent me unto you: and they shall say unto me, What is his name? What shall I say unto them?
> And God said unto Moses, I AM THAT I AM: and he said, Thus shalt thou say unto the children of Israel, I AM hath sent me unto you.

If there is a truth hidden away in the age-old idea that the human being was created in the image of God – in other words that our existence has meaning and purpose rather than being the result of purely random processes and events – then it would seem central to our destiny to have gradually arrived at the experience of being able to say, as did the Being with whom Moses spoke, 'I AM'.

Through such scriptures one can see how the Jews were the first people to understand history as a developmental process; it was a task that in itself warrants the label 'chosen', whatever else one might believe, or not believe, about a young Jewish carpenter as the first human being ready and worthy to fully unite with his divine potential through the incarnation of the being we call Christ.

I myself had a brief and, for me, profound glimpse into what I am trying to describe about our individual and evolving identity – as conveyed in those words 'I am' – when I was diagnosed with cancer some years ago. It was certainly a shock; but then I experienced on and off for the next few days what I am tempted to call euphoria – perhaps elation is a better word. It sounds absurd. I was not at all pleased to have cancer. It certainly had nothing to do with heroics. My overwhelming feeling, however, was that I am not my physical body and therefore that I am essentially all right. My body may have problems, but I remain intact. I exist and I will continue to exist.

I have to say that the euphoria didn't last, and that all the usual fears and depression set in, particularly when the cancer slowly started to reappear after I had undergone major surgery. Despite the wobbles, however, that initial reaction has never entirely left me. It is certainly what I believe in theory – that in essence I am independent of my physicality. But this was more than just intellectualising the situation, and the experience has left me with a very real, lasting, and welcome acceptance of fate in relation to all aspects of my mortal life.

One description of what I've called the continuity, or signature, that runs through each of our otherwise ever-changing lives – and perhaps through many lifetimes – is very movingly conveyed in Michael Mayne's book *The Enduring Melody*. In it he reflects on what remained constant for him throughout the pain and fear that accompanied his illness and the treatment he underwent during the last year of his life. Michael was at one time head of Religious Programmes in BBC Radio, and was Dean at Westminster Abbey when Alan Bennett and I made our films there.

'The enduring melody' is a translation of the Latin term *cantus firmus* – what we know as Gregorian chant or plainsong, the music of the monasteries in the Middle Ages. It is composed of one line of melody which later developed into many different voices singing in harmony and counterpoint around that main melody. 'Bach is the past master in the use of 'cantus firmus', wrote Michael in his book. 'His fugues are built on a structure of melody in the home key, the 'cantus firmus', which he then decorates, turns upside down, plays with, but always comes back to in the end.'

Michael Mayne's 'cantus firmus' – the particular thread that ran through his life and which became ever more apparent to him during his final illness – could be summed up as his faith, as a Christian, in the power and significance of love. 'I believe that the creation is an endless sequence of variations on the unchanging theme of God's love,' he wrote. For Michael love was 'at the heart of our universe'; and it is this love, he believed, 'which we are invited to discover for ourselves. Freedom, the only condition in which love can act, has to be part of the deal.'

In Michael's book he acknowledges that his life, like everyone else's, is a complex mixture of harmony and dissonance, 'but it is uniquely mine'. Perhaps it is only as we grow old, he suggests, that we can discern the 'cantus firmus' of which we can say 'This has been mine and mine alone.' He defines his own as having three strands: 'the experience of love and friendship; recurring experiences of beauty and order; and a few undeniable experiences of transcendence in our search for our elusive God'.

I suspect that many people, including those who don't necessarily call themselves Christians, would have no problem identifying with Michael Mayne's 'enduring melody'. Others might express it differently; but everyone, I believe, has a sense – sometimes buried deep – of their own authentic self that isn't really taken in by the trends and fashions of the day – a melody, in other words, which endures through all the disharmonies which we both create or confront and in which at times we become distressingly entangled.

One response I have to my earlier question: 'Does it matter that thoughts and ideas about a spiritual existence are not more written about and discussed?' is 'Yes, it does', though I realise that it is usually 'between the lines of life', between the words, that such intimations emerge most appropriately and effectively.

One of the main reasons why I believe it is increasingly important to take these matters seriously is my sense that the relationship between those of us who are so-called 'alive', and those who are seemingly no longer present, is of the utmost significance for our further evolution, and thus for the fulfilment of the tasks that are unique to humanity. Nowadays the idea of angels and the souls of the dead has become so remote from our actual experience and understanding that we tend to think of 'spirits' – if we think of them at all – as physically distant, way up in the sky and among the stars. However, in considering a purely spiritual dimension of reality I have gradually come to realise that distance – like time – is meaningless.

In a collection of lectures by Steiner, most sensitively edited and introduced by Christopher Bamford under the title *Staying Connected*, Steiner returns repeatedly to this theme of the interdependence of those who have died with those who are still alive on earth; 'a certain part of the ordering of the world and of all human progress', says Steiner, 'depends on this working of the dead into the life of earthly human beings, inspiring them'.

In addressing this highly mysterious and sensitive subject, however, the words 'alive' and 'dead' are already, for me, extremely misleading – especially the word 'dead'. As I have made clear, I share with millions of others throughout history the belief that the actual essence of our being never dies: the core – the one that Pier Gynt searched for as he peeled the onion – endures, as does Michael Mayne's 'melody'. In this sense the little boy Colin in Frances Compton Burnett's *The Secret Garden*, is not hopelessly idealistic when, having recovered from a serious illness, he declares euphorically: 'I shall live forever, and ever, and ever.' The French writer Antoine de Saint-Exupéry clearly shared this belief. The little prince says to the stranded pilot he has met in the north African desert and from whom he is finally about to part:

> It was wrong of you to come. You will suffer. I shall look as if I were dead; and that will not be true ... You understand ... It is too far. I

cannot carry this body with me. It is too heavy ... But it will be like an old abandoned shell. There is nothing sad about old shells ...

One initially surprising insight of Steiner's, shared with an audience in Bergen in 1913 and recorded in Bamford's anthology, is that knowledge of the spiritual worlds, 'which means more than vision, more than mere looking-on, can arise only on earth'. Earlier that same year, in Stuttgart, he said: 'It is a deep misconception to believe that souls become wise as soon as they pass through the gate of death.' In his autobiography Jung wrote something similar:

> People have the idea that the dead know far more than we, for Christian doctrine teaches that in the hereafter we shall 'see face to face'. Apparently, however, the souls of the dead 'know' only what they knew at the moment of death, and nothing beyond that ... I frequently have the feeling that they are standing directly behind us waiting to hear what answer we will give to them, and what answer to destiny.

In other words, perhaps only here during our earthly lives can we kindle the light that will illumine the existence not only between incarnations, but also in the 'time' we spend asleep every night. In his poem 'African Elegy', Ben Okri wrote of 'secret miracles at work / that only Time will bring forth'. Those, therefore, who are as it were in the dark, or in varying degrees of darkness after their death, depend in part on their relationship with those with whom they were connected on earth and who still live here on earth, in order to further orientate themselves to a quite other state of being. Our 'inner world' becomes their 'outer world'. We, therefore, have an enormous responsibility to take an interest in deeper questions of existence, not just for our own spiritual well-being, but for the sake of others whom we have loved and continue to love. They are dependant on us for help with all that they have not made conscious during their time on earth.

Steiner describes, for example, how our thoughts during the day can come to life at night as potential nourishment for those who have died; but he also speaks about the devastating silence that can ensue for those close to us if we are wholly absorbed by all that is shallow and superficial in life. He goes on to say that it is part of humanity's evolution that the 'dead' are cut off so dramatically in our present age; but that it is that same evolution which must lead to a rediscovery of our connection with them. Meanwhile, it seems, we have to accept – particularly on the death of someone we love – that time and space are meaningful though often distressing illusions.

Yet as we gradually become more open and sensitive to such matters, we can start to benefit profoundly from what Steiner calls the 'imaginations' and the 'unfulfilled thoughts' that those who have died can send us. 'Our work for our fellow human beings does not cease with our passage through the gate of death,' he told a gathering in Bern in 1916. As Florence Nightingale herself believed, it is a time of 'immense activity'. Many of the views and ideas that we experience as our own, suggests Steiner, are constantly influenced by 'those long-dead'. As Vernon Watkins wrote at the conclusion of his poem 'Gravestones': 'For the dead live / And I am of their kind.'

Two years later, speaking on the same theme in Berlin, Steiner said: 'Wait watchfully, until far down in the soul, thoughts arise that clearly distinguish themselves as given, not of our own making … an objective, universal web of thought … common ground where we can "meet" the dead'. This common ground is also cultivated, he suggests, to the extent that we feel gratitude for all our experiences, including unpleasant ones; this, together with 'a feeling of community with everything in existence' helps to build a bridge. It is precisely what Jung as an old man, in his letter to Laurens van der Post, called 'a feeling of kinship with all things'.

Thus, if we nurture such thoughts, alongside a fond and grateful awareness of those who have died, 'ordinary life may be enriched'. Indeed Steiner goes so far as to say that 'life is impoverished when the dead are forgotten.' For me it is as though those who have died physically are saying: 'I can no longer be where you are, but you can come where I am.' This message has become ever more real to me, particularly in relation to my mother, but also when I think about the many other people I know and love who are, in Beryl Bainbridge's words, 'no longer answering the phone'. In this sense I find it interesting that many people, particularly as they get older, start to take an interest in their family tree and often research their genealogy in great detail. Such activity seems to indicate an unconscious wish to connect with their ancestors, just as that Chinese family I filmed in Taiwan do every spring at the festival of Ching Ming.

However, it is perhaps well to remember in all this potential communion beyond the grave that, depending on our disposition, we are open to influence not only from those with whom we were close and from spiritual beings more evolved than us, but also from rebellious and discordant forces that seek to undermine humanity's evolution – much in the same way that we can be led astray by discordance in seemingly human form here on earth. We know that when we are physically run-down we are vulnerable to whatever virus or germs are in the air; likewise, if we are morally and spiritually diminished, demonic entities of all sorts can move in to fill the vacuum.

On this subject of negative forces, Steiner spoke on a number of occasions of how, after death, all that was critical in our attitude to one another slowly starts to fall away as we begin to understand why each person behaves in the way they do, influenced as they are by forces over which they have only limited control. Alexander Solzhenitsyn had a similar insight into this change of heart that can arise while he was a cancer patient at a clinic in Tashkent, during his exile in neighbouring Kasakhstan. He starts by describing how a person can cross the threshold of death while still occupying a body that is not yet dead: 'Your blood still circulates and your stomach digests things, but psychologically you have completed all your preparations for death and lived through death itself.' He then writes: 'Although you never regarded yourself as a Christian – sometimes, indeed, the opposite – now you suddenly notice that you have already forgiven everyone who has insulted you.'

Before I write further about what Steiner called 'the riddle of death', I want to look again at what is sometimes referred to as 'the little death', namely sleep; though you could equally look upon death as the big, or longer sleep. On the whole we have no memory of what, if anything, takes place during those seven or eight hours each night, nor indeed of any existence between incarnations, or of past lives. For me, as I have already written, that doesn't have to mean that there is simply nothing to remember, but rather that it is an indication of the limitation of our consciousness, at this stage of its evolution, in holding on to such experiences. Even in everyday life we don't remember everything we've seen or heard or read, but that, too, doesn't mean that those experiences aren't retained unconsciously in who we are and how we behave.

That dreams, too – however powerful they are at the time – are so quickly forgotten, seems another clear indication of our inability to remember consciously everything that we've experienced. Such forgetfulness probably enables us to better concentrate on the here and now, and all that it – and it alone – can teach us. However, I don't believe we are unaffected by what has taken place during sleep just because it is not in our consciousness, any more than we are untouched by past lives we cannot remember. And our potential connection during sleep with those who have died is one important source of the guidance and inspiration we can receive, if we are sufficiently open to the direction in which our daimon or angel is constantly trying to nudge us. The fact that we often say, in relation to important decisions that have to be made, 'I must sleep on it', seems to me a confirmation of the fact that unconsciously we are wiser than we realise. Who knows what distances we travel in our sleep.

In Chapter Twenty-Three I wrote about the significance of the moment we fall asleep, and then the moment of waking; and about Steiner's use of the word 'simultaneous' in relation to questions and answers we put to, and receive from, the 'spiritual world' even though the dialogue is seemingly interrupted by many hours of sleep. There is a legend about the prophet Mohammed that throws light on the mysterious nature of time to which Steiner alludes.

It concerns an event known as the Night Journey. Mohammed is woken by the archangel Gabriel, and in getting out of bed knocks over a cup of water. Gabriel then takes him on a journey, on the back of a white beast, from Mecca to Jerusalem, and thence through the seven heavens into the presence of Allah. On his return Mohammed is in time to catch that same cup of water before it hits the ground.

If we take such stories seriously, including our own occasional experiences of a similar nature, and if Steiner is therefore correct in using that word 'simultaneous', then perhaps this is another important clue to the mystery of sleep and death; for such occurrences seem to be pointing us towards a realisation that when we are asleep every night, as well as between incarnations, we do truly exist outside of time and space in a purely supersensible dimension. It is why I keep suggesting that our existence after death will not be the sort of surprise that many people expect, since we dip into that reality every night while we sleep – though in both cases only with the degree of consciousness that we forged during our waking, earthly existence.

This alternation between time and timelessness, between sleeping and waking, and between one incarnation and another, is just one expression of the great rhythms that permeate all existence at every level – of day and night, summer and winter, breathing in and breathing out. On a visit to London in the summer of 1922 Rudolf Steiner spoke to his audience about what he called 'the obligation of modern initiation' in contrast to old forms of clairvoyance, 'to seek as knowledge the rhythmical relationship of heaven and earth'. In his introduction to *Staying Connected*, Christopher Bamford sums up his understanding of Steiner's message concerning this twofold nature of the human being with these words:

> visible beings embodied in space and time, and invisible beings of soul and spirit. We live and work and have being in both realms. In both, we are at home. Yet these two – heaven and earth – are in a sense not really two but one: a single reality in two forms.

In his conversation with the broadcaster Joan Bakewell for her anthology *Belief*, John O'Donohue describes his understanding of this tightrope along which we walk with these words: 'The presence of the divine in us is actually what creates huge poignancy in us. We're such threshold creatures, we're neither here nor there – we're in between.' But as creatures who are 'in between', we not only step backwards and forwards across the daily thresholds of sleeping and waking, but also, periodically, across those two other great thresholds of birth and death.

'Decay is the midwife of very great things', wrote Paracelsus. 'It brings about the birth and rebirth of forms a thousand times improved. This is the highest mystery of God.' In Plutarch's *Moralia*, he too writes how 'every mortal creature, situated between birth and passing away, manifests merely an appearance, a feeble and uncertain image of itself'. Everything, therefore, seems to be not only caught up in 'the rhythmical relationship of heaven and earth', but as a result is in a constant state of flux, arising and passing away. Becoming never ceases or stands still. Plutarch continues:

> Change begins in the germ and forms an embryo; then appears a child, a youth, a man, an old man; the early and successive ages are continually annulled by the ensuing ones. Hence it is ridiculous to fear one death, when we have already died in so many ways and are still dying.

Plutarch then quotes Heraclitus who points out that not only is 'the death of fire the birth of air, and the death of air the birth of water', but that this process is even more apparent in the human being. No person endures. Change allows us to become something else. 'Because we have no knowledge of true being', says Heraclitus, 'sense-perception has led us astray into taking appearance for reality.'

I have always imagined, or rather hoped, that the experience of death in old age – providing one is not in too much pain – is similar to the feeling at the end of a long and busy day. However enjoyable that day has been, you've had enough; you're ready to sleep. But I also realise that life is not always so kind. Though perhaps one shouldn't use words like 'kind' and 'cruel' to describe events that may be prompted by a wisdom way beyond our understanding.

In what I think is one of Tolstoy's greatest stories, *The Death of Ivan Ilych*, he writes about death in far more detail than in those few concluding lines about Nikita's death in *Master and Man*. The death he describes is a slow and agonising one – emotionally as well as physically. But it brings the sufferer to a realisation and peace that would otherwise have eluded him. Ivan Ilych is a judge, an ordinary man living an ordinary life. But like most of the people who surround him – his family, colleagues and friends – he is essentially shallow and selfish. He doesn't really care deeply about anyone, and no one really cares about him. If they were honest enough to admit it, they are thankful that it is his life and not theirs that is ebbing away.

Tolstoy's great genius was not only his ability to feel himself into the skin of another person, but also to recognise that however base we seem to be, we are all redeemable – capable of discovering within ourselves something nobler, something that is basically unselfish. Having experienced a multitude of emotions, including fear, false hope and anger – and despite the increasing pain

– Ivan Ilych gradually starts to see his life in all its emptiness, and to feel that if he could have it over again, he would live it very differently. He also begins to feel sorry for the people around him, and for the disruption and suffering that his agonised screams are causing them. 'Yes, I am making them wretched', he thought. 'They are sorry, but it will be better for them when I die. He wished to say this but had not the strength to utter it'. Ivan Ilych then suddenly becomes aware that what has been oppressing him is starting to fall away:

> He was sorry for them, he must act so as not to hurt them; release them and free himself from these sufferings. 'How good and how simple!' he thought. 'And the pain?' he asked himself; 'What has become of it? Where are you, pain?'
> He turned his attention to it.
> 'Yes, here it is. Well, what of it? Let the pain be.'
> 'And death ... where is it?'
> He sought his former accustomed fear of death and did not find it. 'Where is it? What death?' There was no fear because there was no death.
> In place of death there was light.
> 'So that's what it is!' he suddenly exclaimed aloud. 'What joy!'
> To him all this happened in a single instant and the meaning of that instant did not change. For those present his agony continued for another two hours. Something rattled in his throat, his emaciated body twitched, then the gasping and rattle became less and less frequent.
> 'It is finished!' said someone near him.
> He heard these words and repeated them in his soul.
> 'Death is finished', he said to himself. 'It is no more.'
> He drew in a breath, stopped in the midst of a sigh, stretched out, and died.

Some of the most profound words about death that I have come across were written by Steiner in *Knowledge of the Higher Worlds*, first published in the early years of the 20th century. Christopher Bamford calls Rudolf Steiner 'a twentieth-century representative of a long line of what the Koran calls "Warners", who remind us of our divine destiny in the language and manner appropriate to our time.' Steiner's book is an attempt to describe a modern path of initiation, beginning with the exercises I wrote about briefly in Chapter Three. He also emphasises throughout the importance of moral development keeping pace with the acquisition of spiritual knowledge and experiences. Towards the end of the book he then tries to describe a certain stage on this path of self-development when the pupil seeking initiation is confronted by what he calls the Guardian of the Threshold; an encounter with a terrifying being who represents and embodies all that is still unfulfilled and base in his character, 'a supersensible being he has himself brought into existence, and whose body is made up of the consequences, hitherto invisible to him, of his own acts, feelings and thoughts'. It can be a traumatic experience, demanding all the courage and presence of mind that we would need to have developed during our training, for previously we would have been protected from the full impact of such self-knowledge by beings far wiser and more evolved than us. Toynbee, in his autobiographical journal, acknowledges the help he received, in response to prayer at a low point in his life, as being 'chiefly in the recognition that God shows me my miserable faults and failings to just the extent that I can bear to accept them'.

The encounter with the Guardian that Steiner evokes reminds me in many ways of Mary Shelley's descriptions of Dr Frankenstein's confrontation with the hideous creature he has brought into existence in his laboratory. Frankenstein is morally and emotionally unprepared for such an experience, and therefore rejects what in part is a projection of his own considerable shortcomings. But his creation is not so easily disposed of; instead, in response to rejection and denial, it gradually turns into a monster – becoming ugly inwardly as well as outwardly – and so sets about destroying its maker, whose cleverness and hubris far exceeds his maturity as a human being.

Through this encounter with the Guardian that Steiner describes, we experience consciously what previously worked unconsciously through our karma. The individual's essential being, he writes, 'now stands to a certain extent openly revealed before him'. We can recognise, for example, the source of our inclinations and habits; why we love one thing and hate another; and what were the origins of the fate that life has brought us.

It is then, in this most fundamental of Steiner's books, that he writes from yet another angle on the interrelationship between what he calls 'the spiritual world' and the world that we know during our waking life on earth, and by this means he tries to throw light on the significance and meaning of death. Decay as 'the midwife of very great things' was Paracelsus's way of expressing what Steiner strives to elucidate in the final pages of this book.

The earth, like all living things, will eventually die; so too, writes Steiner, might the supersensible world itself: a sobering thought indeed. He then points to what is potentially 'a higher stage of the supersensible world – a stage that will be enriched with fruits brought to maturity in the sense-world'. What follows is even more revelatory – or off the radar – depending on your psychic disposition:

> Death is nothing other than an expression of the fact that the supersensible world, as it once was, reached a point from which it

could not progress by itself. Universal death would inevitably have overtaken it if it had not received a new influx of life. And this new life has become a battle against universal death. Out of the remnants of a dying, inwardly rigidifying world the seeds of a new world came to flower. That is why we have death and life in the world.

In other words the forces of renewal have to be kindled and nurtured here in a world that, like the cosmos itself, is also in a process of dying. We know from astronomers that stars are dying all the time; even our own sun will not last forever – not that this gives us an excuse to hasten the whole process by continuing to plunder and abuse our miraculous planet and all that sustains it.

What is extraordinary to contemplate, however, is that the supersensible world – assuming you can connect to Steiner's picture – will also die if left bereft of new creativity; and it will do so, despite the fact that all existence has its origins in this realm. And this further creativity can only come into being not in the heavens above, but in the heaven that we manage very slowly to create here on earth.

This whole process of dying and becoming is manifest most clearly in the human being. In this sense we are indeed both mortal and immortal, both old and new; as human beings we are dying along with all creation, but we are also the source of potential renewal. And this polarity of life and death plays itself out in every individual person. We do inevitably die physically, but what we have created that is new and of worth will live on. Our efforts and failures will affect the future. Such thoughts have helped me to gradually understand what Christ's pronouncements about everlasting life might mean. There really is, it appears, a path that can lead from death to life. If we could commune with ourselves in the hour of death, these are the words that Steiner imagines we might say:

> The dying world was my teacher. That I am dying is a result of the whole past with which I am interwoven. But the field of mortality has brought to maturity within me the seeds of immortality. I bear these seeds with me into another world. If it depended only on the past I could never have been born. The life of the past came to an end with birth. Life in the sense world is wrested from universal death by the newly formed seed of life. The time between birth and death is only the expression of how much the new life could wrest from the dying past. And illness is nothing but the continuing effect of the dying parts of the past.

The picture I am left with is one I have hinted at throughout these pages – namely the importance of what we forge here on earth and what it signifies for the evolution of the entire cosmos, both visible and invisible. What we achieve, whether good or bad, will affect and be incorporated into the whole of creation, for better or worse. In that sense not just the earth, but the divine realms from which it evolved and which can help to transform it further, will be either enriched or polluted not just by what we do or fail to do ecologically, but also by how we are morally. As Johannes Tauler warned over seven hundred years ago, Herod is not just an historical figure, but a force in the world that is constantly trying to destroy the child in us – the essential purity that each one of us has to nurture and bring to maturity. We therefore have a very great responsibility – one increasingly recognised today in relation to our stewardship of this small, but maybe not insignificant planet.

Emil Bock, one of the young theologians close to Rudolf Steiner, summed up this whole challenge for greater sensitivity and consciousness with these words:

> We have to learn two things: a sense for what is dying, so we can recognise it; and a sense for what is emerging, so we can cultivate it. The outer conditions of the world are doomed; everything transitory, everything time-bound, is essentially dying. But there are also signs of something new emerging. To see the first rays of eternity glimmer through the cracks and crevices of the bursting sense world: this gives us the strength to calmly give over to the abyss what is dying, and to welcome that which is arising.

This thought reminds me of something that Fritz Schumacher used to say about the multinationals and other huge and impersonal corporations that seem to threaten our very humanity. We mustn't worry, he believed. He compared them to the dinosaurs, saying that they incorporated within themselves the seeds of their own obsolescence. 'Cultivate the antelopes!' was his slogan.

————————————

These profound insights into the nature and meaning of death that I have been describing are revealed to the initiate through an inner encounter with what Steiner describes in *Knowledge of the Higher Worlds* as 'an exalted being of light'. He called it the Greater Guardian, saying that 'the beauty of this being is difficult to describe in human language'. In contrast to the Lower Guardian, who reminds us so disturbingly of all our shortcomings, the Greater Guardian – at an even higher stage of our development – gives us a glimpse and reminder of what we might become.

Here again Steiner imagines a dialogue of sorts – words with which the Greater Guardian addresses the pupil who has achieved the spiritual maturity for such an encounter. They are, however, words of warning – a warning of the temptation to wallow, as it were, in our own bliss. 'You will someday be able to unite yourself with me', the Greater Guardian tells the pupil, 'but I cannot find blessedness as long as others are still unredeemed.'

Initiation is thus revealed as inseparable from one's concern and obligation to others. It is a truth that the 'other wise man' sensed instinctively, but only fully understood at the very end of his life. Although the path of those seeking enlightenment is inevitably and essentially a lonely one, salvation is only achieved by realising that nothing and no one is finally separate, and that our well-being at every level of existence is dependant on the other: that our destinies are intrinsically interwoven with all creation. In other words we have a responsibility for one another, and indeed for all the kingdoms of nature. Aldous Huxley recognised the danger of the path opened up by a substance such as mescalin, isolating you as it can from concern for other people. In Steiner's language this is falling too far into the clutches of Lucifer – that polarity in our make-up that individualises us, but on its own leads us into a cul-de-sac of pride, vanity and blissful or torturous self-absorption.

For Buddhists, likewise, lack of compassion for the suffering of others means the goal of Nirvana is always in danger of becoming an escape rather than an ultimate and sublime achievement. Mindfulness is not introspection. We need to look outwards and to recognise how our feelings, thoughts and actions affect others. It is the here and now that matters. Transformation takes place in time and space.

As the Buddha's message spread across India some two and a half thousand years ago, people came to him asking who he was. 'Are you a god?' they asked. 'No.' 'A saint?' 'No.' 'Then what are you?' they asked. Buddha answered: 'I am awake.' It's a message reaffirmed in 19th-century America by Henry Thoreau in his classic book, *Walden*: 'To be awake is to be alive.'

Chapter 36

Heaven and Earth

The sublime and challenging message from what Steiner called the Greater Guardian, who warns against a spirituality that is escapist and fundamentally egotistical, brings us firmly back down to earth, which is exactly where I want to end this book. So, too, does the message about the importance of compassion in our daily lives, as emphasised and practised by the Buddha and by many fine people from all cultures – whatever their beliefs about what may or may not await us after death.

'Free To Love' was the title of one of my early chapters in which I explored the meaning of a consciousness that seems to separate us from everything and everyone else. Through the alienation and loneliness that arises, there awakens our own sense of self, and thereby the capacity for empathy – that growing instinct to feel ourselves into the situation of the other person, and therefore to suffer or rejoice on their behalf. Michael Mayne wrote about the love 'we are invited to discover for ourselves'. Part of what he called 'the deal' is freedom, 'the only condition in which love can act'.

For some people God and love are synonymous: 'God is Love'. For Gandhi, it was 'God is Truth'. Neither statement has any ambivalence. The divine is incapable of not loving, and personifies the truth we seek. Yet although Michael Mayne equates our human potential to love with the love of God, the implication of our freedom *not* to love but to hate, to make mistakes and to be untruthful, indicates for me the birth of something quite new in the universe: a freedom that sets us apart from what we call God, and yet is intimately connected with those words about 'the seeds of new life' that the Greater Guardian reveals to the initiate. And central to this challenge we face are the words contained in that phrase 'a selfless self', which John Davy's Screwtape describes as such a 'disgusting paradox'.

So what are we doing with this freedom, and where is the evidence of any shift in our human sensibilities and the emergence of a selfless self? Certainly it's fashionable these days to say that human nature never changes, and there is, of course, plenty of evidence in the last hundred years or so to suggest that we are not only as brutal as we've always been, but possibly worse.

It is a view that Malcolm Muggeridge, among others, held very strongly.

In an article in *The Times* (October 30th 2008) Ben Okri addresses what he calls the moral bankruptcies of our age with some powerful words. 'The crisis affecting our economy', he writes, 'is a crisis of our civilisation.' And he points his finger not at the bankers and politicians, but at ourselves: 'We are all implicated. We have drifted to this dark unacceptable place together.' And it is a place where he sees artists as 'more appreciated for scandal than for important revelations about our lives':

> Writers are entertainers, provocateurs or, if truly serious – more or less ignored. The Church speaks with a broken voice. Politicians are more guided by polls than by vision. We have disembowelled our oracles. Anybody who claims to have something to say is immediately suspect.

It is our material success, so Okri believes, that has brought us to this 'strange spiritual and moral bankruptcy'. He concludes his article by reminding us that every society has a legend about a treasure that has been lost. It is the same vision that so preoccupied Cecil Collins. Our challenge, Okri believes, is to find that 'Grail', to find 'the values that were so crucial to the birth of our civilisation, but were lost in the intoxication of its triumphs'.

It would be naïve of me to turn a blind eye to what Okri is saying, or to our seemingly inherent egotism, and to the horrors and cruelty we are all capable of. But these tragedies and the flaws in our make-up are only one side of the picture – and often disproportionately emphasised by the media, and by those who wish not to warn, but to satisfy and to profit from our appetite for sensational or violent fodder. There's a Russian definition of a pessimist that calls him 'a well-informed optimist'. I like to think of myself as reasonably well-informed, but I'm still an optimist.

In relation to the other side of the picture, therefore, I was interested to read an article recently by a Camphill co-worker, Andrew Hoy, in their journal *Camphill Correspondence*, in which he draws attention to Newton's Third Law of Motion: to every action, there is an equal and opposite reaction. Hoy suggests that every cultural trend will be counteracted by some balancing influence. His analogy with Newton's law is helpful up to a point, but more directly relevant are the self-correcting processes that exist throughout nature: biological and ecological laws that come into play when something goes too far in one direction, so that the body, organism or ecosystem restores the balance. Another example is the self-regulating system in the human psyche as observed by Jung in relation to our conscious and unconscious thoughts and feelings, particularly as revealed in dreams. Hoy goes on to suggest in his article that the counter-force to the concept 'survival of the fittest' – a description coined by Darwin's contemporary Herbert Spenser – is our enhanced compassion for the underdog, for endangered species, and for those who, for example, suffer from physical or mental disabilities.

We talk about life as a rat race, and refer still to the law of the jungle, but the world is not just a jungle. It was one of Darwin's great contributions to our understanding of life, through his diligent observations of the evolutionary process at work, to undermine the idea that life remains static. We may once have lived a jungle-like existence, remnants of which remain with us still, but essentially humanity is on the move, as we always have been. In fact in *Darwin's Lost Theory*, the psychologist and evolutionary systems scientist David Loye points out that in *The Descent of Man* the word 'cooperation' crops up far more frequently than 'competition'; indeed nature is palpably full of examples of symbiotic development, such as the relationship between bees and flowers. In an article in *Network Review* (Spring 2009) Loye maintains that for Darwin 'the prime driver for evolution – and the completion for his theory of evolution – was and is not natural selection, or "survival of the fittest", as popularised. It is our capacity for the "moral sense", i.e. moral sensitivity, an evolutionary inbuilt thrust within us for the development of a sense of right versus wrong.'

John Betjeman, with his nostalgia for an England 'before the arrival of the internal combustion engine', said to me once that the only improvement in his lifetime was in dentistry. He knew it was a remark that was funnier than it was true, for he understood and appreciated very well the times in which he lived, and the positive shifts that were taking place. He was suspicious of the news on television because he felt instinctively that it wasn't telling us the whole truth about what was really going on in the world. The soap opera *Coronation Street* was for him a far better source of insight into the all-important ups and downs of people's lives, above all into the way that their humanity comes shining through in circumstances that are often dire.

Less than a mile from where I live in Gloucestershire, and a little over a hundred years ago, a man was hanged for stealing a sheep to feed his starving family. Such punishment, not just here, but in more and more countries all over the world, is unthinkable today. The death penalty itself is increasingly rejected. There is, in general, a growing aversion to settling disputes by violent means. In the case of the war in Vietnam, and other conflicts since then, there have been many people reluctant to automatically fight for their country if they feel the cause is unjust.

Such a shift in human sensitivity is, I believe, a sign of our growing awareness of the suffering and injustices that affect not only those on our own doorstep, but the whole of humanity. More and more people, for example, are starting to ask about the conditions of workers who produce the cheap clothes and food we buy. Cynics might say that we actually do very little about all this, except perhaps send off the odd cheque to some appeal, or take our perfectly good but discarded belongings to the nearest charity shop. For me it is profoundly significant that this awareness and concern exists at all. We may not yet be prepared to change our over-indulgent way of life fundamentally, but at least our capacity to empathise is stirring, and that surely has to be the first step. Organisations like the Samaritans, Oxfam, and Médécins sans Frontières are obvious examples, as are all those who voluntarily, and largely anonymously, counsel the bereaved, visit prisoners, or simply care for others who are neither family, nor even perhaps from the same culture or background. Increasingly the word 'neighbour' no longer just applies to those living next door.

'Although the six o'clock news is usually concerned with the death of strangers, millions of people work on behalf of strangers', writes Paul Hawken in his book *Blessed Unrest*. He describes how for him curiosity slowly grew into a hunch that 'something larger was afoot, a significant social movement that was eluding the radar of mainstream culture'. I found Hawken's book an inspiring survey of what he calls 'a global humanitarian movement' – people who are 'fiercely independent', working on the whole in small groups and NGOs, and all determined to heal what he calls 'the wounds of the earth'. They share no unifying ideology, follow no single charismatic leader and are mostly unrecognised by politicians and the media. He suggests that this network of non-profit organisations can be seen as 'humanity's immune response to toxins like political corruption, economic disease, and ecological degradation'. Another American writer, Bill McKibben, has called *Blessed Unrest* 'the first full account of the real news of our time', and exactly the opposite of the official account:

> The movers and shakers on our planet aren't the billionaires and the generals – they are the incredible numbers of people around the world filled with love for neighbor and for the earth who are resisting, remaking, restoring, renewing, revitalizing.

Another indication of this shift in people's sensibilities is the desire of many young people not just to travel before going to university or starting a career, but to travel to places where they might be of help. To go to India just to shoot tigers is nowadays unthinkable – and not just because there are hardly any tigers left.

It's true, of course, that there have always been those who cared deeply about the welfare of others – often, though not always, within the various religious orders – but never on such a vast scale as now. Above all, my own experiences of meeting many different people on my travels has given me a sense that altruism is very much more alive than the headlines convey, and that Gandhi's slogan 'an eye for an eye makes the world blind' resonates for an increasing number of us all; so too does another of his pertinent comments: 'We must become the change we want to see in the world.'

Responding to *Blessed Unrest*, anthropologist Jane Goodall writes: 'Paul Hawken states eloquently all that I believe so passionately to be true: that there is inherent goodness at the heart of our humanity, that collectively we can – and are – changing the world.' I too am heartened that the society into which I was born has already transformed itself so dramatically, particularly in terms of the distribution of wealth, not only within my own lifetime but very much more so since, for example, the 'hard times' that Charles Dickens wrote about. Enormous inequalities remain, but we have made huge strides. And the greater compassion that has evolved over the last hundred years or so in countries like Britain will, I believe, gradually happen on a world scale. Why on earth not? In the words of the 20th-century French political philosopher Raymond Aron, 'with humanity on the way to unification, inequality between peoples takes on the significance that inequality between classes once had.' But these changes will happen peacefully only to the extent that we who live in affluent societies are honest enough to recognise ourselves in the role of Dickens's famous tyrant, the beadle Mr Bumble, and see that more than half the world's population is, like Oliver Twist, justifiably asking for more.

Many Victorians probably felt as remote from the children who swept their chimneys, the people who dug coal out of the ground, or who ploughed their fields, as we might still feel about the children in the slums of Rio, or the millions of people in Africa and elsewhere who do not have enough to eat and get very limited access to education and health care. These people may be further away from us physically than the workhouses or factories were from the prosperous few in 19th-century society, but in the end what counts is not distance but consciousness – and consciousness has no limits to its outreach. Meanwhile ease of travel is playing its part in undermining the illusion of separateness, and our ignorance and prejudices about other cultures. Radio and television at their best, and now the internet, have opened up new possibilities of communication on a world scale.

I have sometimes used the word 'signature' to identify what is unique in each individual. The notion of a 'folk soul' can likewise be seen as an expression of a certain signature that defines each culture, nation or race. And if such observations have a reality, then perhaps there also exists a 'time spirit' – what the Germans call the *Zeitgeist* – that characterises the signature of a particular age. (The word 'zeitgeist' is actually in my English dictionary, which is perhaps another sign of the times.) Steiner identified our current zeitgeist with the archangel Michael, whom he saw as influencing the increasing recognition and experience of our interconnectedness. One outcome is concern for 'the other', to which I have already referred, along with greater reluctance to harm or kill as we have done so often in the past. The world is changing because we as individuals are changing – slowly, and often reluctantly, but ultimately through our own volition.

Yet if we ourselves make the first move, perhaps we are helped to a far greater extent than we realise consciously – particularly if the zeitgeist *is* an actual being and not an abstract concept. Maybe we are helped too by something even more powerful in the background of all our lives: a loving, inspiring and essentially invisible presence, not just for those who call themselves Christians but, as from the outset, for everyone who struggles to heed and to honour their inner voice. 'I shall be with you always, even unto the end of time' was Christ's message which has become increasingly meaningful for me. In this sense, I wonder sometimes if what is called the 'Second Coming' has already taken place.

For Steiner – who was not brought up in a particularly Christian household, but more in what he called 'a free-thinking atmosphere' – the profound significance of what he frequently referred to as 'the mystery of Golgotha' became ever more central to what he was trying to communicate about human evolution. In a lecture he gave in Oslo on October 3rd 1913, published in *The Fifth Gospel*, he shared with his audience 'the feeling of what Christ's sacrifice really signified'. This sacrifice, so Steiner suggests, was the forsaking of the sublime realms in which he dwelt, in order to unite with us on our evolutionary journey: 'He made the earth his heaven.' It is the presence of that power, whatever name you like to give it, that is – so many believe – also helping us edge forward towards fulfilling our human potential.

The capacity that we all have to make a shift in how we live out our lives can manifest in all sorts of small ways. For me it has been powerfully captured in a number of films that have touched me deeply. In one, a Brazilian production called *Central Station*, a woman who is certainly no saint, is gradually prompted, through a casual encounter with a child whose mother has just been run over and killed, to put another person before herself. She makes her living writing letters at Rio's main railway station for those who are illiterate. She charges a dollar for her services, but frequently doesn't bother to post the letters, thereby avoiding the cost of a stamp. At first she even tries to make money out of the boy's plight. Although changes gradually take place in how she behaves – she eventually takes the boy on a long and complicated journey to find his father – the story contains no dramatic transformation, and this is what makes the film so honest and powerful. A small shift is all that most of us are capable of achieving, but it is a shift nonetheless.

Likewise, in an American film called *About Schmidt*, the main character – superbly played by Jack Nicholson – is jogged into discovering new and deeper aspects of himself. Schmidt is at the point of retirement from a soulless career in the insurance business. Everything about him – his routine, the state of his marriage, and indeed his whole life is in a huge and depressing rut. But things then start to happen which, although threatening, disruptive and even tragic, do wake him up. Schmidt certainly doesn't end up some all-American hero, but changes take place that are both credible and moving, above all in his own self-esteem and in his sensitivity to other people.

Another film that explores this same theme – of shift rather than transformation – has its setting in the squalid and tough world of the South African townships. Tsotsi – also the name of the film (the word means 'thug') – is someone who appears to have no feeling for others, not even for members of his own gang. One of his exploits is to steal yet another car, but he then discovers a baby on the back seat. As in *Central Station* we gradually learn more about the character's background, for through his encounter with the baby and the problem of caring for it, we the audience, along with Tsotsi, experience glimpses of his own abandonment as a child, glimpses that are potential awakeners for Tsotsi himself.

All three films are, among other things, important reminders not to judge anyone by what you meet superficially, whether they are a ruthless-looking thug, a boring middle-aged American or simply someone out to con you. Like many of Tolstoy's tales the films are also powerful confirmations of our potential to be something else, something more.

One of the most interesting and encouraging books to have appeared in recent years on the subject of change, and new ways of looking at the world and at us as onlookers, is called *The Cultural Creatives*, written by husband and wife team Paul Ray and Sherry Ruth Anderson. Over a period of thirteen years they conducted a survey of a hundred thousand Americans, focusing essentially on the values that people hold most dear. They found that three main groupings emerged, which they called Moderns, Traditionals, and Cultural Creatives. The Moderns make up around fifty per cent of the population and are the people who basically run things – government, judiciary, the military and the media. They are also all those who more or less go along with the status quo. 'The Moderns are the people who accept the commercialised urban-industrial world as the obvious right way to live', write Ray and Anderson. 'They're not looking for alternatives.'

The Traditionals are those who are concerned at the destruction and disappearance of the world they remember – small-town life and rural simplicity. They tend to be older, poorer and less educated that other Americans, and make up about twenty-five per cent of the population, and according to the survey their numbers are on the decline.

Then there are the twenty-five per cent called the Cultural Creatives, people from every walk of life who tend to reject Left / Right labels. Around sixty per cent of these are women, and all of them tend to share what are often described as feminine values in relation to family life, education, relationships, responsibilities and caring in general. They are also the people whom Paul Hawken recognises and applauds for creating 'blessed unrest'. Many of them, each in their own way, are searching to discover what Arthur Zajonc, in his book on meditation, calls 'a deep stillness beyond self or personal concerns'.

Many, I imagine, are among those who have been helped and inspired by Eckhart Tolle's latest book *A New Earth* and his subsequent series of television dialogues with Oprah Winfrey based on the book. 'All people have a spiritual teacher', he said to her in one programme, 'for many that teacher is suffering.' Along with his wise words, he has all the serenity, humility and authenticity of someone who practises what they preach. His central message – finding the timeless dimension within yourself – resonates for an increasing number of people, though in acknowledging 'the power of now', and the danger of living either too much in the past or too much in the future, it's important to remember that there are also dangers of living entirely in the moment. To reflect, to dream and to hope are capacities that define us as human beings.

To learn from the past, to plan for a better future, and to do something about it right now seems to be what's asked of us. 'In the twenty-first century', write Ray and Anderson, 'the biggest challenges are to preserve and sustain life on the planet and find a new way past the overwhelming spiritual and psychological emptiness of modern life. The Cultural Creatives are responding to these challenges by creating a new culture.' It is a movement whose seeds I already glimpsed in Theodore Roszak's book *The Making of a Counter Culture* and while shooting our film in California for *The Long Search* in the mid-seventies. It is now recognisable not only in the States, but in all cultures where affluence is producing what the psychologist Oliver James has called 'affluenza'. I came across a small but significant example of this 'new culture' here in Britain in a promotional film called *Banking on People* that I made for Hermes Films about ethical banking. Lending money, at a low rate of interest, to support projects and initiatives that are small, idealistic but vulnerable, is a good example of people wanting to use their money in a new, more imaginative and less selfish way. Mercury Provident has since become part of a similar and larger Dutch initiative called Triodos Bank.

What I find particularly interesting in the American survey, but not at all surprising, is that these Cultural Creatives tend to feel themselves individually alone and very much in the minority, whereas in fact there are a great many of them – or should I say us. In one reaction to the book, the American author Joan Borysenko wrote of being astounded at 'the good news that we are not lone voices crying in the wilderness'. Indeed, if Ray and Anderson are correct in their findings, there are over fifty million such people in the USA alone, 'but they have not yet formed a sense of "us" as a collective identity', she writes, 'they don't yet see themselves in their diverse totality and so they fail to recognise their own potential for creating a new world.'

Yet, in this phrase 'diverse totality' lies another important challenge: the awareness and aspirations that Ray and Anderson have described have almost inevitably to be forged individually and often painfully. We need allies, of course, and the company of like-minded people, but not at the expense of falling back into some cosy clan in which a new orthodoxy starts to assert itself. In other words it's that old dilemma of the 'selfless self' that can maintain its autonomy while at the same time being a part of the whole and acting accordingly.

This realisation is beautifully expressed by Tolstoy towards the end of *War and Peace*, at the moment when his idealistic hero, Pierre Bezukhov, suddenly feels called upon 'to give a new direction to the whole of Russian society and the whole world'. Pierre then says to Natasha Rostov:

> Thoughts that have important consequences are always simple. All my thinking could be summed up with these words; since corrupt people unite among themselves to constitute a force, honest people must do the same. It's as simple as that.

This is the sort of idealism that someone like Barack Obama has clearly tapped into in the United States, and elsewhere – particularly among young people. He is undoubtedly a remarkable person, but what I find just as significant is that he's helped to awaken the remarkable person that lives in each one of us.

The last book I want to mention is another American publication, called *Towards a New World View*. It's a collection of interviews that Russell E. DiCarlo conducted with a distinguished collection of scientists, theologians, psychologists, doctors and economists – all of whom are recognisable as belonging to the category that Ray and Anderson identified as Cultural Creatives: people who share a conviction that the traditional, dominant and prevailing world view is, in DiCarlo's words 'hopelessly obsolete'. As Václav Havel, while President of the Czech Republic, said in a speech he gave in the USA back in 1984:

> I think there are good reasons for suggesting that the modern age has ended. Today many things indicate that we are going through a transitional period, when it seems that something is on the way out and something else is painfully being born. It is as if something were crumbling, decaying, and exhausting itself – while something else, still indistinct, were rising from the rubble.

The conversations in DiCarlo's book return again and again to what many recognise as an underlying and profound revolution in human consciousness itself – taking place not just in warm and cosy corners of California, in Totnes and Amsterdam, or in New York's Greenwich Village, but all over the world. And with it come quite new perspectives on questions like 'Who am I?' and 'What kind of universe do I live in?' – in other words a realignment of our most basic assumptions and beliefs about what constitutes reality. In his preface, DiCarlo writes of this emerging world view as 'a shift from seeing the universe as a mechanical device with no mind or will of its own, to seeing it as intelligent, self-organising, and ever evolving'. In his opinion it's a view that is 'like the human mind which creates it, in a state of dynamic evolution and development'.

In his conversation with Richard Tarnas – whose writings and whose company have been such an inspiration to me in recent years – DiCarlo asks him who he thinks have been some of the more prominent personalities in this unfolding drama. 'It depends how far back we want to take it', is Tarnas's reply. In certain respects, he suggests, you can go back all the way to people like Socrates and Moses: 'They are still affecting us in terms of the basic Promethean impulse of rebelling against oppressive structures and creating moral and intellectual autonomy for the human being.'

Richard Tarnas at Stonehenge

Many of the people I have written about and quoted have been courageous enough, each in their own way, to rock the boat and, like Socrates, to ask awkward questions. Such heretics, writes Bernard Lievegoed in his book *Phases*, are 'the hope of our culture'. They listen to their inner voice rather than being guided solely by convention and tradition. 'They are always persecuted', he continues, 'and always will be persecuted. In the past they have been given poison cups or have been burned at the stake; nowadays they are ignored.'

One of the most courageous 'heretics' in recent years was Pierre Teilhard de Chardin, who was harshly criticised by many of his own colleagues – by the Church he strove to serve – and must therefore have experienced the bleakest wilderness of all. And it was he who wrote: 'Some day, when we have mastered the winds, the tides and gravity, we will harness the energies of love. Then, for the second time in the history of the world, man will have discovered fire.'

It is hard to follow on from words like those, for they express so perfectly and so beautifully the thought that runs through everything I have tried to convey in this book: that what matters at the end of the day, at the end of our lives, is not how clever or successful or even independent we have become, but the extent to which we have walked in the steps of the Good Samaritan, rather than passed by on the other side; and this irrespective of how often we say our prayers or acknowledge the existence of a god, by whatever name. For what will survive of us to ease and lighten the way ahead is, I suspect, the love we have expressed, received, and demonstrated in our relationships with one another, and the degree to which the encounter with our fellow human beings has prompted that question which Parzival – not out of curiosity but out of compassion – took so long to ask the wounded King Amfortas: 'Friend, what ails thee?'

I believe therefore that the answer to my question: 'Where on earth is heaven?' is contained in the question itself. As Elizabeth Browning wrote in her *Aurora Leigh*: 'Earth's crammed with heaven / And every common bush afire with God.' Thus, heaven can slowly become a reality, not as some eternal resting place elsewhere, but here on earth amidst all the obstacles through which we learn and grow; an earth which, like the universe which surrounds it and like we who inhabit it, is infinitely more complex and many-layered than most of us can at present either know or even imagine; and a world, too, that incorporates the gods whom we have, until now, always tended to experience as elsewhere and separate. And the peace of mind we long for, and that is within our capability, is indeed what Jesus called the kingdom of heaven. All this, I imagine, might have been the essence of that secret carved on the green stick which Tolstoy's brother told him was buried in the forest surrounding their home.

So where am I in all this? What do I get up to these days, besides writing this book? I continue to read other books, go to the cinema and for walks. I have a wonderful family and many dear friends. I love to visit Paris and Scotland, California and Botton Village; to stroll through London and twenty years of memories; and whenever possible to walk by the Thames where I grew up, and by the sea in Cornwall. I am grateful to *The Guardian* newspaper and to *Channel Four News* for keeping me in touch with places and people I cannot meet or visit; and I try to understand what unfolds from day to day, particularly the tragedies and conflicts, in the light of the broader picture I have attempted to describe in this book. I certainly haven't finished with trying to juggle words and images in ways that might be interesting and helpful for others.

'Writing is a way of talking without being interrupted' is a remark made over a hundred years ago by the French writer and wit Jules Renard. In a way he's right, and yet what I have attempted to describe in this book is the outcome of a long dialogue with very many people – and therefore many interruptions – and of encounters in which at times, as a film-maker, I have tried to simply watch and listen. But as well as drawing on the wise and at times paradoxical ideas and insights of others, I have also tried – by way of a bridge into sometimes more learned sources – to share some of my own intimations as they have arisen along the way.

What more can we do? For me what sometimes helps is to simply sing out loud (when no one is listening!) the opening lines from that beautiful hymn:

Dear Lord and Father of Mankind
Forgive our foolish ways.

Other people must have similarly profound words and music that they remember from their early years. 'The Day Thou gavest, Lord is ended' is another hymn I love. For me it is a celebration of the fact that although night follows day, it is not the end, and that what its composer John Ellerton calls 'God's throne' shall never 'like earth's proud empires pass away'. It's a thought that reminds me of the inscription in Latin over the door of Jung's home in Küsnacht: 'Called or not called, God will be there.'

The third verse of Ellerton's evening hymn leads me perfectly into my final thoughts:

As o'er each continent and island
The dawn leads on another day,
The voice of prayer is never silent,
Nor dies the strain of praise away.

I would like to conclude, therefore, by emphasising my own deep conviction that on this journey we all make there is, in fact, no ending; there is only life. And life – as John Betjeman experienced as an old man and struggled to put into words on that Cornish cliff top – is eternal, one chapter after another in a longer story. Life is also, in essence, invisible; for our eyes, magnificent as they are, are blind to reality in its fullest sense, and blind at times to the fact that all the stages on our heavenly journey are here, interwoven with all that we know as daily life. And despite all the sorrow and pain that accompanies it, I recognise that death is no more than a moment in the rhythmical process of sleeping and waking, whereby that same life-force is renewed and continues to evolve. As the little prince told his friend in the desert, there is nothing sad about old abandoned shells. Indeed we all but abandon those shells every night while we sleep in order to commune not only with those we love, but with the creative energy that underlies and inspires all existence.

Increasingly real to me in this whole, unfolding saga is that we ourselves are our ancestors. They were us. History is not about other people long ago. We did and said all those things we read about, and made those treasures we dig up; history fascinates us because we are hearing about our own biographies – not just the collective biography of humanity, but our own individual stories. We were there. Now we walk down old streets and cobbled alleyways, and into ancient buildings, with a certain nostalgia; we gaze at timeless nature, and at the sea in particular; we read about other lives, many of which are strangely familiar, and something stirs in us – not yet a memory as such, but certainly a bond of sorts. The world that Tolstoy wanted to make 'more beautiful and more joyous' both for his contemporaries and for those who came after him, is the same world where he will one day live again.

And so we wake up each morning, and each new lifetime, to continue the adventure and the task of continuing to ask the questions that we have asked throughout human history; and not always to settle for the answers we came up with in the past. It is tempting to see ourselves in all this as once wiser than we are now; not cleverer, but wiser – like the Pueblo Indians whom Jung met and the bushmen of southern Africa about whom Laurens van der Post wrote so admiringly. But we have moved on, and are moving still, from unconsciousness to consciousness – from tribal to individual identity. And here lies the challenge; for our sense of being separate and seemingly isolated individuals creates a situation in which we are potentially at war – or certainly in competition – with everyone else, including members of our own tribe and even family. Egotism and human intelligence, when severed from morality, are lethal indeed. How then do we 'harness the energies of love' that Teilhard believed in? Such an evolutionary step can only come about, it would seem – as it did so clearly for someone like Gandhi – through a heightened degree of empathy, whereby it is impossible to be at peace while another person suffers.

The other great challenge involves recognising our interconnectedness not only with each other, as members of one great human family, but with all that exists on earth and in the cosmos at large – an ecology that embraces the whole of Creation. 'How much I like the phrase "all the company of Heaven"', wrote Philip Toynbee. Only thus will we slowly start to experience consciously what all the great initiates throughout the ages have taught – that we are, each one of us, a microcosm of the macrocosm. This is what Pierre Bezukhov, in Tolstoy's great novel, experienced when he had a revelation of infinity and eternity that was also a revelation of his own infinite and eternal self. After his capture by the French, he gazes up at the star-filled sky and thinks: 'And all this is mine, and all this is in me, and all this is me.' The creativity that animates the universe also lives in us. This idea was touchingly expressed by the writer Henning Mankell, son-in-law of Ingmar Bergman, shortly after the death of that great Swedish film director: 'Ingmar found the meaning of life in creativity. If he did have a God, then that was it; the creative force that gave purpose to an otherwise troubled life.'

Yet if the laws at work in the universe, and which pervade nature itself, express order and harmony, what are we human beings up to? Why do we have such troubled lives? Is it simply growing pains? Or is there also discord as well as harmony in that creative force itself – in the macrocosm at large; a duality that is mirrored in each of us as microcosm? If so, then the essence of the ultimate challenge we face is a choice: harmony or conflict? Love is harmony made conscious; and that is a task that we can only fulfil individually. No god or angel can do it for us.

In his book *The Cherubinic Wanderer*, the medieval mystic Angelus Silesius wrote the words I quoted earlier: 'Stop, whither are you running? Heaven is in you; if you seek God elsewhere you will forever miss Him.' And it is the words with which Silesius ends his great book that I would like to use to end mine: 'Friend, it is enough now. If you wish to read more, go and become yourself the writing and the essence.'

Acknowledgements

First I would like to thank all those mentioned in this book, including some I never actually met but to whom I nonetheless feel very close. They have each in their own way helped and inspired me. My story only exists because of them.

I would also like to thank the BBC for its support and trust over many years, and my colleagues throughout the television industry for their professionalism, creativity and companionship.

For early encouragement with my writing, I am most grateful to Laurens van der Post, Emilios Bourantinos and Gene Gollogly; and also to Elisabeth Collins, who long before I actually started work on this project would often ask: 'How's the book coming along?'

Once it was underway I became hugely indebted to the following for their helpful comments and suggestions at various stages of the writing: Karen Armstrong, Peter Bark, Elizabeth Bryan, Denise Bryer, Friedwart Bock, Diana Carey, James Dyson, Viven della Negra, Michael Evans, Sevak Gulbenkian, Ronald Higgins, Christopher Moore, Jeremy Naydler, Ben Okri, Urs Pohlmann, Tom Raines, Richard Ramsbotham, Christine Reddaway, Theodore Roszak, Nomi Rowe, Richard Tarnas, Nick Thomas, John Thomson, Mark Tully, Guy Vassall-Adams, Janet Watts, and Arthur Zajonc; also my brother and fellow pilgrim David Bryer, my thoughtful son Thomas, and finally my sister Dede Bark – not only for finding time in her busy life to look at my manuscript, but for her loving support over very many years.

During the three years that I was writing the book I also owed a great deal to Alex Barakan, and more recently to his sister Thais Downman, for inspiring conversations that encouraged me to believe that I had something worth trying to share; and to my witty and perceptive daughter Ellie for her loving and playful reminders of what is sometimes best kept to myself.

In the final months I received extremely helpful suggestions, as well as many welcome grammatical corrections, from my conscientious and sensitive editor Matthew Barton. I have also much appreciated the skill and patience of my book designer Lucy Guenot at Bookcraft, and the trust and support throughout of my publisher Martin Large.

I owe very special thanks to Jessica Lewers who, with great patience and good humour – chapter after chapter, night after night, while her children slept – typed out the original draft from my handwritten pages; and more recently to my wife Jackie who then helped me to make friends with a computer and thus to rework the material over many months. Jackie also held my hand when that same computer seemed to have ideas of its own and quite a different book in mind. She also brought a clear and helpful perspective to some of my more obscure ramblings. And it was a colleague of Jackie's at Oxford, Professor Siegbert Prawer, who when he learned of my forthcoming book wrote to me: 'As to the question your title asks, there is a simple answer. Heaven on Earth is wherever Jackie happens to be.' Well, if heaven is being with someone who knows you very well and still loves you and respects your endeavours, then Siegbert is right.

ILLUSTRATIONS: 'Sir John Betjeman's Funeral' by Joan Cockett; the work of Cecil Collins's © Tate, London 2009; drawing of the author by Saied Dai; Don Quixote by Gustav Doré; 'Malcolm Muggeridge' by Wally Fawkes (Trog); diagrams by Allmut ffrench; 'Illustration –William ran into Hubert Lane at the corner of the road' by Thomas Henry Fisher from *William and the Brains Trust* by Richmal Crompton (© Thomas Henry Fisher 1945) is reproduced by permission of PFD (www.pfd.co.uk) on behalf of The Estate of Thomas Henry Fisher; 'The Other Wise Man' by David Newbatt; 'The Shepherds of Arcadia' by Nicolas Poussin, Musée du Louvre, Paris; 'The Alchemist' from *When We Were Very Young* and 'Christopher Robin and Pooh' from *The House at Pooh Corner* by E.H. Shepard, copyright © The Estate of E.H. Shepard, reproduced with permission of Curtis Brown Group Ltd, London; the Weber family in Cornwall by Posy Simmonds; 'Easter Saturday' by Ninetta Sombart; 'Christ in the Wilderness: the Scorpion' by Stanley Spencer © ADAGP, Paris and DACS, London 2009; 'St Francis with the Leper' and 'Meeting the Lady' by Greg Tricker; 'John Betjeman' by Julia Whatley.

PHOTOGRAPHS: Fritz Schumacher by Sophie Baker; Laurens van der Post by Jane Bown, © Guardian News and Media Ltd 1975; An Arundel tomb by Mark Bridges; Lindsay Clarke, Val Pommier, and Peter Spink by Carol Bruce; *Clouds of Glory* transmission card photograph by Tore Gill; Pierre Teilhard de Chardin by Philippe Halsmann, reproduced with permission of Magnum Press Ltd; photographic reproductions of Cecil Collins's work by the Tate and by Clive Hicks; 'Yasnaya Polyana in the snow' by Aleksei Kolyaskin reproduced with kind permission of Leo Tolstoy Museum Estate, Yasnaya Polyana; Alistair Macmillan by Peter Mernagh; 'The Shepherds of Arcadia' © RMN/René-Gabriel Ojéda; John Davy by Malcolm Powell; Ronald Duncan © Ronald Duncan Literary Foundation; Francis Edmunds, reproduced with kind permission of Angela Locher; M.K. Gandhi © The Gandhi Museum, Delhi; 'Karl König with Camphill pupil' from the Karl König archive at the Camphill Rudolf Steiner Schools, Aberdeen; Sir Bernard Lovell, © Manchester University, Jodrell Bank; Peter and Kate Roth, reproduced with kind permission of Simon Roth; Rudolf Steiner © Rietmann / Dokumentation am Goetheanum; First Goetheanum © Staatsarchiv Basel Stadt; Leo Tolstoy and family, reproduced with kind permission of Leo Tolstoy Museum Estate, Yasnaya Polyana; E.L. Grant Watson, reproduced with kind permission of Hugh Spence; Arthur Zajonc, reproduced with kind permission of the subject.

The remaining photographs were taken by the author, with the exception of the following which were commissioned by the BBC in relation to his productions: Patrick Barlow and Jim Broadbent in *Revolution*, John Betjeman with John and Myfwany Piper; Ron Eyre with Gillian Limb; Mark Tully in Pakistan; Thomas Weihs; Laurens van der Post with bushman in southern Africa.

Bibliography

Some of these books have been reprinted in many editions. They are listed here with publisher and year of the first English edition, except for books or lectures by Rudolf Steiner where the latest editions are given.

Adie, Kate, *The Kindness of Strangers*, Headline, 2002
Albom, Mitch, *The Five People You Meet in Heaven*, Hyperion, 2003
Alliluyeva, Svetlana, *20 Letters to a Friend*, World Books, 1967
Andersen, Hans Christian, *Fairy Tales*, Flensteds Forlag, 1960
Anderson, William, *Cecil Collins: the Quest for the Great Happiness*, Barrie and Jenkins, 1988
Anglican authors (various), *Moral Problems: Questions on Christianity with Answers,* Mowbray, 1952
Armstrong, Karen, *A History of God*, Vintage, 1999
— —, *A Short History of Myth*, Canongate Books, 2005
— —, *The Great Transformation: the World in the Time of Buddha, Socrates, Confucius and Jeremiah*, Atlantic Books, 2006
Arnold, Matthew, *New Poems*, Macmillan, 1867
Ashe, Geoffrey, *Gandhi: a Study in Revolution*, Heinemann, 1968
Astor, Stella (ed.), *Angels: Cecil Collins*, Fools Press, 2004

Bakewell, Joan (ed.), *Belief*, Duckworth Overlook, 2005
Ball, Philip, *The Devil's Doctor: Paracelsus and the World of Renaissance Magic and Science*, William Heinemann, 2006
Barfield, Owen, *Romanticism Comes of Age*, Rudolf Steiner Press, 1944
— —, *Saving the Appearances: a Study in Idolatry*, Faber and Faber, 1957
— —, *Worlds Apart*, Wesleyan University Press, 1963
Belyi, Andrei; Turgenieff, Aasya; Voloschin, Margarita, *Reminiscences of Rudolf Steiner*, Adonis Press, 1987
Bennett, Alan, *Writing Home*, Faber and Faber, 1994
Berlin, Isaiah, *The Roots of Romanticism*, Chatto and Windus, 1999
Betjeman, John, *John Betjeman's Collected Poems*, John Murray, 1958
— —, *Summoned by Bells*, John Murray, 1960
Black, Jonathan, *The Secret History of the World*, Quercus, 2007
Blake, William, *The Poems of William Blake*, edited by W.H. Stevenson, Longman, 1971
Bock, Friedwart (ed.), *The Builders of Camphill: Lives and Destinies of the Founders,* Floris Books, 2004

Bohm, David, *Wholeness and the Implicate Order*, Routledge and Kegan Paul, 1980

du Boulay, Shirley, *Beyond the Darkness: a Biography of Bede Griffiths*, O Books, 2003

Briggs, K.M., *The Fairies in Tradition and Literature*, Routledge and Kegan Paul, 1967

Briggs, Raymond, *Father Christmas*, Hamish Hamilton, 1973

Bronowski, J, *The Ascent of Man*, British Broadcasting Corporation, 1973

Browning, Elizabeth, *The Poetical Works of Elizabeth Barrett Browning*, Oxford, 1906

Browning, Robert, *Robert Browning: a Selection of Poems*, Cambridge, 1911

Bucke, Richard Maurice, *Cosmic Consciousness*, Innes and Sons, 1901

Bunyan, John, *Pilgrim's Progress*, London, 1795

Burnett, Frances Hodgson, *The Secret Garden*, William Heinemann, 1911

Capra, Fritjof, *The Tao of Physics*, Wildwood House, 1975

Carroll, Lewis, *Alice in Wonderland*, Macmillan, 1865

Castaneda, Carlos, *A Separate Reality*, Bodley Head, 1971

Cavafy, C.P., *Poems by C.P. Cavafy*, Chatto and Windus, 1951

Cervantes, Miguel, *Don Quixote*, London, 1620

Chetwode, Penelope, *Kulu: the End of the Habitable World*, John Murray, 1972

Clarke, Lindsay, *The Chymical Wedding*, Cape, 1989

— —, *Parzifal and the Stone from Heaven*, HarperCollins, 2001

Clayton, Philip and Davies, Paul (eds), *The Re-Emergence of Emergence*, Oxford University Press, 2006

Coelho, Paulo, *The Alchemist*, Thorsons, 1993

Colereidge, Samuel Taylor, *Biographia Literaria*, J.M. Dent and Sons, 1906

Collins, Cecil, *The Vision of the Fool and Other Writings*, Golgonooza Press, 1994

Corbin, Henry, *The Voyage and the Messenger: Iran and Philosophy*, North Atlantic books, 1998

Cottingham, John (ed.), *Western Philosophy*, Blackwell Publishing, 1996

Crankshaw, Edward, *The Fall of the House of Hapsburg*, Longmans, 1963

Crompton, Richmal, *William the Detective*, George Newnes, 1935

Darwin, Charles, On *the Origin of Species*, John Murray, 1859

Davies, W.H., *The Collected Poems of W.H. Davies*, Jonathan Cape, 1928

Davy, John, Hope, *Evolution and Change*, Hawthorn Press, 1985

Dawkins, Richard, *The Selfish Gene*, Oxford University Press, 1976

— —, *River out of Eden*, Wiedenfeld and Nicolson, 1995

— —, *The God Delusion*, Bantam Press, 2006

DiCarlo, Russell E. (ed.), *Towards a New World View: Conversations at the Leading Edge,* Epic Publishing, 1996

Dickinson, Emily, *Complete Poems of Emily Dickinson,* Martin Secker, 1924

Donne, John, *Devotions upon Emergent Occasions,* London, 1634

Dostoyevsky, Fyodor, *The Possessed,* Heinemann, 1914

Duncan, Ronald, *This Way to the Tomb,* Faber and Faber, 1946

— —, *All Men are Islands,* Rupert Hart-Davis, 1964

— —, *How to Make Enemies,* Rupert Hart-Davis, 1968

— —, *Man Part One,* Rebel Press, 1970

— —, and Weston-Smith, Miranda, *The Encyclopaedia of Ignorance,* Pergamon Press, 1977

Edwards, Lawrence, *The Field of Form,* Floris Books, 1982

Eckhart, Meister Johannes, *Treatises and Sermons,* Faber and Faber, 1958

Eliot, T.S., *Collected Poems 1909–1935,* Faber and Faber, 1936

Emerson, Ralph Waldo, *Emerson's Complete Works,* G. Routledge, 1883–84

Evans, Michael and Rodger, Iain, *Anthroposophical Medicine: Healing for Body, Soul and Spirit,* Thorsons, 1992

Eyre, Ronald, *Ronald Eyre on the Long Search,* Fount Paperbacks, 1979

Franck, Frederick, *The Zen of Seeing,* Vintage Books, 1973

Freud, Sigmund, *The Interpretation of Dreams,* G. Allen and Unwin, 1954

Frost, Robert, *The Poetry of Robert Frost,* edited by Edward Connery Lathem, Holt Rinehart and Winston, 1969

Gandhi, M.K., *The Story of My Experiments with Truth,* Beacon, 1957

Gebser, Jean, *The Ever Present Origin,* Ohio University Press, 1985

Geldard, Richard, *The Spiritual Teachings of Ralph Waldo Emerson,* Lindisfarne Books, 2001

Golding, William, *Lord of the Flies,* Faber and Faber, 1954

Goodrick-Clarke, Nicholas, *The Western Esoteric Traditions: a Historical Introduction,* Oxford University Press, 2008

Grahame, Kenneth, *The Wind in the Willows,* Charles Scribner's Sons, 1908

Green, Dorothy (ed.), *Descent of Spirit: Writings of E.L. Grant Watson,* Primavera Press, 1990

Gulbenian, Sevak Edward, *In the Belly of the Beast,* Hampton Roads, 2004

Harwood, A.C., *The Recovery of Man in Childhood: a Study in the Educational Work of Rudolf Steiner,* Hodder and Stoughton, 1958

Hawken, Paul, *Blessed Unrest,* Viking, 2007

Heisenberg, Werner, *Physics and Philosophy,* George Allen and Unwin, 1959

— —, *Natural Law and the Structure of Matter,* Rebel Press, 1970

Hemleben, Johannes, *Rudolf Steiner: a Documentary Biography*, Henry Goulden, 1975

Hesse, Hermann, *Narziss and Golmund*, Peter Owen, 1959

— —, *Siddhartha*, Peter Owen, 1954

Higgins, Ronald, *The Seventh Enemy*, Hodder and Stoughton, 1978

Hillier, Bevis, *Betjeman: the Bonus of Laughter*, John Murray, 2004

Hillman, James, *The Soul's Code: in Search of Character and Calling*, Random House, 1996

Hodson, Geoffrey, *Fairies at Work and Play*, The Theosophical Publishing House, 1925

Holmes, Richard, *Coleridge: Darker Reflections*, HarperCollins, 1998

— —, *Coleridge: Early Visions*, HarperCollins, 1989

— —, *The Age of Wonder: How the Romantic Generation discovered the Beauty and Terror of Science*, Harper Press, 2008

Hopkins, Gerard Manley, *Poems of Gerard Manley Hopkins*, H. Milford, 1918

Humphrys, John, *In God We Doubt: Confessions of a Failed Atheist*, Hodder and Stoughton, 2007

Hunt, James Henry Leigh, *The Poetical Works of Leigh Hunt*, Ward, Lock and Co, 1884

Huxley, Aldous, *Brave New World*, Chatto and Windus, 1932

— —, *The Doors of Perception*, Chatto and Windus, 1954

Ibsen, Henrik, *Peer Gynt*, J.M. Dent and Sons, 1920

Ingrams, Richard, *Muggeridge: the Biography*, HarperCollins, 1995

James, Henry, *The Wings of the Dove*, Archibald Constable,1902

Jones, J.D.F., *Storyteller: the Many Lives of Laurens van der Post*, John Murray, 2001

Jung, C.G., *Modern Man in Search of a Soul*, Routledge and Kegan Paul, 1933

— —, *Collected Works of C.G. Jung*, Routledge and Kegan Paul, 1953–79

— —, *Memories, Dreams, Reflections*, Random House, 1961

King, Ursula, *Towards a New Mysticism: Teilhard de Chardin and Eastern Religions*, Collins, 1980

Kübler-Ross, Elizabeth, *On Death and Dying*, Tavistock Publications, 1970

Kuhn, Thomas, *The Structure of Scientific Revolutions*, University of Chicago Press, 1962

Lachman, Gary, *A Secret History of Consciousness*, Lindisfarne Books, 2003

— —, *Rudolf Steiner: an Introduction to his Life and Work*, Tarcher/Penguin, 2007

Ladinsky, Daniel, *I Heard God Laughing: Poems of Hope and Joy*, Sufism Reoriented, 1996

Laing, R.D., *The Divided Self*, Tavistock Publications, 1950

Large, Martin, *Set Free Childhood: Coping with Computers and TV*, Hawthorn Press, 2003

Larkin, Philip, *The Whitsun Weddings*, Faber and Faber, 1964

— —, *Collected Poems*, Faber and Faber, 1988

Lawrence, T.E., *Seven Pillars of Wisdom*, Alden Press, 1935

Lee, Harper, *To Kill a Mockingbird*, Heinemann, 1960

Lewis, C.S., *The Screwtape Letters*, Bles, 1942

— —, *Chronicles of Narnia*, Collins, 1950 onwards

Lissau, Rudi, *Rudolf Steiner: Life, Work, Inner Path and Social Initiatives*, Hawthorn Press, 1987

Lievegoed, Bernard, *Phases, Crisis and Development in the Individual*, Pharos Books, 1979

Lorimer, David (ed.), *Thinking Beyond the Brain: a Wider Science of Consciousness*, Floris Books, 2001

Lovell, Bernard, *In the Center of Immensities*, Harper and Row, 1978

Lovelock, J.E., *Gaia, A New Look at Life on Earth*, Oxford University Press, 1979

Loye, David, *Darwin's Lost Theory*, Benjamin Franklin Press, 2007

Lycett Green, Candida (ed.), *John Betjeman Letters, 3 vols*, Methuen, 1994

— —, *John Betjeman Coming Home: an Anthology of Prose*, Methuen, 1997

Magee, Bryan, *The Great Philosophers*, BBC Books, 1987

Mayne, Michael, *The Enduring Melody*, Darton Longman and Todd, 2006

McDermott, Robert A., *The Essential Steiner*, Harper and Row, 1984

Merton, Thomas, *The Seven Storey Mountain*, Harcourt Brace Jovanovich, 1948

Meyer, Rudolf, *The Wisdom of Fairy Tales*, Floris Books, 1988

Milne, A.A., *When We Were Very Young*, Methuen, 1924

— —, *Now We Are Six*, Methuen, 1927

— —, *The House at Pooh Corner*, Methuen, 1928

Milosz, Czeslaw, *New and Collected Poems, 1931–2001*, Allen Lane the Penguin Press, 2001

Monk, Ray, *Ludwig Wittgenstein: the Duty of Genius*, Vintage, 1990

Moody, Raymond, *Life After Life*, Mockingbird Books, 1975

Morgan, Charles, *The River Line*, Macmillan, 1949

Mowl, Timothy, *Stylistic Cold Wars: Betjeman versus Pevsner*, John Murray, 2000

Muggeridge, Malcolm, *Winter in Moscow*, Eyre and Spottiswoode, 1934

— —, *Muggeridge through the Microphone*, British Broadcasting Corporation, 1967; republished as *Muggeridge Ancient and Modern*, 1981

— —, *Something Beautiful for God: Mother Teresa of Calcutta*, Collins, 1971

— —, *Chronicles of Wasted Time Part I: the Green Stick*, Collins, 1972

— —, *A Twentieth Century Testimony*, Nelson, 1978

Muir, Edwin, *Collected Poems*, Faber and Faber, 1960

Mukherjee, Rudgrangshu (ed.), *The Penguin Gandhi Reader*, Penguin, 1993

Naydler, Jeremy (ed.), *Goethe on Science: an Anthology of Goethe's Scientific Writings,* Floris Books, 1996

Nietzsche, Friedrich Wilhelm, *Thus spake Zarathustra*, London, 1901

Noble, Denis, *The Music of Life: Biology beyond Genes*, Oxford University Press, 2006

O'Donohue, John, *Anam Cara: Spiritual Wisdom from the Celtic World*, Bantam Press, 1997

Okri, Ben, *The Famished Road*, Cape, 1991

— —, *An African Elegy*, Cape, 1992

Orwell, George, *Nineteen Eighty-Four*, Secker and Warburg, 1949

Ouspensky, P.D., *In Search of the Miraculous*, Routledge and Kegan Paul, 1950

— —, *Tertium Organum: the Third Canon of Thought*, Routledge and Kegan Paul, 1957

Pietzner, Cornelius (ed.), *A Candle on the Hill*, Floris Books, 1990

Popplebaum, Hermann, *Man and Animal: their Essential Difference (Considered in Five Aspects),* Anthroposophical Publishing Co., 1931

Pottiez, Jean-Marc (ed.), *A Walk with a White Bushman*, Chatto and Windus, 1986

Postman, Neil, *The Disappeareance of Childhood: How TV is Changing Children's Lives,* Comet Books, 1985

— —, *Amusing Ourselves to Death*, Heinemann, 1986

Pullman, Philip, *His Dark Materials*, Scholastic Press, 2008

Raine, Kathleen, *Cecil Collins: Painter of Paradise*, Golgonooza Press, 1979

Ravindra, Ravi, *The Yoga of Christ*, Element, 1990

Ray, Paul H. and Anderson, Sherry Ruth, *The Cultural Creatives*, Three Rivers Press, 2000

Rinpoche, Sogyal, *The Tibetan Book of Living and Dying*, Rider Books, 1992

Robinson, John A.T., *Honest to God*, SCM Press, 1963

Roszak, Theodore, *The Making of a Counter Culture*, Faber and Faber, 1968

— —, *Where the Wasteland Ends*, Doubleday, 1972

Rowe, Nomi (ed.), *In Celebration of Cecil Collins: Visionary Artist and Educator,* Foolscap, 2008

Ruskin, John, *Fors clavigera: Letters to the Workmen and Labourers of Great Britain,* London, 1871–84

— —, *Unto this Last: Four Essays on the Principles of Political Economy,* George Allen, 1901

Sacks, Jonathan, *The Dignity of Difference: How to Avoid the Clash of Cultures,* Continuum, 2003

Saint-Exupéry, Antoine de, *The Little Prince,* William Heinemann, 1945

Scharmer, C. Otto, *Theory U: Leading from the Future as it Emerges,* Berret Koehler, 2009

Schumacher, E.F., *Small is Beautiful: a Study of Economics as if People Mattered,* Blond and Briggs, 1973

— —, *A Guide for the Perplexed,* Jonathan Cape, 1977

Schwenk, Theodor, *Sensitive Chaos,* Rudolf Steiner Press, 1965

Sheldrake, Rupert, *A New Science of Life,* Blond and Briggs, 1981

— —, *The Presence of the Past,* Collins, 1988

Shelley, Mary, *Frankenstein,* Dent, 1912

Shelley, Percy Bysshe, *The Poetical Works of Percy Bysshe Shelley,* Edward Moxon, 1840

Shepherd, A.P., *A Scientist of the Invisible,* Hodder and Stoughton, 1954

Silesius, Angelus, *Angelus Silesius: Selections from the Cherubinic Wanderer,* Allen and Unwin, 1932

Simmons, Ernest J., *Leo Tolstoy,* John Lehman, 1949

Skinner, B.F., *Beyond Freedom and Dignity,* Alfred A. Knopf, 1971

Smith, Huston, *The Illustrated World's Religions,* Labyrinth Publishing, 1994

Spenser, Edmund, *The Faerie Queen,* London, 1611

Spink, Peter, *Beyond Belief,* Judy Piatkus, 1996

Steiner, Rudolf, *Agriculture Course: the Birth of the Biodynamic Method,* Rudolf Steiner Press, 2004

— —, *Anthroposophical Leading Thoughts,* Rudolf Steiner Press, 1999

— —, *Autobiography: Chapters in the Course of my Life 1861–1907,* Rudolf Steiner Press, 2006

— —, *Evil,* Rudolf Steiner Press, 2003

— —, *From Comets to Cocaine,* Rudolf Steiner Press, 2000

— —, *From Crystals to Crocodiles,* Rudolf Steiner Press, 2002

— —, *Karmic Relationships, 8 vols,* Rudolf Steiner Press, 1997–2009

— —, *Knowledge of the Higher Worlds: How is it Achieved?,* Rudolf Steiner Press, 2009; also translated as *How to Know Higher Worlds,* Anthroposophic Press, 1993

— —, *Manifestations of Karma,* Rudolf Steiner Press, 2000

— —, *Modern Art of Education,* Rudolf Steiner Press, 2004

— —, *Mystics after Modernism*, Rudolf Steiner Press, 2000; previously published as *Eleven European Mystics and Mysticism at the Dawn of the Modern Age*

— —, *Nature Spirits*, Rudolf Steiner Press, 2003

— —, *Occult Science: an Outline*, Rudolf Steiner Press, 2005; also translated as *An Outline of Esoteric Science,* Anthroposophic Press, 1997

— —, *Philosophy of Freedom*, Rudolf Steiner Press, 1999; also translated as *Intuitive Thinking as a Spiritual Path,* Anthroposophic Press, 1995

— —, *Rosicrucian Wisdom*, Rudolf Steiner Press, 2000; previously published as *The Theosophy of the Rosicrucians,* Rudolf Steiner Publishing, 1953

— —, *Staying Connected*, Rudolf Steiner Press, 2000

— —, *The Fifth Gospel: from the Akashic Record*, Rudolf Steiner Press, 1998

— —, *Theosophy*, Rudolf Steiner Press, 2005

Storr, Anthony, *Feet of Clay: a Study of Gurus*, HarperCollins, 1996

Tarnas, Richard, *The Passion of the Western Mind*, Harmony Books, 1991

— —, *Cosmos and Psyche: Intimations of a New World View*, Viking, 2006

Teilhard de Chardin, Pierre, *The Phenomenon of Man*, Collins, 1959

— —, *Le Milieu Divin*, Collins, 1960

— —, *Letters from a Traveller*, Collins, 1962

— —, *Hymn of the Universe*, Collins, 1965

— —, *Science and Christ*, Collins, 1968

— —, *Christianity and Evolution*, Collins, 1971

Tennyson, Hallam, *India's Walking Saint: the Story of Vinoba Bhave*, Doubleday, 1955

Thomas, Dylan, *Collected Poems 1934–1952*, J.M. Dent and Sons, 1952

Thomas, Nick, *Space and Counterspace: a New Science of Gravity, Time and Light,* Floris Books, 2008

Thoreau, Henry D., *Walden, or Life in the Woods*, Clarkson N. Potter, 1970

Tillich, Paul, *The Shaking of the Foundations*, SCM Press, 1949

Tocqueville, Alexis de, *Democracy in America*, Saunders and Otley, 1835

Tolkein, J.R.R., *The Hobbit*, Allen and Unwin, 1937

— —, *The Lord of the Rings*, Allen and Unwin, 1954–55

Tolle, Eckhart, *The Power of Now*, Hodder and Stoughton, 1999

— —, *A New Earth*, Michael Joseph, 2005

Tolstoy, Leo, *Tolstoy Centenary Edition*, Oxford University Press, 1932

Toynbee, Philip, *Part of a Journey: an Autobiographical Journal 1977–79,* William Collins, 1981

Tremain, Rose, *Restoration*, Hamish Hamilton, 1989

— —, *Music and Silence*, Chatto & Windus, 1999

Troyat, Henri, *Tolstoy*, W.H. Allen, 1968

Tully, Mark, *India's Unending Journey*, Rider, 2007

van Dyke, Henry, *The Story of the Other Wise Man*, Harper and Brothers, 1907
van der Post, Laurens, *In a Province*, Hogarth Press, 1934
— —, *Venture into the Interior*, Hogarth Press, 1952
— —, *The Lost World of the Kalahari*, Hogarth Press, 1958
— —, *The Heart of the Hunter*, Hogarth Press, 1961
— —, *The Seed and the Sower*, Hogarth Press, 1963
— —, *Journey into Russia*, Hogarth Press, 1964
— —, *Jung and the Story of our Time*, Hogarth Press, 1976
— —, *Yet Being Someone Other*, Hogarth Press, 1982
Voloschin, Margarita, *Die grüne Schlange*, Verlag Freies Geistesleben, 1954

Watkins, Vernon, *The Collected Poems of Vernon Watkins*, Golgonooza Press, 1945
— —, *New Selected Poems*, Carcanet Press, 2006
Watson, E.L. Grant, *Enigmas of Natural History*, Cresset Press, 1936
— —, *But to What Purpose*, Cresset Press, 1946
— —, *The Leaves Return*, Country Life, 1947
— —, *Nature Abounding*, Faber and Faber, 1951
— —, *The Mystery of Physical Life*, Abelard Schuman, 1964
— —, *Animals in Splendour*, John Baker, 1967
— —, *Descent of Spirit*, Primavera Press, 1990
Watson, Lyall, *Supernature: the Natural History of the Supernatural*, Hodder and Stoughton, 1973
Wehr, Gerhard, *Jung and Steiner: the Birth of a New Psychology*, Anthroposophic Press, 1990
Weihs, Thomas, *Children in Need of Special Care*, Souvenir Press, 1971
— —, *Embryogenesis and Myth in Science*, Floris Books, 1986
Welburn, Andrew, *The Beginnings of Christianity*, Floris Books, 1991
— —, *Rudolf Steiner's Philosophy and the Crisis of Contemporary Thought*, Floris Books, 2004
Wesker, Arnold, *Roots*, Penguin Books, 1959
Whitman, Walt, *Leaves of Grass*, Thayer and Eldridge, 1860
Wilde, Oscar, *De profundis*, New York, 1905
Wilkes, A.J., *Flowforms: the Rhythmic Power of Water*, Floris Books, 2003
Williams, H.A., *The True Wilderness*, Constable, 1965
— —, *Some Day I'll Find You*, Mitchell Beazley, 1982
Williams, Tennessee, 'The Timeless World of a Play', foreword to *The Rose Tattoo*, Penguin Books, 1958
Wilson, Colin, *The Outsider*, Victor Gollancz, 1956
Wittgenstein, Ludwig, *Tractatus logico-philosophicus*, Kegan Paul, 1922
Wordsworth, William, *The Poems of William Wordsworth*, Methuen, 1908

Zajonc, Arthur, *Catching the Light: the Entwined History of Light and Mind*, Bantam Press, 1993

— —, (ed.), *The New Physics and Cosmology: Dialogues with the Dalai Lama*, Oxford University Press, 2004

— —, *Meditation as Contemplative Enquiry*, Lindisfarne Books, 2009

I am often asked about the availability of my films, either to buy, rent or loan. Apart from my 1989 trilogy *Candle on the Hill* (which can be purchased from Camphill Literature Services through vivangriffiths@talktalk.net, telephone 015395 31003) the majority of the films are held in the archives of the BBC who own the copyright. Until now, for reasons of rights, cost, etc., very few such documentaries have been made available on VHS or DVD. However, with advances in technology, the BBC plans – in the words of its first Director of Archive Content – 'to increase public access' to this huge library in the years ahead.

Index